IMMANUEL KANT

Critique of the Power of Judgment

The *Critique of the Power of Judgment* (a more accurate rendition of what has hitherto been translated into English as the *Critique of Judgment*) is the third of Kant's great *Critiques*, following the *Critique of Pure Reason* and the *Critique of Practical Reason*. In the third *Critique* Kant unified the principles of human cognition and conduct expounded in the first two *Critiques*. He argued that in scientific inquiry, in moral and practical conduct, and even in the experience of such aesthetic phenomena as the beautiful and the sublime as well as in the creation of art, human beings must be understood as autonomous agents whose thoughts and actions are grounded on principles independent of experience but who are also at home and effective in nature. Kant thus revealed a deep unity where previously the causal realm of nature and the free domain of human intentions had been thought unrelated. The third *Critique* argues against the division of human thought and conduct and offers an integrated picture of the human condition in which we can make sense of ourselves only if we believe that our autonomy of will and imagination can be effective in nature. This powerful new description of the human condition was to exert a deep influence on such writers as Schiller and Schopenhauer, and would also shape conceptions of science from Goethe to the present day.

This entirely new translation of Kant's masterpiece follows the principles and high standards of all other volumes in The Cambridge Edition of the Works of Immanuel Kant with extensive annotation, glossaries, and an index. This volume includes the indispensable first draft of Kant's introduction to the work. It is the only English edition to note the many differences between the first (1790) and second (1793) editions of the work, and among the copious citations and sources are references to the relevant passages on aesthetics in Kant's lectures on anthropology recently published for the first time in German.

All in all, this new edition offers the serious student of Kant a dramatically richer, more complete, and more accurate translation than has ever been available in English.

THE CAMBRIDGE EDITION OF THE WORKS OF IMMANUEL KANT

General editors: Paul Guyer and Allen W. Wood

Advisory board: Henry Allison
Reinhard Brandt
Ralf Meerbote
Charles D. Parsons
Hoke Robinson
J. B. Schneewind

IMMANUEL KANT

Critique of the power of judgment

EDITED BY

PAUL GUYER
University of Pennsylvania

TRANSLATED BY

PAUL GUYER
University of Pennsylvania

ERIC MATTHEWS
University of Aberdeen

CAMBRIDGE
UNIVERSITY PRESS

PUBLISHED BY THE PRESS SYNDICATE OF THE UNIVERSITY OF CAMBRIDGE
The Pitt Building, Trumpington Street, Cambridge, United Kingdom

CAMBRIDGE UNIVERSITY PRESS
The Edinburgh Building, Cambridge CB2 2RU, UK   http//www.cup.cam.ac.uk
40 West 20th Street, New York, NY 10011-4211, USA   http://www.cup.org
10 Stamford Road, Oakleigh, Melbourne 3166, Australia
Ruiz de Alarcón 13, 28014 Madrid, Spain

© Cambridge University Press 2000

First published 2000

Printed in the United States of America

Typeface Janson 10/12 pt.   *System* DeskTopPro$_{/UX}$ [BV]

A catalog record for this book is available from the British Library.

Library of Congress Cataloging in Publication data
Kant, Immanuel, 1724–1804.
[Kritik der Urteilskraft. English]
Critique of the power of judgment/edited by Paul Guyer; translated by Paul Guyer &
Eric Matthews.
p. cm. – (The Cambridge edition of the works of Immanuel Kant)
Includes bibliographical references and index.
ISBN 0-521-34447-6
1. Judgment (Logic) – Early works to 1800. 2. Judgment (Aesthetics) – Early works to
1800. 3. Aesthetics – Early works to 1800. 4. Teleology – Early works to 1800. I. Guyer,
Paul, 1948– II. Title.
B2783.E5 G89 2000
121–dc21
99-088501

ISBN 0 521 34447 6 hardback

Contents

General editors' preface

Within a few years of the publication of his *Critique of Pure Reason* in 1781, Immanuel Kant (1724–1804) was recognized by his contemporaries as one of the seminal philosophers of modern times – indeed as one of the great philosophers of all time. This renown soon spread beyond German-speaking lands, and translations of Kant's work into English were published even before 1800. Since then, interpretations of Kant's views have come and gone and loyalty to his positions has waxed and waned, but his importance has not diminished. Generations of scholars have devoted their efforts to producing reliable translations of Kant into English as well as into other languages.

There are four main reasons for the present edition of Kant's writings:

1. *Completeness.* Although most of the works published in Kant's lifetime have been translated before, the most important ones more than once, only fragments of Kant's many important unpublished works have ever been translated. These include the *Opus postumum*, Kant's unfinished *magnum opus* on the transition from philosophy to physics; transcriptions of his classroom lectures; his correspondence; and his marginalia and other notes. One aim of this edition is to make a comprehensive sampling of these materials available in English for the first time.

2. *Availability.* Many English translations of Kant's works, especially those that have not individually played a large role in the subsequent development of philosophy, have long been inaccessible or out of print. Many of them, however, are crucial for the understanding of Kant's philosophical development, and the absence of some from English-language bibliographies may be responsible for erroneous or blinkered traditional interpretations of his doctrines by English-speaking philosophers.

3. *Organization.* Another aim of the present edition is to make all Kant's published work, both major and minor, available in comprehensive volumes organized both chronologically and topically, so as to facilitate the serious study of his philosophy by English-speaking readers.

4. Consistency of translation. Although many of Kant's major works have been translated by the most distinguished scholars of their day, some of these translations are now dated, and there is considerable terminological disparity among them. Our aim has been to enlist some of the most accomplished Kant scholars and translators to produce new translations, freeing readers from both the philosophical and literary preconceptions of previous generations and allowing them to approach texts, as far as possible, with the same directness as present-day readers of the German or Latin originals.

In pursuit of these goals, our editors and translators attempt to follow several fundamental principles:

1. As far as seems advisable, the edition employs a single general glossary, especially for Kant's technical terms. Although we have not attempted to restrict the prerogative of editors and translators in choice of terminology, we have maximized consistency by putting a single editor or editorial team in charge of each of the main groupings of Kant's writings, such as his work in practical philosophy, philosophy of religion, or natural science, so that there will be a high degree of terminological consistency, at least in dealing with the same subject matter.

2. Our translators try to avoid sacrificing literalness to readability. We hope to produce translations that approximate the originals in the sense that they leave as much of the interpretive work as possible to the reader.

3. The paragraph, and even more the sentence, is often Kant's unit of argument, and one can easily transform what Kant intends as a continuous argument into a mere series of assertions by breaking up a sentence so as to make it more readable. Therefore, we try to preserve Kant's own divisions of sentences and paragraphs wherever possible.

4. Earlier editions often attempted to improve Kant's texts on the basis of controversial conceptions about their proper interpretation. In our translations, emendation or improvement of the original edition is kept to the minimum necessary to correct obvious typographical errors.

5. Our editors and translators try to minimize interpretation in other ways as well, for example, by rigorously segregating Kant's own footnotes, the editors' purely linguistic notes, and their more explanatory or informational notes; notes in this last category are treated as endnotes rather than footnotes.

We have not attempted to standardize completely the format of individual volumes. Each, however, includes information about the context in which Kant wrote the translated works, a German–English glossary, an English–German glossary, an index, and other aids to comprehension. The general introduction to each volume includes an explanation of specific principles of translation and, where necessary, principles of selection of works included in that volume. The pagination of the standard German edition of Kant's works, *Kant's Gesammelte Schriften*, edited by the Royal Prussian (later German) Academy of Sciences (Berlin: Georg Reimer, later Walter de Gruyter & Co., 1900–), is indicated throughout by means of marginal numbers.

Our aim is to produce a comprehensive edition of Kant's writings, embodying and displaying the high standards attained by Kant scholarship in the English-speaking world during the second half of the twentieth century, and serving as both an instrument and a stimulus for the further development of Kant studies by English-speaking readers in the century to come. Because of our emphasis on literalness of translation and on information rather than interpretation in editorial practices, we hope our edition will continue to be usable despite the inevitable evolution and occasional revolutions in Kant scholarship.

PAUL GUYER
ALLEN W. WOOD

Editor's introduction

BACKGROUND: THE POSSIBILITY OF
A CRITIQUE OF TASTE AND TELEOLOGY

The *Critique of the Power of Judgment* was published at the Leipzig book fair at the end of April 1790, in the week following Immanuel Kant's sixty-sixth birthday (Kant lived from 1724 to 1804). The book completed the series of Kant's three great *Critiques*, begun with the *Critique of Pure Reason* in 1781 and continued with the *Critique of Practical Reason* in 1788. However, Kant clearly had no plan for such a series of works on the foundations of philosophy when he published the first edition of the *Critique of Pure Reason* nor even when he was writing the *Critique of Practical Reason* during 1787, which itself began life in 1786 merely as part of the work for the revision of the first *Critique*, the second edition of which appeared in the spring of 1787. Kant's original assumption was that the *Critique of Pure Reason* alone would provide the foundation on which he could erect a system of theoretical and practical philosophy, or as he called them the metaphysics of nature and the metaphysics of morals (the first of which Kant did indeed provide in the 1786 work entitled *The Metaphysical Foundations of Natural Science*, and the second of which he finally provided, after a decade of delay occasioned not only by the *Critique of the Power of Judgment* but also by the 1793 *Religion within the Boundaries of Mere Reason* and such political works as the 1795 essay *Toward Perpetual Peace*, in the 1797 *Metaphysics of Morals*, which is comprised of two parts, named in analogy to the work on the foundations of natural science, *The Metaphysical Foundations of the Doctrine of Right*, containing Kant's legal and political philosophy, and *The Metaphysical Foundations of the Doctrine of Virtue*, containing the final form of Kant's account of our noncoercively enforceable duties of respect and love to ourselves and others). Yet only a few weeks after completing the manuscript for the *Critique of Practical Reason* Kant suddenly announced, in a letter to the young Jena professor Karl Leonhard Reinhold (1757–1823), whose *Letters on the Kantian Philosophy* of 1786–87 were doing a great deal to popularize Kant's philosophy,[1] that a third *Critique* was in the offing. Here are his words:

My inner conviction grows, as I discover in working on different topics that not only does my system remain self-consistent but I find also, when sometimes

I cannot see the right way to investigate a certain subject, that I need only look back at the general picture of the elements of knowledge, and of the mental powers pertaining to them, in order to make discoveries I had not expected. I am now at work on the critique of taste, and I have discovered a new sort of *a priori* principles, different from those heretofore observed. For there are three faculties of the mind: the faculty of cognition, the faculty of feeling pleasure and displeasure, and the faculty of desire. In the *Critique of Pure* (theoretical) *Reason*, I found *a priori* principles for the first of these, and in the *Critique of Practical Reason a priori* principles for the third. I tried to find them for the second as well, and although I thought it impossible to find such principles, the analysis of the previously mentioned faculties of the human mind allowed me to discover something systematic, which has given me ample material at which to marvel and if possible to explore, sufficient to last me for the rest of my life, and has put me on the path now to recognize three parts of philosophy, each of which has its *a priori* principles, which can be enumerated and for which one can precisely determine the scope of the knowledge that is possible through them – theoretical philosophy, teleology, and practical philosophy, of which the second is, to be sure, the least rich in *a priori* grounds of determination. I hope to have a manuscript on this completed although not in print by Easter, under the title of the "Critique of Taste."[2]

This makes it sound as if both the plan to write a "Critique of Taste" and even the tripartite division of the human mind into faculties of cognition, feeling, and desire (the last of which can be governed by reason), which could explain the need for three *Critiques*, one for each fundamental faculty of the mind, are entirely new. At the same time, it appears to shift the subject matter of a "critique of taste" from what one would expect, namely the ancient branch of philosophy, dating back to Plato but first dubbed "aesthetics" by the German philosopher Alexander Gottlieb Baumgarten (1714–1762) in 1735, which studies the feelings of beauty and sublimity produced by works of both nature and human art and the principles of judgments about such feelings,[3] to something quite different, the "part of natural philosophy that explicates the purposes [*finis*] of things," which had first been named "teleology" by Christian Wolff (1679–1754) just a few years earlier.[4] But all of this is, to put it mildly, at least somewhat misleading. Kant had been interested in both aesthetics and teleology from very early in his philosophical career, and had accepted the tripartite division of human mental powers for at least two decades if not longer before the letter to Reinhold. And the *Critique of the Power of Judgment* that he would finish just over twenty-four months after writing this letter would hardly *replace* aesthetics with teleology, as the letter might seem to suggest, although it would certainly try to *connect* them. So just what could Kant have newly discovered in the few weeks before writing this letter?

A brief review of some of Kant's earlier thinking about both aesthetics and teleology may help us to see what is new and what is not in the *Critique of the Power of Judgment*. As mentioned, both aesthetics and teleology figured among Kant's philosophical concerns from very early in his career. Kant's first group of publications, in 1755–56, had focused on science and metaphysics, and did not include anything on either aesthetics or teleology.[5] However, works in Kant's next main group of publications, written between 1762 and 1766, touched on both aesthetics and teleology. Kant took a cautious position on teleology in his 1763 work on *The Only Possible Basis for a Proof of the Existence of God*, which included, in addition to a version of Kant's critique of Descartes's famous "ontological" argument, that is, the attempt to prove the existence of God directly from the concept of him as a completely perfect being, a detailed critique of the popular argument from design, that is, the attempt to infer to an intelligent author of nature from the evidence of intelligent design within nature; Kant touched upon teleology when he argued that although no such argument could prove the existence of a perfect being as conceived by theology, such a being, if proven to exist on other grounds, could certainly be conceived of as working to achieve its purposes *through* the mechanical and regular laws of nature that we could discover by means of natural science.[6] Then in 1764, in addition to an essay upon philosophical method that is his first real exploration of the foundational questions that would lead to the *Critique of Pure Reason*[7] and another on "negative quantities," which introduced a clear distinction between "logical" and "real" relations, such as the logical relation of ground and consequence and the real relation of cause and effect, which marked a fundamental step in Kant's break with the rationalist philosophy of Leibniz and Wolff,[8] Kant published a work called *Observations on the Feeling of the Beautiful and Sublime*.[9] The title of this book was clearly influenced by Edmund Burke's 1757 *A Philosophical Enquiry into the Original of Our Ideas of the Sublime and the Beautiful*,[10] although Kant does not provide an extensive psychological and physiological analysis of these feelings, as Burke did, but is instead primarily concerned with differences in the capacities for these feelings between the two sexes and among diverse cultures and nations.

Kant also discussed questions of aesthetics in his lecture courses (of which, given that he had no income except what students paid him directly, he offered a great variety!) from a very early point. In the printed announcement of his courses for the winter semester of 1765–66, Kant offered courses on metaphysics, logic, ethics, and physical geography, and explained why his course on logic would also include some discussion of aesthetics:

I shall be lecturing on logic of the first type [a critique and canon of *sound understanding*]. To be more specific, I shall base my lectures on *Meier's* handbook,[11] for he . . . stimulates us to an understanding, not only of the cultivation of reason in its more refined and learned form, but also of the development of the ordinary understanding, which is nonetheless active and sound. The former serves the life of contemplation, while the latter serves the life of action and society. And in this, the very close relationship of the materials under examination leads us at the same time, in the *critique of reason*, to pay some attention to the *critique of taste*, that is to say, *aesthetics*. The rules of the one at all times serve to elucidate the rules of the other. Defining the limits of the two is a means to a better understanding of them both.[12]

Meier (1718–1777), following Leibniz, Wolff, and Baumgarten, had distinguished aesthetic response from logical thought as "confused" (or perhaps better "fused") rather than "distinct" cognition, a form of cognition in which what is important is the richness of associations rather than analytical clarity, and Kant intended to explore this distinction in his lectures. The evidence that we have of his logic lectures from 1770 onward show that he did just that;[13] and the 1765–66 announcement shows that Kant considered the "critique of taste" as part of his subject from this early period, although it does not imply that at that time he had already formulated an intention to write a book that would carry that title.

Kant included more extensive discussion of topics in aesthetics in the subject that he entitled "anthropology" on which he lectured beginning in the winter semester of 1772–73.[14] By "anthropology," Kant certainly did not mean what we now call physical anthropology; but on the other hand, he did not strictly limit himself to what we would now call cultural anthropology either, although this was certainly part of his interest. Instead, these lectures, for which Kant used as his text the chapter on "Empirical Psychology" from Baumgarten's *Metaphysica*, the book that was also the basis for his metaphysics lectures,[15] concerned both the proper and aberrant functioning of human cognition, feeling, and desire, with an emphasis on both individual and cultural differences in the function and use of these faculties. Thus, as early as 1772–73 Kant already organized his thought about the human mind around the tripartite division into the powers of cognition, feeling, and desire that he mentions in the letter to Reinhold as if it were a new discovery. In these lectures, issues in aesthetics are discussed at several places, as Kant was stimulated to touch upon them by Baumgarten's topics. Thus, the nature of poetic invention, differences among the arts, and genius as the source of artistic creation were discussed in the first part of the lectures, on the faculties of cognition, where Baumgarten treated them – although the discussion of genius was considerably enlarged after the 1776 German translation of Alexander Gerard's

Essay on Genius of 1774.[16] The main discussion of the subject of taste, however, is found from the outset squarely in the middle of the second section on the faculty of feeling, by which Kant means above all the feeling of pleasure or displeasure. Thus, the association between taste and the faculty of pleasure that Kant mentions in the letter to Reinhold was hardly new, but had been the basis for Kant's aesthetic theorizing for the better part of two decades. Indeed, what was to become the central thought of the analysis of aesthetic judgment in the *Critique of the Power of Judgment*, the idea that in a judgment of taste a person can claim intersubjective validity for the feeling of pleasure that she experiences in response to a beautiful object because that pleasure is produced, in an attitude of disinterested contemplation, not by a practical concern for utility or advantage in the possession of the object, but by the free and harmonious play of the cognitive faculties of imagination and understanding that the beautiful object induces, and that she can rightly claim such validity for her feeling because we all share these cognitive faculties and they must work pretty much the same way in all of us, was already well developed in these lectures, if not at the outset in 1772–73 then certainly by the middle of the 1770s, at least a decade before the letter to Reinhold.[17]

Again, the prominence of taste as a topic in Kant's anthropology lectures does not prove that he had formulated the intention to write a "Critique of Taste" prior to December of 1787. However, there is separate evidence that even Kant's idea of writing a "Critique of Taste" was by no means new, but dated back to a time at least some months prior to the commencement of his first course on anthropology. In his epochal letter of 21 February 1772 to his prize student Marcus Herz, then studying medicine in Berlin, in which he first announced his intention of writing what would become the *Critique of Pure Reason*,[18] Kant clearly included the subject matter of aesthetics in the scope of his plans. He wrote:

I had already previously made considerable progress in the effort to distinguish the sensible from the intellectual in the field of morals and the principles that spring therefrom. I had also long ago outlined, to my tolerable satisfaction, the principles of feeling, taste, and power of judgment, with their effects – the pleasant, the beautiful and the good – and was then making plans for a work that might perhaps have the title, *The Limits of Sensibility and Reason*. I planned to have it consist of two parts, a theoretical and a practical. The first part would have two sections, (1) general phenomenology and (2) metaphysics, but this only with regard to its nature and method. The second part likewise would have two sections, (1) the universal principles of feeling, taste, and sensuous desire and (2) the universal principles of morality. As I thought through the theoretical part, considering its whole scope and the reciprocal relations of all its parts, I noticed that I still lacked something essential, something that in my long metaphysical studies, I, as well as others, had failed to consider and which in fact constitutes the key to the whole secret of metaphysics, hitherto still hidden from itself.[19]

Now, there need be nothing surprising about the fact that in spite of this statement in 1772, it was the end of 1787 before Kant was ready to start writing a systematic treatise on the "universal principles of feeling [and] taste": It would take Kant nearly a decade to write the first part of what he described to Herz as the treatment of "general phenomenology" and the "nature and method" of metaphysics that would become the *Critique of Pure Reason* of 1781; and then Kant would be constantly occupied until a few weeks before the letter to Herz with the defense of the first *Critique* in the *Prolegomena to any future Metaphysics* of 1783 and the revision for its second edition on which he worked in 1786, with the *Metaphysical Foundations of Natural Science* published in 1786, and with laying the foundations for his moral philosophy in the *Groundwork for the Metaphysics of Morals* that he published in 1785 and in the *Critique of Practical Reason* that he wrote in 1787. So Kant could hardly have started any serious work on a third critique on taste much before the date of his letter to Reinhold. But that still does not explain the air of discovery that we sense in the letter. Why did it apparently come as a *surprise* to Kant, more than twenty years after he had announced his intention to lecture on the "critique of taste," that he should now be in a position to write one?

In the famous letter to Herz, Kant had clearly assumed that a *single* work on the "nature and method" of metaphysics would be all that was needed before he could construct his practical philosophy, which would deal with the principles of both taste and morality. At that time, then, he did not envision writing three *Critiques*, but only one. This was clearly still his assumption when he wrote the *Critique of Pure Reason*, since he thought that upon its completion he could quickly proceed to write the systematic metaphysics of nature and morality.[20] So at this point he might have thought that he could write a systematic treatment of the principles of feeling and taste akin to the metaphysics of nature and morals, but not that he would need to preface any such treatment with a *critique* of the faculty of feeling any more than he would need an additional critique of the faculty of desire or practical reason before he could write his metaphysics of morals. However, this is not exactly what Kant thought when he wrote the first *Critique*: not only did he not see the need for a separate *critique* of taste, but now he was not even sure that there was room for any systematic treatment of the principles of taste at all. At least that seems to be the implication of a striking footnote to the "Transcendental Aesthetic" of the first *Critique*, the section in which Kant presents his theory of space and time as nothing but the pure forms of the human mind for the intuition of external objects and our own inner states.[21] In explaining why he felt he could appropriate Baumgarten's coinage to label his exposition of his theory of our *a priori* knowledge of the properties of space and time, which has nothing to do with the traditional subjects of aesthetics at all, Kant had gone so far as to write this:

The Germans are the only ones who now employ the word "aesthetics" to designate that which others call the critique of taste. The ground for this is a failed hope, held by the excellent analyst Baumgarten, of bringing the critical judging of the beautiful under principles of reason, and elevating its rules to a science. But this effort is futile. For the putative rules or criteria are merely empirical as far as their sources are concerned, and can therefore never serve as *a priori* rules according to which our judgments of taste must be directed, rather the latter constitutes the genuine touchstone of the correctness of the former. For this reason it is advisable again to desist from the use of this term and to save it for that doctrine which is true science.[22]

In other words – and this is quite consistent with what Kant usually held in his lectures on anthropology – judgments of taste, even though they make claims about how others can be expected to respond to objects on the basis of our own feelings of pleasure (or displeasure) in them, are *empirical*: they do not rest on any *a priori* concepts or principles; rather we learn to make them in a fairly reliable way by observing the responses of those around us and correlating them to our own responses. Indeed, for this reason Kant had frequently maintained that people could not learn how to make judgments of taste except by growing up in society; someone growing up in the circumstances of a Robinson Crusoe could never learn how to determine whether his own responses corresponded to those of others, even if the idea of doing so somehow occurred to him.[23] Thus, it seems, in 1781 Kant no longer thought there could be a systematic philosophical treatment of the principles of feeling and taste, let alone a critique of taste, which if it were to be anything like a critique of pure reason would have to discover foundations for *a priori* principles of taste. And while in revising the first *Critique* in 1786 Kant ameliorated this harsh assessment to the extent of adding that the rules of taste are merely empirical as far as their "most prominent" sources are concerned and allowing that the term "aesthetics" might be "shared" with transcendental philosophy, taking it "partly in a transcendental meaning, partly in a psychological meaning,"[24] he still gave no indication that he intended to avail himself of this loophole in order to write a critique of taste.

Kant's 1785 *Groundwork for the Metaphysics of Morals* was not meant as a separate critique of practical reason; Kant's primary intention in this work was to provide a sufficiently clear formulation of the fundamental principle of morality – a principle which he took every person to be tacitly aware of and inherently to acknowledge, although not in a sufficiently clear form to prevent its corruption by temptations also present in ordinary human nature[25] – to allow him to proceed to the detailed formulation of our legal and ethical rights and obligations, in what would eventually become the *Metaphysics of Morals*. The reception of this work, particularly of its attempt to derive the binding force of the moral law from the freedom of the human will in its section III, convinced Kant that he had to do enough additional work on foundational questions to merit a separate *Critique of Practical Reason*, although this had not been part of his original plan of 1772. This new *Critique* greatly amplified Kant's treatment of the problem of freedom of the will, and reversed the argument of the *Groundwork* by holding that the fact of the freedom of the will could only be inferred from our awareness of the binding obligation of the moral law, rather than the validity of the moral law being inferred from any independent proof of the freedom of the will. But while this amplified the argument of the *Critique of Pure Reason* by showing how the actuality and not merely the possibility of the freedom of the will could be established on moral rather than theoretical grounds, it did not fundamentally alter the argument of the first *Critique* in any way, *a fortiori* it did not alter that work's negative assessment of the possibilities for a critique of taste. The second *Critique* in fact almost ends with an allusion to what would become the central argument of Kant's treatment of taste in the third: in contrasting pleasure in the beauty of objects with a moral interest in their existence based in pure practical reason, Kant characterizes the former, pleasure in beauty, as "a consciousness of the harmony of our powers of representation . . . in which we feel our entire cognitive faculty (understanding and imagination) strengthened . . . a satisfaction that can also be communicated to others."[26] However, this substantive view about the nature of aesthetic experience, which Kant had already held in very much this form since the time of the first *Critique*,[27] did not signal a change in Kant's recent view about the possibility of a *critique* of taste; once again, nothing said in the second *Critique* gives any indication that Kant intended to write a third one, let alone immediately start working on it.

So we return to where we began, and ask again what Kant could suddenly have discovered in the few weeks after finishing the second *Critique* that persuaded him that a third one was possible and necessary after all. We know now that it could not have been simply the connection between taste and the faculty of feeling, as contrasted to the faculties of cognition and desire, for that division had been part of Kant's views for close to two decades. However, we also now know what obstacle Kant believed he had to overcome in order to write a critique of taste: the *Critique of Pure Reason* had dashed Baumgartian hopes for a philosophy of taste on the ground that taste permitted only empirical generalizations, not *a priori* principles; so for Kant suddenly to have embarked on a critique of taste, he must have become persuaded that in some way or other taste does have some kind of *a priori* principle. Yet the reader will quickly see from the third *Critique* itself that Kant did not change the view, frequently evinced in his lectures, that there can be no mechanical and determinate rules for individual judgments of taste, such as the supposedly Aristotelian rule of dramaturgy that all the action of a play must transpire within twenty-four hours, which could guide aesthetic judgment in the same way that one geometrical theorem can lead to the next.[28] So what kind of *a priori* principle for taste could there be?

Here is where the connection between taste and teleology to which Kant alludes in the letter to Reinhold may come in. The letter is certainly too brief for us to know precisely what Kant had in mind in writing it, and ultimately it can only be the published work itself that tells us how Kant thought he could finally put the critique of taste on an adequate philosophical footing and connect it in an illuminating way with teleology – a subject about which he had largely been silent since his comments almost twenty-five years earlier in the *Only Possible Basis*. But the thought naturally suggests itself that in reflecting upon the connection between aesthetics and teleology Kant somehow came up with the idea of a new *kind* of *a priori* principle that would let him write a critique of taste without undermining his scruples about determinate rules for judgments on the beauty of objects. And what would such a new kind of principle be like? It would have to be one that can ground judgments about similarities among human minds, for that is what judgments of taste claim, without depending upon determinate predicates of particular objects, for that is what Kant abjures. And perhaps this is what in the most general way teleology suggested to Kant: an *a priori* principle about the relation between the human mind and the nature that surrounds it, including other human minds, that can give us confidence in the validity of our judgments without directly giving us new concepts of objects.

The two versions of the introduction to the *Critique of the Power of Judgment* suggest that Kant did indeed see the formulation of a new kind of *a priori* principle as the key to a critique of both taste and teleology, but also that it was no simple task for him to formulate such a principle;[29] and whether he did succeed in doing so has certainly been one of the fundamental issues in the interpretation of the third *Critique*. Kant's introduction will also reveal another connection between judgments of taste and teleology that appears to be quite new in Kant's philosophy, namely the idea that both judgments of taste and judgments about the purposiveness of natural objects are forms of a hitherto unrecognized kind of judgment, which Kant calls *reflecting judg-*

ment. This is not mentioned in the letter to Reinhold, but at least seems to play a central role in Kant's account in the work itself of why he has linked what had hitherto seemed the unrelated topics of taste and teleology. While previously he had recognized the ordinary function of judgment as that of subsuming a particular under a universal that is antecedently given to us, such as a pure concept in mathematics or an empirical concept in scientific classification, he now calls that function "determining judgment," in order to distinguish it from the quite different case of "reflecting judgment," in which we are not given a concept under which to subsume a particular but are instead given a particular for which we must seek to find a universal, a concept or rule of some kind that we are not immediately given.[30] Another fundamental question for the interpretation of the third *Critique* is certainly how this notion is to be understood, how well it succeeds in connecting aesthetic and teleological judgments, and in particular, given how much of Kant's detailed analysis of the character of judgments of taste had been in place for so many years, whether this notion really adds anything substantive to Kant's longstanding views.

Kant's deepest connection between taste and teleology, however, may be something he does not hint at in the letter to Reinhold at all, although it would explain why he became convinced of not only the possibility but also the necessity for a third *Critique* so soon after finishing the second. In the concluding section of the published introduction to the work, Kant claims that "the power of judgment provides the mediating concept between the concepts of nature and the concept of freedom, which makes possible the transition from the purely theoretical to the purely practical, from lawfulness in accordance with the former to the final end in accordance with the latter, in the concept of a **purposiveness** of nature; for thereby is the possibility of the final end, which can become actual only in nature and in accord with its laws, cognized."[31] The meaning of this statement can hardly be immediately clear, but it is enough to suggest that Kant had become convinced that both aesthetics and teleology have something profound to teach us about the relation between nature and morality, and that the foundations of his philosophy would not be complete until he had fully explored what this is. Somehow, without violating the distinction between the beautiful and the morally good that he had long advocated or the exclusion of human or superhuman aims from scientific explanation of natural phenomena that he had likewise long accepted, Kant suddenly saw how he could take the existence of both natural and artistic beauty and our sense of the purposiveness in the organization of nature as evidence that human beings as moral agents can nevertheless be at home in nature, and even as of value in preparing ourselves for the exercise of our moral agency. Indeed, it may have been precisely this insight that, after a decade of already enormous labor, during most of which he had been skeptical about the possibility of a critique of taste, gave Kant the strength to write an ambitious and complex third *Critique* in less than a quarter of the time it had taken him to write the first – an extraordinary accomplishment.

This introduction is not the place to expound a detailed interpretation of the motivation and meaning of the work to be presented.[32] What follows offers a succinct outline of the main themes of the work and then a brief account of the actual circumstances of its composition and publication.

II.
AN OUTLINE OF THE WORK

Introduction(s). Both the first draft of Kant's introduction and the version that he finally published are translated in the present volume (the circumstances that left us two versions will be explained in the next section). The first draft consists of twelve sections, while the published version has only nine, and only about half as many words. But the main points of the argument are similar, and may in each case be reduced to four main steps. In the first part of each introduction, Kant correlates the tripartite division of the higher faculty of cognition – as contrasted to the lower faculty of cognition, which, in the tradition of Baumgarten, is assumed to consist of sensibility and imagination – into understanding, judgment, and reason – a division already assumed in the first *Critique* – with the tripartite division of the powers of the mind more generally into cognition, feeling, and desire, and then suggests, as an hypothesis, that since understanding has been found to furnish *a priori* principles for cognition and reason the *a priori* principle for the faculty of desire (the moral law), perhaps the faculty of judgment will be shown to supply an *a priori* principle for our ability to feel pleasure and displeasure.[33] By describing this correlation as provisional,[34] Kant makes it clear that it can be proven only by the detailed arguments that will comprise the body of the work, thus that he does not expect the persuasiveness of the work as a whole to depend upon this highly abstract and one might well think artificial maneuver. Kant concludes the first part of the introduction by introducing his new distinction between the "determining" (*bestimmend*) and "reflecting" (*reflectirend*) uses of the power of judgment. In the determining use of judgment, we are supposed to be given a universal, such as a concept of pure mathematics or physics, and to have the task of finding an individual to subsume under it, while in the "reflecting" use of judgment, we are supposed to be presented with an individual, such as a beautiful scene or an intricate organism, and to seek a universal under which to subsume it.[35] It will turn out, however, that the kinds of universals that may be sought by reflecting judgment will have to be understood broadly: while in teleological judgment of an intricate organism the universal that we seek may be understood to be the concept of purpose, such as the purpose of a particular organ within the internal economy of the organism, in the case of aesthetic judgment Kant will explicitly deny that we seek to subsume the object under any particular or determinate concept at all. In this case, as Kant's argument will reveal, the only universal that we seek is the idea of interpersonal agreement in pleasure in a beautiful object or in awe at a sublime one (which is actually both awful and pleasurable). Much of the detail of Kant's account of judgments of beauty in particular was worked out long before Kant introduced this new conception of reflecting judgment, and it is an issue of continuing debate just how much of a role this notion plays in the body of the text.

Although the main body of the *Critique of the Power of Judgment* is divided into two parts, the "Critique of the Aesthetic Power of Judgment" and the "Critique of the Teleological Power of Judgment," the introductions actually consider not two but three main forms of reflecting judgment. The second of these is aesthetic judgment, which Kant initially treats as if it is directed only at beautiful objects in nature, although it will eventually turn out to comprise both the beautiful and the sublime in both nature and in art; and the third of them is teleological judgment, initially presented as concerning only purposiveness in the internal organization of organisms although it will later turn out to include judgment about the purposiveness of nature as a whole. But the first form of reflecting judgment that Kant considers, which is not subsequently treated in the main body of the book at all, is judgment about the systematicity of the body of our scientific concepts and laws itself. Here Kant's argument, presented in Sections IV through VII of the first draft and in Sections IV and V of the published version of the Introduction, is as follows. The *Critique of Pure Reason* is taken to have assured us that we can always bring the particular items in our experience under some concepts and laws, and to have provided us with the most general forms of concepts for the objects of our experiences in the categories or pure concepts of the understanding (concepts such as those of substance or causation) as well as with the most general laws of nature in the form of the principles of empirical thinking (such as the principle that every event has a cause). But all of this still leaves us the task of finding more particular concepts under which to subsume our experiences – for example, more concrete concepts of causation such as the concepts of crystallization or reproduction – and of organizing these concepts and the natural laws associated with them into a system with various formal properties that Kant spells out.[36] The tasks of seeking such particular concepts intermediate between the categories and our actual observations or empirical intuitions and of organizing them into a coherent system are assigned to the reflecting power of judgment as an instance of its general task of seeking to find universals for given concepts, and Kant assumes that reflecting judgment has to have an *a priori* principle by which to be guided in carrying out these tasks. But he is careful to make clear that this *a priori* principle of reflecting judgment is indeed of a different character from the *a priori* principles of understanding or reason. It does not directly determine what kinds of properties our experiences must have in order to represent objects (e.g., being experiences of enduring substances) or what our maxims of action must be like in order to be morally acceptable (i.e., universalizable). Instead, it amounts only to the general assumption, supposed to be necessary for guiding and encouraging the conduct of our scientific inquiry, that nature itself has the kind of systematic organization that we seek to find in it. As Kant puts it in the first draft of the introduction, the *a priori* principle of reflecting judgment is simply that "Nature specifies its general laws into empirical ones, in accordance with the form of a logical system, in behalf of the power of judgment."[37] This principle merely confirms our authorization to seek for systematicity in our concepts and laws, or is what the published Introduction calls a principle of the "heautonomy" of judgment, a law prescribed not so much to nature as to judgment itself.[38]

One question that suggests itself at this stage in Kant's argument is just how much of a model this sort of *a priori* principle can provide for the *a priori* principles of aesthetic and teleological judgment that are subsequently to be sought. Another question is, what has become of the connection between judgment and the feeling of pleasure that was the starting point for Kant's argument? In the first draft of the introduction, Kant does not address this question at all. In the published introduction, perhaps having noticed the omission, Kant does address it, arguing that since the attainment of every aim is accompanied with pleasure, success in realizing our objective of finding systematicity in our concepts and laws of nature must also have been accompanied by pleasure, although we take this success so much for granted that we barely notice this pleasure.[39] This argument seems perfunctory, but it provides an important premise for the account of aesthetic judgment that Kant next introduces: It implies that if pleasure is always the result of the attainment of an end, and if, further, universally valid pleasure must be the result of the realization of a universally valid objective,[40] then there must be some universally valid objective that is fulfilled in the case of our pleasure in beauty as well.

Kant's ensuing account of aesthetic judgment is thus the third main stage of both introductions. Section VIII in the first draft and Section

VII of the published introduction present a capsule summary of the account that will be expounded in detail in the "Analytic of the Beautiful" of the main text. Kant begins by connecting aesthetic judgment or the judgment of taste to what he calls "subjective" purposiveness, a condition in which a fundamental purpose of the cognitive subject is fulfilled, but fulfilled in such a way that it is accompanied by a feeling of pleasure, the only kind of sensation that we do not automatically transform into a predicate of objects and thus interpret exclusively as a sign of our own mental condition.[41] Kant's basic idea is then that when the free play of the imagination with the representations offered to us by an object, unguided and unconstrained by any predetermined concept of what the object is or ought to be in order to serve any particular theoretical or practical purpose, nevertheless seems to us to satisfy the general aim of the understanding to find unity in all of our experience, we respond to this fulfillment of the underlying aim of cognition with pleasure, and a pleasure that is noticeable and enduring because the satisfaction of our general cognitive aim in these circumstances seems contingent and is not taken for granted by us. This is Kant's famous conception of the response to beauty as a free and harmonious play of imagination – our ability to take in and reproduce sensory impressions and images – and understanding.[42] Kant then signals that he intends to argue in the main text that since we all have the same cognitive faculties and they can be expected to work in the same way – this premise is, in fact, the *a priori* principle of aesthetic judgment as a form of reflecting judgment – it is reasonable for us to expect that at least in ideal circumstances others will have the same responses to objects that we do, and thus we can claim universal validity for our pleasure by means of a judgment of taste.[43]

After this brief account of the judgment of beauty, Kant moves directly (in Section IX of the first draft and Section X of the published version) to the last of the three main forms of reflecting judgment that he considers in the Introduction, teleological judgment on the purposiveness of some objects in nature, the ones we now call organisms but that Kant tended to call "organized beings." Here Kant does not tell us as much about what is to follow as he does in the case of aesthetic judgment; he contrasts aesthetic judgment on the *form* of particular objects as such with teleological judgments about the "correspondence of [an object's] form with the possibility of the thing itself, in accordance with a concept of it which precedes and contains the ground of this form."[44] What this means is obscure, and we have to wait until the main body of the text to learn that Kant means that organisms have a kind of internal organization that is for various reasons difficult for us to understand unless we see it as the product of an antecedent concept of the object on the part of a designer of it, and that once we introduce the idea of a designer it becomes inevitable for us to see the organism and even nature as a whole as having some sort of rational purpose – although the principle that nature has a purpose, which is the unstated *a priori* principle of teleological judgment, can only be a regulative principle for reflecting judgment, not a constitutive principle for determining judgment that actually contributes to our scientific knowledge of nature. (It may also be noted that neither here nor in the body of the text does Kant attempt to draw any special connection between teleological judgment and the feeling of pleasure.)

In the published introduction, Kant concludes with the claim already alluded to at the end of the previous section, that the faculty of judgment allows us to bridge the gulf between the legislations and domains of theoretical knowledge on the one hand and freedom on the other.[45] What he means by this is again unexplained at this stage, although the sequel will show that he has a number of claims in mind: that our disinterested affection for beauty prepares us for the non–self-regarding respect and love for mankind that is required of us by morality; that the existence of beauty in nature gives us a hint that nature is hospitable to human morality; and that we can only give content to the idea of a purpose for nature that we are led to by our reflection on the purposiveness of organisms by thinking of human moral development as the ultimate end of nature.[46] These links between beauty and purposiveness on the one hand and Kant's moral vision of the place of mankind in the world on the other are the substantive links between aesthetics and teleology that lie behind and give importance to their superficial connection by means of the technical conception of reflecting judgment.

Having discussed only the judgment of beauty in the body of the introduction, Kant surprises us at the end of the first draft by dividing aesthetic judgment into judgment on the beautiful and on the sublime, and teleological judgment into judgment on the internal purposiveness of organisms and on the relative or external purposiveness of them, or their contribution to the purposiveness of nature as a whole.[47] The first of these distinctions is reflected in the division of the "Critique of the Aesthetic Power of Judgment," the first main part of the whole *Critique*, into two books, the "Analytic of the Beautiful" and the "Analytic of the Sublime." The second distinction is not reflected so explicitly in the organization of the second main part of the *Critique*, the "Critique of the Teleological Power of Judgment," but in fact underlies the division between its "Analytic" and its "Methodology" (which are separated by a "Dialectic"). We will now briefly describe the contents of these parts of the main text of the *Critique*.

"Critique of the Aesthetic Power of Judgment": "Analytic of the Beautiful." The twenty-two numbered sections of this part of the

Critique present the detailed account of judgments on beauty that Kant sketched in the Introduction. The argument is organized into four "moments," mirroring the four headings for functions of judgment and categories that Kant introduced in the *Critique of Pure Reason*, namely quality, quantity, relation, and modality; this organization illuminates what Kant has to say in some ways and obscures it in others. Under the rubric of "quality," Kant begins his discussion by premising that judgments of taste are disinterested, that is, arise solely from the contemplation of their objects without regard to any purposes that can be fulfilled or interests that can be served by their existence (§ 2). In this way, judgments of taste differ from judgments about the mere agreeableness of the sensory stimulation offered by objects and the consumption of them, which do create an empirical interest in the existence of (more) objects of the relevant type (§ 3), and also from judgments about the goodness of objects, which depend upon antecedent concepts of the mediate or immediate use or the moral value of objects, and also create an interest in their existence (§ 4). Kant does not think that aesthetic judgments involve a different *kind* of pleasure from judgments about the agreeable and the good, but a different *relation* of their objects to pleasure, that is, a difference in the way in which objects produce pleasure (§ 5).

The disinterestedness of judgments of taste is not an uncontroversial premise for Kant's entire argument: although it had been given prominence earlier in the century by the Earl of Shaftesbury and Francis Hutcheson, it had by no means been universally accepted.[48] It also does not lead to Kant's next point as seamlessly as Kant would like: Kant infers the "quantity" of judgments of taste, their "universal subjective validity," from their disinterestedness (§ 6), even though this does not strictly follow – a judgment could be disinterested and yet still be arbitrary or idiosyncratic. But Kant introduces two key independent arguments under the heading of "quality," and in many ways this part of the "Analytic of the Beautiful" (§§ 6–9) can be considered the real starting point of Kant's entire account. First Kant appeals to common parlance to support the claim that in judgments of taste we speak with a "universal voice"[49] while in judgments of agreeableness we do not: we can say, "This wine is agreeable to me," thus defeating any expectation that others must also find it so; but we do not add "to me" when we say, "This flower is beautiful" or "This painting is beautiful" (§ 7), and thus allow the claim to interpersonal agreement that we ordinarily imply in our description of objects to stand. Thus in aesthetic judgments we claim "subjective universal validity," that is, although we can never claim that every object in a certain class – a certain kind of flower, a certain kind of poem or musical composition – is beautiful just because it fulfills the criteria for membership in that class, and thus cannot claim "objective universal validity" for judgments of taste, we can reasonably claim that at least under appropriate circumstances (which of course cannot always be realized) everyone else who experiences an object that we find beautiful should experience the same pleasure in it that we do. In the section that he describes as "the key to the critique of taste" (§ 9), Kant then introduces his theory of the free play of imagination and understanding as the cause of our pleasure in beauty. A subsequent "deduction" of judgments of taste (§§ 21 and 38) will then argue that because of the shared nature of human cognitive capacities, this free play can be expected to occur in the same way in everyone, and so the judgment of taste's claim to speak with a universal voice can be sustained.

In the next part of the "Analytic," on the moment of "relation" in the judgment of taste, Kant makes some of his most controversial but also some of his most revealing points. Kant's general claim here is that our pleasure in a beautiful object is related to our perception of the form of purposiveness in it (§ 11). This makes it sound as if a beautiful object is one that at least appears to us to have been designed, as if there were some characteristic way that designed objects look. But Kant does not mean this; rather, he just means that a beautiful object satisfies our subjective purpose in cognition without serving any other, more concrete purpose. However, by what appears to be a sleight of hand, Kant equates a beautiful object's form of purposiveness with the "purposiveness of its form" (§ 13),[50] understood as a property of the spatiotemporal form of objects narrowly understood. Thus Kant maintains, for example, that in the pictorial and plastic arts it is always the design but never the color that is beautiful, while in an art like music it is the formal structure of the composition but not the tones of the instrumentation that is crucial (§ 14).[51] This "formalism" has dominated the popular conception of Kant's aesthetics, but it is not justified by anything in Kant's premises nor motivated by anything other than his desire to minimize sources of disagreement in the objects of taste; moreover, when Kant later turns to his detailed discussion of the fine arts, he clearly takes this narrow version of formalism back, arguing that a work of art is beautiful when we respond with a free play of our imagination and understanding to a harmony among *all* of its perceptible features as well as to its content and intellectual associations as well.[52] The tenuousness of Kant's commitment to formalism is also evident in the last two sections of this third "moment," which instead hint at fundamental connections between works of art and moral significance. In § 16, Kant introduces a distinction between "free" and "adherent" beauty: the former is beauty that is found in an object without any concept of its purpose at all, while the latter is a form of beauty that is perceived when the form of an object is felt to cohere freely with its intended purpose, as in a work of architecture, or even its moral end, as in the case of human beauty. There is a difference between these two kinds of beauty, to be sure, but Kant couldn't call the latter a kind of beauty at all if he held rigidly to the view that beauty always concerns the form of an object alone. Finally, in § 17 Kant discusses what he calls the "ideal of beauty." An object is an ideal of beauty when it is not merely one among many that are beautiful for everyone, but is in some way uniquely or paradigmatically beautiful. Kant argues that only the human figure seen as an expression of the incomparable worth of human morality can be seen as an ideal of beauty.[53] Again, Kant could not call this a form of beauty at all unless the harmony between the perceivable form of a human being and the abstract idea of moral worth were a fit subject for the free play of imagination and understanding.

In the fourth and last part of the "Analytic of the Beautiful," Kant discusses the "modality" of the judgment of taste. In part, this discussion reiterates what Kant had already said under the rubric of quantity: the modality of the judgment of taste is "the necessity of the assent of **all** to a judgment that is regarded as an example of a universal rule that cannot be given."[54] But this formulation also introduces a theme that Kant will emphasize more later, namely, that in aesthetic judgment upon nature and art but also in the production of works of art we do not have *rules* that we can mechanically follow, but at most *examples* that can, especially in the case of art, provide us with models not for imitation but for inspiration.[55] This is what Kant calls the "exemplary" necessity of the aesthetic – of beauty itself as well as the judgment on beauty. Kant then goes on to make explicit the argument that underlies the earlier "key to the critique of taste," namely the argument that we can speak with a universal voice on matters of taste because of the underlying similarity of our cognitive faculties (§ 21). Kant will return to this argument later in the *Critique* – obviously he felt it needs more support than it gets here, which it certainly does, although whether he succeeds in proving it is another question of continuing debate.

"Critique of the Aesthetic Power of Judgment": "Analytic of the Sublime." Here Kant expands upon the theme of the sublime, which was a well-established topic in eighteenth-century aesthetics, but which he had hardly mentioned in the introduction.[56] Once again Kant says that he will organize his discussion around the four headings of quantity, quality, relation, and modality,[57] but this division is overlaid with another distinction, that between the mathematical and dynamical sublime, which may make it hard at first to see how Kant is using the four original categories. In fact, his account of the mathematical sublime is organized around the concepts of quantity and quality while the discussion of the dynamical sublime represents the application of the concepts of relation and modality.

The experience of the mathematical sublime (§§ 25–6) arises when we try to get a grasp of something vast, not by the ordinary mathematical means of quantifying it with an arbitrarily chosen unity of measurement reiterated as often as necessary, but rather by taking it in, aesthetically, as if it were a single, absolutely great whole.[58] In fact, this is an impossible task, but the very fact that we even try it reveals that we possess not just imagination and understanding, the faculties we ordinarily use for mathematical tasks like measurement, but also the faculty of reason, which is what gives us the idea of an absolutely great whole in the first place.[59] And this is what leads to the special quality of the experience of the sublime: unlike the experience of beauty, it is not an unalloyed pleasure, but a complex feeling, consisting first of frustration at the inability of the understanding to grasp an absolute whole with the assistance of the imagination, followed by pleasure at the realization of the fact that our imagination also reflects the demands of our reason (§ 27). This complexity of the feeling of the sublime is akin to the complexity of the moral feeling of respect,[60] and leads Kant to the discussion of the dynamical sublime.

The dynamical sublime (§ 28) represents the application of the concept of relation to the experience of the sublime. The experience of the dynamical sublime is produced by the experience of vast forces in nature, such as those of towering seas or mountain ranges, in relation to which we realize that our own physical powers are puny. At the same time, however, the experience of our insignificance in relation to such physical forces also leads us to the realization that there is another force in us, the faculty of practical reason and the freedom of the will that it gives us, which gives us a value that cannot be damaged even by forces which would suffice for our physical destruction.[61] This again produces a complex mix of displeasure and pleasure, which is even closer to the moral feeling of respect. Finally, under the rubric of modality, Kant argues that we have ground to expect universal subjective validity in the experience of the sublime as well as in that of beauty (§ 29), although in the case of the sublime Kant emphasizes that the ground of agreement lies in a potential for moral sensitivity that each of us has innately but that each of us must actively *cultivate*[62] as part of our moral development. Commonality in the experience of the sublime is thus a product of our active effort to a degree that agreement about the beautiful apparently is not.

Kant's account of the sublime has drawn a great deal of interest in recent years, especially among European philosophers as well as both European and American literary theorists,[63] who have taken the Kantian sublime to provide an image for the quintessentially postmodern experience of the incomprehensibility of the world by any traditional model of rationality. It should be clear from what has just been said, however, that Kant's insistence on the complexity of the experience of the sublime precludes enlisting him in this postmodern cause: any feeling of incomprehensibility belongs only to the first stage of the feeling of the sublime, to be followed and replaced by a deep feeling of satisfaction at the power of our own reason to create moral order in the world. This should also be evident from the "General Remark" on both the beautiful and the sublime that follows § 29, in which Kant argues that "the beautiful prepares us to love something, even nature, without interest; the sublime, to esteem it, even contrary to our (sensible) interest."[64] This is Kant's first intimation of a deep connection between aesthetics and teleology in their common support for morality, which does not depend upon the abstract idea of reflecting judgment – which, as we have now seen, plays virtually no role at all in the details of Kant's accounts of the beautiful and sublime.

"Critique of the Aesthetic Power of Judgment": Deduction and Theory of Fine Art. The next twenty-five sections of the first part of the book, although they look like a continuation of the "Analytic of the Sublime," do not belong to that at all, but return to the question of the universal subjective validity of judgments of the beautiful (§§ 30–40), and then, switching gears entirely, develop Kant's theory of the fine arts (§§ 43–54). The first part of this discussion seems to go over ground well trodden in the "Analytic of the Beautiful," but the second part is a rich trove of insights for aesthetic theory that is often overlooked under the spell of the formalism of the earlier "Analytic."

Formalism plays a role in Kant's introduction of this part of the work, in which he argues that judgments on the sublime, unlike judgments on the beautiful, do not need any deduction beyond their initial exposition because they are induced by the formlessness rather than the form of their objects, and thus in a way are not about objects outside us at all. This would carry weight if the point of the following deduction were to prove that we are justified in applying a certain predicate to objects, or even to proving that objects of a certain sort (e.g., beautiful objects) must exist – but it is not, since Kant specifically abjures any attempt "to explain why nature has spread beauty so extravagantly everywhere."[65] Instead, the point of the deduction is to prove that we are justified in expecting agreement in judgments of taste because of the shared character of our cognitive capacities, and it would seem that if this still has to be shown in the case of judgments about the beautiful that it would also still need to be shown in the case of judgments on the sublime. In fact, it is not clear that this still needs to be shown at all, nor that Kant's official "deduction of judgments of taste" in § 38 adds very much to what was earlier argued in § 21.

Yet there is much in this part of the work that clarifies even if it does not substantially augment what has already been said. In §§ 32 and 33, Kant simplifies the previous four moments of aesthetic judgment into two "logical peculiarities" of judgments of taste. Such judgments are peculiar first because they claim the agreement of everyone even though they concern mere feelings of pleasure (§ 32) and second because they claim such agreement even though they cannot be proven by any traditional rules of criticism (§ 33). Both of these peculiarities can be understood, Kant argues, if we understand the pleasure in beauty as the product of the free play of the faculties of imagination and understanding (§ 35, which reiterates the arguments of the introduction and § 9). In the next two sections, Kant then clarifies the kind of apriority that is involved in a judgment of taste: we can never know in advance of the experience of an object that we will find it pleasing, thus the connection of pleasure to the object is empirical; but if we do think that our pleasure in an object is due to the harmony of imagination and understanding, then we feel justified in expecting that pleasure in everyone else, and *that* expectation is *a priori* (§§ 36–7). Then, in § 38, Kant repeats his assertion that under ideal circumstances an object that produces the harmony of our cognitive faculties in one person can reasonably be expected to do so in everyone else, because it must be assumed that our cognitive faculties all work in the same way. Kant does not in fact add to his previous reasons for assuming this somewhat dubious premise, but he does usefully clarify one point, namely, that errors in assigning particular experiences of pleasure to the harmony of the faculties as their cause need not undermine our general right to make aesthetic judgments, any more than the occasional error in any kind of empirical judgment or even in mathematics undermines our right to make that sort of judgment altogether.[66] Kant's distinction between what is empirical and what is *a priori* in a judgment of taste has prepared the way for this clarification.

Kant also clarifies the point that in making judgments of taste we do not just expect agreement *from* other people but to a certain degree also expect agreement *of* them, that is, regard it "as it were a duty."[67] To explain this, some connection between taste and morality must be found, although this connection cannot be so direct that it would undermine the freedom of imagination that is the essence of the experience of beauty by any obvious didacticism. Kant considers two possible bases for this connection. First (§ 41) he notes that beautiful objects naturally gratify our inclination to sociability: we like to agree with other people, so we like objects about which we can agree. Kant dismisses this as the basis for a merely "empirical interest in the beautiful"; and although he has not explained why an interest in (as opposed to a judgment about) the beautiful has to be *a priori*, this topic does provide him with a useful occasion for pointing out how easily a perfectly natural desire to agree with others can degenerate into a rather disagreeable tendency to pride ourselves on the beautiful things that we own. However, he does argue that we can find a ground for a more purely "intellectual interest" (§ 42) in the beautiful insofar as we take the natural existence of beautiful objects, which serve our fundamental cognitive purpose, as a kind of evidence that nature is hospitable to the realization of our ultimate moral purposes as well.[68] This is obviously a deep point of connection between Kant's aesthetics and his teleology.

The next main part of the work is Kant's treatment of fine art, in which he radically revises the apparent formalism of the "Analytic of the Beautiful" by making clear that what is essential to all art is that it result from and produce a free play between the imagination, understanding, and even reason, not that it restrict our response to the perceptual form of its products in any narrow sense. Kant begins by distinguishing fine art from nature (§ 43), handicraft (§ 44), and natural science (§ 47), but the heart of his argument lies in his claim that fine art is always a product of genius (§ 46). This discussion, although deeply influenced by the popularity of this topic in the eighteenth century,[69] is given a characteristically Kantian twist. Kant argues (§ 49) that genius is what gives a work "spirit" or "soul" (*Geist*),[70] and that it does this by finding for a work an "aesthetic idea" – a central image – which on the one hand makes palpable and animates a "rational idea" such as a moral concept and on the other leads to an inexhaustible wealth of more concrete sensory images and experiences.[71] Genius thus consists in the ability to come up with both content for works of art and forms for the expression of this content that will at the same time manifest the freedom of the imagination of the artist and yet leave room for and stimulate the freedom of the imagination of the audience[72] – a tall order, of course, which is why genius is rare.

Kant stresses that genius is a gift of nature,[73] which raises the question of why the existence of artistic genius isn't as much evidence of nature's hospitality to mankind as the existence of natural beauty, and thus why art isn't just as appropriate a subject for the intellectual interest in the beautiful as nature. Kant does not answer this question. Instead, the last few sections of his treatment of the fine arts classify them (§ 51) and compare their merits (§ 53) on the basis of their varying potential for the expression of aesthetic ideas. This was an exercise of longstanding fascination for Kant,[74] and his final version of it should dispel any assumption that Kant supported a formalist theory of art.

"Critique of the Aesthetic Power of Judgment": "Dialectic." The inclusion of a "Dialectic" in Kant's treatment of judgments of taste seems like an arbitrary imposition upon it of the form of the *Critique of Pure Reason*, and it seems as if Kant is once again just going over well-trodden ground. He sets up the dialectic as an "antinomy" between two "commonplaces" about taste, on the one hand that "Everyone has his own taste" and thus that there can be no "disputing" about taste (deciding about it "by means of proofs"), on the other hand that it is certainly reasonable to "argue" about judgments of taste, which must imply some sort of connection to concepts.[75] Kant says that this antinomy can only be resolved by showing that judgments of taste depend on an *indeterminate* concept, which makes debate reasonable but does not provide any criteria for evaluating objects that can be mechanically applied to them.[76] One would have thought that the concept of the free play of imagination and understanding was just such a concept, which does not offer us any way to prove our judgments of taste but still makes it rational to expect agreement in them and to seek it by means of discussion; but now Kant instead introduces the idea of a supersensible substratum of both human nature and nature at large – a thing in itself lying behind the appearance of our difference from each other and from the rest of nature – as that which plays this role.[77] This step seems unmotivated, but is another anticipation of the argument of the "Critique of the Teleological Power of Judgment," in which Kant will argue that the experience of organization in nature inevitably leads us to the idea of a designer and purpose beyond nature, which has no scientific value but has great moral value in leading us to see our own moral development as the only possible ultimate purpose of nature.

The "Dialectic" is also valuable for its concluding section (§ 59), in which Kant argues that the beautiful is a symbol of the morally good because our *experience* of beauty is an experience of the freedom of the imagination that is in many ways similar though by no means identical to moral freedom, of which we do not have any direct experience at all.[78] Here aesthetic experience again seems to prepare us for morality by making the possibility of the freedom that we have to exercise in morality palpable to us, although in the one-section "Methodology" that follows and concludes the "Critique of the Aesthetic Power of Judgment" Kant seems to contradict this claim by saying that "the true propaedeutic for the grounding of taste is the development of moral ideas and the cultivation of the moral feeling."[79] In the end, it seems that Kant can only possibly conclude that the development of taste and the development of morality are mutually supportive and reinforcing.

"Critique of the Teleological Power of Judgment": "Analytic."
The second half of the book is shorter than the first and its argument
more focused, so it can be more briefly described. This should hardly
be taken to imply that Kant's teleology is less important than his
aesthetics: on the contrary, it is precisely Kant's teleology that deserves
the title of "the Crowning Phase of the Critical Philosophy."[80]

Kant begins the "Analytic of Teleological Judgment" by distinguishing between the "relative" and "internal purposiveness" of things
in nature. Relative purposiveness would be one thing's existence for
the sake of another, and on the face of it we have no reason to think
that it is an objective fact that anything in nature is relatively purposive
for anything else: it may seem natural for us to think that plants exist
for the sake of herbivores, and herbivores for the sake of carnivores,
and all of them ultimately for the sake of omnivores like ourselves; but
if we confine ourselves to an entirely naturalistic view of things then
for all we know everything else exists to trim or fertilize the plants
(§ 63). Internal purposiveness, however, is what obtains when certain
parts or organs of an organism exist for the sake of others, and where
indeed the parts are both the cause and effect of the whole; and, Kant
argues, certain properties and functions of organisms force us to look
at them as having internal purposiveness (§ 64); for instance, we cannot
but see the leaves of a tree as both contributing to the health of the
whole and yet depending for their own existence on the health of the
whole.[81] But because the human mind is limited to a unidirectional
comprehension of causality, we cannot in fact understand how the
whole can be both cause and effect of its parts; we can only see it as
the effect. The only way we can make internal purposiveness comprehensible to ourselves is by analogizing it to human intentional or
artistic production, where an antecedent *concept* of the object can be
seen as the cause of the existence of the parts that are in turn the cause
of the whole.[82] Thus, the recognition of the internal purposiveness of
organisms in nature inevitably leads us to the idea of a designer and
thus a plan for those organisms, and once we have formed this idea, of
an author of organisms, it is natural for us to think of it as the idea of
an author of nature as a whole as well[83] – and once we have gotten this
far, it will be inevitable for us to try to think of a point or purpose for
nature as a whole, for we can hardly think of a planner without a point
for its plans. Thus our experience of internal purposiveness leads us to
reintroduce the concept of the relative purposiveness of nature after
all. However, Kant stresses, such thoughts can play no role in natural
science at all, but are only a reflection of the limitations of our scientific
comprehension – limits which seem inescapable for us but which we
cannot ascribe to nature itself (§ 78).

"Critique of the Teleological Power of Judgment": "Dialectic."
Kant pursues this argument – which, it must be noted, has made no attempt to connect teleological judgment with the feeling of pleasure at all – in the "Dialectic." Here he sets up another antinomy, now between the maxims that "All generation of material things is possible in accordance with merely mechanical laws" and "Some generation of such things is not possible in accordance with merely mechanical laws."[84] Here finally appealing to his introductory distinction between determining and reflective uses of judgment, Kant argues that if we were to take these to be constitutive principles of determining judgment, they would be in outright contradiction, but that if we take them to be merely regulative principles of reflecting judgment, we can acknowledge that there may be limits to our powers to explain things according to purely mechanical laws – ones on which all properties and changes in the whole are due to antecedent properties and changes in their parts – yet that we should still seek to press our mechanical explanations, which are the essence of natural science, as far as they can go (§ 71). This solution is somewhat unsatisfactory, for it begins to become unclear just why we should assume that there is any definite limit to our powers of mechanical explanation at all. And as Kant continues, his solution seems to shift back to something more like the original position of his early essay on *The Only Possible Basis for a Proof of the Existence of God*, with one addition: Kant now seems to argue that (§ 78) once we have been led to the idea of an intelligent author of nature by our experience of the unique internal purposiveness of organisms, we can even imagine being able to give a complete mechanical explanation of everything in nature while also conceiving that the completely mechanical laws of nature are themselves the means by which the author of nature achieves his ultimate purpose.[85] In other words, organisms teach us to think of nature at two levels, as governed by natural law and as having a point that can be achieved through natural law. (This argument follows two dense but fascinating sections [§§ 76–77] in which Kant argues that the existence of organisms is another example of the *contingency* that is ineliminable from our understanding of reality given the insuperable difference between our intuitions and concepts: our concepts can never fully comprehend the reality we can only intuit.)

"Critique of the Teleological Power of Judgment": "Methodology." Unlike the "Critique of the Aesthetic Power of Judgment," the "Critique of the Teleological Power of Judgment" has a long and intricate "Methodology on the Application of Teleological Judgment," not one section but twelve that occupy more pages than the preceding "Analytic" and "Dialectic" combined, and that in many ways represent

Kant's final statement of his most fundamental philosophical testament. Kant begins with several sections on the theory of organic reproduction, in which he almost but not quite argues for the possibility of a proto-Darwinian theory of evolution: he argues that merely mechanical means (adaptation, although not yet natural selection) could account for variations in the form of living species, but not for the origins of life itself (§ 80). The heart of this part of the work, however, concerns the question of how we are to apply the idea of a purpose for nature as a whole to which we have been led by the preceding arguments. Again Kant reminds us that if we take a purely naturalistic view of nature, we cannot pick out anything in it, even mankind considered as one more natural species, as its ultimate end or purpose (§§ 82–3); the experience of organisms can lead us to the idea of a purpose, but, as an idea of the merely reflecting power of judgment, cannot by itself make this idea determinate. In order to make the idea of a purpose for nature determinate, we need to introduce an end that has *unconditional* value, something that can only be an end and not in turn a means for something else – and the only candidate for this is humanity itself, not as a merely natural species but as a moral being (§ 84). To be an end of nature, however, mankind in its moral capacity must be thought of as existing *in* nature, and this means that it cannot be merely human *virtue* that is the end of nature, but a natural condition, namely human happiness, although happiness as the product of human virtue. In other words, it must be what Kant calls the "highest good," the maximal possible human happiness as the product of human virtue, that is seen as the ultimate end of nature.[86] Once again, of course, Kant stresses that this is not a theoretical claim about nature, but a regulative principle that can lead us to apply our powers in behalf of this end, which is already set for us by morality itself.[87]

This is a new argument for Kant: previously he had argued only that morality itself requires us to think of nature as suitable for the realization of the moral object of the highest good,[88] but now he argues that what starts out as a purely *scientific* experience, the observation of organisms in nature, inevitably leads us to the thought of a purpose for nature that can only be provided by morality. The "crowning phase" of the critical philosophy is thus the recognition that science and morality ultimately bring us to the same place: starting from either, we come to see that nature can and must be seen as the sphere in which human beings not only can but must attempt to establish an order in which each can work for happiness in harmony with the happiness of all. Aesthetics can prepare us for morality, but teleology reveals the full power of its demand.

The remainder of the "Methodology" explores the limits of teleology as the basis for a theoretical proof of the existence of God (§ 85) and its power as the basis for a moral proof of the existence of God (§§ 86–91). In these sections Kant expands upon arguments given in the first two *Critiques*, such as his argument that only the need to postulate the existence of God as the condition for the possibility of realizing the highest good can justify us in attributing omniscience, omnipotence, and omnibenevolence to our conception of him.[89] He then concludes with one of his most detailed discussions of what he means by a moral rather than theoretical proof (§§ 90–1), complementing his discussions of this issue in the first two *Critiques*[90] and also in the *Jäsche Logic*. These sections merit careful study by every student of Kant – as does indeed the whole *Critique of the Power of Judgment*.

III.

THE COMPOSITION AND PUBLICATION OF THE WORK

We know very little about the timing and sequence of Kant's work on the *Critique of the Power of Judgment* between his letter to Reinhold in December 1787 and his transmission of the first major piece of manuscript to his new publisher in Berlin, François Théodore de Lagarde,[91] on 21 January 1790. We do have at least one note that is clearly an attempt at an outline for the work – which shows a definite division between the treatments of the beautiful and the sublime, and hints that the introduction must concern the "divisions" of our mental powers, while making no mention of teleology at all – but the editor of Kant's posthumous materials, Erich Adickes, was not able to date this note more precisely than the general period 1785–89, so that tells us little.[92] A letter from Kant's longtime Riga publisher Johann Friedrich Hartknoch dated 6 January 1788 shows that Hartknoch expected Kant to deliver both "the critique of beautiful taste and that of practical reason" to his printer Grunert (in Halle) shortly,[93] but clearly Kant was to deliver in the near future only the *Critique of Practical Reason*, which Hartknoch published that spring. Only four letters written by Kant during 1788 survive; two of these are brief letters on academic business, and neither of the two more substantial letters (one to Reinhold and one to Johann Schultz) refer to work on the third *Critique* at all. A letter to Marcus Herz on 26 May 1789 suggests that Kant was certainly working on the book at that time: he gently chides Herz for sending him a large manuscript by Salomon Maimon, saying, "What are you thinking of, dearest friend, in sending me a large package of the most subtle investigations . . . I who in my 66th year am still burdened with the extensive work of completing my plan (partly in producing the last part of the critique, namely that of the *power of judgment*, which should appear soon)" (however, the rest of the letter shows that in spite of his complaint Kant read Maimon's manuscript quite carefully).[94] On 2 October 1789, Kant wrote to Lagarde that the manuscript had been completed for "several weeks," but that the "final sheets still needed to be gone through and transcribed," which other business had prevented him from doing.[95] On 15 October, Kant wrote to Lagarde again, now telling him that he would have to postpone the remaining work until the end of November, though repeating that the manuscript "is for my part already finished and needs only transcription and collation"; this letter is also significant because in it Kant asks Lagarde to hire his former student Johann Gottfried Carl Christian Kiesewetter (1766–1819) as "corrector" for the printing of the book, which would take place in Berlin.[96] (In his letter of 19 November Kiesewetter tells Kant that Lagarde had indeed offered him the job.)[97] On 9 January 1790, Lagarde wrote Kant with "the most pressing request" that Kant send him the manuscript, because one of the best printers in Berlin (Wegener) was holding a press open for the work but could not do so much longer. On 21 January Kant wrote him back, saying that he had sent the first part of the manuscript with that day's post: 40 out of 84 sheets, not including 17 sheets of introduction (which Kant says he "might yet abbreviate"), and promises that the remainder would be in the mail in 14 days – "which you can count on." In spite of not having delivered the whole manuscript, Kant then proceeds to press Lagarde to have the book ready for the Leipzig Easter book fair, and to tell Kiesewetter at once if that was going to be a problem. Finally, the letter spells out Kant's terms for letting Lagarde publish the book: twenty free copies, four of them on fine paper, and two ducats per sheet for the first edition of one thousand copies.[98] That same day, Kant also wrote to Kiesewetter, telling him that the manuscript was on its way and urging him too to press Lagarde to have the book ready by Easter. He also told Kiesewetter to make sure that Lagarde is not "cheap" with him.[99] On 29 January Lagarde wrote Kant that the manuscript had arrived, reassured him that it would be printed by Easter, and agreed to Kant's terms.[100] On 9 February, Kant wrote Lagarde that he had sent another 40 sheets of manuscript, leaving only three sheets that he had not yet corrected and an introduction, which he now expected to be "12 sheets strong," and which he expected to send in another 14 days.[101] The next day, obviously not having gotten Kant's latest letter or manuscript, Lagarde sent Kant the first two printed sheets of the work, although it was still expected that Kiesewetter would have primary responsibility for proofreading in Berlin.[102] Lagarde sent another sheet on 14 February, and on 16 February acknowledged the receipt of the second package of manuscript. On 9 March, Kant sent the final portion of the manuscript, now sheets 81 through 89, to Lagarde, but once again told him that he still needed a little more time to finish the preface and introduction, now saying that "the already finished introduction that lies before me, since it has turned out to be too extensive, must be abbreviated."[103] Finally, on 25 March, Kant wrote Lagarde that on 22 March he had sent the final portion of the manuscript, "consisting of 10 sheets of introduction and preface together with 2 sheets of title," and listing some of the people who should receive complimentary copies of the published book, including Friedrich Heinrich Jacobi, Reinhold, Marcus Herz, and of course Kiesewetter.[104] Lagarde wrote back on 1 April that he had received the material, and, one is tempted to say miraculously, had the printed books ready for the Leipzig book fair in the last week of the same month.[105] Lagarde wrote Kant again on 22 May, after his return from Leipzig, telling Kant that he had distributed the free copies as directed, and sending Kant a total of 201 Reichs dollars in fulfillment of their contract. (That was clearly a substantial amount of money, nearly equal to the 220-dollar annual raise for which Kant had personally thanked King Friedrich Wilhelm II, who would later cause Kant much grief for his views on religion, on 27 March 1789.)[106] Lagarde also apologized to Kant for the numerous typographical errors caused by the speed with which the work had been printed.

There has been a great deal of speculation about the sequence in which Kant wrote the several parts of the third *Critique*. The most prominent hypothesis holds that Kant first wrote the "Analytic of the Beautiful" and the "Deduction of Pure Aesthetic Judgments," probably in 1788, followed by the first draft of the introduction (the 17-sheet version), in which he first introduced the distinction between determining and reflecting judgment, and only then wrote the "Analytic of the Sublime" and the "Critique of the Teleological Power of Judgment."[107] This hypothesis is based entirely on internal evidence, most notably the lack of use of the concept of reflecting judgment in the "Analytic of the Beautiful" – which could also be explained simply by the fact that, as the recent publication of the anthropology lectures now makes clear, Kant was there and in the treatment of fine art (§§ 43–54) expounding views he held long before attempting to connect aesthetics and teleology. In any case, as the present review of Kant's correspondence makes clear, the only thing that we can say with certainty is that Kant did write two different versions of the introduction to the book, the 17-sheet version that he referred to on 21 January 1790, but that was presumably already finished in October 1789, when Kant said that the whole manuscript was finished, and the ten-sheet version that Kant finally sent to Lagarde on 22 March. These are the two versions of the introduction, the first draft or so-called first introduction, and the published version, which are presented in this volume.

A few words on the history of the first draft of the introduction are in order here. At one point Kant presumably expected to use this version as the introduction to the published work, since the manuscript copy that exists is a fair copy in another hand, apparently that of Kiesewetter,[108] which Kant must have had prepared with the expectation of giving it to the printer; it also has corrections and additions in Kant's own hand. (If it was transcribed by Kiesewetter, that would confirm that it was prepared before the fall of 1789, when Kiesewetter was already in Berlin.) Kant's reason for rejecting this version seems to have been simply that it was too long, as he said several times in his letters to Lagarde. After writing the final version and publishing the book, Kant apparently set the manuscript of the original introduction aside, without any intention of using it further. However, several years later, when another of Kant's students, Jakob Sigismund Beck (1761–1840), was preparing several volumes of excerpts from the master's works and asked if Kant had any unpublished material he could use, Kant sent him the manuscript with this explanation: "In behalf of your future excerpt from the *Critique of the Power of Judgment* I will send you, in the next post, a packet of the manuscript of my originally written **Introduction** to it, which I rejected solely on account of its disproportionate extensiveness for the text, but which still seems to me to contain much that can contribute to a fuller understanding of the concept of a purposiveness of nature, for use as you see fit."[109] After a reminder, Kant finally sent Beck the manuscript on 18 August 1793, repeating that he had rejected it only on account of its length and telling Beck that he could use it as he saw fit.[110] Beck did then include excerpts from the manuscript in the second volume of his *Erläuternder Auszug aus den critischen Schriften des Herrn Prof. Kant auf Anrathen desselben* (Explanatory excerpts from the critical writings of Professor Kant, with his advice).[111] Beck entitled the material "Comments on the introduction to the *Critique of the Power of Judgment*," and did make it plain that what he had was an earlier version of the published introduction that Kant had rejected on account of its length. But this connection was lost during the course of the nineteenth century, and Beck's version appeared in such collections as the Rosenkranz-Schubert edition of Kant's works (1838) under the title "On Philosophy in General." The first person to recognize the original connection to the introduction of the *Critique* again was the great scholar Benno Erdmann, who included Beck's excerpts, under the proper title "Beck's excerpt from Kant's original version of the introduction to the *Critique of the Power of Judgment*," in his edition of the *Critique* in 1880.[112] Meanwhile, the manuscript passed into the library of the university in Rostock, where Beck had become a professor, where it was found several years later by Wilhelm Dilthey. However, although Dilthey was one of the original instigators of the Prussian Academy edition of Kant's works, which began publication in 1900 (volumes 10 and 11, the first two volumes of correspondence, appeared that year, prior to volume 1 of the published works, which did not appear until 1902), Wilhelm Windelband, the editor of volume 5 (1908), which contained the second and third *Critiques*, still knew only Beck's excerpts, and did not include them in his edition. Ernst Cassirer's edition of Kant's works was the first to publish the whole first draft of the introduction in 1914,[113] and the draft was first published in the Academy edition in volume 20, a wartime volume that appeared in 1942, edited by Gerhard Lehmann. The present translation gives the Academy edition pagination, as do all volumes in the Cambridge Edition of the Works of Immanuel Kant,[114] but is actually based on the facsimile edition and transcription edited by Norbert Hinske, Wolfgang Müller-Lauter, and Michael Theunissen in 1965 (see note 104). Readers must decide for themselves whether the two versions differ only in length or if there are significant differences in substance.

We can now return to a few further comments about the first edition of the book. On 3 March 1790, Kiesewetter wrote to Kant that he had been sick in bed for two weeks, and was behind in the corrections of the proofs (another party seems to have helped out). He also wrote that he had been having some problems with Kant's manuscript, particularly with titles in the manuscript, which didn't match what Kant had written on a card (*Zettel*) that he had included with the manuscript. In both the manuscript and the card, Kant had divided the "Analytic of the Aesthetic Power of Judgment" into two books, "First Book: Analytic of the Beautiful" and "Second Book: Analytic of the Sublime." However, in the manuscript Kiesewetter came upon "Third Section of the Analytic of the Aesthetic Power of Judgment: Deduction of aesthetic judgments," which was missing from Kant's card listing the table of contents. So Kiesewetter had added the title "Third Book: Deduction of Aesthetic Judgments" above § 30 in the proofs.[115] However, Kant wrote to him on 20 April, Kiesewetter's letter had been included in a packet of proofs that Lagarde had sent Kant on 10 March, which Kant had set aside to look at once all the proofs had arrived, and thus he had not seen it earlier. He then thanked Kiesewetter for the correction of errors, sent him a list of some he had found himself, and then said, rather confusingly,

I wish that I had noticed the error (Third Section of the Analytic of the Aesthetic Power of Judgment) myself, and had entirely stricken this title; but otherwise you have quite appropriately altered it to: Third Book: Deduction, etc. But now this must also be altered in the table of division that will be appended to the preface, or rather to the introduction. However, if there is still time, then I request that *the title that has been altered by you should be noted at the end among the typographical errors and the table of division should be left as it has been set and only 2 books in the first part should be named.* However, I doubt that there is still time for this.[116]

This is confusing, because Kant seems both to accept Kiesewetter's division of the *Critique of the Aesthetic Power of Judgment* into three books and then to reject it; and the first edition reflects this confusion, using the title "Third Book" at the start of the "Deduction of aesthetic judgments" (§ 30, p. 129 in the original edition), yet then retracting it in the errata list (following p. 476): "P. 129: The title Third Book: Deduction, etc., is stricken." But it is clear that Kant recognized that the material beginning with the deduction of aesthetic judgments and continuing through the theory of fine art was not part of the "Analytic of the Sublime," even though he did not want to call this material a third "book," which would have destroyed the symmetry of his division of the treatment of the beautiful and the sublime into two books.[117] Kant then left the whole matter unresolved in the second edition by simply introducing the title "Deduction of pure aesthetic judgments" in large type over "§ 30" and its specific title, but without any other title such as "book," "part," or "division" (p. 131 of the second edition). Nevertheless, in spite of this confusion it should be clear both from the format and the content that the material beginning in § 30 is not a continuation of the "Analytic of the Sublime" – after all, Kant immediately says that the sublime does not need any deduction beyond the exposition already given[118] – and the practice of previous English translations of continuing the running head "Analytic of the Sublime" over §§ 30 through 54 is an error.[119]

One last observation about the publication of the first edition of the third *Critique* casts some not entirely flattering light on Kant's character. Both the *Critique of Pure Reason* and the *Critique of Practical Reason* had been published in Riga by Johann Friedrich Hartknoch, who had in fact already been a co-publisher of Kant's work *Dreams of a Spirit-Seer* in 1766. On 25 April 1789, Hartknoch's son, also named Johann Friedrich Hartknoch, wrote Kant with the sad news that his father had died on 1 April after a brief illness, and told Kant that he and his mother would continue his father's business, and hoped for Kant's support. In August, the younger Hartknoch wrote Kant again, telling him that he was publishing new editions of 1,000 copies of the first *Critique* and 2,000 of the second, and also wrote that he had found among his father's papers "a little memorandum concerning the printing of a critique of beautiful taste," begging Kant for the favor of indeed being granted the privilege of publishing this work.[120] On 5 September, Kant put him off, writing only that "he would not gladly break old connections" and "would give him further news of the work he had in hand as soon as it is finished."[121] Another letter from Hartknoch on 29 September shows that at that time the young publisher still expected to publish Kant's new work. However, Kant's letter to Lagarde on 2 October clearly implies that Kant was already negotiating with Lagarde for the publication of the book,[122] a fact of which Kant neither then nor later bothered to inform Hartknoch. Kant had apparently chosen Lagarde, a much more prominent publisher, in the expectation that he would be able to print and distribute the new book quickly, an expectation in which, as we have seen, Kant was not disappointed. But Hartknoch certainly was disappointed. He seems to have learned that Kant had chosen another publisher only after the book was published,[123] and to have been able to bring himself to write to Kant about it only when he had to write to him anyway in order to report that the new edition of the *Critique of Practical Reason* had sold out and that he was planning yet another. Although it pained him to do so, he wrote, "I am just a beginner, whose chief support was your preeminent writings, and hoped to do honor to my business by the continuation of your favor, and now, at the beginning of my career, I see myself forsaken by one of the oldest and worthiest friends of my blessed father."[124] Hartknoch continued as publisher of Kant's first two *Critiques*, and continued faithfully to pay Kant his honoraria for the new editions, but there is no record that Kant ever even replied to this letter, nor did he ever give Hartknoch another book, turning instead to Friedrich Nicolovius, another young Riga publisher, for his later works.

Finally, a few words about the second edition of the third *Critique*. As early as 5 July 1791, Lagarde wrote to Kant that he had only 122 copies of the first edition left, and that he hoped to publish a second edition by the next Easter book fair, by which time he expected these copies to be gone; to meet this deadline he asked Kant to send him a revised copy by the end of October.[125] Kant wrote back on 2 August, asking for an interleaved copy on which to make his corrections,[126] which Lagarde duly sent. On 28 October, however, Kant wrote Lagarde that he could not send the revisions before the end of November.[127] However, Kant missed this deadline too. On 30 March 1792, Kant wrote to Lagarde to thank him for the 200 dollars he had already received for the new edition, and now promised him the corrections "soon after Easter."[128] Finally, on 12 June 1792, Kant wrote to Lagarde to say that the corrected copy, except for the preface and introduction, had been sent two days earlier; Kant stated that he had made no additions to the text except to add a sentence to the note on page 462 (5:471).[129] It was not until 2 October that Kant finally sent the revised introduction, which added a long footnote to its section III (5:177–8).[130] Kant did not write a new preface for the second edition, although he did make minor changes and improvements throughout the work, including breaking up some (but by no means all!) of his long sentences. Kant received eight copies of the new edition from Lagarde on 2 November 1792, although the title page bore the date "1793." Some errors remained in this new edition, and as previously noted Kant left the question of a title for §§ 30–54 unresolved. A few more corrections were made for a third edition published in 1799, though by whose hand is not clear (no correspondence related to it survives), and there were no substantive additions. The present translation is based on the second edition. All significant changes between the first and second editions have been noted. In a very few places, readings from the first edition have been preferred, and in one or two places a correction from the third edition has been incorporated.

One anecdote about the second edition can put Kant's intellectual if not his commercial interests in a more flattering light. After putting off a decision about what to do with the 12 free copies of the new edition that he was still owed,[131] in the following September Kant finally asked Lagarde if he could have a few other titles from Lagarde's list instead of unneeded copies of his own work. The works that Kant asked for were a translation of a now forgotten work, *Travels of the younger Anacharis through Greece*, by Abbé Jean Jacques Barthélemy,[132] and a new translation by Johann Joachim Bode of Montaigne's *Thoughts and Opinions*.[133] Apparently Kant intended to spend some time in his waning years reading Montaigne – a wise choice for anyone. Lagarde was happy to comply, sending Kant the works asked for as well as one that Kant had not even requested, but which Lagarde assumed he would be interested in, Lucius Junius Frey's *Philosophie sociale, dédiée au peuple français*.[134] Kant thanked Lagarde for the first installment of books on 24 November 1794.[135] Lagarde later also sent a gift of porcelain, for which Kant thanked him on 30 March 1795,[136] but Kant did not publish another book with him either. Lagarde, like Hartknoch, was clearly hurt by this, although in his position he could afford to be less plaintive about it.[137]

IV.
NOTE ON THE TRANSLATION

The present project was originally begun by Eva Schaper and Eric Matthews. It was undertaken outside of the framework of the Cambridge Kant edition, and was indeed one of the projects in hand that spurred Cambridge University Press to launch the larger enterprise. Schaper and Matthews prepared samples of a translation of the first introduction and "Analytic of the Beautiful" and Paul Guyer, in his capacity as General Co-Editor of the Cambridge edition, had made some comments on these samples before Professor Schaper's untimely death in 1992. After Professor Schaper's death, it was decided that Paul

Guyer would step in for her, and that the project would be completed by Guyer and Matthews, even though this would entail a delay while Guyer and Allen Wood finished the *Critique of Pure Reason*. In the end, Matthews prepared a translation of the introductions and "Critique of the Aesthetic Power of Judgment" while Guyer translated the "Critique of Teleological Judgment" and then revised the whole translation for stylistic uniformity as well as consistency with the Guyer–Wood first *Critique*. The notes and editor's introduction are by Guyer. The final version of the translation benefited from careful readings not only by Matthews but also by Allen Wood, though final responsibility remains with Guyer.

The present work is an entirely new translation: the three previous English translations of the whole work as well as the two previous translations of the first draft of the introduction (these will be listed in Section V below) have been consulted on occasion, but our translation cannot be considered a revision of any of them. In particular, the translations of a number of Kant's central terms depart from previous practice.

The most striking of our changes will undoubtedly be the decision to use "determining" and "reflecting" for the translation of *bestimmend* and *reflectirend* as modifiers of the term "power of judgment" (*Urtheilskraft*). It seemed desirable to translate these terms in a way that mirrors their common grammatical structure, which excludes J. C. Meredith's choice of "reflective" but "determinant"; in a way that involves no new English coinage, which excludes Werner Pluhar's "reflective" and "determinative"; and in a way that acknowledges that these two terms are present participles that can be pressed into service as adjectives as well as adverbs, and by so doing keeps the sense of activity that is present in Kant's terms, thus the sense that Kant is talking about two different uses or applications of the power of judgment, but not two different faculties of mind. We hope our choice will do that. There are some contexts in which Kant's constructions could well have been rendered as "the power of determining" or "reflecting judgment," but this was not possible in all cases, so for the sake of consistency we have always used "determining" or "reflecting power of judgment."

Another major departure from past practice is our treatment of the verb *beurteilen* and the noun *Beurteilung*. While Meredith translated these as "to estimate" and "estimation," and Eva Schaper originally proposed to translate them as "to appraise" and "appraisal," as indeed Mary J. Gregor had done in her translations of the *Groundwork* and *Critique of Practical Reason*,[138] the General Co-Editors felt that these were misleadingly specific translations for what are simply the transitive form of the verb *urteilen* and its associated nominative; we have thus simply translated *beurteilen* as "to judge" (something), and *Beur-*

teilung as "the judging" (of something). We have noted all uses of *beurteilen* and its related forms in the footnotes, so that the reader may be clear that it is not *urteilen* or one of its variants that is being translated. (We have not followed the practice of the Guyer–Wood first *Critique* in noting the difference between Kant's uses of *Objekt* and *Gegenstand*, however, since in the third *Critique* Kant seems to use these terms interchangeably and no one has ever argued that there is a significant philosophical difference between them in this work.)

The terms *Zweck* and *Zweckmäßigkeit* are also a traditional source of problems. For reasons of symmetry, previous translators have tended to translate them as matched pairs, i.e., "purpose" and "purposive" or "end" and "finality." But we found neither of these pairings satisfactory, because "purpose" for *Zweck* obscures the connection between Kant's aesthetics and his ethics, where *Zweck* is always translated as "end," while "finality" in the context of this work is a neologism constructed on the Latin stem *fin-*, and is easily confused with its ordinary English meaning of "conclusiveness." So we have opted for "end" as the translation of *Zweck* but "purposiveness" for *Zweckmäßigkeit*.

Kant's many terms connected with pleasure and pain also presented problems. Meredith's "delight" for *Wohlgefallen*, which Kant uses as his most generic term for positive rather than negative feeling, seemed dated and too specific, and Pluhar's use of "liking" as a noun seemed unnatural. We have chosen to translate the nouns *Wohlgefallen* and *Mißfallen* as "satisfaction" and "dissatisfaction" respectively,[139] using "pleasure" and "displeasure" for *Lust* and *Unlust*, "enjoyment" for *Genießen*, and "gratification" for *Vergnügen*.

Kant's many terms – nouns, verbs, adjectives, and adverbs – based on the stem *stimmen* also presented problems. We did not want to use "harmony," "harmonious," or "harmonize" for any of these, since Kant also uses the words *Harmonie* and *harmonisch*, and we wanted to sort them out from each other, but this could not always be done with a single English equivalent for each term. Our primary choices for the noun forms have been: "assent" for *Beistimmung*, "consensus" for *Einstimmigkeit*, "accord" for *Einstimmung*, "correspondence" for *Übereinstimmung*, and "agreement" for *Zusammenstimmung*, while the related word *Einhelligkeit* has usually been translated as "unanimity" but sometimes as "unison." Further variants for some of these terms are listed in the Glossary.

Kant's several terms for the kind of claims made by aesthetic judgments are also difficult to translate: it seems confusing to translate both *ansinnen* and *zumuten* as "to require," but to translate *zumuten* as "to impute," as Meredith does, makes it sound excessively legalistic. We have chosen to translate *ansinnen* usually as "to require," though some-times as "to ascribe," *erwarten* as "to expect," and *zumuten* as "to expect (something) of (someone)." Other related verbs, such as *fordern* and *verlangen*, are translated as indicated in the Glossary.

Finally, we have generally followed the Cambridge Edition practice of using English terms based on Latin equivalents of German terms where Kant gives them, most notably in the cases of "cognition" (*cognitio*) for *Erkenntnis* and "representation" (*representatio*) for *Vorstel-lung*. However, it did not always seem natural to translate *Darstellung* as "exhibition" (the "exhibition of an idea" sounds peculiar) even though Kant does equate it with *exhibitio*; here we have usually pre-ferred "presentation."

These choices and variants are all reflected in the Glossary, which should be consulted for other terms as well.

It should be noted here that since our translation is based on the original editions of 1793 and 1790, we have followed the original orthography in our footnotes, e.g. *Beurtheilung* instead of *Beurteilen* or *frey* instead of *frei*. In the following bibliography, the original orthog-raphy of each entry is preserved.

One point about typography should also be mentioned. In the orig-inal editions of Kant's works, the bulk of the text is set in *Fraktur* (so-called Gothic type); words that Kant regarded as foreign, including *a priori*, are set in roman type; and headings as well as words that Kant emphasized are set in *Fettdruck*, that is, larger and heavier letters than the normal type, whether *Fraktur* or roman. To reproduce as closely as possible the look of Kant's original pages, as well as to make clear the distinction between words Kant emphasized and words he regarded as foreign, we have used italics where he used roman type and boldface where he indicated emphasis by *Fettdruck* (though we have not tried to distinguish among the several sizes of *Fettdruck* that are variously used). We have also followed the original editions as closely as possible in the division of lines within section titles and in the location on the page of major divisions of the work. We have used only Kant's own running heads.

V.
BIBLIOGRAPHY

The secondary literature on the *Critique of the Power of Judgment*, especially on Kant's aesthetics, has become vast, especially since the 1970s, and any list that could be given here would be limited and quickly outdated. This bibliography will list German editions of Kant's text, translations that have been consulted, and a few secondary sources that themselves contain extensive bibliographies of the secondary literature.

1. German editions

KANT, IMMANUEL. *Critik der Urtheilskraft.* Berlin und Libau: bey Lagarde und Friederich, 1790. (Facsimile reprint, with a brief introduction by Lewis White Beck; London: Routledge/Thoemmes Press, 1994.)

KANT, IMMANUEL. *Critik der Urtheilskraft.* Zweyte Auflage. Berlin: F. T. Lagarde, 1793. (Facsimile reprint, with a brief introduction by Lewis White Beck; London: Routledge/Thoemmes Press, 1994. The present translation is based on this edition.)

KANT, IMMANUEL. *Critik der Urtheilskraft.* Dritte Auflage. Berlin: F. T. Lagarde, 1799.

KANT, IMMANUEL. *Erste Einleitung in die Kritik der Urteilskraft: Faksimile und Transkription.* Edited by Norbert Hinske, Wolfgang Müller-Lauter, and Michael Theunissen. Stuttgart-Bad Canstatt: Fromann (Holzboog), 1965. (The present translation of the first introduction is based on this edition.)

KANT, IMMANUEL. *Immanuel Kant's Kritik der Urtheilskraft.* Edited by Benno Erdmann. Leipzig: Leopold Voss, 1880. (This was the first edition to include the first introduction and to collate the variations among the three editions published in Kant's lifetime.)

Kant's gesammelte Schriften, Herausgegeben von der Königlich Preußischen Akademie der Wissenschaften. Band V. Erste Abtheilung: Werke, Fünfter Band: Kritik der praktischen Vernunft, Kritik der Urtheilskraft. Berlin: Georg Reimer, 1908 (first edition), 1913 (second edition). (The *Kritik der Urtheilskraft* was edited by Wilhem Windelband. The variants among the first three editions are recorded in the endnotes, in an extremely inaccessible format. The pagination of this edition has become standard, and is provided in our margins in accordance with the practice of the Cambridge Edition.)

Kant's gesammelte Schriften. Herausgegeben von der Preußischen Akademie der Wissenschaften. Band XX: Dritte Abteilung: Handschriftlicher Nachlaß, Siebenter Band. Edited by Gerhard Lehmann. Berlin: Walter de Gruyter & Co., 1942. (Contains Lehmann's edition of the first draft of the introduction. The pagination of this edition has been provided in the present translation.)

KANT, IMMANUEL. *Kritik der Urteilskraft.* Edited by Gerhard Lehmann. Stuttgart: Philipp Reclam Jun., 1963. (This edition records the variants among the original editions in a helpful format, and was of assistance in preparing the present edition.)

KANT, IMMANUEL. *Kritik der Urteilskraft: Kants Schriften zur Ästhetik und Naturphilosophie – kritisch geprüfte Texte mit umfassender Kommentierung. Bibliothek deutscher Klassiker, 135.* Edited by Manfred Frank and Véronique Zanetti. Frankfurt am Main: Deutscher Klassiker Verlag, 1996. (This edition reproduces Windelband's text from the Academy edition, but also contains useful selections from Kant's notes on anthropology and from

l

the *Logik Philippi* as well as a number of Kant's other works. Its notes were helpful in the preparation of ours.)

2. Translations

KANT, IMMANUEL. *Critique of Judgment.* Translated with an introduction by J. H. Bernard. London: Macmillan, 1892. Second edition revised, 1914.

KANT, IMMANUEL. *Kant's Critique of Aesthetic Judgment.* Translated with seven introductory essays, notes, and analytical index by James Creed Meredith. Oxford: Clarendon Press, 1911.

KANT, IMMANUEL. *Kant's Critique of Teleological Judgment.* Translated with an introduction, notes, and analytical index by James Creed Meredith. Oxford: Clarendon Press, 1928.

KANT, IMMANUEL. *The Critique of Judgment.* Translated with analytical indexes by James Creed Meredith. Oxford: Clarendon Press, 1952. (One-volume reprint of the previous two translations, without the introductions and notes.)

KANT, IMMANUEL. *Analytic of the Beautiful, from The Critique of Judgment, with excerpts from Anthropology from a Pragmatic Viewpoint.* Translated with an introduction, comments, and notes by Walter Cerf. Indianapolis: Bobbs-Merrill, 1963.

KANT, IMMANUEL. *First Introduction to the Critique of Judgment.* Translated by James Haden. Indianapolis: Bobbs-Merrill, 1965.

KANT, IMMANUEL. *Critique of Judgment, Including the First Introduction.* Translated with an introduction by Werner S. Pluhar. With a foreword by Mary J. Gregor. Indianapolis: Hackett Publishing Company, 1987. (This edition was helpful in the preparation of our notes.)

The following Italian translation was also helpful in the preparation of our notes:

KANT, IMMANUEL. *Critica della facoltà di giudizio.* Edited by Emilio Garroni and Hansmichael Hohenegger. Biblioteca Einaudi, 58. Turin: Einaudi, 1999.

3. Bibliographical resources

The Pluhar translation (above) contains an extensive bibliography.

For early materials, including original editions of Kant's works and works by innumerable early expositors and opponents, consult:

ADICKES, ERICH. *German Kantian Bibliography: Bibliography of Writings by and on Kant which have appeared in Germany up to the end of 1887.* New York: Burt Franklin, 1970. (The material originally appeared in *The Philosophical Review* in 1893–96.)

The following works also have extensive bibliographies, including much more recent material:

COHEN, TED, AND PAUL GUYER, EDS. *Essays in Kant's Aesthetics*. Chicago: University of Chicago Press, 1982.

GUYER, PAUL, ED. *The Cambridge Companion to Kant*. Cambridge: Cambridge University Press, 1992.

GUYER, PAUL. *Kant and the Experience of Freedom*. Cambridge: Cambridge University Press, 1993.

KULENKAMPFF, JENS. *Materialen zu Kants >Kritik der Urteilskraft<*. Frankfurt am Main: Suhrkamp, 1974. (Includes extracts of material relevant to Kant's aesthetics from Georg Friedrich Meier to Frank Sibley.)

MEERBOTE, RALF, AND HUD HUDSON, EDS. *Kant's Aesthetics*. North American Kant Society Studies in Philosophy, Volume 1. Atascadero, Cal.: Ridgeview Publishing Co., 1991. (The bibliography in this volume was intended to update that in Cohen and Guyer, which went up to 1980.)

PARRET, HERMAN, ED. *Kants Ästhetik – Kant's Aesthetics – L'esthétique de Kant*. Berlin and New York: Walter de Gruyter, 1998.

RUFFING, MARGIT, ED. *Kant-Bibliographie 1999*. Frankfurt am Main: Vittorio Klostermann, 1945–90. (This bibliography is continued periodically in the journal *Kant-Studien*.)

ZAMMITO, JOHN H. *The Genesis of Kant's Critique of Judgment*. Chicago: University of Chicago Press, 1992.

First Introduction
to the
Critique of the Power of Judgment

I.
On philosophy as a system.

If philosophy is the **system** of rational cognition[a] through concepts, it is thereby already sufficiently distinguished from a critique of pure reason, which, although it contains a philosophical investigation of the possibility of such cognition, does not belong to such a system as a part, but rather outlines and examines the very idea of it in the first place.

The division of the system can at first only be that into its formal and material parts, of which the first (the logic) concerns merely the form of thinking in a system of rules, while the second (the real[b] part) systematically takes under consideration the objects which are thought about, insofar as a rational cognition of them from concepts is possible.

Now this real system of philosophy itself, given the original distinction of its objects and the essential difference, resting on them, of the principles of a science that contains them, cannot be divided except into **theoretical** and **practical** philosophy; thus, the one part must be the philosophy of nature, the other that of morals,[c] the first of which is also empirical, the second of which, however (since freedom absolutely cannot be an object of experience), can never contain anything other than pure principles *a priori*.

However, there is a great misunderstanding, which is even quite disadvantageous to the way in which the science is handled, about what should be held to be **practical** in a sense[d] in which it deserves to be taken up into a **practical philosophy**. Statesmanship and political economy, rules of good housekeeping as well as those of etiquette, precepts for good health and diet, of the soul as well as of the body (indeed why not all trades and arts?), have been believed to be able to be counted as practical philosophy, because they all contain a great many practical propositions. But while practical propositions certainly differ from theoretical ones, which contain the possibility of things and

[a] *Vernunfterkenntnis*
[b] *reale*
[c] *Sitten*
[d] *Bedeutung*

20: 196

their determination, in the way in which they are presented, they do not on that account differ in their content, except only those which consider **freedom** under laws. All the rest are nothing more than the theory of that which belongs to the nature of things, only applied to the way in which they can be generated by us in accordance with a principle, i.e., their possibility is represented through a voluntary[a] action (which belongs among natural causes as well). Thus the solution to the problem in mechanics of finding the respective lengths of the arms of a lever by means of which a given force will be in equilibrium with a given weight, is of course expressed as a practical formula, but it contains nothing other than the theoretical proposition that the length of the arms is in inverse proportion to the force and the weight if these are in equilibrium; only this relation, as far as its origin is concerned, is represented as possible through a cause whose determining ground is the **representation** of that relation (our choice). It is exactly the same with all practical propositions that concern merely the production of objects. If precepts for the promotion of one's happiness are given, and, e.g., the issue is only what one has to do in one's own case in order to be susceptible to happiness, then all that is represented are the inner conditions of the possibility of such happiness – in contentment, in moderation of the inclinations so they will not become passions, etc. – as belonging to the nature of the subject, and at the same time the manner of generating this equilibrium as a causality possible through ourselves alone, hence all of this is represented as an immediate consequence from the theory of the object in relation to the theory of our own nature (ourselves as cause): hence the practical precept here differs from a theoretical one in its form, but not in its content, and thus a special kind of philosophy is not required for insight into the connection of grounds with their consequences. – In a word: all practical propositions that[b] derive that which nature can contain from the faculty of choice as a cause collectively belong to theoretical philosophy, as cognition of nature; only those propositions which give the law to freedom are specifically distinguished from the former in virtue of their content.[c] One can say of the former that they constitute the practical part of a **philosophy of nature**, but the latter alone ground[d] a special **practical philosophy.**

20: 197

---

[a] *willkürlich*
[b] Here Kant crossed out the words: "are also possible through empirical determining grounds (e.g., those of the theory of happiness)."
[c] Here Kant crossed out the words: "and are determining grounds only in so far as they are *a priori* grounds."
[d] Here Kant crossed out "belong to."

Remark

It is very important to determine the parts of philosophy precisely and to that end not to include among the members of the division of philosophy, as a system, that which is merely a consequence or an application of it to given cases, requiring no special principles.

Practical propositions are distinguished from theoretical ones either in regard to principles or to consequences. In the latter case they do not constitute a special part of the science, but belong to the theoretical part, as a special kind of its consequences. Now the possibility of things in accordance with natural laws is essentially distinct in its principles from that in accordance with laws of freedom. This distinction, however, does not consist in the fact that in the latter case the cause is placed in a will, but in the former case outside of the will, in the things themselves. For even if the will follows no other principles than those by means of which the understanding has insight into the possibility of the object in accordance with them, as mere laws of nature, then the proposition which contains the possibility of the object through the causality of the faculty of choice may still be called a practical proposition, yet it is not at all distinct in principle from the theoretical propositions concerning the nature of things, but must rather derive   20: 198
its own content from the latter in order to exhibit the representation of an object in reality.

Practical propositions, therefore, the content of which concerns merely the possibility of a represented object (through voluntary action), are only applications of a complete theoretical cognition and cannot constitute a special part of a science. A practical geometry, as a separate science, is an absurdity, although ever so many practical propositions are contained in this pure science, most of which, as problems, require a special instruction for their solution. The problem of constructing a square with a given line and a given right angle is a practical proposition, but a pure consequence of the theory. And the art of surveying (*agrimensoria*) cannot in any way presume to the name of a practical **geometry** and be called a special part of geometry in general, but rather belongs among the scholia of the latter, namely the use of this science for business.*

---

* This pure and for that very reason sublime science seems to forgo some of   20: 198
its dignity if it concedes that, as elementary geometry, it needs *tools*, even if only two, for the construction of its concepts, namely the compass and the ruler, which construction alone it calls geometrical, while those of higher geometry on the contrary it calls mechanical, since for the construction of the concepts of the latter more complex machines are required. But what is

20: 199 Even in a science of nature, insofar as it rests on empirical principles, namely in physics proper, the practical procedures for discovering hidden laws of nature, under the name of experimental physics, can in no way justify the designation of a practical physics (which is likewise an absurdity) as a part of natural philosophy. For the principles in accordance with which we set up experiments must themselves always be derived from the knowledge of nature, hence from theory. The same is true of practical precepts, which concern the voluntary production of a certain state of mind in us (e.g., that of the stimulation[a] or restraint of the imagination, the gratification or weakening of the inclinations). There is no practical **psychology** as a special part of the philosophy of human nature. For the principles of the possibility of its state by means of art must be borrowed from those of the possibility of our determinations from the constitution of our nature and, although the former consist of practical propositions, still they do not constitute a practical part of empirical psychology, because they do not have any special principles, but merely belong among its scholia.

In general, practical propositions (whether they are pure *a priori* or empirical), if they immediately assert the possibility of an object through our faculty of choice, always belong to the knowledge of nature and to the theoretical part of philosophy. Only those which directly exhibit the determination of an action as necessary merely through the representation of its form (in accordance with laws in general), without regard to[b] the means[c] of the object that is thereby to be realized, can and must have their own special principles (in the idea of freedom); and, although they ground the concept of an object of the will (the highest good) on these very principles, still this belongs only indirectly, as a consequence, to the practical precept (which is henceforth called moral). Further, there can be no insight into its possibility through the knowledge of nature (theory). Thus only those propositions alone belong to a special part of a system of rational cognitions, under the name of practical philosophy.

20: 200 All other propositions of practice, whatever science they might be attached to, can, if one is perhaps worried about ambiguity, be called

meant by the former is not the actual tools (*circinus et regula*), which can never give those shapes with mathematical precision, rather they are to signify only the simplest kinds of exhibition of the imagination *a priori*, which cannot be matched by any instrument.

[a] *Bewegung*
[b] Crossed out: "a determinate."
[c] Cassirer suggests "matter" (*Materie*).

6

technical rather than practical propositions. For they belong to the **art** of bringing about that which one wishes should exist, which in the case of a complete theory is always a mere consequence and not a self-subsistent part of any kind of instruction. In this way, all precepts of skill belong to **technique***[1] and hence to the theoretical knowledge of nature as its consequences. However, we shall in the future also use the expression "technique" where objects of nature are sometimes merely **judged**[a] as if their possibility were grounded in art, in which cases the judgments are neither theoretical nor practical (in the sense   20: 201 just adduced), since they do not **determine** anything about the constitution of the object nor the way in which to produce it; rather through them nature itself is judged,[b] but merely in accordance with the analogy with an art, and indeed in subjective relation to our cognitive faculty, not in objective relation to the objects.[c] Now here we will not indeed call the judgments themselves technical, but rather the power of judgment, on whose laws they are grounded, and in accordance with it we will also call nature technical; further, this technique, since it contains no objectively determining propositions, does not constitute any part of doctrinal philosophy, but only a part of the critique of our faculty of cognition.

---

* This is the place to correct an error which I committed in the *Groundwork*   20: 200 *for the Metaphysics of Morals*. For after I had said that imperatives of skill command only conditionally, under the condition of merely possible, i.e., *problematic*, ends, I called such practical precepts problematic imperatives, an expression in which a contradiction certainly lurks. I should have called them *technical* imperatives, i.e., imperatives of art. The *pragmatic* imperatives, or rules of prudence, which command under the condition of an *actual* and thus even subjectively necessary end, also stand under the technical imperatives (for what is prudence other than the skill of being able to use for one's intentions free human beings and among these even the natural dispositions and inclinations in oneself?). Only the fact that the end which we ascribe to ourselves and to others, namely that of our own happiness, does not belong among the merely arbitrary ends justifies a special designation for these technical imperatives; for the problem does not merely, as in the case of technical imperatives, require the manner of the execution of an end, but also the determination of that which constitutes this end itself (happiness), which in the case of technical imperatives in general must be presupposed as known.

[a] *beurtheilt*
[b] *beurtheilt*
[c] Here Kant crossed out the following marginal note: "Now since such judgments are not cognitive judgments at all, it can be understood why the concept of technical judgments lies outside the field of the logical division (into theoretical and practical) and can find its place only in a critique of the origin of our cognition."

II.
On the system of the higher cognitive faculties,
which grounds philosophy.

If the issue is not the division of a **philosophy**, but of our **faculty of *a priori* cognition through concepts** (of our higher faculty of cognition), i.e., of a critique of pure reason, but considered only with regard to its faculty for thinking (where the pure kind of intuition is not taken into account), then the systematic representation of the faculty for thinking is tripartite: namely, first, the faculty for the cognition of the **general**[a] (of rules), **the understanding**; second, the faculty for the **subsumption of the particular** under the general, **the power of judgment**; and third, the faculty for the **determination** of the particular through the general (for the derivation from principles), i.e., **reason**.

20: 202 The critique of pure **theoretical** reason, which was dedicated to the sources of all cognition *a priori* (hence also to that in it which belongs to intuition), yielded the laws of **nature**, the critique of **practical** reason the law of **freedom**, and so the *a priori* principles for the whole of philosophy already seem to have been completely treated.

But now if the understanding yields *a priori* laws of nature, reason, on the contrary, laws of freedom, then by analogy one would still expect that the power of judgment, which mediates the connection between the two faculties, would, just like those, add its own special principles *a priori* and perhaps ground a special part of philosophy, even though philosophy as a system can have only two parts.

Yet the power of judgment is such a special faculty of cognition, not at all self-sufficient, that it provides neither concepts, like the understanding, nor ideas, like reason, of any object at all, since it is a faculty merely for subsuming under concepts given from elsewhere. Thus if there is to be a concept or a rule which arises originally from the power of judgment, it would have to be a concept of things in **nature insofar as nature conforms to our power of judgment**, and thus a concept of a property of nature such that one cannot form any concept of it except that its arrangement conforms to our faculty for subsuming the particular given laws under more general ones even though these are not given;[b] in other words, it would have to be the concept of a purposiveness of nature in behalf of our faculty for cognizing it, insofar as for this it is required that we be able to judge[c] the particular as

[a] *des Allgemeinen.* The term *allgemein* can be translated as either "general" or "universal"; we will generally use the former where there is a contrast with "particular," and the latter when a claim to the assent of all is contrasted to an idiosyncratic or private judgment.
[b] The remainder of the paragraph was added in the margin.
[c] *beurtheilen*

contained under the general and subsume*a* it under the concept of a 20: 203
nature.

Now such a concept is that of an experience **as a system in accordance with empirical laws**. For although experience constitutes a system in accordance with **transcendental laws**, which contain the condition of the possibility of experience in general, there is still possible such an **infinite multiplicity** of empirical laws and such a **great heterogeneity of forms** of nature, which would belong to particular experience, that the concept of a system in accordance with these (empirical) laws must be entirely alien to the understanding, and neither the possibility, let alone the necessity, of such a whole can be conceived. Nevertheless particular experience, thoroughly interconnected in accordance with constant principles, also requires this systematic interconnection of empirical laws, whereby it becomes possible for the power of judgment to subsume the particular under the general, however empirical it may be, and so on, right up to*b* the highest empirical laws and the forms of nature corresponding to them, and thus to regard the **aggregate** of particular experiences as a **system** of them; for without this presupposition no thoroughly lawlike interconnection,* i.e., empirical unity of these experiences can obtain.

---

* The possibility of an experience in general is the possibility of empirical 20: 203
cognitions as synthetic judgments. It therefore cannot be drawn **analytically** from mere comparison of perceptions (as is commonly believed), for the combination of two different perceptions in the concept of an object (for the cognition of it) is a **synthesis**, which does not make an empirical **cognition**, i.e., experience, possible otherwise than in accordance with principles of the synthetic unity of the appearances, i.e., in accordance with principles through which they are brought under the categories. Now these empirical cognitions constitute, in accordance with what they necessarily have in common (namely 20: 204
those transcendental laws of nature), an analytic unity of all experience, but not that synthetic unity of experience as a system in which the empirical laws, even with regard to what is different in them (and where their multiplicity can go on to infinitude), are bound together under a principle. What the category is with regard to each particular experience, that is what the purposiveness or fitness of nature to our power of judgment is (even with regard to its particular laws), in accordance with which it is represented not merely as mechanical but also as technical; a concept which certainly does not determine the synthetic unity objectively, as does the category, but which still yields subjective principles that serve as a guideline for the investigation of nature.*c*

---

a Here Kant crossed out "so" and "consequently," having originally written "and so subsume, consequently,".
b Here Kant crossed out "yet higher, likewise to".
c This footnote appears to be an addition to the fair copy.

20: 204   This lawfulness, in itself (in accordance with all concepts of the understanding) contingent, which the power of judgment presumes of nature and presupposes in it (only for its own advantage), is a formal purposiveness of nature, which we simply **assume** in it, but through which neither a theoretical cognition of nature nor a practical principle of freedom is grounded, although a principle for the judging*a* and investigation of nature is given, in order to seek for particular experiences the general rules in accordance with which we have to arrange them in order to bring out that systematic connection which is necessary for an interconnected experience and which we have to assume *a priori*.

The concept which originally arises from the power of judgment and is proper to it is thus that of nature as **art**, in other words that of the **technique** of nature with regard to its **particular** laws, which concept does not ground any theory and does not, any more than logic, contain cognition of objects and their constitution, but only gives a principle for progress in accordance with laws of experience, whereby
20: 205   the investigation of nature becomes possible.*b* But this does not enrich the knowledge of nature by any particular objective law, but rather only grounds a maxim for the power of judgment, by which to observe nature and to hold its forms together.*c*

*d*Philosophy, as a doctrinal system of the cognition of nature as well as freedom, does not hereby acquire a new part; for the representation of nature as art is a mere idea, which serves as a principle, merely for the subject, for our investigation of nature, so that we can where possible bring interconnection, as in a system, into the aggregate of empirical laws as such, by attributing to nature a relation to this need of ours. On the contrary, our concept of a technique of nature, as a heuristic principle in the judgment*e* of it, will belong to the critique of our faculty of cognition, which indicates what occasion we have to

---

a *Beurtheilung*

b Here Kant crossed out "for us" (*uns*).

c Here Kant crossed out the following paragraph:

Philosophy, as a real **system of cognition of nature** *a priori* through concepts, thus does not acquire a new part; for that consideration belongs to its theoretical part. But the critique of the **pure faculties of cognition** does indeed acquire such a new part, and indeed one that is very necessary, by means of which, first, judgments about nature whose determining ground could easily be counted among the empirical ones are separated from these, and, second, others, which could easily be taken for **real** and held to be determination of the objects of nature, are distinguished from these and cognized as **formal**, i.e., rules for mere reflection on things in nature, not for the determination of these in accordance with objective principles.

d This paragraph appears to have been added to the fair copy.

e *Beurtheilung*

10

make such a representation of it to ourselves, what origin this idea has, whether it is to be found in an *a priori* source, and also what the scope and boundary of its use are; in a word, such an inquiry will belong as a part to the system of the critique of pure reason, but not to doctrinal philosophy.

III.

On the system
of all the faculties of the human mind.

We can trace all faculties of the human mind without exception back to these three: the **faculty of cognition**, the **feeling of pleasure and displeasure**, and the **faculty of desire**. To be sure, philosophers who otherwise deserve nothing but praise for the thoroughness of their way of thinking have sought to explain this distinction as merely illusory and to reduce all faculties to the mere faculty of cognition.[2] But it can easily be demonstrated, and has already been understood for some time,[3] that this attempt to bring unity into the multiplicity of faculties, although undertaken in a genuinely philosophical spirit, is futile. For there is always a great difference between representations belonging to cognition, insofar as they are related merely to the object and the unity of the consciousness of it, and their objective relation where, considered as at the same time the cause of the reality of this object, they are assigned to the faculty of desire, and, finally,[a] their relation merely to the subject, where they are considered merely as grounds for preserving their own existence in it and to this extent in relation to the feeling of pleasure; the latter is absolutely not a cognition, nor does it provide one, although to be sure it may presuppose such a cognition as a determining ground.

    The connection between the cognition of an object and the feeling of pleasure and displeasure in its existence, or the determination of the faculty of desire to produce it, is certainly empirically knowable; but since this interconnection is not grounded in any principle *a priori*, to this extent the powers of the mind constitute only an **aggregate** and not a system. Now it is surely enough to produce a connection *a priori* between the feeling of pleasure and the other two faculties if we connect a cognition *a priori*, namely the rational concept of freedom, with the faculty of desire as its determining ground, at the same time subjectively finding in this objective determination a feeling of pleasure contained in the determination of the will.[b],[4] But in this way the faculty

20: 206

20: 207

---

[a] "finally" crossed out by Kant.

[b] Crossed out by Kant: "as in fact found to be identical with the former."

of cognition is not combined with the faculty of desire **by means of the pleasure or displeasure**, for this does not precede the latter faculty,[a] but either first succeeds the determination of it, or else is perhaps nothing other than the sensation of the determinability of the will through reason itself, thus not a special feeling and distinctive receptivity that requires a special section under the properties of the mind. Now since in the analysis[b] of the faculties of the mind in general a feeling of pleasure which is independent of the determination of the faculty of desire, which indeed is rather able to supply a determining ground for that faculty, is incontrovertibly given, the connection of which with the other two faculties in a system nevertheless requires that this feeling of pleasure, like the other two faculties, not rest on merely empirical grounds but also on *a priori* principles, there is thus required for the idea of philosophy as a system (if not a doctrine then still) a **critique of the feeling of pleasure and displeasure** insofar as it is not empirically grounded.

Now the **faculty of cognition** in accordance with concepts has its *a priori* principles in the pure understanding (in its concept of nature), the **faculty of desire**, in pure reason (in its concept of freedom), and there remains among the properties of mind in general an intermediate faculty or receptivity, namely the **feeling of pleasure and displeasure**, just as there remains among the higher faculties of cognition an intermediate one, the power of judgment. What is more natural than to suspect that the latter will also contain *a priori* principles for the former?[c]

Without yet deciding anything about the possibility of this connection, a certain suitability of the power of judgment to serve as the determining ground for the feeling of pleasure, or to find one in it, is already unmistakable, insofar as, while in the **division of faculties of cognition through concepts** understanding and reason relate their representations to objects, in order to acquire concepts of them, the power of judgment is related solely to the subject and does not produce any concepts of objects for itself alone. Likewise, if in the general **division of the powers of the mind** overall the faculty of cognition as well as the faculty of desire contain an **objective** relation of representations, so by contrast the feeling of pleasure and displeasure is only the receptivity of a determination of the subject,[d] so that if the power of judgment is to determine anything for itself alone, it could not be

20: 208

---

[a] Crossed out by Kant: "As inner perceptions exhibit in so many cases."
[b] Crossed out: "in inner observation."
[c] Question mark added.
[d] Kant substituted "of the subject" for the phrase "of the state of mind" (*Gemüthszustandes*) in the fair copy, and then added the remainder of the sentence.

anything other than the feeling of pleasure, and, conversely, if the latter is to have an *a priori* principle at all, it will be found only in the power of judgment.[5]

IV.
On experience
as a system for the power of judgment.

We have seen in the critique of pure reason[a] that the whole of nature as the totality of all objects of experience constitutes a system in accordance with transcendental laws, namely those that the understanding itself gives *a priori* (for appearances, namely, insofar as they, combined in one consciousness, are to constitute experience). For that very reason, experience, in accordance with general as well as particular laws, insofar as it is considered objectively to be possible in general, must also constitute (in the idea) a system of possible empirical cognitions. For that is required by the unity of nature, in accordance with a principle of the thoroughgoing connection of everything contained in this totality of all appearances. To this extent experience in general in accordance with transcendental laws of the understanding is to be regarded as a system and not as a mere aggregate.

20: 209

But it does not follow from this that nature even in accordance with **empirical** laws is a system that **can be grasped**[b] by the human faculty of cognition, and that the thoroughgoing systematic interconnection of its appearances in one experience, hence the latter itself as a system, is possible for human beings. For the multiplicity and diversity of empirical laws could be so great that it might be possible for us to connect perceptions to some extent[c] in accordance with particular laws discovered on various occasions into one experience, but never to bring these empirical laws themselves to the unity of kinship under a common principle, if, namely, as is quite possible in itself (at least as far as the understanding can make out *a priori*), the multiplicity and diversity of these laws, along with the natural forms corresponding to them, being infinitely great, were to present to us a raw chaotic aggregate and not the least trace of a system, even though we must presuppose such a system in accordance with transcendental laws.

For **unity of nature in time and space** and unity of the experience possible for us are identical, since the former is a totality of mere appearances (kinds of representations), which can have its objective

---

[a] Presumably this means the book, the *Critique of Pure Reason*, but the words are not underlined in the fair copy.
[b] *faßliches*
[c] *theilweise*

reality only in experience, which, as itself a system in accordance with empirical laws, must be possible if one is to think of the former as a system (as must indeed be done). Thus it is a subjectively*ª* necessary transcendental **presupposition** that such a disturbingly unbounded diversity of empirical laws and heterogeneity of natural forms does not pertain to nature, rather that nature itself, through the affinity of particular laws under more general ones, qualifies for an experience, as an empirical system.

Now this presupposition is the transcendental principle of the power of judgment. For this is not merely a faculty for subsuming the particular under the general (whose concept is given), but is also, conversely, one for finding the general for the particular. The understanding, however, abstracts in its transcendental **legislation** for nature from all multiplicity of possible empirical laws; in that legislation, it takes into consideration only the conditions of the possibility of an experience in general as far as its form is concerned. In it, therefore, that principle of the affinity of particular laws of nature is not to be found. Yet the power of judgment, which is obliged to bring particular laws, even with regard to what differentiates them under the same general laws of nature, under higher, though still empirical laws, must ground its procedure on such a principle. For by groping about among forms of nature whose agreement with each other under common empirical but higher laws appeared entirely contingent to the power of judgment, it would be even more contingent if **particular perceptions** were luckily to be qualified for an empirical law; it would be all the more contingent if multiple empirical laws were to fit into a systematic unity of the cognition of nature in a possible experience **in their entire interconnection** without presupposing such a form in nature through an *a priori* principle.

All of the stock formulae: nature takes the shortest route – **she does nothing in vain – she makes no leaps in the manifold of forms** (*continuum formarum*) – **she is rich in species but sparing with genera**, etc.[6] – are nothing other than this very same transcendental expression of the power of judgment in establishing a principle for experience as a system and hence for its own needs. Neither understanding nor reason can ground such a law of nature *a priori*. For while it may readily be understood that nature should be directed by our understanding in its merely formal laws (by means of which it is an object of experience in general), with regard to particular laws, in their multiplicity and diversity, it is free from all the restrictions of our law-giving faculty of cognition, and it is a mere presupposition of the power of

ª The word "subjectively" was added to the fair copy.

judgment, in behalf of its own use, always to ascend from empirical, particular laws to more general[a] but at the same time still empirical ones, for the sake of the unification of empirical laws, which grounds that principle. And one can by no means charge such a principle to the account of experience, because only under the presupposition of it is it possible to organize experiences in a systematic way. 20: 211

V.
On the reflecting power of judgment.

The power of judgment can be regarded either as a mere faculty for **reflecting** on a given representation, in accordance with a certain principle, for the sake of a concept that is thereby made possible, or as a faculty for **determining** an underlying concept through a given **empirical** representation. In the first case it is the **reflecting**, in the second case the **determining power of judgment**. **To reflect** (to consider),[b] however, is to compare and to hold together given representations either with others or with one's faculty of cognition, in relation to a concept thereby made possible. The reflecting power of judgment is that which is also called the faculty of judging[c] (*facultas diiudicandi*).[7]

Reflecting (which goes on even in animals, although only instinctively, namely not in relation to a concept which is thereby to be attained but rather in relation to some inclination which is thereby to be determined) in our case requires a principle just as much as does determining, in which the underlying concept of the object prescribes the rule to the power of judgment and thus plays the role of the principle.

The principle of reflection on given objects of nature is that for all things in nature empirically determinate **concepts** can be found,*

---

* On first glance, this principle does not look at all like a synthetic and tran-   20: 211
scendental proposition, but seems rather to be tautological and to belong to mere logic. For the latter teaches how one can compare a given representation with others, and, by extracting what it has in common with others, as a characteristic for general use, form a concept. But about whether for each object nature has many others to put forth as objects of comparison, which   20: 212
have much in common with the first in their form, it teaches us nothing; rather, this condition of the possibility of the application of logic to nature is a principle of the representation of nature as a system for our power of judgment, in which the manifold, divided into genera and species, makes it

---

[a] The next two clauses were added to the fair copy.
[b] **Reflectiren** (*überlegen*)
[c] *Beurtheilungsvermögen*

which is to say the same as that in all of its products one can always presuppose a form that is possible for general laws cognizable by us. For if we could not presuppose this and did not ground our treatment of empirical representations on this principle, then all reflection would become arbitrary and blind, and hence would be undertaken without any well-grounded expectation of its agreement with nature.

With regard to the general concepts of nature, under which a concept of experience (without specific empirical determination) is first possible at all, reflection already has its directions in the concept of a nature in general, i.e., in the understanding, and the power of judgment requires no special principle of reflection, but rather **schematizes** this *a priori* and applies these schemata to every empirical synthesis, without which no judgment of experience*a* would be possible at all. The power of judgment in its reflection is here also determining and its transcendental schematism serves it at the same time as a rule under which given empirical intuitions*b* are subsumed.

But for those concepts which must first of all be found for given empirical intuitions, and which presuppose a particular law of nature, in accordance with which alone **particular** experience is possible, the power of judgment requires a special and*c* at the same time transcendental principle for its reflection, and one cannot refer it in turn to already known empirical concepts and transform reflection into a mere comparison with empirical forms for which one already has concepts.

possible to bring all the natural forms that are forthcoming*d* to concepts (of greater or lesser generality) through comparison. Now of course pure understanding already teaches (but also through synthetic principles) how to think of all things in nature as contained in a transcendental **system in accordance with *a priori* concepts** (the categories); only the (reflecting) power of judgment, which also seeks concepts for empirical representations, as such, must further assume for this purpose that nature in its boundless multiplicity has hit upon a division of itself into genera and species that makes it possible for our power of judgment to find consensus in the comparison of natural forms and to arrive at empirical concepts, and their interconnection with each other, through ascent to more general but still empirical concepts; i.e., the power of judgment presupposes a system of nature which is also in accordance with empirical laws and does so *a priori*, consequently by means of a transcendental principle.

a This phrase replaces "perception of an object" in the fair copy.
b Kant replaces "representations" in the fair copy with "intuitions."
c *Und* in the fair copy crossed out by Kant.
d Kant replaces *empirische Vorstellungen* ("empirical representations") in the fair copy with *alle vorkommende Naturformen*.

*For it is open to question how one could hope to arrive at empirical concepts of that which is common to the different natural forms through the comparison of perceptions, if, on account of the great diversity of its empirical laws, nature (as it is quite possible to think) has imposed on these natural forms such a great diversity that all or at least most comparison would be useless for producing consensus and a hierarchical order of species and genera under it. All comparison of empirical representations in order to cognize empirical laws in natural things and **specific** forms matching these, which however through their comparison with others are also **generically corresponding** forms, presuppose that even with regard to its empirical laws nature has observed a certain economy suitable to our power of judgment and a uniformity that we can grasp, and this presupposition, as an *a priori* principle of the power of judgment, must precede all comparison.

The reflecting power of judgment thus proceeds with given appearances, in order to bring them under empirical concepts of determinate natural things, not schematically, but **technically**, not as it were merely 20: 214
mechanically, like an instrument, but **artistically**, in accordance with the general but at the same time indeterminate principle of a purposive arrangement of nature in a system, as it were for the benefit of our power of judgment, in the suitability of its particular laws (about which understanding has nothing to say) for the possibility of experience as a system, without which presupposition we could not hope to find our way in a labyrinth of the multiplicity of possible empirical particular laws. Thus the power of judgment itself makes the **technique of nature** into the principle of its reflection *a priori*, without however being able to explain this or determine it more precisely or having for this end an objective determining ground for the general concepts of nature (from a cognition of things in themselves),*b* but only in order to be able to reflect in accordance with its own subjective law, in accordance with its need,*c* but at the same time in accord with laws of nature in general.

The principle of the reflecting power of judgment, through which nature is thought of as a system in accordance with empirical laws, is however merely a principle **for the logical use of the power of**

---

a The remainder of this paragraph is Kant's replacement for the following in the fair copy: "For it is also rightly open to question about these [empirical forms] how and through what reflection we have arrived at them as lawful natural forms. Laws cannot be perceived, but rather presuppose principles in accordance with which perceptions must be able to be compared, which, if under them alone experience is possible, are transcendental principles."
b Kant added the phrase *an sich selbst* to the fair copy.
c Kant added the phrase *nach ihrem Bedürfniß* to the fair copy.

judgment, a transcendental principle, to be sure, in terms of its origin,[a] but only for the sake of regarding nature *a priori* as qualified for a **logical system** of its multiplicity under empirical laws.[8]

The logical form of a system consists merely in the division of given general concepts (of the sort which that of a nature in general is here), by means of which one thinks the particular (here the empirical) with its variety as contained under the general, in accordance with a certain principle. To this there belongs, if one proceeds empirically and ascends from the particular to the general, a **classification** of the manifold, i.e., a comparison with each other of several classes, each of which stands under a determinate concept, and, if they are complete with regard to the common characteristic, their subsumption[b] under higher classes (genera), until one reaches the concept that contains the principle of the entire classification (and which constitutes the highest genus). If, on the contrary, one begins with the general concept, in order to descend to the particular through a complete division, then the action is called the **specification** of the manifold under a given concept, since the progression is from the highest genus to lower (subgenera or species) and from species to subspecies. This would be expressed more correctly if, instead of saying (as in common usage) that one must specify the particular which stands under a general concept, it were instead said that one **specifies the general concept** by adducing the manifold under it. For the genus is (considered logically) as it were the matter, or the raw substratum, which nature works up into particular species and subspecies through various determinations, and thus it can be said, in analogy with the use of this word by jurists, when they speak of the specification of certain raw materials, that **nature specifies itself** in accordance with a certain principle (or the idea of a system).*[9]

Now it is clear that the reflecting power of judgment, given its

20: 215

20: 215 *[c]The Aristotelian school also called the **genus** matter, but the **specific difference** the form.

20: 216 [d]Could Linnaeus have hoped to outline a system of nature if he had had to worry that if he found a stone that he called granite, this might differ in its internal constitution from every other stone which nevertheless looked just like it, and all he could hope to find were always individual things, as it were isolated for the understanding, and never a class of them that could be brought under concepts of genus and species[?]

[a] Kant added the phrase *seinem Ursprung nach* to the fair copy.
[b] Kant added the words *ihrer Subsumtion* to the fair copy.
[c] Kant added this footnote to the fair copy.
[d] He then added this in the margin next to the note.

18

nature, could not undertake to **classify** the whole of nature according to its empirical differences if it did not presuppose that nature itself **specifies** its transcendental laws in accordance with some sort of principle. Now this principle can be none other than that of the suitability for the capacity[a] of the power of judgment itself for finding in the immeasurable multiplicity of things in accordance with possible empirical laws sufficient kinship among them to enable them to be brought under empirical concepts (classes) and these in turn under more general laws (higher genera) and thus for an empirical system of nature to be reached. – Now since such a classification is not a common experiential cognition, but an artistic one, nature, to the extent that it is thought of as specifying itself in accordance with such a principle, is also regarded as **art**, and the power of judgment thus necessarily carries with it *a priori* a principle of the **technique** of nature, which is distinct from the **nomothetic** of nature in accordance with transcendental laws of understanding in that the latter can make its principle valid as a law but the former only as a necessary presupposition.

The special principle of the power of judgment is thus: **Nature specifies its general laws into[b] empirical ones, in accordance with the form of a logical system, in behalf of the power of judgment.** 20: 216

Now here arises the concept of a **purposiveness** of nature, indeed as a special concept of the reflecting power of judgment, not of reason; for the end is not posited in the object at all, but strictly in the subject and indeed in its mere capacity[c] for reflecting. – For we call purposive that the existence of which seems to presuppose a representation of that same thing; natural laws, however, which are so constituted and related to each other as if they had been designed by the power of judgment for its own need, have a similarity with the possibility of things that presuppose a representation of themselves as their ground. Thus through its principle the power of judgment thinks of a purposiveness of nature in the specification of its forms through empirical laws.

However, these forms themselves are not thereby thought of as purposive, but only their relation to one another and their fitness, even in their great multiplicity, for a logical system of empirical concepts. – Now if nature showed us nothing more than this logical purposiveness, we would indeed already have cause to admire it for this, since we cannot suggest any ground for this in accordance with the general laws of the understanding; only hardly anyone other than a transcendental

---

[a] *Vermögen*
[b] Kant crossed out *durch die* (through the) and replaced it with *zu* (into).
[c] *Vermögen*

philosopher would be capable of this admiration, and even he[a] would not be able to name any determinate case where this purposiveness proved itself *in concreto*, but would have to think of it only in general.

20: 217

VI.
On the purposiveness
of the forms of nature
as so many particular systems.

That nature in its empirical laws should specify itself as is requisite for a possible experience, as **a system** of empirical cognition – this form of nature contains a logical purposiveness, namely of its conformity to the subjective conditions of the power of judgment with regard to the possible interconnection of empirical concepts in the whole of an experience. Now this, however, yields no inference to its usefulness for a real purposiveness in its products, i.e., for producing individual things in the form of systems: for the latter could always, as far as intuition is concerned, be mere aggregates and nevertheless be possible in accordance with empirical laws interconnected with others in a system **of logical division**, without a concept specially instituted as the condition for their particular possibility having to be assumed, hence without a purposiveness of nature as its ground. In this way we see soils, stones, minerals, etc., without any purposive form, as mere aggregates, but nevertheless as so related in the inner character and grounds for the cognition of their possibility that they are suitable for the classification of things in a system of nature under empirical laws yet do not display the form of a system[b] **in themselves**.

Hence I understand by an **absolute purposiveness** of natural forms such an external shape as well as inner structure that are so constituted that their possibility must be grounded in an idea of them in our power of judgment. For purposiveness is a lawfulness of the contingent as such.[c] With regard to its products as aggregates, nature proceeds **mechanically, as mere nature**; but with regard to its products as systems, e.g., crystal formations, various shapes of flowers, or the inner structure of plants and animals, it proceeds **technically**, i.e., as at the same time an **art**. The distinction between these two ways of judging[d]

20: 218

---

[a] The words from the last semicolon to here replace the single word "we" (*wir*) in the original fair copy.

[b] *eine Form des Systems*

[c] In the fair copy, this sentence originally read: "For purposiveness is a lawfulness which is at the same time contingent with respect to general laws of nature that are necessary for experience."

[d] *beurtheilen*

natural beings is made merely by the **reflecting** power of judgment, which perfectly well can and perhaps even must allow to happen what the **determining** power of judgment (under principles of reason) would not concede with regard to the possibility of the objects themselves, and which would perhaps even like to know everything to be traced back to a mechanical sort of explanation; for it is entirely consistent that the **explanation** of an appearance, which is an affair of reason in accordance with objective principles of reason, be **mechanical**, while the rule for the **judging**ᵃ of the same object, in accordance with subjective principles of reflection on it, should be **technical**.

Now although the principle of the power of judgment concerning the purposiveness of nature in the specifications of its general laws by no means extends so far as to imply the generation **of natural forms that are purposive in themselves** (because even without them the system of nature in accordance with empirical laws, which is all that the power of judgment has a basis for postulating, is possible), and this must therefore be given solely through experience, nevertheless, because we already have a ground for ascribing to nature in its particular laws a principle of purposiveness, it is always **possible** and permissible, if experience shows us purposive forms in its products, for us to ascribe this to the same ground as that on which the first may rest.

Although even*ᵇ* this ground itself may lie in the supersensible and beyond the sphere of the insights into nature that are possible for us, we have still already won something by having ready in the power of judgment a transcendental principle of the purposiveness of nature for the purposiveness of the natural forms that may be found in experience, which, even though it is not sufficient to explain the possibility of such forms, nevertheless makes it permissible for us to apply such a special concept as that of purposiveness to nature and its lawfulness, although it cannot of course be an objective concept of nature, but is rather derived merely from the subjective relation of nature to a faculty of the mind.

VII.

On the technique of the power of judgment
as the ground of the idea of a technique of nature.

20: 219

As was shown above, the power of judgment first makes it possible, indeed necessary, to conceive in nature, over and above its mechanical necessity, a purposiveness without the presupposition of which system-

---

ᵃ *Beurtheilung*
ᵇ Kant added *auch* to the fair copy.

atic unity in the thoroughgoing classification*a* of particular forms in accordance with empirical laws*b* would not be possible. It has just been shown that since this principle of purposiveness is only a subjective principle of the division and specification of nature, it does not determine anything with regard to the forms of the products of nature. In this way, this purposiveness would merely remain in concepts and supply a maxim of the unity of nature in its empirical laws for the logical use of the power of judgment in experience, in behalf of the use of reason about its objects, but by this particular kind of systematic*c* unity, namely that in accordance with the representation of a purpose, no objects in nature, as products corresponding to it in their form, would be given. – Now I would call the **causality** of nature with regard to the form of its products as ends the **technique** of nature. It is opposed to the mechanics of nature, which consists in its causality through the combination of the manifold without a concept lying at the ground of its manner of unification, roughly as we would call certain tools, e.g., a lever or an inclined plane, which have their effect in an end without a concept having to be their ground, machines but not works of art; *d*for they can certainly be used for ends, but are not possible solely in relation to them.

Now the first question here is: How can the technique of nature in its products **be perceived**? The concept of purposiveness is not a constitutive concept of experience at all, not a determination of an appearance belonging to an empirical **concept** of the object; for it is not a category.*e* In our power of judgment we perceive purposiveness insofar as it merely reflects upon a given object, whether in order to bring the empirical intuition of that object under some concept (it is indeterminate which), or in order to bring the laws which the concept of experience itself contains under common principles. Thus the **power of judgment** is properly technical; nature is represented technically only insofar as it conforms to that procedure of the power of judgment and makes it necessary.*f* We will shortly indicate the way in which the concept of the reflecting power of judgment, which makes possible*g* the inner perception of a purposiveness of representations,

20: 220

---

a Kant crossed out *Verknüpfung* (connection) and replaced it with "classification."
b Kant substituted *Formen nach empirischen Gesetzen* for *Erfahrung und ihren Gesetzen* (experience and its laws).
c Kant added "systematic" to the fair copy.
d Kant added the remainder of this sentence to the fair copy.
e Kant added the last clause to the fair copy.
f Written in the margin next to this sentence, in a hand that does not appear to be either Kant's or Kiesewetter's: "We put, it is said, final causes into things, and do not as it were draw them out of their perception."
g Kant substituted *möglich macht* for "permits" (*verstattet*) in the fair copy.

can also be applied to the representation of the object as contained under it.

To every empirical concept, namely, there belong three actions of the self-active faculty of cognition: 1. the **apprehension**[a] (*apprehensio*) of the manifold of intuition; 2. the **comprehension**,[b] i.e., the synthetic unity of the consciousness of this manifold in the concept of an object (*apperceptio comprehensiva*); 3. the **presentation**[c] (*exhibitio*) of the object corresponding to this concept in intuition. For the first action imagination is required, for the second understanding, for the third the power of judgment, which, if it is an empirical concept that is at issue, would be the determining power of judgment.

But since in the mere reflection on a perception it is not a matter of a determinate concept, but in general only of reflecting on the rule concerning a perception in behalf of the understanding, as a faculty of concepts, it can readily be seen that in a merely reflecting judgment imagination and understanding are considered in the relation to each other in which they must stand in the power of judgment in general, as compared with the relation in which they actually stand in the case of a given perception.

If, then, the form of a given object in empirical intuition is so constituted that the **apprehension** of its manifold in the imagination agrees with the **presentation** of a concept of the understanding (though which concept be undetermined), then in the mere reflection understanding and imagination mutually agree for the advancement of their business, and the object will be perceived as purposive merely for the power of judgment, hence the purposiveness itself will be considered as merely subjective; for which, further, no determinate concept of the object at all is required nor is one thereby generated,[d] and the judgment itself is not a cognitive judgment. – Such a judgment is called an **aesthetic**[e] **judgment of reflection**.

In contrast, if empirical concepts and even empirical laws are already given in accordance with the mechanism of nature and the power of judgment compares such a concept of the understanding with reason and its principle of the possibility of a system, then, if this form is found in the object, the purposiveness is judged[f] **objectively** and the thing is called a **natural end**, whereas previously things were judged[g]

20:221

---

[a] *Auffassung*
[b] *Zusammenfassung*
[c] *Darstellung*
[d] Kant added the words *noch dadurch erzeugt* to the fair copy.
[e] This word is doubly underlined in the manuscript.
[f] *beurtheilt*
[g] *beurtheilt*

as indeterminately*ᵃ* purposive **natural forms**. The judgment about the objective purposiveness of nature is called **teleological**.*ᵇ* It is a **cognitive judgment**, but still belonging only to the reflecting, not to the determining power of judgment. For in general the technique of nature, whether it be merely **formal** or **real**, is only a relation of things to our power of judgment, in which alone can be found the idea of a purposiveness of nature, and which is ascribed to nature only in relation to that power.

VIII.
On the aesthetic
of the faculty of judging.*ᶜ*

The expression "an aesthetic **kind of representation**" is entirely unambiguous if we understand by it the relation of the representation to an object, as an appearance, for the cognition of that object; for then the expression "**aesthetic**" signifies only that the form of sensibility (how the subject is affected) necessarily adheres to such a representation and that this is unavoidably carried over to the object (but only as phenomenon). Hence there could be a transcendental aesthetic as a science belonging to the faculty of cognition.[10] But it has been customary for some time also to call a kind of representation aesthetic in a sense*ᵈ* in which what is meant is the relation of a representation not to the cognitive faculty but to the feeling of pleasure and displeasure. Now even though we are also used to calling this feeling (in accordance with this designation) a sense (modification of our state) for the lack of another expression, yet it is not an objective sense, whose determination would be used for the **cognition** of an object (for to intuit something with pleasure or otherwise cognize it is not a mere relation of the representation to the object, but rather a receptivity of the subject), which contributes nothing at all to the cognition of the object.[11] For that very reason, since all determinations of feeling are merely of subjective significance, there cannot be an aesthetic of feeling as a science as there is, say, an aesthetic of the faculty of cognition. Thus there always remains an unavoidable ambiguity in the expression "an aesthetic kind of representation," if by that one sometimes understands that which arouses the feeling of pleasure and displeasure, sometimes that which merely concerns the faculty of cognition insofar as sensible

20: 222

ᵃ Kant inserted this word in the fair copy.
ᵇ This word is doubly underlined in the manuscript.
ᶜ *Beurtheilungsvermögen*
ᵈ *Bedeutung*

intuition is found in it, which allows us to cognize objects only as appearances.

However, this ambiguity can be removed if the expression "aesthetic" is applied neither to intuition nor, still less, to representations of the understanding, but only to the actions of the **power of judgment**. An **aesthetic judgment**, if one would use it for an objective determination, would be so patently contradictory that one is sufficiently insured against misinterpretation by this expression. For intuitions can certainly be sensible, but **judgments** belong absolutely only to the understanding (taken in a wider sense), and **to judge** aesthetically or sensibly, insofar as this is supposed to be **cognition** of an object, is itself a contradiction even if sensibility meddles in the business of the understanding and (through a *vitium subreptionis*[a])[12] gives the understanding a false direction; rather, an **objective** judgment is always made by the understanding, and to that extent cannot be called aesthetic. Hence our transcendental aesthetic of the faculty of cognition could very well speak of sensible intuitions, but could nowhere speak of aesthetic judgments; for since it has to do only with cognitive judgments, which determine the object, its judgments must all be logical. By the designation "an aesthetic judgment about an object" it is therefore immediately indicated that a given representation is certainly related to an object[b] but that what is understood in the judgment is not the determination of the object but of the subject and its feeling. For in the power of judgment understanding and imagination are considered in relation to each other, and this can, to be sure, first be considered objectively, as belonging to cognition (as happened in the transcendental schematism of the power of judgment);[13] but one can also consider this relation of two faculties of cognition merely subjectively, insofar as one helps or hinders the other in the very same representation and thereby affects the **state of mind**, and [is] therefore a relation which is **sensitive**[c] (which is not the case in the separate use of any other faculty of cognition). Now although this sensation[d] is not a sensible representation of an object,[e] still, because it is subjectively connected with the process of making the concepts of the understanding sensible[f] by means of the power of judgment, it can, as a sensible

20: 223

---

[a] the vice of subreption
[b] Kant inserted in the margin but then crossed out the words "as its determination" (*als Bestimmung desselben*).
[c] *empfindbar*
[d] *Empfindung*
[e] *Objects*
[f] *Versinnlichung der Verstandesbegriffe*

representation of the state of the subject who is affected by an act of that faculty, be reckoned to sensibility, and a judgment can be called aesthetic, i.e., sensible (as far as its subjective effect, not its determining ground is concerned),*a* although judging (that is, objectively) is an action of the understanding (as the higher cognitive faculty in general) and not of sensibility.

Every **determining** judgment is **logical** because its predicate is a given objective concept. A merely **reflecting** judgment about a given individual object, however, **can be aesthetic** if (before its comparison with others is seen), the power of judgment, which has no concept ready for the given intuition, holds the imagination (merely in the apprehension of the object) together with the understanding (in the presentation of a concept in general) and perceives a relation of the two faculties of cognition which constitutes the subjective, merely sensitive condition of the objective use of the power of judgment in general (namely the agreement of those two faculties with each other).*b* However, an aesthetic judgment of sense is also possible, if, namely, the predicate of the judgment **cannot be** a predicate of an object at all, because it does not belong to the faculty of cognition at all, e.g., the wine is pleasant, for then the predicate expresses the relation of the representation immediately to the feeling of pleasure and not to the faculty of cognition.

An aesthetic judgment in general can therefore be explicated as that judgment whose predicate can never be cognition (concept of an object) (although it may contain the subjective conditions for a cognition in general). In such a judgment the determining ground is sensation. However, there is only one so-called sensation that can never become a concept of an object, and this is the feeling of pleasure and displeasure. This is merely subjective, whereas all other sensation can be used for cognition.[14] Thus an aesthetic judgment is that whose determining ground lies in a sensation that is immediately connected with the feeling of pleasure and displeasure. In the aesthetic judgment of sense it is that sensation which is immediately produced by the empirical intuition of the object, in the aesthetic judgment of reflection, however, it is that sensation which the harmonious play of the two faculties of cognition in the power of judgment, imagination and understanding, produces in the subject insofar as in the given representation the faculty of the apprehension of the one and the faculty of presentation of the other are reciprocally expeditious,*c* which relation in such a case produces through this mere form a sensation that is the determining

20: 224

---

a Kant added the parenthetical phrase to the fair copy.
b Kant added the parenthetical phrase to the fair copy.
c *beförderlich*

ground of a judgment which for that reason is called aesthetic and as subjective purposiveness (without a concept) is combined with the feeling of pleasure.[15]

The aesthetic judgment of sense contains material purposiveness, the aesthetic judgment of reflection formal purposiveness. But since the former is not related to the faculty of cognition at all, but is related immediately through sense to the feeling of pleasure, only the latter is to be regarded as grounded in special principles of the power of judgment.[16] For if the reflection on a given representation precedes the feeling of pleasure (as the determining ground of the judgment), then the subjective purposiveness is **thought** before it is **felt**[a] in its effect, and to this extent, namely in terms of its principles, the aesthetic judgment belongs to the higher faculty of cognition and indeed to the power of judgment, under whose subjective but nevertheless still universal[b] conditions the representation of the object is subsumed. However, since a merely subjective condition of a judgment does not permit a determinate concept of that judgment's determining ground, this can only be given in the feeling of pleasure, so that the aesthetic judgment is always a judgment of reflection; while on the contrary one which presupposes no comparison of the representation with the faculties of cognition that operate in unity[c] in the power of judgment is an aesthetic judgment of sense, which relates a given representation (but not by means of the power of judgment and its principle) to the feeling of pleasure. The criterion[d] by which to decide this distinction can only be given in the treatise itself and consists in the claim of the judgment to universal validity and necessity;[17] for if the aesthetic judgment carries such a claim with it, then it also makes a claim that its determining ground must lie **not merely**[e] **in the feeling** of pleasure and displeasure in itself alone, but **at the same time in a rule** of the higher faculty of cognition, in this case, namely, in the rule of the power of judgment, which is thus legislative with regard to the conditions of reflection *a priori*, and demonstrates **autonomy**;[f] this autonomy is not, however (like that of the understanding, with regard to the theoretical laws of nature, or of reason, in the practical laws of freedom), valid objectively, i.e., through concepts of things or possible actions, but is merely subjectively valid,[g] for the judgment from feeling, which, if it

20: 225

---

[a] *empfunden*
[b] *allgemeine*
[c] Kant inserted the word *vereinigt* in the fair copy, replacing *verbunden* (in combination).
[d] *Merkmal*
[e] Kant inserted *bloß* in the fair copy.
[f] "Autonomy" is doubly underlined.
[g] Kant inserted *gültig* into the fair copy, thereby changing *objectiv* and *subjectiv* from adjectives modifying "autonomy" into adverbs modifying "valid."

can make a claim to universal validity, demonstrates its origin grounded in *a priori* principles. Strictly speaking, one must call this legislation **heautonomy**, since the power of judgment does not give the law to nature nor to freedom, but solely to itself, and it is not a faculty for producing concepts of objects, but only for comparing present cases to others that have been given to it and thereby indicating the subjective conditions of the possibility of this combination *a priori*.

20: 226

From this it may also be understood why the power of judgment, in an action that it exercises for itself (without any concept of the object for its ground), as the merely reflecting power of judgment, instead of relating the given representation to its own rule with consciousness of it, relates reflection immediately only to sensation, which, like all sensations, is always accompanied with pleasure or displeasure (which does not happen in the case of any other higher faculty of cognition): because, namely, the rule itself is only subjective and correspondence with it can be recognized only in that which always merely expresses relation to the subject, namely sensation, as the criterion and determining ground of the judgment; hence it is also called aesthetic, and consequently all our judgments, in accordance with the order of the higher cognitive faculties, can be divided into **theoretical**, **aesthetic**, and **practical**, whereby aesthetic judgments are understood only the judgments of reflection, which alone are related to a principle of the power of judgment, as a higher faculty of cognition, since the aesthetic judgments of sense, on the contrary, have to do immediately only with the relation of representations to the inner sense, insofar as that is feeling.

Remark

Now here it is particularly necessary to elucidate the explanation of pleasure as the sensible representation of the **perfection** of an object.[18] According to this explanation, an aesthetic judgment of sense or reflection would always be a cognitive judgment of the object; for perfection is a determination that presupposes a concept of the object, because of which, therefore, the judgment which ascribes perfection to the object would not be distinguished from other logical judgments at all, except perhaps, as some claim, through the confusion that attaches to the concept (which some presume to call sensibility), which however absolutely cannot constitute a specific distinction among judgments.[19] For otherwise an endless host of judgments, not only of the understanding but even of reason, would have to be called aesthetic, since in them an object is determined through a concept that is confused, as in, e.g., judgments about right and wrong;[a] for how many people (or even philosophers) have a distinct concept of what is right.* The sensible representation of perfection is an express contradiction, and if the agreement of the manifold as a unity[b] is to be called perfection, then it must be represented through a concept, or else it cannot carry the name of a perfection. If one wants to say that pleasure and displeasure should be nothing but mere cognitions of things through the understanding (which would only not be consciousness of its concepts) and that they only seem to us to be mere sensations, then one would have to call the judging[c] of things by this means not aesthetic (sensible) but generally intellectual, and the senses would be at bottom nothing but a judging understanding (although one without adequate consciousness of its own actions), the aesthetic kind of representation would not be specifically different from the logical, and thus, since it would then be impossible to draw the boundary between the two in a determinate way, this difference in denomination would be entirely useless. (Not to mention anything here about this mystical kind of representation of the things of the world, which does not admit as sensible at all any intuition that is distinct from concepts, where thus nothing would be left for the former except an intuitive understanding.)[21]

Still one might ask: Doesn't our concept of a purposiveness of nature signify exactly the same as the concept of **perfection**, and isn't

20: 227

---

* One can say, in general, that things must never be considered to be **specifically different** because of a quality that merges into another through mere increase or decrease in its degree. Now the distinction between distinctness and confusion of concepts comes down solely to the degree of consciousness of the marks, corresponding to the amount of attention directed to them, and thus to this extent one mode of representation is not specifically different from the other. Intuition and concept, however, are specifically distinguished from each other, for they do not merge into one another, no matter how the consciousness of each and of its marks may grow or diminish. For even the greatest lack of distinctness of a mode of representation by concepts (e.g., that of right) still retains the specific difference of the latter in regard to its origin in the understanding, and the greatest distinctness of intuition does not in the least bring the latter nearer to the former, because the latter mode of representation has its seat in sensibility. Logical distinctness is also totally different from aesthetic distinctness, and the latter can obtain even though we do not represent the object to ourselves by means of concepts at all, that is, even though the representation, as intuition, is sensible.[20]

20: 227

[a] *Recht und Unrecht*
[b] *zu Einem*
[c] *Beurtheilung*

the empirical consciousness of subjective purposiveness, or the feeling of pleasure in certain objects, therefore the sensible intuition of a perfection, just as some would explain pleasure in general?

20: 228   I reply: **Perfection**, as mere completeness of the many, insofar as together it constitutes a one, is an ontological concept, which is the same as that of the totality (allness)*a* of something composite (through coordination of the manifold in an aggregate, or at the same time its subordination as grounds and consequences in a series), and has not the least to do with the feeling of pleasure or displeasure. **The** perfection of a thing in the relation of its manifold to a concept of it is merely formal. If, however, I speak of **a** perfection (of which there can be many in a thing under the same concept of it), then it is always grounded in the concept of something, as an end, to which that ontological concept, of the agreement of the manifold as a unity,*b* is applied. This end, however, need not always be a practical end, which presupposes or includes a pleasure in the existence of the object, but can also belong to technique, and thus concerns merely the possibility of things and **the lawfulness of an intrinsically contingent combination of the manifold** in the object. An example might be the purposiveness that one necessarily thinks in the possibility of a regular hexagon, since it is entirely contingent that six equal lines on a plane should intersect at precisely equal angles, for this lawlike combination presupposes a concept which, as principle, makes it possible. The same kind of objective purposiveness observed in things in nature (especially in organized beings) is now thought as objective and material and necessarily carries with it the concept of an end of nature (either real or imputed to it), in relation to which we also attribute perfection to the things; judgment about this is called teleological and does not carry a feeling of pleasure with it at all, just as in general this should not be sought in judgment about mere causal combination.

In general, therefore, the concept of perfection as objective purposiveness has nothing at all to do with the feeling of pleasure, and the latter has nothing to do with the former. A **concept** of the object necessarily belongs to the judging*c* of the former, while such a concept is not necessary at all for the judging of the latter, which can be created by merely empirical intuition. By contrast, the representation of a subjective purposiveness of an object is even identical with the feeling of pleasure (without even involving an abstract concept of a purposive relation), and between the latter and the former there is a very great gap. For whether what is subjectively purposive is also objectively

20: 229

---

a Kant added the parenthetical word *Allheit* to the fair copy.
b *zu Einem*
c *Beurtheilung*

purposive requires an often extensive investigation, not only in practical philosophy but also in technique, whether in nature or in art, i.e., to find perfection in a thing requires reason, to find agreeableness requires mere sense, and to discover beauty in it requires nothing but mere reflection (without any concept) on a given representation.[a]

Thus the faculty of aesthetic reflection judges only about the subjective purposiveness (not about the perfection) of the object: and the question arises whether it judges only **by means** of the pleasure or displeasure which is felt in it,[b] or whether it rather judges **about** these, so that the judgment at the same time determines that pleasure or displeasure **must** be combined with the representation of the object.

As was already mentioned above, this question cannot yet be adequately decided here. It must only emerge from the exposition of this sort of judgment in the treatise whether it carries with it a universality and necessity which qualifies it for derivation from a determining ground *a priori*. In this case the judgment would certainly determine something *a priori* by means of the sensation of pleasure or displeasure, but it would also at the same time determine something *a priori*, through the faculty of cognition (namely, the power of judgment), about the universality of the rule for combining it with a given representation. If, on the contrary, the judgment contained nothing but the relation of the representation to the feeling (without the mediation of a cognitive principle), as is the case in the aesthetic judgment of sense (which is neither a cognitive judgment nor a judgment of reflection), then all aesthetic judgments would belong merely to the empirical department.

Provisionally, it can also be noted that no transition from cognition to the feeling of pleasure and displeasure takes place **through concepts** of objects (so far as the latter are to stand in relation to the former), and one thus cannot expect[c] to determine *a priori* the influence that a given representation has on the mind, as we previously noticed in the *Critique of Practical Reason*, where the representation of a universal lawfulness of willing must at one and the same time determine the will and thereby also arouse the feeling of respect, as a law contained, and indeed contained *a priori*, in our moral judgments, even though this feeling could nonetheless not be derived from concepts.[22] In just the same way the resolution of the aesthetic judgment of reflection will display the concept of the formal but subjective purposiveness of the object, resting on an *a priori* principle, which is fundamentally identical

20: 230

---

[a] Here Kant crossed out the further sentence: "Perfection sensibly represented is a *contradictio in adjecto*."
[b] *der dabey empfundenen Lust oder Unlust*
[c] Here Kant crossed out "*a priori*."

with the feeling of pleasure, but which cannot be derived from concepts, and to the possibility of which in general the power of representation is related when it affects the mind in reflection on an object.

An explanation of this feeling considered in general, **without regard to the distinction whether it accompanies sensation, reflection or the determination of the will**, must be transcendental.* It can go like

20: 230

* *ª*It is useful to attempt a transcendental definition of concepts which are used as empirical principles, if one has cause to suspect that they have kinship with the pure faculty of cognition *a priori*. One then proceeds like the mathematician, who makes it much easier to solve his problem by leaving its empirical data undetermined and bringing the mere synthesis of them under the expressions of pure arithmetic.*ᵇ* But the following objection has been made to a similar explanation of the faculty of desire (*Critique of Practical Reason*, Preface, p. 16): that it cannot be defined as **the faculty for being, through its representations, the cause of the reality of the objects of these representations**, since mere **wishes** would also be desires, which, it is nevertheless admitted, cannot bring forth their objects. However, this proves nothing more than that there are also determinations of the faculty of desire in which it is in contradiction with itself: a phenomenon which is certainly noteworthy for empirical psychology (like noticing the influence that prejudices have on the understanding is for logic), but one which must not influence the definition of the faculty of desire considered objectively, that is, as it is in itself, before it is deflected from its determination by something else. In fact, a person may desire something in the most lively and persistent way even

20: 231

though he is convinced that he cannot accomplish it or even that it is absolutely impossible: e.g., to wish that which has been done to be undone, to yearn for the more rapid passage of a burdensome time, etc. It is important for morality to warn emphatically against such empty and fantastic desires, which are frequently nourished by novels, and sometimes also by mystical representations, similar to novels, of superhuman perfections and fantastical bliss. But even the effect which such empty desires and yearnings, over-exciting and enfeebling the heart, have on the mind, weakening it by exhausting its powers, are sufficient to prove that these powers are in fact repeatedly strained by representations in order to make their object real, but just as often let the mind sink back into consciousness of its incapacity. For anthropology it is also a not unimportant task to investigate why nature has implanted in us a disposition to such a fruitless expenditure of our powers as empty wishes and yearnings are (which certainly play a great role in human life). In this, as in all else, nature seems to me to have made its arrangements wisely. For if we were not determined to apply our powers by the representation of an object until we had made sure of the adequacy of our capacity*ᶜ*

ª Kant added this footnote to the fair copy.
ᵇ Here Kant crossed out "One cannot know how far this procedure may be taken, or whether an inventive mind may not perhaps succeed with it."
ᶜ Vermögen

this: **Pleasure** is a **state** of the mind in which a representation is in agreement with itself, as a ground, either merely for preserving this state itself (for the state of the powers of the mind reciprocally pro- 20: 231 moting each other in a representation preserves itself),[a] or for produc- ing its object.[24] If it is the former, then the judgment on the given object is an aesthetic judgment of reflection; however, if it is the latter, then it is an aesthetic-pathological or an aesthetic-practical judgment. 20: 232 It can be readily seen here that pleasure or displeasure, since they are not kinds of cognition, cannot be explained by themselves[b] at all, and are felt, not understood; hence they can be only inadequately explained through the influence that a representation has on the activity of the powers of the mind by means of this feeling.

IX.
On teleological judging.[c]

By a **formal** technique of nature, I understand its purposiveness in intuition; by its **real** technique, however, I understand its purposiveness in accordance with concepts. The first provides purposive shapes[d] for the power of judgment, i.e., the form in the representation of which imagination and understanding agree mutually and of themselves for the possibility of a concept. The second signifies the concept of things as ends of nature, i.e., as such that their internal possibility presupposes an end, hence a concept which, as a condition, grounds the causality of their generation.

The power of judgment itself can provide and construct purposive forms of intuition *a priori* if, namely, it invents such forms for appre- hension as are suitable for the presentation of a concept. But ends, i.e., representations that are themselves regarded as conditions of the cau- sality of their objects (as effects), must in general be given from some- where before the power of judgment occupies itself with the conditions

for producing it, then the latter would remain mostly unused. For we com- monly learn to know our powers only by trying them out. Nature has therefore combined the determination of our power with the representation of the object even prior to knowledge of our capacity, which is often first brought forth precisely by this striving, which initially seemed to the mind itself to be an empty wish. Now wisdom is obliged to set limits for this instinct, but it would never succeed in eradicating it, nor will it ever even demand to do so.[23]

[a] This parenthetical remark was added by Kant to the fair copy.
[b] *für sich*
[c] *Beurtheilung*
[d] *Gestalten*

for bringing the manifold into agreement with such ends, and if they are to be ends of nature, then certain things in nature must be able to be considered as if they were products of a cause whose causality could only be determined through a **representation** of the object. However, we cannot determine how and in how many ways things are possible through their causes *a priori*; for this laws of experience are necessary.

20: 233

The judgment about the purposiveness in things in nature, which is considered as a ground of their possibility (as ends of nature), is called a **teleological judgment**. Now although aesthetic judgments themselves are not possible *a priori*, nevertheless *a priori* principles are given in the necessary idea of an experience, as a system, which contain the concept of a formal purposiveness of nature for our power of judgment, and from which the possibility of aesthetic judgments of reflection, as such, which are grounded on *a priori* principles, is illuminated *a priori*. Nature is necessarily harmonious not merely with our **understanding**, in regard to its transcendental laws, but also, in its empirical laws, with the **power of judgment** and its capacity[a] for exhibiting those laws in an empirical apprehension of its forms through the imagination, and that indeed only for the sake of experience, and so its formal purposiveness can still be shown as necessary with regard to the latter accord (with the power of judgment). But now, as object of a teleological judging,[b] it is also to be thought of as corresponding, in its causality, with **reason**, in accordance with the concept that it forms of an end; that is more than can be expected of the power of judgment alone, which can certainly contain its own principles *a priori* for the form of intuition, but not for the concepts of the generation of things. The concept of a real **end of nature** therefore lies entirely outside the field of the power of judgment if that is considered by itself, and since this, as a separate power of cognition, considers only two faculties, imagination and understanding, as in relation in a representation prior to any concept, and thereby perceives the subjective purposiveness of the object for the faculty of cognition in the apprehension of that object (through the imagination), in the teleological purposiveness of things, as ends of nature, which can only be represented through concepts, it must set the understanding into relation with reason (which is not necessary for experience in general) in order to make things representable as ends of nature.

The aesthetic judging[c] of natural forms, without a basis in a concept of the object, was able to find certain objects occurring in nature purposive in the mere empirical apprehension of the intuition, namely merely in relation to the subjective condition of the power of judg-

---

[a] *Vermögen*
[b] *Beurtheilung*
[c] *Beurtheilung*

ment. Aesthetic judging^a thus required no concept of the object nor did it bring one forth; hence it explained these objects not as **ends of nature**, in an objective judgment, but only as **purposive** for the power of representation, in a subjective relation, which purposiveness of forms can be called **figurative**, and the technique of nature with regard to such forms can also be so called (*technica speciosa*).^{b,25}   20: 234

The teleological judgment, by contrast, presupposes a concept of the object and makes a judgment about its possibility in accordance with a law of the connection of causes and effects. This technique of nature could thus be called **plastic**, if it had not already become fashionable to use this word in a more general sense, namely for natural beauty as well as natural intentions; hence it may, if you like, be called the **organic technique** of nature, which expression then designates the concept of purposiveness not merely for the manner of representation, but for the possibility of the things themselves.

What is most essential and important in this section, however, is the proof that the concept of **final causes** in nature, which separates the teleological judging^c of nature from that in accordance with general, mechanical laws, is a concept belonging merely to the power of judgment, and not to the understanding or to reason, i.e., the proof that while one can also use the concept of a natural end in an objective sense, as a **natural intention**, such a use, as already sophistical,^d is absolutely not grounded in experience, which certainly exhibits ends, but that these are at the same time intentions cannot be proved in any way; hence whatever may be found in experience to belong to teleology contains merely the relation of its objects to the power of judgment and indeed to a principle of it by means of which it is legislative for itself (not for nature), namely as a reflecting power of judgment.

The concept of ends and of purposiveness is of course a concept of reason, insofar as one ascribes the ground of the possibility of an object to it. But purposiveness in nature, as well as the concept of things as natural ends, places reason as cause into a relation with such things, as the ground of their possibility, in a way which we cannot know through any experience. For we can be conscious of the causality of reason in objects, which on that account are called purposive or ends, only in the case of **products of art**, and to call reason technical in regard to them is appropriate to the experience of the causality of our own capacity.^e But to represent nature as technical, like a reason (and so to attribute   20: 235

---

^a *Beurtheilung*
^b a technique of appearance
^c *Beurtheilung*
^d *vernünftelnd*
^e *Vermögen*

purposiveness and even ends **to nature**), is a special concept, which we cannot encounter in experience and which only the power of judgment introduces into its reflection on objects, in order to treat experience, following its direction, in accordance with special laws, namely those of the possibility of a system.

That is, all purposiveness in nature can be regarded either as **natural** (*forma finalis naturae spontanea*)[a] or as **intentional** (*intentionalis*). Mere experience justifies only the first way of representing purposiveness; the second is a hypothetical way of explaining it, which is additional to the first concept of things as natural ends. The first concept of things, as natural purposes, originally belongs to the **reflecting** power of judgment (although not to the aesthetically but to the logically reflecting power of judgment), the second to the **determining** power of judgment. For the first, to be sure, reason is also required, but only for the sake of an experience that is to be arranged according to principles (thus in its **immanent** use), but for the second there is required a reason that ascends into extravagance (in transcendent use).

We can and should be concerned to investigate nature, so far as lies within our capacity,[b] in experience, in its causal connection in accordance with merely mechanical laws: for in these lie the true physical grounds of explanation, the interconnection of which constitutes scientific cognition of nature through reason. But now we find among the products of nature special and very widely distributed genera, which contain within themselves a combination of efficient causes that we must ground in the concept of an end, even if we wish to employ only experience, i.e., observation in accordance with a principle suitable to their inner possibility. If we wished to judge[c] their form and its possibility merely in accordance with mechanical laws, in which the idea of the effect must not be taken as the ground of the possibility of their cause, but vice versa, then it would be impossible to obtain even one experiential concept of the specific form of these natural things which would put us in the position to move from their inner disposition as cause to the effect, since the parts of these machines, not insofar as each has a separate ground of its possibility but rather only insofar as all together have a common ground, are the cause of the effect that is

20: 236   visible in them. Now since it is entirely contrary to the nature of physical-mechanical causes that the whole should be the cause of the possibility of the causality of the parts, rather the latter must be given first in order for the possibility of a whole to be comprehended from it; since, further, the particular representation of a whole which pre-

---

[a] the form of a spontaneous end in nature
[b] *Vermögen*
[c] *beurtheilen*

cedes the possibility of the parts is a mere idea and this, if it is regarded as the ground of causality, is called an end: it is clear that if there are such products of nature, it would be impossible to investigate their character and their cause only in experience (let alone explain them by reason), without representing their form and causality as determined in accordance with a principle of ends.

Now it is clear that in such cases the concept of an objective purposiveness of nature serves only **for the sake of reflection** on the object, not for the **determination** of the object through the concept of an end, and the teleological judgment on the inner possibility of a natural product is a merely reflecting, not a determining judgment. E.g., by saying that the crystalline lens in the eye has the **end** of reuniting, by means of a second refraction of the light rays, the rays emanating from one point at one point on the retina, one says only that the representation of an end in the causality of nature is conceived in the production of the eye because such an idea serves as a principle for guiding the investigation of the eye as far as the part that has been mentioned is concerned, with regard to the means that one can think up to promote that effect. No cause acting in accordance with the representation of purposes, i.e., no **intentionally** acting cause, is thereby attributed to nature, which would be a determining teleological judgment and as such transcendent, since it would suggest a causality that lies beyond the bounds of nature.

The concept of natural ends is therefore strictly a concept of the reflecting power of judgment for its own behalf, in order to pursue the causal connection in objects of experience. A teleological principle for explaining the inner possibility of certain natural forms leaves it undetermined whether their purposiveness is **intentional** or **unintentional**. A judgment which asserted one of these two would no longer be merely reflecting, but determining, and the concept of a natural end would also no longer be a mere **concept of the power of judgment**, for immanent (experiential) use, but would be connected with a **concept of reason** of an intentionally acting cause, posited beyond nature, the use of which is transcendent, regardless of whether in this case one would judge affirmatively or negatively.

20: 237

X.
On the search for a principle of the technical power of judgment.

If what is to be found is merely the ground for the explanation of that which happens, then this can be either an empirical principle, or an *a priori* principle, or even a composite of the two, as one can see in physical-mechanical explanations of events in the corporeal world, which find their principles in part in the general (rational) science of nature, and partly in those sciences which contain the empirical laws of motion.[26] Something similar takes place when one seeks for psychological grounds of explanation for what goes on in our mind, only with this difference that, as far as I am aware, the principles for this are all empirical, with only one exception, namely the law of the *continuity* of all changes (since time, which has only one dimension, is the formal condition of inner intuition), which is the *a priori* ground of these perceptions, but which is virtually useless for the sake of explanation, since the general theory of time, unlike the pure theory of space (geometry), does not yield sufficient material for an entire science.

So if the concern were to explain how that which we call taste first arose among human beings, why it was these objects rather than others that occupied them and brought about the judgment on beauty under these or those circumstances of place and society, by what causes it could have grown into a luxury, and so on, then the principles for such an explanation would have to be sought for the most part in psychology (by which is always meant in such a case empirical psychology). Thus the moralists[a] require the psychologists to explain the strange phenomenon of miserliness, which places an absolute value on the mere possession of the means for well-being (or some other aim) but with the resolve never to make use of them, or of the desire for honor, which believes that this is found in mere reputation without any further aim, so that they can direct their precepts, not to the moral laws themselves, but to the removal of hindrances that oppose their influence; though one must admit that the situation of psychological explanations is quite pitiable compared to that of physical explanations, that they are endlessly hypothetical and that for three different grounds of explanation it is very easy to think up a fourth, equally plausible one, and that hence there is a host of so-called psychologists of this sort, who know how to propose causes for every affection or movement of the mind aroused by plays, poetic representations, and objects of nature and even call their wit philosophy, who yet fail to give a glimpse of even the ability let alone knowledge of how to explain scientifically the most common natural event in the corporeal world. To make psychological observations (as Burke does in his book on the beautiful and the sublime),[27] and thus to gather material for rules of experience that will be systematically connected in the future, without yet seeking to comprehend them,[b] is certainly the only true obligation of empirical psychology, which only with difficulty could ever lay claim to the rank of a philosophical science.

[a] *Sittenlehrer*
[b] Kant added this clause to the fair copy.

If, however, a judgment gives itself out to be universally valid and therefore asserts a claim to **necessity**, then, whether this professed necessity rests on concepts of the object *a priori* or on subjective conditions for concepts, which ground them *a priori*, it would be absurd, if one concedes to such a judgment a claim of this sort, to justify it by explaining the origin of the judgment psychologically. For one would thereby be acting contrary to one's own intention, and if the attempted explanation were completely successful it would prove that the judgment could make absolutely no claim to necessity, precisely because its empirical origin can be demonstrated.

Now aesthetic judgments of reflection (which we shall subsequently analyze under the name of judgments of taste) are of the kind mentioned above. They lay claim to necessity and say, not that everyone does so judge – that would make their explanation a task for empirical psychology – but that everyone **ought** to so judge, which is as much as to say that they have an *a priori* principle for themselves. If the relation to such a principle were not contained in such judgments, even though they*ᵃ* lay claim to necessity, then one would have to assume that one can assert that a judgment ought to be universally valid because, as observation proves, it is universally valid, and, vice versa, that it follows from the fact that everyone does judge in a certain way that he too **ought** so to judge, which is an obvious absurdity.

Now it is of course a difficulty in aesthetic judgments of reflection that they cannot in any way be grounded on concepts and therefore cannot be derived from any determinate principle, since they would otherwise be logical; the subjective representation of purposiveness, however, should not in any way be a concept of an end. But still the **relation** to an *a priori* principle can and must be present where the judgment lays claim to necessity, and it is only such a claim and its possibility that is at issue here, for it is precisely that which causes a critique of reason to search for the principle which does ground it even though it is indeterminate – and it can also succeed in finding such a principle and recognizing it as one that does ground the judgment subjectively and *a priori*, even though it can never provide a determinate concept of the object.

20: 239

* *
*

One must likewise admit that the teleological judgment is grounded on a principle *a priori* and would be impossible without such a principle,

---

ᵃ The text actually uses the singular here (*es . . . macht*).

although in such judgments we discover the end of nature solely through experience and without that we could not know^a that things of this sort are even possible. That is, the teleological judgment, although it connects a determinate concept of an end, on which it grounds the possibility of certain natural products, with the representation of the object (which does not happen in the aesthetic judgment), is nevertheless always only a judgment of reflection, just like the former. It does not presume at all to assert that in this objective purposiveness nature (or another being acting through nature) in fact proceeds **intentionally**, i.e., that in it, or its cause, the thought of an end determines the causality, but rather only that we must utilize the mechanical laws of nature in accordance with this analogy (relations of causes and effects), in order to cognize the possibility of such objects and to acquire a concept of them which can provide them with an interconnection in an experience that can be systematically arranged.

A teleological judgment compares the concept of a product of nature as it is with one of what it **ought to be.** Here the judging^b of its possibility is grounded in a concept (of the end) that precedes it *a priori.* There is no difficulty in representing the possibility of products of art in such a way. But to think of a product of nature that there is something that it **ought to be** and then to judge^c whether it really is so already presupposes a principle that could not be drawn from experience (which teaches only what things are).

That we can see with the eye we experience immediately, as we do the outer and internal structure of the eye, which contain the conditions for its possible use, and therefore its causality in accordance with mechanical laws. But I can also use a stone, either in order to crush something upon it, or to build something upon it, etc., and these effects can also be related to their causes as ends, although I cannot on that account say that it ought to have served for building.^{d} Only of the eye do I judge that it **ought** to have been suitable for seeing, and although its figure, the character of all its parts and their composition, judged^e in accordance with merely mechanical laws of nature, is entirely contingent for my power of judgment, I nevertheless think in its form and in its construction a necessity for being formed in a certain way, namely in accordance with a concept that precedes the formative causes of this organ, without which the possibility of this product of nature is not comprehensible for me in accordance with any mechanical natural law

^{a} *erkennen*
^{b} *Beurtheilung*
^{c} *beurtheilen*
^{d} Kant added this clause to the fair copy.
^{e} *beurtheilt*

(which is not the case with the stone). Now this ought contains a necessity which is clearly distinguished from physical-mechanical necessity, in accordance with which a thing is possible in accordance with mere laws of efficient causes (without any preceding idea of that thing), 20: 241 and can no more be determined through merely physical (empirical) laws than the necessity of the aesthetic judgment can be determined through psychological ones, but instead requires its own *a priori* principle in the power of judgment, insofar as it is reflecting, under which the teleological judgment stands and by means of which both its validity and its limitation must also be determined.

Thus all judgments about the purposiveness of nature, be they aesthetic or teleological, stand under principles *a priori*, and indeed such as belong especially and exclusively to the power of judgment, since they are merely reflecting and not determining[a] judgments. Precisely because of this they also belong within the critique of pure reason (taken in the most general sense), which the latter need more than the former, since left to themselves they invite reason to make inferences which can become lost in extravagance, whereas the former require a painstaking investigation merely in order to prevent them from limiting themselves, even in their principle, strictly to the empirical, and thereby nullifying their claims to universal validity for everyone.[b]

XI.
Encyclopedic introduction
of the critique of the power of judgment
into the system of the critique of pure reason.

Any introduction of a discourse is either that of a proposed doctrine or of the doctrine itself into a system, in which it belongs as a part. The former precedes the doctrine, the latter should properly only constitute its conclusion, in order to assign it, in accordance with fundamental principles,[c] its place in the body of doctrines with which it is interconnected by common principles. The former is a **propaedeutic** introduction, the latter can be called an **encyclopedic** one.

Propaedeutic introductions are the customary ones, preparing the way for a doctrine that is to be presented by adducing the precognition which is necessary for that from doctrines or sciences already to hand, in order to make the transition possible. If they are aimed at carefully 20: 242 distinguishing the principles proper to the new doctrine (*domestica*)

---

[a] Here Kant replaced the word *beständige* (constant), an obvious mistake, with *bestimmende*.
[b] Kant added the last clause to the fair copy.
[c] *Grundsätze*

from those which belong to another one (*peregrinis*),[a] then they serve for determining the boundaries between sciences, a precaution which cannot be too highly commended, since without it no thoroughness is to be hoped for, especially in philosophical cognition.

An encyclopedic introduction, however, presupposes not some related doctrine which prepares the way for the newly announced one, but the idea of a system which will first become complete through the latter. Now since such a system is not made possible by rummaging about and gathering up the many things that have been found during the course of inquiry, but is possible only if one is in a position to present completely the subjective or objective sources of a certain sort of cognition, through the formal concept of a whole that at the same time contains in itself *a priori* the principle of a complete division, one can readily grasp why encyclopedic introductions, useful as they may be, are yet so unusual.

Since that faculty whose unique principle is here to be sought and discussed (the power of judgment) is of such a special kind that by itself[b] it does not produce any cognition at all (neither theoretical nor practical) and, despite its *a priori* principle, provides no part of transcendental philosophy as an objective doctrine, but only constitutes the connection between two other higher faculties of cognition (the understanding and reason), I may be allowed, in the determination of the principles of such a faculty, which is not susceptible of any doctrine but only of a critique, to depart from the order which is otherwise necessary everywhere else and to go ahead with a short encyclopedic introduction to it, not in the system of the **sciences** of pure reason but merely in the **critique** of all faculties of the mind that are determinable *a priori*, insofar as they constitute among themselves a system in the mind, and in this way to unite the propaedeutic introduction with the encyclopedic one.

The introduction of the power of judgment into the system of the pure faculties of cognition through concepts rests entirely on its transcendental principle, which is peculiar to it: that nature [in] the specification of the transcendental laws of understanding (principles of its possibility as nature in general), i.e., in the manifold of its empirical laws, proceeds in accordance with the idea of a system of their division for the sake of the possibility of experience as an empirical system. – This is what first gives us the concept of an objectively contingent but subjectively (for our faculty of cognition) necessary lawfulness, i.e., a purposiveness of nature, and indeed does so *a priori*.

20: 243

---

[a] of a foreigner
[b] *für sich*

Now although this principle does not, of course, determine anything with regard to the particular forms of nature, but the purposiveness of the latter must always be given empirically, the judgment about these forms nevertheless wins a claim to universality and necessity, as merely reflective judgment, through the relation of the subjective purposiveness of the given representation for the power of judgment to that *a priori* principle of the power of judgment, of the purposiveness of nature in its empirical lawfulness in general, and thus an aesthetic reflecting judgment can be regarded as resting on a principle *a priori* (although it is not determining), and the power of judgment in it can be justified in finding a place in the critique of the higher pure faculties of cognition.

But since the concept of a purposiveness of nature (as a technical purposiveness, which is essentially distinct from practical purposiveness), if it is not to be a merely surreptitious substitution of **what we make out of nature** for what **nature is**, is a concept separate from all dogmatic philosophy (theoretical as well as practical), which is grounded solely on that principle of the power of judgment that precedes all empirical laws and first makes possible their agreement in the unity of a system, it can be seen from this that of the two kinds of use of the reflecting power of judgment (the aesthetic and the teleological) that only the judgment which precedes all concepts of the object, hence the aesthetic reflecting judgment, has its determining ground in the power of judgment, unmixed with any other faculty of cognition, while the teleological judgment, although it uses the concept of a natural end in the judgment itself only as a principle of the reflecting, not of the determining power of judgment, nevertheless cannot be made except through the combination of reason with empirical concepts. Hence the possibility of a teleological judgment about nature can easily be shown, without having to ground it in a special principle of the power of judgment, for this merely follows the principle of reason. By contrast, the possibility of an aesthetic judgment which is nevertheless a judgment of mere reflection grounded on a principle *a priori*, i.e., a judgment of taste, if it can be shown that this is really justified in its claim to universal validity, absolutely requires a critique of the power of judgment as a faculty with its own special transcendental principles (like understanding and reason), and only in this way is it qualified to be included in the system of the pure faculties of cognition; the ground for which is that the aesthetic judgment, without presupposing a concept of its object, nevertheless ascribes purposiveness to it, and indeed does so with universal validity, the principle for which must therefore lie in the power of judgment itself, while the teleological judgment presupposes a concept of the object which reason brings under the

20: 244

principle of a connection to an end, only this concept of a natural end is used by the power of judgment merely in reflecting, not in determining judgment.

It is therefore properly only in taste, and especially with regard to objects in nature, in which alone the power of judgment reveals itself as a faculty that has its own special principle and thereby makes a well-founded claim to a place in the general critique of the higher faculties of cognition, which one would perhaps not have entrusted to it. However, once the capacity[a] of the power of judgment to institute *a priori* principles for itself is granted, then it is also necessary to determine the scope of this capacity, and for this completeness in critique it is required that its aesthetic faculty be recognized[b] as contained in one faculty together with the teleological and as resting on the same principle, for the teleological judgment about things in nature also belongs, just as much as the aesthetic, to the reflecting (not the determining) power of judgment.

But the critique of taste, which is otherwise used only for the improvement or confirmation of taste itself, discloses, when treated from a transcendental point of view, by the way in which it fills in a gap in the system of our cognitive faculties, a striking and in my view very promising prospect for a complete system of all the powers of the mind, insofar as they are related in their vocation[c] not only to the sensible but also to the supersensible, yet without upsetting the border posts which a strict critique has imposed on the latter use of them. Perhaps it may help the reader to gain a more perspicuous overview of the interconnection between the following investigations if I here sketch an outline of this systematic connection, which, to be sure, like the whole present section, should properly have its place only at the conclusion of the treatise.

20: 245

The faculties of the mind, namely, can all be reduced to the following three:

Faculty of cognition
Feeling of pleasure and displeasure
Faculty of desire

The exercise of all of them, however, is always grounded in the faculty of cognition, although not always in cognition (since a representation belonging to the faculty of cognition can also be an intuition, pure or empirical, without concepts). Thus, insofar as the issue is the faculty of

[a] *Vermögen*
[b] *erkannt*
[c] *Bestimmung*

44

cognition in accordance with principles, the following higher powers take their place beside the powers of the mind in general:

Faculty of cognition	**Understanding**
Feeling of pleasure and displeasure	**Power of Judgment**
Faculty of desire	**Reason**

It turns out that the understanding contains its own special principles *a priori* for the faculty of cognition, the power of judgment only for the feeling of pleasure and displeasure, but reason merely for the faculty of desire. These formal principles ground a necessity which is partly objective, partly subjective, but partly also, just because it is subjective, at the same time of objective validity, in accordance with which, by means of the higher faculties that stand beside them, they determine these corresponding powers of the mind:

Faculty of cognition	**Understanding**	**Lawfulness**
Feeling of pleasure and displeasure	**Power of judgment**	**Purposiveness**
Faculty of desire	**Reason**	Purposiveness that is at the same time law **(Obligation)**

Finally, the following are associated with the adduced *a priori* grounds of the possibility of forms, as their products: 20: 246

Faculty of the mind	**Higher cogni- tive faculties**	*A priori* **principles**	**Products**[a]
Faculty of cognition	**Understanding**	**Lawfulness**	**Nature**
Feeling of pleasure and displeasure	**Power of judgment**	**Purposiveness**	**Art**
Faculty of desire	**Reason**	Purposiveness that is at the same time law **(Obligation)**	**Morals**[b]

Thus **nature**[c] grounds its **lawfulness** on *a priori* **principles** of the **understanding** as a **faculty of cognition**; **art**[d] is guided *a priori* in its **purposiveness** in accordance with the **power of judgment** in relation to the **feeling of pleasure and displeasure**; finally **morals**[e] (as prod-

---

[a] The headings on this line are doubly underlined.
[b] *Sitten*
[c] This word is doubly underlined.
[d] Doubly underlined.
[e] *Sitten*, doubly underlined.

uct of freedom) stand under the idea of a form of **purposiveness** that is qualified for universal law, as a determining ground of **reason** with regard to the **faculty of desire**. The judgments that arise in this way from *a priori* principles peculiar to each of the fundamental faculties of the mind are **theoretical, aesthetic** and **practical** judgments.

There is thus revealed a system of the powers of mind, in their relation to nature and freedom, both of which have their own special, **determining** principles *a priori* and therefore constitute the two parts of philosophy (the theoretical and the practical) as a doctrinal system, and at the same time a transition by means of the power of judgment, which connects the two parts through its own special principle, namely from the **sensible** substratum of the first part of philosophy to the **intelligible** substratum of the second, through the critique of a faculty (the power of judgment) which serves only for connecting and which hence cannot provide any cognition of its own nor make any contribution to doctrine, whose judgments, however, under the name of **aesthetic** (whose principles are merely subjective), insofar as they differ from all those, under the name of **logical**, whose fundamental principles[a] must be objective (whether they are theoretical or practical), are of such a special sort that they relate sensible intuitions to the idea of nature, whose lawfulness cannot be understood without their relation to a supersensible substratum – the proof of which will be provided in the treatise itself.

We shall call the critique of this faculty with regard to the first sort of judgments, not **aesthetics** (as if it were a doctrine of sense), but a **critique of the aesthetic power of judgment**, because the former expression has too broad a meaning, since it could also signify the sensibility of **intuition**, which belongs to theoretical cognition and furnishes the material for logical (objective) judgments; that is why we have already restricted[b] the expression "aesthetic" exclusively to the predicate that belongs to intuition in cognitive judgments.[28] However, to call a power of judgment aesthetic because it does not relate the representation of an object to concepts, and thus does not relate the judgment to cognition (because it is not determining at all, but only reflecting) occasions no concern about misinterpretation; since for the logical power of judgment intuitions, even if they are merely sensible (aesthetic), must first be raised to concepts in order to serve for cognition of the object, which is not the case with the aesthetic power of judgment.

20: 247

[a] *Grundsätze*
[b] *bestimmt*

46

XII.
Division of the
Critique of the Power of Judgment

The division of a domain of cognitions of a certain sort, in order to make it representable as a system, is important in a way that is inadequately understood as well as difficult in a way that is equally often underestimated. If one regards the parts for such a possible whole as already completely given, then the division proceeds **mechanically**, as the consequence of mere comparison, and the whole becomes an **aggregate** (as cities do if, without regard to regulation,[a] a territory is divided according to the preferences of the would-be settlers). But if one can and should presuppose the idea of a whole in accordance with a certain principle prior to the determination of the parts, then the division must proceed **scientifically**, and only in this way does the whole become a system. The latter requirement always holds when what is at issue is a domain of *a priori* cognition (which, together with its principles, rests on a special legislative faculty of the subject), since here the domain of the use of these laws is likewise determined *a priori* through the special constitution of this faculty, as are the number and the relation of the parts to a whole of cognition. But one cannot make a well-founded division without at the same time **making** the whole itself and antecedently exhibiting it in all its parts, although to be sure only in accordance with the rule of the **critique**; subsequently to bring this into the systematic form of a **doctrine** (which can always be done given the nature of this cognitive faculty) nothing more is required than to connect with it **exhaustiveness** in the application to the particular and the elegance of **precision**.

20: 248

Now the division a critique of the power of judgment (which faculty is precisely one that, although grounded on principles *a priori*, still never yields the material for a doctrine), must be grounded on the distinction that it is not the determining but only the reflecting power of judgment that has its own principles *a priori*; that the former operates only **schematically**, under laws of another faculty (the understanding),[29] while the latter operates only **technically** (in accordance with its own laws), and that the latter procedure is grounded on a principle of the technique of nature, hence on the concept of a purposiveness, which one must presuppose in it *a priori*; which indeed is necessarily presupposed, in accordance with the principle of the reflecting power of judgment, as only subjective, i.e., relatively to this faculty itself, but yet brings along it with the concept of a **possible** objective purposiveness, i.e., of the lawfulness of the things in nature as natural ends.

---

[a] *Policei*, i.e., "police" in the sense of provisions for public well-being.

A purposiveness judged[a] merely subjectively, which is therefore not grounded on any concept, nor can be so grounded insofar as it is judged[b] merely subjectively, is the relation to the feeling of pleasure and displeasure, and the judgment concerning this is **aesthetic** (and at the same time the only possible way of judging aesthetically). But since if this feeling were to accompany merely the sensible representation of the object, i.e., the sensation of it, the aesthetic judgment would be empirical and require, certainly, a certain receptivity, but no special power of judgment, and since, further, if the latter were assumed to be determining, it would have to be grounded on a concept of an end, and the purposiveness would thus have to be judged[c] not aesthetically but logically, then, by the aesthetic power of judgment as a special faculty necessarily nothing else can be meant than the **reflecting power of judgment**, and the feeling of pleasure (which is identical with the representation of **subjective purposiveness**) must not be regarded as the sensation in an empirical representation of the object, nor as its concept, but must be regarded as dependent only on reflection and its form (the special action of the power of judgment), by means of which it strives to rise from intuitions to concepts in general, and as connected with it in accordance with a principle *a priori*. Thus, the **aesthetic** of the reflecting power of judgment will occupy one part of the critique of this faculty, just as the **logic** of the same faculty, under the name of **teleology**, will constitute its other part. In both parts, however, nature itself will be considered as technical, i.e., purposive in its products, in the first case subjectively, with regard to the mere manner of representation of the subject, in the second case, however, as objectively purposive in relation to the possibility of the object itself. We shall see in the sequel that the purposiveness of form in appearance is beauty, and the faculty for judging[d] it is **taste**. Now from this it would seem to follow that the division of the critique of the power of judgment into the aesthetic and the teleological would have to comprise only the **theory of taste** and the **theory of physical ends** (the theory of the judging[e] of the things in the world as natural ends).

But one can divide all **purposiveness**, whether it is subjective or objective, into **internal** and **relative** purposiveness, the first of which is grounded in the representation of the object in itself, the second merely in the contingent **use** of it.[f] In accordance with this the form

20: 249

---

[a] *beurtheilte*
[b] *beurtheilt*
[c] *beurtheilt*
[d] *Beurtheilungsvermögen*
[e] *Beurtheilung*
[f] *derselben*, literally meaning the use of the representation rather than of the object

of an object can, **first**, already be perceived as purposive for the reflecting power of judgment by itself, i.e., in the mere intuition without any concept, and then the subjective purposiveness is attributed to the thing and to nature itself; **second**,[a] the object may, in perception, have[b] nothing at all purposive for reflection in the determination of its form in itself, although its representation, when applied to a purposiveness lying in the subject *a priori*, for the arousal of its feeling (that, say, 20: 250 of the supersensible determination of the powers of the mind of the subject), can ground an aesthetic judgment, which is related to a principle *a priori* (although to be sure only a subjective one), not, as in the first case, in accordance with a **purposiveness of nature** in regard to the subject, but only in regard to a possible purposive **use** of certain sensible intuitions in accordance with their form by means of the merely reflecting power of judgment. Thus if the first judgment attributes **beauty** to the objects of nature, but the second attributes to it **sublimity**, and both, indeed, only through aesthetic (reflecting) judgments, without concepts of the object, merely with respect to subjective purposiveness, then no special technique of nature is to be presupposed for the latter, because it is merely a matter of a contingent use of the representation, not for the sake of cognition of the object, but rather with a view to another feeling, namely that of the inner purposiveness in the disposition of the powers of the mind. Nevertheless the judgment on the sublime in nature is not to be excluded from the division of the aesthetic of the reflecting power of judgment, because it also expresses a subjective purposiveness which is not based on a concept of the object.

It is the same with the objective purposiveness of nature, i.e., the possibility of things as natural ends, the judgment about which is made only in accordance with concepts of these, i.e., not aesthetically (in relation to the feeling of pleasure or displeasure) but rather logically, and is called teleological. The objective purposiveness is grounded either on the internal possibility of the object, or on the relative possibility of its external consequences. In the first case the teleological judgment considers the **perfection** of a thing in accordance with an end that lies in it itself (since the manifold elements in it are related to each other reciprocally as end and means); in the second the teleological judgment about a natural object concerns only its **usefulness**, namely its correspondence to an end that lies in other things.

Accordingly the critique of the aesthetic power of judgment contains first the critique of **taste** (the faculty for judging[c] the beautiful), and

---

[a] Kant replaces *oder* (or) in the fair copy with *zweytens* (second).
[b] Kant substitutes *mag . . . haben* (may have) for *hat* (has) in the fair copy.
[c] *Beurtheilungsvermögen*

20: 251

second the critique of the **feeling of spirit**,[a] for thus I provisionally[b] call the capacity[c] for representing a sublimity in objects. – Since the teleological power of judgment relates its representation of purposiveness to the object not by means of feelings but through concepts, the distinction of the capacity for internal as well as relative (but in both cases objective purposiveness) contained in it does not require any special designations; this is because it relates its reflection entirely to reason (not to feeling).

It should be noted, further, that it is the technique in nature and not that of the causality of the powers of representation of human beings which is what is called *art* (in the proper sense of the word), with regard to which purposiveness will be investigated as a regulative concept of the power of judgment, and that is not the principle of artistic beauty or of an artistic perfection that is being sought, even though if nature is considered technically (or plastically), on account of an analogy which its causality must be represented as having with that of art, its procedure can be called technical, i.e., as it were artistic. For what is at issue is the principle of the merely reflecting, not the determining power of judgment (such as grounds all human works of art), in which, therefore, the purposiveness should be considered **unintentional**, and which can therefore pertain only to nature. The judging[d] of artistic beauty will subsequently have to be considered as a mere consequence of the same principles which ground the judgment of natural beauty.

The critique of the reflecting power of judgment with regard to nature will therefore consist of two parts, the critique of the **aesthetic** and of the **teleological power of judging**[e] things in nature.

The first part will contain two books, the first of which will be the critique of **taste** or of the judging[f] of the **beautiful**, the second the critique of the **feeling of spirit** (in mere reflection on an object) or of the judging[g] of the **sublime**.

The second part likewise contains two books, the first of which will bring under principles the judging[h] of things as natural ends with regard to their **internal possibility**, but the other the judgment about their **relative purposiveness**.[30]

---

[a] *des Geistesgefühls*
[b] Kant inserted this word into the fair copy.
[c] *Vermögen*
[d] *Beurtheilung*
[e] *Beurtheilungsvermögen*
[f] *Beurtheilung*
[g] *Beurtheilung*
[h] *Beurtheilung*

Each of these books will contain in two sections an **analytic** and a **dialectic** of the power of judging.[a]

The analytic will seek, in the same number of chapters, to execute first the **exposition** and then the **deduction** of the concept of a purposiveness of nature.

[a] *Beurtheilungsvermögen*

Critique
of the
Power of Judgment

by

Immanuel Kant

Second Edition

Berlin,

F. T. Lagarde, 1793

Preface
to the first edition, 1790^a

The faculty of cognition from *a priori* principles can be called **pure reason**, and the investigation of its possibility and boundaries in general can be called the critique of pure reason; although by this faculty only reason in its theoretical use is understood, as was also the case in the first work under this title,[1] without bringing into the investigation its capacity*^b* as practical reason, in accordance with its special principles. The former pertains solely to our faculty for cognizing things *a priori*, and thus concerns itself only with the **faculty of cognition**, excluding the feeling of pleasure and displeasure and the faculty of desire; and among the faculties of cognition it concerns itself only with the **understanding** in accordance with its *a priori* principles, excluding the **power of judgment** and **reason** (as faculties likewise belonging to theoretical cognition), because in the course of that work it turns out that no faculty of cognition except for the understanding can yield constitutive principles of cognition *a priori*.*^c* Thus the critique, which looks to the faculties of cognition*^d* as a whole, concerned with the contribution that each of the other faculties might profess to make to the bare possession of cognition from its own source,*^e* is left with nothing but what the **understanding** prescribes *a priori* as law for nature, as the sum of appearances (whose form is likewise given *a priori*); but it refers all other pure concepts to the ideas, which are an extravagance for our theoretical faculty of cognition, but not thereby useless or dispensable, but which rather serve*^f* as regulative principles: partly in order to restrain the worrisome pretensions of the understanding, as if (in virtue of being able to furnish *a priori* the conditions

---

^a Kant added the words "to the first edition, 1790" in the second edition of 1793. But he did not add a new preface to the second edition; as elsewhere throughout the work, he made only minor changes and corrections to the text.

^b *Vermögen*

^c In the first edition, this sentence ends with a semicolon instead of a period, and the next sentence is introduced with *so, daß* (so that) instead of *also* (therefore).

^d Kant has the pronoun *sie*; since there is no singular feminine antecedent for this in the previous sentence, presumably it refers to the several faculties of cognition just mentioned.

^e *Wurzel*, i.e., root.

^f The verb *dienen* was added in the second edition.

5: 168   of the possibility of all things that it can cognize) it has thereby also confined the possibility of all things in general within these boundaries, and partly in order to guide itself in the contemplation of nature in accordance with a principle of a completeness to which it can never attain, and thereby to further the final aim^a of all cognition.

Thus it was strictly speaking the **understanding**, which has its proper domain indeed in the **faculty of cognition**, insofar as it contains constitutive principles of cognition *a priori*, which was to be established in secure and unique possession against all other competitors by means of the critique of pure reason, so named in general terms. In just the same way **reason**, which contains constitutive principles *a priori* nowhere except strictly with regard to the **faculty of desire**, was directed to its territory in the critique of practical reason.[2]

Now whether the **power of judgment**, which in the order of our faculties of cognition constitutes an intermediary between understanding and reason, also has *a priori* principles for itself; whether these are constitutive or merely regulative (and thus do not prove the power of judgment to have its own domain), and whether the feeling of pleasure and displeasure, as the intermediary between the faculty of cognition and the faculty of desire, gives the rule *a priori* (just as the understanding prescribes *a priori* laws to the former, but reason to the latter): it is this with which the present critique of the power of judgment is concerned.

A critique of pure reason, i.e., of our faculty for judging in accordance with *a priori* principles, would be incomplete if the power of judgment, which also claims to be a faculty of cognition, were not dealt with as a special part of it, even though its principles may not constitute a special part of a system of pure philosophy, between the theoretical and the practical part, but can occasionally be annexed to either of them in case of need. For if such a system, under the general name of metaphysics, is ever to come into being (the complete production of which is entirely possible and highly important for the use of reason in all respects), then the critique must previously have probed the ground for this structure down to the depth of the first foundations of the faculty of principles independent of experience, so that it should not sink in any part, which would inevitably lead to the collapse of the whole.

5: 169   It can, however, easily be inferred from the nature of the power of judgment (the correct use of which is so necessary and generally required that nothing other than this very faculty is meant by the name "sound understanding") that great difficulties must be involved in find-

---

^{a} *Endabsicht*

ing a special principle for it (which it must contain in itself *a priori*, for otherwise, it would not, as a special faculty of cognition, be exposed even to the most common critique), which nevertheless must not be derived from concepts *a priori*; for they belong to the understanding, and the power of judgment is concerned only with their application. It therefore has to provide a concept itself, through which no thing is actually cognized, but which only serves as a rule for it, but not as an objective rule to which it can conform its judgment, since for that yet another power of judgment would be required in order to be able to decide whether it is a case of the rule or not.[3]

This embarrassment about a principle (whether it be subjective or objective) is found chiefly in those judgings[a] that are called aesthetic, which concern the beautiful and the sublime in nature or in art. And likewise the critical investigation of a principle of the power of judgment in these cases is the most important part of a critique of this faculty. For although by themselves they contribute nothing at all to the cognition of things, still they belong to the faculty of cognition alone, and prove an immediate relation of this faculty to the feeling of pleasure or displeasure in accordance with some *a priori* principle, without mixing up the latter with that which can be the determining ground of the faculty of desire, since this has its *a priori* principles in concepts of reason. – But in the case of the logical[b] judging[c] of nature, where experience imposes on things a conformity to law that the understanding's general concept of the sensible is not sufficient to understand or explain, and where the power of judgment can derive from itself a principle for the relation of the thing in nature to the uncognizable supersensible but can only use it with respect to itself for the cognition of nature, there indeed such an *a priori* principle can and must be applied for the **cognition** of the beings in the world and at the same time opens up prospects that are advantageous for practical reason; but it has no immediate relation to the feeling of pleasure and displeasure, which is precisely what is puzzling in the principle of the power of judgment and what makes a special division for this faculty necessary in the critique, since logical judging[d] in accordance with concepts (from which an immediate inference to the feeling of pleasure and displeasure can never be drawn), together with a critical restriction of it, could always have been appended to the theoretical part of philosophy.

Since the investigation of the faculty of taste, as the aesthetic power

5: 170

<hr>

[a] *Beurtheilungen*
[b] *logische*. From what follows, it appears that Kant should have written *teleologische*.
[c] *Beurtheilung*
[d] *Beurtheilung*

of judgment, is here undertaken not for the formation and culture of taste (for this will go its way in the future, as in the past, even without any such researches), but only from a transcendental point of view, it will, I flatter myself, be judged[a] leniently with regard to its deficiencies for the former end. But in what concerns the latter aim it must be made firm against the most rigorous examination. But even there the great difficulty in solving a problem which nature has made so involuted may, I hope, serve to excuse some not entirely avoidable obscurity in the solution, as long as it can be shown clearly enough that the principle has been correctly stated; granted that the way in which the phenomenon is derived from the power of judgment does not have all the distinctness that one can rightly demand elsewhere, namely from a cognition in accordance with concepts, which I also believe myself to have achieved in the second part of this work.

Thus with this I bring my entire critical enterprise to an end. I shall proceed without hindrance to the doctrinal part, in order, if possible, to win yet from my increasing age some time still favorable to that. It is self-evident that there will be no special part for the power of judgment in that, since in regard to that critique serves instead of theory; rather, in accordance with the division of philosophy into theoretical and practical parts, and the division of pure philosophy into the very same parts, the metaphysics of nature and of morals will constitute that enterprise.

[a] *beurtheilt*

I.
On the division of philosophy.

If one divides philosophy, insofar as it contains principles of rational cognition of things by means of concepts (not merely, like logic, principles of the form of thinking in general*a* without distinction of objects), into **theoretical** and **practical**, as is customary, then one proceeds entirely correctly. But then the concepts that refer the principles of this rational cognition to its object must also be specifically distinct, since otherwise they would not justify any division, which always presupposes an opposition between the principles of the rational cognition belonging to the different parts of a science.

There are, however, only two sorts of concepts that allow an equal number of distinct principles of the possibility of their objects: namely the **concepts of nature** and the **concept of freedom**. Now since the former make possible a **theoretical** cognition of nature in accordance with *a priori* principles, but the latter includes within its concept in that regard only a negative principle (of mere opposition), while on the contrary it attains ampliative principles for the determination of the will, which on that account are called practical: thus philosophy is justifiably divided into two parts, entirely distinct as far as their principles are concerned, namely, the theoretical, as **philosophy of nature**, and the practical, as **moral philosophy** (for thus is the practical legislation of reason in accordance with the concept of freedom named). Hitherto, however, a great misuse of these expressions for the division of the different principles, and with them also of philosophy, has prevailed: for that which is practical in accordance with concepts of nature has been taken to be the same as that which is practical in accordance with the concept of freedom, and thus, under the same designations of theoretical and practical philosophy, a division has been made through which, in fact (since both parts could have the same principles), nothing has been divided.   5: 172

The will, as the faculty of desire, is one of the many kinds of natural causes in the world, namely that which operates in accordance with

---

a In the first edition: "like logic does, which contains the form of thinking in general . . ."

concepts; and everything that is represented as possible (or necessary) through a will is called practically possible (or necessary), in distinction from the physical possibility or necessity of an effect to which the cause is not determined to causality through concepts (but rather, as in the case of lifeless matter, through mechanism, or, in the case of animals, through instinct). – Now here it is left indeterminate with regard to the practical whether the concept that gives the rule to the causality of the will is a concept of nature or a concept of freedom.

However, the latter distinction is essential. For if the concept determining the causality is a concept of nature, then the principles are **technically practical**, but if it is a concept of freedom, then these are **morally practical**; and since in the division of a rational science what is at issue is entirely this sort of difference of objects, the cognition of which requires distinct principles, the former will belong to theoretical philosophy (as a doctrine of nature), while the latter[a] will entirely by itself constitute the second part, namely practical philosophy (as a doctrine of morals).[b]

All technically practical rules (i.e., those of art and skill in general, as well as those of prudence, as a skill in influencing human beings and their will), so far as their principles rest on concepts, must be counted only as corollaries of theoretical philosophy. For they concern only the possibility of things in accordance with concepts of nature, to which belong not only the means thereto that are to be encountered in nature, but even the will (as a faculty of desire, hence as a natural faculty), insofar as it can be determined through natural incentives in accordance with those rules. Hence practical rules of that kind are not called laws (like, say, physical laws), but only precepts: and precisely because the will does not merely stand under the concept of nature, but also under the concept of freedom, in relation to which its principles are called laws, and alone constitute, together with their consequences, the second part of philosophy, namely the practical.

Thus, as little as the solution of the problems of pure geometry belongs to a special part of it, or as little as the art of surveying deserves the name of a practical geometry, as a second part of geometry in general in contrast to pure geometry, even less should the mechanical or chemical art of experiments or observations be counted as a practical part of the doctrine of nature, or, finally, should domestic, agrarian and political economy, the art of social intercourse, the prescriptions of dietetics, the general doctrine of happiness itself or even the mastery of inclinations and the control of affects for the sake of the latter be counted as practical philosophy, or the latter constitute the second part

[a] In the first edition, "the second."
[b] *Sittenlehre*

of philosophy as a whole; since all of these contain only rules of skill, which are thus only technically practical, for producing an effect that is possible in accordance with natural concepts of causes and effects which, since they belong to theoretical philosophy, are subject to[a] these precepts as mere corollaries of it (of natural science), and thus cannot demand a place in a special philosophy which is called practical. By contrast, the morally practical precepts, which are grounded entirely on the concept of freedom to the complete exclusion of the determining grounds of the will from nature, constitute an entirely special kind of precept: which are also, like the rules that nature obeys, simply called laws, but which do not, like the latter, rest on sensible conditions, but on a supersensible principle, and require a second part of philosophy for themselves alone, alongside the theoretical part, under the name of practical philosophy.

It can be seen from this that a set of practical precepts provided by philosophy does not constitute a special part of it, alongside its theoretical part, just because they are practical; for they could be that even if their principles were derived entirely from the theoretical cognition of nature (as technically practical rules); rather they constitute such a special part when and if their principle is not borrowed from the concept of nature, which is always sensibly conditioned, and hence rests on the supersensible, which the concept of freedom alone makes knowable through formal laws, and they are therefore morally practical, i.e., not merely precepts and rules for this or that purpose, but laws, without prior reference to ends and aims.

II.
On the domain of philosophy in general.

5: 174

The use of our cognitive faculty in accordance with principles, and with this philosophy, extend as far as *a priori* concepts have their application.

However, the set of all objects to which those concepts are related, in order where possible to bring about a cognition of them, can be divided in accordance with the varying adequacy or inadequacy of our faculties for this purpose.

Concepts, insofar as they are related to objects, regardless of whether a cognition of the latter is possible or not, have their field, which is determined merely in accordance with the relation which their object has to our faculty of cognition in general. – The part of this field within which cognition is possible for us is a territory (*ter-*

---

[a] The words "are subject to" in this clause, and "and thus" in the next, are added in the second edition.

ritorium) for these concepts and the requisite faculty of cognition. The part of the territory in which these are legislative is the domain (*ditio*) of these concepts and of the corresponding faculty of cognition. Thus empirical concepts do indeed have their territory in nature, as the set of all objects of sense, but no domain (only their residence, *domicilium*); because they are, to be sure, lawfully generated, but are not legislative, rather the rules grounded on them are empirical, hence contingent.

Our cognitive faculty as a whole has two domains, that of the concepts of nature and that of the concept of freedom; for it is *a priori* legislative through both. Philosophy is also divided accordingly into the theoretical and the practical. But the territory on which their domain is established and[a] their legislation **exercised** is always only the set of objects of all possible experience, insofar as they are taken as nothing more than mere appearances; for otherwise no legislation of the understanding with regard to them could be conceived.

Legislation through concepts of nature takes place through the understanding, and is theoretical. Legislation through the concept of freedom takes place through reason, and is merely practical. Only in the practical alone can reason be legislative; with regard to theoretical cognition (of nature) it can only (by being well-versed in law by means of the understanding) draw inferences from given laws to conclusions that still always stop at nature. Conversely, however, where rules are practical, reason is not on that account immediately **legislative**, since they[b] can also be technically practical.

Understanding and reason thus have two different legislations on one and the same territory of experience, without either being detrimental to the other. For just as little as the concept of nature influences legislation through the concept of freedom does the latter disturb the legislation of nature. – The possibility of at least conceiving without contradiction the coexistence[c] of the two legislations and the faculties pertaining to them in one and the same subject was proved by the *Critique of Pure Reason*, when it annihilated the objections to this by exposing the dialectical illusion in them.[4]

But that these two different domains, which are inevitably limited[d] not to be sure in their legislation but still in their effects in the sensible world, do not constitute **one** domain, stems from this: that the concept

5: 175

---

[a] The first edition adds "on which" here.
[b] In the third edition, "the former."
[c] *Zusammenbestehen*
[d] "which were . . . limited" in the first edition.

of nature certainly makes its objects representable in intuition, but not as things in themselves, rather as mere appearances, while the concept of freedom in its object makes a thing representable in itself but not in intuition, and thus neither of the two can provide a theoretical cognition of its object (and even of the thinking subject) as a thing in itself, which would be the supersensible, the idea of which must underlie the possibility of all those objects of experience, but which itself can never be elevated and expanded into a cognition.

There is thus an unlimited but also inaccessible field for our faculty of cognition as a whole, namely the field of the supersensible, in which we find no territory for ourselves, and thus cannot have on it a domain for theoretical cognition either for the concepts of the understanding or for those of reason, a field that we must certainly occupy with ideas for the sake of the theoretical as well as the practical use of reason, but*a* for which, in relation to the laws from the concept of freedom, we can provide nothing but a practical reality, through which, accordingly, our theoretical cognition is not in the least extended to the supersensible.

Now although there is an incalculable gulf fixed between the domain of the concept of nature, as*b* the sensible, and the domain of the concept of freedom, as the supersensible, so that from the former to the latter (thus by means of the theoretical use of reason) no transition is possible, just as if there were so many different worlds, the first of which can have no influence on the second: yet the latter **should** have an influence on the former, namely the concept of freedom should*c* make the end that is imposed by its laws real*d* in the sensible world; and nature must consequently also be able to be conceived in such a way that the lawfulness of its form is at least in agreement with the possibility of the ends that are to be realized*e* in it in accordance with the laws of freedom. – Thus there must still be a ground of the **unity** of the supersensible that grounds nature with that which the concept of freedom contains practically, the concept of which, even if it does not suffice for cognition of it either theoretically or practically, and thus has no proper domain of its own, nevertheless makes possible the transition from the manner of thinking in accordance with the principles of the one to that in accordance with the principles of the other.

5: 176

---

a *aber* added in the second edition.
b In the first edition, this word is *also* rather than *als*, i.e., "thus" instead of "as."
c Added in the second edition.
d *wirklich*
e *zu bewirkenden*

III.
On the critique of the power of judgment, as a
means for combining the two parts of
philosophy into one whole.

The critique of the faculties of cognition with regard to what they can accomplish *a priori* has, strictly speaking, no domain with regard to objects, because it is not a doctrine, but only has to investigate whether and how a doctrine is possible through it given the way it is situated with respect to our faculties. Its field extends to all the presumptions of that doctrine, in order to set it within its rightful limits. However, what cannot enter into the division of philosophy can nevertheless enter as a major part into the critique of the pure faculty of cognition in general if, namely, it contains principles that are for themselves fit neither for theoretical nor for practical use.

The concepts of nature, which contain the ground for all theoretical cognition *a priori*, rested on the legislation of the understanding. – The concept of freedom, which contains the ground for all sensibly unconditioned practical precepts *a priori*, rested on the legislation of reason. Both faculties thus have, in addition to the fact that in accordance with logical form they can be applied to principles whatever their origin might be, their own legislation concerning content, beyond which there is no other (*a priori*), which hence justifies the division of philosophy into the theoretical and the practical.

5: 177

But in the family of the higher faculties of cognition there is still an intermediary between the understanding and reason. This is the **power of judgment**, about which one has cause to presume, by analogy, that it too should contain in itself *a priori*, if not exactly its own legislation, then still a proper principle of its own for seeking laws, although a merely subjective one; which, even though it can claim no field of objects as its domain, can nevertheless have some territory and a certain constitution*a* of it, for which precisely this principle only might be valid.

To this, however (to judge by analogy), a fresh ground is added for bringing the power of judgment into association with another ordering of our powers of representation, which seems to be of still greater importance than that of its kinship with the family of faculties of cognition. For all faculties or capacities of the soul can be reduced to the three that cannot be further derived from a common ground: the **faculty of cognition**, the **feeling of pleasure and displeasure**, and

---

a *Beschaffenheit*

the **faculty of desire.*** For the faculty of cognition only the under-   5: 178
standing is legislative, if (as must be the case if it is considered for
itself, without being mixed up with the faculty of desire), it is related
as a faculty of a **theoretical cognition** to nature, with regard to which
alone (as appearance) it is possible for us to give laws through *a priori*

---

* *a*"It is useful to attempt a transcendental definition for concepts that are used   5: 177
as empirical principles if one has cause to conjecture that they have an affinity
with the pure faculty of cognition *a priori*, on account of this relation: a
definition, that is, through pure categories, insofar as these alone already
yield the distinction between the concept in question and others. In this one
follows the example of the mathematician, who leaves the empirical data of
his problem undetermined and brings only their relation in their pure synthesis under the concepts of pure arithmetic and thereby generalizes their
solution. – An objection has been made to me on the basis of a similar
procedure (*Critique of Practical Reason*, p. 16 of the preface),[5] and the definition
of the faculty of desire as **the faculty for being through one's representations the cause of the reality of the objects of these representations** has
been criticized because mere **wishes** are also desires, but yet everyone would
concede that he could not produce their object by their means alone. – This,
however, proves nothing more than that there are also desires in a human
being as a result of which he stands in contradiction with himself, in that he
works toward the production of the object by means of his representation
alone, from which he can however expect no success, because he is aware
that his mechanical powers (if I may so name those that are not psychological), which have to be determined through that representation in order to   5: 178
realize the object (hence mediately), are either inadequate or even aimed at
something impossible, e.g., to make what has happened not have happened
(*O mihi praeteritos,*[b] etc.), or, when impatiently waiting, to make the time until
the wished-for moment disappear. – Although in the case of such fantastic
desires we are aware of the inadequacy of our representations (or their un-
suitability) to be **causes** of their objects, nevertheless their relation as causes,
hence the representation of their **causality**, is contained in every **wish**, and it
is especially visible if this is an affect, namely **longing**. For the latter prove
by the fact that they expand the heart and make it flaccid and thus exhaust
our powers that the powers are repeatedly strained by means of representations, but the mind, in view of the impossibility, is inexorably allowed to sink
back into exhaustion. Even the prayers for the avoidance of great and so far
as one can see unavoidable evil and many superstitious means for the attainment of naturally impossible ends prove the causal relation of representations

---

a The footnote was added to the second edition.
b Kant's reference is to Virgil's *Aeneid*, Book VIII, line 560, "*O mihi praeteritos referat si
Juppiter annos*" ("If only Jupiter would give me back/The past years and the man I
was"); translation by Robert Fitzgerald, *Virgil: The Aeneid* (New York: Random House,
1983), p. 249.

concepts of nature, which are, strictly speaking, pure concepts of the understanding. – For the faculty of desire, as a higher faculty in accordance with the concept of freedom, reason alone (in which alone this concept has its place) is legislative *a priori*. – Now between the faculty of cognition and that of desire there is the feeling of pleasure, just as the power of judgment is contained between the understanding and reason. It is therefore to be suspected at least provisionally that the power of judgment likewise contains an *a priori* principle for itself, and, since pleasure or displeasure is necessarily combined with the faculty of desire (whether, as in the case of the lower faculty of desire, it

5: 179   precedes the principle of that faculty or, as in the case of the upper, it follows only from the determination of that faculty through the moral law), it will likewise effect a transition from the pure faculty of cognition, i.e., from the domain of the concepts of nature, to the domain of the concept of freedom, just as in its logical use it makes possible the transition from understanding to reason.

Thus even if philosophy can be divided into only two parts, the theoretical and the practical; even if everything that we might have to say about the proper principles of the power of judgment must be counted as belonging to the theoretical part, i.e., to rational cognition in accordance with concepts of nature; still, the critique of pure reason, which must constitute all this before undertaking that system, for the sake of its possibility, consists of three parts: the critique of the pure understanding, of the pure power of judgment, and of pure reason, which faculties are called pure because they are legislative *a priori*.

IV.
On the power of judgment as an *a priori* legislative faculty.

The power of judgment in general is the faculty for thinking of the particular as contained under the universal.[a] If the universal (the rule,

---

to their objects, which cannot be held back from striving to achieve their effect even by the consciousness of their inadequacy for it. – Why there is this tendency in our nature to consciously vain desires is an anthropological-teleological question. It appears that if we were not to be determined to the application of our powers until we had assured ourselves of the adequacy of our faculties for the production of an object, then these powers would remain largely unemployed. For ordinarily we learn to know our powers only by first trying them out. This illusion in empty wishes is therefore only the consequence of a beneficent arrangement in our nature.

---

[a] *dem Allgemeinen.* In this section, the term *das Allgemeine* is frequently used as a nominative, which can only be translated as "the universal," and the adjective *allgemein* will

the principle, the law) is given, then the power of judgment, which subsumes the particular under it (even when, as a transcendental power of judgment, it provides the conditions *a priori* in accordance with which alone anything can be subsumed under that universal), is **determining**. If, however, only the particular is given, for which the universal is to be found, then the power of judgment is merely **reflecting**.[6]

The determining power of judgment under universal transcendental laws, given by the understanding, merely subsumes; the law is sketched out for it *a priori*, and it is therefore unnecessary for it to think of a law for itself in order to be able to subordinate the particular in nature to the universal. – But there is such a manifold of forms in nature, as it were so many modifications of the universal transcendental concepts of nature that are left undetermined by those laws that the pure understanding gives *a priori*, since these pertain only to the possibility of a nature (as object of the senses) in general, that there must nevertheless also be laws for it which, as empirical, may seem to be contingent in accordance with the insight of **our** understanding, but which, if they are to be called laws (as is also required by the concept of a nature), must be regarded as necessary on a principle of the unity of the manifold, even if that principle is unknown to us.[7] – The reflecting power of judgment, which is under the obligation of ascending from the particular in nature to the universal, therefore requires a principle that it cannot borrow from experience, precisely because it is supposed to ground the unity of all empirical principles under equally empirical but higher principles, and is thus to ground the possibility of the systematic subordination of empirical principles under one another. The reflecting power of judgment, therefore, can only give itself such a transcendental principle as a law, and cannot derive it from anywhere else (for then it would be the determining power of judgment), nor can it prescribe it to nature: for reflection on the laws of nature is directed by nature, and nature is not directed by the conditions in terms of which we attempt to develop a concept of it that is in this regard entirely contingent.

5: 180

Now this principle can be nothing other than this: that since universal laws of nature have their ground in our understanding, which prescribes them to nature (although only in accordance with the universal concept of it as nature), the particular empirical laws, in regard to that which is left undetermined in them by the former, must be considered in terms of the sort of unity they would have if an understanding (even if not ours) had likewise given them for the sake of our faculty of cognition, in order to make possible a system of experience

correspondingly be translated as "universal" rather than "general" in this and the following sections of the Introduction unless otherwise noted.

in accordance with particular laws of nature. Not as if in this way such an understanding must really be assumed (for it is only the reflecting power of judgment for which this idea serves as a principle, for reflecting, not for determining); rather this faculty thereby gives a law only to itself, and not to nature.[8]

Now since the concept of an object insofar as it at the same time contains the ground of the reality of this object is called an **end**, and the correspondence of a thing with that constitution of things that is possible only in accordance with ends is called the **purposiveness** of its form, thus the principle of the power of judgment in regard to the form of things in nature under empirical laws in general is the **purposiveness of nature** in its multiplicity. I.e., nature is represented through this concept as if an understanding contained the ground of the unity of the manifold of its empirical laws.

The purposiveness of nature is thus a special *a priori* concept that has its origin strictly in the reflecting power of judgment. For we cannot ascribe to the products of nature anything like a relation of nature in them to ends, but can only use this concept in order to reflect on the connection of appearances in nature that are given in accordance with empirical laws.[9] This concept is also entirely distinct from that of practical purposiveness (of human art as well as of morals), although it is certainly conceived of in terms of an analogy with that.

V.
The principle of the formal purposiveness of nature is a transcendental principle of the power of judgment.

A transcendental principle is one through which the universal *a priori* condition under which alone things can become objects of our cognition at all is represented. By contrast, a principle is called metaphysical if it represents the *a priori* condition under which alone objects whose concept must be given empirically can be further determined *a priori*. Thus the principle of the cognition of bodies as substances and as alterable substances is transcendental if what is meant by that is that their alteration must have a cause; it is metaphysical, however, if what is meant by that is that their alteration must have an **external** cause: for in the first case the body may be conceived of only through ontological predicates (pure concepts of the understanding), e.g., as substance, in order for the proposition to be cognized *a priori*; in the second case, however, the empirical concept of a body (as a movable thing in space) must be made the ground of this proposition, from which, however, it can then be understood fully *a priori* that the latter predicate (of motion only through an external cause) applies to the body.[10] – Thus, as I shall show forthwith, the principle of the purposiveness of nature (in the multiplicity of its empirical laws) is a transcendental principle. For the concept of the objects insofar as they are thought as standing under this principle is only the pure concept of objects of possible experiential cognition in general, and contains nothing empirical. By contrast, the principle of practical purposiveness which must be conceived of in the idea of the **determination** of a free **will** would be a metaphysical principle, because the concept of a faculty of desire as a will must still be given empirically (it does not belong among the transcendental predicates). Both principles are nevertheless not empirical but *a priori* principles, because the combination of the predicate with the empirical concept of the subject of their judgments requires no further experience, but can be understood entirely *a priori*.

5: 182

That the concept of a purposiveness of nature belongs among the transcendental principles can readily be seen from the maxims of the power of judgment, which are laid down *a priori* as the basis for research into nature, but which nevertheless pertain to nothing other than the possibility of experience, hence of the cognition of nature, but not merely as nature in general, but rather as nature as determined by a manifold of particular laws. – They are to be found often enough in the course of this science, but only scattered about, as pronouncements of metaphysical wisdom, on the occasion of various rules whose necessity cannot be demonstrated from concepts. "Nature takes the shortest way" (*lex parsimoniae*);[a] "it makes no leaps, either in the sequence of its changes or in the juxtaposition of specifically different forms" (*lex continui in natura*);[b] "the great multiplicity of its empirical laws is nevertheless unity under a few principles" (*principia praeter necessitatem non sunt multiplicanda*);[c] and so on.[11]

However, if one wants to give the origin of these fundamental principles and attempts to do so in a psychological way, this is entirely contrary to their sense. For they do not say what happens, i.e., in accordance with which rule our powers of cognition actually perform their role and how things are judged, but rather how they ought to be judged;[d] and this logical objective necessity is not forthcoming if the principles are merely empirical. Thus the purposiveness of nature for our cognitive faculties and for their use, which is obvious in them, is a transcendental principle of judgments and therefore also requires a transcendental deduction, by means of which the ground for judging in this way must be sought in the sources of cognition *a priori*.

---

[a] the law of parsimony
[b] law of continuity in nature
[c] principles are not to be multiplied beyond necessity
[d] *nicht . . . wie geurtheilt wird, sondern wie geurtheilt werden soll*

5: 183   That is, we first find in the grounds of the possibility of an experience something necessary, namely the universal laws without which
nature in general (as object of the senses) could not be conceived; and
these rest on the categories, applied to the formal conditions of all
intuition that is possible for us, insofar as it is likewise given to us *a
priori*.[a] Now under these laws the power of judgment is determining,
for it has nothing to do but subsume under given laws. E.g., the
understanding says: All alteration has its cause (universal law of nature);
now the transcendental power of judgment has nothing further to do
than to provide the condition of subsumption under the *a priori* concept of the understanding that has been laid down for it: and that is
the succession of the determinations of one and the same thing.[12] Now
for nature in general (as the object of possible experience) that law is
cognized as absolutely necessary. – Now, however, the objects of empirical cognition are still determined or, as far as one can judge *a priori*,
determinable in so many ways apart from that formal time-condition
that specifically distinct natures, besides what they have in common as
belonging to nature in general, can still be causes in infinitely many
ways; and each of these ways must (in accordance with the concept of
a cause in general) have its rule, which is a law, and hence brings
necessity with it, although given the constitution and the limits of our
faculties of cognition we have no insight at all into this necessity. Thus
we must think of there being in nature, with regard to its merely
empirical laws, a possibility of infinitely manifold empirical laws, which
as far as our insight goes are nevertheless contingent (cannot be cognized *a priori*); and with regard to them we judge[b] the unity of nature
in accordance with empirical laws and the possibility of the unity of
experience (as a system in accordance with empirical laws) as contingent.[13] But since such a unity must still necessarily be presupposed and
assumed, for otherwise no thoroughgoing interconnection of empirical
cognitions into a whole of experience would take place, because the
universal laws of nature yield such an interconnection among things
with respect to their genera, as things of nature in general, but not
specifically, as such and such particular beings in nature, the power of
judgment must thus assume it as an *a priori* principle for its own use
that what is contingent for human insight in the particular (empirical)
laws of nature nevertheless contains a lawful unity, not fathomable by
5: 184   us but still thinkable, in the combination of its manifold into one
experience possible in itself. Consequently, since the lawful unity in a
combination that we cognize as in accordance with a necessary aim (a

---

[a] In the first edition, there is a comma rather than a period here, and the next sentence
  is a further clause of this one, introduced with an "and."
[b] *beurtheilen*

need) of the understanding but yet at the same time as contingent in itself is represented as a purposiveness of the objects (in this case, of nature), thus the power of judgment, which with regard to things under possible (still to be discovered) empirical laws is merely reflecting, must think of nature with regard to the latter in accordance with a **principle of purposiveness** for our faculty of cognition, which is then expressed in the maxims of the power of judgment given above. Now this transcendental concept of a purposiveness of nature is neither a concept of nature nor a concept of freedom, since it attributes nothing at all to the object (of nature), but rather only represents the unique way in which we must proceed in reflection on the objects of nature with the aim of a thoroughly interconnected experience, consequently it is a subjective principle (maxim) of the power of judgment; hence we are also delighted (strictly speaking, relieved of a need) when we encounter such a systematic unity among merely empirical laws, just as if it were a happy accident which happened to favor our aim, even though we necessarily had to assume that there is such a unity, yet without having been able to gain insight into it and to prove it.

In order to be convinced of the correctness of this deduction of the concept that is before us and of the necessity of assuming it as a transcendental principle of cognition, one need only consider the magnitude of the task of making an interconnected experience out of given perceptions of a nature that in the worst case contains an infinite multiplicity of empirical laws, a task that lies in our understanding *a priori*. The understanding is of course in possession *a priori* of universal laws of nature, without which nature could not be an object of experience at all; but still it requires in addition a certain order of nature in its particular rules, which can only be known to it empirically and which from its point of view are contingent. These rules, without which there would be no progress from the general[a] analogy of a possible experience in general to the particular, it must think as laws (i.e., as necessary), because otherwise they would not constitute an order of nature, even though it does not and never can cognize their necessity. Thus although it cannot determine anything *a priori* with regard to those (objects), it must yet, in order to investigate these empirical so-called laws, ground all reflection on nature on an *a priori* principle, the principle, namely, that in accordance with these laws a cognizable order of nature is possible – the sort of principle that is expressed in the following propositions: that there is in nature a subordination of genera and species that we can grasp; that the latter in turn converge in accordance with a common principle, so that a tran-

5: 185

---

[a] *allgemeinen*

sition from one to the other and thereby to a higher genus is possible; that since it seems initially unavoidable for our understanding to have to assume as many different kinds of causality as there are specific differences of natural effects, they may nevertheless stand under a small number of principles with the discovery of which we have to occupy ourselves, etc.[14] This agreement of nature with our faculty of cognition is presupposed *a priori* by the power of judgment in behalf of its reflection on nature in accordance with empirical laws, while at the same time the understanding recognizes it objectively as contingent, and only the power of judgment attributes it to nature as transcendental purposiveness (in relation to the cognitive faculty of the subject): because without presupposing this, we would have no order of nature in accordance with empirical laws, hence no guideline for an experience of this in all its multiplicity and for research into it.

For it may certainly be thought that, in spite of all the uniformity of things in nature in accordance with the universal laws, without which the form of an experiential cognition in general would not obtain at all, the specific diversity of the empirical laws of nature together with their effects could nevertheless be so great that it would be impossible for our understanding to discover in them an order that we can grasp, to divide its products into genera and species in order to use the principles for the explanation and the understanding of one for the explanation and comprehension of the other as well, and to make an interconnected experience out of material that is for us so confused (strictly speaking, only infinitely manifold and not fitted for our power of comprehension).

The power of judgment thus also has in itself an *a priori* principle for the possibility of nature, though only in a subjective respect, by means of which it prescribes a law, not to nature (as autonomy), but to

5: 186

itself (as heautonomy) for reflection on nature, which one could call the **law of the specification of nature** with regard to its empirical laws, which it does not cognize in nature *a priori* but rather assumes in behalf of an order of nature cognizable for our understanding in the division that it makes of its universal laws when it would subordinate a manifold of particular laws to these.[15] Thus if one says that nature specifies its universal laws in accordance with the principle of purposiveness for our faculty of cognition, i.e., into suitability for human understanding in its necessary business of finding the universal for the particular that is offered to it by perception and then further connection in the unity of the principle for all that is different (though universal for each species), then one is thereby neither prescribing a law to nature nor learning one from it by means of observation (although that principle can be confirmed by the latter). For it is not a principle of the determining but rather merely of the reflecting power of judgment; one means only that, however nature may be arranged as far as its universal laws are concerned, we must always seek out its empirical laws in accordance with that principle and the maxims that are grounded on it, because only so far as that takes place can we make progress in experience and acquire cognition by the use of our understanding.

VI.
On the combination of the feeling of pleasure with the concept of the purposiveness of nature.

This correspondence of nature in the multiplicity of its particular laws with our need to find universality of principles for it must be judged,[a] as far as our insight goes, as contingent but nevertheless indispensable for the needs of our understanding, and hence as a purposiveness through which nature agrees with our aim, but only as directed to cognition. – The universal laws of the understanding, which are at the same time laws of nature, are equally as necessary to it (though they have originated from spontaneity) as the laws of motion are to matter; and their generation presupposes no intention with regard to our faculty of cognition, since only through them do we first obtain a concept of what cognition of things (of nature) is, and they necessarily pertain to nature as object of our cognition in general. Yet that the order of nature in its particular laws, although its multiplicity and diversity at least possibly surpass all our power of comprehension, is yet fitted to it, is, as far as we can see, contingent; and its discovery is a task for the understanding, which is aimed at an end that is necessary for it, namely to introduce into it unity of principles – which purpose must be attributed to nature by the power of judgment, because the understanding cannot prescribe to it any law on this matter.

5: 187

The attainment of every aim is combined with the feeling of pleasure; and, if the condition of the former is an *a priori* representation, as in this case a principle for the reflecting power of judgment in general, then the feeling of pleasure is also determined through a ground that is *a priori* and valid for everyone; and indeed merely through the relation of the object to the faculty of cognition, without the concept of purposiveness in this case having the least regard to the faculty of desire, and thus being entirely distinct from any practical purposiveness of nature.

In fact, although in the concurrence of perceptions with laws in

[a] *beurtheilt*

accordance with universal concepts of nature (the categories) we do not encounter the least effect on the feeling of pleasure in us nor can encounter it, because here the understanding proceeds unintentionally, in accordance with its nature, by contrast the discovered unifiability of two or more empirically heterogeneous laws of nature under a principle that comprehends them both is the ground of a very noticeable pleasure, often indeed of admiration, even of one which does not cease though one is already sufficiently familiar with its object. To be sure, we no longer detect any noticeable pleasure in the comprehensibility of nature and the unity of its division into genera and species, by means of which alone empirical concepts are possible through which we cognize it in its particular laws; but it must certainly have been there in its time, and only because the most common experience would not be possible without it has it gradually become mixed up with mere cognition and is no longer specially noticed. – It thus requires study to make us attentive to the purposiveness of nature for our understanding in our judging*a* of it, where possible bringing heterogeneous laws of nature under higher though always still empirical ones, so that if we succeed in this accord of such laws for our faculty of cognition, which we regard as merely contingent, pleasure will be felt.[16] Conversely, a representation of nature that foretold that even in the most minor investigation of the most common experience we would stumble on a heterogeneity in its laws that would make the unification of its particular laws under universal empirical ones impossible for our understanding would thoroughly displease us; because this would contradict the principle of the subjective-purposive specification of nature in its genera and our reflecting power of judgment with respect to the latter.

5: 188

This presupposition of the power of judgment is, however, so indeterminate on the question of how far that ideal purposiveness of nature for our faculty of cognition should be extended that if someone were to tell us that a deeper or more extensive acquaintance with nature through observation must finally stumble upon a multiplicity of laws that no human understanding can trace back to one principle, we would be content with this, although we would rather listen if another gives us hope that the more we become acquainted with what is innermost in nature or could compare it with external members as yet unknown to us, the simpler and more perspicuous would we find it in the apparent heterogeneity of its empirical laws the farther our experience progressed. For it is a command of our power of judgment to proceed in accordance with the principle of the suitability of nature to our faculty of cognition as far as it reaches, without (since it is not a

a Beurtheilung

74

determining power of judgment that gives us this rule) deciding whether or not it somewhere has its boundaries: because we can certainly determine boundaries with regard to the rational use of our cognitive faculties, but in the empirical field no determination of boundaries is possible.

VII.
On the aesthetic representation of the purposiveness of nature.

What is merely subjective in the representation of an object, i.e., what constitutes its relation to the subject, not to the object, is its aesthetic property; but that in it which serves for the determination of the object (for cognition) or can be so used is its logical validity. In the cognition of an object of the senses both relations are present together. In the sensible representation of things outside me the quality of the space in which we intuit them is the merely subjective aspect of my representation of them (through which what they might be as objects in themselves remains undetermined), on account of which relation the object is also thereby thought of merely as appearance; space, however, in spite of its merely subjective quality, is nevertheless an element in the cognition of things as appearances. **Sensation** (in this case external) likewise expresses the merely subjective aspect of our representations of things outside us, but strictly speaking it expresses the material (the real) in them (through which something existing is given), just as space expresses the mere *a priori* form of the possibility of their intuition; and the former is likewise used for the cognition of objects outside us.

5: 189

However, the subjective aspect in a representation **which cannot become an element of cognition at all** is the **pleasure** or **displeasure** connected with it; for through this I cognize nothing in the object of the representation, although it can well be the effect of some cognition or other.[17] Now the purposiveness of a thing, insofar as it is represented in perception, is also not a property of the object itself (for such a thing cannot be perceived), although it can be derived from a cognition of things. Thus the purposiveness that precedes the cognition of an object, which is immediately connected with it even without wanting to use the representation of it for a cognition, is the subjective aspect of it that cannot become an element of cognition at all. The object is therefore called purposive in this case only because its representation is immediately connected with the feeling of pleasure; and this representation itself is an aesthetic representation of the purposiveness. – The question is only whether there is such a representation of purposiveness at all.

If pleasure is connected with the mere apprehension (*apprehensio*) of the form of an object of intuition without a relation of this to a concept for a determinate cognition, then the representation is thereby related not to the object, but solely to the subject, and the pleasure can express nothing but its suitability to the cognitive faculties that are in play in the reflecting power of judgment, insofar as they are in play, and thus merely a subjective formal purposiveness of the object.[18] For that apprehension of forms in the imagination can never take place without the reflecting power of judgment, even if unintentionally, at least comparing them to its faculty for relating intuitions to concepts. Now if in this comparison the imagination (as the faculty of *a priori* intuitions) is unintentionally brought into accord with the understanding, as the faculty of concepts, through a given representation and a feeling of pleasure is thereby aroused, then the object must be regarded as purposive for the reflecting power of judgment. Such a judgment is an aesthetic judgment on the purposiveness of the object, which is not grounded on any available concept of the object and does not furnish one. That object the form[a] of which (not the material aspect of its representation, as sensation) in mere reflection on it (without any intention of acquiring a concept from it) is judged[b] as the ground of a pleasure in the representation of such an object – with its representation this pleasure is also judged to be necessarily combined, consequently not merely for the subject who apprehends this form but for everyone who judges at all. The object is then called beautiful; and the faculty for judging through such a pleasure (consequently also with universal validity) is called taste. For since the ground of the pleasure is placed merely in the form of the object for reflection in general, hence not in any sensation of the object and also without relation to a concept that contains any intention, it is only the lawfulness in the empirical use of the power of judgment in general (unity of imagination with the understanding) in the subject with which the representation of the object in reflection, whose *a priori* conditions are universally valid, agrees; and, since this agreement of the object with the faculties of the subjective is contingent, it produces the representation of a purposiveness of the object with regard to the cognitive faculties of the subject.

Now here is a pleasure which, like all pleasure or displeasure which is not produced through the concept of freedom (i.e., through the antecedent determination of the higher faculty of desire through pure reason), can never be understood through concepts to be necessarily combined with the representation of an object, but must always be cognized to be connected with this only through reflected perception,

5: 190

5: 191

---

[a] In the first edition, "An object whose form . . ."
[b] *beurtheilt*

and consequently, like all empirical judgments, cannot promise any objective necessity and make a claim to *a priori* validity. But the judgment of taste, like every other empirical judgment, also only makes a claim to be valid for everyone, which, in spite of its intrinsic contingency, is always possible. What is strange and anomalous is only this: that it is not an empirical concept but rather a feeling of pleasure (consequently not a concept at all) which, through the judgment of taste, is nevertheless to be expected of everyone[a] and connected with its representation, just as if it were a predicate associated with the cognition of the object.

An individual judgment of experience, e.g., one made by someone who perceives a mobile droplet of water in a rock crystal, rightly demands that anyone else must also find it so, since he has made this judgment, in accordance with the general conditions of the determining power of judgment, under the laws of a possible experience in general. In just the same way, someone who feels pleasure in mere reflection on the form of an object, without regard to a concept, rightly makes claim to the assent of everyone else, even though this judgment is empirical and is an individual judgment, since the ground for this pleasure is to be found in the universal though subjective condition of reflecting judgments, namely the purposive correspondence of an object (be it a product of nature or of art) with the relationship[b] of the cognitive faculties among themselves (of the imagination and the understanding) that is required for every empirical cognition. The pleasure in the judgment of taste is therefore certainly dependent on an empirical representation, and cannot be associated *a priori* with any concept (one cannot determine *a priori* which object will or will not suit taste, one must try it out); but it is nevertheless the determining ground of this judgment only in virtue of the fact that one is aware that it rests merely on reflection and on the general although only subjective conditions of its correspondence for the cognition of objects in general, for which the form of the object is purposive.

That is the reason why judgments of taste are also subject to a critique with regard to their possibility, since this presupposes an *a priori* principle, though this principle is neither a cognitive principle for the understanding nor a practical principle for the will, and thus is not *a priori* determining at all.   5: 192

The susceptibility to a pleasure from reflection on the form of things (of nature as well as art), however, indicates not only a purposiveness of objects in relation to the reflecting power of judgment, in

[a] *jedermann zugemuthet*; the verb *zumuthen* will generally be translated as "expect of [someone]," while *erwarten* will be translated simply as "expect [that]."
[b] *Verhältnis*

accordance with the concept of nature, in the subject, but also, conversely, one of the subject, due to the concept of freedom, with regard
to the objects, concerning their form or even their lack of form; and
thereby it happens that the aesthetic judgment is related not only to
the beautiful, merely as judgment of taste, but also, as one that has
arisen from a feeling of spirit,[a] to the **sublime**, and thus the critique
of the aesthetic power of judgment must be divided into two principal
parts corresponding to this distinction.[19]

VIII.
On the logical representation of the purposiveness of nature.

In an object given in experience purposiveness can be represented
either on a merely subjective ground, as a correspondence of its form
in its **apprehension** (*apprehensio*) prior to any concept with the faculties
of cognition, in order to unite the intuition with concepts for a cognition in general, or on an objective ground, as a correspondence of its
form with the possibility of the thing itself, in accordance with a
concept of it which precedes and contains the ground of this form. We
have seen that the representation of the first sort of purposiveness rests
on the immediate pleasure in the form of the object in mere reflection
on it; thus the representation of the second kind of purposiveness,
since it relates the form of the object not to the cognitive faculties of
the subject in the apprehension of it but to a determinate cognition of
the object under a given concept, has nothing to do with a feeling of
pleasure in things but rather with the understanding in judging[b] them.
If the concept of an object is given, then the business of the power of
judgment in using it for cognition consists in **presentation** (*exhibitio*),
i.e., in placing a corresponding intuition beside the concept – whether
this be done through our own imagination, as in art, when we realize
an antecedently conceived concept of an object that is an end for us,
or through nature, in its technique (as in the case of organized bodies),
when we ascribe to it our concept of an end for judging[c] its product,
in which case what is represented is not merely a **purposiveness** of
nature in the form of the thing, but this product of it is represented as
a **natural end**. – Although our concept of a subjective purposiveness of
nature in its forms, in accordance with empirical laws, is not a concept
of the object at all, but only a principle of the power of judgment for
providing concepts in the face of this excessive multiplicity in nature

5: 193

---

[a] *Geistesgefühl*
[b] *Beurtheilung*
[c] *Beurtheilung*

(in order to be able to be oriented in it), we nevertheless hereby ascribe to it as it were a regard to our faculty of cognition, in accordance with the analogy of an end; and thus we can regard **natural beauty** as the **presentation** of the concept of formal (merely subjective) purposiveness and **natural ends** as the presentation of the concept of a real (objective) purposiveness, one of which we judge*a* through taste (aesthetically, by means of the feeling of pleasure), the other through understanding and reason (logically, in accordance with concepts).

On this is grounded the division of the critique of the power of judgment into that of the **aesthetic** and **teleological** power of judgment; by the former is meant the faculty for judging*b* formal purposiveness (also called subjective) through the feeling of pleasure or displeasure, by the latter the faculty for judging the real purposiveness (objective) of nature through understanding and reason.

In a critique of the power of judgment the part that contains the aesthetic power of judgment is essential, since this alone contains a principle that the power of judgment lays at the basis of its reflection on nature entirely *a priori*, namely that of a formal purposiveness of nature in accordance with its particular (empirical) laws for our faculty of cognition, without which the understanding could not find itself in it; whereas no *a priori* ground at all can be given why there must be objective ends of nature, i.e., things that are possible only as natural ends, indeed not even the possibility of such things is obvious from the concept of a nature as an object of experience in general as well as in particular; rather the power of judgment, without containing a principle for this in itself *a priori*, in order to make use of the concept of ends in behalf of reason, merely contains in some cases that come before it (certain products) the rule by which that transcendental principle has already prepared the understanding to apply the concept of an end (at least as far as form is concerned) to nature.   5: 194

The fundamental transcendental principle, however, for representing a purposiveness of nature in subjective relation to our faculty of cognition in the form of a thing as a principle for judging*c* it leaves it entirely undetermined where and in which cases I have to undertake the judging*d* of this form as that of a product in accordance with a principle of purposiveness and not rather merely in accordance with general laws of nature, and leaves it to the **aesthetic** power of judgment to make out, in taste, the suitability of the thing (of its form) to our cognitive faculties (insofar as these decide not through correspon-

---

a *beurtheilen*
b Here and in the next clause: *beurtheilen*.
c *Beurtheilung*
d *Beurtheilung*

dence with concepts but through feeling). By contrast, the teleologically employed power of judgment provides the determinate conditions under which something (e.g., an organized body), is to be judged[a] in accordance with the idea of an end of nature; but it cannot adduce any fundamental principle from the concept of nature, as object of experience, that would warrant ascribing to it *a priori* a relation to ends or even warrant merely indeterminately assuming anything of the sort about the actual experience of such products: the reason for which is that many particular experiences must be arranged and considered under the unity of their principle in order to be able to cognize even empirically an objective purposiveness in a particular object. – The aesthetic power of judgment is thus a special faculty for judging[b] things in accordance with a rule but not in accordance with concepts. The teleological power of judgment is not a special faculty, but only the reflecting power of judgment in general, insofar as it proceeds in accordance with concepts, as is always the case in theoretical cognitions, but, with regard to certain objects in nature, in accordance with particular principles, namely those of a power of judgment that is merely reflecting and is not determining objects; thus as far as its application is concerned it belongs to the theoretical part of philosophy, and on account of its special principles, which are not determining, as must be the case in a doctrine, must also constitute a special part of the critique; whereas the aesthetic power of judgment contributes nothing to the cognition of its objects and thus must be counted **only** as part of the critique of the judging subject and its cognitive faculties, insofar as these are capable of *a priori* principles, whatever their use (theoretical or practical) might otherwise be, which is the propaedeutic of all philosophy.

5: 195

IX.
On the connection of the legislations
of understanding and reason through
the power of judgment.

The understanding legislates *a priori* for nature, as object of the senses, for a theoretical cognition of it in a possible experience. Reason legislates *a priori* for freedom and its own causality, as the supersensible in the subject, for an unconditioned practical cognition. The domain of the concept of nature under the one legislation and that of the concept of freedom under the other are entirely barred from any mutual influence that they could have on each other by themselves (each in accor-

[a] *zu beurtheilen sei*
[b] *zu beurtheilen*

dance with its fundamental laws) by the great chasm that separates the supersensible from the appearances. The concept of freedom determines nothing in regard to the theoretical cognition of nature; the concept of nature likewise determines nothing in regard to the practical laws of freedom: and it is to this extent not possible to throw a bridge from one domain to the other. – But although the determining grounds of causality in accordance with the concept of freedom (and the practical rules that it contains) are not found in nature, and the sensible cannot determine the supersensible in the subject, nevertheless the converse is possible (not in regard to the cognition of nature, of course, but in regard to the consequences of the former on the latter) and is already contained in the concept of a causality through freedom, whose **effect** in accordance with its formal laws is to take place in the world, although the word **cause**, when used of the supersensible, signifies only the **ground** for determining the causality of natural things to an effect that is in accord with their*a* own natural laws but yet at the same time is also in unison with the formal principle of the laws of reason, the possibility of which cannot of course be understood, although the objection that there is an alleged contradiction in it can be adequately refuted.* – The effect in accordance with the concept of freedom is the   5: 196
final end, which (or its appearance in the sensible world) should exist, for which the condition of its possibility in nature (in the nature of the subject as a sensible being, that is, as a human being) is presupposed. That which presupposes this *a priori* and without regard to the practical, namely, the power of judgment, provides the mediating concept between the concepts of nature and the concept of freedom, which makes possible the transition from the purely theoretical to the purely

---

* One of the various alleged contradictions in this whole distinction between   5: 195
the causality of nature and that through freedom is that which objects that if I speak of the **hindrances** that nature lays in the way of causality through the laws of freedom (the moral laws) or of its **promotion** of this causality, I still concede an **influence** of the former on the latter. But if one would simply   5: 196
understand what has been said, this misinterpretation can very easily be avoided. The resistance or the promotion is not between nature and freedom, but between the former as appearance and the **effects** of the latter as appearances in the sensible world; and even the causality of freedom (of pure and*b* practical reason) is the causality of a natural cause (of the subject, as a human being, thus considered as an appearance) subordinated to the former, the ground of the **determination** of which is contained in the intelligible that is thought under freedom, in a way that is otherwise inexplicable (just as is that which constitutes the supersensible substrate of nature).

a In the first edition, "these their . . ."
b The word "and" was added in the second edition.

practical, from lawfulness in accordance with the former to the final
end in accordance with the latter, in the concept of a **purposiveness**
of nature; for thereby is the possibility of the final end, which can
become actual only in nature and in accord with its laws, cognized.

Through the possibility of its *a priori* laws for nature the understanding gives a proof that nature is cognized by us only as appearance,
and hence at the same time an indication of its supersensible substratum; but it leaves this entirely **undetermined**. The power of judgment,
through its *a priori* principle for judging^a nature in accordance with
possible particular laws for it, provides for its supersensible substratum
(in us as well as outside us) **determinability through the intellectual
faculty**. But reason provides **determination** for the same substratum
through its practical law *a priori*; and thus the power of judgment
makes possible the transition from the domain of the concept of nature
to that of the concept of freedom.

In regard to the faculties of the soul in general, insofar as they are
considered as higher faculties, i.e., as ones that contain an autonomy,
the understanding is the one that contains the **constitutive** principles
a priori for the **faculty of cognition** (the theoretical cognition of nature); for the **feeling of pleasure and displeasure** it is the power of
judgment, independent of concepts and sensations that are related to
the determination of the faculty of desire and could thereby be immediately practical; for the **faculty of desire** it is reason, which is practical
without the mediation of any sort of pleasure, wherever it might come
from, and determines for this faculty, as a higher faculty, the final end,
which at the same time brings with it the pure intellectual satisfaction
in the object. – The power of judgment's concept of a purposiveness
of nature still belongs among the concepts of nature, but only as a
regulative principle of the faculty of cognition, although the aesthetic
judgment on certain objects (of nature or of art) that occasions it is a
constitutive principle with regard to the feeling of pleasure or displeasure. The spontaneity in the play of the faculties of cognition, the
agreement of which contains the ground of this pleasure, makes that
concept suitable for mediating the connection of the domain of the
concept of nature with the concept of freedom in its consequences, in
that the latter at the same time promotes the receptivity of the mind
for the moral feeling. – The following table can facilitate the overview
of all the higher faculties in accordance with their systematic unity.*

5: 197

* It has been thought suspicious that my divisions in pure philosophy almost
always turn out to be threefold. But that is in the nature of the matter. If a
division is to be made *a priori*, then it will either be **analytic**, in accordance

^a *der Beurtheilung*

All the faculties of the mind	**Faculty of cognition**	*A priori principles*	**Application to**
Faculty of cognition	Understanding	Lawfulness	Nature
Feeling of pleasure and displeasure	Power of judgment	Purposiveness	Art
Faculty of desire	Reason	Final end	Freedom

with the principle of contradiction, and then it is always twofold (*quodlibet ens est aut A aut non A*[a]). Or it is **synthetic**; and if in this case it is to be derived from **concepts** *a priori* (not, as in mathematics, from the *a priori* intuition corresponding to the concept), then, in accordance with what is requisite for synthetic unity in general, namely (1) a condition, (2) something conditioned, (3) the concept that arises from the unification of the conditioned with its condition, the division must necessarily be a trichotomy.

[a] "Anything is either A or not A."

Division
of the entire work

First Part
Critique of the Aesthetic Power of Judgment

First Section
Analytic of the Aesthetic Power of Judgment

First Book
Analytic of the Beautiful

Second Book
Analytic of the Sublime

Second Section
Dialectic of the Aesthetic Power of Judgment

Second Part
Critique of the Teleological Power of Judgment

First Division
Analytic of the Teleological Power of Judgment

Second Division
Dialectic of the Teleological Power of Judgment

Appendix
Methodology of the Teleological Power of Judgment

Critique of the Power of Judgment
First Part

Critique of the Aesthetic Power of Judgment

First Section

Analytic
of the Aesthetic Power of Judgment
First Book
Analytic of the Beautiful[1]

First Moment
of the judgment of taste,* concerning its quality.

§ 1.
The judgment of taste is aesthetic.

[handwritten: Bestimmungsgrund]

In order to decide whether or not something is beautiful, we do not relate the representation by means of understanding to the object for cognition, but rather relate it by means of the imagination (perhaps combined with the understanding) to the subject and its feeling of pleasure or displeasure. The judgment of taste is therefore not a cognitive judgment, hence not a logical one, but is rather aesthetic, by which is understood one whose determining ground **cannot** be **other than subjective**. Any relation of representations, however, even that of sensations, can be objective (in which case it signifies what is real in an empirical representation); but not the relation to the feeling of pleasure and displeasure, by means of which nothing at all in the object is designated, but in which the subject feels itself as it is affected by the representation.[2]

To grasp a regular, purposive structure with one's faculty of cognition (whether the manner of representation be distinct or confused) is something entirely different from being conscious of this repre-

---

* The definition of taste that is the basis here is that it is the faculty for the judging*a* of the beautiful. But what is required for calling an object beautiful must be discovered by the analysis of judgments of taste. In seeking the moments to which this power of judgment attends in its reflection, I have been guided by the logical functions for judging (for a relation to the understanding is always contained even in the judgment of taste). I have considered the moment of quality first, since the aesthetic judgment on the beautiful takes notice of this first.

a Beurtheilung

sentation with the sensation of satisfaction. Here the representation is related entirely to the subject, indeed to its feeling of life,[3] under the name of the feeling of pleasure or displeasure, which grounds an entirely special faculty for discriminating and judging[a] that contributes nothing to cognition but only holds the given representation in the subject up to the entire faculty of representation, of which the mind becomes conscious in the feeling of its state. Given representations in a judgment can be empirical (hence aesthetic); however, the judgment that is made by means of them is logical if in the judgment they are related to the object. Conversely, however, even if the given representations were to be rational but related in a judgment solely to the subject (its feeling), then they are to that extent always aesthetic.

§ 2.

The satisfaction that determines the judgment of taste
is without any interest.

The satisfaction that we combine with the representation of the existence of an object is called interest. Hence such a satisfaction always has at the same time a relation to the faculty of desire, either as its determining ground or else as necessarily interconnected with its determining ground. But if the question is whether something is beautiful, one does not want to know whether there is anything that is or that could be at stake, for us or for someone else, in the existence of the thing, but rather how we judge[b] it in mere contemplation (intuition or reflection).[4] If someone asks[c] me whether I find the palace that I see before me beautiful, I may well say that I don't like that sort of thing, which is made merely to be gaped at, or, like the Iroquois sachem, that nothing in Paris pleased him better than the cook-shops;[5] in true **Rousseauesque** style I might even vilify the vanity of the great who waste the sweat of the people on such superfluous things;[6] finally I could even easily convince myself that if I were to find myself on an uninhabited island, without any hope of ever coming upon human beings again, and could conjure up such a magnificent structure through my mere wish, I would not even take the trouble of doing so if I already had a hut that was[d] comfortable enough for me. All of this might be conceded to me and approved; but that is not what is at issue here. One only wants to know whether the mere representation of the

5: 205

---

[a] *Unterscheidungs- und Beurtheilungsvermögen*
[b] *beurtheilen*
[c] In the first edition, "were to ask . . ."
[d] In the first edition, "is."

object is accompanied with satisfaction in me, however indifferent I might be with regard to the existence of the object of this representation. It is readily seen that to say that it is **beautiful** and to prove that I have taste what matters is what I make of this representation in myself, not how I depend on the existence of the object. Everyone must admit that a judgment about beauty in which there is mixed the least interest is very partial and not a pure judgment of taste. One must not be in the least biased in favor of the existence of the thing, but must be entirely indifferent in this respect in order to play the judge in matters of taste.

We can find no better way of elucidating this proposition, however, which is of the utmost importance, than by contrasting to the pure disinterested* satisfaction in the judgment of taste that which is combined with interest, especially if we can be certain that there are not more kinds of interest than those that are to be mentioned now.

§ 3.
The satisfaction *in the agreeable* is
combined with interest.

The agreeable is that which pleases the senses in sensation.[7] Now here there is an immediate opportunity to reprove and draw attention to a quite common confusion of the double meaning that the word "sensation" can have. All satisfaction (it is said or thought) is itself sensation (of a pleasure). Hence everything that pleases, just because it pleases, is agreeable (and, according to its different degrees or relations to other agreeable sensations, **graceful, lovely, enchanting, enjoyable,** etc.). But if this is conceded, then impressions of the senses, which determine inclination, or principles of reason, which determine the will, or merely reflected forms of intuition, which determine the power of judgment, are all entirely the same as far as the effect on the feeling of pleasure is concerned. For this would be the agreeableness in the sensation of one's state, and, since in the end all the effort of our faculties is directed to what is practical and must be united in it as their goal, one could not expect of them any other assessment of things and their value than that which consists in the gratification that they promise. In the end, how they achieve this does not matter at all, and

5: 206

---

* A judgment on an object of satisfaction can be entirely **disinterested** yet still very **interesting**, i.e., it is not grounded on any interest but it produces an interest; all pure moral judgments are like this. But the pure judgment of taste does not in itself even ground any interest. Only in society does it become **interesting** to have taste, the reason for which will be indicated in the sequel.

5: 205

since*a* the choice of means alone can make a difference here, people could certainly blame one another for foolishness and incomprehension, but never for baseness and malice: for all of them, each seeing things his own way, would be after one goal, which for everyone is gratification.

If a determination of the feeling of pleasure or displeasure is called sensation, then this expression means something entirely different than if I call the representation of a thing (through sense, as a receptivity belonging to the faculty of*b* cognition) sensation. For in the latter case the representation is related to the object, but in the first case it is related solely to the subject, and does not serve for any cognition at all, not even that by which the subject **cognizes** itself.

In the above explanation, however, we understand by the word "sensation" an objective representation of the senses; and in order not always to run the risk of being misinterpreted, we will call that which must always remain merely subjective and absolutely cannot constitute a representation of an object by the otherwise customary name of "feeling." The green color of the meadows belongs to **objective** sensation, as perception of an object of sense; but its agreeableness belongs to **subjective** sensation, through which no object is represented, i.e., to feeling, through which the object is considered as an object of satisfaction (which is not a cognition of it).

5: 207 Now that my judgment about an object by which I declare it agreeable expresses an interest in it is already clear from the fact that through sensation it excites a desire for objects of the same sort, hence the satisfaction presupposes not the mere judgment about it but the relation of its existence to my state insofar as it is affected by such an object. Hence one says of the agreeable not merely that it **pleases** but that it **gratifies**. It is not mere approval that I give it, rather inclination is thereby aroused; and any judgment about the constitution of the object belongs so little to that which is agreeable in the liveliest way that those who are always intent only on enjoyment (for this is the word that signifies intensity of gratification) gladly put themselves above all judging.

§ 4.
The satisfaction *in the good* is combined with interest.

That is **good** which pleases by means of reason alone, through the mere concept. We call something **good for something** (the useful)

---

a The first edition inserts the word "only" here.
b The word *Vermögen* (faculty of) was added in the second edition.

that pleases only as a means; however, another thing is called **good in itself** that pleases for itself. Both always involve the concept of an end, hence the relation of reason to (at least possible) willing, and consequently a satisfaction in the **existence** of an object or of an action, i.e., some sort of interest.[8]

In order to find something good, I must always know what sort of thing the object is supposed to be, i.e., I must have a concept of it. I do not need that in order to find beauty in something. Flowers, free designs, lines aimlessly*a* intertwined in each other under the name of foliage, signify nothing, do not depend on any determinate concept, and yet please. The satisfaction in the beautiful must depend upon reflection on an object that leads to some sort of concept (it is indeterminate which), and is thereby also distinguished from the agreeable, which rests entirely on sensation.

In many cases, to be sure, the agreeable seems to be identical to the good. Thus it is commonly said that all gratification (especially if it is durable) is good in itself, which means roughly that to be durably agreeable is the same as to be good. But one can quickly see that this is merely an erroneous verbal confusion, since the concepts that are properly attached to these expressions can in no way be exchanged for each other. The agreeable, which as such represents the object solely in relation to sense, must first be brought under principles of reason through the concept of an end before it can be called good as an object of the will. But that there is an entirely different relation to satisfaction when I call something that gratifies at the same time **good** can be seen from the fact that in the case of the good there is always the question whether it is merely mediately good or immediately good (whether it is useful or good in itself), while in contrast this cannot be a question at all in the case of the agreeable, since the word always signifies something that pleases immediately. (This is exactly the same in the case of that which I call beautiful.)

Even in the most common speech the agreeable is distinguished from the good. Of a dish that stimulates the taste through spices and other flavorings one may say without hesitation that it is agreeable and yet at the same time concede that it is not good; because while it immediately **appeals to**[b] the senses, considered mediately, i.e., by reason, which looks beyond to the consequences, it displeases. Even in judging[c] health this difference can be noticed. It is immediately agreeable to anyone who possesses it (at least negatively, i.e., as the absence of all bodily pains). But in order to say that it is good it must still be

a ohne Absicht
b **behagt**
c der Beurtheilung

referred by reason to ends, as a state, namely, that makes us fit for all our tasks. In respect to^a happiness, finally, everyone believes that the greatest sum (in terms of number as well as duration) of the agreeableness of life can be called a true good, indeed even the highest good. But reason also balks at this. Agreeableness is enjoyment. But if this were all that is at stake, then it would be foolish to be scrupulous with regard to the means for providing ourselves with it, that is, whether it is obtained passively, from the generosity of nature, or through self-activity and our own effort. But that the existence of a human being who lives merely **for enjoyment** (however busy he might be in this respect) should have a value in itself,^{b} even if as a means to this he was as helpful as possible to others who were likewise concerned only with enjoyment, because he participated in all gratification through sympathy: of this reason could never be persuaded. Only through that which he does without regard to enjoyment, in full freedom and independently of that which nature could passively provide for him, does he

5: 209   give his being as the existence of a person an absolute value; and happiness, in all the fullness of its agreeableness, is far from being an unconditional good.*

But despite all this difference between the agreeable and the good, the two still agree in this: that they are always combined with an interest in their object, not only the agreeable (§ 3) and the mediately good (the useful), which pleases as a means to some agreeableness or other, but also that which is good absolutely and in all respects, namely the morally good, which carries the highest interest with it. For the good is the object of the will (i.e., of a faculty of desire that is determined by reason). But to will something and to have satisfaction in its existence, i.e., to take an interest in it, are identical.

§ 5.
Comparison of the three specifically different
kinds of satisfaction.^{9}

The agreeable and the good both have a relation to the faculty of desire, and to this extent bring satisfaction with them, the former a pathologically conditioned satisfaction (through stimuli, *stimulos*), the

---

5: 209   * An obligation to enjoyment is a patent absurdity. The same thing must also be true of an alleged obligation in all actions that have mere enjoyment as their goal, however spiritually refined (or embellished) this may be, even if it were a mystical, so-called heavenly enjoyment.

^{a} In the first edition, "But of . . ."
^{b} The words "in itself" were added in the second edition.

latter a pure practical satisfaction, which is determined not merely through the representation of the object but at the same time through the represented connection of the subject with the existence of the object. Not merely the object but also its existence please.*a* Hence the judgment of taste is merely **contemplative**, i.e., a judgment that, indifferent with regard to the existence of an object, merely connects its constitution together with the feeling of pleasure and displeasure. But this contemplation itself is also not directed to concepts; for the judgment of taste is not a cognitive judgment (neither a theoretical nor a practical one),*b* and hence it is neither **grounded** on concepts nor **aimed** at them.

The agreeable, the beautiful, and the good therefore designate three different relations of representations to the feeling of pleasure and displeasure, in relation to which we distinguish objects or kinds of representations from each other.[10] The expressions appropriate to each of these, by means of which one designates the pleasure*c* in each of them, are also not the same. **Agreeable** is that which everyone calls what **gratifies** him; **beautiful**, what merely **pleases** him; **good,** what is **esteemed, approved,**d i.e., that on which he sets an objective value.[11] Agreeableness is also valid for nonrational animals; beauty is valid only for human beings, i.e., animal but also rational beings,*e* but not merely as the latter (e.g., spirits), rather as beings who are at the same time animal; the good, however, is valid for every rational being in general;[12] a proposition, which can receive its complete justification and explanation only in the sequel. One can say that among all these three kinds of satisfaction only that of the taste for the beautiful is a disinterested and **free** satisfaction; for no*f* interest, neither that of the senses nor that of reason, extorts approval. Hence it could be said of satisfaction that it is related in the three cases mentioned to **inclination**, to **favor**, or to **respect**. For **favor** is the only free satisfaction. An object of inclination and one that is imposed upon us by a law of reason for the sake of desire leave us no freedom to make anything into an object of pleasure ourselves. All interest presupposes a need or produces one; and as a determining ground of approval it no longer leaves the judgment on the object free.

Concerning the interest of inclination in the case of the agreeable, everyone says that hunger is the best cook, and people with a healthy

5: 210

---

a This sentence was added in the second edition.
b The words in parentheses were added in the second edition.
c *Complacenz*, i.e., Latin *complacentia*, which Kant often gives as an equivalent of *Lust*.
d This word (*gebilligt*) added in the second edition.
e The words from here to the next semicolon were added in the second edition.
f In the second edition, "no" (*kein*) replaces "an" (*ein*).

appetite relish everything that is edible at all; thus such a satisfaction demonstrates no choice in accordance with taste. Only when the need is satisfied can one distinguish who among the many has taste or does not. Likewise, there are mores*a* (conduct)*b* without virtue, politeness without benevolence, propriety without honorableness, etc. For where the moral*c* law speaks there is, objectively,*d* no longer any free choice with regard to what is to be done; and to show taste in one's conduct (or in judging*e* that of others) is something very different from expressing one's moral*f* mode of thinking; for the latter contains a command and produces a need, while modish*g* taste by contrast only plays with the objects of satisfaction without attaching itself to any of them.

Definition of the beautiful derived from the first moment.

Taste is the faculty for judging*h* an object or a kind of representation through a satisfaction or dissatisfaction **without any interest**. The object of such a satisfaction is called **beautiful**.[13]

Second Moment
of the judgment of taste, concerning its quality.
§ 6.
The beautiful is that which, without concepts, is represented as the object of a *universal* satisfaction.[14]

This definition of the beautiful can be deduced from the previous explanation of it as an object of satisfaction without any interest. For one cannot judge*i* that about which he is aware that the satisfaction in it is without interest in his own case in any way except that it must contain a ground of satisfaction for everyone. For since it is not grounded in any inclination of the subject (nor in any other underlying interest), but rather the person making the judgment feels himself completely **free** with regard to the satisfaction that he devotes to the

---

a *Sitten.* In this paragraph, Kant contrasts mere mores or manners (*Sitten*) with genuine morality (*moralische Denkungsart*), but uses the adjective *sittlich* ambiguously, meaning both genuinely moral but also merely modish.
b *Conduite*
c *sittliche*
d The word "objectively" is added in the second edition.
e *in Beurtheilung*; "in" added in the second edition.
f *moralische*
g *sittliche*
h *Beurtheilungsvermögen*
i *beurtheilen*

object, he cannot discover as grounds of the satisfaction any private conditions, pertaining to his subject alone, and must therefore regard it as grounded in those that he can also presuppose in everyone else; consequently he must believe himself to have grounds for expecting a similar pleasure of everyone. Hence he will speak of the beautiful as if beauty were a property[a] of the object and the judgment logical (constituting a cognition of the object through concepts of it), although it is only aesthetic and contains merely a relation of the representation of the object to the subject, because it still has the similarity with logical judgment that its validity for everyone can be presupposed. But this universality cannot originate from concepts. For there is no transition from concepts to the feeling of pleasure or[b] displeasure (except in pure practical laws, which however bring with them an interest of the sort that is not combined with the pure judgment of taste). Consequently there must be attached to the judgment of taste, with the consciousness of an abstraction in it from all interest, a claim to validity for everyone without the universality that pertains to objects, i.e., it must be combined with a claim to subjective universality.

5:212

§ 7.
Comparison of the beautiful with the agreeable and the good through the above characteristic.

With regard to the **agreeable**, everyone is content that his judgment, which he grounds on a private feeling, and in which he says of an object that it pleases him, be restricted merely to his own person.[15] Hence he is perfectly happy if, when he says that sparkling wine from the Canaries is agreeable, someone else should improve his expression and remind him that he should say "It is agreeable **to me**"; and this is so not only in the case of the taste of the tongue, palate, and throat, but also in the case of that which may be agreeable to someone's eyes and ears. For one person, the color violet is gentle and lovely, for another dead and lifeless. One person loves the tone of wind instruments, another that of stringed instruments. It would be folly to dispute the judgment of another that is different from our own in such a matter, with the aim of condemning it as incorrect, as if it were logically opposed to our own; thus[c] with regard to the agreeable, the principle **Everyone has his own**[d] taste (of the senses) is valid.

---

[a] *Beschaffenheit*
[b] In the first edition, "and."
[c] The word "thus" in the second edition replaces "and" in the first.
[d] The word "own" (*eigenen*) in the second edition replaces the word "special" or "particular" (*besondern*) in the first.

With the beautiful it is entirely different. It would be ridiculous if (the precise converse) someone who prided himself on his taste thought to justify himself thus: "This object (the building we are looking at, the clothing someone is wearing, the poem that is presented for judging)[a] is beautiful **for me**." For he must not call it **beautiful** if it pleases merely him. Many things may have charm and agreeableness for him, no one will be bothered about that; but if he pronounces that something is beautiful, then he expects the very same satisfaction of others: he judges not merely for himself, but for everyone, and speaks of beauty as if it were a property of things. Hence he says that the **thing**[b] is beautiful, and does not count on the agreement of others with his judgment of satisfaction because he has frequently found them to be agreeable with his own, but rather **demands** it from them. He rebukes them if they judge otherwise, and denies that they have taste, though he nevertheless requires that they ought to have it; and to this extent one cannot say, "Everyone has his special taste." This would be as much as to say that there is no taste at all, i.e., no aesthetic judgment that could make a rightful claim to the assent of everyone.

Nevertheless, one also finds with regard to the agreeable that unanimity in their judging[c] of it may be encountered among people, in view of which taste is denied of some of them but conceded to others, and not indeed with the meaning of an organic sense, but as a faculty for judging[d] with regard to the agreeable in general. Thus one says of someone who knows how to entertain his guests with agreeable things (of enjoyment through all the senses), so that they are all pleased, that he has taste. But here the universality is understood only comparatively, and in this case there are only **general**[e] rules (like all empirical rules are),[f] not **universal**[g] ones, the latter of which the judgment of taste about the beautiful ventures or claims. It is a judgment in relation to sociability insofar as it rests on empirical rules. With regard to the good, to be sure, judgments also rightly lay claim to validity for everyone; but the good is represented as an object of a universal satisfaction only **through a concept**, which is not the case either with the agreeable or with the beautiful.

5: 213

---

[a] *Beurtheilung*
[b] *Sache*
[c] *Beurtheilung*
[d] *Beurtheilungsvermögen*
[e] *generale*
[f] The words in parentheses were added in the second edition.
[g] *universale*

§ 8.
The universality of the satisfaction is
represented in a judgment of taste
only as subjective.

This particular determination of the universality of an aesthetic judgment that can be found in a judgment of taste is something remarkable, not indeed for the logician, but certainly for the transcendental philosopher, the discovery of the origin of which calls for no little effort on his part, but which also reveals a property of our faculty of cognition that without this analysis would have remained unknown.

First, one must be fully convinced that through the judgment of taste (on the beautiful) one ascribes the satisfaction in an object **to everyone**, yet without grounding it on a concept (for then it would be the good), and that this claim to universal validity so essentially belongs to a judgment by which we declare something to be **beautiful** that without thinking this it would never occur to anyone to use this expression, rather everything that pleases without a concept would be counted as agreeable, regarding which everyone can be of his own mind, and no one expects assent to his judgment of taste of anyone else, although this is always the case in judgments of taste about beauty. I can call the first the taste of the senses, the second the taste of reflection,[16] insofar as the first makes merely private judgments about an object, while the second makes supposedly generally valid (public) judgments, but both make aesthetic (not merely practical judgments) about an object, regarding merely*a* the relation of its representation to the feeling of pleasure and displeasure. Now it is nevertheless strange that in the case of the taste of the senses experience not only shows that its judgment (of pleasure or displeasure in something) is not universally valid, but also that everyone is intrinsically so modest as not even to ascribe this assent to others (even though a quite extensive unanimity is often found in these judgments as well), whereas the taste of reflection, which, as experience teaches, is often enough rejected in its claim to the universal validity of its judgment (about the beautiful), can nevertheless find it possible (as it also actually does) to represent judgments that could demand such assent universally, and does in fact expect it of everyone for each of its judgments, while those who make those judgments do not find themselves in conflict over the possibility of such a claim, but only find it impossible to agree on the correct application of this faculty in particular cases.

Here it should first of all be noted that a universality that does not

5:214

---

a Added in the second edition.

rest on concepts of objects (even if only empirical ones) is not logical at all, but aesthetic, i.e., it does not contain an objective quantity of judgment, but only a subjective one, for which I also use the expression **common validity**,[a] which does not designate[b] the validity for every subject of the relation of a representation to the faculty of cognition but rather to the feeling of pleasure and displeasure. (The same expression can, however, also be used for the logical quantity of the judgment provided only that one adds to it **objective** universal validity to distinguish it from the merely subjective, which is always aesthetic.)[17]

5: 215

Now an **objectively universally valid** judgment is also always subjectively so, i.e., if the judgment is valid for everything that is contained under a given concept then it is also valid for everyone who represents an object through this concept. But from a **subjectively universal validity**, i.e., from aesthetic universal validity, which does not rest on any concept, there cannot be any inference at all to logical universal validity; because the first kind of judgment does not pertain to the object at all. For that very reason, however, the aesthetic universality that is ascribed to a judgment must also be of a special kind, since the predicate of beauty is not connected with the concept of the **object** considered in its entire logical[c] sphere, and yet it extends it over the whole sphere of **those who judge.**

In regard to logical quantity all judgments of taste are **singular** judgments. For since I must immediately hold the object up to my feeling of pleasure and displeasure, and yet not through concepts, it cannot have the quantity of an objectively generally valid judgment, although if the singular representation of the object of the judgment of taste in accordance with the conditions that determine the latter is transformed into a concept through comparison, then a logically universal judgment can arise from it: e.g., by means of a judgment of taste I declare the rose that I am gazing at to be beautiful. By contrast, the judgment that arises from the comparison of many singular ones, that roses in general are beautiful, is no longer pronounced merely as an aesthetic judgment, but as an aesthetically grounded logical judgment. Now the judgment that the rose is (in its use)[d] agreeable is also, to be sure, an aesthetic and singular judgment, but not a judgment of taste, rather a judgment of the senses. That is to say, it differs from the former in that the judgment of taste carries with it

---

[a] *Gemeingültigkeit*
[b] The verb "designate" (*bezeichnet*) was added in the second edition.
[c] The word "logical" was added in the second edition.
[d] *im Gebrauche*; in the Academy edition, Windelband suggests *im Geruche* (in its smell).

an **aesthetic quantity** of universality, i.e., validity for everyone, which cannot be found in the judgment about the agreeable. Only judgments about the good alone, although they also determine the satisfaction in an object, have logical and not merely aesthetic validity, for they are valid of the object, as cognitions of it, and are therefore valid for everyone.

If one judges[a] objects merely in accordance with concepts, then all representation of beauty is lost. Thus there can also be no rule in accordance with which someone could be compelled to acknowledge something as beautiful. Whether a garment, a house, a flower is beautiful: no one allows himself to be talked into[b] his judgment about that by means of any grounds or fundamental principles. One wants to submit the object to his own eyes, just as if his satisfaction depended on sensation; and yet, if one then calls the object beautiful, one believes oneself to have a universal voice, and lays claim to the consent of everyone, whereas any private sensation would be decisive only for him alone and his satisfaction.[18]

5: 216

Now here it can be seen that in the judgment of taste nothing is postulated except such a **universal voice** with regard to satisfaction without the mediation of concepts, hence the **possibility** of an aesthetic judgment that could at the same time be considered valid for everyone. The judgment of taste does not itself **postulate** the accord of everyone (only a logically universal judgment can do that, since it can adduce grounds); it only **ascribes** this agreement to everyone, as a case of the rule with regard to which it expects confirmation not from concepts but only from the consent of others.[19] The universal voice is thus only an idea (what it rests on will not yet be investigated here). Whether someone who believes himself to be making a judgment of taste is in fact judging in accordance with this idea can be uncertain; but that he relates it to that idea, thus that it is supposed to be a judgment of taste, he announces through the expression of beauty. Of that he can be certain for himself through the mere consciousness of separation of everything that belongs to the agreeable and the good from the satisfaction that remains to him; and this is all for which he promises himself the assent of everyone: a claim which he would also be justified in making under these conditions, if only he were not often to offend against them and thereby make an erroneous judgment of taste.[c]

---

[a] *beurtheilt*
[b] *beschwatzen*; the first edition has *abschwatzen* (talked out of).
[c] In the first edition, this clause was in the past indicative and not in the subjunctive mood.

§ 9.
Investigation of the question: whether in the judgment of taste the feeling of pleasure precedes the judging[a] of the object or the latter precedes the former.

The solution of this problem is the key to the critique of taste, and hence worthy of full attention.

5: 217   If the pleasure in the given object came first, and only its universal communicability[b] were to be attributed in the judgment of taste to the representation of the object, then such a procedure would be self-contradictory. For such a pleasure would be none other than mere agreeableness in sensation,[c] and hence by its very nature could have only private validity, since it would immediately depend on the representation through which the object **is given.**

Thus it is the universal capacity for the communication[d] of the state of mind in the given representation which, as the subjective condition of the judgment of taste, must serve as its ground and have the pleasure in the object as a consequence.[20] Nothing, however, can be universally communicated except cognition and representation so far as it belongs to cognition. For only so far is the latter objective, and only thereby does it have a universal point of relation with which everyone's faculty of representation is compelled to agree. Now if the determining ground of the judgment on this universal communicability of the representation is to be conceived of merely subjectively, namely without a concept of the object, it can be nothing other than the state of mind that is encountered in the relation of the powers of representation to each other insofar as they relate a given representation to **cognition in general.**

The powers of cognition that are set into play by this representation are hereby in a free play, since no determinate concept restricts them to a particular rule of cognition.[21] Thus the state of mind in this representation must be that of a feeling of the free play of the powers of representation in a given representation for a cognition in general. Now there belongs to a representation by which an object is given, in order for there to be cognition of it in general, **imagination** for the composition of the manifold of intuition and **understanding** for the unity of the concept that unifies the representations.[e] This state of a

---

[a] *Beurtheilung*
[b] *Mittheilbarkeit*
[c] *Sinnenempfindung*
[d] *Mittheilungsfähigkeit*
[e] In the first edition, this clause ends with a comma, and the next sentence is a further clause of the present one, introduced with an "and."

free play of the faculties of cognition with a representation through which an object is given must be able to be universally communicated, because cognition, as a determination of the object with which given representations (in whatever subject it may be) should agree, is the only kind of representation that is valid for everyone.[22]

The subjective universal communicability of the kind of representation in a judgment of taste, since it is supposed to occur without presupposing a determinate concept, can be nothing other than the state of mind in the free play of the imagination and the understanding (so far as they agree with each other as is requisite for a **cognition in general**): for we are conscious that this subjective relation suited to cognition in general must be valid for everyone and consequently universally communicable, just as any determinate cognition is, which still always rests on that relation as its subjective condition.   5: 218

Now this merely subjective (aesthetic) judging*ª* of the object, or of the representation through which the object is given, precedes the pleasure in it, and is the ground of this pleasure in the harmony of the faculties of cognition; but on that universality of the subjective conditions of the judging*ᵇ* of objects alone is this universal subjective validity of satisfaction, which we combine with the representation of the object that we call beautiful, grounded.

That being able to communicate one's state of mind, even if only with regard to the faculties of cognition, carries a pleasure with it, could easily be established (empirically and psychologically) from the natural tendency of human beings to sociability. But that is not enough for our purposes. When we call something beautiful, the pleasure that we feel is expected of everyone else in the judgment of taste as necessary, just as if it were to be regarded as a property of the object that is determined in it in accordance with concepts; but beauty is nothing by itself, without relation to the feeling of the subject. However, we must reserve the discussion of this question until we have answered another: how and whether aesthetic judgments *a priori* are possible.

For now we shall still concern ourselves with the lesser question: in what way do we become conscious of a mutual subjective correspondence of the powers of cognition with each other*ᶜ* in the judgment of taste – aesthetically, through mere inner sense and sensation, or intellectually, through the consciousness of our intentional activity through which we set them in play?*ᵈ*

If the given representation, which occasions the judgment of taste,

---

ª *Beurtheilung*
ᵇ *Beurtheilung*
ᶜ The words "with each other" (*untereinander*) were added in the second edition.
ᵈ Question mark added.

5: 219

were a concept, which united understanding and imagination in the judging*a* of the object into a cognition of the object, then the consciousness of this relationship would be intellectual (as in the objective schematism of the power of judgment, which was dealt with in the critique).[23] But in that case the judgment would not be made in relation to pleasure and displeasure, hence it would not be a judgment of taste. Now the judgment of taste, however, determines the object, independently of concepts, with regard to satisfaction and the predicate of beauty. Thus that subjective unity of the relation can make itself known only through sensation. The animation*b*,[24] of both faculties (the imagination and the understanding)*c* to an activity that is indeterminate but yet, through the stimulus of the given representation, in unison,*d* namely that which belongs to a cognition in general, is the sensation whose universal communicability is postulated by the judgment of taste. Of course, an objective relation can only be thought, but insofar*e* as it is subjective as far as its conditions are concerned it can still be sensed in its effect on the mind; and further, in the case of a relation that is not grounded in any concept (like that of the powers of representation to a faculty of cognition in general), no other consciousness of it is possible except through sensation of the effect that consists in the facilitated play of both powers of the mind (imagination and understanding), enlivened*f* through mutual agreement. A representation which, though singular and without comparison to others, nevertheless is in agreement with the conditions of universality, an agreement that constitutes the business of the understanding in general, brings the faculties of cognition into the well-proportioned disposition that we require for all cognition and hence also regard as valid for everyone (for*g* every human being) who is determined to judge by means of understanding and sense in combination.

The definition of the beautiful drawn from the second moment.

That is **beautiful** which pleases universally without a concept.

a Beurtheilung
b Belebung
c The words in parentheses were added in the second edition.
d einhelliger
e In the first edition, "if."
f belebten
g The word "for" added in the second edition.

Third Moment
of judgments of taste, concerning the *relation*
of the ends that are taken into
consideration in them.

§ 10.
On purposiveness in general.

If one would define what an end is in accordance with its transcendental determinations (without presupposing anything empirical, such as the feeling of pleasure), then an end is the object of a concept insofar   5: 220
as the latter is regarded as the cause of the former (the real ground of its possibility); and the causality of a **concept** with regard to its **object** is purposiveness (*forma finalis*).[a] Thus where not merely the cognition of an object but the object itself (its form or its existence) as an effect is thought of as possible only through a concept of the latter, there one thinks of an end. The representation of the effect is here the determining ground of its cause, and precedes the latter. The consciousness of the causality of a representation with respect to the state of the subject, **for maintaining** it in that state, can here designate in general what is called pleasure; in contrast to which displeasure is that representation that contains the ground for determining the state of the representations to their own opposite (hindering or getting rid of them).[b,25]

The faculty of desire, insofar as it is determinable only through concepts, i.e., to act in accordance with the representation of an end, would be the will.[26] An object or a state of mind or even an action, however, even if its possibility does not necessarily presuppose the representation of an end, is called purposive merely because its possibility can only be explained and conceived by us insofar as we assume as its ground a causality in accordance with ends, i.e., a will that has arranged it so in accordance with the representation of a certain rule. Purposiveness can thus exist without an end, insofar as we do not place the causes[c] of this form in a will, but can still make the explanation of its possibility conceivable to ourselves only by deriving it from a will. Now we do not always necessarily need to have insight through reason (concerning its possibility) into what we observe. Thus we can at least observe a purposiveness concerning form, even without basing it in an end (as the matter of the *nexus finalis*),[d] and notice it in objects, although in no other way than by reflection.

---

[a] purposive form
[b] The words in parentheses were added in the second edition.
[c] This word was singular in the first edition.
[d] purposive connection

§ 11.

The judgment of taste has nothing but the
form of the purposiveness of an object
(or of the way of representing it)
as its ground.

Every end, if it is regarded as a ground of satisfaction, always brings an interest with it, as the determining ground of the judgment about the object of the pleasure. Thus no subjective end can ground the judgment of taste. But further no representation of an objective end, i.e., of the possibility of the object itself in accordance with principles of purposive connection, hence no concept of the good, can determine the judgment of taste, because it is an aesthetic judgment and not a cognitive judgment, which thus does not concern any **concept** of the constitution and internal or external possibility of the object, through this or that cause, but concerns only the relation of the powers of representation to each other insofar as they are determined by a representation.

Now this relation in the determination of an object as a beautiful one is combined with the feeling of pleasure that is at the same time declared to be valid for everyone through the judgment of taste; consequently an agreeableness accompanying the representation can contain the determining ground just as little as the representation of[a] the perfection of the object and the concept of the good can. Thus nothing other than the subjective purposiveness in the representation of an object without any end (objective or subjective), consequently the mere form of purposiveness in the representation through which an object is **given** to us, insofar as we are conscious of it, can constitute the satisfaction that we judge,[b] without a concept, to be universally communicable, and hence the determining ground of the judgment of taste.

§ 12.

The judgment of taste rests on
a priori grounds.

To establish *a priori* the connection of the feeling of a pleasure or displeasure as an effect with some representation (sensation or concept) as its cause is absolutely impossible, for that would be a [c]causal relation, which (among objects of experience) can only ever be cognized *a posteriori* and by means of experience itself. To be sure, in the critique of

---

[a] The words "the representation of" were added in the second edition.
[b] *beurtheilen*
[c] The second edition omits the word "particular" (*besonderes*) that precedes "causal" in the first edition.

practical reason we actually derived the feeling of respect (as a special and peculiar modification of this feeling, which will not coincide exactly either with the pleasure or with the displeasure that we obtain from empirical objects) from universal moral concepts *a priori*.[27] But there we could also step beyond the bounds of experience and appeal to a causality that rests on a supersensible property of the subject, namely that of freedom. But even there we did not actually derive this **feeling** from the idea of the moral as a cause, rather it was merely the determination of the will that was derived from the latter. The state of mind of a will determined by something, however, is in itself already a feeling of pleasure and is identical with it, thus it does not follow from it as an effect: the latter would only have to be assumed if the concept of the moral as a good preceded the determination of the will by the law, for in that case it would be pointless for the pleasure that would be connected with the concept to be derived from it as a mere cognition.

Now it is similar with the pleasure in the aesthetic judgment, except that here it is merely contemplative and does not produce an interest in the object, while in the moral judgment it is practical.[a] The consciousness of the merely formal purposiveness in the play of the cognitive powers of the subject in the case of a representation through which an object is given is the pleasure itself, because it contains a determining ground of the activity of the subject with regard to the animation of its cognitive powers, thus an internal causality (which is purposive) with regard to cognition in general, but without being restricted to a particular cognition, hence it contains a mere form of the subjective purposiveness of a representation in an aesthetic judgment. This pleasure is also in no way practical, neither like that from the pathological ground of agreeableness nor like that from the intellectual ground of the represented good. But yet it has a causality in itself, namely that of **maintaining** the state of the representation of the mind and the occupation of the cognitive powers without a further aim. We **linger** over the consideration of the beautiful because this consideration strengthens and reproduces itself, which is analogous to (yet not identical with) the way in which we linger when a charm in the representation of the object repeatedly attracts attention, where the mind is passive.

§ 13.

The pure judgment of taste is independent from
charm and emotion.[28]

Any interest spoils the judgment of taste and deprives it of its impartiality, especially if the purposiveness does not precede the feeling of

---

[a] In the first edition, "moral but practical."

pleasure, as in the interest of reason, but is instead grounded on it, which always happens in the aesthetic judgment about something insofar as it is gratifying or painful. Hence judgments that are so affected can make no claim at all to universal satisfaction or as little claim as can be made when those sorts of sensations are found among the determining grounds of taste. Taste is always still barbaric when it needs the addition of **charms** and **emotions** for satisfaction, let alone if it makes these into the standard for its approval.

And yet charms are not only often included with beauty (which should properly concern merely form) as a contribution to the aesthetic universal satisfaction, but are even passed off as beauties in themselves, hence the matter of satisfaction is passed off for the form: a misunderstanding which, like many others that yet always have something true as their ground, can be eliminated by careful determination of these concepts.

A judgment of taste on which charm and emotion have no influence (even though these may be combined with the satisfaction in the beautiful), which thus has for its determining ground merely the purposiveness of the form, is a **pure judgment of taste.**[29]

§ 14.
Elucidation by means of examples.

Aesthetic judgments can be divided, just like theoretical (logical) ones, into empirical and pure. The first are those which assert agreeableness or disagreeableness, the second those which assert beauty of an object or the way of representing it; the former are judgments of sense (material aesthetic judgments), the latter (as formal)[a] are alone proper judgments of taste.

5: 224   A judgment of taste is thus pure only insofar as no merely empirical satisfaction is mixed into its determining ground. This always happens, however, if charm or emotion has any share in the judgment by which something is to be declared to be beautiful.

Now here there may arise many objections, pretending that charm is not merely a necessary ingredient of beauty, but even entirely sufficient by itself to be called beautiful. A mere color, e.g., the green of a lawn, a mere tone (in distinction from sound and noise), say that of a violin, is declared by most people to be beautiful in itself, although both seem to have as their ground merely the matter of the representations, namely mere sensation, and on that account deserve to be called only agreeable. Yet at the same time one will surely note that

---

[a] The parenthesis "(as formal)" was added in the second edition.

the sensations of color as well as of tone justifiably count as beautiful only insofar as both are **pure**, which is a determination that already concerns form, and is also the only thing that can be universally communicated about these representations with certainty: because the quality of the sensations themselves cannot be assumed to be in accord in all subjects, and it cannot easily be assumed that the agreeableness of one color in preference to another or of the tone of one musical instrument in preference to another will be judged[a] in the same way by everyone.

If one assumes, with Euler, that the colors are vibrations (*pulsus*) of the air immediately following one another, just as tones are vibrations of the air disturbed by sound, and, what is most important, that the mind does not merely perceive, by sense, their effect on the animation of the organ, but also, through reflection, perceives the regular play of the impressions (hence the form in the combination of different representations) (about which I have very little doubt),[b,30] then colors and tones would not be mere sensations, but would already be a formal determination of the unity of a manifold of them, and in that case could also be counted as beauties in themselves.

The purity of a simple kind of sensation, however, means that its uniformity is not disturbed and interrupted by any foreign sensation, and belongs merely to the form; for in that case one can abstract from the quality of that kind of sensation (from whether and what color or whether and what tone it represents). Hence all simple colors, insofar as they are pure, are held to be beautiful; those that are mixed do not have this advantage since, precisely because they are not simple, one has no standard for judging[c] whether they should be called pure or impure.[31]   5: 225

As for the opinion that the beauty that is attributed to the object on account of its form may well be heightened by charm, this is a common error and one that is very detrimental to genuine, uncorrupted, well-grounded taste, although charms may certainly be added beside beauty in order to interest the mind through the representation of the object beyond dry satisfaction, and thus to serve to recommend taste and its cultivation,[d] especially when it is still crude and unpracticed. But they actually do damage to the judgment of taste if they attract attention to

---

[a] *beurtheilt*
[b] Here we follow the third edition, which prints "*woran ich doch gar nicht zweifle*," rather than the first and second editions, which read "*woran ich doch gar sehr zweifle*," i.e., "which I very much doubt." For explanation of this departure from the second edition, see the endnote.
[c] *der Beurtheilung*
[d] *Kultur*

themselves as grounds for the judging^a of beauty. For it is so far from being true that they contribute to taste that, if taste is still weak and unpracticed, they must rather be accepted cautiously, as foreigners, only to the extent that they do not disturb that beautiful form.[32]

In painting and sculpture, indeed in all the pictorial arts,^{b} in architecture[33] and horticulture insofar as they are fine arts, the **drawing** is what is essential, in which what constitutes the ground of all arrangements for taste is not what gratifies in sensation but merely what pleases through its form. The colors that illuminate the outline belong to charm; they can of course enliven^c the object in itself for sensation, but they cannot make it worthy of being intuited and beautiful, rather, they are often even considerably restricted by what is required by beautiful form, and even where charm is permitted it is ennobled only through the former.^{d}

All form of the objects of the senses (of the outer as well as, mediately, the inner) is either **shape**^{e} or **play**: in the latter case, either play of shapes (in space, mime, and dance), or mere^f play of sensations (in time). The **charm** of colors or of the agreeable tones of instruments can be added, but **drawing** in the former and composition in the latter constitute the proper object of the pure judgment of taste; and that the purity of colors as well as of tones as well as their multiplicity and their contrast seem to contribute to beauty does not mean that they as it were supply a supplement of the same rank to the satisfaction in the form because they are agreeable by themselves, but rather they do so because they merely make the latter more precisely, more determinately, and more completely intuitable, and also enliven the representation^g through their charm, thereby awakening and sustaining^h attention to the object itself.

5: 226

Even what one calls **ornaments** (*parerga*),^{i} i.e., that which is not internal to the entire representation of the object as a constituent, but

---

^{a} *Beurtheilungsgründe*

^{b} *bildenden Künste*

^{c} Following the second edition, reading *belebt . . . machen* rather than *beliebt* (make it beloved).

^{d} In the first edition, Kant explicitly refers to "beautiful form" rather than merely "the former" here.

^{e} *Gestalt*

^{f} The word "mere" added in the second edition.

^{g} The phrase "enliven the representation" added in the second edition; the first edition would read "and through their charm awaken and elevate . . ."

^{h} In the first edition, "elevating" (*erheben* rather than *erhalten*).

^{i} The parenthetical term *parerga*, a word in both Latin and Greek meaning something subordinate or incidental, is added in the second edition.

only belongs to it externally as an addendum and augments the satisfaction of taste, still does this only through its form: like the borders of paintings,[a] draperies on statues, or colonnades around magnificent buildings. But if the ornament itself does not consist in beautiful form, if it is, like a gilt frame, attached merely in order to recommend approval for the painting through its charm – then it is called **decoration**, and detracts from genuine beauty.

Emotion, a sensation in which agreeableness is produced only by means of a momentary inhibition followed by a stronger outpouring of the vital force, does not belong to beauty at all. Sublimity (with which the feeling of emotion is combined), however, requires another standard for judging[b] than that on which taste is grounded; and thus a pure judgment of taste has neither charm nor emotion, in a word no sensation, as matter of the aesthetic judgment, for its determining ground.

§ 15.
The judgment of taste is entirely independent from the concept of perfection.

Objective purposiveness can be cognized only by means of the relation of the manifold to a determinate end, thus only through a concept. From this alone it is already clear that the beautiful, the judging[c] of which has as its ground a merely formal purposiveness, i.e., a purposiveness without an end, is entirely independent of the representation of the good, since the latter presupposes an objective purposiveness, i.e., the relation of the object to a determinate end.

Objective purposiveness is either external, i.e., the **utility** of the object, or internal, i.e., its **perfection**. That the satisfaction in an object on account of which we call it beautiful could not rest on the representation of its utility is sufficiently obvious from the two preceding main sections,[d] since in that case it would not be an immediate satisfaction in the object, which latter is the essential condition of the judgment about beauty. But an objective inner purposiveness, i.e., perfection, already comes closer to the predicate of beauty, and has therefore been held to be identical with beauty even by philosophers of repute, though with the proviso **if it is thought confusedly**.[34] It is of the greatest

5: 227

---

[a] This example was added in the second edition.
[b] *Beurtheilung*
[c] *Beurtheilung*
[d] That is, the first and second moments of the "Analytic of the Beautiful."

importance in a critique of taste to decide whether beauty is really reducible to the concept of perfection.

To judge[a] objective purposiveness we always require the concept of an end, and [if that purposiveness is not to be an external one (utility), but an internal one],[b] we require the concept of an internal end, which contains the ground of the internal possibility of the object. Now as an end in general is that the **concept** of which can be regarded as the ground of the possibility of the object itself, thus in order to represent an objective purposiveness in a thing the concept of **what sort of thing it is supposed to be** must come first; and the agreement of the manifold in the thing with this concept (which supplies the rule for the combination of the manifold in it) is the **qualitative perfection** of a thing.[c] **Quantitative** perfection, as the completeness of any thing in its own kind, is entirely distinct from this, and is a mere concept of magnitude (of totality), in which **what the thing is supposed to be** is thought of as already determined and it is only asked whether **everything** that is requisite for it exists.[35] What is formal in the representation of a thing, i.e., the agreement of the manifold with a unity (leaving undetermined what it is supposed to be) does not by itself allow any cognition of objective purposiveness at all, because since abstraction is made from this unity, **as an end** (what the thing is supposed to be), nothing remains but the subjective purposiveness of representations in the mind of the beholder,[d] which indicates a certain purposiveness of the representational state of the subject, and in this an ease in apprehending a given form in the imagination, but not the perfection of any object, which is here not conceived through any concept of an end. E.g., if I encounter in the forest a plot of grass around which the trees stand in a circle, and I do not represent a purpose for it, say that it is to serve for country dancing, then not the slightest concept of perfection is given through the mere form. But to represent a formal **objective** purposiveness without an end, i.e., the mere form of a **perfection** (without any material and **concept** of that with which it is to agree, even if it were only the idea of a lawfulness in general),[e] is a veritable contradiction.

Now the judgment of taste is an aesthetic judgment, i.e., one that rests on subjective grounds, and its determining ground cannot be a concept, and thus not a concept of a determinate end. Thus by beauty,

5: 228

---

[a] *beurtheilen*
[b] The square brackets are Kant's.
[c] In the first edition, there is a comma here, and the next sentence continues as a dependent clause.
[d] *des Anschauenden*, i.e., the one who intuits
[e] This clause was added in the second edition.

as a formal subjective purposiveness, there is not conceived any perfection of the object as a supposedly formal but yet also objective purposiveness, and the distinction between the concepts of the beautiful and good, as if both differed only in logical form, the former being merely a confused but the latter a distinct concept of perfection while they were otherwise identical in content and origin, is null, because in that case there would be no **specific** difference between them, rather a judgment of taste would be just as much a cognitive judgment as the judgment whereby something is declared to be good – just as when the ordinary man, when he says that deception is unjust, grounds his judgment on confused principles, while the philosopher grounds his on distinct ones, but at bottom these are identical principles of reason. But I have already pointed out that an aesthetic judgment is of a unique[a] kind, and affords absolutely no cognition (not even a confused one) of the object, which happens only in a logical judgment; while the former, by contrast, relates the representation by which an object is given solely to the subject, and does not bring to our attention any property of the object, but only the purposive form in the determination[b] of the powers of representation that are occupied with it. The judgment is also called aesthetic precisely because its determining ground is not a concept but the feeling (of inner sense) of that unison in the play of the powers of the mind, insofar as they can only be sensed.[c] By contrast, if one were to call confused concepts and the objective judgment that is grounded in them aesthetic, one would have an understanding that judged by sense or a sense that represented its object through concepts, both of which are self-contradictory. The faculty of concepts, be they confused or distinct, is the understanding; and although understanding also belongs to the judgment of taste, as an aesthetic judgment (as in all judgments), it does not belong to it as a faculty for the cognition   5: 229
of an object, but as the faculty for the determination of the judgment and its representation (without a concept) in accordance with the relation of the representation to the subject and its internal feeling, and indeed insofar as this judgment is possible in accordance with a universal rule.

---

[a] Here reading *einzig* with the third edition rather than *einig* ("unitary") as in the first two.
[b] The words "in the determination" were added in the second edition.
[c] *empfunden*

§ 16.
The judgment of taste through which an object is declared to be beautiful under the condition of a determinate concept is not pure.

There are two kinds of beauty: free beauty (*pulchritudo vaga*) or merely adherent[a] beauty (*pulchritudo adhaerens*). The first presupposes no concept of what the object ought to be; the second does presuppose such a concept and the perfection of the object in accordance with it. The first are called (self-subsisting) beauties of this or that thing; the latter, as adhering to a concept (conditioned beauty), are ascribed to objects that stand under the concept of a particular end.[36]

Flowers are free natural beauties. Hardly anyone other than the botanist knows what sort of thing a flower is supposed to be; and even the botanist, who recognizes in it the reproductive organ of the plant, pays no attention to this natural end if he judges the flower by means of taste. Thus this judgment is not grounded on any kind of perfection, any internal purposiveness to which the composition of the manifold is related. Many birds (the parrot, the hummingbird, the bird of paradise) and a host of marine crustaceans are beauties in themselves, which are not attached to a determinate object in accordance with concepts regarding its end, but are free and please for themselves. Thus designs *à la grecque*,[37] foliage for borders or on wallpaper, etc., signify nothing by themselves: they do not represent anything, no object under a determinate concept, and are free beauties. One can also count as belonging to the same kind what are called in music fantasias (without a theme), indeed all music without a text.

In the judging[b] of a free beauty (according to mere form) the judgment of taste is pure. No concept of any end for which the manifold should serve the given object and thus which the latter should represent is presupposed, by which the imagination, which is as it were at play in the observation of the shape, would merely be restricted.

But the beauty of a human being (and in this species that of a man, a woman, or a child), the beauty of a horse, of a building (such as a church, a palace, an arsenal, or a garden-house) presuppose a concept of the end that determines what the thing should be, hence a concept of its perfection, and is thus merely adherent[c] beauty. Now just as the combination of the agreeable (of sensation) with beauty, which properly concerns only form, hindered the purity of the judgment of taste,

---

[a] *anhängende*; the Latin equivalent shows that Kant means the same by this as by the term *adhärirende*, which he uses later in this section.
[b] *Beurtheilung*
[c] *adhärierende*

so the combination of the good (that is, the way in which the manifold is good for the thing itself, in accordance with its end) with beauty does damage to its purity.[38]

One would be able to add much to a building that would be pleasing in the intuition of it if only it were not supposed to be a church; a figure could be beautified with all sorts of curlicues and light but regular lines, as the New Zealanders[a] do with their tattooing, if only it were not a human being; and the latter could have much finer features and a more pleasing, softer outline to its facial structure if only it were not supposed to represent a man, or even a warrior.

Now the satisfaction in the manifold in a thing in relation to the internal purpose that determines its possibility is a satisfaction grounded on a concept; the satisfaction in beauty, however, is one that presupposes no concept, but is immediately combined with the representation through which the object is given (not through which it is thought). Now if the judgment of taste in regard to the latter is made dependent on the purpose in the former, as a judgment of reason, and is thereby restricted, then it is no longer a free and pure judgment of taste.

To be sure, taste gains by this combination of aesthetic satisfaction with the intellectual in that it becomes fixed and, though not universal, can have rules prescribed to it in regard to certain purposively deter-mined objects. But in this case these are also not rules of taste, but merely rules for the unification of taste with reason, i.e., of the beauti-ful with the good, through which the former becomes usable as an instrument of the intention with regard to the latter, so that the deter-mination of the mind that sustains itself and is of subjective universal validity can underlie that which can only be sustained through strenu-ous resolve but is objectively universally valid. Strictly speaking, how-ever, perfection does not gain by beauty, nor does beauty gain by perfection; rather, since in comparing the representation by which an object is given to us with the object (with regard to what it ought to be) we cannot avoid at the same time holding it together with the subject, the **entire faculty** of the powers of representation gains if both states of mind are in agreement. 5: 231

A judgment of taste in regard to an object with a determinate internal end would thus be pure only if the person making the judg-ment either had no concept of this end or abstracted from it in his judgment. But in that case, although this person would have made a correct judgment of taste, in that he would have judged[b] the object as a free beauty, he would nevertheless be criticized and accused of a false

---

[a] That is, the Maori aborigines in New Zealand.
[b] *beurtheilete*

taste by someone else, who considered beauty in the object only as an adherent property (who looked to the end of the object), even though both judge correctly in their way: the one on the basis of what he has before his sense, the other on the basis of what he has in his thoughts. By means of this distinction one can settle many disputes about beauty between judges of taste, by showing them that the one is concerned[a] with free beauty, the other with adherent beauty, the first making a pure, the second an applied judgment of taste.

§ 17.
On the ideal of beauty.[39]

There can be no objective rule of taste that would determine what is beautiful through concepts. For every judgment from this source is aesthetic, i.e., its determining ground is the feeling of the subject and not a concept of an object. To seek a principle of taste that would provide the universal criterion of the beautiful through determinate concepts is a fruitless undertaking, because what is sought is impossible and intrinsically self-contradictory. The universal communicability of the sensation (of satisfaction or dissatisfaction), and indeed one that occurs without concepts, the unanimity, so far as possible, of all times and peoples about this feeling in the representation of certain objects: although weak and hardly sufficient for conjecture, this is the empirical criterion of the derivation of a taste, confirmed by examples, from the common ground, deeply buried in all human beings, of unanimity in the judging[b] of forms under which objects are given to them.

5: 232

Hence some products of taste are regarded as **exemplary** – not as if taste could be acquired by imitating others.[40] For taste must be a faculty of one's own; however, whoever imitates a model certainly shows, so far as he gets it right, a skill, but he shows taste only insofar as he can judge[c] this model himself.* From this, however, it follows that the highest model, the archetype of taste, is a mere idea, which everyone must produce in himself, and in accordance with which he must judge[d]

5: 232

* Models of taste with regard to the arts of discourse must be composed in a dead and learned language: the former, in order not to have to suffer the alterations that unavoidably affect living languages, which make noble expressions flat, common ones outmoded, and newly created ones of only brief currency; the latter, so that it should have a grammar that is not subject to any willful change of fashion but has its own unalterable rules.

[a] In the second edition, the verb *halte* replaces *wende* (turning to), used in the first.
[b] *Beurtheilung*
[c] *beurtheilen*
[d] *beurtheilen*

everything that is an object of taste, or that is an example of judging[a] through taste, even the taste of everyone. **Idea** signifies, strictly speaking, a concept of reason, and **ideal** the representation of an individual being as adequate to an idea. Hence that archetype of taste, which indeed rests on reason's indeterminate idea of a maximum, but cannot be represented through concepts, but only in an individual presentation, would better be called the ideal of the beautiful, something that we strive to produce in ourselves even if we are not in possession of it. But it will be merely an ideal of the imagination, precisely because it does not rest on concepts but on presentation, and the faculty of presentation is the imagination. – Now how do we attain such an ideal of beauty? *A priori* or empirically? Likewise, what species of beauty admits of an ideal?

First, it should be noted that the beauty for which an idea is to be sought must not be a **vague**[b] beauty, but must be a beauty **fixed** by a concept of objective purposiveness, consequently it must not belong to the object of an entirely pure judgment of taste, but rather to one of[c] a partly intellectualized judgment of taste. I.e., in whatever kind of grounds for judging[d] an ideal is supposed to occur, at its basis there must lie some idea of reason in accordance with determinate concepts, which determines *a priori* the end on which the internal possibility of the object rests. An ideal of beautiful flowers, of beautiful furnishings, of a beautiful view, cannot be conceived. However, an ideal of a beauty adhering to determinate ends, e.g., of a beautiful residence, a beautiful tree, beautiful gardens, etc., is also incapable of being represented, presumably because the ends are not adequately determined and fixed by their concept, and consequently the purposiveness is almost as free as in the case of **vague** beauty. Only that which has the end of its existence in itself, the **human being**, who determines his ends himself through reason, or, where he must derive them from external perception can nevertheless compare them to essential and universal ends and in that case also aesthetically judge[e] their agreement with them: this **human being** alone is capable of an ideal of **beauty**, just as the humanity in his person, as intelligence, is alone among all the objects in the world capable of the ideal of **perfection.**

5: 233

But there are two elements involved here: **first**, the aesthetic **normal**

---

[a] *Beurtheilung*

[b] *vage*; in § 16, Kant used the Latin word *vaga* as a parenthetical synonym of "free" in the expression "free beauty."

[c] Following the first edition rather than the second, which omits the words "one of" (*dem eines*).

[d] *Beurtheilung*

[e] *beurtheilen*

idea, which is an individual intuition (of the imagination) that represents the standard for judging[a] it as a thing belonging to a particular species of animal; **second**, the **idea of reason**, which makes the ends of humanity insofar as they cannot be sensibly represented into the principle for the judging[b] of its figure, through which, as their effect in appearance, the former are revealed. The normal idea must take its elements for the figure of an animal of a particular species from experience; but the greatest purposiveness in the construction of the figure, which would be suitable as a universal standard for the aesthetic judging[c] of every individual of this species, the image which has as it were intentionally grounded the technique of nature, to which only the species as a whole but not any separate individual is adequate, lies merely in the idea of the one who does the judging,[d] which, however, with its proportions, can be represented fully *in concreto* as an aesthetic idea in a model image. In order to make it somewhat comprehensible how this happens (for who can entirely unlock its secret from nature?), we shall attempt a psychological explanation.

5: 234   It should be noted that the imagination does not only know how to recall for us occasionally signs of concepts, even after a long time, in a way that is entirely incomprehensible to us; it also knows how to reproduce the image and shape of an object out of an immense number of objects of different kinds, or even of one and the same kind; indeed, when the mind is set on making comparisons, it even knows how, by all accounts actually if not consciously,[e] as it were to superimpose one image on another and by means of the congruence of several of the same kind to arrive at a mean that can serve them all as a common measure. Someone has seen a thousand grown men. Now if he would judge what should be estimated as their comparatively normal size, then (in my opinion) the imagination allows a great number of images (perhaps all thousand) to be superimposed on one another, and, if I may here apply the analogy of optical presentation, in the space where the greatest number of them coincide and within the outline of the place that is illuminated by the most concentrated colors, there the **average size** becomes recognizable, which is in both height and breadth equidistant from the most extreme boundaries of the largest and smallest statures; and this is the stature for a beautiful man.[41] (One could get the same result mechanically if one measured all thousand men, added up their heights, widths (and girths) and then divided the

---

[a] *Beurtheilung*
[b] *Beurtheilung*
[c] *Beurtheilung*
[d] *des Beurtheilenden*
[e] The second edition here omits the phrase "to reproduce" from the first.

sum by a thousand. But the imagination does just this by means of a dynamic effect, which arises from the repeated apprehension of such figures on the organ of inner sense.) Now if in a similar way there is sought for this average man the average head, the average nose, etc., then this shape is the basis for the normal idea of the beautiful man in the country where this comparison is made; hence under these empirical conditions[a] a Negro must necessarily have a different normal idea[b] of the beauty of a figure than a white, a Chinese person a different idea from a European. It will be exactly the same with the model of a beautiful horse or dog (of a certain breed). – This **normal idea** is not derived from the proportions taken from experience, **as determinate rules**; rather it is in accordance with it that rules for judging[c] first become possible. It is the image for the whole species, hovering among all the particular and variously diverging intuitions of the individuals, which nature used as the archetype underlying her productions in the same species, but does not seem to have fully achieved in any individual. It is by no means the entire[d] **archetype** of **beauty** in this species, but only the form that constitutes the indispensable condition of all beauty, and so merely the **correctness** in the presentation of the species. It is, as was said of **Polycletus's** famous **Doryphorus**, the **rule** (and **Myron's** cow could be used in the same way in its species).[42] For that very reason it cannot contain anything specifically characteristic, for then it would not be the **normal idea** for the species. Its presentation also does not please because of beauty, but merely because it does not contradict any condition under which alone a thing of this species can be beautiful. The presentation is merely academically correct.*

5 : 235

* One will find that a perfectly regular face, which a painter might ask to sit for him as a model, usually says nothing: because it contains nothing characteristic, and thus expresses more the idea of the species than anything specific to a person. What is characteristic in this way, when it is exaggerated, i.e., when it itself breaks with the normal idea (of the purposiveness of the species), is called **caricature.** Experience also shows that such completely regular faces usually betray an inwardly only average human being, presumably for this reason (if it may be assumed that nature expresses in the exterior the proportions of the interior), that if none of the mental characteristics stand out beyond those proportions that are required merely to constitute a faultless human being, then nothing may be expected of that which is called **genius,** in which nature seems to depart from its usual relations among the powers of the mind in favor of a particular one.

5 : 235

[a] The phrase "under these empirical conditions" was added in the second edition.
[b] In the first edition, the word "normal" was omitted.
[c] *Beurtheilung*
[d] This word was added in the second edition.

Yet there is still a distinction between the **normal idea** of the beautiful and its **ideal**, which on the grounds already introduced can be expected only in the **human figure**.[43] In the latter the ideal consists in the expression of the **moral**, without which the object would not please universally and moreover positively (not merely negatively in an academically correct presentation). The visible expression of moral ideas, which inwardly govern human beings, can of course be drawn only from experience; but as it were to make visible in bodily manifestation (as the effect of what is inward) their combination with everything that our understanding connects with the morally good in the idea of the highest purposiveness – goodness of soul, or purity, or strength, or repose, etc. – this requires pure ideas of reason and great force of imagination united in anyone who would merely judge[a] them, let alone anyone who would present them. The correctness of such an ideal of beauty is proved by the fact that no sensory charm is allowed to be mixed into the satisfaction in its object, while it nevertheless allows a great interest to be taken in it, which then proves that judging[b] in accordance with such a standard can never be purely aesthetic, and judging in accordance with an ideal of beauty is no mere judgment of taste.

5: 236

Definition of the beautiful inferred from this third moment.

Beauty is the form of the **purposiveness** of an object, insofar as it is perceived in it **without representation of an end.** *[44]

5: 236

* It might be adduced as a counterexample to this definition that there are things in which one can see a purposive form without[c] cognizing an end in them, e.g., the stone utensils often excavated from ancient burial mounds, which are equipped with a hole, as if for a handle, which, although they clearly betray by their shape a purposiveness the end of which one does not know, are nevertheless not declared to be beautiful on that account. Yet the fact that they are regarded as a work of art is already enough to require one to admit that one relates their shape to some sort of intention and to a determinate purpose. Hence there is also no immediate satisfaction at all in their intuition. A flower, by contrast,[d] e.g., a tulip, is held to be beautiful because a certain purposiveness is encountered in our perception of it which, as we judge[e] it, is not related to any end at all.

[a] *beurtheilen*
[b] *Beurtheilung* here and in the next clause of this sentence.
[c] The second edition here omits the word "also" from the first.
[d] In the first edition, "however."
[e] *beurtheilen*

Fourth Moment
of the judgment of taste, concerning the modality
of the satisfaction in the object.

§ 18.
What the modality of a judgment
of taste is.

Of every representation I can say that it is at least **possible** that it (as a cognition) be combined with a pleasure. Of that which I call **agreeable** I say that it **actually** produces a pleasure in me. Of the **beautiful**, however, one thinks that it has a necessary relation to satisfaction. Now this necessity is*ª* of a special kind: not a theoretical objective necessity, where it can be cognized *a priori* that everyone **will feel** this satisfaction in the object called beautiful by me, nor a practical necessity, whereby means of concepts of a pure will, serving as rules for freely acting beings, this satisfaction is a necessary consequence of an objective law and signifies nothing other than that one absolutely (without a further aim) ought to act in a certain way. Rather, as a necessity that is thought in an aesthetic judgment, it can only be called **exemplary**, i.e., a*ᵇ* necessity of the assent of **all** to a judgment that is regarded as an example of a universal rule that one cannot produce.[45] Since an aesthetic judgment is not an objective and cognitive judgment, this necessity cannot be derived from determinate concepts, and is therefore not apodictic. Much less can it be inferred from the universality of experience (from a complete unanimity in judgments about the beauty of a certain object). For not only would experience hardly supply sufficient evidence of this, but it is also impossible to ground any concept of the necessity of these judgments on empirical judgments.[46]

5: 237

cf 149

§ 19.
The subjective necessity that we ascribe to the
judgment of taste is conditioned.

The judgment of taste ascribes assent to everyone, and whoever declares something to be beautiful wishes that everyone **should** approve of the object in question and similarly declare it to be beautiful. The **should** in aesthetic judgments of taste is thus pronounced only conditionally even given all the data that are required for the judging.*ᶜ* One solicits assent from everyone else because one has a ground for it that

---

ª The second edition here omits the word "however" present in the first.
ᵇ In the first edition, "the."
ᶜ *Beurtheilung*

is common to all; one could even count on this assent if only one were always sure that the case were correctly subsumed under that ground as the rule of approval.

§ 20.
The condition of the necessity that is alleged by a judgment of taste is the idea of a common sense.

5: 238

If judgments of taste (like cognitive judgments) had a determinate objective principle, then someone who made them in accordance with the latter would lay claim to the unconditioned necessity of his judgment. If they had no principle at all, like those of mere sensory taste, then one would never even have a thought of their necessity. They must thus have a subjective principle, which determines what pleases or displeases only through feeling and not through concepts, but yet with universal validity. Such a principle, however, could only be regarded as a **common sense**, which is essentially different from the common understanding that is sometimes also called common sense (*sensus communis*),[47] since the latter judges not by feeling but always by concepts, although commonly only in the form of[a] obscurely represented principles.

Thus only under the presupposition that there is a common sense (by which, however, we do not mean any external sense but rather the effect of the free play of our cognitive powers), only under the presupposition of such a common sense, I say, can the judgment of taste be made.

§ 21.
Whether one has good reason to presuppose a common sense.

Cognitions and judgments must, together with the conviction that accompanies them, be able to be universally communicated, for otherwise they would have no correspondence with the object: they would all be a merely subjective play of the powers of representation, just as skepticism insists. But if cognitions are to be able to be communicated, then the mental state, i.e., the disposition of the cognitive powers for a cognition in general, and indeed that proportion which is suitable for making cognition out of a representation (whereby an object is given to us) must also be capable of being universally communicated; for

---

[a] In the first edition, "although commonly in accordance with the latter [concepts], as only obscurely represented principles."

without this, as the subjective condition of cognizing, the cognition, as an effect, could not arise. And this actually happens every time when, by means of the senses, a given object brings the imagination into activity for the synthesis[a] of the manifold, while the imagination brings the understanding into activity for the unification of the manifold into concepts. But this disposition of the cognitive powers has a different proportion depending on the difference of the objects that are given. Nevertheless, there must be one in which this inner relationship is optimal for the animation of both powers of the mind (the one through the other) with respect to cognition (of given objects) in general; and this disposition cannot be determined except through the feeling (not by concepts). Now since this disposition itself must be capable of being universally communicated, hence also the feeling of it (in the case of a given representation), but since the universal communicability of a feeling presupposes a common sense, the latter must be able to be assumed with good reason, and indeed without appeal to psychological observations, but rather as the necessary condition of the universal communicability of our cognition, which is[b] assumed in every logic and every principle of cognitions that is not skeptical.

5: 239

§ 22.
The necessity of the universal assent
that is thought in a judgment of taste
is a subjective necessity,
which is represented as objective under the presupposition
of a common sense.

In all judgments by which we declare something to be beautiful, we allow no one to be of a different opinion, without, however, grounding our judgment on concepts, but only on our feeling, which we therefore make our ground not as a private feeling, but as a common one. Now this common sense cannot be grounded on experience for this purpose, for it is to justify judgments that contain a "should": it does not say that everyone **will** concur with our judgment but that everyone **should** agree with it. Thus the common sense, of whose judgment I here[c] offer my judgment of taste as an example and on account of which I ascribe **exemplary** validity to it, is a merely ideal norm, under the presupposition of which one could rightfully make a judgment that agrees with it and the satisfaction in an object that is expressed in it into a rule for everyone: since the principle, though only subjective, is

---

[a] *Zusammensetzung*
[b] In the first edition, "must be."
[c] Following the second edition in reading *hier* rather than *mir* (to myself).

nevertheless assumed to be subjectively universal (an idea necessary for everyone), which, as far as the unanimity of different judges is concerned, could demand universal assent just like an objective one – if only one were certain of having correctly subsumed under it.

This indeterminate norm of a common sense is really presupposed by us: our presumption in making judgments of taste proves that.[48] Whether there is in fact such a common sense, as a constitutive principle of the possibility of experience, or whether a yet higher principle of reason only makes it into a regulative principle for us first to produce a common sense in ourselves for higher ends, thus whether taste is an original and natural faculty, or only the idea of one that is yet to be acquired and is artificial, so that a judgment of taste, with its expectation of a universal assent, is in fact only a demand of reason to produce such a unanimity in the manner of sensing, and whether the "should," i.e., the objective necessity of the confluence of the feeling of everyone with that of each, signifies only the possibility of coming to agreement about this, and the judgment of taste only provides an example of the application of this principle – this we would not and cannot yet investigate here; for now we have only to resolve the faculty of taste into its elements and to unite them ultimately in the idea of a common sense.

The definition of the beautiful drawn from the fourth moment.

That is **beautiful** which is cognized without a concept as the object of a **necessary** satisfaction.

* *
*

General remark on the first section of the Analytic.

If one draws the conclusion from the above analyses, it turns out that everything flows from the concept of taste as a faculty for judging[a] an object in relation to the **free lawfulness** of the imagination. But if in the judgment of taste the imagination must be considered in its freedom, then it is in the first instance taken not as reproductive, as subjected to the laws of association, but as productive and self-active (as the authoress of voluntary[b] forms of possible intuitions);[49] and although in the apprehension of a given object of the senses it is of course bound to a determinate form of this object and to this extent has no free play (as in invention),[c] nevertheless it is still quite conceivable that the

[a] *Beurtheilungsvermögen*
[b] *willkührlicher*
[c] *Dichten*

object can provide it with a form that contains precisely such a composition of the manifold as the imagination would design in harmony with the **lawfulness of the understanding** in general if it were left free by itself. Yet for the **imagination** to be **free** and yet **lawful by itself**, i.e., that it carry autonomy with it, is a contradiction.[50] The understanding alone gives the law. But when the imagination is compelled to proceed in accordance with a determinate law, then how its product should be, as far as its form is concerned, is determined through concepts; but then, as was said above, the satisfaction is not that in the beautiful, but in the good (of perfection, in any case merely the formal kind), and the judgment is not a judgment by means of taste. Thus only a lawfulness without law and a subjective correspondence of the imagination to the understanding without an objective one – where the representation is related to a determinate concept of an object – are consistent with the free lawfulness of the understanding (which is also called purposiveness without an end) and with the peculiarity of a judgment of taste.

Now geometrically regular shapes – a circle, a square, a cube, etc. – are commonly adduced by critics of taste as the simplest and most indubitable examples of beauty; and yet they are called regular precisely because they cannot be represented except by being regarded as mere presentations of a determinate concept, which prescribes the rule for that shape (in accordance with which it is alone possible). Thus one of the two must be wrong: either the judgment of the critics that attributes beauty to such shapes, or ours, which finds purposiveness without a concept to be necessary for beauty.

No one is likely to think it necessary for a person to have taste in order to find more satisfaction in the shape of a circle than in a scribbled outline, or more in an equilateral and equiangular quadrilateral than in one that is lopsided and irregular, as it were deformed; for this takes only common understanding and no taste at all. Where there is an aim in view, e.g., judging[a] the magnitude of an area or grasping the relation of the parts in a division to each other and to the whole, there regular shapes, and indeed those of the simplest kind, are necessary, and the satisfaction does not rest immediately on the view of the shape, but on its usefulness for all sorts of possible aims. A room whose walls form oblique angles, a garden of a similar sort, even any injury to symmetry in the shape of animals (e.g., having one eye) as well as in buildings or floral arrangements displeases, because it is contrapurposive, not only practically, with regard to a determinate use of these things, but also for judging[b] with respect to all sorts of possible aims; this is not the case in the judgment of taste, which, if it is pure, immediately connects satisfaction or dissatisfaction to the mere **consideration** of the object without respect to use or to an end.

The regularity that leads to the concept of an object is of course the indispensable condition (*conditio sine qua non*) of grasping the object in a single representation and determining the manifold in its form. This determination is an end with regard to cognition; and in relation to this it is also always

[a] *beurtheilen*
[b] *Beurtheilung*

connected with satisfaction (which accompanies the accomplishment of any aim, even a merely problematic one). But then it is merely the approval of the solution that answers a problem, and not a free and indeterminately purposive entertainment of the mental powers with that which we call beautiful, where the understanding is in the service of the imagination and not vice versa.

In a thing that is possible only through an intention, in a building, even in an animal, the regularity that consists in symmetry must express the unity of the intuition, which accompanies the concept of the end and belongs to the cognition. But where only a free play of the powers of representation (although under the condition that the understanding does not thereby suffer any offense) is to be maintained, in pleasure gardens, in the decoration of rooms, in all sorts of tasteful utensils and the like, regularity that comes across as constraint is to be avoided as far as possible; hence the English taste in gardens or the baroque taste in furniture pushes the freedom of the imagination almost to the point of the grotesque, and makes this abstraction from all constraint by rules the very case in which the taste can demonstrate its greatest perfection in projects of the imagination.

5: 243

All stiff regularity (whatever approaches mathematical regularity) is of itself contrary to taste: the consideration of it affords no lasting entertainment, but rather, insofar as it does not expressly have cognition or a determinate practical end as its aim, it induces boredom. By contrast, that with which the imagination can play in an unstudied and purposive way is always new for us, and we are never tired of looking at it. In his description of Sumatra, **Marsden**[51] remarks that the free beauties of nature everywhere surround the observer there and hence have little attraction for him any more; by contrast, a pepper garden where the stakes on which the plants were trained formed parallel rows had much charm for him when he encountered it in the middle of a forest; and from this he infers that wild, to all appearances irregular beauty is pleasing only as a change for one who has had enough of the regular kind. But he needed only to have made the experiment of spending one day in his pepper garden to realize that once the understanding has been disposed by means of the regularity to the order that it always requires the object would no longer entertain him, but would rather impose upon the imagination a burdensome constraint, whereas nature, which is there extravagant in its varieties to the point of opulence, subject to no coercion from artificial rules, could provide his taste with lasting nourishment. – Even the song of the bird, which we cannot bring under any musical rules, seems to contain more freedom and thus more that is entertaining for taste than even a human song that is performed in accordance with all the rules of the art of music: for one grows tired of the latter far more quickly if it is repeated often and for a long time. But here we may well confuse our sympathy with the merriment of a beloved little creature with the beauty of his song, which, when it is exactly imitated by a human being (as is sometimes done with the notes of the nightingale) strikes our ear as utterly tasteless.

Further, beautiful objects are to be distinguished from beautiful views of objects (which on account of the distance can often no longer be distinctly cognized). In the latter, taste seems to fasten not so much on what the imagi-

126

nation **apprehends** in this field as on what gives it occasion to **invent**,[a] i.e., on what are strictly speaking the fantasies with which the mind entertains itself while it is being continuously aroused by the manifold which strikes the eye, as for instance in looking at the changing shapes of a fire in a hearth or of a rippling brook, neither of which are beauties, but both of which carry with them a charm for the imagination, because they sustain its free play.

5: 244

[a] *zu dichten*

Second Book
Analytic of the Sublime

§ 23.
Transition from the faculty for judging[a]
the beautiful to that for judging the sublime.

The beautiful coincides with the sublime in that both please for themselves.[1] And further in that both presuppose neither a judgment of sense nor a logically determining judgment, but a judgment of reflection: consequently the satisfaction does not depend on a sensation, like that in the agreeable, nor on a determinate concept, like the satisfaction in the good; but it is nevertheless still related to concepts, although it is indeterminate which, hence the satisfaction is connected to the mere presentation or to the faculty for that, through which the faculty of presentation or the imagination is considered, in the case of a given intuition, to be in accord with the **faculty of concepts** of the understanding or of reason, as promoting the latter. Hence both sorts of judgments are also **singular**, and yet judgments that profess to be universally valid in regard to every subject, although they lay claim merely to the feeling of pleasure and not to any cognition of the object.

But notable differences between the two also strike the eye. The beautiful in nature concerns the form of the object, which consists in limitation; the sublime, by contrast, is to be found in a formless object insofar as **limitlessness** is represented in it, or at its instance, and yet it is also thought as a totality: so that the beautiful seems to be taken as the presentation of an indeterminate concept of the understanding, but the sublime as that of a similar concept of reason. Thus the satisfaction is connected in the first case with the representation of **quality**, but in this case with that of **quantity**. Also the latter pleasure is very different in kind from the former, in that the former (the beautiful)[b] directly brings with it a feeling of the promotion of life,[2] and hence is

compatible with charms and an imagination at play, while the latter (the feeling of the sublime)[c] is a pleasure that arises only indirectly, being generated, namely, by the feeling of a momentary inhibition of

---

[a] *Beurtheilungsvermögen*
[b] The parenthetical phrase was added in the second edition.
[c] The parenthetical phrase was added in the second edition.

the vital powers and the immediately following and all the more powerful outpouring of them; hence as an emotion it seems to be not play but something serious in the activity of the imagination. Hence it is also incompatible with charms, and, since the mind is not merely attracted by the object, but is also always reciprocally repelled by it, the satisfaction in the sublime does not so much contain[a] positive pleasure as it does admiration or respect, i.e., it deserves to be called negative pleasure.[3]

The most important and intrinsic difference between the sublime and the beautiful, however, is this: that if, as is appropriate, we here consider first only the sublime in objects of nature (that in art is, after all, always restricted to the conditions of agreement with nature),[4] natural beauty (the self-sufficient kind) carries with it a purposiveness in its form, through which the object seems as it were to be predetermined for our power of judgment, and thus constitutes an object of satisfaction in itself, whereas that which, without any rationalizing, merely in apprehension, excites in us the feeling of the sublime, may to be sure[b] appear in its form to be contrapurposive for our power of judgment, unsuitable for our faculty of presentation, and as it were doing violence to our imagination, but[c] is nevertheless judged all the more sublime for that.

But from this one immediately sees that we express ourselves on the whole incorrectly if we call some **object of nature** sublime, although we can quite correctly call very many of them beautiful; for how can we designate with an expression of approval that which is apprehended[d] in itself as contrapurposive? We can say no more than that the object serves for the presentation of a sublimity that can be found in the mind; for what is properly sublime cannot be contained in any sensible form, but concerns only ideas of reason, which, though no presentation adequate to them is possible, are provoked and called to mind precisely by this inadequacy, which does allow of sensible presentation. Thus the wide ocean, enraged by storms, cannot be called sublime. Its visage is horrible; and one must already have filled the mind with all sorts of ideas if by means of such an intuition it is to be put in the mood for a feeling which is itself sublime, in that the mind is incited to abandon sensibility and to occupy itself with ideas that contain a higher purposiveness.

5: 246

The self-sufficient beauty of nature reveals to us a technique of nature, which makes it possible to represent it as a system in accor-

---

[a] This verb was added in the second edition.
[b] In the second edition, *zwar*; in the first edition, *gar* (even).
[c] Added in the second edition.
[d] *aufgefaßt*; in the first edition, *abgefaßt* (conceived).

dance with laws the principle of which we do not encounter anywhere in our entire faculty of understanding, namely that of a purposiveness with respect to the use of the power of judgment in regard to appearances, so that this must be judged[a] as belonging not merely to nature in its purposeless mechanism but rather also to the analogy with[b] art. Thus it actually expands not our cognition of natural objects, but our concept of nature, namely as a mere mechanism, into the concept of nature as art: which invites profound investigations into the possibility of such a form. But in that which we are accustomed to call sublime in nature there is so little[c] that leads to particular objective principles and forms of nature corresponding to these that it is mostly rather in its chaos or in its wildest and most unruly disorder and devastation, if only it allows a glimpse of magnitude and might, that it excites the ideas of the sublime. From this we see that the concept of the sublime in nature is far from being as important and rich in consequences as that of its beauty, and that in general it indicates nothing purposive in nature itself, but only in the possible **use** of its intuitions to make palpable in ourselves a purposiveness that is entirely independent of nature. For the beautiful in nature we must seek a ground outside ourselves, but for the sublime merely one in ourselves and in the way of thinking that introduces sublimity into the representation of the former – a very necessary introductory remark, which entirely separates the ideas of the sublime from that of a purposiveness of **nature**, and makes of the theory of the sublime a mere appendix to the aesthetic judging[d] of the purposiveness of nature, since by this means no particular form is represented in the latter, but only a purposive use that the imagination makes of its representation is developed.

5: 247

§ 24.
On the division of an investigation of the feeling of the sublime.

As far as the division of the moments of the aesthetic judging[e] of objects in relation to the feeling of the sublime is concerned, the analytic will be able to proceed in accordance with the same principle that was used in the analysis of judgments of taste. For as a judgment of the aesthetic reflecting power of judgment, the satisfaction in the sublime, just like that in the beautiful, must be represented as univer-

---

[a] *beurtheilt*
[b] The words "the analogy with" were added in the second edition.
[c] Following the first edition in reading *so gar nichts* instead of *sogar nichts* (even nothing).
[d] *Beurtheilung*
[e] *Beurtheilung*

sally valid in its **quantity**, as without interest in its **quality**, as subjective purposiveness in its **relation**, and the latter, as far as its **modality** is concerned, as necessary. Thus the method here will not depart from that in the preceding section,[a] though some account must be taken of the fact that there, where the aesthetic judgment concerned the form of the object, we began with the investigation of quality, but here, in view of the formlessness that can pertain to that which we call sublime, we will begin with quantity as the first moment of the aesthetic judgment on the sublime; the ground for which, however, is to be seen from the preceding §.

But one division is necessary in the analysis of the sublime which that of the beautiful did not require, namely that into the **mathematically** and the **dynamically sublime**.[5]

For since the feeling of the sublime brings with it as its characteristic mark a **movement** of the mind connected with the judging[b] of the object, whereas the taste for the beautiful presupposes and preserves the mind in **calm** contemplation, yet this movement is to be judged[c] as subjectively purposive (because the sublime pleases), thus this movement is related through the imagination either to the **faculty of cognition** or to the **faculty of desire**, but in both relations the purposiveness of the given representation is judged[d] only with regard to this **faculty** (without an end or interest): for then the first is attributed to the object as a **mathematical**, the second as a **dynamical** disposition of the imagination, and thus the object is represented as sublime in the twofold manner intended.

A.

On the mathematically sublime

§ 25.
Nominal definition of the sublime.

5: 248

We call **sublime** that which is **absolutely great**.[e] However, to be great[f] and to be a magnitude[g] are quite different concepts (*magnitudo*

---

[a] That is, the "Analytic of the Beautiful."

[b] *Beurtheilung*

[c] *beurtheilt*

[d] *beurtheilt*

[e] *schlechthin groß*

[f] *Groß-sein*

[g] *eine Größe sein*; since Kant equates *Größe* with *quantitas* and contrasts that with *magnitudo*, it would seem natural to translate *Größe* as "quantity" rather than "magnitude." However, he also equates it with *quantum*; in § 23 he has used *Quantität* as a distinct German word; and in many of the claims that follow, "magnitude" will be a more

and *quantitas*). Likewise, **simply**[a] (*simpliciter*) **to say** that something is great is also something entirely different from saying that it is **absolutely**[b] great (*absolute, non comparative magnum*).[c] The latter is that **which is great beyond all comparison.** – So what does the expression that something is great or small or medium-sized say? It is not a pure concept of the understanding that is thereby designated,[d] still less an intuition of sense, and just as little a concept of reason, since it does not bring with it any principle of cognition at all. It must therefore be a concept of the power of judgment, or derive from such a concept, and be grounded in a subjective purposiveness of the representation in relation to the power of judgment. That something is a magnitude (*quantum*) may be cognized from the thing itself, without any comparison with another; if, that is, a multitude of homogeneous elements together constitute a unity. But **how great** it is always requires something else, which is also a magnitude, as its measure. However, since in the judging[e] of magnitude not merely the multitude (number) but also the magnitude of the unit (of the measure) is involved, and the magnitude of this latter in turn always needs something else as a measure with which it can be compared, we see that any determination of the magnitude of appearances is absolutely[f] incapable of affording an absolute[g] concept of a magnitude but can afford at best only a comparative concept.

Now if I simply say that something is great, it seems that I do not have in mind any comparison at all, at least not with any objective measure, since it is not thereby determined at all how great the object is. However, even though the standard for comparison is merely subjective, the judgment nonetheless lays claim to universal assent;[h] the judgments "The man is beautiful" and "He is great" do not restrict themselves merely to the judging subject, but, like theoretical judgments, demand everyone's assent.

5: 249

But because in a judgment by which something is described simply as great it is not merely said that the object has a magnitude, but rather this is attributed to it to a superior extent than to many others of the

---

natural translation than "quantity." We will therefore follow the practice of all the previous English translators in using "magnitude."

[a] *schlechtweg*
[b] *schlechthin*
[c] absolutely, not comparatively great
[d] The words "that is thereby designated" were added in the second edition.
[e] *Beurtheilung*
[f] *schlechterdings*
[g] *absoluten*
[h] Reading *Beistimmung* with the second edition rather than *Bestimmung* (determination) with the first.

same kind, yet without this superiority being given determinately, this judgment is certainly grounded on a standard that one presupposes can be assumed to be the same for everyone, but which is not usable for any logical (mathematically determinate) judging[a] of magnitude, but only for an aesthetic one, since it is a merely subjective standard grounding the reflecting judgment on magnitude. It may be, by the way,[b] empirical, as in the case of the average magnitude of the people known to us, of animals of a certain species, of trees, houses, mountains, etc., or a standard given *a priori*, which because of the deficiencies of the judging[c] subject is restricted to subjective conditions of presentation *in concreto*: as in the practical sphere, the magnitude of a certain virtue, or of public freedom and justice in a country; or in the theoretical sphere, the magnitude of the accuracy or inaccuracy of an observation or measurement that has been made, and so on.

Now it is noteworthy here that even if we have no interest at all in the object, i.e., its existence is indifferent to us, still its mere magnitude, even if it is considered as formless, can bring with it a satisfaction that is universally communicable, hence it may contain a consciousness of a subjective purposiveness in the use of our cognitive faculties: but not a satisfaction in the object, as in the case of the beautiful (since it can be formless), where the reflecting power of judgment finds itself purposively disposed in relation to cognition in general; rather in the enlargement of the imagination in itself.

If (under the above-mentioned restriction) we say of an object absolutely[d] that it is great, this is not a mathematically determining judgment but a mere judgment of reflection about its representation, which is subjectively purposive for a certain use of our cognitive powers in the estimation of magnitude, and in that case we always combine a kind of respect with the representation, just as we combine contempt with that which we call absolutely small. Moreover, the judging[e] of things as great or small applies to everything, even to all their properties; hence we call even beauty great or small; the reason for which is to be sought in the fact that whatever we may present in intuition in accordance with the precept of the power of judgment (and hence represent aesthetically) is entirely appearance, and hence is also a quantum.

If, however, we call something not only great, but simply, absolutely[f] great, great in every respect (beyond all comparison), i.e., sub-

5: 250

---

[a] *Beurtheilung*
[b] The word *übrigens* in the second edition replaces *nun* (now) in the first.
[c] The word *beurtheilenden* was inserted here in the second edition.
[d] Here and at the end of the sentence, *schlechtweg*.
[e] *Beurtheilung*
[f] *schlechthin-, absolut-*

lime, then one immediately sees that we do not allow a suitable standard for it to be sought outside of it, but merely within it. It is a magnitude that is equal only to itself. That the sublime is therefore not to be sought in the things of nature but only in our ideas follows from this; but in which of these it lies must be saved for the deduction.[6]

The above explanation can also be expressed thus: **That is sublime in comparison with which everything else is small.** Here one readily sees that nothing can be given in nature, however great it may be judged[a] to be by us, which could not, considered in another relation, be diminished down to the infinitely small; and conversely, there is nothing so small which could not, in comparison with even smaller standards, be amplified for our imagination up to the magnitude of a world. The telescope has given us rich material for making the former observation, the microscope rich material for the latter.[b] Thus nothing that can be an object of the senses is, considered on this footing, to be called sublime. But just because there is in our imagination a striving to advance to the infinite, while in our reason there lies a claim to absolute totality, as to a real idea, the very inadequacy of our faculty for estimating the magnitude of the things of the sensible world awakens the feeling of a supersensible faculty in us; and the use that the power of judgment naturally makes in behalf of the latter (feeling), though not the object of the senses, is absolutely great, while in contrast to it any other use is small.[c] Hence it is the disposition of the mind resulting from a certain representation occupying the reflective judgment, but not the object, which is to be called sublime.

Thus we can also add this to the foregoing formulation of the explanation of the sublime: **That is sublime which even to be able to think of demonstrates a faculty of the mind that surpasses every measure of the senses.**

5: 251

§ 26.
On the estimation of the magnitude of things of nature that is requisite for the idea of the sublime.

The estimation of magnitude by means of numerical concepts (or their signs in algebra) is mathematical, but that in mere intuition (measured by eye) is aesthetic. Now we can, to be sure, obtain determinate concepts of **how great** something is only by means of numbers (or at any rate through approximations by means of numerical series progressing to infinity), whose unit is the measure; and to this extent all logical

---

[a] *beurtheilt*
[b] In the first edition, "telescope" and "microscope" were plural rather than singular.
[c] In the first edition there is a comma rather than a period here.

estimation of magnitude is mathematical. But since the magnitude of the measure must still be assumed to be known, then, if this in turn is to be estimated only by means of numbers whose unit would have to be another measure, and so mathematically, we can never have a primary or basic fundamental measure, and hence we can never have a determinate concept of a given magnitude. Thus the estimation of the magnitude of the basic measure must consist simply in the fact that one can immediately grasp it in an intuition and use it by means of imagination for the presentation of numerical concepts – i.e., in the end all estimation of the magnitude of objects of nature is aesthetic (i.e., subjectively and not objectively determined).[7]

Now for the mathematical estimation of magnitude there is, to be sure, no greatest (for the power of numbers goes on to infinity);[8] but for the aesthetic estimation of magnitude there certainly is a greatest; and about this I say that if it is judged[a] as an absolute measure, beyond which no greater is subjectively (for the judging[b] subject) possible, it brings with it the idea of the sublime, and produces that emotion which no mathematical estimation of magnitudes by means of numbers can produce (except insofar as that aesthetic basic measure is vividly preserved in the imagination), since the latter always presents only relative magnitude through comparison with others of the same species, but the former presents magnitude absolutely, so far as the mind can grasp it in one intuition.

To take up a quantum in the imagination intuitively, in order to be able to use it as a measure or a unit for the estimation of magnitude by means of numbers, involves two actions of this faculty: **apprehension**[c] (*apprehensio*) and **comprehension**[d] (*comprehensio aesthetica*). There is no difficulty with apprehension, because it can go on to infinity; but comprehension becomes ever more difficult the further apprehension advances, and soon reaches its maximum, namely the aesthetically greatest basic measure for the estimation of magnitude. For when apprehension has gone so far that the partial representations of the intuition of the senses that were apprehended first already begin to fade in the imagination as the latter proceeds on to the apprehension of further ones, then it loses on one side as much as it gains on the other, and there is in the comprehension a greatest point beyond which it cannot go.

5: 252

This makes it possible to explain a point that Savary[9] notes in his report on Egypt: that in order to get the full emotional effect of the

---

[a] *beurtheilt*
[b] *beurtheilenden*
[c] *Auffassung*
[d] *Zusammenfassung*

magnitude of the pyramids one must neither come too close to them nor be too far away. For in the latter case, the parts that are apprehended (the stones piled on top of one another) are represented only obscurely, and their representation has no effect on the aesthetic judgment of the subject. In the former case, however, the eye requires some time to complete its apprehension from the base level to the apex, but during this time the former always partly fades before the imagination has taken in the latter, and the comprehension is never complete. – The very same thing can also suffice to explain the bewilderment or sort of embarrassment that is said to seize the spectator on first entering St. Peter's in Rome. For here there is a feeling of the inadequacy of his imagination for presenting the ideas*a* of a whole, in which the imagination reaches its maximum and, in the effort to extend it, sinks back into itself, but is thereby transported into an emotionally moving satisfaction.

I shall not yet add anything about the basis for this satisfaction, which is associated with a representation from which one should least expect it, namely one that makes us notice the inadequacy, consequently also the subjective non-purposiveness of the representation for the power of judgment in the estimation of magnitude; rather I only note that if the aesthetic judgment is to be **pure (not mixed up with anything teleological** as judgments of reason) and if an example of that is to be given which is fully appropriate for the critique of the **aesthetic** power of judgment, then the sublime must not be shown in products of art (e.g., buildings, columns, etc.), where a human end determines the form as well as the magnitude,[10] nor in natural things **whose concept already brings with it a determinate end** (e.g., animals of a known natural determination), but rather in raw nature (and even in this only insofar as it by itself brings with it neither charm nor emotion from real danger), merely insofar as it contains magnitude. For in this sort of representation nature contains nothing that would be monstrous (or magnificent or terrible); the magnitude that is apprehended may grow as large as one wants as long as it can be comprehended in one whole by the imagination. An object is **monstrous** if by its magnitude it annihilates the end which its concept constitutes.[11] The mere presentation of a concept, however, which is almost too great for all presentation (which borders on the relatively monstrous) is called **colossal**, because the end of the presentation of a concept is made more difficult if the intuition of the object is almost too great for our faculty of apprehension. – A pure judgment on the sublime, however, must have no end of the object as its determining ground if it is

---

a Reading *Ideen* as in the second edition, rather than the singular *Idee* as in the first.

to be aesthetic and not mixed up with any judgment of the understanding or of reason.

* *
*

Since everything that is to please the merely reflecting power of judgment without interest must involve in its representation subjective and as such universally valid purposiveness, though here no purposiveness of the **form** of the object (as in the case of the beautiful) is the basis for the judging,[a] the question arises: what is this subjective purposiveness? and how is it prescribed as a norm that provides a ground for universally valid satisfaction in the mere estimation of magnitude, and indeed where that has been pushed almost to the point of the inadequacy of our faculty of imagination in the presentation of the concept of a magnitude?

The imagination, by itself, without anything hindering it, advances to infinity in the composition that is requisite for the representation of magnitude; the understanding, however, guides this by numerical concepts, for which the former must provide the schema;[12] and in this procedure, belonging to the logical estimation of magnitude, there is certainly something objectively purposive[b] in accordance with the concept of an end (such as all measuring is), but nothing that is purposive and pleasing for the aesthetic power of judgment. There is also in this intentional purposiveness nothing that would necessitate pushing the magnitude of the measure and hence the **comprehension** of the many in one intuition to the boundaries of the faculty of imagination and as far as the latter might reach in presentations. For in the understanding's estimation of magnitudes (in arithmetic) one gets equally far whether one pushes the composition of the units up to the number 10 (in the decadic system) or only to 4 (in the tetradic system);[13] the further generation of magnitude in composition, or, if the quantum is given in intuition, in apprehension, proceeds merely progressively (not comprehensively) in accordance with an assumed principle of progression. In this mathematical estimation of magnitude the understanding is equally well served and satisfied whether the imagination chooses for its unit a magnitude that can be grasped in a single glance, e.g., a foot or a rod, or whether it chooses a German mile or even a diameter of the earth, whose apprehension but not composition is possible in an intuition of the imagination (not through *comprehensio aesthetica* though

5: 254

---

[a] *Beurtheilung*
[b] In the first edition, this reads "there is something that is certainly objectively purposive."

certainly through *comprehensio logica* in a numerical concept). In both cases the logical estimation of magnitude proceeds unhindered to infinity.

But now the mind hears in itself the voice of reason, which requires totality for all given magnitudes, even for those that can never be entirely apprehended although they are (in the sensible representation) judged[a] as entirely given, hence comprehension in **one** intuition, and it demands a **presentation** for all members of a progressively increasing numerical series, and does not exempt from this requirement even the infinite (space and past time), but rather makes it unavoidable for us to think of it (in the judgment of common reason) as **given entirely** (in its totality).

The infinite, however, is absolutely (not merely comparatively) great. Compared with this, everything else (of the same kind of magnitude) is small. But what is most important is that even being able to think of it as **a whole** indicates a faculty of the mind which surpasses every standard of sense. For this would require a comprehension that yielded as a measure a unit that has a determinate relation to the infinite, expressible in numbers, which is impossible. But **even to be able to think** the given[b] infinite without contradiction requires a faculty in the human mind that is itself supersensible. For it is only by means of this and its idea of a noumenon, which itself admits of no intuition though it is presupposed as the substratum of the intuition of the world as mere appearance, that the infinite of the sensible world is **completely** comprehended in the pure intellectual estimation of magnitude **under** a concept, even though it can never be completely thought in the mathematical estimation of magnitude **through numerical concepts**. Even a faculty for being able to think the infinite of supersensible intuition as given (in its intelligible substratum) surpasses any standard of sensibility, and is great beyond all comparison even with the faculty of mathematical estimation, not, of course, from a theoretical point of view, in behalf of the faculty of cognition, but still as an enlargement of the mind which feels itself empowered[c] to overstep the limits of sensibility from another (practical) point of view.

Nature is thus sublime in those of its appearances the intuition of which brings with them the idea of its infinity. Now the latter cannot happen except through the inadequacy of even the greatest effort of our imagination in the estimation of the magnitude of an object. Now, however, the imagination is adequate for the mathematical estimation of every object, that is, for giving an adequate measure for it, because

5: 255

---

[a] *beurtheilt*
[b] The word "given" was added in the second edition.
[c] *vermögend*

the numerical concepts of the understanding, by means of progression, can make any measure adequate for any given*a* magnitude. Thus it must be the **aesthetic** estimation of magnitude in which is felt the effort at comprehension which exceeds the capacity*b* of the imagination to comprehend the progressive apprehension in one whole of intuition, and in which is at the same time perceived the inadequacy of this faculty, which is unbounded in its progression, for grasping a basic measure that is suitable for the estimation of magnitude with the least effort of the understanding and for using it for the estimation of magnitude. Now the proper unalterable basic measure of nature is its absolute whole, which, in the case of nature as appearance, is infinity comprehended. But since this basic measure is a self-contradictory concept (on account of the impossibility of the absolute totality of an endless progression), that magnitude of a natural object on which the imagination fruitlessly expends its entire capacity*c* for comprehension must lead the concept of nature to a supersensible substratum (which grounds both it and at the same time our faculty for thinking), which is great beyond any standard of sense and hence allows not so much the object as rather the disposition of the mind in estimating it to be judged*d* **sublime**.

5: 256

Thus, just as the aesthetic power of judgment in judging*e* the beautiful relates the imagination in its free play to the **understanding**, in order to agree with its **concepts** in general (without determination of them), so in judging*f* a thing to be sublime the same faculty is related to **reason**, in order to correspond subjectively with its **ideas** (though which is undetermined), i.e., in order to produce a disposition of the mind which is in conformity with them and compatible with that which the influence of determinate (practical) ideas on feeling would produce.

It is also evident from this that true sublimity must be sought only in the mind of the one who judges, not in the object in nature, the judging*g* of which occasions this disposition in it. And who would want to call sublime shapeless mountain masses towering above one another in wild disorder with their pyramids of ice, or the dark and raging sea, etc.? But the mind feels itself elevated in its own judging*h* if, in the consideration of such things, without regard to their form, abandoning itself to the imagination and to a reason which, although it is associated

---

a The word "given" was added in the second edition.
b *Vermögen*
c *Vermögen*
d *beurtheilen*
e *Beurtheilung*
f *Beurtheilung*
g *Beurtheilung*
h *Beurtheilung*

with it entirely without any determinate end, merely extends it, it nevertheless finds the entire power of the imagination inadequate to its ideas.

Examples of the mathematically sublime in nature in mere intuition are provided for us by all those cases where what is given to us is not so much a greater numerical concept as rather a great unity as measure (for shortening the numerical series) for the imagination. A tree that we estimate by the height of a man may serve as a standard for a mountain, and, if the latter were, say, a mile high, it could serve as the unit for the number that expresses the diameter of the earth, in order to make the latter intuitable; the diameter of the earth could serve as the unit for the planetary system so far as known to us, this for the Milky Way, and the immeasurable multitude of such Milky Way systems, called nebulae, which presumably constitute such a system among themselves in turn, does not allow us to expect any limits here.[14] Now in the aesthetic judging[a] of such an immeasurable whole, the sublime does not lie as much in the magnitude of the number as in the fact that as we progress we always arrive at ever greater units; the

5: 257 systematic division of the structure of the world contributes to this, representing to us all that is great in nature as in its turn small, but actually representing our imagination in all its boundlessness, and with it nature, as paling into insignificance beside the ideas[b] of reason if it is supposed to provide a presentation adequate to them.

§ 27.
On the quality of the satisfaction in the judging[c] of the sublime.

The feeling of the inadequacy of our capacity[d] for the attainment of an idea **that is a law for us** is **respect**.[15] Now the idea of the comprehension of every appearance that may be given to us into the intuition of a whole is one enjoined on us by a law of reason, which recognizes no other determinate measure, valid for everyone and inalterable,[e] than the absolute whole. But our imagination, even in its greatest effort with regard to the comprehension of a given object in a whole of intuition (hence for the presentation of the idea of reason) that is demanded of it, demonstrates its limits and inadequacy, but at the same

---

[a] *Beurtheilung*
[b] In the first edition this was singular.
[c] *Beurtheilung*
[d] *Vermögens*
[e] In the first edition, this word was "alterable."

time its vocation[a] for adequately realizing that idea as a law. Thus the feeling of the sublime in nature is respect for our own vocation, which we show to an object in nature through a certain subreption (substitution of a respect for the object instead of for the idea of humanity in our subject), which as it were makes intuitable the superiority of the rational vocation of our cognitive faculty over the greatest faculty of sensibility.

The feeling of the sublime is thus a feeling of displeasure from the inadequacy of the imagination in the aesthetic estimation of magnitude for the estimation[b] by means of reason, and a pleasure that is thereby aroused at the same time from the correspondence of this very judgment of the inadequacy of the greatest sensible faculty in comparison with ideas of reason, insofar as striving for them is nevertheless a law for us. That is, it is a law (of reason) for us and part of our vocation to estimate everything great that nature contains as an object of the senses for us as small in comparison with ideas of reason; and whatever arouses the feeling of this supersensible vocation in us is in agreement with that law. Now the greatest effort of the imagination in the presentation of the unity for the estimation of magnitude is a relation to something **absolutely great**, and consequently also a relation to the law of reason to adopt this alone as the supreme measure of magnitude. Thus the inner perception of the inadequacy of any sensible standard for the estimation of magnitude by reason corresponds with reason's laws, and is a displeasure that arouses the feeling of our supersensible vocation in us, in accordance with which it is purposive and thus a pleasure to find every standard of sensibility inadequate for the ideas of the understanding.[c]

5: 258

The mind feels itself **moved** in the representation of the sublime in nature, while in the aesthetic judgment on the beautiful in nature it is in **calm** contemplation. This movement (especially in its inception) may be compared to a vibration, i.e., to a rapidly alternating repulsion from and attraction to one and the same object. What is excessive for the imagination (to which it is driven in the apprehension of the intuition) is as it were an abyss, in which it fears to lose itself, yet for reason's idea of the supersensible to produce such an effort of the imagi-

---

[a] *Bestimmung*. Some occurrences of this word in this and the following sections could be translated as "determination," but some can only be translated as "vocation," so for the sake of consistency all will be translated that way.

[b] The second edition repeats the word "estimation" (*Schätzung*) instead of just using the pronoun "that" (*die*).

[c] Following the second edition, which prints "of understanding" (*des Verstandes*) instead of "of reason" (*der Vernunft*).

nation is not excessive but lawful, hence it is precisely as attractive as it was repulsive for mere sensibility. Even in this case, however, the judgment itself remains only aesthetic because, without having a determinate concept of the object as its ground, it represents merely the subjective play of the powers of the mind (imagination and reason) as harmonious even in their contrast. For just as imagination and **understanding** produce subjective purposiveness of the powers of the mind in the judging of the beautiful through their unison, so do imagination and **reason** produce subjective purposiveness through their conflict: namely, a feeling that we have pure self-sufficient reason, or[a] a faculty for estimating magnitude, whose preeminence cannot be made intuitable through anything except the inadequacy of that faculty which is itself unbounded in the presentation of magnitudes (of sensible objects).

5: 259
The measurement of a space (as apprehension) is at the same time the description of it, thus an objective movement in the imagination and a progression; by contrast, the comprehension of multiplicity in the unity not of thought but of intuition, hence the comprehension in one moment of that which is successively apprehended, is a regression, which in turn cancels the time-condition in the progression of the imagination and makes **simultaneity** intuitable. It is thus (since temporal succession is a condition of inner sense and of an intuition) a subjective movement of the imagination, by which it does violence to the inner sense, which must be all the more marked the greater the quantum is which the imagination comprehends in one intuition. Thus the effort to take up in a single intuition a measure for magnitudes, which requires an appreciable time for its apprehension, is a kind of apprehension which, subjectively considered, is contrapurposive, but which objectively, for the estimation of magnitude, is necessary, hence purposive; in this way, however, the very same violence that is inflicted on the subject by the imagination is judged[b] as purposive **for the whole vocation** of the mind.

The **quality** of the feeling of the sublime is that it is a feeling of displeasure concerning the aesthetic faculty of judging[c] an object that is yet at the same time represented as purposive, which is possible because the subject's own incapacity[d] reveals the consciousness of an unlimited capacity[e] of the very same subject, and the mind can aesthetically judge[f] the latter only through the former.

---

[a] The word "or" was added in the second edition.
[b] *beurtheilt*
[c] *Beurtheilungsvermögen*
[d] *Unvermögen*
[e] *Vermögens*
[f] *beurtheilen*

In the logical estimation of magnitude, the impossibility of ever attaining to absolute totality through the progression of the measurement of the things of the sensible world in time and space was recognized as objective, i.e., as an impossibility of **thinking** the infinite as even given, and not as merely subjective, i.e., as an incapacity[a] for **grasping** it; for there nothing at all turns on the degree of comprehension in one intuition as a measure, but everything comes down to a numerical concept. But in an aesthetic estimation of magnitude the numerical concept must drop out or be altered, and the comprehension of the imagination in respect of the unity of measure (so that the concept of a law of the successive generation of concepts of magnitude is avoided) is alone purposive for it. – Now if a magnitude almost reaches the outermost limit of our faculty of comprehension in one intuition, and yet the imagination is by means of numerical concepts (our capacity[b] for which we are aware is unlimited) summoned to aesthetic comprehension in a greater unity, then we feel ourselves in our mind as aesthetically confined within borders; but with respect to the necessary enlargement of the imagination to the point of adequacy to that which is unlimited in our faculty of reason, namely the idea of the absolute whole, the displeasure and thus the contrapurposiveness of the faculty of imagination is yet represented as purposive for the ideas of reason and their awakening. It is precisely in this way, however, that the aesthetic judgment itself becomes purposive for reason, as the source of ideas, i.e., for an intellectual comprehension for which all aesthetic comprehension is small; and the object is taken up as sublime with a pleasure that is possible only by means of a displeasure.

5: 260

B.
On the Dynamically Sublime in Nature

§ 28.
On nature as a power.

Power is a capacity[c] that is superior to great obstacles. The same thing is called **dominion** if it is also superior to the resistance of something that itself possesses power. Nature considered in aesthetic judgment as a power that has no dominion over us is **dynamically sublime.**

If nature is to be judged[d] by us dynamically as sublime, it must be represented as arousing fear (although, conversely, not every object

[a] *Unvermögen*
[b] *Vermögens*
[c] *Vermögen*
[d] *beurtheilt*

143

that arouses fear is found sublime in our aesthetic judgment). For in aesthetic judging[a] (without a concept) the superiority over obstacles can only be judged[b] in accordance with the magnitude of the resistance. However, that which we strive to resist is an evil, and, if we find our capacity[c] to be no match for it, an object of fear. Thus, for the aesthetic power of judgment[d] nature can count as a power,[e] thus as dynamically sublime, only insofar as it is considered an object of fear.

We can, however, consider an object as **fearful** without being afraid of it, if, namely, we judge[f] it in such a way that we merely **think** of the case in which we might wish to resist it and think that in that case all resistance would be completely futile. Thus the virtuous man fears God without being afraid of him, because he does not think of the case of wishing to resist God and his commands as anything that is worrisome for **him.** But since he does not think of such a case as impossible in itself, he recognizes God as fearful.

Someone who is afraid can no more judge about the sublime in nature than someone who is in the grip of inclination and appetite can judge about the beautiful. The former flees from the sight of an object that instills alarm in him, and it is impossible to find satisfaction in a terror that is seriously intended. Hence the agreeableness in the cessation of something troublesome is **joyfulness.** But this joyfulness on account of liberation from a danger is accompanied with the proviso that one never again be exposed to that danger; indeed one may well be reluctant to think back on that sensation, let alone seek out the opportunity for it.

Bold, overhanging, as it were threatening cliffs, thunder clouds towering up into the heavens, bringing with them flashes of lightning and crashes of thunder, volcanoes with their all-destroying violence, hurricanes with the devastation they leave behind, the boundless ocean set into a rage, a lofty waterfall on a mighty river, etc., make our capacity[g] to resist into an insignificant trifle in comparison with their power. But the sight of them only becomes all the more attractive the more fearful it is, as long as we find ourselves in safety, and we gladly call these objects sublime because they elevate the strength of our soul above its usual level, and allow us to discover within ourselves a capacity[h] for

[a] *Beurtheilung*
[b] *beurtheilt*
[c] *Vermögen*
[d] *Urtheilskraft*
[e] *Macht*
[f] *beurtheilen*
[g] *Vermögen*
[h] *Vermögen*

144

resistance of quite another kind, which gives us the courage to measure ourselves against the apparent all-powerfulness of nature.

For just as we found our own limitation in the immeasurability of nature and the insufficiency of our capacity[a] to adopt a standard proportionate to the aesthetic estimation of the magnitude of its **domain**, but nevertheless at the same time found in our own faculty of reason another, nonsensible standard, which has that very infinity under itself as a unit against which everything in nature is small, and thus found in our own mind a superiority over nature itself even in its immeasurability: likewise the irresistibility of its power certainly makes us, considered as natural beings, recognize our physical[b] powerlessness, but at the same time it reveals a capacity[c] for judging[d] ourselves as independent of it and a superiority over nature on which is grounded a self-preservation of quite another kind than that which can be threatened and endangered by nature outside us, whereby the humanity in our person remains undemeaned even though the human being must submit to that dominion. In this way, in our aesthetic judgment nature is judged[e] as sublime not insofar as it arouses fear, but rather because it calls forth our power[f] (which is not part of nature) to regard those things about which we are concerned (goods, health and life) as trivial, and hence to regard its power[g] (to which we are, to be sure, subjected in regard to these things) as not the sort of dominion over ourselves and our authority to which we would have to bow if it came down to our highest principles and their affirmation or abandonment. Thus nature is here called sublime merely because it raises the imagination to the point of presenting those cases in which the mind can make palpable to itself the sublimity of its own vocation even over nature.

This self-esteem is not diminished by the fact that we must see ourselves as safe in order to be sensible of this inspiring satisfaction, in which case (it might seem), because the danger is not serious, the sublimity of our spiritual capacity[h] is also not to be taken seriously.[16] For the satisfaction here concerns only the **vocation** of our capacity[i] as it is revealed to us in such a case, just as the predisposition to it lies in our nature; while the development and exercise of it is left to us and

5: 262

[a] *Vermögens*
[b] The word "physical" was added in the second edition.
[c] *Vermögen*
[d] *beurtheilen*
[e] *beurtheilt*
[f] *Kraft*
[g] *Macht*
[h] *Geistesvermögen*
[i] *Vermögens*

remains our responsibility.[a] And there is truth here, however much the person, if he takes his reflection this far, may be conscious of his present actual powerlessness.

To be sure, this principle seems far-fetched and subtle, hence excessive for an aesthetic judgment; but the observation of human beings shows the opposite, that it can be the principle for the most common judgings[b] even though one is not always conscious of it. For what is it that is an object of the greatest admiration even to the savage? Someone who is not frightened, who has no fear, thus does not shrink before danger but energetically sets to work with full deliberation. And even in the most civilized[c] circumstances this exceptionally high esteem for the warrior remains, only now it is also demanded that he at the same time display all the virtues of peace, gentleness, compassion and even proper care for his own person, precisely because in this way the incoercibility of his mind by danger can be recognized. Hence however much debate there may be about whether it is the statesman or the general who deserves the greater respect in comparison to the other, aesthetic judgment decides in favor of the latter. Even war, if it is conducted with order and reverence for the rights of civilians, has something sublime about it, and at the same time makes the mentality of the people who conduct it in this way all the more sublime, the more dangers it has been exposed to and before which it has been able to assert its courage; whereas a long peace causes the spirit of mere commerce to predominate, along with base selfishness, cowardice and weakness, and usually debases the mentality of the populace.

5: 263

This analysis of the concept of the sublime, to the extent that it is ascribed to power, seems to run counter to the fact that we usually represent God as exhibiting himself in anger but at the same time in his sublimity in thunder, storm, earthquake etc., where to imagine that our minds have any superiority over the effects and as it seems even over the intentions of such a power would seem to be at once both foolishness and outrage. Here it seems to be not a feeling of the sublimity of our own nature but rather submission, dejection, and a feeling of complete powerlessness that is the appropriate disposition of the mind to the appearance of such an object, and which is also usually associated with the idea of it in the case of natural occurrences of this sort. In religion in general submission, adoration with bowed head, and remorseful and anxious gestures and voice, seem to be the only appropriate conduct in the presence of the Deity, and so to have been

[a] In the first edition, this period was a comma, and the sentence continued to the end of the paragraph.
[b] Beurtheilungen
[c] allergesittesten

adopted and still observed by most people. But this disposition of the mind is far from being intrinsically and necessarily connected with the idea of the **sublimity** of a religion and its object. Someone who is genuinely afraid because he finds cause for that within himself, because he is conscious of having offended with his contemptible disposition^a a power whose will is irresistible and at the same time just, certainly does not find himself in the right frame of mind to marvel at the greatness of God, for which a mood of calm contemplation and an entirely free^b judgment is requisite. Only when he is conscious of his upright, God-pleasing disposition do those effects of^c power serve to awaken in him the idea of the sublimity of this being, insofar as he recognizes in himself a sublimity of disposition suitable to God's will, and is thereby raised above the fear of such effects of nature, which he does not regard as outbursts of God's wrath. Even humility, as the pitiless judging^d of one's own failings, which otherwise, given consciousness of good dispositions, could easily be covered with the mantle of the fragility of human nature, is a sublime state of mind, that of voluntarily subjecting oneself to the pain of self-reproach in order gradually to eliminate the causes of it. In this way alone does religion internally distinguish itself from superstition, the latter not providing a basis in the mind for reverence^e for the sublime, but only for fear^f and anxiety before the being of superior power, to whose will the terrified person sees himself as subjected without holding him in great esteem; from which of course nothing can arise but the attempt to curry favor and ingratiate oneself, instead of a religion of the good conduct of life.[17]

5: 264

Thus sublimity is not contained in anything in nature, but only in our mind, insofar as we can become conscious of being superior to nature within us and thus also to nature outside us (insofar as it influences us). Everything that arouses this feeling in us, which includes the **power**^g of nature that calls forth our own powers,^h is thus (although improperly) called sublime; and only under the presupposition of this idea in us and in relation to it are we capable of arriving at the idea of the sublimity of that being who produces inner respect in us not merely through his power, which he displays in nature, but even more by the

---

^a *Gesinnung*
^b In the second edition, *freyes*; in the first edition, *zwangfreyes* (uncoerced or free from coercion).
^c *der*; in the first edition, *seiner*, that is, God's power.
^d *Beurtheilung*
^e *Ehrfurcht*
^f *Furcht*
^g *Macht*
^h *Kräfte*

capacity*a* that is placed within us for judging*b* nature without fear and thinking of our vocation as sublime in comparison with it.

§ 29.
On the modality of the judgment on the
sublime in nature.

There are innumerable things in beautiful nature concerning which we immediately require consensus with our own judgment from everyone else and can also, without being especially prone to error, expect it; but we cannot promise ourselves that our judgment concerning the sublime in nature will so readily find acceptance by others. For a far greater culture, not merely of the aesthetic power of judgment, but also of the cognitive faculties on which that is based, seems to be requisite in order to be able to make a judgment about this excellence of the objects of nature.

5: 265   The disposition of the mind to the feeling of the sublime requires its receptivity to ideas; for it is precisely in the inadequacy of nature to the latter, thus only under the presupposition of them, and of the effort of the imagination to treat nature as a schema for them, that what is repellent for the sensibility, but which is at the same time attractive for it, consists, because it is a dominion that reason exercises over sensibility only in order to enlarge it in a way suitable for its own proper domain (the practical) and to allow it to look out upon the infinite, which for sensibility is an abyss. In fact, without the development of moral ideas, that which we, prepared by culture, call sublime will appear merely repellent to the unrefined person. He will see in the proofs of the dominion of nature given by its destructiveness and in the enormous measure of its power, against which his own vanishes away to nothing, only the distress, danger, and need that would surround the person who was banished thereto. Thus the good and otherwise sensible Savoyard peasant (as Herr de Saussure relates) had no hesitation in calling all devotees of the icy mountains fools.[18] And who knows whether that would have been entirely unjust if that observer had undertaken the dangers to which he there exposed himself, as most travelers usually do, merely as a hobby, or in order one day to be able to describe them with pathos? But his intention was the edification of mankind, and this excellent man experienced the elevating sentiment*c* that he gave to the readers of his travels as part of the bargain.

But just because the judgment on the sublime in nature requires

a *Vermögen*
b *beurtheilen*
c *seelenerhebende Empfindung*

culture (more so than that on the beautiful), it is not therefore first generated by culture and so to speak introduced into society merely as a matter of convention; rather it has its foundation in human nature, and indeed in that which can be required of everyone and demanded of him along with healthy understanding, namely in the predisposition to the feeling for (practical) ideas, i.e., to that which is moral.[a]

This is the ground for the necessity of the assent of the judgment of other people concerning the sublime to our own, which we at the same time include in the latter. For just as we reproach someone who is indifferent in judging[b] an object in nature that we find beautiful with lack of **taste**, so we say of someone who remains unmoved by that which we judge to be sublime that he has no **feeling.** We demand both, however, of every human being, and also presuppose it in everyone who has any culture – only with this difference, that we immediately require the former of everyone because in it the power of judgment relates the imagination merely to the understanding, as the faculty of concepts, but because the latter relates the imagination to reason, as the faculty of ideas, we require it only under a subjective presupposition (which, however, we believe ourselves to be justified in demanding of everyone), namely that of the moral feeling in the human being,[c] and so we also[d] ascribe necessity to this aesthetic judgment.

5: 266

In this modality of aesthetic judgments, namely their presumed necessity, lies a principal moment for the critique of the power of judgment. For it makes us cognizant of an *a priori* principle in them, and elevates them out of empirical psychology, in which they would otherwise remain buried among the feelings of enjoyment and pain (only with the meaningless epithet of a **more refined** feeling),[e,19] in order to place them and by their means the power of judgment in the class of those which have as their ground *a priori* principles, and as such to transpose them into transcendental philosophy.

General remark on the exposition of aesthetic reflective judgments.[20]

In relation to the feeling of pleasure an object is to be counted either among the **agreeable** or the **beautiful** or the **sublime** or the (absolutely) **good** (*iucundum, pulchrum, sublime, honestum*).

---

[a] *dem moralischen*; in the first edition, *den moralischen*, which would refer back to the previous clause and thus be translated as "to the moral ideas."
[b] *Beurtheilung*
[c] The words "in the human being" were added in the second edition.
[d] The word "also" was added in the second edition.
[e] The parenthetical remark was added in the second edition.

The **agreeable**, as an incentive for the desires, is of the same kind throughout, no matter where it comes from and how specifically different the representation (of sense and of sensation, objectively considered) may be.[21] Hence in judging[a] of its influence on the mind it is only a matter of the number[b] of the charms (simultaneous and successive), and as it were only of the mass of the agreeable sensation; and thus this cannot be made intelligible except by **quantity**. It also does not contribute to culture, but is simply a matter of enjoyment. – The **beautiful**, by contrast, requires the representation of a certain **quality** of the object, which also makes itself intelligible, and can be brought to concepts (although in the aesthetic judgment it is not brought to that); and it does contribute to culture, in that it at the same time teaches us to attend to purposiveness in the feeling of pleasure. – The **sublime** consists merely in the **relation** in which the sensible in the representation of nature is judged[c] as suitable for a possible supersensible use of it. – The **absolutely good**, judged[d] subjectively in terms of the feeling that it instills (the object of the moral feeling) as the determinability of the powers of the subject by means of the representation of an **absolutely necessitating** law, is distinguished chiefly by the **modality** of a necessity resting on concepts *a priori*, which contains in itself not merely a **claim** but also a **command** that everyone should assent, and belongs in itself not to the aesthetic but to the pure intellectual[e] power of judgment; it is also ascribed, not in a merely reflecting but in a determining judgment, not to **nature** but to **freedom**.[22] But the **determinability of the subject** by means of this idea, and indeed of a subject that can sense in itself **obstacles** in sensibility but at the same time superiority over them through overcoming them as a **modification of its condition**, i.e., the moral feeling, is nevertheless related to the aesthetic power of judgment and its **formal conditions** to the extent that it can serve to make the lawfulness of action out of duty representable at the same time as aesthetic, i.e., as sublime, or also as beautiful, without sacrificing any of its purity; which would not be the case if one would place it in natural combination with the feeling of the agreeable.

5: 267

If one draws the result from the exposition thus far of the two kinds of aesthetic judgment, the outcome would be the following brief explanations:

That is **beautiful** which pleases in the mere judging[f] (thus not by means of the sensation of sense in accordance with a concept of the understanding). From this it follows of itself that it must please without any interest.

That is **sublime** which pleases immediately through its resistance to the interest of the senses.

Both, as explanations of aesthetically universally valid judging,[g] are related to subjective grounds, namely on the one hand to those of sensibility, as it is

---

[a] *Beurtheilung*
[b] *Menge*
[c] *beurtheilt*
[d] *beurtheilt*
[e] In the first edition, the words "but to the pure intellectual" were enclosed in parentheses.
[f] *Beurtheilung*
[g] *Beurtheilung*

purposive in behalf of the contemplative understanding, on the other, **in op-position** to those, as purposive for the ends of practical reason; and yet both, united in the same subject, are purposive in relation to the moral feeling. The beautiful prepares us to love something, even nature, without interest; the sublime, to esteem it, even contrary to our (sensible) interest.[23]

One can describe the sublime thus: it is an object (of nature) **the represen-** 5: 268
tation of which determines the mind to think of the unattainability of nature as a presentation of ideas.

Taken literally, and considered logically, ideas cannot be presented. But if we extend our empirical faculty of representation (mathematically or dynami-cally) for the intuition of nature, then reason inevitably comes in as a faculty of the independence of the absolute totality, and produces the effort of the mind, though it is in vain, to make the representation of the senses adequate to that. This effort, and the feeling of the unattainability of the idea by means of the imagination, is itself a presentation of the subjective purposiveness of our mind in the use of the imagination for its supersensible vocation, and compels us to **think** nature itself in its totality, as the presentation of something supersensible, subjectively, without being able to produce this presentation **objectively.**

For we quickly realize that nature falls completely short of the uncondi-tioned in space and time, and thus of absolute magnitude, even though this is demanded by the commonest reason. And precisely by this are we reminded that we have to do only with a nature as appearance, and that this itself must be regarded as the mere presentation of a nature in itself (which reason has in the idea). This idea of the supersensible, however, which of course we cannot further determine, so that we cannot **cognize** nature as a presentation of it but can only **think** it, is awakened in us by means of an object the aesthetic judging[a] of which stretches imagination to its limit, whether that of enlarge-ment (mathematically) or of its power over the mind (dynamically), in that it is grounded in the feeling of a vocation of the mind that entirely oversteps the domain of the former (the moral feeling), in regard to which the representation of the object is judged[b] as subjectively purposive.

In fact a feeling for the sublime in nature cannot even be conceived without connecting it to a disposition of the mind that is similar to the moral disposi-tion; and, although the beautiful in nature likewise presupposes and cultivates a certain **liberality** in the manner of thinking, i.e., independence of the satis-faction from mere sensory enjoyment, nevertheless by means of it freedom is represented more as in **play** than as subject to a lawful **business**, which is the 5: 269
genuine property of human morality, where reason must exercise dominion over sensibility; it is just that in the aesthetic judgment on the sublime this dominion is represented as being exercised by the imagination itself, as an instrument of reason.

The satisfaction in the sublime in nature is thus also only **negative** (whereas that in the beautiful is **positive**), namely a feeling of the deprivation of the

---

[a] *Beurtheilung*
[b] *beurtheilt*

deren Grund aber ihr selbst verborgen ist

ab-yss
cd|4|
130

freedom of the imagination by itself, insofar as it is purposively determined in accordance with a law other than that of empirical use. It thereby acquires an enlargement and power which is greater than that which it sacrifices, but whose ground is hidden from it, whereas it **feels** the sacrifice or deprivation and at the same time the cause to which it is subjected. The **astonishment** bordering on terror, the horror and the awesome shudder, which grip the spectator in viewing mountain ranges towering to the heavens, deep ravines and the raging torrents in them, deeply shadowed wastelands inducing melancholy reflection, etc., is, in view of the safety in which he knows himself to be, not actual fear, but only an attempt to involve ourselves in it by means of the imagination, in order to feel the power of that very faculty, to combine the movement of the mind thereby aroused with its calmness, and so to be superior to nature within us, and thus also that outside us, insofar as it can have an influence on our feeling of well-being. For the imagination, in accordance with the law of association, makes our state of contentment physically dependent; but the very same imagination, in accordance with principles of the schematism of the power of judgment (consequently to the extent that it is subordinated to freedom), is an instrument of reason and its ideas, but as such a power to assert our independence in the face of the influences of nature, to diminish the value of what is great according to these,*a* and so to place what is absolutely great only in its (the subject's) own vocation. This reflection of the aesthetic power of judgment, elevating itself to adequacy to reason (yet without a determinate concept of the latter), represents the object, precisely by means of the objective inadequacy of the imagination in its greatest extension to reason (as a faculty of ideas), as subjectively purposive.

5: 270

Here one must attend above all to what was already pointed out above, that in the transcendental aesthetic of the power of judgment it is strictly pure aesthetic judgments that are at issue, consequently the examples must not be drawn from those beautiful or sublime objects of nature that presuppose the concept of an end; for in that case it would be either teleological or grounded in mere sensations of an object (gratification or pain), and thus in the first case would not be an aesthetic purposiveness and in the second case not a merely formal purposiveness. Thus, if someone calls the sight of the starry heavens **sublime**, he must not ground such a judging*b* of it on concepts of worlds inhabited by rational beings, taking the bright points with which we see the space above us to be filled as their suns, about which they move in their purposively appointed orbits, but must take it, as we see it, merely as a broad, all-embracing vault; and it must be merely under this representation that we posit the sublimity that a pure aesthetic judgment attributes to this object. In just the same way, we must not take the sight of the ocean as we **think** it, enriched with all sorts of knowledge (which are not, however, contained in the immediate intuition), for example as a wide realm of water creatures, as the great storehouse of water for the evaporation which impregnates the air with

---

a The first and second editions have *der ersteren*, the third *der letzteren*; in either case, the reference is back to "the influences of nature."
b *Beurtheilung*

clouds for the benefit of the land, or as an element that separates parts of the world from one another but at the same time makes possible the greatest community among them, for this would yield merely teleological judgments; rather, one must consider the ocean merely as the poets do, in accordance with what its appearance shows, for instance, when it is considered in periods of calm, as a clear watery mirror bounded only by the heavens, but also when it is turbulent, an abyss threatening to devour everything, and yet still be able to find it sublime. The same is to be said about the sublime and the beautiful in the human figure, where we do not look to concepts of the ends **for which** all its members exist for determining grounds of our judgment and must not let agreement with them **influence** our aesthetic judgment (which in that case would no longer be pure), though that they do not conflict with those ends is of course a necessary condition even of aesthetic satisfaction.[24] Aesthetic purposiveness is the lawfulness of the power of judgment in its **freedom.** The satisfaction in the object depends on the relation in which we would place the imagination: namely, that it entertain the mind by itself in free activity. If, on the contrary, something else determines the judgment, whether it be a sensation of the senses or a concept of the understanding, then it is certainly lawful but not the judgment of a **free** power of judgment.

    Thus if one speaks of an intellectual beauty or sublimity, then, **first**, these expressions are not entirely correct, because they are kinds of aesthetic representation that would not be found in us at all if we were simply pure intelligences (or even if we were to transform ourselves into such in our thoughts); **second**, although both, as objects of an intellectual (moral) satisfaction, are certainly compatible with the aesthetic insofar as they do not **rest** on any interest, nevertheless they are still difficult to unite with the aesthetic because they are supposed to **produce** an interest which, if the presentation is to agree with the satisfaction in aesthetic judging,[a] would never occur except by means of an interest of the senses, which is combined with it in the presentation, through which, however, damage would be done to the intellectual purposiveness and it would become impure.

    The object of a pure and unconditioned intellectual satisfaction is the moral law in all its power, which it exercises in us over each and every incentive of the mind **antecedent to it**; and, since this power actually makes itself aesthetically knowable only through sacrifices (which is a deprivation, although in behalf of inner freedom, but also reveals in us an unfathomable depth of this supersensible faculty together with its consequences reaching beyond what can be seen),[b] the satisfaction on the aesthetic side (in relation to sensibility) is negative, i.e., contrary to this interest, but considered from the intellectual side it is positive, and combined with an interest. From this it follows that the intellectual, intrinsically purposive (moral) good, judged[c] aesthetically, must not be represented so much as beautiful but rather as sublime, so that it arouses more the feeling of respect (which scorns charm) than that of love and intimate

5: 271

---

[a] *Beurtheilung*
[b] The parentheses around this part of the sentence were added in the second edition.
[c] *beurtheilt*

affection, since human nature does not agree with that good of its own accord, but only through the dominion that reason exercises over sensibility. Conversely, even that which we call sublime in nature outside us or even within ourselves (e.g., certain affects) is represented only as a power of the mind to soar above **certain**[a] obstacles of sensibility by means of moral[b] principles, and thereby to become interesting.

5: 272   I should like to dwell a little on the last point. The idea of the good with affect is called **enthusiasm.**[c,25] This state of mind seems to be sublime, so much so that it is commonly maintained that without it nothing great can be accomplished. Now, however, every affect* is blind, either in the choice of its end, or, even if this is given by reason, in its implementation; for it is that movement of the mind that makes it incapable of engaging in free consideration of principles, in order to determine itself in accordance with them.[d] Thus it cannot in any way merit a satisfaction of reason. Nevertheless, enthusiasm is aesthetically sublime, because it is a stretching of the powers through ideas, which give the mind a momentum that acts far more powerfully and persistently than the impetus given by sensory representations. But (what seems strange) even **affectlessness** (*apatheia, phlegma in significactu bono*)[e] in a mind that emphatically pursues its own inalterable principles is sublime, and indeed in a far superior way, because it also has the satisfaction of pure reason on its side.[27] Only such a mentality is called **noble** – an expression subsequently also applied to things, e.g., buildings, costume, a literary style, a bodily posture, etc., if it arouses not so much **astonishment** (an affect in the representation of novelty that exceeds expectation)[28] as **admiration** (an astonishment that does not cease when the novelty is lost), which happens when ideas in their presentation unintentionally and without artifice agree with aesthetic satisfaction.

Every affect of the **courageous sort** (that is, which arouses the consciousness of our powers to overcome any resistance (*animi strenui*)[f]) is **aesthetically sublime**, e.g., anger, even despair (that is, the **enraged**, not the **despon-**

---

* **Affects** are specifically different from **passions**. The former are related merely to feeling; the latter belong to the faculty of desire, and are inclinations that make all determinability of the faculty of choice by means of principles difficult or impossible. The former are tumultuous and unpremeditated, the latter sustained and considered; thus indignation, as anger, is an affect, but as hatred (vindictiveness), it is a passion. The latter can never, in any circumstances, be called sublime, because while in the case of an affect the freedom of the mind is certainly **hampered**, in the case of passion it is removed.[26]

---

[a] The emphasized word "certain" (*gewisse*) in the second edition replaces "the" in the first.
[b] Reading *moralische* with the first edition rather than *menschliche* with the second.
[c] Here Kant uses the word "*Enthusiasm*," not, as he usually does, "*Schwarmerei*."
[d] In the first edition, "that makes it incapable of determining itself through principles in accordance with free consideration."
[e] apathy, being phlegmatic in a positive sense
[f] vigorous spirits or mental powers

dent kind). Affect of the **yielding** kind, however (which makes the effort at resistance itself into an object of displeasure (*animum languidum*)*ᵃ*) has nothing **noble** in it, although it can be counted as belonging to beauty of the sensory kind.[29] Hence the **emotions** that can reach the strength of an affect are also quite diverse. We have **brave** as well as **tender** emotions. The latter, if they reach the level of an affect, are good for nothing at all; the tendency toward them is called **oversensitivity**.[30] A sympathetic pain that will not let itself be consoled, or with which, when it concerns invented evils, we consciously become involved, to the point of being taken in by the fantasy, as if it were real, proves and constitutes a tenderhearted but at the same time weak soul, which reveals a beautiful side, and which can certainly be called fantastic but not even enthusiastic. Novels, sentimental plays, shallow moral precepts, which make play with (falsely) so-called noble dispositions, but in fact enervate the heart, and make it unreceptive to the rigorous precept of duty and incapable of all respect for the dignity of humanity in our own person and the right of human beings (which is something entirely different from their happiness), and in general incapable of all firm principles; even a religious sermon that preaches a groveling, base currying of favor and self-ingratiation, which abandons all confidence in our own capacity*ᵇ* for resistance against evil, instead of the energetic determination to seek out the powers that still remain in us, despite all our frailty, for overcoming inclinations; the false humility that finds the only way to be pleasing to the supreme being in self-contempt, in whimpering, feigned remorse and a merely passive attitude of mind – none of these have anything to do with that which can be counted as the beauty, let alone the sublimity, of a mentality.[31]

5: 273

But even tumultuous movements of the mind, whether they be associated with ideas of religion, under the name of edification, or, as belonging merely to culture, with ideas that contain a social interest, no matter how much they stretch the imagination, can in no way claim the honor of being a **sublime** presentation, if they do not leave behind a disposition of mind that, even if only indirectly, has influence on the consciousness of its strength and resolution in regard to that which brings with it intellectual purposiveness (the supersensible). For otherwise all these emotions belong only to the **motion***ᶜ* that we are glad to have for the sake of health. The agreeable exhaustion that follows such an agitation by the play of affects is an enjoyment of the well-being resulting from the equilibrium of the various vital forces that is thus produced in us, which in the end comes down to the same thing as that which the voluptuaries of the Orient find so comforting when they have their bodies as it were kneaded, and all their muscles and joints softly pressed and flexed; only in the first case the moving principle is for the most part in us, while in the latter it is entirely outside us. Now many a person does believe himself to be edified by a sermon in which, however, nothing (no system of good maxims) has been erected, or improved by a tragedy when he is merely glad about a

5: 274

ᵃ enfeebled spirit
ᵇ *Vermögen*
ᶜ Here Kant uses the Latinate word *Motion* instead of *Bewegung* (movement).

lucky escape from boredom. Thus the sublime must always have a relation to the **manner of thinking,** i.e., to maxims for making the intellectual and the ideas of reason superior to sensibility.

There need be no anxiety that the feeling of the sublime will lose anything through such an abstract presentation, which becomes entirely negative in regard to the sensible; for the imagination, although it certainly finds nothing beyond the sensible to which it can attach itself, nevertheless feels itself to be unbounded precisely because of this elimination of the limits of sensibility; and that separation is thus a presentation of the infinite, which for that very reason can never be anything other than a merely negative presentation, which nevertheless expands the soul. Perhaps there is no more sublime passage in the Jewish Book of the Law than the commandment: Thou shalt not make unto thyself any graven image, nor any likeness either of that which is in heaven, or on the earth, or yet under the earth, etc.[32] This commandment alone can explain the enthusiasm that the Jewish people felt in its civilized[a] period for its religion when it compared itself with other peoples, or the pride that Mohammedanism inspired. The very same thing also holds of the representation of the moral law and the predisposition to morality in us. It is utterly mistaken to worry that if it were deprived of everything that the senses can recommend it would then bring with it nothing but cold, lifeless approval and no moving force or emotion. It is exactly the reverse: for where the senses no longer see anything before them, yet the unmistakable and inextinguishable idea of morality remains, there it would be more necessary to moderate the momentum of an unbounded imagination so as not to let it reach the point of enthusiasm,[b][33] rather than, from fear of the powerlessness of these ideas, to look for assistance for them in images and childish devices. That is why even governments have gladly allowed religion to be richly equipped with such supplements and thus sought to relieve the subject[c] of the bother but at the same time also of the capacity[d] to extend the powers of his soul beyond the limits that are arbitrarily set for him and by means of which, as merely passive, he can more easily be dealt with.

This pure, elevating,[e] merely negative presentation of morality, by contrast, carries with it no risk of **visionary rapture,**[f] which is **a delusion of being able to see**[g] **something beyond all bounds of sensibility,**[h] i.e., to dream in accordance with principles (to rave with reason), precisely because the presentation in this case is merely negative. For the **inscrutability of the idea of freedom** entirely precludes any positive presentation;[34] but the moral law is sufficient in itself in us and originally determining, so that it does not even

5: 275

---

[a] *gesitteten*
[b] Here and in the next paragraph, *Enthusiasm.*
[c] *Unterthan*
[d] *Vermögen*
[e] *seelenerhebende*, literally "soul-elevating."
[f] *Schwärmerei*
[g] This word is set in spaced *Fettdruck* in Kant's text.
[h] Following the second edition in reading *Sinnlichkeit* instead of *Sittlichkeit* (morality) as in the first.

allow us to look around for a determining ground outside it. If enthusiasm can be compared with the **delusion of sense**,[a] then visionary rapture is to be compared with the **delusion of mind**,[b] the latter of which is least of all compatible with the sublime, since it is brooding and absurd. In enthusiasm, as an affect, the imagination is unreined; in visionary rapture, as a deep-rooted, oppressive passion, it is unruled. The former is a passing accident, which occasionally affects the most healthy understanding; the latter is a disease that destroys it.

Simplicity (artless purposiveness) is as it were the style of nature in the sublime, and so also of morality, which is a second (supersensible) nature, of which we know only the laws, without being able by intuition to reach the supersensible faculty in ourselves that contains the ground of this legislation.

It should further be remarked that, although the satisfaction in the beautiful, as much as that in the sublime, is not only clearly distinguished among the other aesthetic judgings[c] by means of universal **communicability**, but also, by means of this property, acquires an interest in relation to society (in which it can be communicated), nevertheless the **separation from all society** is also regarded as something sublime if it rests on ideas that look beyond all sensible interest. To be self-sufficient, hence not to need society, yet without being unsociable, i.e., fleeing it, is something that comes close to the sublime, just like any superiority over needs. In contrast, to flee from human beings out of **misanthropy**, because one is hostile to them, or out of **anthropophobia** (fear of people), because one fears them as enemies, is in part hateful and in part contemptible. Nevertheless there is a kind of misanthropy (very improperly so called), the predisposition to which is often found in the mind of many well-thinking people as they get older, which is certainly philanthropic enough as far as their **benevolence** is concerned, but is because of long, sad experience far removed from any **pleasure**[d] in human beings; evidence of this is to be found in the tendency to withdraw from society, the fantastic wish for an isolated country seat, or even (in young people) the dream of happiness in being able to pass their life on an island unknown to the rest of the world with a small family, which the novelists or poets who write Robinsonades[35] know so well how to exploit. Falsehood, ingratitude, injustice, the childishness in ends that we ourselves hold to be important and great, in the pursuit of which people do every conceivable evil to each other, so contradict the idea of what they could be if they wanted to, and are so opposed to the lively wish to take a better view of them that, in order not to hate them, since one cannot love them, doing without all social joys seems to be only a small sacrifice. This sadness, not about the evil that fate imposes on other human beings (which is caused by sympathy), but over that which they do to themselves (which is based on antipathy in fundamental principles) is, since it rests on ideas, sublime,

5: 276

---

[a] *Wahnsinn*
[b] *Wahnwitz*
[c] *Beurtheilungen*
[d] Here *Wohlgefallen*, in contrast to *Wohlwollen* ("benevolence") in the previous clause.

whereas the former can at best only count as beautiful. – Saussure,[36] as inspired as he is thorough, in the description of his travels in the Alps says of Bonhomme, one of the mountains of Savoy: "There reigns there a certain **tedious sadness.**" But he also knew of an **interesting** sadness, which is instilled by the view of a wasteland to which human beings would move in order to hear or experience nothing more of the world, but which nevertheless must not be so completely inhospitable that it would offer human beings only an extremely burdensome refuge. – I make this remark only with the intention of recalling that even sorrow (not dejected sadness) can be counted among the **vigorous** affects if it is grounded in moral ideas, but if it is grounded in sympathy, and, as such, is also lovable, it belongs merely to the **mellowing** affects, only in order to draw attention to the disposition of the mind that is **sublime** only in the former case.

* *
*

5: 277   The transcendental exposition of aesthetic judgments that has now been completed can be compared with the physiological[a] exposition, as it has been elaborated by a **Burke** and many acute men among us, in order to see whither a merely empirical exposition of the sublime and the beautiful would lead. **Burke,**[*] who deserves to be named as the foremost author in this sort of approach, brings out in this manner (p. 223 of his work) "that the feeling of the sublime is grounded on the drive to self-preservation and on **fear,** i.e., a pain, which, since it does not go as far as the actual destruction of bodily parts, produces movements which, since they cleanse the finer or cruder vessels of dangerous and burdensome stoppages, are capable of arousing agreeable sensations, not, to be sure, pleasure, but a kind of pleasing horror, a certain tranquility that is mixed with terror."[38] The beautiful, which he grounds on love (which, however, he would have known as separate from desire), he traces (pp. 251–52) "to the relaxation, loosening and slackening of the fibers of the body, hence to a softening, a dissolution, an enervation, a sinking away, a dying away, a melting away of gratification."[39] And now he confirms this sort of explanation through cases in which the imagination is able to arouse the feeling of the beautiful as well as the sublime not only in association with the understanding, but even in association with sensory sensations. – As psychological remarks, these analyses of the phenomena of our mind are extremely fine,[b] and provide rich materials for the favorite researches of empirical anthropology. Moreover, it cannot be denied that all representations in us, whether they are

---

[*] According to the German translation of his essay, *Philosophische Untersuchungen über dem Ursprung unserer Begriffe vom Schönen und Erhabenen* (Riga: Hartknoch, 1773).[37]

---

[a] In the first edition, the word printed here was "psychological."
[b] *schön*

objectively merely sensible or else entirely intellectual, can nevertheless subjectively be associated with gratification or pain, however unnoticeable either might be (because they all affect the feeling of life, and none of them, insofar as it is a modification of the subject, can be indifferent), or even that, as Epicurus maintained, **gratification** and **pain** are always[a] ultimately corporeal,[40] whether they originate from the imagination or even from representations of the understanding: because life without the feeling of the corporeal organ is merely consciousness of one's existence, but not a feeling of well- or ill-being, i.e., the promotion or inhibition of the powers of life; because the mind for itself is entirely life (the principle of life itself), and hindrances or promotions must be sought outside it, though in the human being himself, hence in combination with his body.

5: 278

If, however, one locates the satisfaction in the object entirely in the fact that it gratifies by means of charm and emotion, then one must not expect of **others** that they will assent to the aesthetic judgments that **we** make; for about that everyone is justified in consulting only his own private sense. In that case, however, all criticism[b] of taste also ceases entirely; for one would then have to make the example that others give by means of the contingent correspondence among their judgments into a **command** for assent from us, in opposition to which principle, however, we would presumably struggle and appeal to the natural right to subject the judgment that rests on the immediate feeling of our own well-being to our own sense, and not to that of others.

If, therefore, the judgment of taste must not be counted as **egoistic**, but necessarily, in accordance with its inner nature, i.e., of itself, not for the sake of the examples that others give of their taste, as **pluralistic**, if one evaluates it as one that may at the same time demand that everyone should consent to it, then it must be grounded in some sort of *a priori* principle (whether objective or subjective), which one can never arrive at by scouting about among empirical laws of the alterations of the mind: for these allow us to cognize only how things are judged, but never to prescribe how they ought to be judged, particularly in such a way that the command is **unconditioned**; though it is something of this sort that the judgments of taste presuppose when they would have the satisfaction known to be **immediately** connected with a representation. Thus the empirical exposition of aesthetic judgments may always make a start at furnishing the material for a higher investigation, yet a transcendental discussion of this faculty is still possible and essential for the critique of taste.[c] For unless this has *a priori* principles, it could not possibly guide the judgments of others and make claims[d] to approve or reject them with even a semblance of right.

What belongs to the remainder of the analytic of the aesthetic power of judgment contains first of all the:[e]

---

[a] In the first edition, "all."

[b] *Censur*

[c] In the first edition, the next sentence followed after a comma rather than a period.

[d] In the first edition, "judgments."

[e] This lead-in to the next section was added in the second edition.

Deduction of pure aesthetic
judgments[a],[1]

§ 30.
The deduction of aesthetic judgments concerning
the objects of nature may not be directed towards
that which we call sublime among them,
but only to the beautiful.

The claim of an aesthetic judgment to universal validity for every subject, as a judgment that must be based on some principle *a priori*, needs a deduction (i.e., a legitimation of its presumption), which must be added to its exposition, if, that is, it concerns a satisfaction or dissatisfaction in the **form of the object**. The judgments of taste concerning the beautiful in nature are of this sort. For in this case the purposiveness has its ground in the object and its shape,[b] even if it does not indicate the relation of the object to others in accordance with concepts (for judgments of cognition), but rather generally concerns merely the apprehension of this form insofar as it shows itself in the mind to be suitable to the **faculty** both of concepts and of the presentation of them (which is one and the same as that of apprehension). Hence one can also raise many questions in regard to the beautiful in nature, concerning the cause of this purposiveness of its forms: e.g., how is one to explain why nature has spread beauty so extravagantly everywhere, even at the bottom of the ocean, where it is only seldom that the human eye (for which alone, after all, it is purposive) penetrates? and so on.

Only the sublime in nature – if we make a pure aesthetic judgment about it, which is not mixed with concepts of perfection, as objective purposiveness, in which case it would be a teleological judgment – can be considered as entirely formless or shapeless, but nevertheless as the object of a pure satisfaction, and can demonstrate subjective purposiveness in the given representation; and the question now arises, whether in the case of this kind of aesthetic judgment, beyond the exposition of what is thought in it, a deduction of its claim to some sort of (subjective) principle *a priori* could also be demanded.

It will serve as an answer to this that the sublime in nature is only improperly so called, and should properly be ascribed only to the manner of thinking, or rather to its foundation in human nature.[c] The

---

[a] In the first edition, the heading "Third Book" (*Drittes Buch*) preceded this title.
[b] *Gestalt*
[c] In the first edition, there was a comma rather than a period here, and the sentence continued thus: "for which the apprehension . . . merely provides the occasion."

apprehension of an otherwise formless and nonpurposive object merely provides the occasion for becoming conscious of this, which in this way is **used** in a subjectively purposive way, but is not judged to be such **for itself** and on account of its form (as it were *species finalis accepta, non data*).[a] Hence our exposition of the judgments on the sublime in nature was at the same time their deduction. For when we analyzed the reflection of the power of judgment in these, we found in them a purposive relation of the cognitive faculties, which must ground the faculty of ends (the will) *a priori*, and hence is itself purposive *a priori*, which then immediately contains[b] the deduction, i.e., the justification of the claim of such a judgment to universally necessary validity.

We shall thus have to seek only the deduction of judgments of taste, i.e., of the judgments about the beauty of things in nature, and by this means accomplish the task for the whole of the aesthetic power of judgment in its entirety.

§ 31.
On the method of the deduction of judgments of taste.

The obligation to provide a deduction, i.e., the guarantee of the legitimacy, of a kind of judgment arises only if the judgment makes a claim to necessity, which is the case even if it demands subjective universality, i.e., the assent of all, in spite of the fact that it is not a judgment of cognition, but only of the pleasure or displeasure in a given object, i.e., a presumption of a subjective purposiveness that is throughout valid for everyone, which is not supposed to be grounded in any concept of the thing, because it is a judgment of taste.

Since in the latter case we do not have before us a judgment of cognition, neither a theoretical one, grounded in the concept of a **nature** in general through the understanding, nor a (pure) practical one, grounded in the idea of **freedom** as given *a priori* by reason, and thus have to justify *a priori* the validity of neither a judgment that represents what a thing is nor one that I, in order to produce it, ought to perform something, it is only the **universal validity** of a **singular** judgment, which expresses the subjective purposiveness of an empirical representation of the form of an object, that has to be shown for the faculty of judgment in general in order to explain how it is possible that something could please merely in the judging[c] (without a sensa-

5: 281

---

[a] The appearance of finality is assigned, not given.
[b] In the first edition, "is."
[c] *Beurtheilung*

tion of the senses or a concept) and that, just as the judging[a] of an object for the sake of a **cognition** in general has universal rules, the satisfaction of one[b] can also be announced as a rule for everyone else.

Now if this universal validity is not to be grounded on collecting votes and asking around among other people about the sort of sensations they have, but is as it were to rest on an autonomy of the subject judging about the feeling of pleasure in the given representation, i.e., on his own taste, but yet is also not to be derived from concepts, then such a judgment has – as the judgment of taste in fact does – a twofold and indeed logical peculiarity: namely, **first**, universal validity *a priori*, yet not a logical universality in accordance with concepts, but the universality of a singular judgment; **second**, a necessity (which must always rest on *a priori* grounds), which does not, however, depend on any *a priori* grounds of proof, by means of the representation of which the approval that the judgment of taste requires of everyone could be compelled.

The resolution of these logical peculiarities, in which a judgment of taste differs from all judgments of cognition, if we here initially abstract from all its content, namely the feeling of pleasure, and merely compare the aesthetic form with the form of objective judgments, as logic prescribes it, will by itself be sufficient for the deduction of this unusual faculty. We will therefore first of all offer a representation of these characteristic properties of taste, elucidated by means of examples.

§ 32.
First peculiarity of the judgment of taste.

The judgment of taste determines its object with regard to satisfaction (as beauty) with a claim to the assent of **everyone**, as if it were objective.

To say "This flower is beautiful" is the same as merely to repeat its own claim to everyone's satisfaction. On account of the agreeableness of its smell it has no claims at all. For one person is enraptured by this smell, while another's head is dizzied by it. Now what should one infer from this except that the beauty must be held to be a property of the flower itself, which does not correspond to the difference of heads and so many senses, but to which instead the latter must correspond if they would judge it? And yet this is not how it is. For the judgment of taste consists precisely in the fact that it calls a thing beautiful only in accordance with that quality in it by means of which it corresponds with our way of receiving it.

---

[a] *Beurtheilung*
[b] The phrase "of one" (*eines Jeden*) was added in the second edition.

Moreover, it is required of every judgment that is supposed to prove the taste of the subject that the subject judge for himself, without having to grope about by means of experience among the judgments of others[a] and first inform himself about their satisfaction or dissatisfaction in the same object, and thus that he should pronounce his judgment not as imitation, because a thing really does please universally, but *a priori*.[2] One would think, however, that an *a priori* judgment must contain a concept of the object, for the cognition of which it contains the principle; the judgment of taste, however, is not grounded on concepts at all, and is above all not cognition, but only an aesthetic judgment.

Hence a young poet does not let himself be dissuaded from his conviction that his poem is beautiful by the judgment of the public nor that of his friends, and, if he does give them a hearing, this is not because he now judges[b] it differently, but rather because, even if (at least in his view) the entire public has a false taste, he nevertheless (even against his judgment) finds cause to accommodate himself to the common delusion in his desire for approval. Only later, when his power of judgment has been made more acute by practice, does he depart from his previous judgment of his own free will, just as he does with those of his judgments that rest entirely on reason. Taste makes claim merely[c] to autonomy. To make the judgments of others into the determining ground of one's own would be heteronomy.

That the works of the ancients are rightly praised as models, and their authors called classical, like a sort of nobility among writers, who give laws to the people through their precedence, seems to indicate *a posteriori* sources of taste and to contradict the autonomy of taste in every subject. But one could just as well say that the ancient mathematicians, who have been regarded until now as nearly indispensable models of the greatest thoroughness and elegance of the synthetic method, also demonstrate an imitative reason on our part and its incapacity to produce from its own resources strict proofs, with the greatest intuitive evidence,[d] by means of the construction of concepts. There is no use of our powers at all, however free it might be, and even of reason (which must draw all its judgments from the common source *a priori*), which, if every subject always had to begin entirely from the raw predisposition of his own nature, would not fall into mistaken attempts if others had not preceded him with their own, not

5: 283

---

[a] In the first edition, this clause could be translated as "to grope about . . . among others for their judgments."

[b] *beurtheilt*

[c] The word "merely" (*bloß*) was added in the second edition.

[d] *mit der größten Intuition*

in order to make their successors into mere imitators, but rather by means of their method[a] to put others on the right path for seeking out the principles in themselves and thus for following their own, often better, course. Even in religion, where, certainly, each must derive the rule of his conduct from himself, because he also remains responsible for it himself and cannot shift the guilt for his transgressions onto others, whether as teachers or as predecessors, general precepts, which one may either have acquired from priests or philosophers or drawn from oneself, never accomplish as much as an example of virtue or holiness, which, established in history, does not make the autonomy of virtue out of one's own original idea of morality (*a priori*) dispensable or transform this into a mechanism of imitation.[3] **Succession**, related to a precedent, not imitation, is the correct expression for any influence that the products of an exemplary author[b] can have on others, which means no more than to create from the same sources from which the latter created, and to learn from one's predecessor[c] only the manner of conducting oneself in so doing. But among all the faculties and talents, taste is precisely the one which, because its judgment is not determinable by means of concepts and precepts, is most in need of the examples of what in the progress of culture has longest enjoyed approval if it is not quickly to fall back into barbarism and sink back into the crudity of its first attempts.

§ 33.
Second peculiarity of the judgment of taste.

The judgment of taste is not determinable by grounds of proof at all, just as if it were merely **subjective.**

If someone does not find a building, a view, or a poem beautiful, then, **first**, he does not allow approval to be internally imposed upon himself by a hundred voices who all praise it highly. He may of course behave[d] as if it pleased him as well, in order not to be regarded as lacking in taste; he can even begin to doubt whether he has adequately formed his taste by acquaintance with a sufficient number of objects of a certain kind (just as one who believes himself to recognize something in the distance as a forest, which everyone else regards as a town, doubts the judgment of his own eyes). But what he does see clearly is this: that the approval of others provides no valid proof for the judging

[a] *Verfahren*
[b] *Urhebers*
[c] In the first edition, "predecessors."
[d] In the second edition, *stellen*; in the first edition, *anstellen*.

of beauty,[a] that others may perhaps see and observe for him, and that what many have seen in one way what he believes himself to have seen otherwise, may serve him as a sufficient ground of proof for a theoretical, hence a logical judgment, but that what has pleased others can never serve as the ground of an aesthetic judgment. The judgment of others, when it is unfavorable to our own, can of course rightly give us reservations about our own, but can never convince us of its incorrectness. Thus there is no empirical **ground of proof** for forcing the judgment on anyone.

Second, an *a priori* proof in accordance with determinate rules can determine the judgment on beauty even less.[4] If someone reads me his poem or takes me to a play that in the end fails to please my taste, then he can adduce **Batteux**[5] or **Lessing**,[6] or even older and more famous critics of taste, and adduce all the rules they established as proofs that his poem is beautiful; certain passages, which are the very ones that displease me, may even agree with rules of beauty (as they have been given there and have been universally recognized): I will stop my ears, listen to no reasons and arguments, and would rather believe that those rules of the critics are false or at least that this is not a case for their application than allow that my judgment should be determined by means of *a priori* grounds of proof, since it is supposed to be a judgment of taste and not of the understanding or of reason.[7]

It seems that this is one of the chief causes on account of which this faculty of aesthetic judging[b] has been given the very name of "taste." For someone may list all the ingredients of a dish for me, and remark about each one that it is otherwise agreeable to me, and moreover even rightly praise the healthiness of this food; yet I am deaf to all these grounds, I try the dish with **my** tongue and my palate, and on that basis (not on the basis of general principles) do I make my judgment.

In fact, the judgment of taste is always made as a singular judgment about the object. The understanding can make a universal judgment by comparing how satisfying the object is with the judgments of others, e.g., all tulips are beautiful; but in that case that is not a judgment of taste, but a logical judgment, which makes the relation of an object to taste into a predicate of things of a certain sort in general; but that by means of which I find a single given tulip beautiful, i.e., find my satisfaction in it universally valid, is the judgment of taste alone. Its peculiarity, however, consists in this: that although it has merely subjective validity, it nevertheless makes a claim on **all** subjects of a kind

5: 285

---

[a] In the second edition, *Beurtheilung der Schönheit*; in the first edition, *Schönheits-Beurtheilung*.
[b] *ästhetische Beurtheilungsvermögen*

that could only be made if it were an objective judgment resting on cognitive grounds and capable of being compelled by means of a proof.

§ 34.
No objective principle of taste
is possible.

By a principle of taste would be understood a fundamental proposition*a* under the condition of which one could subsume the concept of an object and then by means of an inference conclude that it is beautiful. But that is absolutely impossible.[8] For I must be sensitive of the pleasure immediately in the representation of it, and I cannot be talked into it by means of any proofs.*b* Thus although critics, as Hume says, can reason more plausibly than cooks, they still suffer the same fate as them.[9] They cannot expect a determining ground for their judgment from proofs, but only from the reflection of the subject on his own state (of pleasure or displeasure), rejecting all precepts and rules.

5: 286

However, what critics nonetheless can and should reason about, in a way that is useful for correcting and broadening our judgments of taste, is this: not the exposition of the determining ground of this sort of aesthetic judgments in a universally usable formula, which is impossible, but the investigation of the faculties of cognition and their functions in these judgments and laying out in examples the reciprocal subjective purposiveness, about which it has been shown above that its form in a given representation is the beauty of its object. Thus the critique of taste itself is only subjective, with regard to the representation by means of which an object is given to us: that is, it is the art or science of bringing under rules the reciprocal relation of the understanding and the imagination to each other in the given representation (without relation to an antecedent sensation or concept), and consequently their concord or discord, and of determining it with regard to its conditions. It is **art** if it shows this only in examples; it is **science** if it derives the possibility of such a judging*c* from the nature of this faculty as a faculty of cognition in general. It is with the latter, as transcendental critique, that we are here alone concerned. It should develop and justify the subjective principle of taste as an *a priori* principle of the power of judgment. Criticism,*d* as an art, merely seeks to apply the physiological (here psychological) and hence em-

a *Grundsatz*
b *Beweisgründe*
c *Beurtheilung*
d *Die Critik*

pirical rules, according to which taste actually proceeds to the judging[a] of its objects (without reflecting on its possibility), and criticizes the products of fine art just as the **former** criticizes the faculty of judging[b] them itself.

§ 35.
The principle of taste is the subjective principle of the power of judgment in general.

The judgment of taste differs from logical judgment in that the latter subsumes a representation under concepts of the object, but the former does not subsume under a concept at all, for otherwise the necessary universal approval could be compelled by proofs. All the same, however, it is similar to the latter in that it professes a universality and necessity, though not in accordance with concepts of the object, and hence a merely subjective one. Now since the concepts in a judgment constitute its content (that which pertains to the cognition of the object), but the judgment of taste is not determinable by means of concepts, it is grounded only on the subjective formal condition of a judgment in general. The subjective condition of all judgments is the faculty for judging[c] itself, or the power of judgment. This, employed with regard to a representation by means of which an object is given, requires the agreement of two powers of representation: namely, the imagination (for the intuition and the composition of the manifold of intuition), and the understanding (for the concept as representation of the unity of this composition). Now since no concept of the object is here the ground of the judgment, it can consist only in the subsumption of the imagination itself (in the case of a representation by means of which an object is given) under the condition that the understanding in general advance from intuitions to concepts. I.e., since the freedom of the imagination consists precisely in the fact that it schematizes without a concept, the judgment of taste must rest on a mere sensation of the reciprocally animating imagination in its **freedom** and the understanding with its **lawfulness**, thus on a feeling that allows the object to be judged[d] in accordance with the purposiveness of the representation (by means of which an object is given) for the promotion of the faculty of cognition in its free play; and taste, as a subjective power of judgment, contains a principle of subsumption, not of intui-

5: 287

---

[a] *Beurtheilung*
[b] *Beurtheilung*
[c] *beurtheilen*
[d] *beurtheilen läßt*

tions under **concepts**, but of the **faculty** of intuitions or presentations (i.e., of the imagination) under the **faculty** of concepts (i.e., the understanding), insofar as the former **in its freedom** is in harmony with the latter **in its lawfulness.**

Now in order to discover this justifying ground through a deduction of judgments of taste, only the formal peculiarities of this kind of judgments, that is, only insofar as it is merely their logical form that is considered, can serve as our guideline.

§ 36.
On the problem for a deduction of
judgments of taste.

The perception of an object can be immediately combined with the concept of an object in general, for which the former contains the empirical predicates, for a judgment of cognition, and a judgment of experience can thereby be produced. Now this is grounded in *a priori* concepts of the synthetic unity of the manifold, in order to think it as the determination of an object; and these concepts (the categories) require a deduction, which, moreover, was given in the *Critique of Pure Reason*, by means of which the solution to the problem "How are synthetic *a priori* judgments of cognition possible?" was provided.[10] This problem thus concerned the *a priori* principles of pure understanding and its theoretical judgments.

However, a perception can also be immediately combined with a feeling of pleasure (or displeasure) and a satisfaction that accompanies the representation of the object and serves it instead of a predicate, and an aesthetic judgment, which is not a cognitive judgment, can thus arise. Such a judgment, if it is not a mere judgment of sensation but a formal judgment of reflection, which requires this satisfaction of everyone as necessary, must be grounded in something as an *a priori* principle, even if only a merely subjective principle (if an objective principle for this kind of judgment would be impossible), but which, as such a principle, also requires a deduction, by means of which it may be comprehended how an aesthetic judgment could lay claim to necessity. This is the basis of the problem with which we are now concerned: How are judgments of taste possible? This problem thus concerns the *a priori* principles of the pure power of judgment in **aesthetic** judgments, i.e., in those where it does not (as in theoretical judgments) merely have to subsume under objective concepts of the understanding and stands under a law, but where it is itself, subjectively, both object as well as law.

This problem can also be represented thus: How is a judgment possible which, merely from **one's own** feeling of pleasure in an object,

5: 288

independent of its concept, judges[a] this pleasure, as attached to the representation of the same object **in every other subject**, *a priori*, i.e., without having to wait for the assent of others?

That judgments of taste are synthetic is readily seen, because they go beyond the concept and even the intuition of the object, and add to that as a predicate something that is not even cognition at all, namely the feeling of pleasure (or displeasure). However, that such judgments, even though the predicate (of **one's own** pleasure that is combined with the representation) is empirical, are nevertheless, as far as the requisite assent **of everyone** is concerned, *a priori* judgments, or would be taken as such, is already implicit in the expressions of their claim; and thus this problem of the critique of the power of judgment belongs under the general problem of transcendental philosophy: How are synthetic *a priori* judgments possible?

5: 289

§ 37.
What is really asserted *a priori* of an object in a judgment of taste?

That the representation of an object is immediately combined with a pleasure can be perceived only internally, and would, if one wanted to indicate nothing more than this, yield a merely empirical judgment. For I cannot combine a determinate feeling (of pleasure or displeasure) *a priori* with any representation, except where my ground is an *a priori* principle of reason determining the will; for then the pleasure (in the moral feeling) is the consequence of it, but precisely on that account it cannot be compared with the pleasure in taste at all, since it requires a determinate concept of a law, while the judgment of taste, by contrast, is to be combined immediately with the mere judging,[b] prior to any concept. Hence all judgments of taste are also singular judgments, since they combine their predicate of satisfaction not with a concept but with a given singular empirical representation.

Thus it is not the pleasure but **the universal validity of this pleasure** perceived in the mind as connected with the mere judging[c] of an object that is represented in a judgment of taste as a universal rule for the power of judgment, valid for everyone. It is an empirical judgment that I perceive and judge[d] an object with pleasure. But it is an *a priori* judgment that I find it beautiful, i.e., that I may require that satisfaction of everyone as necessary.[11]

---

[a] *beurtheilte*
[b] *Beurtheilung*
[c] *Beurtheilung*
[d] *beurtheile*

§ 38.
Deduction of judgments of taste.

If it is admitted that in a pure judgment of taste the satisfaction in the object is combined with the mere judging*ᵃ* of its form, then it is nothing other than the subjective purposiveness of that form for the power of judgment that we sense as combined with the representation of the object in the mind. Now since the power of judgment in regard to the formal rules of judging,*ᵇ* without any matter (neither sensation*ᶜ* nor concept), can be directed only to the subjective conditions of the use of the power of judgment in general (which is restricted*ᵈ* neither to the particular kind of sense nor to a particular concept of understanding), and thus to that subjective element that one can presuppose in all human beings (as requisite for possible cognitions in general), the correspondence of a representation with these conditions of the power of judgment must be able to be assumed to be valid for everyone *a priori*. I.e., the pleasure or subjective purposiveness of the representation for the relation of the cognitive faculties in the judging*ᵉ* of a sensible object in general can rightly be expected of everyone.*

5: 290

Remark

This deduction is so easy because it is not necessary for it to justify any objective reality of a concept; for beauty is not a concept of the object, and the judgment of taste is not a judgment of cognition. It asserts only that we are

5: 290   * In order to be justified in laying claim to universal assent for judgments of the aesthetic power of judgment resting merely on subjective grounds, it is sufficient to admit: 1) In all human beings, the subjective conditions of this faculty, as far as the relation of the cognitive powers therein set into action to a cognition in general is concerned, are the same, which must be true, since otherwise human beings could not communicate their representations and even cognition itself. 2) The judgment has taken into consideration solely this relation (hence the **formal condition** of the power of judgment), and is pure, i.e., mixed with neither concepts of the object nor with sensations as determining grounds. If an error is made with regard to the latter, that concerns only the incorrect application to a particular case of the authority that a law gives us, by which the authority in general is not suspended.

    ᵃ *Beurtheilung*
    ᵇ *Beurtheilung*
    ᶜ *Sinnenempfindung*
    ᵈ Here we follow the first edition, which has *eingeschränkt*, rather than the second, which prints *eingerichtet* (arranged for or equipped for).
    ᵉ *Beurtheilung*

justified in presupposing universally in every human being the same subjective conditions of the power of judgment that we find in ourselves; and then only if we have correctly subsumed the given object under these conditions.[a] Now although this latter has unavoidable difficulties that do not pertain to the logical power of judgment (because in the latter one subsumes under concepts, but in the aesthetic power of judgment one subsumes under a relation that is merely a matter of sensation, that of the imagination and the understanding reciprocally attuned to each other in the represented form of the object, where the subsumption can easily be deceptive);[b] yet nothing is thereby taken away from the legitimacy of the claim of the power of judgment in counting on universal assent, which only comes down to this: the correctness of the principle for validly judging for everyone on subjective grounds. For as far as the difficulty and the doubt about the correctness of the subsumption under that principle is concerned, it makes the legitimacy of the claim to this validity of an aesthetic judgment in general, and thus the principle itself, no more doubtful than the equally (although not as often and as easily) erroneous subsumption of the logical power of judgment under its principle can make the latter, which is objective, doubtful. But if the question were to be "How is it possible[c] to assume nature as a sum of objects of taste *a priori*?," then this problem is related to teleology, because producing forms that are purposive for our power of judgment would have to be regarded as an end of nature that pertains to its concept essentially. But the correctness of this assumption is still very dubious, whereas the reality of the beauties of nature is open[d] to experience.

5: 291

§ 39.
On the communicability of a sensation.

If sensation, as the real in perception, is related to cognition, it is called sensory sensation;[e] and its specific quality can be represented as completely communicable in the same way only if one assumes that everyone has a sense that is the same as our own – but this absolutely cannot be presupposed in the case of a sensory sensation. Thus, to someone who lacks the sense of smell, this kind of sensation cannot be communicated; and, even if he does not lack this sense, one still cannot be sure that he has exactly the same sensation from a flower that we have from it. Still more, however, we must represent people as differing with regard to the **agreeableness** or **disagreeableness** of the sensation of one and the same object of the sensations; and it is absolutely not to be demanded that pleasure in the same objects be conceded to every-

---

[a] In the first edition, there was a comma instead of a period here, and the sentence continued "which has unavoidable . . ."
[b] In the first edition, this clause was not enclosed in parentheses.
[c] The first edition here includes the word *auch* (also), omitted from the second.
[d] The first edition has *bloß* (merely) instead of *offen*.
[e] *Sinnenempfindung*

5: 292 one. Pleasure of this kind, since it comes into the mind through the senses and we are therefore passive with regard to it, can be called the pleasure of **enjoyment.**

The satisfaction in an action on account of its moral quality is by contrast not a pleasure of enjoyment, but of self-activity and of its appropriateness to the idea of its vocation. This feeling, however, which is called moral, requires concepts; and does not exhibit a free, but rather a lawful purposiveness, and therefore also cannot be universally communicated other than by means of reason, and, if the pleasure is to be of the same kind in everyone, by means of very determinate practical concepts of reason.

The pleasure in the sublime in nature, as a pleasure of contemplation involving subtle reasoning,*a* also lays claim to universal participation, yet already presupposes another feeling, namely that of its supersensible vocation, which, no matter how obscure it might be, has a moral foundation.*b* But that other human beings will take regard of it and find a satisfaction in the consideration of the brute magnitude of nature (which cannot be truthfully ascribed to the sight of it, which is rather terrifying) is not something that I am justified in simply presupposing. Nevertheless, in consideration of what should be taken account of in those moral predispositions on every appropriate occasion, I can still require even that satisfaction of everyone, but only by means of the moral law, which for its part is in turn grounded on concepts of reason.

By contrast, the pleasure in the beautiful is neither a pleasure of enjoyment, nor of a lawful activity, and not even of a contemplation involving subtle reasoning in accordance with ideas, but of mere reflection.*c* Without having any purpose or fundamental principle for a guide, this pleasure accompanies the common apprehension of an object by the imagination, as a faculty of intuition, in relation to the understanding, as a faculty of concepts, by means of a procedure of the power of judgment, which it must also exercise for the sake of the most common experience: only in the latter case it is compelled*d* to do so for the sake of an empirical objective concept, while in the former case (in the aesthetic judging)*e* it is merely for the sake of perceiving the suitability of the representation for the harmonious (subjectively purposive) occupation of both cognitive faculties in their freedom, i.e., to sense the representational state with pleasure. This pleasure must nec-

---

a *vernünftelnde Contemplation*
b In the first edition, there is a comma rather than a period here.
c In the first edition, there is a comma and the word *und* (and) rather than a period here.
d The word *genötigt* (compelled or necessitated) was added in the second edition.
e *Beurtheilung*

172

essarily rest on the same conditions in everyone, since they are subjective conditions of the possibility of a cognition in general, and the proportion of these cognitive faculties that is required for taste is also requisite for the common and healthy understanding that one may presuppose in everyone. For this very reason, one who judges with taste (as long as he does not err in this consciousness, and does not take the matter for the form, the charm for beauty) may also require the subjective purposiveness, i.e., his satisfaction in the object, of everyone else, and may assume his feeling to be universally communicable, even without the mediation of concepts.

§ 40.
On taste as a kind of *sensus communis*.[12]

The power of judgment, when what is noticed is not so much its reflection as merely the result of that, is often called a sense, and there is talk of a sense of truth, a sense for propriety, for justice, etc., although one surely knows, or at least properly ought to know, that these concepts cannot have their seat in a sense, and that even less could such a sense have the slightest capacity for the expression of universal rules, but rather that a representation of truth, suitability, beauty, or justice could never enter our thoughts if we could not elevate ourselves above the senses to higher cognitive faculties. **The common human understanding**, which, as merely healthy (not yet cultivated) understanding, is regarded as the least that can be expected from anyone who lays claim to the name of a human being, thus has the unfortunate honor of being endowed with the name of common sense (*sensus communis*), and indeed[a] in such a way that what is understood by the word **common** (not merely in our language, which here really contains an ambiguity, but in many others as well) comes to the same as the *vulgar*,[b] which is encountered everywhere, to possess which is certainly not an advantage or an honor.

By "*sensus **communis**,*"[c] however, must be understood the idea of a **communal** sense, i.e., a faculty for judging[d] that in its reflection takes account (*a priori*) of everyone else's way of representing in thought, in order **as it were** to hold its judgment up to human reason as a whole and thereby avoid the illusion which, from subjective private conditions that could easily be held to be objective, would have a detrimental

---

[a] "Indeed" (*zwar*) added in the second edition.
[b] Kant prints the Latin word *vulgare*.
[c] Kant prints the first word in roman type and the second in italics, presumably meaning to add emphasis to the word "*communis*."
[d] *Beurtheilungsvermögen*

5: 294

influence on the judgment. Now this happens by one holding his judgment up not so much to the actual as to the merely possible judgments of others, and putting himself into the position of everyone else, merely by abstracting from the limitations that contingently attach to our own judging;[a] which is in turn accomplished by leaving out as far as is possible everything in one's[b] representational state that is matter, i.e., sensation, and attending solely to the formal peculiarities of his representation or his representational state. Now perhaps this operation of reflection seems much too artificial to be attributed to the faculty that we call the **common** sense; but it only appears thus if we express it in abstract formulas; in itself, nothing is more natural than to abstract from charm and emotion if one is seeking a judgment that is to serve as a universal rule.

The following maxims of the common human understanding do not belong here, to be sure, as parts of the critique of taste, but can nevertheless serve to elucidate its fundamental principles. They are the following: 1. To think for oneself; 2. To think in the position of everyone else; 3. Always to think in accord with oneself.[13] The first is the maxim of the **unprejudiced** way of thinking, the second of the **broad-minded** way, the third that of the **consistent** way. The first is the maxim of a reason that is never **passive**. The tendency toward the latter, hence toward heteronomy of reason, is called **prejudice**; and the greatest prejudice of all is that of representing reason as if it were not subject to the rules of nature on which the understanding grounds it by means of its own essential law:[c] i.e., **superstition.** Liberation from superstition is called **enlightenment,*** since, although this designation is also applied to liberation from prejudices in general, it is

5: 294

* One readily sees that while enlightenment is easy *in thesi, in hypothesi* it is a difficult matter that can only be accomplished slowly; for while not being passive with his reason but always being legislative for himself is something that is very easy for the person who would only be adequate to his essential end and does not demand to know that which is beyond his understanding, nevertheless, since striving for the latter is hardly to be forbidden and there will never be lacking many who confidently promise to be able to satisfy this desire for knowledge, it must be very difficult to maintain or establish the merely negative element (which constitutes genuine enlightenment) in the manner of thinking (especially in that of the public).

[a] *Beurtheilung*
[b] In the first edition, "in our" (*in unserm*).
[c] Following the second edition; the first edition has *unter welchen das größte, die Natur sich Regeln, die der Verstand ihr durch . . . zum Grunde liegt,* which would imply that it is nature rather than reason which in the case of prejudice fails to be subjected to the essential law of understanding.

superstition above all (*in sensu eminenti*) that deserves to be called a prejudice, since the blindness to which superstition leads, which indeed it even demands as an obligation, is what makes most evident the need to be led by others, hence the condition of a passive reason.[14] As far as the second maxim of the way of thinking is concerned, we are accustomed to calling someone limited (**narrow-minded**, in contrast to **broad-minded**) whose talents do not suffice for any great employment (especially if it is intensive). But the issue here is not the faculty of cognition, but the **way of thinking** needed to make a purposive use of it, which, however small the scope and degree of a person's natural endowment may be, nevertheless reveals a man of a **broad-minded way of thinking** if he sets himself apart from the subjective private conditions of the judgment, within which so many others are as if bracketed, and reflects on his own judgment from a **universal standpoint** (which he can only determine by putting himself into the standpoint of others). The third maxim, namely that of the **consistent** way of thinking, is the most difficult to achieve, and can only by achieved through the combination of the first two and after frequent observance of them has made them automatic. One can say that the first of these maxims is that maxim of the understanding, the second that of the power of judgment, the third that of reason. –

5: 295

I take up again the thread that has been laid aside through this digression, and say that taste can be called *sensus communis* with greater justice than can the healthy understanding, and that the aesthetic power of judgment rather than the intellectual can bear the name of a communal sense,* if indeed one would use the word "sense" of an effect of mere reflection on the mind: for there one means by "sense" the feeling of pleasure. One could even define taste as the faculty for judging[a] that which makes our feeling in a given representation **universally communicable** without the mediation of a concept.

The aptitude of human beings for communicating their thoughts also requires a relation between the imagination and the understanding in order to associate intuitions with concepts and concepts in turn with intuitions, which flow together into a cognition; but in that case the agreement of the two powers of the mind is **lawful**, under the constraint of determinate concepts. Only where the imagination in its freedom arouses the understanding, and the latter, without concepts, sets the imagination into a regular[b] play is the representation commu-

5: 296

---

* One could designate taste as *sensus communis aestheticus*, common human understanding as *sensus communis logicus*.

5: 295

[a] *Beurtheilungsvermögen*
[b] *regelmäßiges*

nicated, not as a thought, but as the inner feeling of a purposive state of mind.

Taste is thus the faculty for judging[a] *a priori* the communicability of the feelings that are combined with a given representation (without the mediation of a concept).

If one could assume that the mere universal communicability of his feeling must in itself already involve an interest for us (which, however, one is not justified in inferring from the constitution of a merely reflective power of judgment), then one would be able to explain how it is that the feeling in the judgment of taste is expected of everyone as if it were a duty.[15]

§ 41.
On the empirical interest in the beautiful.[16]

That the judgment of taste, by which something is declared to be beautiful, must have no interest **for its determining ground** has been adequately demonstrated above. But from that it does not follow that after it has been given as a pure aesthetic judgment no interest can be combined with it. This combination, however, can always be only indirect, i.e., taste must first of all be represented as combined with something else in order to be able to connect with the satisfaction of mere reflection on an object a further **pleasure in** its **existence** (as that in which all interest consists). For what is said of cognitive judgments (of things in general) also holds here in the aesthetic judgment: *a posse ad esse non valet consequentia.*[b] Now this other element can be something empirical, namely, an inclination that is characteristic of human nature, or something intellectual, as a property of the will of being determinable *a priori* through reason; both of which contain a satisfaction in the existence of an object, and can thus provide the ground for an interest in that which has already pleased for itself and without respect to any sort of interest.[17]

The beautiful interests empirically only in **society**; and if the drive to society is admitted to be natural to human beings, while the suit-

5: 297

ability and the tendency toward it, i.e., **sociability**, are admitted to be necessary for human beings as creatures destined for society, and thus as a property belonging to **humanity**, then it cannot fail that taste should also be regarded as a faculty for judging[c] everything by means of which one can communicate even his **feeling** to everyone else, and

---

[a] *zu beurtheilen*
[b] There is no valid inference from possibility to actuality.
[c] *Beurtheilungsvermögen*

hence as a means for promoting what is demanded by an inclination natural to everyone.

For himself alone a human being abandoned on a desert island would not adorn either his hut or himself, nor seek out or still less plant flowers in order to decorate himself;[18] rather, only in society does it occur to him to be not merely a human being but also, in his own way, a refined human being (the beginning of civilization): for this is how we judge[a] someone who is inclined to communicate his pleasure to others and is skilled at it, and who is not content with an object if he cannot feel his satisfaction in it in community with others. Further, each expects and requires of everyone else a regard to universal communication, as if from an original contract dictated by humanity itself; and thus, at first to be sure only charms, e.g., colors for painting oneself (roucou among the Caribs and cinnabar among the Iroquois),[19] or flowers, mussel shells, beautifully colored birds' feathers, but with time also beautiful forms (as on canoes, clothes, etc.) that do not in themselves provide any gratification, i.e., satisfaction of enjoyment, become important in society and combined with great interest, until finally civilization that has reached the highest point makes of this almost the chief work of refined inclination, and sensations have value only to the extent that they may be universally communicated; at that point, even though the pleasure that each has in such an object is merely inconsiderable and has in itself no noticeable interest, nevertheless the idea of its universal communicability almost infinitely increases its value.

However, this interest, attached to the beautiful indirectly, through an inclination to society, and thus empirical, is of no importance for us here, for we must find that importance only in what may be related to the judgment of taste *a priori*, even if only indirectly. For even if in this latter form an interest combined with it should be revealed, then taste would reveal in our faculty for judging[b] a transition from sensory enjoyment to moral feeling; and not only would one thereby be better guided in the purposive employment of taste, but also a mediating link in the chain of human faculties *a priori*, on which all legislation must depend, would thereby be exhibited as such. This much can certainly be said about the empirical interest in objects of taste and in taste itself, namely, that since the latter indulges inclination, although this may be ever so refined, it also gladly allows itself to blend in with all the inclinations and passions that achieve their greatest variety and highest level in society, and the interest in the beautiful, if it is grounded on this, could afford only a very ambiguous transition from the agreeable

5: 298

---

[a] *beurtheilt*
[b] *Beurtheilungsvermögen*

to the good.[a] But whether the latter could not perhaps be promoted by taste, if it is taken in its purity, we have cause to investigate.

§ 42.
On the intellectual interest in the beautiful.

It has been with a good intention that those who would gladly direct all of the occupations of human beings to which these are driven by their inner natural predisposition to the ultimate end of humanity, namely the morally good, have taken it as a sign of a good moral character to take an interest in the beautiful in general. But they have been contradicted by others, not without ground, who have appealed to the experience that virtuosi of taste, who are not only often but even usually vain, obstinate, and given to corrupting passions, could perhaps even less than others lay claim to the merit of devotion to moral principles; and so it appears that the feeling for the beautiful is not only specifically different from the moral feeling (as it actually is), but also that the interest that can be combined with it can be united with the moral interest with difficulty, and by no means through an inner affinity.

Now I gladly concede that the interest in the **beautiful in art** (as part of which I also count the artful use of the beauties of nature for decoration, and thus for vanity) provides no proof of a way of thinking that is devoted to the morally good or even merely inclined to it.[b] By contrast, however, I do assert that to take an **immediate interest** in the beauty of **nature** (not merely to have taste in order to judge[c] it) is always a mark of a good soul, and that if[d] this interest is habitual, it at least indicates a disposition of the mind that is favorable to the moral feeling, if it is gladly combined with the **viewing of nature.** It must be remembered, however, that I mean here strictly the beautiful **forms** of nature, and by contrast set to one side the **charms** that it usually combines so abundantly with them, since the interest in them is to be sure also immediate, but nevertheless empirical.

Someone who alone (and without any intention of wanting to communicate his observations to others) considers the beautiful shape of a wildflower, a bird, an insect, etc., in order to marvel at it, to love it, and to be unwilling for it to be entirely absent from nature, even though some harm might come to him from it rather than there being

---

[a] In the first edition, there was a comma rather than a period here, and the next sentence was a dependent clause introduced with a "which."
[b] In the first edition, there was a comma rather than a period here.
[c] *beurtheilen*
[d] The first edition says simply "if" instead of "and that if."

any prospect of advantage to him from it, takes an immediate and certainly intellectual interest in the beauty of nature. I.e., not only the form of its product but also its existence pleases him, even though no sensory charm has a part in this and he does not combine any sort of end with it.

However, it is worth noting here that if someone had secretly deceived this lover of the beautiful and had planted artificial flowers (which can be manufactured to look entirely similar to natural ones) or had placed artfully carved birds on the twigs of trees, and he then discovered the deception, the immediate interest that he had previously taken in it would immediately disappear, though perhaps another, namely the interest of vanity in decorating his room with them for the eyes of others, would take its place. The thought that nature has produced that beauty must accompany the intuition and reflection, and on this alone is grounded the immediate interest that one takes in it.[a] Otherwise there remains either a mere judgment of taste without any interest, or only one combined with a mediate interest, namely one related to society:[b] which latter affords no sure indications of a morally good way of thinking.

This preeminence of the beauty of nature over the beauty of art in alone awakening an immediate interest,[c] even if the former were to be surpassed by the latter in respect of form, is in agreement with the refined and well-founded thinking of all human beings who have cultivated their moral feeling. If a man who has enough taste to judge about products of beautiful art[d] with the greatest correctness and refinement gladly leaves the room in which are to be found those beauties that sustain vanity and at best social joys and turns to the beautiful in nature, in order as it were to find here an ecstasy for his spirit in a line of thought that he can never fully develop, then we would consider this choice of his with esteem and presuppose in him a beautiful soul, to which no connoisseur and lover of art can lay claim on account of the interest that he takes in his objects. – Now what is the distinction between such different assessments of two sorts of objects, which in the mere judgment of taste would scarcely compete for preeminence over each other?

5: 300

---

[a] In the first edition, this period was a comma.
[b] In the first edition, this colon was a period.
[c] In the first edition, "in that in the former alone an interest is taken."
[d] *Produkte der schönen Kunst*. In the eighteenth century, the German phrases *schöne Kunst* and *schöne Künste* were used like the English phrases "fine art" and "fine arts," and could easily be translated that way here. But since there are passages, such as the first paragraph of § 44, where this would require us to translate *schön* two different ways, we will use the literal rather than more idiomatic translation.

We have a faculty of merely aesthetic judgment,[a] for judging of forms without concepts and for finding a satisfaction in the mere judging[b] of them which we at the same time make into a rule for everyone without this judgment being grounded on an interest or producing one. – Alternatively, we also have a faculty of intellectual judgment,[c] for determining *a priori* for mere forms of practical maxims (insofar as they qualify in themselves for universal legislation) a satisfaction which we make into a law for everyone without our judgment being grounded on any interest, **although it produces one.** The pleasure or displeasure in the first judgment is called that of taste, in the second that of moral feeling.

But since it also interests reason that the ideas (for which it produces an immediate interest in the moral feeling) also have objective reality, i.e., that nature should at least show some trace or give a sign that it contains in itself some sort of ground for assuming a lawful correspondence of its products with our satisfaction that is independent of all interest (which we recognize *a priori* as a law valid for everyone, without being able to ground this on proofs), reason must take an interest in every manifestation in nature of a correspondence similar to this; consequently the mind cannot reflect on the beauty of **nature** without finding itself at the same time to be interested in it.[20] Because of this affinity, however, this interest is moral, and he who takes such an interest in the beautiful in nature can do so only insofar as he has already firmly established his interest in the morally good. We thus have cause at least to suspect a predisposition to a good moral disposition in one who is immediately interested in the beauty of nature.

It will be said that this explanation of aesthetic judgments in terms of their affinity with moral feeling looks much too studied to be taken as the true interpretation of the cipher by means of which nature figuratively speaks to us in its beautiful forms. But, first, this immediate interest in the beautiful in nature is not actually common, but belongs only to those whose thinking is either already trained to the good or especially receptive to such training; and then, even without clear, subtle, and deliberate reflection, the analogy between the pure judgment of taste, which, without depending on any sort of interest, allows a pleasure to be felt and at the same time to be represented *a priori* as proper for mankind in general, and the moral judgment, which does the same thing on the basis of concepts, leads to an equally immediate interest in the object of the former as in that of the latter – only the former is a free interest, the latter one grounded on objective laws. To

5: 301

---

[a] *Vermögen der bloß ästhetischen Urtheilskraft*
[b] *Beurtheilung*
[c] *Vermögen einer intellectuellen Urtheilskraft*

that is further added the admiration of nature, which in its beautiful products shows itself as art, not merely by chance, but as it were intentionally, in accordance with a lawful arrangement and as purposiveness without an end, which latter, since we never encounter it externally, we naturally seek within ourselves, and indeed in that which constitutes the ultimate end of our existence, namely the moral vocation (the question of the ground of possibility of such a purposiveness of nature, however, will first be investigated in the Teleology).[21]

That the satisfaction in beautiful art in the pure judgment of taste is not combined with an immediate interest in the same way as that in beautiful nature is also easy to explain. For the former is either such an imitation of the latter that it is deceptive, and in that case it has the effect of natural beauty (which it is taken to be); or else it is an art that is obviously intentionally directed toward our satisfaction, in which case the satisfaction in this product would, to be sure, occur immediately by means of taste, but would arouse[a] only a mediate interest in the cause on which it is grounded, namely an art that can interest only through its end and never in itself. One will perhaps say that this is also the case if an object of nature interests through its beauty only insofar as a moral idea is associated with it; but it is not this, but rather the quality inherent in it by means of which it qualifies for such an association, which thus pertains to it internally, that interests immediately.

5: 302

The charms in beautiful nature, which are so frequently encountered as it were melted together with the beautiful form, belong either to the modifications of the light (in the coloring) or of the sound (in tones). For these are the only sensations which permit not merely sensory feeling but also reflection on the form of these modifications of the senses, and thus as it were contain a language that nature brings to us and that seems to have a higher meaning.[b] Thus the white color of the lily seems to dispose the mind to ideas of innocence, and the seven colors, in their order from red to violet, to the ideas 1) of sublimity, 2) of audacity, 3) of candor, 4) of friendliness, 5) of modesty, 6) of steadfastness, and 7) of tenderness. The song of the bird proclaims joyfulness and contentment with its existence. At least this is how we interpret nature, whether anything of the sort is its intention or not. But this interest, which we here take in beauty, absolutely requires that it be the beauty of nature; and it disappears entirely as soon as one notices that one has been deceived and that it is only art, so much so that even taste can no longer find anything beautiful in it or sight anything charming. What is more highly extolled by poets than the

[a] The word "arouse" (*erwecken*) was added in the second edition.
[b] *Sinn*

bewitchingly beautiful song of the nightingale, in a lonely stand of bushes, on a still summer evening, under the gentle light of the moon? Yet there have been examples in which, where no such songbird was to be found, some jolly landlord has tricked the guests staying with him, to their complete satisfaction, by hiding in a bush a mischievous lad who knew how to imitate this song (with a reed or a pipe in his mouth) just like nature. But as soon as one becomes aware that it is a trick, no one would long endure listening to this song, previously taken to be so charming; and the same is true with every other songbird. It must be nature, or taken to be nature by us, for us to be able to take such an immediate **interest** in the beautiful, and even more so if we are to be at all able to expect of others that they should take this interest in it; which in fact happens, as we consider coarse and ignoble the thinking of those who have no **feeling** for beautiful nature (for this is what we call the receptivity to an interest in its contemplation), and who confine themselves to the enjoyment of mere sensory sensations at table or from the bottle.

5: 303

§ 43.
On art in general.[22]

1) **Art** is distinguished from **nature** as doing (*facere*) is from acting or producing[a] in general (*agere*), and the product or consequence of the former is distinguished as a **work** (*opus*) from the latter as an effect[b] (*effectus*).

By right, only production through freedom, i.e., through a capacity for choice that grounds its actions in reason, should be called art. For although people are fond of describing the product of the bees (the regularly constructed honeycombs) as a work of art, this is done only on account of the analogy with the latter; that is, as soon as we recall that they do not ground their work on any rational consideration of their own, we say that it is a product of their nature (of instinct), and as art it is ascribed only to their creator.

If someone searching through a moorland bog finds, as sometimes happens, a piece of carved wood, he does not say that it is a product of nature, but of art; the cause that produced it conceived of an end, which the wood has to thank for its form. In other cases too one sees an art in everything that is so constituted that a representation of it in its cause must have preceded its reality (as even in the case of bees), although it may not exactly have **thought of** the effect; but if something is called a work of art without qualification, in order to distin-

[a] *Wirken*
[b] *Wirkung*

guish it from an effect of nature, then by that is always understood a work of human beings.

2) **Art** as a skill of human beings is also distinguished from **science** (**to be able** from **to know**), as a practical faculty is distinguished from a theoretical one, as technique is distinguished from theory (as the art of surveying is distinguished from geometry).[23] And thus that which one **can** do as soon as one **knows** what should be done is not exactly called art. Only that which one does not immediately have the skill to do even if one knows it completely belongs to that extent to art. **Camper**[24] describes quite precisely how the best shoe must be made, but he certainly was not able to make one.*

5: 304

3) **Art** is also distinguished from **handicraft**: the first is called **liberal**,[a] the second can also be called **remunerative art**.[26] The first is regarded as if it could turn out purposively (be successful) only as play, i.e., an occupation that is agreeable in itself; the second is regarded as labor, i.e., an occupation that is disagreeable (burdensome) in itself and is attractive only because of its effect (e.g., the remuneration), and hence as something that can be compulsorily imposed. Judging[b] whether, in the hierarchy of the guilds, clockmakers should be counted as artists but smiths as craftsmen requires a different standpoint than the one adopted here, namely, the proportion of the talents on which the one or the other of these occupations must be grounded. Further, I will not here discuss whether among the so-called seven liberal[c] arts there may not have been included some that are to be counted among the sciences, and several others that are to be compared with crafts. But it is not inadvisable to recall that in all liberal arts there is nevertheless required something compulsory, or, as it is called, a **mechanism**, without which the **spirit**, which must be **free**[d] in the art and which alone animates the work, would have no body at all and would entirely evaporate (e.g., in the art of poetry, correctness and richness of diction as well as prosody and meter), since many modern teachers believe that they can best promote a liberal art if they remove all compulsion from it and transform it from labor into mere play.

---

* In my region, the common man, when confronted with a problem like that of Columbus and his egg, says **That is not an art, it is just a science.** I.e., if one **knows** it, then one **can** do it; and he says the same thing about all the putative arts of the conjuror. But he would never refuse to call those of the tightrope walker art.[25]

5: 304

[a] *freye*
[b] *Beurtheilung*
[c] *freyen*
[d] *frey*

§ 44.
On beautiful art.[a]

5: 305There is neither a science of the beautiful, only a critique, nor beautiful science, only beautiful art.[27] For if the former existed, then it would be determined in it scientifically, i.e., by means of proofs, whether something should be held to be beautiful or not; thus the judgment about beauty, if it belonged to a science, would not be a judgment of taste. As for the second, a science which, as such, is supposed to be beautiful, is absurd. For if in it, as a science, one were to ask for grounds and proofs, one would be sent packing with tasteful expressions (*bons mots*). – What has given rise to the customary expression **beautiful sciences**[28] is without doubt nothing but the fact that it has been quite rightly noticed that for beautiful art in its full perfection much science is required, such as, e.g., acquaintance with ancient languages, wide reading of those authors considered to be classical, history, acquaintance with antiquities, etc., and for that reason these historical sciences, because they constitute the necessary preparation and foundation for beautiful art, and also in part because acquaintance with the products of beautiful art (rhetoric and poetry) is even included within them, have because of a verbal confusion themselves been called beautiful sciences.

If art, adequate for the **cognition** of a possible object, merely performs the actions requisite to make it actual, it is **mechanical**; but if it has the feeling of pleasure as its immediate aim, then it is called **aesthetic** art. This is either **agreeable** or **beautiful** art. It is the former if its end is that pleasure accompany the representations as mere **sensations**, the latter, if its end is that it accompany these as **kinds of cognition**.

Agreeable arts are those which are aimed merely at enjoyment; of this kind are all those charms that can gratify the company at a table, such as telling entertaining stories, getting the company talking in an open and lively manner, creating by means of jokes and laughter a certain tone of merriment, in which, as is said, much can be chattered about and nobody will be held responsible for what he says, because it is only intended as momentary entertainment, not as some enduring material for later reflection or discussion. (Also included here is the way in which the table is set out for enjoyment, or even, at big parties, the table-music – an odd thing, which is supposed to sustain the mood

---

[a] *Von der schönen Kunst.* As noted in the previous section, an idiomatic translation of Kant's expression *schöne Künste* would be "fine arts," but in order to preserve the logic of his argument, as in the first sentence of the following paragraph, we have preferred a literal to an idiomatic translation.

of joyfulness merely as an agreeable noise, and to encourage the free conversation of one neighbor with another without anyone paying the least attention to its composition.) Also included here are all games   5: 306
that involve no interest beyond that of making time pass unnoticed.

Beautiful art, by contrast, is a kind of representation that is purposive in itself and, though without an end, nevertheless promotes the cultivation^a of the mental powers for sociable communication.[29]

The universal communicability of a pleasure already includes in its concept that this must not be a pleasure of enjoyment, from mere sensation, but one of reflection; and thus aesthetic art, as beautiful art, is one that has the reflecting power of judgment and not mere sensation^b as its standard.

§ 45.
Beautiful art is an art to the extent that it seems
at the same time to be nature.

In a product of art one must be aware that it is art, and not nature; yet the purposiveness in its form must still seem to be as free from all constraint by arbitrary rules as if it were a mere product of nature. On this feeling of freedom in the play of our cognitive powers, which must yet at the same time be purposive, rests that pleasure which is alone universally communicable though without being grounded on concepts. Nature was beautiful, if at the same time it looked like art; and art can only be called beautiful if we are aware that it is art and yet it looks to us like nature.[30]

For we can generally say, whether it is the beauty of nature or of art that is at issue: **that is beautiful which pleases in the mere judging**^c (neither in sensation nor through a concept). Now art always has a determinate intention of producing something. If however this were a mere sensation (something merely subjective) that is supposed to be accompanied with pleasure, then this product would please, in the judging,^d only by means of the feeling of sense. If the intention were aimed at the production of a determinate object, then, if it were achieved through art, the object would please only through concepts. But in either case the art would not please **in the mere judging**,^e i.e., it would not please as beautiful but as mechanical art.

Thus the purposiveness in the product of beautiful art, although it

^a *Cultur*
^b *Sinnenempfindung*
^c *Beurtheilung*
^d *Beurtheilung*
^e *Beurtheilung*

5: 307

is certainly intentional, must nevertheless not seem intentional; i.e., beautiful art must be **regarded** as nature, although of course one is aware of it as art. A product of art appears as nature, however, if we find it to agree **punctiliously** but not **painstakingly** with rules in accordance with which alone the product can become what it ought to be, that is, without the academic form showing through,[a] i.e., without showing any sign that the rule has hovered before the eyes of the artist and fettered his mental powers.

§ 46.
Beautiful art is art of genius.

Genius is the talent (natural gift) that gives the rule to art. Since the talent, as an inborn productive faculty of the artist, itself belongs to nature, this could also be expressed thus: **Genius** is the inborn predisposition of the mind (*ingenium*) **through which** nature gives the rule to art.[31]

Whatever the case may be with this definition, and whether it is merely arbitrary or is adequate to the concept which is usually associated with the word **genius** or not (which is to be discussed in the following sections), it can nevertheless already be proved at the outset that, according to the significance of the word assumed here, beautiful arts must necessarily be considered as arts of **genius**.

For every art presupposes rules which first lay the foundation by means of which a product that is to be called artistic is first represented as possible. The concept of beautiful art, however, does not allow the judgment concerning the beauty of its product to be derived from any sort of rule that has a **concept** for its determining ground, and thus has as its ground a concept of how it is possible.[b] Thus beautiful art cannot itself think up the rule in accordance with which it is to bring its product into being. Yet since without a preceding rule a product can never be called art, nature in the subject (and by means of the disposition of its faculties) must give the rule to art, i.e., beautiful art is possible only as a product of genius.

From this one sees: That genius 1) is a **talent** for producing that for which no determinate rule can be given, not a predisposition of skill for that which can be learned in accordance with some rule, consequently that **originality** must be its primary characteristic. 2) That since there can also be original nonsense, its products must at the same time be models, i.e., **exemplary**, hence, while not themselves the result

5: 308

---

[a] This clause was added in the second edition.

[b] In the first edition, "and thus does not have have as its foundation any concept of how it is possible."

of imitation, they must yet serve others in that way, i.e., as a standard or a rule for judging.[a] 3) That it cannot itself describe or indicate scientifically how it brings its product into being, but rather that it gives the rule as **nature**, and hence the author of a product that he owes to his genius does not know himself how the ideas for it come to him, and also does not have it in his power to think up such things at will or according to plan, and to communicate to others precepts that would put them in a position to produce similar products. (For that is also presumably how the word "genius" is derived from *genius*,[b] in the sense of the particular spirit given to a person at birth, which protects and guides him, and from whose inspiration those original ideas stem.) 4) That by means of genius nature does not prescribe the rule to science but to art, and even to the latter only insofar as it is to be beautiful art.

§ 47.
Elucidation and confirmation of the above explanation of genius.

Everyone agrees that genius is entirely opposed to the **spirit of imitation**.[32] Now since learning is nothing but imitation, even the greatest aptitude for learning, facility for learning (capacity) as such, still does not count as genius. But even if one thinks or writes[c] for himself, and does not merely take up what others have thought, indeed even if he invents a great deal for art and science, this is still not a proper reason for calling such a great **mind** (in contrast to someone who, because he can never do more than merely learn and imitate, is called a **blockhead**) a **genius**, since just this sort of thing **could** also have been learned, and thus still lies on the natural path of inquiry and reflection in accordance with rules, and is not specifically distinct from that which can be acquired with effort by means of imitation.[33] Thus everything that Newton expounded in his immortal work on the principles of natural philosophy,[34] no matter how great a mind it took to discover it, can still be learned; but one cannot learn to write inspired poetry, however exhaustive all the rules for the art of poetry and however excellent the models for it may be. The reason is that Newton could make all the steps that he had to take, from the first elements of geometry to his great and profound discoveries, entirely intuitive not only to himself but also to everyone else, and thus set them out for posterity quite determinately; but no Homer or Wieland[35] can indicate

5: 309

---

[a] *Beurtheilung*
[b] That is, the German word *Genie* is derived from the Latin word *genius*.
[c] *dichtet*

how his ideas, which are fantastic and yet at the same time rich in thought, arise and come together in his head, because he himself does not know it and thus cannot teach it to anyone else either. In the scientific sphere, therefore, the greatest discoverer differs only in degree from the most hard working imitator and apprentice, whereas he differs in kind from someone who is gifted by nature for beautiful art. This is not to belittle those great men, to whom the human race owes so much, in comparison to those favorites of nature with respect to their talent for beautiful art. In their very talent for ever advancing greater perfection of cognition and all the utility that depends on it, and likewise in the education of others for the acquisition of the same knowledge, lies the great advantage of such people over those who have the honor of being called geniuses: since for the latter art somewhere comes to a halt, because a limit is set for it beyond which it cannot go, which presumably has also long since been reached and cannot be extended any more; and moreover such a skill cannot be communicated, but is apportioned to each immediately from the hand of nature, and thus dies with him, until nature one day similarly endows another, who needs nothing more than an example in order to let the talent of which he is aware operate in a similar way.

Since the gift of nature must give the rule to art (as beautiful art), what sort of rule is this? It cannot be couched in a formula to serve as a precept, for then the judgment about the beautiful would be determinable in accordance with concepts; rather, the rule must be abstracted from the deed, i.e. from the product, against which others may test their own talent, letting it serve them as a model not for **copying**[a] but for **imitation**.[b,36] How this is possible is difficult to explain. The ideas of the artist arouse similar ideas in his apprentice if nature has equipped him with a similar proportion of mental powers. The models

5: 310

of beautiful art are thus the only means for transmitting these to posterity, which could not happen through mere descriptions (especially not in the field of the arts of discourse); and even in the latter case it is only those in old and dead languages, now preserved only as learned ones, that can become classical.[37]

Although mechanical and beautiful art, the first as a mere art of diligence and learning, the second as that of genius, are very different from each other, still there is no beautiful art in which something mechanical, which can be grasped and followed according to rules, and thus something **academically correct**, does not constitute the essential condition of the art.[38] For something in it must be thought of as an end, otherwise one cannot ascribe its product to any art at all; it would

[a] *Nachmachung*
[b] *Nachahmung*

be a mere product of chance. But in order to aim at an end in the work, determinate rules are required, from which one may not absolve oneself. Now since the originality of his talent constitutes one (but not the only) essential element of the character of the genius, superficial minds believe that they cannot show that they are blossoming geniuses any better than by pronouncing themselves free of the academic constraint of all rules, and they believe that one parades around better on a horse with the staggers than one that is properly trained. Genius can only provide rich **material** for products of art; its elaboration and **form** require a talent that has been academically trained, in order to make a use of it that can stand up to the power of judgment. But when someone speaks and decides like a genius even in matters of the most careful rational inquiry, then it is completely ridiculous; one does not rightly know whether one should laugh more at the charlatan who spreads about himself such a mist that one cannot judge[a] clearly but can indulge in imagination all the more, or at the public, which trustingly imagines that its incapacity to recognize clearly and grasp the masterpiece of insight comes from the fact that whole masses of new truths are being thrown at it, in contrast with which detail (achieved by careful explanations and the academically correct examination of fundamental principles) seems to be merely the work of amateurs.

§ 48.
On the relation of genius to
taste.

5: 311

For the **judging**[b] of beautiful objects, as such, **taste** is required; but for beautiful art itself, i.e., for **producing** such objects, **genius** is required.[39]

If genius is considered as a talent for beautiful art (which the proper meaning of the word implies), and with this in mind it is to be analyzed into the faculties that must come together to constitute such a talent, then it is necessary first to determine precisely the difference between the beauty of nature, the judging[c] of which requires only taste, and the beauty of art, the possibility of which (which must also be taken account of in the judging[d] of such an object) requires genius.

A beauty of nature is a **beautiful thing**; the beauty of art is a **beautiful representation** of a thing.[40]

---

[a] *beurtheilen*
[b] ***Beurtheilung***
[c] *Beurtheilung*
[d] *Beurtheilung*

In order to judge[a] a beauty of nature as such, I do not need first to have a concept of what sort of thing the object is supposed be, i.e., it is not necessary for me to know the material purposiveness (the end), but the mere form without knowledge of the end pleases for itself in the judging.[b] But if the object is given as a product of art, and is as such supposed to be declared to be beautiful, then, since art always presupposes an end in the cause (and its causality), a concept must first be the ground of what the thing is supposed to be, and, since the agreement of the manifold in a thing with its inner determination as an end is the perfection of the thing, in the judging of the beauty of art the perfection of the thing will also have to be taken into account, which is not even a question in the judging of a natural beauty (as such). – To be sure, in the judging especially of living objects in nature, e.g., a human being or a horse, objective purposiveness is also commonly taken into account for judging[c] its beauty; but in that case the judgment is also no longer purely aesthetic, i.e., a mere judgment of taste. Nature is no longer judged as it appears as art, but to the extent that it really **is** art (albeit superhuman); and the teleological judgment serves as the foundation for the aesthetic and as a condition of which the latter must take account. In such a case, if, e.g., it is said "That is a beautiful woman," then in fact one thinks nothing other than that in her figure nature represents the ends in the feminine physique beautifully, for it is necessary to look beyond the mere form to a concept with which the object is thought in such a way through a logically conditioned aesthetic judgment.

Beautiful art displays its excellence precisely by describing beautifully things that in nature would be ugly or displeasing. The furies, diseases, devastations of war, and the like can, as harmful things, be very beautifully described, indeed even represented in painting; only one kind of ugliness cannot be represented in a way adequate to nature without destroying all aesthetic satisfaction, hence beauty in art, namely, that which arouses **loathing.** For since in this strange sensation, resting on sheer imagination, the object is represented as if it were imposing the enjoyment which we are nevertheless forcibly resisting, the artistic representation of the object is no longer distinguished in our sensation itself from the nature of the object itself, and it then becomes impossible for the former to be taken as beautiful. The art of sculpture, since in its products art is almost confused with nature, has

---

[a] *beurtheilen*; except where noted, further forms of the verb "to judge" in this paragraph are translations of this verb.
[b] *Beurtheilung*; all occurrences of the noun "judging" throughout the rest of this paragraph translate this term.
[c] *urtheilen*

also excluded the representation of ugly objects from its images,[a] and thus permits, e.g., death (in a beautiful genius) or the spirit of war (in the person of Mars) to be represented through an allegory or attributes that look pleasing, hence only indirectly by means of an interpretation of reason, and not for the aesthetic power of judgment alone.[41]

So much for the beautiful representation of an object, which is really only the form of the presentation of a concept by means of which the latter is universally communicated. – To give this form to the product of beautiful art, however, requires merely taste, to which the artist, after he has practiced and corrected it by means of various examples of art or nature, holds up his work, and after many, often laborious attempts to satisfy it, finds the form that contents him; hence this is not as it were a matter of inspiration or a free swing of the mental powers, but a slow and indeed painstaking improvement, in order to let it become adequate to the thought and yet not detrimental to the freedom in the play of the mental powers.

5: 313

Taste, however, is merely a faculty for judging,[b] not a productive faculty; and what is in accordance with it is for that very reason not a work of beautiful art, although it can be a product belonging to a useful and mechanical art or even to science, conforming to determinate rules which can be learned and which must be precisely followed. But the pleasing form which one gives to it is only the vehicle of communication and a manner, as it were, of presentation, in regard to which one still remains[c] to a certain extent free, even if one is otherwise bound to a determinate end. Thus one demands that table settings, or a moral treatise, or even a sermon must have in themselves this form of beautiful art, though without seeming **studied**; but they are not on this account called works of beautiful art. Among the latter, however, are counted a poem, a piece of music, a picture gallery, and so on; and there, in one would-be work of beautiful art, one can often perceive genius without taste, while in another, taste without genius.

§ 49.
On the faculties of the mind that constitute genius.

One says of certain products, of which it is expected that they ought, at least in part, to reveal themselves as beautiful art, that they are without **spirit**, even though one finds nothing in them to criticize as far as taste is concerned. A poem can be quite pretty and elegant, but

---

[a] *Bildungen*
[b] *Beurtheilungs-*
[c] In the first edition, "is" (*ist*) instead of "remains" (*bleibt*).

without **spirit**. A story is accurate and well organized, but without spirit. A solemn oration is thorough and at the same time flowery, but without spirit. Many a conversation is not without entertainment, but is still without spirit; even of a woman one may well say that she is pretty, talkative and charming, but without spirit. What is it then that is meant here by "spirit"?

Spirit, in an aesthetic significance, means the animating principle in the mind. That, however, by which this principle animates the soul, the material which it uses for this purpose, is that which purposively sets the mental powers into motion, i.e., into a play that is self-maintaining and even strengthens the powers to that end.[42]

Now I maintain that this principle is nothing other than the faculty for the presentation of **aesthetic ideas**; by an aesthetic idea, however, I mean that representation of the imagination that occasions much thinking though without it being possible for any determinate thought, i.e., **concept**, to be adequate to it, which, consequently, no language fully attains or can make intelligible. – One readily sees that it is the counterpart (pendant) of an **idea of reason**, which is, conversely, a concept to which no **intuition** (representation of the imagination) can be adequate.

The imagination (as a productive cognitive faculty) is, namely, very powerful in creating, as it were, another nature, out of the material which the real one gives it. We entertain ourselves with it when experience seems too mundane to us; we transform the latter, no doubt always in accordance with analogous laws, but also in accordance with principles that lie higher in reason (and which are every bit as natural to us as those in accordance with which the understanding apprehends empirical nature); in this we feel our freedom from the law of association (which applies to the empirical use of that faculty), in accordance with which material can certainly be lent to us by nature, but the latter can be transformed by us into something entirely different, namely into that which steps beyond nature.

One can call such representations of the imagination **ideas**:[43] on the one hand because they at least strive toward something lying beyond the bounds of experience, and thus seek to approximate a presentation of concepts of reason (of intellectual ideas), which gives them the appearance of an objective reality; on the other hand, and indeed principally, because no concept can be fully adequate to them, as inner intuitions. The poet ventures to make sensible rational ideas of invisible beings, the kingdom of the blessed, the kingdom of hell, eternity, creation, etc., as well as to make that of which there are examples in experience, e.g., death, envy, and all sorts of vices, as well as love, fame, etc., sensible beyond the limits of experience, with a completeness that goes beyond anything of which there is an example in nature, by means of an imagination that emulates the precedent of reason in attaining to a maximum; and it is really the art of poetry in which the faculty of aesthetic ideas can reveal itself in its full measure. This faculty, however, considered by itself alone, is really only a talent (of the imagination).

Now if we add to a concept a representation of the imagination that belongs to its presentation, but which by itself stimulates so much thinking that it can never be grasped in a determinate concept, hence which aesthetically enlarges the concept itself in an unbounded way, then in this case the imagination is creative, and sets the faculty of intellectual ideas (reason) into motion, that is, at the instigation of a representation it gives more to think about than can be grasped and made distinct in it (although it does, to be sure, belong to the concept of the object). 5: 315

Those forms which do not constitute the presentation of a given concept itself, but, as supplementary representations of the imagination, express only the implications connected with it and its affinity with others, are called (aesthetic) **attributes** of an object whose concept, as an idea of reason, cannot be adequately presented. Thus Jupiter's eagle, with the lightning in its claws, is an attribute of the powerful king of heaven, as is the peacock of the splendid queen of heaven. They do not, like **logical attributes**, represent what lies in our concepts of the sublimity and majesty of creation, but something else, which gives the imagination cause to spread itself over a multitude of related representations, which let one think more than one can express in a concept determined by words; and they yield an **aesthetic idea**, which serves that idea of reason instead of logical presentation, although really only to animate the mind by opening up for it the prospect of an immeasurable field of related representations. Beautiful art, however, does this not only in painting or sculpture (where the names of the attributes are commonly used); rather, poetry and oratory also derive the spirit which animates their works solely from the aesthetic attributes of the objects, which go alongside the logical ones, and give the imagination an impetus to think more, although in an undeveloped way, than can be comprehended in a concept, and hence in a determinate linguistic expression. – For the sake of brevity, I must limit myself to only a few examples.

When the great king expressed himself in one of his poems thus: "Let us depart from life without grumbling and without regretting anything, leaving the world behind us replete with good deeds. Thus does the sun, after it has completed its daily course, still spread a gentle light across the heavens; and the last rays that it sends forth into the sky are its last sighs for the well-being of the world,"[44] he animates his idea of reason of a cosmopolitan disposition even at the end of life by 5: 316

means of an attribute that the imagination (in the recollection of everything agreeable in a beautiful summer day, drawn to a close, which a bright evening calls to mind) associates with that representation, and which arouses a multitude of sensations and supplementary representations for which no expression is found. Conversely, even an intellectual concept can serve as the attribute of a representation of sense, and so animate the latter by means of the idea of the supersensible; but only insofar as the aesthetic, which is subjectively attached to the consciousness of the latter, is used to this end. Thus, e.g., a certain poet says in the description of a beautiful morning: "The sun streamed forth, as tranquillity streams from virtue."[45] The consciousness of virtue, when one puts oneself, even if only in thought, in the place of a virtuous person, spreads in the mind a multitude of sublime and calming feelings, and a boundless prospect into a happy future, which no expression that is adequate to a determinate concept fully captures.*

In a word, the aesthetic idea is a representation of the imagination, associated with a given concept, which is combined with such a manifold of partial representations in the free use of the imagination that no expression designating a determinate concept can be found for it, which therefore allows the addition to a concept of much that is unnameable, the feeling of which animates the cognitive faculties and combines spirit with the mere letter of language.

The mental powers, then, whose union (in a certain relation) constitutes **genius**, are imagination and understanding. Only in the use of the imagination for cognition, the imagination is under the constraint of the understanding and is subject to the limitation of being adequate to its concept; in an aesthetic respect, however, the imagination is free to provide, beyond that concord with the concept, unsought extensive undeveloped material for the understanding, of which the latter took no regard in its concept, but which it applies, not so much objectively, for cognition, as subjectively, for the animation of the cognitive powers, and thus also indirectly to cognitions; thus genius really consists in the happy relation, which no science can teach and no diligence learn, of finding ideas for a given concept on the one hand and on the other hitting upon the **expression** for these, through which the subjective disposition of the mind that is thereby produced, as an accompaniment

5: 317

5: 316 * Perhaps nothing more sublime has ever been said, or any thought more sublimely expressed, than in the inscription over the temple of **Isis** (Mother **Nature**): "I am all that is, that was, and that will be, and my veil no mortal has removed." **Segner** made use of this idea by means of a vignette, **rich in sense**, placed at the beginning of his theory of nature, in order at the outset to fill his pupil, whom he was ready to lead into this temple, with the holy fear that should dispose the mind to solemn attentiveness.[46]

of a concept, can be communicated to others. The latter talent is really that which is called spirit, for to express what is unnameable in the mental state in the case of a certain representation and to make it universally communicable, whether the expression consist in language, or painting, or in plastic art – that requires a faculty for apprehending the rapidly passing play of the imagination and unifying it into a concept (which for that very reason is original and at the same time discloses a new rule, which could not have been deduced from any antecedent principles or examples), which can be communicated without the constraint of rules.*

* *
*

If, after these analyses, we look back to the explanation given above of what is called **genius**, then we find: **first**, that it is a talent for art, not for science, in which rules that are distinctly cognized must come first and determine the procedure in it; **second**, that, as a talent for art, it presupposes a determinate concept of the product, as an end, hence understanding, but also a representation (even if indeterminate) of the material, i.e., of the intuition, for the presentation of this concept, hence a relation of the imagination to the understanding; **third**, that it displays itself not so much in the execution of the proposed end in the presentation of a determinate **concept** as in the exposition or the expression of **aesthetic ideas**, which contain rich material for that aim, hence the imagination, in its freedom from all guidance by rules, is nevertheless represented as purposive for the presentation of the given concept; finally, **fourth**, that the unsought and unintentional subjective purposiveness in the free correspondence of the imagination to the lawfulness of the understanding presupposes a proportion and disposition of this faculty that cannot be produced by any following of rules, whether of science or of mechanical imitation, but that only the nature of the subject can produce.⁴⁷ 5: 318

According to these presuppositions, genius is the exemplary originality of the natural endowment of a subject for the **free** use of his cognitive faculties. In this way the product of a genius (in respect of that in it which is to be ascribed to genius, not to possible learning or schooling) is an example, not for imitation (for then that which is genius in it and constitutes the spirit of the work would be lost),ᵇ but for emulation by another genius, who is thereby awakened to the feeling of his own originality, to exercise freedom from coercion in his

---

ᵃ The words "of rules" were added in the second edition.
ᵇ In the second edition, *verlorengehen*; in the first, *wegfallen* (disappear).

art in such a way that the latter thereby itself acquires a new rule, by which the talent shows itself as exemplary. But since the genius is a favorite of nature, the likes of which one has to regard as only a rare phenomenon, his example for other good minds gives rise to a school, i.e., a methodical instruction in accordance with rules, insofar as it has been possible to extract them from those products of spirit and their individuality; and for these beautiful art is to that extent imitation, to which nature gave the rule through a genius.

But this imitation becomes **aping** if the student **copies** everything, even down to that which the genius had to leave in, as a deformity, only because it could not easily have been removed without weakening the idea. This courage is a merit only in a genius, and a certain **boldness** in expression and in general some deviation from the common rule is well suited to him, but is by no means worthy of imitation, but always remains in itself a defect which one must seek to remove, but for which*a* the genius is as it were privileged, since what is inimitable in the impetus of his spirit would suffer from anxious caution. **Mannerism** is another sort of aping, namely that of mere **individuality** (originality) in general, in order to distance oneself as far as possible from imitators, yet without having the talent thereby to be **exemplary** at the same time. – There are in general, to be sure, two ways (*modus*) of putting thoughts together in a presentation, one of which is called a **manner** (*modus aestheticus*) and the other of which is called a **method**

5: 319 (*modus logicus*), which differ from each other in that the former has no other standard than the **feeling** of unity in the presentation, while the latter follows determinate **principles** in this; for beautiful art, therefore, only the first is valid. But one calls a product of art **mannered** only if the presentation of its idea in that product is **aimed** at singularity rather than being made adequate to the idea. The ostentatious (precious), the stilted and the affected, intended only to distinguish oneself from the vulgar*b* (but without any spirit), are like the behavior of someone of whom it is said that he is fond of the sound of his own voice, or who stands and moves as if he were on a stage, in order to be gaped at, which always betrays a bungler.

§ 50.
On the combination of taste with genius in products of beautiful art.[48]

If the question is whether in matters of beautiful art it is more important whether genius or taste is displayed, that is the same as asking

---

a In the first edition, "for the likes of which" (*dergleichen*).
b *dem Gemeinen*

whether imagination or the power of judgment counts for more in them. Now since it is in regard to the first of these that an art deserves to be called **inspired**,[a] but only in regard to the second that it deserves to be called a **beautiful** art, the latter, at least as an indispensable condition (*conditio sine qua non*), is thus the primary thing to which one must look in the judging[b] of art as beautiful art. To be rich and original in ideas is not as necessary for the sake of beauty as is the suitability of the imagination in its freedom to the lawfulness of the understanding. For all the richness of the former produces, in its lawless freedom, nothing but nonsense; the power of judgment, however, is the faculty for bringing it in line with the understanding.

Taste, like the power of judgment in general, is the discipline (or corrective) of genius, clipping its wings and making it well behaved or polished; but at the same time it gives genius guidance as to where and how far it should extend itself if it is to remain purposive; and by introducing clarity and order into the abundance of thoughts it makes the ideas tenable, capable of an enduring and universal approval, of enjoying a posterity among others and in an ever progressing culture. Thus if anything must be sacrificed in the conflict of the two properties in one product, it must rather be on the side of genius: and the power of judgment, which in matters of beautiful art makes its pronouncements on the basis of its own principles, will sooner permit damage to the freedom and richness of the imagination than to the understanding.

5: 320

For beautiful art, therefore, **imagination, understanding, spirit** and **taste** are requisite.*

$\S$ 51.
On the division of the beautiful arts.[50]

Beauty (whether it be beauty of nature or of art) can in general be called the **expression** of aesthetic ideas:[51] only in beautiful art this idea must be occasioned by a concept of the object, but in beautiful nature the mere reflection on a given intuition, without a concept of what the object ought to be, is sufficient for arousing and

---

* The first three faculties first achieve their **unification** through the fourth. **Hume** in his history gives the English to understand that, although in their works they do not yield anything to any nation in the world with regard to evidence of the first three properties considered **separately**, nevertheless in that which unifies them they must come in second to their neighbors, the French.[49]

5: 320

[a] *geistreiche*
[b] *Beurtheilung*

communicating the idea of which that object is considered as the **expression**.

Thus if we wish to divide the beautiful arts, we can, at least as an experiment, choose no easier principle than the analogy of art with the kind of expression that people use in speaking in order to communicate to each other, i.e., not merely their concepts, but also their sensations.* – This consists in the **word**, the **gesture**, and the **tone** (articulation, gesticulation, and modulation). Only the combination of these three kinds of expression constitutes the speaker's complete communication. For thought, intuition, and sensation are thereby conveyed to the other simultaneously and united.

5: 321 There are thus only three kinds of beautiful arts: the art of **speech**, **pictorial** art,*a* and the art **of the play of sensations** (as external sensory impressions). One could also arrange this division as a dichotomy, so that beautiful art would be divided into that of the expression of thoughts or of intuitions, and the latter in turn in accordance with their form or their matter (of sensation). But then it would look too abstract and not as suitable to ordinary concepts.

1) The arts of **speech** are **rhetoric** and **poetry**. **Rhetoric** is the art of conducting a business of the understanding as a free play of the imagination; **poetry** that of carrying out a free play of the imagination as a business of the understanding.[52]

The **orator** thus announces a matter of business and carries it out as if it were merely a **play** with ideas in order to entertain the audience.*b* The **poet** announces merely an entertaining **play** with ideas, and yet as much results for the understanding as if he had merely had the intention of carrying on its business. The combination and harmony of the two cognitive faculties, the sensibility and the understanding, which to be sure cannot manage without each other but which nevertheless cannot readily be united with each other without constraint and mutual harm, must seem to be unintentional and to happen on their own; otherwise it is not **beautiful** art. Hence everything contrived and laborious in it must be avoided; for beautiful art must be free art in a double sense: it must not be a matter of remuneration, a labor whose magnitude can be judged,*c* enforced, or paid for in accor-

---

5: 320 * The reader will not judge of*d* this outline for a possible division of the beautiful arts as if it were a deliberate theory. It is only one of the several experiments that still can and should be attempted.

a die **bildende** Kunst
b Zuschauer; in the first edition, Zuhörer (listeners).
c beurtheilen
d beurtheilen

dance with a determinate standard; but also, while the mind is certainly occupied, it must feel itself to be satisfied and stimulated (independently of remuneration) without looking beyond to another end.

The orator thus certainly provides something which he does not promise, namely an entertaining play of the imagination; but he also takes something away from what he does promise, namely the purposive occupation of the understanding. The poet, by contrast, promises little and announces a mere play with ideas, but accomplishes something that is worthy of business, namely providing nourishment to the understanding in play, and giving life to its concepts through the imagination: hence the former basically provides less than he promises, the latter more.[a]

2) The **pictorial** arts or those of the expression of ideas in **sensible intuition** (not through representations of the mere imagination, which are evoked through words) are either those of **sensible truth** or of **sensible illusion**.[53] The first are called the **plastic** arts, the second **painting.** Both make shapes in space into expressions of ideas: the former makes shapes knowable by two senses, sight and feeling (although in the case of the latter, to be sure, without regard to beauty), the latter only for the first of these. The aesthetic idea (archetype, prototype[b]) is for both grounded in the imagination; the shape, however, which constitutes its expression (ectype, afterimage)[c] is given either in its corporeal extension (as the object itself exists) or in accordance with the way in which the latter is depicted in the eye (in accordance with its appearance[d] on a plane); or else, whatever the former is, either the relation to a real end or just the appearance[e] of one is made into a condition for reflection.

The **plastic** arts, as the first kind of beautiful pictorial arts, include **sculpture** and **architecture**. The **first** is that which presents corporeal concepts of things as they **could exist in nature** (although, as a beautiful art, with regard to aesthetic purposiveness); the **second** is the art of presenting, with this intention but yet at the same time in an aesthetically purposive way, concepts of things that are possible **only through art**, and whose form has as its determining ground not nature but a voluntary end. In the latter a certain **use** of the artistic object is the main thing, to which, as a condition, the aesthetic ideas are restricted. In the former the mere **expression** of aesthetic ideas is the chief aim. Thus statues of humans, gods, animals, etc., are of the first

5: 322

[a] The clause following the colon was added in the second edition.
[b] *Archetypon, Urbild*
[c] *Nachbild*
[d] *Apparenz*
[e] *Anschein*

sort; but temples, magnificent buildings for public gatherings, as well as dwellings, triumphal arches, columns, cenotaphs, and the like, erected as memorials, belong to architecture. Indeed, all domestic furnishings (the work of the carpenter and the like things for use) can be counted as belonging[a] to the latter, because the appropriateness of the product to a certain use is essential in a **work of architecture**,[b] while by contrast a mere **picture**,[c] which is made strictly for viewing and is to please for itself, is, as a corporeal presentation, a mere imitation of nature, though with respect to aesthetic ideas: where, then, **sensible truth** should not go so far that it stops looking like art and a product of the power of choice.

5: 323   The **art of the painter**, as the second kind of pictorial art, which presents **sensible illusion** in artful combination with ideas, I would divide into that of the beautiful **depiction** of nature and that of the beautiful **arrangement** of its **products**. The first would be **painting proper**, the second **the art of pleasure gardens**. For the former gives only the illusion of corporeal extension; the latter certainly gives this in truth, but gives only the illusion of employment and use for ends other than merely the play of the imagination in the viewing of its forms.* The latter is nothing other than the decoration of the ground with the same variety (grasses, flowers, bushes and trees, even

---

5: 323   * That the art of pleasure gardens could be considered as a kind of painting, although of course it presents its forms corporeally, seems strange; but since it actually takes its forms from nature (the trees, bushes, grasses and flowers from woods and field, at least to begin with), and to that extent is not an art like the plastic arts, and also has no concept of the object and its end (as in architecture) as the condition of its arrangement, but merely the free play of the imagination in the contemplation, to that extent it coincides with merely aesthetic painting, which has no determinate theme (which puts air, land, and water together by means of light and shadows in an entertaining way). – In general, the reader is to judge[d] this only as an attempt to judge of[e] the combination of the beautiful arts under one principle, which in this case is to be that of the expression of aesthetic ideas (in accordance with the analogy[f] of a language), and not regard it as a derivation of them that is meant to be definitive.[54]

[a] Reading *gezählt*, with the first edition, rather than *gewählt* (chosen) with the second.
[b] *Bauwerks*
[c] *Bildwerk*
[d] *beurtheilen*
[e] *beurtheilen*
[f] Reading *Analogie*, with the first edition, rather than *Anlage* (predisposition) with the second and third.

water, hills and valleys) with which nature presents it to intuition, only arranged differently and suited to certain ideas. The beautiful arrangement of corporeal things, however, is also given only for the eye, like painting; the sense of touch, however, cannot furnish any intuitable representation of such a form. To painting in the broad sense I would also assign the decoration of rooms by means of wallpaper, moldings, and all kinds of beautiful furnishings, which merely serve to be **viewed**; likewise the art of dressing with taste (rings, pill boxes, etc.).[a] For a terrace with all kinds of flowers, a room with all sorts of decorations (even including the finery of the ladies) constitute, at a splendid party, a kind of painting, which, just like painting properly so called (which does not have the aim, say, of **teaching** history or knowledge of nature), is there merely to be viewed,[b] in order to entertain the imagination in free play with ideas and to occupy the power of aesthetic judgment without a determinate end. The work in all these decorations may be, mechanically, quite different, and require very different artists; but the judgment of taste concerning what is beautiful in this art is determined in a single way: namely, to judge of[c] only the forms (without regard to an end) as they are offered to the eye, individually or in their interconnection, in accordance with the effect that they have on the imagination. – But how pictorial art can be counted (by analogy) as gesture in a language is justified by the fact that the spirit of the artist gives a corporeal expression through these shapes to what and how he has thought, and makes the thing itself speak as it were in mime: a very common play of our fantasy, which attributes to lifeless things, in accordance with their form, a spirit that speaks from them.

5: 324

3) The art of the **beautiful play of sensations** (which are generated from the outside), which must nevertheless be able to be universally communicated, can concern nothing other than the proportion of the different degrees of the disposition (tension) of the sense to which the sensation belongs, i.e., its tone; and in this extended meaning of the word it can be divided into the artistic play of the sensations[d] of hearing and of sight, and thus into **music** and the **art of colors**.[55] – It is remarkable that these two senses, besides the susceptibility to sensations to the extent that that is required in order to arrive by their means at concepts of external objects, are also capable of a special sensation connected with that, about which it cannot rightly be made

---

[a] In the first edition there is a comma rather than a period here.
[b] The first edition adds an "and" here.
[c] *beurtheilen*
[d] In the first edition, "play with the tone of the sensation."

out whether it has as its ground sense or reflection; and that this affectability can yet sometimes be lacking, although as far as its use for the cognition of objects is concerned the sense is not at all defective otherwise, but is rather exceptionally acute. That is, one cannot say with certainty whether a color or a tone (sound) is merely agreeable sensations or is in itself already a beautiful play of sensations, which as such involves a satisfaction in the form in aesthetic judging.[a] If one considers the rapidity of the vibrations of the light, or, in the second case, of the air, which probably far exceeds all our capacity for judging[b] immediately in perception the proportion of the division of time, then one would have to believe that it is only the **effect** of these vibrations on the elastic parts of our body that is sensed, but

5: 325   that the **division of time** by means of them is not noticed and drawn into the judging,[c] hence that in the case of colors and tones there is associated only agreeableness, not beauty of their composition. But if one considers, on the contrary, **first**, what can be said mathematically about the proportion of the oscillations in music and of the judging of[d] them, and judges of[e] contrasts among colors, as is appropriate, in analogy with the latter, and if one takes into account, **second**, those admittedly rare examples of human beings who, with the best sight in the world, cannot distinguish colors and, with the most acute hearing, cannot distinguish tones, and also, for those who can do this, the perception of an altered quality (not merely of the degree of the sensation) in various positions on the scale of colors or tones, and further that the number of these is determinate for **comprehensible** distinctions: then one may see oneself as compelled to regard the sensations of both not as mere sensory impressions, but as the effect of a judging of[f] the form in the play of many sensations.[56] The difference between the one or the other opinion in the judging of[g] music, however, would only alter the definition to this extent, that it would be explained, as we have done, as the beautiful play of sensations (through hearing), or as **agreeable** sensations. Only on the first definition would music be represented completely as a **beautiful** art; on the second, however, it would be represented as an **agreeable** art (at least in part).

[a] *Beurtheilung*
[b] *zu beurtheilen*
[c] *Beurtheilung*
[d] *Beurtheilung*
[e] *beurtheilt*
[f] *Beurtheilung*
[g] *Beurtheilung*

§ 52.
On the combination of the beautiful arts in
one and the same product.

Rhetoric can be combined with a painterly presentation of its subjects as well as objects in a **play**; poetry with music in **song**; this, in turn, with a painterly (theatrical) presentation in an **opera**; the play of the sensations in a piece of music with the play of shapes in **dance**, etc. Further, the presentation of the sublime, so far as it belongs to beautiful art, can be united with beauty in a **verse tragedy**, a **didactic poem**, an **oratorio**; and in these combinations beautiful art is all the more artistic, although whether it is also more beautiful (since so many different kinds of satisfaction are crisscrossed with each other) can be doubted in some of these cases. Yet in all beautiful art what is essential consists in the form, which is purposive for observation and judging,^{a} where the pleasure is at the same time culture and disposes the spirit to ideas, hence makes it receptive to several sorts of pleasure and entertainment – not in the matter of the sensation (the charm or the emotion), where it is aimed merely at enjoyment, which leaves behind it nothing in the idea, and makes the spirit dull, the object by and by^b loathsome, and the mind, because it is aware that its disposition is contrapurposive in the judgment of reason, dissatisfied with itself and moody.

5: 326

If the beautiful arts are not combined, whether closely or at a distance, with moral ideas, which alone carry with them a self-sufficient satisfaction, then the latter is their ultimate fate. They then serve only for diversion, which one increasingly needs the more one uses them to banish the mind's dissatisfaction with itself, by which one makes oneself ever more useless and dissatisfied with oneself. In general, the beauties of nature are most compatible with the first aim if one has become accustomed early to observing, judging,^{c} and admiring them.

§ 53.
Comparison of the aesthetic value of the
beautiful arts with each other.[57]

The **art of poetry** (which owes its origin almost entirely to genius, and will be guided least by precept or example) claims the highest rank of all.[58] It expands the mind by setting the imagination free and present-

^{a} *Beurtheilung*
^{b} The words "by and by" (*nach und nach*) were added in the second edition.
^{c} *zu beurtheilen*

ing, within the limits of a given concept and among the unbounded manifold of forms possibly agreeing with it, the one that connects its presentation with a fullness of thought to which no linguistic expression is fully adequate, and thus elevates itself aesthetically to the level of ideas. It strengthens the mind by letting it feel its capacity[a] to consider and judge of[b] nature, as appearance, freely, self-actively, and independently of determination by nature, in accordance with points of view that nature does not present by itself in experience either for sense or for the understanding, and thus to use it for the sake of and as it were as the schema of the supersensible. It plays with the illusion which it produces at will, yet without thereby being deceitful; for it itself declares its occupation to be mere play, which can nevertheless be purposively employed by the understanding for its own business. – Rhetoric, insofar as by that is understood the art of persuasion, i.e., of deceiving by means of beautiful illusion (as an *ars oratoria*), and not merely skill in speaking (eloquence and style), is a dialectic, which borrows from the art of poetry only as much as is necessary to win minds over to the advantage of the speaker before they can judge[c] and to rob them of their freedom; thus it cannot be recommended either for the courtroom or for the pulpit. For when it is a matter of civil laws concerning the rights of individual persons, or of the lasting instruction and determination of minds to correct knowledge and conscientious observation of their duty, then it is beneath the dignity of such an important business to allow even a trace of exuberance of wit and imagination to be glimpsed, let alone of the art of persuasion and taking someone in for the advantage of someone else.[d] For even if it can sometimes be applied to purposes that are in themselves legitimate and praiseworthy, it is nevertheless still objectionable that the maxims and dispositions be subjectively corrupted in this way, even if the deed is objectively lawful: for it is not enough to do what is right, but it is also to be performed solely on the ground that it is right. Further, the merely distinct concept of these sorts of human affairs, combined with a lively presentation in examples, and without offense against the rules of euphony in speech or of propriety in expression, for ideas of reason (which together constitute eloquence), already has in itself sufficient influence on human minds, without[e] it being necessary also to bring to bear the machinery of persuasion, which, since it can also be used

5: 327

---

[a] *Vermögen*
[b] *zu beurtheilen*
[c] *vor der Beurtheilung*
[d] In the first edition, this period was a comma, and the sentence continued, "which, even though . . ."
[e] Following the first edition, reading *ohne daß* instead of *als daß*.

for glossing over or concealing vice and error, can never entirely erad-
icate the deep-seated suspicion of artful trickery. In poetry, everything
proceeds honestly and uprightly. It declares that it will conduct a
merely entertaining play with the imagination, and indeed concerning
form, in concord with the laws of the understanding, and does not
demand that the understanding be deceived and embroiled through
sensible presentation.*

After poetry, I would, **if what is at issue is charm and movement
of the mind**, place that which comes closest to it among the arts of
speech and may also very naturally be united with it, namely **the art of
tone.** For, although of course it speaks through mere sensations without concepts, and hence does not, like poetry, leave behind something
for reflection, yet it moves the mind in more manifold and, though
only temporarily, in deeper ways; but it is, to be sure, more enjoyment
than culture (the play of thought that is aroused by it in passing is
merely the effect of an as it were mechanical association); and it has,
judged*a* by reason, less value than any other of the beautiful arts.
Hence it demands, like any other enjoyment, frequent change, and
cannot bear frequent repetition without inducing antipathy. Its charm,
which can be communicated so universally, seems to rest on this: that
every expression of language has, in context, a tone that is appropriate
to its sense; that this tone more or less designates an affect of the
speaker and conversely also produces one in the hearer, which then in
turn arouses in the latter the idea that is expressed in the language by

5: 328

---

* I must confess that a beautiful poem has always given me a pure enjoyment,
whereas reading the best speech of a Roman popular speaker or a contemporary speaker in parliament or the pulpit has always been mixed with the
disagreeable feeling of disapproval of a deceitful art, which understands how
to move people, like machines, to a judgment in important matters which
must lose all weight for them in calm reflection. Eloquence and well-
spokenness (together, rhetoric) belong to beautiful art; but the art of the
orator (*ars oratoria*), as the art of using the weakness of people for one's own
purposes (however well intentioned or even really good these may be) is not
worthy of any **respect** at all. Further, both in Athens and in Rome it reached
its highest level only at a time when the state was rushing toward its ruin and
a truly patriotic way of thinking had been extinguished. He who has at his
command, along with clear insight into the facts, language in all its richness
and purity, and who, along with a fruitful imagination capable of presenting
his ideas, feels a lively sympathy for the true good, is the *vir bonus dicendi
peritus,*b the speaker without art but full of vigor, as **Cicero** would have him,
though he did not himself always remain true to this ideal.[59]

5: 327
5: 328

a *beurtheilt*
b the good man, powerful in speech

205

means of such a tone; and that, just as modulation is as it were a language of sensations universally comprehensible to every human being, the art of tone puts that language into practice for itself alone, in all its force, namely as a language of the affects, and so, in accordance with the law of association, universally communicates the aesthetic ideas that are naturally combined with it; however, since those aesthetic ideas are not concepts nor determinate thoughts, the form of the composition of these sensations (harmony and melody) serves only, instead of the form of a language, to express, by means of a proportionate disposition of them (which, since in the case of tones it rests on the relation of the number of the vibrations of the air in the same time, insofar as the tones are combined at the same time or successively, can be mathematically subsumed under certain rules), the aesthetic ideas of a coherent whole of an unutterable fullness of thought, corresponding to a certain theme, which constitutes the dominant affect in the piece. On this mathematical form, although not represented by determinate concepts, alone depends the satisfaction that the mere reflection on such a multitude of sensations accompanying or following one another connects with this play of them as a condition of its beauty valid for everyone; and it is in accordance with it alone that taste may claim for itself a right to pronounce beforehand about the judgment of everyone.

However, mathematics certainly has not the least share in the charm and the movement of the mind that music produces; rather, it is only the indispensable condition (*conditio sine qua non*) of that proportion of the impressions, in their combination as well as in their alternation, by means of which it becomes possible to grasp them together and to prevent them from destroying one another, so that they instead agree in a continuous movement and animation of the mind by means of consonant affects and hereby in a comfortable self-enjoyment.

If, on the contrary, one estimates the value of the beautiful arts in terms of the culture that they provide for the mind and takes as one's standard the enlargement of the faculties that must join together in the power of judgment for the sake of cognition, then to that extent music occupies the lowest place among the beautiful arts (just as it occupies perhaps the highest place among those that are estimated according to their agreeableness), because it merely plays with sensations. The pictorial arts therefore far surpass it in this respect; for while they set the imagination into a free play that is nevertheless also suitable for the understanding, at the same time they conduct a business by bringing about a product that serves the concepts of the understanding as an enduring and self-recommending vehicle for its unification with sensibility and thus as it were for promoting the urbanity of the higher powers of cognition. The two sorts of arts take completely different paths: the former from sensations to indeterminate ideas, the latter,

5: 329

5: 330

however, from determinate ideas to sensations. The latter are of **lasting** impression, the former only of a **transitory** one. The imagination can recall the former and agreeably entertain itself with them; but the latter are either entirely extinguished or, if they are involuntarily recalled by the imagination, are burdensome rather than agreeable to us. Further, there is a certain lack of urbanity in music, in that, primarily because of the character of its instruments, it extends its influence further (into the neighborhood) than is required, and so as it were imposes itself, thus interfering with the freedom of others, outside of the musical circle, which the arts that speak to the eyes do not do, since one need only turn one's eyes away if one would not admit their impression. It is almost the same here as in the case of the delight from a widely pervasive smell. Someone who pulls his perfumed handkerchief out of his pocket treats everyone in the vicinity to it against their will, and forces them, if they wish to breathe, to enjoy it at the same time; hence it has also gone out of fashion.* – Among the pictorial arts, I would give the palm to **painting**, partly because, as the art of drawing, it is the basis of all the other pictorial arts, partly because it can penetrate much further into the region of ideas and also expand the field of intuition in accordance with these much further than is possible for the rest.

Remark*^a*

Between that **which pleases merely in the judging**^b and that which **gratifies** (pleases in the sensation) there is, as we have often shown, an essential difference. The latter is something that one cannot, like the former, require of everyone. Gratification (even if its cause may lie in ideas) always seems to consist in a feeling of the promotion of the total life of the human being, consequently also of bodily well-being, i.e., of health; so that Epicurus, who made out all gratification as at bottom bodily sensation, may to that extent perhaps not have been mistaken, and only misunderstood himself when he counted intellectual and even practical satisfaction as gratification.⁶¹ If one keeps the latter distinction before one's eyes, one can explain how a gratifica-

5: 331

---

* Those who have recommended the singing of spiritual songs as part of the domestic rites of worship have not considered that by means of such a **noisy** (and precisely for that reason usually pharisaical) form of worship they have imposed a great inconvenience on the public, for they have forced the neighborhood either to join in their singing or to give up their own train of thought.⁶⁰

5: 330

^a Neither the first nor the second edition print "§ 54" here, although the next section (the first section of the Dialectic) is labeled "§ 55" in both.
^b *Beurtheilung*

tion can even displease the one who feels^a it (like the joy of a needy but right-thinking person over the inheritance from his loving but tightfisted father), or how a deep pain can still please the one who suffers it (the sadness of a widow at the death of her praiseworthy husband), or how a gratification can in addition please (like that in the sciences that we pursue) or a pain (e.g., hatred, envy, or vengefulness) can in addition displease us. The satisfaction or dissatisfaction here rests on reason, and is the same as **approval** or **disapproval**; gratification and pain, however, can rest only on the feeling or the prospect (whatever its basis might be) of a possible state of **well-** or **ill-being.**

All changing free play of sensations (which is not grounded in any intention) gratifies, because it promotes the feeling of health, whether or not we take satisfaction in the rational judging^b of its object and even in this gratification; and this gratification can rise to the level of an affect, although we take no interest in the object itself, at least not one that would be proportionate to the degree of the latter.[62] We can divide it into the **play of chance**, the **play of tone,** and the **play of thoughts.** The **first** requires an **interest,** whether it be of vanity or of selfishness, which is, however, far from as great as the interest in the way in which we seek to satisfy it; the **second** requires merely the change of **sensations,** each of which has its relation to affect, but not the degree of an affect, and arouses aesthetic ideas; the **third** arises merely from the change in the representations, in the faculty of judgment, by means of which, to be sure, no thought that involves any sort of interest is generated, but the mind is nevertheless animated.

5: 332

How gratifying these games^c must be, without there being any need to ground them in an interested intention, is shown by all of our evening social gatherings, for without games hardly anyone finds these entertaining. But the affects of hope, of fear, of joy, of anger, of scorn are here at play, changing their role every moment,^{d} and are so lively that as a result the entire business of bodily life, as an inner motion, seems to be promoted, as is proved by the cheerfulness of mind that is thereby generated, even though nothing has been either gained or learned. But since games of chance are not a beautiful play,^{e} we shall here set it aside. By contrast,^{f} music and material for laughter are two kinds of play with aesthetic ideas or even representations of the understanding, by which in the end nothing is thought, and which can gratify merely through their change, and nevertheless do so in a lively fashion;^{g} by which they make it fairly evident that the animation in both cases is merely corporeal, although it is aroused by ideas of the mind, and that the feeling of health resulting from a movement of the viscera corresponding to that play constitutes the whole gratification in a lively party, which is extolled as so refined and spirited.^{h} It is

---

^{a} *empfindet*
^{b} *Vernunftbeurtheilung*
^{c} *die Spiele*
^{d} In the first edition, Kant says simply "changing every moment."
^{e} *das Glücksspiel kein schönes Spiel ist*
^{f} *Hingegen*; the first edition reads *aber* (however).
^{g} In the first edition, "and can gratify in a lively fashion merely through their change."
^{h} *geistvoll*

not the judging^a of the harmonies in tones or sallies of wit, which with their beauty serve only as the necessary vehicle, but the promotion of the business of life in the body, the affect which moves the viscera and the diaphragm, in a word the feeling of health (which otherwise cannot be felt without such a stimulus), which constitutes the gratification in which one discovers that one can get at the body even through the soul and use the latter as the doctor for the former.

In music, this play proceeds from the sensation of the body to aesthetic ideas (of the objects for affects), and then from them back again, but with united force, to the body. In the joke (which like music deserves to be counted as agreeable rather than as beautiful art) the play begins with thoughts which, as a whole, insofar as they are to be expressed sensibly, also occupy the body; and since the understanding, in this presentation in which it does not find what was expected, suddenly relaxes, ones feels the effect of this relaxation in the body through the oscillation^b of the organs, which promotes the restoration of their balance and has a beneficial influence on health.

In everything that is to provoke a lively, uproarious laughter, there must be something nonsensical (in which, therefore, the understanding in itself can take no satisfaction). **Laughter is an affect resulting from the sudden transformation of a heightened expectation into nothing.**[63] This very transformation, which is certainly nothing enjoyable for the understanding, is nevertheless indirectly enjoyable and, for a moment, very lively. The cause must thus consist in the influence of the representation on the body and its reciprocal effect on the mind; certainly not insofar as the representation is objectively an object of gratification^c (for how can a disappointed expectation be gratifying?), but rather solely through the fact that as a mere play of representations it produces an equilibrium^d of the vital powers in the body.

If someone tells this story: An Indian, at the table of an Englishman in Surat,[64] seeing a bottle of ale being opened and all the beer, transformed into foam, spill out, displayed his great amazement with many exclamations, and in reply to the Englishman's question "What is so amazing here?" answered, "I'm not amazed that it's coming out, but by how you got it all in," we laugh, and it gives us a hearty pleasure: not because we find ourselves cleverer than this ignorant person, or because of any other pleasing thing that the understanding allows us to note here, but because our expectation was heightened and suddenly disappeared into nothing. Or if the heir of a rich relative wants to arrange a properly solemn funeral for him, but laments that he cannot get it quite right, because (he says), "The more money I give my mourners to look sad, the merrier they look," then we laugh out loud, and the reason is that an expectation is suddenly transformed into nothing. Note that it must not be transformed into the positive opposite^e of an expected object – for that is

5: 333

---

^{a} *Beurtheilung*
^{b} In the first edition, this word (*Schwingung*) is in the plural.
^{c} The first edition here includes the clause, omitted from the second edition, "as in the case of one who receives news of a great profit in business."
^{d} *Gleichgewicht*; in the first edition, "play" (*Spiel*).
^{e} The word "positive" (*positive*) was added in the second edition.

always something, and can often be distressing – but into nothing. For if in telling us a story someone arouses a great expectation and at its conclusion we immediately see its untruth, that is displeasing, like, e.g., the story of people whose hair is supposed to have turned gray in a single night because of a great grief. By contrast, if in response to such a story another joker tells a very elaborate story about the grief of a merchant who, returning from India to Europe with all his fortune in merchandise, was forced to throw it all over-board in a terrible storm, and was so upset that in the very same night his **wig** turned gray, then we laugh and it gives us gratification, because for a while we toss back and forth like a ball our own misconception about an object that is otherwise indifferent to us, or rather our own idea that we've been chasing, while we were merely trying to grasp and hold it firm. It's not sending a liar or a dummy packing that arouses the gratification here, for even for itself the latter story, told with an assumed seriousness, would move a party to peals of laughter, and the former would not ordinarily even be worthy of attention.[a]

5: 334

It is noteworthy that in all such cases the joke must always contain some-thing that can deceive for a moment: hence, when the illusion disappears into nothing, the mind looks back again in order to try it once more, and thus is hurried this way and that by rapidly succeeding increases and decreases of tension and set into oscillation: which, because that which as it were struck the string bounces back suddenly (not through a gradual slackening), is bound to cause a movement of the mind and an internal bodily movement[b] in harmony with it, which continues involuntarily, and produces weariness, but at the same time also cheerfulness (the effects of a motion that is beneficial to health).[c]

For if one assumes that all of our thoughts are at the same time harmoni-ously combined with some kind of movement in the organs of the body, then one will have a fair grasp of how to that sudden shift of the mind, first to one and then to another point of view for considering its object, there can corre-spond a reciprocal tensing and relaxing of the elastic parts of our viscera, which communicates itself to our diaphragm (like that which ticklish people feel), so that the lungs expel the air with rapidly succeeding pauses, and thus produce a movement that is conducive to health, which alone, and not what goes on in the mind, is the real cause of a gratification in a thought that at bottom represents nothing. – Voltaire said that Heaven has given us two things as a counterweight against the many burdens of life: **hope** and **sleep**.[65] He could also have added **laughter**, if only the means for provoking it in rational people were so readily available, and the wit or originality of fancy requisite for it were not as rare as the talent is frequent for composing works that **break one's head**, like those of mystical brooders, or **break one's neck**, like those of a genius, or **break one's heart**, like those of sentimental novelists (or for that matter moralists of the same kind).

One can thus, it seems to me, grant to Epicurus that all gratification, even

---

[a] The second edition uses *Aufmerksamkeit* instead of *Mühe* (worth the trouble).
[b] The word "movement" was added in the second edition.
[c] This clause was not enclosed in parentheses in the first edition.

if it is caused by concepts that arouse aesthetic ideas, is **animal**, i.e., bodily sensation,[66] without thereby doing the least damage to the **spiritual** feeling of respect for moral ideas, which is not gratification but self-esteem (of the humanity within us) that elevates us above the need for gratification, without indeed any damage even to the less noble feeling of **taste.**

Something with a bit of both is found in **naïveté**, which is the resistance of the uprightness that is originally natural to humanity against the art of pretense that has become second nature.[67] One laughs at the simplicity that still does not understand how to pretend, and yet also rejoices over the simplicity of nature that here thwarts that art. One expects the normal custom[a] of artificial expression carefully aimed at beautiful illusion, and see! it is uncorrupted, innocent nature, which one was not at all prepared to encounter and which he who allows it to be glimpsed did not even intend to expose. That the beautiful but false illusion, which usually means so much in our judgment, is here suddenly transformed into nothing, that as it were the joker in ourselves is exposed, produces the successive movement of the mind in two opposite directions, which at the same time gives the body a healthy shake. But that something that is infinitely better than every assumed custom, namely purity of thought (or at least the predisposition to it), has not been entirely extinguished in human nature, adds seriousness and high esteem to this play of the power of judgment. But because it is an appearance that manifests itself[b] only for a short time, and the curtain of the art of pretense is soon drawn closed again, it also contains an element of regret, which is an emotion of tenderness, that can very well be combined as play with such good-hearted laughter, and which actually usually is combined with it, and at the same time usually compensates the person who provides the material for it for the embarrassment of not being sharp in the ways of men. – An art for being **naive** is thus a contradiction; but it is certainly possible to represent naïveté in a fictional person, and this is a beautiful although also rare art. Naïveté must not be confused with open-hearted simplicity, which does not artificially conceal nature only because it does not understand what the art of social life is.

Along with what is cheerful, closely related to the gratification from laughter, and part of the originality of spirit, but not on that account part of the talent for beautiful art, there may also be reckoned the **capricious** manner. **Caprice** in the good sense signifies the talent of being able to transpose oneself at will into a certain mental disposition in which everything is judged[c] quite differently from what is usual (even completely reversed), and yet in accordance with certain principles of reason in such a mental disposition. Someone who is involuntarily given to such alterations is **subject to caprice**,[d] but someone who can assume them voluntarily and purposively (for the sake of a lively

---

[a] *Sitte*
[b] The words translated as "that manifests itself" (*sich hervortuende*) were added in the second edition.
[c] *beurtheilt*
[d] *launisch*

presentation by means of a laugh-provoking contrast), such a person and his performance are called **capricious.**[a] This manner however belongs more to agreeable than to beautiful art, because the object of the latter must always display some dignity in itself, and hence requires a certain earnestness in the presentation, just as taste does in its judging.[b]

[a] *launicht*
[b] *Beurtheilung*

Critique of the
Aesthetic Power of Judgment
Second Section
The Dialectic
of the
Aesthetic Power of Judgment

§ 55.[a]

A power of judgment that is to be dialectical must first of all be rationalistic,[b] i.e., its judgments must lay claim to universality, and indeed do so *a priori*,* for the dialectic consists in the opposition of such judgments. Hence the incompatibility of aesthetic judgments of sense (about the agreeable and the disagreeable) is not dialectical. Even the conflict between judgments of taste, insofar as each person appeals merely to his own taste, does not constitute a dialectic of taste, since no one has any thought of making his own judgment into a universal rule. Thus there remains no other concept of a dialectic that could apply to taste except that of a dialectic of the **critique** of taste (not of taste itself) with regard to its **principles**: namely, where mutually conflicting concepts of the basis of the possibility of judgments of taste naturally and unavoidably emerge. A transcendental critique of taste

---

* A rationalistic judgment (*iudicium ratiocinans*)[c] is any judgment that declares itself to be universal, for to that extent it can serve as the major premise in a rational inference. In contrast, only a judgment which is thought as the conclusion of an inference of reason, and consequently as grounded *a priori*, can be called a judgment of reason (*iudicium ratiocinatum*).[d]

[a] This section has no title.
[b] *vernünftelnd*. This term is usually translated as "sophistical," but here Kant uses it to connote only a necessary condition of a sophistical argument, namely that it make a pretense to universality, without yet implying that anything that gives rise to a dialectic is sophistical in the usual, pejorative sense.
[c] Literally, a rationalizing judgment.
[d] Literally, a judgment that has been reached by ratiocination.

will thus contain a part that can bear the name of a dialectic of the aesthetic power of judgment only if there is an antinomy of the principles of this faculty, which makes its lawfulness and hence also its inner possibility doubtful.

5: 338

§ 56.
Representation of the antinomy of taste.

The first commonplace of taste is contained in the proposition by means of which everyone who lacks taste thinks to defend himself against criticism: **Everyone has his own taste.** That amounts to saying that the determining ground of this judgment is merely subjective (gratification or pain), and the judgment has no right to the necessary assent of others.

Its second commonplace, which is also used even by those who concede to judgments of taste the right to pronounce validly for everyone, is: **There is no disputing about taste.** That is as much as to say that the determining ground of a judgment of taste may even be objective, but it cannot be brought to determinate concepts; consequently nothing can be **decided** about the judgment itself by means of proofs, although it is certainly possible and right to **argue** about it. For **to argue**[a] and **to dispute**[b] are certainly alike in this, that they try to bring about unanimity in judgments through their mutual opposition, but they differ in that the latter hopes to accomplish this in accordance with determinate concepts as grounds of proofs, and so assumes **objective concepts** as grounds of the judgment. Where this is considered unfeasible, however, then disputing is also considered unfeasible.

It is easy to see that between these two commonplaces one proposition is missing, which is not, to be sure, a proverb in general circulation, but which nevertheless everyone has some sense of: **It is possible to argue about taste** (but not to dispute). But this proposition implies the opposite of the first proposition above. For wherever it is supposed to be possible to argue, there must be hope of coming to mutual agreement; hence one must be able to count on grounds for the judgment that do not have merely private validity and thus are not merely subjective, which is nevertheless completely opposed to the fundamental principle **Everyone has his own taste.**

There is thus the following antinomy with regard to the principle of taste:

[a] *Streiten*
[b] *Disputieren*

1. **Thesis**. The judgment of taste is not based on concepts, for otherwise it would be possible to dispute about it (decide by means of proofs).
2. **Antithesis.** The judgment of taste is based on concepts, for otherwise, despite its variety, it would not even be possible to argue about it (to lay claim to the necessary assent of others to this judgment).[1]

5: 339

§ 57.
Resolution of the antinomy of taste.

There is no possibility of lifting the conflict between these two principles underlying every judgment of taste (which are nothing other than the two peculiarities of the judgment of taste represented above in the Analytic),[2] except by showing that the concept to which the object is related in this sort of judgment is not taken in the same sense in the two maxims of the aesthetic power of judgment, that this twofold sense or point of view in judging[a] is necessary in our transcendental power of judgment, but also that the semblance[b] involved in the confusion of the one with the other is, as a natural illusion,[c] unavoidable.

The judgment of taste must be related to some sort of concept, for otherwise it could not lay claim to necessary validity for everyone at all. But it need not on that account be demonstrable **from** a concept, because a concept can be either determinable or else in itself indeterminate and also indeterminable. The concept of reason, which is determinable by means of predicates of the sensible intuition that can correspond to it, is of the first sort; of the second sort, however, is the transcendental concept of reason of the supersensible, which is the basis of all that intuition, and which thus cannot be further determined theoretically.[d]

Now the judgment of taste does pertain to objects of the senses, but not in order to determine a **concept** of them for the understanding, for it is not a cognitive judgment. It is thus, as an intuitive singular representation related to the feeling of pleasure, only a private judgment, and to this extent its validity would be limited to the judging individual alone: The object is an object of satisfaction **for me**, it may be different for others; – everyone has his own taste.

Nevertheless, the judgment of taste doubtlessly contains an enlarged

[a] *Beurtheilung*
[b] *Schein*
[c] *Illusion*
[d] The word "theoretically" was added in the second edition.

215

relation of the representation of the object (and at the same time of the subject), on which we base an extension of this kind of judgment, as necessary for everyone, which must thus^a be based on some sort of concept, but a concept that **cannot** be determined by intuition, by which nothing can be cognized, and which thus also **leads to no proof** for the judgment of taste. A concept of this kind, however, is the mere pure rational concept of the supersensible, which grounds the object (and also the judging subject) as an object of sense, consequently as an appearance.[3] For if one did not assume such a point of view, then the claim of the judgment of taste to universal validity could not be saved; if the concept on which it is based were only a merely confused concept of the understanding, of perfection, say, to which one could, correspondingly, assign^b the sensible intuition of the beautiful,[4] then it would be possible, at least in itself, to ground the judgment of taste on proofs, which contradicts the thesis.

But now all contradiction vanishes if I say that the judgment of taste is based on a concept (of a general ground for the subjective purposiveness of nature for the power of judgment), from which, however, nothing can be cognized and proved with regard to the object, because it is in itself indeterminable and unfit for cognition; yet at the same time by means of this very concept it acquires validity for everyone (in each case, to be sure, as a singular judgment immediately accompanying the intuition), because its determining ground may lie in the concept of that which can be regarded as the supersensible substratum of humanity.

The resolution of an antinomy amounts merely to the possibility that two apparently conflicting propositions do not in fact contradict each other, but can be compatible with each other, even though the explanation of the possibility of their concept exceeds our faculty of cognition. That this semblance is also natural and unavoidable for human reason, and thus why it exists and remains, although after the resolution of the apparent conflict it no longer deceives, can also be made comprehensible on this basis.[5]

Namely, we take the concept, on which the universal validity of a judgment must be based, in the same sense in both conflicting propositions, and yet we assert two opposed predicates of it. Thus, the thesis should say that the judgment of taste is not based on **determinate** concepts; but in the antithesis, it should say that the judgment of taste is still based on some, although **indeterminate** concept (namely, of the supersensible substratum of appearances); and then there would be no conflict between them.

---

^a The word "thus" (*daher*) was added in the second edition.
^b In the second edition, *beygeben*; in the first, *geben* (give).

We cannot do any more than remove this conflict in the claims and counterclaims of taste. To provide a determinate objective principle of taste, by means of which its judgments could be guided, examined, and proved, is absolutely impossible; for then it would not be a judgment of taste. The subjective principle, namely the indeterminate idea of the supersensible in us, can only be indicated as the sole key to demystifying this faculty which is hidden to us even in its sources, but there is nothing by which it can be made more comprehensible.

The antinomy that has here been set out and resolved is based on the correct concept of taste, as, namely, a merely reflecting power of aesthetic judgment; and the two apparently conflicting fundamental propositions would here be united with each other insofar as **both can be true**, which is also sufficient. If, by contrast, **agreeableness** were to be assumed as the determining ground of taste (on account of the singularity of the representation that is the basis of the judgment of taste), as it is by some, or the principle of **perfection** were to be assumed, as it is by others (on account of its universal validity), and the judgment of taste were to be fixed accordingly, then from that there would arise an antinomy that could not be resolved at all except by showing that **both** of the opposed (but not merely contradictory) **propositions are false**: which would then prove that the concept on which each is based is self-contradictory. Thus one sees that the removal of the antinomy of the aesthetic power of judgment takes a course similar to that followed by the *Critique*[6] in the resolution of the antinomies of pure theoretical reason, and that in the same way both here and in the *Critique of Practical Reason* one is compelled, against one's will, to look beyond the sensible and to seek the unifying point of all our faculties *a priori* in the supersensible: because no other way remains to make reason self-consistent.[a]

Remark I.

Since in transcendental philosophy we so frequently find occasion to distinguish ideas from concepts of the understanding, it may be of use to introduce terms of art appropriate to their difference. I believe that nobody will object if I propose several. – Ideas in the most general meaning are representations related to an object in accordance with a certain (subjective or objective) principle, insofar as they can nevertheless never become a cognition of that object. They are either related to an intuition in accordance with a merely subjective principle of the correspondence of the faculties of cognition with each other (of imagination and of understanding), and in this case they are called **aesthetic**; or they are related to a concept in accordance with an objec-

5: 342

---

[a] *mit sich selbst einstimmig*

tive principle, yet can never yield a cognition of the object, and are called ideas of reason, in which case the concept is a **transcendent** concept, which is distinct from the concept of the understanding, to which an adequately corresponding experience can always be ascribed, and which is therefore called **immanent**.[7]

An **aesthetic idea** cannot become a cognition, because it is an **intuition** (of the imagination) for which a concept can never be found adequate. An **idea of reason** can never become a cognition, because it contains a **concept** (of the supersensible) for which no suitable intuition can ever be given.

Now I believe that one could call the aesthetic idea an **inexponible** representation of the imagination, the idea of reason, however, an **indemonstrable** concept of reason. Of both it is presupposed that they are not entirely groundless, but rather (in accordance with the above explanation of an idea in general) are generated in accordance with certain principles of the cognitive faculty to which they belong (the former according to subjective principles, the latter to objective ones).

Concepts of the understanding must, as such, always be demonstrable (if by demonstrating, as in anatomy, it is merely **presenting** that is understood);[a] i.e., the object that corresponds to them must always be able to be given in intuition (pure or empirical): for thereby alone can they become cognitions. The concept of **magnitude** can be given in the intuition of space *a priori*, e.g., the intuition of a straight line, etc.; the concept of **cause** in the impenetrability or the impact of bodies, etc. Hence both can be confirmed by an empirical intuition, i.e., the thought of them can be shown (demonstrated, illustrated) in an example, and this must be able to happen: otherwise one will not be certain that the concept is not empty, i.e., without any object.

In logic, the expressions "demonstrable" or "indemonstrable" are ordinarily used only with regard to **propositions**; but the first could better be designated by the term "only mediate" and the latter by the term "**immediately certain**" propositions: for pure philosophy also has propositions of both sorts, if by that is meant true sentences capable of being proved and those incapable of being proved.[b] But from *a priori* grounds it can, as philosophy, certainly prove, but not demonstrate, if one will not depart entirely from the meaning of the words, according to which to demonstrate (*ostendere, exhibere*) means the same as (be it in proofs or even simply in the definition) to present its concept at the same time in intuition – which, if the intuition is *a priori*, is called constructing of the concept, but if it is also empirical nevertheless remains[c] the presentation[d] of the object by means of which the objective reality of the concept is assured. Thus one says of an anatomist that he demonstrates the human eye when he makes the concept that he has previously expounded discursively intuitable by means of the dissection of this organ.

In consequence of this, the rational concept of the supersensible substratum

---

[a] The words in parentheses were added in the second edition.
[b] In the first edition, there is a semicolon rather than a period here.
[c] In the first edition, "is."
[d] Here *Vorzeigung* rather than *Darstellung*.

of all appearances in general, or even of that on which our power of choice in relation to moral laws must be based, namely the idea of transcendental freedom, is already in terms of its species an indemonstrable concept and idea of reason, but virtue is so as a matter of degree: because to the former nothing can be given in experience that corresponds to its quality at all, while in the case of the latter no experiential product of that causality attains the degree that the idea of reason prescribes as a rule.

Just as in the case of an idea of reason the **imagination**, with its intuitions, never attains to the given concept, so in the case of an aesthetic idea the **understanding**, by means of its concepts, never attains to the complete inner intuition of the imagination which it combines with a given representation. Now since to bring a representation of the imagination to concepts is the same as to **expound** it, the aesthetic idea can be called an **inexponible** representation of the imagination (in its free play). In what follows I will have the opportunity to say a little more about ideas of this sort; for now I note only that both sorts of ideas, the ideas of reason as well as the aesthetic ideas, must have their principles, and indeed in both cases in reason, the former in the objective and the latter in the subjective principles of its use.

5: 344

As a result of this, one can also explain **genius** in terms of the faculty of **aesthetic ideas**: by which at the same time is indicated the reason why in products of genius nature (that of the subject), not a deliberate end, gives the rule to art (the production of the beautiful). For since the beautiful must not be judged[a] in accordance with concepts, but rather in accordance with the purposive disposition of the imagination for its correspondence with the faculty of concepts in general, it is not a rule or precept but only that which is merely nature in the subject, i.e., the supersensible substratum of all our faculties (to which no concept of the understanding attains), and so that in relation to which it is the ultimate end given by the intelligible in our nature to make all our cognitive faculties agree, which is to serve as the subjective standard of that aesthetic but unconditioned purposiveness in beautiful art, which is supposed to make a rightful claim to please everyone. Thus alone is it possible that the latter, to which one can prescribe no objective principle, can be grounded on a subjective and yet universally valid principle *a priori*.

Remark II.

The following important comment suggests itself here: namely, that there are **three kinds of antinomy** of pure reason, which, however, all coincide in this, that they force reason to give up the otherwise very natural presupposition that holds objects of the senses to be things in themselves, and rather to count them as appearances, and ascribe to them an intelligible substratum (something supersensible, the concept of which is only an idea and permits no genuine cognition). Without such an antinomy reason would never be able to decide on the assumption of a principle that so narrows the field of its speculation and on sacrifices in which so many otherwise shining hopes must entirely disappear;

---

[a] *beurtheilt*

for even now, when in compensation for these losses an all the greater employ-
5: 345 ment opens up for it in a practical respect, it seems unable to depart from those
hopes and to free itself from its old dependency without pain.

That there are three kinds of antinomy is grounded in the fact that there
are three cognitive faculties – understanding, the power of judgment, and
reason – each of which (as a higher cognitive faculty) must have its *a priori*
principles; for then reason, insofar as it judges concerning these principles
themselves and their use, unremittingly demands with regard to all of them
the unconditioned for the given conditioned, which, however, can never be
found if one considers the sensible as belonging to the things in themselves
rather than ascribing to it, as mere appearance, something supersensible (the
intelligible substratum of nature outside us and within us) as a thing in itself.
There is then 1) an antinomy of reason with regard to the theoretical use of
the understanding extending to the unconditioned **for the faculty of cognition**; 2) an antinomy of reason with regard to the aesthetic use of the power of
judgment **for the feeling of pleasure and displeasure**; 3) an antinomy with
regard to the practical use of reason, which is intrinsically self-legislative, **for
the faculty of desire**, to the extent that all these faculties have their higher
principles *a priori*, and, in accordance with an inescapable requirement of
reason, must also be able to judge and determine their object **unconditionally**
in accordance with these principles.

With regard to two antinomies of those higher cognitive faculties, that of
the theoretical and that of the practical employment, we have already shown
elsewhere their **unavoidability** if judgments of this kind do not look back to a
supersensible substratum of the given objects, as appearances, but also their
resolvability as soon as the latter happens. Now as far as the antinomy in the
use of the power of judgment and the resolution of it given here are concerned,
there is no other means for avoiding it than **either** to deny that the aesthetic
judgment of taste is grounded on any principle *a priori*, so that all claim to the
necessity of universal assent is a groundless, empty delusion, and a judgment
of taste deserves to be held to be correct only insofar as **it happens** that many
people agree about it, and even this, strictly speaking, not because one **suspects**
an *a priori* principle behind this consensus, but rather (as in the taste of the
5: 346 palate) because the subjects are contingently organized in the same way; **or**
one must assume that the judgment of taste is really a concealed judgment of
reason about the perfection that is revealed in a thing and the relation of the
manifold in it to an end, so that it is called aesthetic only on account of the
confusion that attaches to this reflection of ours, although at bottom it is
teleological – in which case one could declare the resolution of the antinomy
by means of transcendental ideas to be unnecessary and void, and thus unite
those laws of taste with the objects of the senses not as mere appearances but
also as things in themselves. But how little the one as well as the other
subterfuge succeeds has been shown in several places in the exposition of the
judgments of taste.

But if it is conceded that our deduction is at least on the right track, even if
it has not been made clear enough in every detail, then three ideas are revealed:
first, that of the supersensible in general, without further determination, as the
substratum of nature; **second**, the very same thing, as the principle of the

220

subjective purposiveness of nature for our faculty of cognition; **third**, the very same thing, as the principle of the ends of freedom and principle of the correspondence of freedom with those ends in the moral sphere.[a]

§ 58.
On the idealism of the purposiveness of nature as well as art, as the sole principle of the power of aesthetic judgment.

The principle of taste, first of all, can either be placed in the fact that taste always judges in accordance with empirical determining grounds, and thus in accordance with those that are given only *a posteriori* by means of the senses, or it can be conceded that it judges on the basis of an *a priori* ground. The first would be the **empiricism** of the critique of taste, the second its **rationalism**. According to the **first**, the object of our satisfaction would not differ from the **agreeable**, and according to the second, if the judgment rested on determinate concepts, it would not differ from the **good**; and so all **beauty** in the world would be denied, and all that would be left in its place would be a special name, perhaps for a certain mixture of the two previously mentioned kinds of satisfaction. But we have shown that there are also grounds of satisfaction *a priori*, which can thus coexist with the principle of rationalism, even though they cannot be grasped in **determinate concepts**.

    The rationalism of the principle of taste is, by contrast, either that of the **realism** of purposiveness or that of its **idealism**. Now since a judgment of taste is not a cognitive judgment and beauty is not a quality of the object considered for itself, the rationalism of the principle of taste can never be based on the fact that the purposiveness in this judgment is thought as objective, i.e., on the fact that the judgment pertains to the perfection of the object theoretically and thus logically (even if only in a confused judging),[b] but rather only on the fact that it pertains to the subject **aesthetically**, to the correspondence of its representation in the imagination with the essential principles of the power of judgment in general. Consequently, even according to the principle of rationalism, the judgment of taste and the distinction between its realism and idealism can be based only on the assumption, in the first case, that that subjective purposiveness is a real (intentional) **end** of nature (or of art) aimed at correspondence with our power of judgment, or, in the second case, that it is, without any end, merely an intrinsically yet contingently manifested purposive correspondence

5: 347

[a] *im Sittlichen*
[b] *Beurtheilung*

with the need of the power of judgment in regard to nature and the forms generated in it in accordance with particular laws.

The beautiful formations[a] in the realm of organized[b] nature speak strongly in behalf of the realism of the aesthetic purposiveness of nature, since one may assume that the production of the beautiful is based on an idea of that in the producing cause, namely an **end** for the benefit of our imagination. The flowers, the blossoms, indeed the shapes of whole plants; the delicacy of animal formations of all sorts of species, which is unnecessary for their own use but as if selected for our own taste; above all the manifold and harmonious composition of colors (in the pheasant, in crustaceans, insects, right down to the commonest flowers), which are so pleasant and charming to our eyes, which seem to have been aimed entirely at outer contemplation, since they concern merely the surface, and even in this do not concern the figure of the creature, which could still be requisite for its inner ends: all of these give great weight to the kind of explanation that involves the assumption of real ends of nature for our power of aesthetic judgment.

However, this assumption is not only contradicted by reason, through its maxims of always avoiding as far as possible the unnecessary multiplication of principles, but also nature displays everywhere in its free formations so much mechanical tendency to the generation of forms that seem as if they have been made for the aesthetic use of our power of judgment without giving us the slightest ground to suspect that it requires for this anything more than its mechanism, merely as nature, by means of which it can be purposive for our judging[c] even without being based on any idea. By a **free formation** of nature, however, I understand that by which, from a **fluid at rest**, as a result of the evaporation or separation of a part of it (sometimes merely of the caloric), the rest assumes upon solidification a determinate shape or fabric (figure or texture) which, where there is a specific difference in the matter, is different, but if the matter is the same is exactly the same. Here is presupposed what is always understood by true fluidity, namely, that the matter in it is to be regarded as fully dissolved, i.e., not as a mere mixture of solid parts merely suspended in it.

The formation in such a case takes place through **precipitation**, i.e., through a sudden solidification, not through a gradual transition from the fluid to the solid state, but as it were through a leap, which transition is also called **crystallization.** The most common example of this sort of formation is freezing water, in which straight raylets of ice form

5: 348

---

[a] *Bildungen*
[b] *organisirten*; as will be seen in the "Critique of Teleological Judgment," Kant uses this term where we would use "organic."
[c] *Beurtheilung*

first, which then join together at angles of 60 degrees, while others attach themselves at every point in exactly the same way, until everything has turned to ice, so that during this time, the water between the raylets of ice does not gradually become more viscous, but remains as completely fluid as it would be if it were at a much higher temperature, and yet is fully as cold as ice. The matter that separates itself, which suddenly escapes at the moment of solidification, is a considerable quantum of caloric, the departure of which, because it was required only for maintaining a fluid state, leaves what is now all ice not the least bit colder than was the water that shortly before was still fluid.[8]

Many salts as well as stones that have a crystalline figure are generated in the same way from some sort of earth which is, by means of who knows what sort of mediation, dissolved in water. The drusy[9] configurations of many minerals,[a] such as cubic galenite,[10] pyrargyrite,[11] and so on, are in all likelihood formed in the same way, in water, by means of the precipitation of their parts, when by some cause they are forced to leave this vehicle and to combine with one another into determinate external shapes.

5: 349

But even internally all materials that were fluid only because of heat and which through cooling have become solid reveal, when broken, a determinate texture, and thus make it possible to judge that if their own weight or contact with air had not prevented it, they would also have displayed their specifically proper shape externally: this sort of thing has been observed in some metals which had hardened externally after melting but were still fluid on the inside, by drawing off the inner, still fluid part and then precipitating calmly the rest which was left behind. Many of these mineral crystallizations, such as spar-druses, hematite or aragonite,[12] often have shapes of extreme beauty, which art could hardly think up; and the halo of the cave on Antiparos is merely the product of water dripping through a bed of gypsum.

The fluid is, to all appearances, older than the solid, and both the plants as well as animal bodies are formed from fluid nutritive matter that has formed itself in a state of rest: in the latter case, to be sure, first and foremost in accordance with a certain original predisposition directed at ends (which, as will be shown in the second part, must be judged of[b] not aesthetically but teleologically, in accordance with the principle of realism);[13] but perhaps also as precipitating and forming itself freely, in accordance with the universal laws of the affinity of materials. Now just as the watery fluids dissolved in an atmosphere, which is a mixture of different types of air, when the former are separated from the latter because of the departure of heat, generate

---

[a] Reading *Mineralien* as in the first edition rather than *Minern* as in the second.
[b] *beurtheilt*

snowflakes[a] which, depending on the difference of the particular mixture of air, often have a very artistic-appearing and extremely beautiful figure, so it may well be thought, without detracting anything from the teleological principle for judging of[b] organization, that as far as the beauty of flowers, of birdfeathers, and seashells is concerned, in terms of both their shape and their color, these can be ascribed to nature and its faculty for forming itself aesthetically and purposively in its freedom, without special ends aimed at that, in accordance with chemical laws, by the deposit of the matter requisite for the organization.

5: 350

However, what downright proves the principle of the **ideality** of the purposiveness in the beautiful in nature as that which is always our basis in the aesthetic judgment itself, and which does not allow us to use any realism of an end in it as an explanatory ground for our power of representation, is that in the judging[c] of beauty in general we seek the standard for it in ourselves *a priori*, and the power of aesthetic judgment, with regard to the judgment whether or not something is beautiful, is itself legislative, which could not be the case on the assumption of the realism of the purposiveness of nature; because then we would have to learn from nature what we have to find beautiful, and the judgment of taste would be subject to empirical principles. For in such judging[d] what is at issue is not what nature is or even what it is for us as a purpose, but how we take it in. It would always be an objective purposiveness of nature if it had created its forms for our satisfaction, and not a subjective purposiveness, which rests on the play of the imagination in its freedom, where it is a favor with which we take nature in and not a favor that it shows to us.[e] That nature has the property of containing an occasion for us to perceive the inner purposiveness in the relationship of our mental powers in the judging of[f] certain of its products, and indeed as something that has to be explained as necessarily and universally valid on the basis of a supersensible ground, cannot be an end of nature, or rather be judged[g] by us as such a thing: because otherwise the judgment that would thereby be determined would be grounded in heteronomy and would not, as befits a judgment of taste, be free and grounded in autonomy.

In beautiful art the principle of the idealism of purposiveness can be recognized even more distinctly. For that here its aesthetic realism by

---

[a] *Schneefiguren*

[b] *Beurtheilung*

[c] *Beurtheilung*

[d] *Beurtheilung*

[e] *nicht Gunst, die sie uns erzeigt*; in the first edition, *nicht eine solche die sie uns erzeugt* (not one that nature generates for us).

[f] *Beurtheilung*

[g] *beurtheilt*

means of sensations (in which case it would be merely agreeable instead of beautiful art) cannot be assumed is something that it has in common with beautiful nature. But that the satisfaction by means of aesthetic ideas must not depend on the attainment of determinate ends (as a mechanically intentional art), consequently that even in the rationalism of the principle the ground must be the ideality of ends, not their reality: that is already evident from the fact that beautiful art, as such, must not be considered as a product of the understanding and of science, but of genius, and thus acquires its rule through **aesthetic** ideas, which are essentially different from rational ideas of determinate ends.

5: 351

Just as the **ideality** of the objects of the senses as appearances is the only way to explain the possibility that their forms can be determined *a priori*, likewise the **idealism** of the purposiveness in judging*ᵃ* of the beautiful in nature and in art is the only presupposition under which the critique can explain the possibility of a judgment of taste, which demands *a priori* validity for everyone (yet without basing the purposiveness that is represented in the object on concepts).

§ 59.
On beauty as a symbol of morality.

To demonstrate the reality of our concepts, intuitions are always required. If they are empirical concepts, then the latter are called **examples.** If they are pure concepts of the understanding, then the latter are called **schemata.** But if one demands that the objective reality of the concepts of reason, i.e., of the ideas, be demonstrated, and moreover for the sake of theoretical cognition of them, then one desires something impossible, since no intuition adequate to them can be given at all.

All **hypotyposis** (presentation, *subjecto sub adspectum*), as making something sensible, is of one of two kinds: either **schematic**, where to a concept grasped by the understanding the corresponding intuition is given *a priori*; or **symbolic**, where to a concept which only reason can think, and to which no sensible intuition can be adequate, an intuition is attributed with which the power of judgment proceeds in a way merely analogous to that which it observes in schematization, i.e., it is merely the rule of this procedure, not of the intuition itself, and thus merely the form of the reflection, not the content, which corresponds to the concept.

ᵃ Beurtheilung

The use of the word **symbolic** in contrast to the **intuitive** kind of representation has, of course, been accepted by recent logicians, but this is a distorted and incorrect use of the word: for the symbolic is merely a species of the intuitive.[14] The latter, namely (the intuitive), can be divided into the **schematic** and the **symbolic** kinds of representation. Both are hypotyposes, i.e., presentations (*exhibitiones*):[a] not mere **characterizations**, i.e., designations of the concepts by means of accompanying sensible signs, which contain nothing at all belonging to the intuition of the object, but only serve them, in accordance with the laws of association of the imagination, and hence in a subjective regard, as a means of reproduction; such things are either words, or visible (algebraic, even mimetic) signs, as mere **expressions** for concepts.*

All intuitions that are ascribed to concepts *a priori* are thus either **schemata** or **symbols**, the first of which contain direct, the second indirect presentations of the concept. The first do this demonstratively, the second by means of an analogy (for which empirical intuitions are also employed), in which the power of judgment performs a double task, first applying the concept to the object of a sensible intuition, and then, second, applying the mere rule of reflection on that intuition to an entirely different object, of which the first is only the symbol. Thus a monarchical state is represented by a body with a soul if it is ruled in accordance with laws internal to the people, but by a mere machine (like a handmill) if it is ruled by a single absolute will, but in both cases it is represented only **symbolically.** For between a despotic state and a handmill there is, of course, no similarity, but there is one between the rule for reflecting on both and their causality. This business has as yet been little discussed, much as it deserves a deeper investigation; but this is not the place to dwell on it. Our language is full of such indirect presentations, in accordance with an analogy, where the expression does not contain the actual schema for the concept but only a symbol for reflection. Examples are the words **ground**[b] (support, basis), **depend**[c] (be held from above), from which **flow** (instead of follow), **substance** (as Locke expresses it: the bearer of accidents),[15] and innumerable other nonschematic but symbolic hypotyposes and expressions for concepts not by means of a direct intuition, but only in accordance with an analogy with it, i.e., the transportation of the

---

* The intuitive in cognition must be contrasted to the discursive (not the symbolic). Now the former is either **schematic**, by means of **demonstration**, or **symbolic**, as a representation based on mere **analogy**.

[a] In the first edition, *exhibitio* in the singular.
[b] *Grund*
[c] *abhängen*

reflection on one object of intuition to another, quite different concept,   5: 353
to which perhaps no intuition can ever directly correspond. If one may
already call a mere kind of representation cognition (which is certainly
permissible if it is a principle not of the theoretical determination of
what an object is in itself, but of the practical determination of what
the idea of it ought to be for us and for the purposive use of it), then
all of our cognition of God is merely symbolic, and anyone who takes
it, along with the properties of understanding, will, etc., which prove
their objective reality only in beings within the world,*a* as schematic,
lapses into anthropomorphism, just as, if he leaves out everything
intuitive, he lapses into deism, by which nothing at all, not even from
a practical point of view, is cognized.[16]

Now I say that the beautiful is the symbol of the morally good, and
also that only in this respect (that of a relation that is natural to
everyone, and that is also expected of everyone else as a duty) does it
please with a claim to the assent*b* of everyone else, in which the mind
is at the same time aware of a certain ennoblement and elevation above
the mere receptivity for a pleasure from sensible impressions, and also
esteems the value of others in accordance with a similar maxim of their
power of judgment. That is the **intelligible**, toward which, as the
preceding paragraph*c* indicated, taste looks, with which, namely, even
our higher faculties of cognition agree, and without which glaring
contradictions would emerge between their nature and the claims that
taste makes. In this faculty the power of judgment does not see itself,
as is otherwise the case in empirical judging,*d* as subjected to a heteronomy of the laws of experience; in regard to the objects of such a
pure satisfaction it gives the law to itself, just as reason does with regard
to the faculty of desire; and it sees itself, both on account of this inner
possibility in the subject as well as on account of the outer possibility
of a nature that corresponds to it, as related to something in the subject
itself and outside of it, which is neither nature nor freedom, but which
is connected with the ground of the latter, namely the supersensible,
in which the theoretical faculty is combined with the practical, in a
mutual and unknown way, to form a unity. We will adduce several
aspects of this analogy, while at the same time not leaving unnoticed
its differences.[17]

1) The beautiful pleases **immediately** (but only in reflecting intui-   5: 354
tion, not, like morality, in the concept). 2) It pleases **without any
interest** (the morally good is of course necessarily connected with an

a *Weltwesen*
b *Beistimmung*; in the first edition, *Bestimmung* (determination).
c That is, § 58.
d *Beurtheilung*

interest, but not with one that precedes the judgment on the satisfaction, but rather with one that is thereby first produced). 3) The **freedom** of the imagination (thus of the sensibility of our faculty) is represented in the judging of[a] the beautiful as in accord with the lawfulness of the understanding (in the moral judgment the freedom of the will is conceived as the agreement of the latter with itself in accordance with universal laws of reason). 4) The subjective principle for judging of[b] the beautiful is represented as **universal**, i.e., valid for everyone, but not as knowable by any universal concept (the objective principle of morality is also declared to be universal, i.e., knowable for all subjects, and at the same time also for all actions of one and the same subject, yet by means of a universal concept). Hence the moral judgment is not only capable of determinate constitutive principles, but is also possible **only** by means of the grounding of its maxims on these principles and their universality.

A regard to this analogy is customary even for the ordinary understanding, and we often designate beautiful objects of nature or of art with names that seem to be grounded in a moral judging.[c] We call buildings or trees majestic and magnificent, or fields smiling and joyful; even colors are called innocent, modest or tender, because they arouse sensations that contain something analogical to the consciousness of a mental state produced by moral judgments. Taste as it were makes possible the transition from sensible charm to the habitual moral interest without too violent a leap by representing the imagination even in its freedom as purposively determinable for the understanding and teaching us to find a free satisfaction in the objects of the senses even without any sensible charm.

§ 60.
Appendix
On the methodology of taste.[18]

The division of a critique into a doctrine of elements and a doctrine of method that precedes the science cannot be applied to the critique of taste, because there cannot be any science of the beautiful and the judgment of taste is not determinable by principles. For as far as the scientific element in any art is concerned, which concerns **truth** in the presentation of its object, this is to be sure the indispensable condition (*conditio sine qua non*) of beautiful art, but not the art itself. For beautiful

5: 355

---

[a] *Beurtheilung*
[b] *Beurtheilung*
[c] *Beurtheilung*

228

art there is thus only a **manner** (*modus*), not a **way of teaching it**[a] (*methodus*). The master must demonstrate what the student is to do and how he should accomplish it; and the universal rules under which he ultimately brings his procedure can serve rather to bring its principal elements to mind as occasion requires than to prescribe them to him. Nevertheless, in so doing there must be regard for a certain ideal that art must have before its eyes, even though in practice it is never fully attained. Only by stimulating the imagination of the student toward suitability for a given concept, by means of the already noted inade-quacy of the expression for the idea, which the concept itself never attains because it is aesthetic, and through severe criticism, can one prevent the examples that are set before him from being immediately taken by him as prototypes and models for imitation, as it were not subject to any higher norm and to his own judging,[b] thus smothering the genius and together with it also the freedom of the imagination even in its lawfulness, without which no beautiful art nor even a correct personal taste for judging of it[c] is possible.

The propaedeutic for all beautiful art, so far as it is aimed at the highest degree of its perfection, seems to lie not in precepts, but in the culture of the mental powers through those prior forms of knowledge that are called *humaniora*, presumably because **humanity** means on the one hand the universal **feeling of participation**[d] and on the other hand the capacity for being able to **communicate**[e] one's inmost self universally, which properties taken together constitute the sociability[f] that is appropriate to humankind, by means of which it distinguishes itself from the limitation of animals. The age as well as the peoples in which the vigorous drive towards the **lawful** sociability by means of which a people constitutes an enduring commonwealth wrestled with the great difficulties surrounding the difficult task of uniting freedom (and thus also equality) with coercion (more from respect and subjec-tion to duty than from fear): such an age and such a people had first of all to discover the art of the reciprocal communication of the ideas of the most educated part with the cruder, the coordination of the breadth and refinement of the former with the natural simplicity and originality of the latter, and in this way to discover that mean between higher

5: 356

---

[a] *Lehrart*
[b] *Beurtheilung*
[c] *ein richtiger sie beurtheilender eigener Geschmack*
[d] *Teilnehmungsgefühl*
[e] *mittheilen*
[f] Reading *Geselligkeit* as in the first edition rather than *Glückseligkeit* (happiness), as in the second.

culture and contented nature which constitutes the correct standard, not to be given by any universal rule, for taste as a universal human sense.

With difficulty will a later age dispense with that model, because it will always be further from nature, and ultimately, without having enduring examples of it, will hardly be in a position to form a concept of the happy union of the lawful constraint of the highest culture with the force and correctness of a free nature, feeling its own worth, in one and the same people.

But since taste is at bottom a faculty for the judging of*[a] the sensible rendering*[b] of moral ideas (by means of a certain analogy of the reflection on both),*[c] from which, as well as from the greater receptivity for the feeling resulting from the latter (which is called the moral feeling) that is to be grounded upon it, is derived that pleasure which taste declares to be valid for mankind in general, not merely for the private feeling of each, it is evident that the true propaedeutic for the grounding of taste is the development of moral ideas and the cultivation of the moral feeling; for only when sensibility is brought into accord with this can genuine taste assume a determinate, unalterable form.[19]

*[a] *Beurtheilungsvermögen*
*[b] *Versinnlichung*
*[c] Parentheses added in the second edition.

Critique
of the
Teleological Power of Judgment

§ 61.
On the objective purposiveness of nature.

One has good reason to assume, in accordance with transcendental principles, a subjective purposiveness of nature in its particular laws, for comprehensibility for the human power of judgment and the possibility of the connection of the particular experiences in one system of nature; where among its many products those can also be expected to be possible which, just as if they had actually been designed for our power of judgment, contain a form so specifically suited for it that by means of their variety and unity they serve as it were to strengthen and entertain the mental powers (which are in play in the use of these faculties), and to which one has therefore ascribed the name of **beautiful** forms.

But that things of nature serve one another as means to ends, and that their possibility itself should be adequately intelligible only through this kind of causality, for that we have no basis at all in the general idea of nature as the sum of the objects of the senses. For in the previous case the representation of things, because it is something in us, could also quite well be conceived of *a priori* as apt and serviceable for the internally purposive disposition of our cognitive faculties; but we have no basis at all for presuming *a priori* that ends that are not our own, and which also cannot pertain to nature (which we cannot assume as an intelligent being), nevertheless can or should constitute a special kind of causality, or at least an entirely unique lawlikeness thereof. Moreover, even experience cannot prove the reality of this to us unless it has been preceded by some sophistry that has merely projected the concept of the end into the nature of things but has not 5: 360 derived it from the objects and the experiential cognition of them, and which is therefore more accustomed to making nature comprehensible to us by means of the analogy with a subjective ground for the connection of representations than to cognizing it from objective grounds.

Further, objective purposiveness, as a principle of the possibility of the things of nature, is so far from being *necessarily* connected with the concept of the latter that it is rather precisely that to which one refers above all in order to prove the contingency of it (of nature) and of its form. For if one adduces, e.g., the structure of a bird, the hollowness of its bones, the placement of its wings for movement and of its tail for steering, etc., one says that given the mere *nexus effectivus*[a] in nature, without the help of a special kind of causality, namely that of ends

---

[a] a nexus of efficient causes

(*nexus finalis*),[a] this is all in the highest degree contingent: i.e., that nature, considered as a mere mechanism, could have formed itself in a thousand different ways without hitting precisely upon the unity in accordance with such a rule, and that it is therefore only outside the concept of nature, not within it, that one could have even the least ground *a priori* for hoping to find such a principle.

Nevertheless, teleological judging[b] is rightly drawn into our research into nature, at least problematically, but only in order to bring it under principles of observation and research in **analogy** with causality according to ends, without presuming thereby to **explain** it. It thus belongs to the reflecting, not to the determining power of judgment. The concept of the combinations and forms of nature in accordance with ends is still at least **one more principle** for bringing its appearances under rules where the laws of causality about the mere mechanism of nature do not suffice. For we adduce a teleological ground when we ascribe causality in regard to an object to a concept of the object as if it were to be found in nature (not in us), or rather we represent the possibility of the object in accordance with the analogy of such a causality (like the kind we encounter in ourselves), and hence we conceive of nature as **technical** through its own capacity;[c] whereas if we did not ascribe such an agency[d] to it, we would have to represent its causality as a blind mechanism. If, however, we were to base nature on **intentionally** acting causes, hence were to ground teleology not merely on a **regulative** principle for the mere **judging**[e] of appearances, to which nature in its particular laws could be thought of as subjected, but rather on a **constitutive** principle for the **derivation** of its products from their causes, then the concept of a natural end would no longer belong to the reflecting, but to the determining power of judgment; in which case, however, it would not in fact properly belong to the power of judgment at all (like the concept of beauty, as a formal subjective purposiveness), but rather, as a concept of reason, it would introduce a new causality into natural science, which, however, we merely borrow from ourselves and ascribe to other beings, yet without wanting to think of them as similar to ourselves.

[a] a nexus of final causes
[b] *Beurtheilung*
[c] *als durch eignes Vermögen*
[d] *Wirkungsart*
[e] *Beurtheilung*

First Division
Analytic
of the
Teleological Power of Judgment

§ 62.
On the objective purposiveness which is merely formal, in distinction to that which is material.

All geometrical figures that are drawn in accordance with a principle display a manifold and often admired objective purposiveness, namely that of serviceability for the solution of many problems in accordance with a single principle, and indeed of each of them in infinitely many different ways. The purposiveness here is evidently objective and intellectual, not, however, merely subjective and aesthetic. For it expresses the suitability of the figure for the generation of many shapes aimed at purposes,*a* and is cognized through reason. But the purposiveness still does not make the concept of the object itself possible, i.e., it is not regarded as possible merely with respect to this use.

In such a simple figure as the circle there lies the basis for the solution of a host of problems, for each of which by itself much preparation would be required, and which as it were arises from this figure itself as one of its many splendid properties. If, e.g., the problem is to construct a triangle from a given baseline and the angle opposite to it, then it is indeterminate, i.e., it can be solved in infinitely many ways. But the circle comprehends them all, as the geometrical locus for all triangles that satisfy this condition. Or two lines are supposed to intersect in such a way that the rectangle constructed from the two parts of the one is equal to the rectangle from the two parts of the other: the solution of this problem looks as if it will be very difficult. But all the lines that intersect within the circle the circumference of which bounds each of them are of themselves divided into this proportion. The other curves yield in turn other purposive solutions that were not thought of at all in the rule that constitutes their construction. All conic sections, by themselves and in comparison with one another, are

---

a *abgezweckten Gestalten*

fruitful in principles for the solution of a host of possible problems, as simple as the definition*a* is which determines their concept. – It is a true joy to see the eagerness with which the ancient geometers investigated the properties of such lines without being distracted by the question of limited minds: for what is this knowledge useful?, e.g., that of the parabola, without knowing the law of terrestrial gravitation, which would have given them its application to the trajectory of heavy bodies (whose gravitational direction in their motion can be seen as parallel);*b* or of the ellipse, without suspecting that there is also gravity in heavenly bodies, and without knowing its law at different distances from points of attraction, which makes them describe these lines in free movement. While these geometers, unbeknownst to themselves, were working for posterity, they delighted in a purposiveness in the essence of things, which they could yet exhibit fully *a priori* in its necessity. Plato, himself a master of this science, was led by such an original constitution of things, in the discovery of which we can dispense with all experience, and by the mental capacity*c* for drawing the harmony of things out of their supersensible principle (to which pertain the properties of numbers, with which the mind plays in music), to the enthusiasm that elevated him beyond the concepts of experience to ideas, which seemed to him explicable only by means of an intellectual communion with the origin of all things.[1] No wonder that he banned from his school those who were ignorant of geometry, for he thought he could derive that which Anaxagoras inferred from objects of experience from the pure intuition internal to the human mind.[2] For in the necessity of that which is purposive and so constituted as if it were intentionally arranged for our use, but which nevertheless seems to pertain originally to the essence of things, without any regard to our use, lies the ground for the great admiration of nature, not outside of us so much as in our own reason; in which case it is surely excusable that through misunderstanding this admiration gradually rose to enthusiasm.

5: 364

This intellectual purposiveness, however, although it is objective (not, like the aesthetic, subjective), can nevertheless be conceived, as far as its possibility is concerned, as merely formal (not real), i.e., as purposiveness that is not grounded in a purpose, for which teleology would be necessary, but only in general. The figure of a circle is an intuition that can be determined by the understanding in accordance with a principle; the unity of this principle, which I assume arbitrarily

a *Erklärung*
b To a parabola, presumably; that is, the actual trajectory of a body is parallel to the geometrical figure of a parabola.
c *Vermögen*

and, as a concept, make into a ground, when applied to a form of intuition (to space) which is to be found in me merely as representation and indeed *a priori*, makes comprehensible the unity of many rules resulting from the construction of that concept, which are purposive in many respects, without an *end* or any other ground having to be the basis of this purposiveness. This is different from finding order and regularity in a sum of *things* outside of me enclosed in certain bounds, e.g., among the trees, flower beds and paths in a garden, which I cannot hope to deduce *a priori* from my demarcation of a space in accordance with an arbitrary rule:[a] for these are existing things, which must be given empirically in order to be cognized, and not a mere representation in me determined in accordance with an *a priori* principle. Hence the latter (empirical) purposiveness, as **real**, is dependent on the concept of an end.

But the reason for the admiration of a purposiveness perceived in the essence of things (insofar as their concept can be constructed) can be quite easily and indeed quite rightly understood. The many rules, the unity of which (from a principle) arouses this admiration, are one and all synthetic, and do not follow from a **concept** of the object, e.g., from that of a circle, but need this object to be given in intuition. But it thereby comes to seem as if this unity empirically possesses an external ground, distinct from our power of representation, for its rules, and thus as if the correspondence of the object with the need for rules, which is characteristic of the understanding, is in itself contingent, hence possible only by means of an end expressly aimed at it. Now of course this very harmony, since it is, in spite of all this purposiveness, cognized not empirically but *a priori*, should bring it home to us that space, by the determination of which (by means of the imagination, in accordance with a concept) the object is alone possible, is not a property of the object outside of me, but merely a kind of representation in me, and thus that I **introduce** the **purposiveness** into the figure that I draw **in accord with a concept**, i.e., into my own way of representing that which is given to me externally, whatever it may be in itself, thus that I am not instructed empirically about this purposiveness by the object, and consequently do not need for this purposiveness any particular end outside of me in the object. But since this reflection already requires a critical use of reason, and hence cannot be immediately contained in the judging[b] of the object in accordance with its properties, the latter gives me immediately nothing other than the unification of heterogeneous rules (united even in that which is diverse in them) in one principle, which, without needing a particular

5: 365

---

[a] In the first edition, "from my arbitrary demarcation of a space."
[b] *Beurtheilung*

ground lying *a priori* beyond my concept and, in general, my representation, can nevertheless be cognized by me *a priori* as truthful. Now **astonishment**[a] is a mental shock at the incompatibility of a representation and the rule that is given through it with the principles already grounded in the mind, which thus produces a doubt as to whether one has seen or judged correctly; but **admiration**[b] is an astonishment that continually recurs despite the disappearance of this doubt. The latter is consequently an entirely natural effect of that purposiveness observed in the essence of things (as appearances), which also cannot be criticized insofar as the compatibility of that form of sensible intuition (which is called space) with the faculty of concepts (the understanding) is not only inexplicable for us insofar as it is precisely thus and not otherwise, but also enlarges the mind, allowing it, as it were, to suspect something lying beyond those sensible representations, in which, although unknown to us, the ultimate ground of that accord could be found.[c] Indeed, it is not necessary for us to know this if it is merely a matter of the formal purposiveness of our *a priori* representations; but even just being compelled to look in that direction fills us with admiration for the object that forces us to do so.

5: 366 It is customary to call the properties of geometrical shapes as well as of numbers that have been mentioned **beauty**, on account of a certain *a priori* purposiveness, not expected from the simplicity of their construction, for all sorts of cognitive use, and to speak of this or that **beautiful** property of, e.g., a circle, which is discovered in this way or that. But it is not an aesthetic judging[d] by means of which we find it purposive, not a judging[e] without a concept, which makes noticeable a merely **subjective** purposiveness in the free play of our cognitive faculties, but an intellectual judging in accordance with concepts, which gives us distinct cognition of an objective purposiveness, i.e., serviceability for all sorts of (infinitely manifold) purposes. One would have to call it a **relative perfection** rather than a beauty of the mathematical figure. The designation of an **intellectual beauty** can also not be allowed at all, for otherwise the word "beauty" would have to lose all determinate meaning, or intellectual satisfaction would have to lose all preeminence over sensible satisfaction. It would be better to be able to call a **demonstration** of such properties beautiful, since by means of

[a] *Verwunderung*

[b] *Bewunderung*

[c] In the first edition, there is no period here, and instead the sentence continues: "which we do not indeed have to know if what is at stake is merely formal purposiveness of our representations *a priori*, even to take notice of which, however, at the same time fills us with admiration for the object that forces us to do that."

[d] *Beurtheilung*

[e] *Beurtheilung*

this the understanding, as the faculty of concepts, and the imagination, as the faculty for exhibiting them, feel themselves strengthened *a priori* (which, together with the precision which is introduced by reason, is called its elegance): for here at least the satisfaction, although its ground lies in concepts, is subjective, whereas perfection is accompanied with an objective satisfaction.

§ 63.
On the relative purposiveness of nature in distinction from internal purposiveness.

Experience leads our power of judgment to the concept of an objective and material purposiveness, i.e., to the concept of an end of nature, only if there is a relation of the cause to the effect to be judged*,[a] which we can understand as lawful only insofar as we find ourselves capable of subsuming the idea of the effect under the causality of its cause as the underlying condition of the possibility of the former. But this can happen in two ways: either if we regard the effect immediately as a product of art or if we regard it only as material for the art of other possible natural beings, thus if we regard it either as an end or as a means for the purposive use of other causes. The latter purposiveness is called usefulness (for human beings) or advantageousness (for every other creature), and is merely relative; while the former is an internal purposiveness of the natural being.

5: 367

Rivers, e.g., carry with them all sorts of soil helpful for the growth of plants, which they sometimes deposit in the middle of the land, sometimes in their deltas. On many coasts, the tide spreads this silt on the land, or deposits it on the bank, and, particularly if human beings help prevent the ebb from carrying it away again, the fruitful land increases, and the vegetable kingdom wins a place where previously fish and shellfish dwelt. Most of these sorts of extension of the land have been produced by nature, and it continues to do so, although slowly. – Now the question arises, is this to be judged[b] as an end of nature, because it is useful for human beings? – for its usefulness for the vegetable kingdom cannot be brought into the balance, because

---

* Since in pure mathematics there can never be an issue of the existence of things, but only of their possibility, namely the possibility of an intuition corresponding to their concept, and hence there can never be an issue of cause and effect, all of the purposiveness that has been noted there must therefore be considered merely as formal, never as a natural end.

5: 366

[a] *zu beurtheilen ist*
[b] *zu beurtheilen sei*

just as much is taken away from the creatures of the sea as is added to the land.[3]

Or, to give an example of the advantageousness of certain natural things as means for other creatures (if one presupposes them as ends[a]): no soil is more favorable to pine trees than a sandy soil. Now the ancient sea, before it withdrew from the land, left so many sandy tracts behind in our northern regions that on this soil, otherwise so useless for any cultivation, extensive pine forests grew up, for the irrational eradication of which we frequently blame our ancestors; and here one can ask whether this ancient deposit of sandy strata was an end of nature for the sake of the pine forests that were possible there. This much is clear: that if one assumes this to be an end of nature, then one would also have to admit that the sand is an end, though only a relative one, for which in turn the ancient beach and the withdrawal of the sea were the means; for in the series of subordinated members of a connection of ends every intermediate member must be considered as an end (although not as the final end), for which its proximate cause is the means. In the same way, if cattle, sheep, horses, etc. were even to exist in the world, then there had to be grass on the earth, and saltwort had to grow in the desert if camels were to thrive, and these and other herbivorous animals had to be found if there were to be wolves, tigers and lions. Hence the objective purposiveness which is grounded on advantageousness is not an objective purposiveness of the things in themselves, as if the sand in itself, as an effect of its cause, the sea, could not be comprehended without ascribing a purpose to the latter and without considering the effect, namely the sand, as a work of art. It is a merely relative purposiveness, contingent in the thing itself to which it is ascribed; and although in the examples we have given the species of grasses themselves are to be judged[b] as organized products of nature, hence as rich in art, nevertheless in relation to the animals which they nourish they are to be regarded as mere raw materials.

If, however, the human being, through the freedom of his causality, finds things in nature completely advantageous for his often foolish aims (colorful bird feathers for the decoration of his clothing, colored soils or juices of plants for painting himself), but sometimes also to his rational ends, as the horse for riding or the ox and in Minorca even the ass and the swine for plowing, one cannot assume here even a relative end of nature (for this use). For the human's reason knows how to bring things into correspondence with his own arbitrary inspi-

[a] In the second edition, this is changed to "means"; the first edition seems preferable here.
[b] zu beurtheilen sind

rations, to which he was by no means predestined by nature. Only **if** one assumes that human beings have to live on the earth would there also have to be at least no lack of the means without which they could not subsist as animals and even as rational animals (in however low a degree); but in that case those things in nature which are indispensable for this purpose*ª* would also have to be regarded as natural ends.

From this it can readily be seen that external purposiveness (advantageousness of one thing for another) can be regarded as an external natural end only under the condition that the existence of that for which it is advantageous, whether in a proximate or a distant way, is in itself an end of nature. This, however, can never be made out by mere contemplation of nature; thus it follows that relative purposiveness, although it gives hypothetical indications of natural ends, nevertheless justifies no absolute teleological judgments.

5: 369

In cold lands the snow protects the seeds*ᵇ* from frost; it facilitates communication among humans (by means of sleds); the Laplanders find animals there that bring about this communication (reindeer), which find adequate nourishment in a sparse moss, which they must even scrape out from under the snow, and yet are easily tamed and readily deprived of the freedom in which they could otherwise maintain themselves quite well. For other peoples*ᶜ* in the same icy regions the sea contains a rich supply of animals which, even beyond the nourishment and clothing that they provide and the wood which the sea as it were washes up for them for houses, also supplies them with fuel for warming their huts. Now here is an admirable confluence of so many relations of nature for one end: and this is the Greenlander, the Lapp, the Samoyed, the Yakut, etc. But one does not see why human beings have to live there at all. Thus to say that moisture falls from the air in the form of snow, that the sea has its currents which float the wood that has grown in warmer lands there, and that great sea animals filled with oil exist **because** the cause that produces all these natural products is grounded in the idea of an advantage for certain miserable creatures would be a very bold and arbitrary judgment. For even if all of this natural usefulness did not exist, we would find nothing lacking in this state of things for the adequacy of natural causes; rather, even merely to demand such a predisposition and to expect such an end of nature would seem to us presumptuous and ill-considered (for only the greatest incompatibility among human beings could have forced them into such inhospitable regions).[4]

ª zu diesem Behuf
ᵇ reading *Saaten* with the first edition rather than *Staaten* (states) with the second.
ᶜ The word "peoples" (*Völker*) was added in the second edition.

§ 64.
On the special character of
things as natural ends.

In order to see that a thing is possible only as an end, i.e., that the causality of its origin must be sought not in the mechanism of nature, but in a cause whose productive capacity[a] is determined by concepts, it is necessary that its form not be possible in accordance with mere natural laws, i.e., ones that can be cognized by us through the understanding, applied to objects of the senses, alone; rather even empirical cognition of their cause and effect presupposes concepts of reason.[5] Since reason must be able to cognize the necessity in every form of a natural product if it would understand the conditions connected with its generation, the **contingency** of their form with respect to all empirical laws of nature in relation to reason is itself a ground for regarding their causality as if it were possible only through reason; but this is then the capacity[b] for acting in accordance with ends (a will); and the object which is represented as possible only on this basis is represented as possible only as an end.

5: 370

If someone were to perceive a geometrical figure, for instance a regular hexagon, drawn in the sand in an apparently uninhabited land, his reflection, working with a concept of it, would become aware of the unity of the principle of its generation by means of reason, even if only obscurely, and thus, in accordance with this, would not be able to judge as a ground of the possibility of such a shape the sand, the nearby sea, the wind, the footprints of any known animals, or any other non-rational cause, because the contingency of coinciding with such a concept, which is possible only in reason, would seem to him so infinitely great that it would be just as good as if there were no natural law of nature, consequently no cause in nature acting merely mechanically, and as if the concept of such an object could be regarded as a concept that can be given only by reason and only by reason compared with the object, thus as if only reason can contain the causality for such an effect, consequently that this object must be thoroughly regarded as an end, but not a natural end, i.e., as a product of **art** (*vestigium hominis video*[c]).[6]

But in order to judge[d] something that one cognizes as a product of nature as being at the same time an end, hence a **natural end**, something more is required if there is not simply to be a contradiction here.

---

[a] *Vermögen zu wirken*
[b] *Vermögen*
[c] I see it as a trace of a human being.
[d] *beurtheilen*

I would say provisionally that a thing exists as a natural end **if it is cause and effect of itself** (although in a twofold sense);*ᵃ* for in this there lies a causality the likes of which cannot be connected with the mere concept of a nature without ascribing an end to it, but which in that case also can be conceived without contradiction but cannot be comprehended. We will first elucidate the determination of this idea of a natural end by means of an example before we fully analyze it.⁷

5: 371

First, a tree generates another tree in accordance with a known natural law. However, the tree that it generates is of the same species;*ᵇ* and so it generates itself as far as the **species** is concerned, in which it, on one side as effect, on the other as cause, unceasingly produces itself, and likewise, often producing itself, continuously preserves itself, as species.

Second, a tree also generates itself as an **individual**. This sort of effect we call, of course, growth; but this is to be taken in such a way that it is entirely distinct from any other increase in magnitude in accordance with mechanical laws, and is to be regarded as equivalent, although under another name, with generation. This plant first prepares the matter that it adds to itself with a quality peculiar to its species, which could not be provided by the mechanism of nature outside of it, and develops itself further by means of material which, as far as its composition is concerned, is its own product. For although as far as the components that it receives from nature outside of itself are concerned, it must be regarded only as an educt, nevertheless in the separation and new composition of this raw material there is to be found an originality of the capacity*ᶜ* for separation and formation in this sort of natural being that remains infinitely remote from all art when it attempts to reconstitute such a product of the vegetable kingdom from the elements that it obtains*ᵈ* by its decomposition or from the material that nature provides for its nourishment.

Third,*ᵉ* one part of this creature also generates itself in such a way that the preservation of the one is reciprocally dependent on the preservation of the other. An eye from the leaf of one tree grafted into the twig of another brings forth a growth of its own kind in an alien stock, and similarly a scion attached to another trunk. Hence one can regard every twig or leaf of one tree as merely grafted or inoculated into it, hence as a tree existing in itself, which only depends on the other and

---

ᵃ The phrase enclosed in these parentheses was added in the second edition.
ᵇ *Gattung*
ᶜ *-vermögens*
ᵈ The word "obtains" (*erhält*) was inserted in the second edition.
ᵉ The words "First" and "Second" in the preceding two paragraphs are not emphasized in Kant's text.

nourishes itself parasitically. At the same time, the leaves are certainly products of the tree, yet they preserve it in turn, for repeated defoliation would kill it, and its growth depends upon their effect on the stem. The self-help of nature in the case of injury in these creatures, where the lack of a part that is necessary for the preservation of the neighboring parts can be made good by the others; the miscarriages or malformations in growth, where certain parts form themselves in an entirely new way because of chance defects or obstacles, in order to preserve that which exists and bring forth an anomalous creature: these I mention only in passing, although they belong among the most wonderful properties of organized creatures.

§ 65.
Things, as natural ends, are organized beings.

According to the characterization of the previous section, a thing that is to be cognized as a natural product but yet at the same time as possible only as a natural end must be related to itself reciprocally as both cause and effect, which is a somewhat improper and indeterminate expression, in need of a derivation from a determinate concept.

The causal nexus,[a] insofar as it is conceived merely by the understanding, is a connection that constitutes a series (of causes and effects) that is always descending; and the things themselves, which as effects presuppose others as their causes, cannot conversely be the causes of these at the same time. This causal nexus is called that of efficient causes (*nexus effectivus*). In contrast, however, a causal nexus can also be conceived in accordance with a concept of reason (of ends), which, if considered as a series, would carry with it descending as well as ascending dependency, in which the thing which is on the one hand designated as an effect nevertheless deserves, in ascent, the name of a cause of the same thing of which it is the effect. In the practical sphere (namely, of art) such a connection can readily be found, e.g., the house is certainly the cause of the sums that are taken in as rent, while conversely the representation of this possible income was the cause of the construction of the house.[8] Such a causal connection is called that of final causes (*nexus finalis*). The first could perhaps more aptly be called the connection of real causes, and the second that of ideal ones, since with this terminology it would immediately be grasped that there cannot be more than these two kinds of causality.

Now for a thing as a natural end it is requisite, **first**, that its parts

[a] *Kausalverbindung*

(as far as their existence and their form are concerned) are possible only through their relation to the whole. For the thing itself is an end, and is thus comprehended under a concept or an idea that must determine *a priori* everything that is to be contained in it. But insofar as a thing is conceived of as possible only in this way it is merely a work of art, i.e., the product of a rational cause distinct from the matter (the parts), the causality of which (in the production and combination of the parts) is determined through its idea of a whole that is thereby possible (thus not through nature outside of it).⁹

But if a thing, as a natural product, is nevertheless to contain in itself and its internal possibility a relation to ends, i.e., is to be possible only as a natural end and without the causality of the concepts of a rational being outside of it, then it is required, **second**, that its parts be combined into a whole by being reciprocally the cause and effect of their form. For in this way alone is it possible in turn for the idea of the whole conversely (reciprocally) to determine the form and combination of all the parts: not as a cause – for then it would be a product of art – but as a ground for the cognition of the systematic unity of the form and the combination of all of the manifold that is contained in the given material for someone who judges*ᵃ* it.

For a body, therefore, which is to be judged*ᵇ* as a natural end in itself and in accordance with its internal possibility, it is required that its parts reciprocally produce each other, as far as both their form and their combination is concerned, and thus produce a whole out of their own causality, the concept of which, conversely, is in turn the cause (in a being that would possess the causality according to concepts appropriate for such a product) of it in accordance with a principle; consequently the connection of **efficient causes** could at the same time be judged*ᶜ* as an **effect through final causes**.

In such a product of nature each part is conceived as if it exists only **through** all the others, thus as if existing **for the sake of the others** and **on account of** the whole, i.e., as an instrument (organ), which is, however, not sufficient (for it could also be an instrument of art, and thus represented as possible at all only as an end); rather it must be thought of as an organ that **produces** the other parts (consequently each produces the others reciprocally), which cannot be the case in any instrument of art, but only of nature, which provides all the matter for instruments (even those of art): only then and on that account can such a product, as an **organized** and **self-organizing** being, be called a **natural end.**

5: 374

ᵃ *beurtheilt*
ᵇ *beurtheilt*
ᶜ *beurtheilt*

In a watch one part is the instrument for the motion of another, but one wheel is not the efficient cause for the production of the other: one part is certainly present for the sake of the other but not because of it. Hence the producing cause of the watch and its form is not contained in the nature (of this matter), but outside of it, in a being that can act in accordance with an idea of a whole that is possible through its causality. Thus one wheel in the watch does not produce the other, and even less does one watch produce another, using for that purpose other matter (organizing it); hence it also cannot by itself replace parts that have been taken from it, or make good defects in its original construction by the addition of other parts, or somehow repair itself when it has fallen into disorder: all of which, by contrast, we can expect from organized nature. – An organized being is thus not a mere machine, for that has only a **motive** power, while the organized being possesses in itself a **formative** power, and indeed one that it communicates to the matter, which does not have it (it organizes the latter): thus it has a self-propagating formative power, which cannot be explained through the capacity for movement alone (that is, mechanism).[10]

One says far too little about nature and its capacity[a] in organized products if one calls this an **analogue of art**: for in that case one conceives of the artist (a rational being) outside of it. Rather, it organizes itself, and in every species of its organized products, of course in accordance with some example in the whole, but also with appropriate deviations, which are required in the circumstances for self-preservation. Perhaps one comes closer to this inscrutable property if one calls it an **analogue of life**: but then one must either endow matter as mere matter with a property (hylozoism) that contradicts its essence, or else associate with it an alien principle **standing in communion** with it (a soul), in which case, however, if such a product is to be a product of nature, organized matter as an instrument of that soul is already presupposed, and thus makes that product not the least more comprehensible, or else the soul is made into an artificer of this structure, and the product must be withdrawn from (corporeal) nature. Strictly speaking, the organization of nature is therefore not analogous with any causality that we know.* Beauty in nature, since it is ascribed

5: 375

5: 375 * One can, conversely, illuminate a certain association, though one that is encountered more in the idea than in reality, by means of an analogy with the immediate ends of nature that have been mentioned. Thus, in the case of a recently undertaken fundamental transformation of a great people into a state, the word **organization** has frequently been quite appropriately used for

[a] *Vermögen*

to objects only in relation to reflection on their **outer** intuition, thus only to the form of their surfaces, can rightly be called an analogue of art. But **inner natural perfection**, as is possessed by those things that are possible only as **natural ends** and hence as organized beings, is not thinkable and explicable in accordance with any analogy to any physical, i.e., natural capacity that is known to us; indeed, since we ourselves belong to nature in the widest sense, it is not thinkable and explicable even through an exact analogy with human art.

The concept of a thing as in itself a natural end is therefore not a constitutive concept of the understanding or of reason, but it can still be a regulative concept for the reflecting power of judgment, for guiding research into objects of this kind and thinking over their highest ground in accordance with a remote analogy with our own causality in accordance with ends; not, of course, for the sake of knowledge of nature or of its original ground, but rather for the sake of the very same practical faculty of reason in us in analogy with which we consider the cause of that purposiveness.

Organized beings are thus the only ones in nature which, even if considered in themselves and without a relation to other things, must nevertheless be thought of as possible only as its ends, and which thus   5: 376 first provide objective reality for the concept of an **end** that is not a practical end but an end of **nature**, and thereby provide natural science with the basis for a teleology, i.e., a way of judging*a* its objects in accordance with a particular principle the likes of which one would otherwise be absolutely unjustified in introducing at all (since one cannot at all understand the possibility of such a kind of causality *a priori*).

§ 66.
On the principle for the judging*b* of the internal purposiveness in organized beings.

This principle, or its definition, states: **An organized product of nature is that in which everything is an end and reciprocally a means**

the institution of the magistracies, etc., and even of the entire body politic. For in such a whole each member should certainly be not merely a means, but at the same time also an end, and, insofar as it contributes to the possibility of the whole, its position and function should also be determined by the idea of the whole.[11]

a *Beurtheilungsart*
b *Beurtheilung*

as well.[12] Nothing in it is in vain, purposeless, or to be ascribed to a blind mechanism of nature.

As for what occasions it, this principle is of course to be derived from experience, that is, experience of the kind that is methodically undertaken and is called observation; but the universality and necessity that it asserts of such a purposiveness cannot rest merely on grounds in experience, but must have as its ground some sort of *a priori* principle, even if it is merely regulative and even if that end lies only in the idea of the one who judges[a] and never in any efficient cause. One can thus call this principle a **maxim** for the judging[b] of the inner purposiveness of organized beings.

It is well known that the anatomists of plants and animals, in order to investigate their structure and to understand for what reason and to what end[c] they have been given such a disposition and combination of parts and precisely this internal form, assume as indispensably necessary the maxim that nothing in such a creature is **in vain**, and likewise adopt it as the fundamental principle of the general doctrine of nature that **nothing** happens **by chance**. In fact, they could just as little dispense with this teleological principle as they could do without the universal physical principle, since, just as in the case of the abandonment[d] of the latter there would remain no experience at all, so in the case of the abandonment of the former principle there would remain no guideline for the observation of a kind of natural thing that we have conceived of teleologically under the concept of a natural end.

5: 377 For this concept leads reason into an order of things entirely different from that of a mere mechanism of nature, which will here no longer satisfy us. An idea has to ground the possibility of the product of nature. However, since this is an absolute unity of the representation, while the matter is a multitude of things, which by itself can provide no determinate unity of composition, if that unity of the idea is even to serve as the determining ground *a priori* of a natural law of the causality of such a form of the composite, then the end of nature must extend to **everything** that lies in its product.[e] For once we have related such an effect in the **whole** to a supersensible determining ground beyond the blind mechanism of nature, we must also judge[f] it entirely in accordance with this principle; and there is no ground for

---

[a] *dem Beurtheilenden*
[b] *Beurtheilung*
[c] *Ende*
[d] *Verlassung*; the first edition had *Veranlassung* (occasion).
[e] In the first edition, there was a semicolon here and the sentence continued to the end of the paragraph.
[f] *beurtheilen*

assuming that the form of such a thing is only partially dependent on the latter, for in such a case, in which two heterogeneous principles are jumbled together, no secure rule for judging*a* would remain at all.

It might always be possible that in, e.g., an animal body, many parts could be conceived as consequences*b* of merely mechanical laws (such as skin, hair, and bones).*c* Yet the cause that provides the appropriate material, modifies it, forms it, and deposits it in its appropriate place must always be judged*d* teleologically, so that everything in it must be considered as organized, and everything is also, in a certain relation to the thing itself, an organ in turn.

§ 67.
On the principle of the teleological judging*e* of nature in general as a system of ends.

We have said above that the **external** purposiveness of natural things offers no sufficient justification for using them at the same time as ends of nature, as grounds for the explanation of their existence, and using their contingently purposive effects, in the idea, as grounds for their existence in accordance with the principle of final causes. Thus because **rivers** promote communication among peoples in inland countries, and **mountains** contain the sources of rivers and stores of snow for their maintenance in times of drought, while the **slope** of the land carries these waters down and allows the land to drain, one cannot immedi-   5: 378 ately take these to be natural ends: for even though this configuration of the surface of the earth was quite necessary for the origination and preservation of the vegetable and animal kingdoms, yet there is nothing in it the possibility of which would require the assumption of a causality in accordance with ends. The same is true of plants that humans use for their needs or diversion, and of animals, such as camels, cattle, horses, dogs, etc., which are so widely used, partly for nourishment and partly for service, and are in great part indispensable. In things that one has no cause to regard as ends for themselves, an external relationship can be judged*f* to be purposive only hypothetically.

To judge*g* a thing to be purposive on account of its internal form is

---

a *Beurtheilung*
b *Concretionen*
c In the first edition, this period was a comma.
d *beurtheilt*
e *Beurtheilung*
f *beurtheilt*
g *beurtheilen*

entirely different from holding the existence of such a thing to be an end of nature. For the latter assertion we need not only the concept of a possible end, but also cognition of the final end (*scopus*)[a] of nature, which requires the relation of nature to something supersensible, which far exceeds all of our teleological cognition of nature; for the end of the existence of nature itself must be sought beyond nature. The internal form of a mere blade of grass can demonstrate its merely possible origin in accordance with the rule of ends in a way that is sufficient for our human faculty for judging.[b] But if one leaves this aside and looks only to the use that other natural beings make of it, then one abandons the contemplation of its internal organization and looks only at its external purposive relations, where the grass is necessary to the livestock, just as the latter is necessary to the human being as the means for his existence; yet one does not see why it is necessary that human beings exist (a question which, if one thinks about the New Hollanders or the Fuegians,[13] might not be so easy to answer); thus one does not arrive at any categorical end, but all of this purposive relation rests on a condition that is always to be found further on, and which, as unconditioned, (the existence of a thing as a final end) lies entirely outside of the physical-teleological way of considering the world. But then such a thing is also not a natural end; for it (or its entire species) is not to be regarded as a natural product.

It is therefore only matter insofar as it is organized that necessarily carries with it the concept of itself as a natural end, since its specific form is at the same time a product of nature. However, this concept necessarily leads to the idea of the whole of nature as a system in accordance with the rule of ends, to which idea all of the mechanism of nature in accordance with principles of reason must now be subordinated (at least in order to test natural appearance by this idea).[14] The principle of reason is appropriate for it only subjectively, i.e., as the maxims that everything in the world is good for something, that nothing in it is in vain; and by means of the example that nature gives in its organic products, one is justified, indeed called upon to expect nothing in nature and its laws but what is purposive in the whole.

It is self-evident that this is not a principle for the determining but only for the reflecting power of judgment, that it is regulative and not constitutive, and that by its means we acquire only a guideline for considering things in nature, in relation to a determining ground that is already given, in accordance with a new, lawful order, and for extending natural science in accordance with another principle, namely

5: 379

[a] a target or object aimed at
[b] *Beurtheilungsvermögen*

250

that of final causes, yet without harm to the mechanism of nature. Moreover, it is by no means determined by this whether something that we judge in accordance with this principle is an **intentional** end of nature – whether grass exists for cattle or sheep, and these and the other things in nature for human beings. It is even good for us to consider in this light things that are unpleasant and in certain relations contrapurposive for us. Thus one could say, e.g., that the vermin that plague humans in their clothes, hair, or bedding are, in accordance with a wise dispensation of nature, an incentive for cleanliness, which is in itself already an important means for the preservation of health. Or the mosquitoes and other stinging insects that make the wilds of America so trying for the savages are so many goads to spur these primitive people to drain the swamps and let light into the thick, airless forests and thereby as well as by the cultivation of the soil to make their abode more salubrious. If it is treated in this way, then even what seems to the human being to be contrary to nature in his internal organization provides an entertaining and sometimes also instructive prospect on a teleological order of things, to which merely physical consideration alone, without such a principle, would not lead us. Just as some judge that a tapeworm is given to the human or the animal in which it resides as if it were to make good a certain defect in its organs, so I would ask whether dreams (from which our sleep is never free, although we rarely remember them) might not be a purposive arrangement in nature, since, when all the motive forces in the body have relaxed, they serve to move the vital organs internally by means of the imagination and its great activity (which in this condition often amount to an affect);[15] and in the case of an overfilled stomach, where this movement during nocturnal sleep is all the more necessary, they commonly play themselves out with all the more liveliness; consequently,[a] without this internal motive force and exhausting unrest, on account of which we often complain about dreams (which nevertheless are in fact perhaps a remedy), sleep, even in a healthy condition, might well amount to a complete extinction of life.[16] Even beauty in nature, i.e., its agreement with the free play of our cognitive faculties in the apprehension and judging[b] of its appearance, can be considered in this way as an objective purposiveness of nature in its entirety, as a system of which the human being is a member, once the teleological judging[c] of nature by means of natural ends, which have been made evident to us by organized beings, has justified us in the idea of a great system of the

5: 380

---

[a] This word was added in the second edition.
[b] Beurtheilung
[c] Beurtheilung

ends of nature. We may consider it as a favor* that nature has done for us that in addition to usefulness it has so richly distributed beauty and charms, and we can love it on that account, just as we regard it with respect because of its immeasurability, and we can feel ourselves to be ennobled in this contemplation – just as if nature had erected and decorated its magnificent stage precisely with this intention.

5: 381

In this section we have meant to say nothing except that once we have discovered in nature a capacity^a for bringing forth products that can only be conceived by us in accordance with the concept of final causes, we may go further and also judge^b to belong to a system of ends even those things (or their relation, however purposive)^c which do not make it necessary to seek another principle of their possibility beyond the mechanism of blindly acting causes; because the former idea already, as far as its ground is concerned, leads us beyond the sensible world, and the unity of the supersensible principle must then be considered as valid in the same way not merely for certain species of natural beings but for the whole of nature as a system.

§ 68.
On the principle of teleology as an internal principle of natural science.

The principles of a science are either internal to it, and are then called indigenous (*principia domestica*), or they are based on princples that can find their place only outside of it, and are *foreign* principles (*peregrina*).^{d} Sciences that contain the latter base their doctrines on auxiliary propositions (*lemmata*), i.e., they borrow some concept, and along with it a basis for order, from another science.[17]

Every science is of itself a system; and it is not enough that in it we build in accordance with principles and thus proceed technically; rather, in it, as a freestanding building, we must also work architecton-

---

5: 380

* In the aesthetic part it was said that **we would look on nature with favor** insofar as we have an entirely free (disinterested) satisfaction in its form. For in this mere judgment of taste there is no regard for the end for which these natural beauties exist, whether to arouse pleasure in us or without any relation to us as ends. In a teleological judgment, however, we do attend to this relation, and then we can **regard** it **as a favor of nature** that by means of the exhibition of so many beautiful shapes it would promote culture.

^{a} *Vermögen*
^{b} *beurtheilen*
^{c} Parentheses added in the second edition.
^{d} foreign

ically, and treat it not like an addition and as a part of another building, but as a whole by itself, although afterwards we can construct a transition from this building to the other or vice versa.

Thus if one brings the concept of God into natural science and its context in order to make purposiveness in nature explicable, and subsequently uses this purposiveness in turn to prove that there is a God, then there is nothing of substance in either of the sciences, and a deceptive fallacy[a] casts each into uncertainty by letting them cross each other's borders.

The expression "an end of nature" is already enough to preclude this confusion so that there is no mix-up between natural science and the occasion that it provides for the **teleological** judging[b] of its objects and the consideration of God, and thus a **theological** derivation; and one must not regard it as unimportant whether one exchanges the former expression for that of a divine purpose in the order of nature or even passes off the latter as more fitting and more suitable for a pious soul because in the end it must come down to deriving every purposive form in nature from a wise author of the world; rather, we must carefully and modestly restrict ourselves to the expression that says only exactly as much as we know, namely that of an end of nature. For even before we ask after the cause of nature itself, we find within nature and the course of its generation products generated in accordance with the known laws of experience within it, in accordance with which natural science must judge[c] its objects and thus seek within itself for their causality in accordance with the rule of ends. Hence natural science must not jump over its boundaries in order to bring within itself as an indigenous principle that to whose concept no experience at all can ever be adequate and upon which we are authorized to venture only after the completion of natural science.

5: 382

Natural properties that can be demonstrated *a priori* and whose possibility can thus be understood from general principles without any assistance from experience, even though they are accompanied with a technical purposiveness, can nevertheless, because they are absolutely necessary, not be counted at all as part of the teleology of nature as a method of solving its problems that belongs within physics. Arithmetical and geometrical analogies as well as universal mechanical laws, no matter how strange and astonishing the unification of different and apparently entirely independent rules in a single principle in them may seem, can make no claim on that account to be teleological grounds of explanation within physics; and even if they deserve to be taken into

[a] *Diallele*
[b] *Beurtheilung*
[c] *beurtheilen*

consideration within the general theory of the purposiveness of things in nature, this would still belong elsewhere, namely in metaphysics, and would not constitute any internal principle of natural science: whereas in the case of the empirical laws of natural ends in organized beings it is not merely permissible but is even unavoidable to use the teleological **way of judging**[a] as the principle of the theory of nature with regard to a special class of its objects.

5: 383

Now in order to remain strictly within its own boundaries, physics abstracts entirely from the question of whether the ends of nature are **intentional** or **unintentional**; for that would be meddling in someone else's business (namely, in that of metaphysics). It is enough that there are objects that are **explicable** only in accordance with natural laws that we can think only under the idea of ends as a principle, and which are even internally **cognizable**, as far as their internal form is concerned, only in this way. In order to avoid even the least suspicion of wanting to mix into our cognitive grounds something that does not belong in physics at all, namely a supernatural cause, in teleology we certainly talk about nature as if the purposiveness in it were intentional, but at the same time ascribe this intention to nature, i.e., to matter, by which we would indicate (since there can be no misunderstanding here, because no intention in the strict sense of the term can be attributed to any lifeless matter) that this term signifies here only a principle of the reflecting, not of the determining power of judgment, and is thus not meant to introduce any special ground for causality, but is only meant to add to the use of reason another kind of research besides that in accordance with mechanical laws, in order to supplement the inadequacy of the latter even in the empirical search for all the particular laws of nature. Hence in teleology, insofar as it is connected to physics, we speak quite rightly of the wisdom, the economy, the forethought, and the beneficence of nature, without thereby making it into an intelligent being (since that would be absurd); but also without daring to set over it, as its architect, another, intelligent being, because this would be presumptuous;* rather, such talk is only meant to designate a

5: 383

* The German word **presumptuous**[b] is a good, meaningful word. A judgment in which we forget to take the proper measure of our powers (of understanding) can sound very modest and yet make great claims and be very presumptuous. Most of the judgments by means of which we purport to exalt the divine wisdom are like this, since in them we ascribe intentions to the works of creation and preservation that are really intended to do honor to our own wisdom as subtle thinkers.

[a] *Beurtheilungsart*
[b] *vermessen*

kind of causality in nature, in accordance with an analogy with our own causality in the technical use of reason, in order to keep before us the rule in accordance with which research into certain products of nature must be conducted.

Why, then, does teleology usually not constitute a proper part of theoretical natural science, but is instead drawn into theology as a propaedeutic or transition? This is done in order to keep the study of the mechanism of nature restricted to what we can subject to our observation or experiments, so that we could produce it ourselves, like nature, at least as far as the similarity of its laws is concerned; for we understand completely only that which we ourselves can make and bring about in accordance with concepts. Organization, however, as the internal end of nature, infinitely surpasses all capacity^a for a similar presentation by art; and as far as natural arrangements that are held to be externally purposive are concerned (e.g., wind, rain, etc.), physics can very well consider their mechanism, but it cannot present their relation to ends, insofar as this is supposed to be a condition necessarily belonging to their cause, at all, because this necessity in the connection pertains entirely to the combination of our concepts and not to the constitution of things.

^{a} *Vermögen*

Second Division
Dialectic
of the
Teleological Power of Judgment

<hr>

§ 69.
What is an antinomy of the power of judgment?

The **determining** power of judgment by itself has no principles that ground **concepts of objects.** It is no autonomy, for it merely **subsumes** under given laws or concepts as principles. For that very reason it is not exposed to any danger from its own antinomy and from a conflict of its principles. Thus the transcendental power of judgment, which contains the conditions for subsuming under categories, was not by itself **nomothetic**, but merely named the conditions of sensible intuition under which a given concept, as a law of the understanding, could be given reality (application) – about which it could never fall into disunity with itself (at least in the matter of principles).[1]

But the **reflecting** power of judgment is supposed to subsume under a law that is not yet given and which is in fact only a principle for reflection on objects for which we are objectively entirely lacking a law or a concept of the object that would be adequate as a principle for the cases that come before us. Now since no use of the cognitive faculties can be permitted without principles, in such cases the reflecting power of judgment must serve as a principle itself, which, since it is not objective, and cannot be presupposed as a sufficient ground for cognition of the intention of the object, can serve as a merely subjective principle for the purposive use of the cognitive faculties, namely for reflecting on one kind of objects. In relation to such cases, the reflecting power of judgment therefore has its maxims, indeed necessary ones, for the sake of the cognition of natural laws in experience, in order to arrive by their means at concepts, even if these are concepts of reason, if it needs these merely in order to come to know nature as far as its empirical laws are concerned. – Now between these necessary maxims of the reflecting power of judgment there can be a conflict, hence an antinomy, on which is based a dialectic which, if each of the two conflicting maxims has its ground in the nature of the cognitive faculties, can be called a natural dialectic and an unavoidable illusion which we must expose and resolve in the critique so that it will not deceive us.

§ 70.

Representation of this antinomy.

Insofar as reason has to do with nature, as the sum of the objects of the outer senses, it can be grounded on laws which are in part pre-scribed *a priori* to nature by the understanding itself, and which can in part be extended beyond what can be foreseen by empirical determi-nations encountered in experience. For the application of the first sort of laws, namely the **universal** laws of material nature in general, the power of understanding needs no special principle of reflection: for in that case it is determining, since an objective principle is given to it by the understanding. But as far as the particular laws that can only be made known to us by experience are concerned, there can be such great diversity and dissimilarity among them that the power of judg-ment itself must serve as a principle even in order merely to investigate the appearances of nature in accordance with a law and spy one out, because it requires one for a guideline if it is to have any hope of an interconnected experiential cognition in accordance with a thorough-going lawfulness of nature or of its unity in accordance with empirical laws. Now in the case of this contingent unity of particular laws the power of judgment can set out from two maxims in its reflection, one of which is provided to it by the mere understanding *a priori*, the other of which, however, is suggested by particular experiences that bring reason into play in order to conduct the judging*a* of corporeal nature and its laws in accordance with a special principle. It may then seem that these two sorts of maxims are not consistent with each other, thus that a dialectic will result that will make the power of judgment go astray in the principle of its reflection.

5: 387

The **first maxim** of the power of judgment is the **thesis**:*b* All generation of material things and their forms must be judged*c* as possible in accordance with merely mechanical laws.

The **second maxim** is the **antithesis**:*d* Some products of material nature cannot be judged*e* as possible according to merely mechanical

---

a *Beurtheilung*
b *Satz*
c *beurtheilt*
d *Gegensatz*
e *beurtheilt*

258

laws (judging*a* them requires an entirely different law of causality, namely that of final causes).

Now if one were to transform these regulative principles for research into constitutive principles of the possibility of the objects themselves, they would run:

Thesis: All generation of material things is possible in accordance with merely mechanical laws.

Antithesis: Some generation of such things is not possible in accordance with merely mechanical laws.

In this latter quality, as objective principles for the determining power of judgment, they would contradict one another, and hence one of the two propositions would necessarily be false; but that would then be an antinomy, though not of the power of judgment, but rather a conflict in the legislation of reason. However, reason can prove neither the one nor the other of these fundamental principles, because we can have no determining principle *a priori* of the possibility of things in accordance with merely empirical laws of nature.

By contrast, the maxims of a reflecting power of judgment that were initially expounded do not in fact contain any contradiction. For if I say that I must **judge**^b the possibility of all events in material nature and hence all forms, as their products, in accordance with merely mechanical laws, I do not thereby say that they **are possible only in accordance with such laws** (to the exclusion of any other kind of causality); rather, that only indicates that I **should** always **reflect** on them **in accordance with the principle** of the mere mechanism of nature, and hence research the latter, so far as I can, because if it is not made the basis for research then there can be no proper cognition of nature. Now this is not an obstacle to the second maxim for searching after a principle and reflecting upon it which is quite different from explanation in accordance with the mechanisms of nature, namely the principle of final causes, on the proper occasion, namely in the case of some forms of nature (and, at their instance, even the whole of nature). For reflection in accordance with the first maxim is not thereby suspended, rather one is required to pursue it as far as one can; it is also not thereby said that those forms would not be possible in accordance with the mechanism of nature. It is only asserted that **human reason**, in the pursuit of this reflection and in this manner, can never discover the least basis for what is specific in a natural end, although it may well be able to discover other cognitions of natural laws; in which case it will remain undetermined whether in the inner ground of nature itself,

5: 388

---

a *Beurtheilung*
b *beurtheilen*

which is unknown to us, physical-mechanical connection and connection to ends may not cohere in the same things, in a single principle: only our reason is not in a position to unify them in such a principle, and thus the power of judgment, as a **reflecting** (on a subjective ground) rather than as a determining (according to an objective principle of the possibility of things in themselves) power of judgment, is forced to think of another principle than that of the mechanism of nature as the ground of the possibility of certain forms in nature.

§ 71.
Preparation for the resolution of the above antinomy.

We can by no means prove the impossibility of the generation of organized products of nature through the mere mechanism of nature, because since the infinite manifold of particular laws of nature that are contingent for us are only cognized empirically, we have no insight into their primary internal ground, and thus we cannot reach the internal and completely sufficient principle of the possibility of a nature (which lies in the supersensible) at all. Whether, therefore, the productive capacity^a of nature may not be as adequate for that which we judge^b as formed or combined in accordance with the idea of ends as well as for that which we believe to need merely the machinery of nature, and whether in fact things as genuine natural ends (as we must necessarily judge^c them) must be based in an entirely different kind of original causality, which cannot be contained at all in material nature or in its intelligible substratum, namely, an architectonic understanding: about this our reason, which is extremely limited with regard to the concept of causality if the latter is supposed to be specified *a priori*, can give us no information whatever. – However, with respect to our cognitive faculty, it is just as indubitably certain that the mere mechanism of nature is also incapable of providing an explanatory ground for the generation of organized beings. It is therefore an entirely correct fundamental principle **for the reflecting power of judgment** that for the evident connection of things in accordance with final causes we must conceive of a causality different from mechanism, namely that of an (intelligent) world-cause acting in accordance with ends, no matter how rash and indemonstrable that would be **for the determining power of judgment.** In the first case, the principle is a mere maxim of the power of judgment, in which the concept of that causality is a mere

5: 389

---

^{a} *Vermögen*
^{b} *beurtheilen*
^{c} *beurtheilen*

idea, to which one by no means undertakes to concede reality, but uses only as a guideline for reflection, which thereby always remains open for any mechanical explanatory grounds, and never strays from the sensible world; in the second case, the fundamental principle would be an objective principle, which would be prescribed by reason and to which the power of judgment would be subjected as determining, in which case, however, it would stray beyond the sensible world into that which transcends it, and would perhaps be led astray.

All appearance of an antinomy between the maxims of that kind of explanation which is genuinely physical (mechanical) and that which is teleological (technical) therefore rests on confusing a fundamental principle of the reflecting with that of the determining power of judgment, and on confusing the **autonomy** of the former (which is valid merely subjectively for the use of our reason in regard to the particular laws of experience) with the **heteronomy** of the latter, which has to conform to the laws given by the understanding (whether general or particular).

§ 72.

On the various systems concerning the
systematicity of nature.

No one has doubted the correctness of the fundamental principle that certain things in nature (organized beings) and their possibility must be judged in accordance with the concept of final causes, even if one requires only a **guideline** for coming to know their constitution through observation without rising to the level of an investigation into their ultimate origin. The question can thus be only whether this fundamental principle is merely subjectively valid, i.e., merely a maxim of our power of judgment, or is an objective principle of nature, according to which there would pertain to it, in addition to its mechanism (in accordance with mere laws of motion) yet another kind of causality, namely that of final causes, under which the first kind (that of moving forces) would stand only as intermediate causes. 5: 390

Now one could leave this question or problem for speculation entirely untouched and unsolved, for if we are satisfied with speculation within the boundaries of the mere cognition of nature, the above maxims are sufficient for studying nature as far as human powers reach and for probing its most hidden secrets. It must therefore be a certain presentiment[a] of our reason, or a hint as it were given to us by nature, that we could by means of that concept of final causes step beyond

---

[a] *Ahnung*; in the first edition, *Ahndung*, an archaic spelling of the same word.

nature and even connect it to the highest point in the series of causes if we were to abandon research into nature (even though we have not gotten very far in that), or at least set it aside for a while, and attempt to discover first where that stranger in natural science,[a] namely the concept of natural ends, leads.

Now here, to be sure, the maxim that was not disputed above must lead to a wide array of controversial problems: whether the connection of ends in nature **proves** a special kind of causality in it; or whether, considered in itself and in accordance with objective principles, it is not instead identical with the mechanism of nature or dependent on one and the same ground, where, however, since in many products of nature this ground is often too deeply hidden for our research, we attempt to ascribe it to nature by analogy with a subjective principle, namely that of art, i.e., causality in accordance with ideas – an expedient that also succeeds in many cases, although it certainly seems to fail in some, but in any case never justifies us in introducing into natural science a special kind of agency[b] distinct from causality in accordance with merely mechanical laws of nature. Insofar as we would call the procedure (the causality) of nature a technique, on account of the similarity to ends that we find in its products, we would divide this into **intentional** technique (*technica intentionalis*) and **unintentional** technique (*technica naturalis*). The former would mean that the productive capacity of nature in accordance with final causes must be held to be a special kind of causality; the latter that it is at bottom entirely identical with the mechanism of nature, and that the contingent coincidence with our concepts of art and their rules, as a merely subjective condition for judging[c] nature, is falsely interpreted as a special kind of natural generation.

If we now speak of the systems for the explanation of nature with regard to final causes, one must note that they all controvert one another dogmatically, i.e., concerning objective principles of the possibility of things, whether through intentionally or even entirely unintentionally acting causes, but[d] not concerning the subjective maxims for merely judging about the causes of such purposive products – in which case **disparate** principles could well be united with each other, unlike the former case, where **contradictorily opposed** principles cancel each other out and cannot subsist together.

The systems with regard to the technique of nature, i.e., of its

---

[a] In the first edition, "that stranger in the concept of natural science."
[b] *Wirkungsart*
[c] *beurtheilen*
[d] "but" replaces "and" in the first edition.

productive force in accordance with the rule of ends, are twofold: those of the **idealism** or of the **realism** of natural ends. The former is the assertion that all purposiveness in nature is **unintentional**, the latter that some purposiveness in nature (in organized beings) is **intentional**, from which there can also be inferred as a hypothesis the consequence that the technique of nature is also intentional, i.e., an end, as far as concerns all its other products in relation to the whole of nature.

1. The **idealism** of purposiveness (I always mean objective purposiveness here) is now either that of the **causality** or of the **fatality** of the determination of nature in the purposive form of its products. The first principle concerns the relation of matter to the physical ground of its form, namely the laws of motion; the second concerns the **hyperphysical** ground of matter and the whole of nature. The system of **causality**, which is ascribed to Epicurus[2] or Democritus,[3] is, if taken literally, so obviously absurd that it need not detain[a] us; by contrast, the system of fatality (of which Spinoza[4] is made the author, although it is to all appearance much older), which appeals to something supersensible, to which our insight therefore does not reach, is not so easy to refute, since its concept of the original being is not intelligible at all. But this much is clear: that on this system the connection of ends in the world must be assumed to be unintentional (because it is derived from an original being, but not from its understanding, hence not from any intention on its part, but from the necessity of its nature and the unity of the world flowing from that), hence the fatalism of purposiveness is at the same time an idealism of it.

5: 392

2. The **realism** of the purposiveness of nature is also either physical or hyperphysical. The **first** bases ends in nature on the analogue of a faculty acting in accordance with an intention, the **life of matter** (in it, or also through an animating inner principle, a world-soul); and is called **hylozoism**.[5] The **second** derives them from the original ground of the world-whole, as an intentionally productive (originally living) intelligent being; and it is **theism**.*

---

* One sees from this that in most speculative matters of pure reason the philosophical schools have usually tried all of the solutions that are possible for a certain question concerning dogmatic assertions. Thus for the sake of the purposiveness of nature either **lifeless matter** or a **lifeless God** as well as **living matter** or a **living God** have been tried. Nothing is left for us except, if need be, to give up all these objective **assertions** and to weigh our judgment critically, merely in relation to our cognitive faculty, in order to provide its principle with the non-dogmatic but adequate validity of a maxim for the reliable use of reason.

5: 392

[a] *aufhalten*; in the first edition, *verweilen*, i.e., "we need not linger over it."

§ 73.
None of the above systems accomplishes what it pretends to do.

What do all these systems want? They want to explain our teleological judgments about nature, but go to work in such a way that some of them deny the truth of these judgments, thus declaring them to be an idealism of nature (represented as an art), while the others acknowledge them to be true, and promise to demonstrate the possibility of a nature in accordance with the idea of final causes.

1) On the one hand, the systems that contend for the idealism of final causes in nature concede to its principle a causality according to laws of motion (through which natural things purposively exist), but they deny **intentionality** to it, i.e., they deny that nature is intentionally determined to its purposive production, or, in other words, that an end is the cause. This is **Epicurus's** kind of explanation, on which the difference between a technique of nature and mere mechanism is completely denied, and blind chance is assumed to be the explanation not only of the correspondence of generated products with our concepts of ends, hence of technique, but even of the determination of the causes of this generation in accordance with laws of motion, hence of their mechanism, and thus nothing is explained, not even the illusion in our teleological judgments, and hence the putative idealism in them is not demonstrated at all.

On the other hand, **Spinoza** would suspend all inquiry into the ground of the possibility of the ends of nature and deprive this idea of all reality by allowing them to count not as products of an original being but as accidents inhering in it, and to this being, as the substratum of those natural things, he ascribes not causality with regard to them but merely subsistence, and (on account of the unconditional necessity of this being, together with all natural things as accidents inhering in it), he secures for the natural forms the unity of the ground that is, to be sure, requisite for all purposiveness, but at the same time he removes their contingency, without which no **unity of purpose** can be thought, and with that removes everything **intentional**, just as he removes all understanding from the original ground of natural things.

However, Spinozism does not accomplish what it wants. It wants to provide a basis for the explanation of the connection of ends (which it does not deny) in the things of nature, and names merely the unity of the subject in which they all inhere. But even if one concedes to it this sort of existence for the beings of the world, still that ontological unity is not immediately a **unity of end**, and in no way makes the latter comprehensible. The latter is a quite special mode of the former, which does not follow at all from the connection of the things (the beings of the world) in one subject (the original being), but which throughout implies relation to a **cause** that has understanding; and even if all these things were united in a simple subject, still no relation to an end would be exhibited unless one conceives of them, first, as internal **effects** of the substance, as a **cause**, and, second, of the latter as a cause **through its understanding.** Without these formal conditions all unity is mere natural necessity, and, if it is nevertheless ascribed to things that we represent as external to one another, blind necessity. If, however, one would call purposiveness in nature that which the academy called the transcendental perfection of things (in relation to their own proper essence), in accordance with which everything must have in itself everything that is necessary in order to be that kind of thing and not any other, then that is merely a childish game played with words instead of concepts. For if all things must be conceived as ends, thus if to be a thing and to be an end are identical, then there is at bottom nothing that particularly deserves to be represented as an end.

5: 394

From this it is readily seen that by tracing our concept of the purposiveness in nature back to the consciousness of ourselves in one all-comprehending (yet at the same time simple) being, and seeking that form merely in the unity of the latter, Spinoza must have intended to assert not the realism but merely the idealism of nature; but he could not accomplish even this, for the mere representation of the unity of the substratum can never produce the idea of even an unintentional purposiveness.

2) Those who intend not merely to assert but also to explain the **realism** of natural ends believe themselves able to understand a special kind of causality, namely that of intentionally acting causes, at least as far as its possibility is concerned; otherwise they could not undertake to try to explain it. For even the most daring hypothesis can be authorized only if at least the **possibility** of that which is assumed to be its ground is **certain**, and one must be able to insure the objective reality of its concept.

However, the possibility of a living matter (the concept of which contains a contradiction, because lifelessness, *inertia*, constitutes its essential characteristic), cannot even be conceived;[6] the possibility of an animated matter and of the whole of nature as an animal can be used at all only insofar as it is revealed to us (for the sake of an hypothesis of purposiveness in nature at large), in experience, in the organization of nature in the small, but its possibility can by no means be understood *a priori*. There must therefore be a circle in the explanation if one would derive the purposiveness of nature in organized beings from the life of matter and in turn is not acquainted with this

5: 395 life otherwise than in organized beings, and thus cannot form any concept of its possibility without experience of them. Hylozism thus does not accomplish what it promises.

Theism, finally, is just as incapable of dogmatically establishing the possibility of natural ends as a key to teleology, although among all the grounds for explaining this it has the advantage that by means of the understanding that it ascribes to the original being it can best rid the purposiveness of nature of idealism and introduce an intentional causality for its generation.

For in order to be justified in placing the ground of the unity of purpose in matter beyond nature in any determinate way, the impossibility of placing this in matter through its mere mechanism would first have to be demonstrated in a way sufficient for the determining power of judgment. But we cannot say more than that given the constitution and the limits of our cognitive capacities (by means of which we cannot understand the primary internal ground of even this mechanism) we must by no means seek for a principle of determinate purposive relations in matter; rather, for us there remains no other way of judging*a* the generation of its products as natural ends than through a supreme understanding as the cause of the world. But that is only a ground for the reflecting, not for the determining power of judgment, and absolutely cannot justify any objective assertion.

§ 74.
The cause of the impossibility of a dogmatic treatment
of the concept of a technique of nature
is the inexplicability of a natural end.

We deal with a concept dogmatically (even if it is supposed to be empirically conditioned) if we consider it as contained under another concept of the object, which constitutes a principle of reason, and determine it in accordance with the latter. But we deal with it merely critically if we consider it only in relation to our cognitive faculties, hence in relation to the subjective conditions for thinking it, without undertaking to decide anything about its object. The dogmatic treatment of a concept is thus that which is lawful for the determining, the critical that which is lawful merely for the reflecting power of judgment.

5: 396 Now the concept of a thing as a natural end is a concept that subsumes nature under a causality that is conceivable only by means of reason, in order to judge, in accordance with this principle, about that

---

a *Beurtheilungsart*

266

which is given by the object in experience. But in order to use it dogmatically for the determining power of judgment, we would first have to be assured of the objective reality of this concept, for otherwise we would not be able to subsume any natural thing under it. The concept of a thing as a natural end, however, is certainly an empirically conditioned concept, i.e., one that is possible only under certain conditions given in experience, but it is still not a concept that can be abstracted from experience, but one that is possible only in accordance with a principle of reason in the judging^a of the object. It thus cannot be understood and dogmatically established at all as in accordance with such a principle of its objective reality (i.e., that an object is possible in accordance with such a principle); and we do not know whether it is merely a rationalistic^b and objectively empty concept (*conceptus ratiocinans*)^c or a concept of reason that grounds cognition and is confirmed by reason (*conceptus ratiocinatus*).^{d} Thus it cannot be treated dogmatically for the determining power of judgment, i.e., not merely can it not be determined whether or not things of nature, considered as natural ends, require for their generation a causality of an entirely special kind (that in accordance with intentions), but this question cannot even be raised, because the objective reality of the concept of a natural end is not demonstrable by means of reason at all (i.e., it is not constitutive for the determining, but is merely regulative for the reflecting power of judgment).

That this concept is not demonstrable is clear from the fact that as a concept of a **natural product** it includes natural necessity and yet at the same time a contingency of the form of the object (in relation to mere laws of nature) in one and the same thing as an end; consequently, if there is not to be a contradiction here, it must contain a basis for the possibility of this thing in nature and yet at the same time a basis of the possibility of this nature itself and its relation to something that is not empirically cognizable nature (supersensible) and thus is not cognizable at all for us, in order to be judged^e in accordance with another kind of causality than that of the mechanism of nature, if its possibility is to be determined. Thus, since the concept of a thing as a natural end is excessive **for the determining power of judgment** if one considers the object by means of reason (although it may be

---

^{a} *Beurtheilung*
^{b} *vernünftelnder*. Here this term could be translated in the usual way as "sophistical," but we have translated it as "rationalistic" in order to preserve the contrast with *Vernunftbegriff* (concept of reason) and *von der Vernunft bestätigter* (confirmed by reason) in the remainder of the sentence.
^{c} rationalizing concept
^{d} concept reached by reason
^{e} *beurtheilt*

5: 397 immanent for the reflecting power of judgment with regard to objects of experience), and thus it cannot be provided with objective reality for determining judgments, it is thereby comprehensible how all the systems that can even be sketched for the dogmatic treatment of the concept of natural ends and of nature as a whole connected by final causes cannot decide anything about it, whether objectively affirmative or objectively negative; because if things are subsumed under a concept that is merely problematic, the synthetic predicates of such a concept (here, e.g., whether the end of nature which we conceive for the generation of things is intentional or unintentional) must yield the same sort of (problematic) judgments of the object, whether they are affirmative or negative, since one does not know whether one is judging about something or nothing. The concept of a causality through ends (of art) certainly has objective reality, as does that of a causality in accordance with the mechanism of nature. But the concept of a causality of nature in accordance with the rule of ends, even more the concept of a being the likes of which is not given to us in experience at all, namely that of a original ground of nature, can of course be thought without contradiction, but is not good for any dogmatic determinations, because since it cannot be drawn from experience and is not requisite for the possibility of experience its objective reality cannot be guaranteed by anything. But even if it could be, how could I count things that are definitely supposed to be products of divine art among the products of nature, whose incapacity for producing such things in accordance with its laws is precisely that which has made necessary the appeal to a cause that is distinct from it?

§ 75.
The concept of an objective purposiveness
of nature is a critical principle of
reason for the reflecting power of judgment.

To say that the generation of certain things in nature or even of nature as a whole is possible only through a cause that is determined to act in accordance with intentions is quite different from saying that **because of the peculiar constitution of my cognitive faculties** I cannot judge
5: 398 about the possibility of those things and their generation except by thinking of a cause for these that acts in accordance with intentions, and thus by thinking of a being that is productive in accordance with the analogy with the causality of an understanding. In the first case I would determine something about the object, and I am obliged to demonstrate the objective reality of a concept that has been assumed; in the second case, reason merely determines the use of my cognitive faculties in accordance with their special character and with the essen-

tial conditions as well as the limits of their domain. The first principle is thus an **objective** fundamental principle for the determining, the second a subjective fundamental principle merely for the reflecting power of judgment, hence a maxim that reason prescribes to it.

It is in fact indispensable for us to subject nature to the concept of an intention if we would even merely conduct research among its organized products by means of continued observation; and this concept is thus already an absolutely necessary maxim for the use of our reason in experience. It is obvious that once we have adopted such a guideline for studying nature and found it to be reliable we must also at least attempt to apply this maxim of the power of judgment to the whole of nature, since by means of it we have been able to discover many laws of nature which, given the limitation of our insights into the inner mechanisms of nature, would otherwise remain hidden from us. But with regard to the latter use this maxim of the power of judgment is certainly useful, but not indispensable, because nature as a whole is not given to us as organized (in the strictest sense of the term adduced above).[a,7] By contrast, this maxim of the reflecting power of judgment is essential for those products of nature which must be judged[b] only as intentionally formed thus and not otherwise, in order to obtain even an experiential cognition of their internal constitution; because even the thought of them as organized things is impossible without associating the thought of a generation with an intention.

Now the concept of a thing whose existence or form we represent as possible[c] under the condition of an end is inseparable from the concept of its contingency (according to natural laws). Hence natural things which we find possible only as ends constitute the best proof of the contingency of the world-whole, and are the only basis for proof valid for both common understanding as well as for philosophers of the dependence of these things on and their origin in a being that exists outside of the world and is (on account of that purposive form) intelligent; thus teleology cannot find a complete answer for its inquiries except in a theology. 5: 399

But what does even the most complete teleology prove in the end? Does it prove anything like that such an intelligent being exists? No; it proves nothing more than that because of the constitution of our cognitive faculties, and thus in the combination of experience with the supreme principles of reason, we cannot form any concept at all of the possibility of such a world except by conceiving of such an **intentionally acting** supreme cause. Objectively, therefore, we cannot establish

[a] The first edition has a semicolon rather than period here.
[b] *beurtheilt*
[c] In the first edition, "as being possible."

the proposition that there is an intelligent original being; we can establish it only subjectively for the use of our power of judgment in its reflection upon the ends in nature, which cannot be conceived in accordance with any other principle than that of an intentional causality of a highest cause.

If we would establish the supreme proposition dogmatically, from teleological grounds, then we would be trapped by[a] difficulties from which we could not extricate ourselves. For then these inferences would have to be based on the proposition that the organized beings in the world are not possible except through an intentionally acting cause. But then we could not avoid asserting that because the causal connection of these things can be pursued and their lawfulness cognized only under the idea of ends we would also be justified in presupposing that this is a necessary condition for every thinking and cognizing being, thus that it is a condition that depends on the object and not just on our own subject. But we cannot get away with such an assertion. For since we do not actually **observe** ends in nature as intentional, but merely **add** this concept as a guideline for the power of judgment in reflection on the products of nature, they are not given to us through the object. It is even impossible for us to justify *a priori* the assumption of the objective reality of such a concept. There is thus left nothing but a proposition resting only on subjective conditions, namely those of a reflecting power of judgment appropriate to our cognitive faculties, which, if one were to express it as objectively and dogmatically valid, would say: There is a God; but all that is allowed to us humans[b] is the restricted formula: We cannot conceive of the purposiveness which must be made the basis even of our cognition of the internal possibility of many things in nature and make it comprehensible except by representing them and the world in general as a product of an intelligent cause (a God).[c]

Now if this proposition, grounded on an indispensably necessary maxim of our power of judgment, is completely sufficient for every speculative as well as practical use of our reason in every **human** respect, I would like to know what we lose by being unable to prove it valid for higher beings, on purely objective grounds (which unfortunately exceed our capacity[d])?[e] For it is quite certain that we can never

5: 400

---

[a] In the first edition, "among."
[b] In the first edition, "to us as humans."
[c] The parenthetical phrase is added in the second edition.
[d] *Vermögen*
[e] Question mark added.

adequately come to know the organized beings and their internal possibility in accordance with merely mechanical principles of nature, let
alone explain them; and indeed this is so certain that we can boldly say
that it would be absurd for humans even to make such an attempt or
to hope that there may yet arise a Newton who could make comprehensible even the generation of a blade of grass according to natural
laws that no intention has ordered; rather, we must absolutely deny
this insight to human beings.[8] But for us to judge in turn that even if
we could penetrate to the principle of nature in the specification of its
universal laws known to us there **could** lie hidden no ground sufficient
for the possibility of organized beings without the assumption of an
intention underlying their generation would be presumptuous: for how
could we know that? Probabilities count for nothing here, where judgments of pure reason are at stake. – Thus we cannot make any objective
judgment at all, whether affirmative or negative, about the proposition
that there is an intentionally acting being as a world-cause (hence as an
author) at the basis of what we rightly call natural ends; only this much
is certain, namely, that if we are to judge at least in accordance with
what it is granted to us to understand through our own nature (in
accordance with the conditions and limits of our reason), we absolutely
cannot base the possibility of those natural ends on anything except an
intelligent being – which is what alone is in accord with the maxims of
our reflecting power of judgment and is thus a ground which is subjective but ineradicably attached to the human race.   5: 401

§ 76.
Remark.

This consideration, which would certainly deserve to be elaborated in detail in
transcendental philosophy, can come in here only as a digression, for elucidation (not for the proof of what has here been expounded).

Reason is a faculty of principles, and in its most extreme demand it reaches
to the unconditioned, while understanding, in contrast, is always at its service
only under a certain condition, which must be given. Without concepts of the
understanding, however, which must be given objective reality, reason cannot
judge at all objectively (synthetically), and by itself it contains, as theoretical
reason, absolutely no constitutive principles, but only regulative ones. One
soon learns that where the understanding cannot follow, reason becomes excessive, displaying itself in well-grounded ideas (as regulative principles) but
not in objectively valid concepts; the understanding, however, which cannot
keep up with it, but which would yet be necessary for validity for objects,
restricts the validity of those ideas of reason solely to the subject, although still
universally for all members of this species, i.e., understanding restricts the

validity of those ideas to the condition which, given the nature of our (human) cognitive faculty or even the concept that **we can form** of the capacity*ª* of a finite rational being in general, we cannot and must not conceive otherwise, but without asserting that the basis for such a judgment lies in the object. We will adduce examples, which are certainly too important as well as too difficult*ᵇ* for them to be immediately pressed upon the reader as proven propositions, but which will still provide material to think over and can serve to elucidate what is our proper concern here.

It is absolutely necessary for the human understanding to distinguish between the possibility and the actuality of things. The reason for this lies in the subject and the nature of its cognitive faculties. For if two entirely heterogeneous elements were not required for the exercise of these faculties, understanding for concepts and sensible intuition for objects corresponding to them,

5: 402 then there would be no such distinction (between the possible and the actual). That is, if our understanding were intuitive, it would have no objects except what is actual. Concepts (which pertain merely to the possibility of an object) and sensible intuitions (which merely give us something, without thereby allowing us to cognize it as an object) would both disappear. Now, however, all of our distinction between the merely possible and the actual rests on the fact that the former signifies only the position of the representation of a thing with respect to our concept and, in general, our faculty for thinking, while the latter signifies the positing of the thing in itself (apart from this concept).*ᶜ,⁹* Thus the distinction of possible from actual things is one that is merely subjectively valid for the human understanding, since we can always have something in our thoughts although it does not exist, or represent something as given even though we do not have any concept of it. The propositions, therefore, that things can be possible without being actual, and thus that there can be no inference at all from mere possibility to actuality, quite rightly hold for the human understanding without that proving that this distinction lies in the things themselves. For that the latter cannot be inferred from the former, hence that those propositions are certainly valid of objects insofar as our cognitive faculty, as sensibly conditioned, is concerned with objects of these senses, but are not valid of objects in general, is evident from the unremitting demand of reason to assume some sort of thing (the original ground)*ᵈ* as existing absolutely necessarily, in which possibility and actuality can no longer be distinguished at all, and for which idea our understanding has absolutely no concept, i.e., can find no way in which to represent such a thing and its way of existing. For if understanding **thinks** it (it can think it as it will), then it is represented as merely possible. If understanding is conscious of it as given in intuition, then it is actual without understanding being able to conceive of its possibility. Hence the concept of an absolutely necessary being is an indispensable idea of reason but an unattainable problematic concept for the human

---

ª Vermögen

ᵇ "as well as too difficult" added in the second edition.

ᶜ The phrase in the parentheses was added in the second edition.

ᵈ Reading *Urgrund* instead of *Urgund*, a typographical error in both the first and second editions.

understanding. It is still valid, however, for the use of our cognitive faculties in accordance with their special constitution, thus not for objects and thereby for every cognitive being: because I cannot presuppose that in every such being thinking and intuiting, hence the possibility and actuality of things, are two different conditions for the exercise of its cognitive faculties. For an understanding to which this distinction did not apply, all objects that I cognize would **be** (exist), and the possibility of some that did not exist, i.e., their contingency if they did exist, as well as the necessity that is to be distinguished from that, would not enter into the representation of such a being at all. What makes it so difficult for our understanding with its concepts to be the equal of reason is simply that for the former, as human understanding, that is excessive (i.e., impossible for the subjective conditions of its cognition) which reason nevertheless makes into a principle belonging to the object. – Now here this maxim is always valid, that even where the cognition of them outstrips the understanding, we should conceive all objects in accordance with the subjective conditions for the exercise of our faculties necessarily pertaining to our (i.e., human) nature; and, if the judgments made in this way cannot be constitutive principles determining how the object is constituted (as cannot fail to be the case with regard to transcendent concepts), there can still be regulative principles, immanent and secure in their use and appropriate for the human point of view.

5: 403

Just as in the theoretical consideration of nature reason must assume the idea of an unconditioned necessity of its primordial ground, so, in the case of the practical, it also presupposes its own unconditioned (in regard to nature) causality, i.e., freedom, because it is aware of its moral command. Now since here, however, the objective necessity of the action, as duty, is opposed to that which it, as an occurrence, would have if its ground lay in nature and not in freedom (i.e., in the causality of reason), and the action which is morally absolutely necessary can be regarded physically as entirely contingent (i.e., what necessarily **should** happen often does not), it is clear that it depends only on the subjective constitution of our practical faculty that the moral laws must be represented as commands (and the actions which are in accord with them as duties), and that reason expresses this necessity not through a **be**[a] (happening) but through a should-be:[b] which would not be the case if reason without sensibility (as the subjective condition of its application to objects of nature) were considered, as far as its causality is concerned, as a cause in an intelligible world, corresponding completely with the moral law, where there would be no distinction between what should be done and what is done, between a practical law concerning that which is possible through us and the theoretical law concerning that which is actual through us. Now, however, although an intelligible world, in which everything would be actual merely because it is (as something good) possible, and even freedom, as its formal condition, is a transcendent concept for us, which is not serviceable for any constitutive principle for determining an object and its objective reality, still, in accordance

5: 404

---

[a] *Seyn*
[b] *Seyn-Sollen*

with the constitution of our (partly sensible) nature, it can serve as a universal **regulative principle** for ourselves and for every being standing in connection with the sensible world, so far as we can represent that in accordance with the constitution of our own reason and capacity,[a] which does not determine the constitution of freedom, as a form of causality, objectively, but rather makes the rules of actions in accordance with that idea into commands for everyone and indeed does so with no less validity than if it did determine freedom objectively.

Likewise, as far as the case before us is concerned, it may be conceded that we would find no distinction between a natural mechanism and a technique of nature, i.e., a connection to ends in it, if our understanding were not of the sort that must go from the universal to the particular, and the power of judgment can thus cognize no purposiveness in the particular, and hence make no determining judgments, without having a universal law under which it can subsume the particular. But now since the particular, as such, contains something contingent with regard to the universal, but reason nevertheless still requires unity, hence lawfulness, in the connection of particular laws of nature (which lawfulness of the contingent is called purposiveness), and the *a priori* derivation of the particular laws from the universal, as far as what is contingent in the former is concerned, is impossible through the determination of the concept of the object, thus the concept of the purposiveness of nature in its products is a concept that is necessary for the human power of judgment in regard to nature but does not pertain to the determination of the objects themselves, thus a subjective principle of reason for the power of judgment which, as regulative (not constitutive), is just as necessarily valid for our **human power of judgment** as if it were an objective principle.

5: 405

§ 77.
On the special character of the human understanding, by means of which the concept of a natural end is possible for us.

In the remark, we have adduced special characteristics of our cognitive faculty (even the higher one) which we may easily be misled into carrying over to the things themselves as objective predicates; but they concern ideas for which no appropriate objects can be given in experience, and which could therefore serve only as regulative principles in the pursuit of experience. It is the same with the concept of a natural end, as far as the cause of the possibility of such a predicate is concerned, which can only lie in the idea; but the consequence that answers to it (the product) is still given in nature, and the concept of a causality of the latter, as a being acting in accordance with ends, seems

[a] *Vermögens*

to make the idea of a natural end into a constitutive principle of nature; and in this it differs from all other ideas.

This difference, however, consists in the fact that the idea at issue is not a principle of reason for the understanding, but for the power of judgment, and is thus merely the application of an understanding in general to possible objects of experience, where, indeed, the judgment cannot be determining, but merely reflecting, hence where the object is, to be sure, given in experience, but where it cannot even be **determinately** (let alone completely appropriately) **judged** in accordance with the idea, but can only be reflected upon.

What is at issue is therefore a special character of **our** (human) understanding with regard to the power of judgment in its reflection upon things in nature. But if that is the case, then it must be based on the idea of a possible understanding other than the human one (as in the *Critique of Pure Reason* we had to have in mind another possible intuition if we were to hold our own to be a special kind, namely one that is valid of objects merely as appearances),[10] so that one could say that certain products of nature, as far as their possibility is concerned, **must**, given the particular constitution of our understanding, **be considered by us** as intentional and generated as ends, yet without thereby demanding that there actually is a particular cause that has the representation of an end as its determining ground, and thus without denying that another (higher) understanding than the human one might be able to find the ground of the possibility of such products of nature even in the mechanism of nature, i.e., in a causal connection for which an understanding does not have to be exclusively assumed as a cause.

5: 406

What is at issue here is thus the relation of **our** understanding to the power of judgment, the fact, namely, that we have to seek a certain contingency in the constitution of our understanding in order to notice this as a special character of our understanding in distinction from other possible ones.

This contingency is quite naturally found in the **particular**, which the power of judgment is to subsume under the **universal** of the concepts of the understanding; for through the universal of **our** (human) understanding the particular is not determined, and it is contingent in how many different ways distinct things that nevertheless coincide in a common characteristic can be presented to our perception. Our understanding is a faculty of concepts, i.e., a discursive understanding, for which it must of course be contingent what and how different might be the particular that can be given to it in nature and brought under its concepts. But since intuition also belongs to cognition, and a faculty of a **complete spontaneity of intuition** would be a cognitive faculty distinct and completely independent from sensibility, and thus an understanding in the most general sense of the term, one can thus also conceive of an **intuitive** understanding (negatively, namely merely as not discursive),[a] which does not go from the universal to the particular and thus to the individual (through concepts), and for which that contingency of the agreement of nature in its products in accordance with **particular** laws for the understanding, which makes it so difficult for ours to bring the manifold of these[b] to the unity of cognition, is not encountered – a job that our understanding can accomplish only through the correspondence of natural characteristics with our faculty of concepts, which is quite contingent, but which an intuitive understanding would not need.

5: 407

Our understanding thus has this peculiarity for the power of judgment, that in cognition by means of it the particular is not determined by the universal, and the latter therefore cannot be derived from the former alone; but nevertheless this particular in the manifold of nature should agree with the universal (through concepts and laws), which agreement under such circumstances must be quite contingent and without a determinate principle for the power of judgment.

Nevertheless, in order for us to be able at least to conceive of the possibility of such an agreement of the things of nature with the power of judgment (which we represent as contingent, hence as possible only through an end aimed at it), we must at the same time conceive of another understanding, in relation to which, and indeed prior to any end attributed to it, we can represent that agreement of natural laws with our power of judgment, which for our understanding is conceivable only through ends as the means of connection, as **necessary**.

Our understanding, namely, has the property that in its cognition, e.g., of the cause of a product, it must go from the **analytical universal** (of concepts) to the particular (of the given empirical intuition), in which it determines nothing with regard to the manifoldness of the latter, but must expect this determination for the power of judgment from the subsumption of the empirical intuition (when the object is a product of nature) under the concept. Now, however, we can also conceive of an understanding which, since it is not discursive like ours but is intuitive, goes from the **synthetically universal** (of the intuition of a whole as such) to the particular, i.e., from the whole to the parts, in which, therefore, and in whose representation of the whole, there is no **contingency** in the combination of the parts, in order to make possible a determinate form of the whole, which is needed by our understanding, which must progress from the parts, as universally con-

---

[a] The words contained in the parentheses were added in the second edition.
[b] *derselben*; this could refer back to any of "nature," "its products," or its "particular laws."

276

ceived grounds, to the different possible forms, as consequences, that can be subsumed under it. In accordance with the constitution of our understanding, by contrast, a real whole of nature is to be regarded only as the effect of the concurrent moving forces of the parts. Thus if we would not represent the possibility of the whole as depending upon the parts, as is appropriate for our discursive understanding, but would rather, after the model of the intuitive (archetypical)^a understanding, represent the possibility of the parts (as far as both their constitution and their combination is concerned) as depending upon the whole, then, given the very same special characteristic of our understanding, this cannot come about by the whole being the ground of the possibility of the connection of the parts (which would be a contradiction in the discursive kind of cognition), but only by the **representation** of a   5: 408
whole containing the ground of the possibility of its form and of the connection of parts that belongs to that. But now since the whole would in that case be an effect (**product**) the **representation** of which would be regarded as the **cause** of its possibility, but the product of a cause whose determining ground is merely the representation of its effect is called an end, it follows that it is merely a consequence of the particular constitution of our understanding that we represent products of nature as possible only in accordance with another kind of causality than that of the natural laws of matter, namely only in accordance with that of ends and final causes, and that this principle does not pertain to the possibility of such things themselves (even considered as phenomena) in accordance with this sort of generation, but pertains only to the judging^b of them that is possible for our understanding. From this we at the same time understand why in natural science we are far from being satisfied with an explanation of the products of nature by means of causality in accordance with ends, since here we are required to judge^c the generation of nature as is appropriate for our faculty for judging^d them, i.e., the power of reflecting judgment, and not according to the things themselves as is appropriate for the determining power of judgment. And further, it is not at all necessary here to prove that such an *intellectus archetypus* is possible, but only that in the contrast of it with our discursive, image-dependent understanding (*intellectus ectypus*) and the contingency of such a constitution we are led to that idea (of an *intellectus archetypus*), and that this does not contain any contradiction.

Now if we consider a material whole, as far as its form is concerned,

---

^{a} *urbildlich*
^{b} *Beurtheilung*
^{c} *beurtheilen*
^{d} *beurtheilen*

as a product of the parts and of their forces and their capacity to combine by themselves (including as parts other materials that they add to themselves), we represent a mechanical kind of generation. But from this there arises no concept of a whole as an end, whose internal possibility presupposes throughout the idea of a whole on which even the constitution and mode of action of the parts depends, which is just how we must represent an organized body. But from this, as has just been shown, it does not follow that the mechanical generation of such a body is impossible; for that would be to say the same as that it is impossible (i.e., self-contradictory) to represent such a unity in the connection of the manifold **for every understanding** without the idea of that connection being at the same time its generating cause, i.e.,

5: 409   without intentional production. Nevertheless, this would in fact follow if we were justified in regarding material beings as things in themselves. For then the unity that constitutes the ground of the possibility of natural formations would be merely the unity of space, which is however no real ground of generatings but only their formal condition; although it has some similarity to the real ground that we seek in that in it no part can be determined except in relation to the whole (the representation of which is thus the basis of the possibility of the parts).[11] But since it is still at least possible to consider the material world as a mere appearance, and to conceive of something as a thing in itself (which is not an appearance) as substratum, and to correlate with this a corresponding intellectual intuition (even if it is not ours), there would then be a supersensible real ground for nature, although it is unknowable for us, to which we ourselves belong, and in which that which is necessary in it as object of the senses can be considered in accordance with mechanical laws, while the agreement and unity of the particular laws and corresponding forms, which in regard to the mechanical laws we must judge[a] as contingent, can at the same time be considered in it, as object of reason (indeed the whole of nature as a system) in accordance with teleological laws, and the material world would thus be judged in accordance with two kinds of principles, without the mechanical mode of explanation being excluded by the teleological mode, as if they contradicted each other.

From this we may also understand what we could otherwise easily suspect but only with difficulty assert as certain and prove, namely, that the principle of a mechanical derivation of purposive products of nature could of course subsist alongside the teleological principle, but could by no means make the latter dispensable; i.e., one could investigate all the thus far known and yet to be discovered laws of mechanical gener-

---

[a] *beurtheilen*

ation in a thing that we must judge^a as an end of nature, and even hope to make good progress in this, without the appeal to a quite distinct generating ground for the possibility of such a product, namely that of causality through ends, ever being canceled out; and absolutely no human reason (or even any finite reason that is similar to ours in quality, no matter how much it exceeds it in degree) can ever hope to understand the generation of even a little blade of grass from merely mechanical causes. For if the teleological connection of causes and effects is entirely indispensable for the possibility of such an object for the power of judgment, even merely for studying it with the guidance of experience; if for outer objects, as appearances, a sufficient ground related to causes cannot even be found, but this, which also lies in nature, must still be sought only in its supersensible substratum, from all possible insight into which we are cut off: then it is absolutely impossible for us to draw from nature itself any explanatory grounds for purposive connections, and in accordance with the constitution of the human cognitive faculty it is necessary to seek the highest ground of such connections in an original understanding as cause of the world.

5: 410

§ 78.
On the unification of the principle of the universal mechanism of matter with the teleological principle in the technique of nature.

It is of infinite importance to reason that it not allow the mechanism of nature in its productions to drop out of sight and be bypassed in its explanations; for without this no insight into the nature of things can be attained. As soon as it is granted to us that a highest architect immediately created the forms of nature as they have always existed or has predetermined those which in their course are continuously formed in accordance with one and the same model, our cognition of nature is not thereby in the least advanced, because we do not know the mode of action of such a being and the ideas which should contain the principles of the possibility of natural beings at all, and we cannot explain nature from that being as if from above (*a priori*). But if, in order to explain the forms of the objects of experience from below (*a posteriori*), we appeal from them to a cause acting in accordance with ends because we believe that we find purposiveness in these forms, then our explanation would be entirely tautological, and reason would be deceived with words, not to mention that where we stray into excess with this sort of explanation, where knowledge of nature cannot follow

---

^{a} *beurtheilen*

us, reason is seduced into poetic enthusiasm, although the avoidance of this is precisely reason's highest calling.

5: 411 On the other hand, it is an equally necessary maxim of reason not to bypass the principle of ends in the products of nature, because even though this principle does not make the way in which these products have originated more comprehensible, it is still a heuristic principle for researching the particular laws of nature, even granted that we would want to make no use of it for explaining nature itself, since although nature obviously displays an intentional unity of purpose we still always call that a merely natural end, i.e., we do not seek the ground of its possibility beyond nature. But since the question of the latter must ultimately still arise, it is just as necessary to conceive of a particular kind of causality for it that is not, unlike the mechanism of natural causes, found in nature, since to the receptivity to various and different forms than those of which matter is capable in accordance with that mechanism there must still be added the spontaneity of a cause (which thus cannot be matter) without which no ground of those forms could be given. Of course, before reason takes this step, it must proceed carefully, and not attempt to explain every technique of nature, i.e., a productive capacity in it which displays purposiveness of form for our mere apprehension in itself (as in the case of regular bodies), as teleological, but must instead always regard these as possible merely mechanically; but to exclude the teleological principle entirely, and always to stick with mere mechanism even where purposiveness, for the rational investigation of the possibility of natural forms by means of their causes, undeniably manifests itself as a relation to another kind of causality, must make reason fantastic and send it wandering about among figments of natural capacities that cannot even be conceived, just as a merely teleological mode of explanation which takes no regard of the mechanism of nature makes it into mere enthusiasm.

The two principles cannot be united in one and the same thing in nature as fundamental principles for the explanation (deduction) of one from the other, i.e., as dogmatic and constitutive principles of insight into nature for the determining power of judgment. If, e.g., I assume that a maggot can be regarded as a product of the mere mechanism of matter (a new formation that it produces for itself when its elements are set free by putrefaction), I cannot derive the very same product
5: 412 from the very same matter as a causality acting according to ends. Conversely, if I assume that the same product is a natural end, I cannot count on a mechanical mode of generation for it and take that as a constitutive principle for the judging*a* of its possibility, thus uniting

---

a *Beurtheilung*

both principles. For one kind of explanation excludes the other, even on the supposition that objectively both grounds of the possibility rest on a single one, but one of which we take no account. The principle which is to make possible the unifiability of both in the judging[a] of nature in accordance with them must be placed in what lies outside of both (hence outside of the possible empirical representation of nature) but which still contains the ground of both, i.e., in the supersensible, and each of these two kinds of explanation must be related to that. Now since we can have no concept of this except the undetermined concept of a ground that makes the judging[b] of nature in accordance with empirical laws possible, but cannot determine this more precisely by any predicate, it follows that the unification of the two principles cannot rest on a ground for the **explanation** (explication) of the possibility of a product in accordance with given laws for the determining power of judgment, but only on a ground for the **elucidation** (exposition) of this for the reflecting power of judgment.[12] – For to explain means to derive from a principle, which one must therefore cognize distinctly and be able to provide. Now of course the principle of the mechanism of nature and that of its causality according to ends in one and the same product of nature must cohere in a single higher principle and flow from it in common, because otherwise they could not subsist alongside one another in the consideration of nature. But if this objectively common principle, which also justifies the commonality of the maxims of natural research that depend upon it, is such that it can be indicated but can never be determinately cognized and distinctly provided for use in actual cases, then from such a principle there can be drawn no explanation, i.e., a distinct and determinate derivation of the possibility of a natural product that is possible in accordance with those two heterogeneous principles. Now, however, the common principle of the mechanical derivation on the one side and the teleological on the other is the **supersensible**, on which we must base nature as phenomenon. But from a theoretical point of view, we cannot form the least affirmative determinate concept of this. Thus how in accordance with this, as a principle, nature (in accordance with its particular laws) constitutes a principle for us, which could be cognized as possible in accordance with the principle of generation from physical as well as from final causes, can by no means be explained; rather, if it happens that we are presented with objects of nature the possibility of which we cannot conceive in accordance with the principle of mechanism (which always has a claim on any natural being) without appeal to teleological principles, then we can only presuppose that we may confidently re-

5: 413

[a] *Beurtheilung*
[b] *Beurtheilung*

search the laws of nature (as far as the possibility of their product is cognizable from one or the other principle of our understanding) in accordance with both of these principles, without being troubled by the apparent conflict between the two principles for judging[a] this product; for at least the possibility that both may be objectively unifiable in one principle (since they concern appearances that presuppose a supersensible ground) is secured.

Thus even though the mechanism as well as the teleological (intentional) technicism[b] of nature can stand, with regard to one and the same product and its possibility, under a common higher principle for the particular laws of nature, still, since this principle is **transcendent**, we cannot, given the limitation of our understanding, unite both principles **in the explanation** of one and the same natural generation, even if the inner possibility of this product is only **intelligible** through a causality according to ends (as is the case with organized matter). The above fundamental principle of teleology thus stands, namely, that given the constitution of the human understanding, only intentionally acting causes for the possibility of organic beings in nature can be assumed, and the mere mechanism of nature cannot be adequate at all for the explanation of these products of it – even though nothing is to be decided with regard to the possibility of such things themselves by means of this fundamental principle.

That is, since this is only a maxim of the reflecting, not of the determining power of judgment, and hence is valid only subjectively for us, not objectively for the possibility of this sort of thing itself (where both sorts of generation could well cohere in one and the same ground); since, further, without the concept of a mechanism of nature that is also to be found together with any teleologically conceived kind of generation such a generation could not be judged[c] as a product of nature at all, the above maxim leads to the necessity of a unification of both principles in the judging[d] of things as natural ends, but not in order to put one wholly or partly in place of the other. For in the place of that which (at least for us) can only be conceived of as possible in accordance with an intention no mechanism can be assumed; and in the place of that which can be cognized as necessary in accordance with the latter, no contingency, which would require an end as its determining ground, can be assumed; rather, the one (mechanism) can only be subordinated to the other (intentional technicism), which, in

5: 414

[a] *Beurtheilung*
[b] *Technicism*
[c] *beurtheilt*
[d] *Beurtheilung*

accordance with the transcendental principle of the purposiveness of nature, can readily be done.

For where ends are conceived as grounds of the possibility of certain things, there one must also assume means the laws of the operation of which do not **of themselves** need anything that presupposes an end, which can thus be mechanical yet still be a cause subordinated to intentional effects. Hence even in organic products of nature, but even more if, prodded to do so by their infinite multitude, we assume that intentionality in the connection of natural causes in accordance with particular laws is also (at least as a permissible hypothesis) the **universal principle** of the reflecting power of judgment for the whole of nature (the world), we can conceive a great and even universal connection of the mechanical laws with the teleological ones in the productions of nature, without confusing the principles for judging[a] it with one another and putting one in the place of the other, because in a teleological judging[b] of matter, even if the form which it assumes is judged[c] as possible only in accord with an intention, still its nature, in accordance with mechanical laws, can also be subordinated as a means to that represented end; likewise, since the ground of this unifiability lies in that which is neither the one nor the other (neither mechanism nor connection to an end) but is the supersensible substratum of nature, of which we can cognize nothing, the two ways of representing the possibility of such objects are not to be fused into one for our (human) reason, but rather we cannot judge[d] them other than as a connection of final causes grounded in a supreme understanding, by which nothing is taken away from the teleological kind of explanation.

But now since how much the mechanism of nature as a means contributes to each final end in it is entirely undetermined and for our reason also forever undeterminable, and, on account of the above mentioned intelligible principle of the possibility of a nature in general, it can be assumed that nature is completely possible in accordance with both of the universally consonant laws (the physical laws and those of final causes), although we can have no insight at all into the way in which this happens, we also do not know how far the mechanical mode of explanation that is possible for us will extend, but are only certain of this much, namely, that no matter how far we ever get with that, it will still always be inadequate for things that we once acknowledge as natural ends, and, given the constitution of our understanding, we must

5: 415

---

[a] *Beurtheilung*
[b] *Beurtheilung*
[c] *beurtheilt*
[d] *beurtheilen*

always subordinate all such mechanical grounds to a teleological principle.

Now on this is grounded the authorization and, on account of the importance that the study of nature in accordance with the principle of mechanism has for our theoretical use of reason, also the obligation to give a mechanical explanation of all products and events in nature, even the most purposive, as far as it is in our capacity^a to do so (the limits of which within this sort of investigation we cannot determine), but at the same time never to lose sight of the fact that those which, given the essential constitution of our reason, we can, in spite of those mechanical causes, subject to investigation only under the concept of an end of reason, must in the end be subordinated to causality in accordance with ends.

---

^{a} *Vermögen*

Appendix^a
Methodology of the Teleological
Power of Judgment

§ 79.
Whether teleology must be treated
as part of the doctrine of nature.

Every science must have its determinate position in the encyclopedia of the sciences. If it is a philosophical science, then we must assign it its position in either its theoretical or its practical part, and, if it has its place in the former, we must assign it its place either in the doctrine of nature, insofar as it examines that which can be an object of experience (consequently, in the doctrine of body, the doctrine of the soul, and universal cosmology), or in theology (concerning the original ground of the world as the sum total of all objects of experience).

Now the question arises: Which position does teleology deserve? Does it belong to natural science (properly so called) or to theology? It must be one or the other, because no science can belong to the transition from one to the other, since that signifies only the articulation or organization of the system and not a place within it.

That it does not belong in theology, as one of its parts, even though the most important use of it can be made within theology, is self-evident. For it has as its object natural productions and their cause, and although it refers to the latter as a ground lying outside of and beyond nature (a divine author), it does not do this for the determining power of judgment, but merely for the reflecting power of judgment in the consideration of nature (for the guidance of the judging^b of the things in the world by means of such an idea, appropriate to the human understanding, as a regulative principle).

But just as little does it seem to belong in natural science, which requires determining and not merely reflecting principles in order to provide objective grounds for natural effects. In fact, nothing is gained for the theory of nature or the mechanical explanation of its phenom-

---

^a The heading "Appendix" does not appear in the first edition, nor is a new page started here.
^b Beurtheilung

ena by its efficient causes when they are considered in light of the relation of ends to one another. Strictly speaking, positing ends of nature in its products, insofar as it constitutes a system in accordance with teleological concepts, belongs only to the description of nature, which is composed in accordance with a particular guideline, in which reason certainly plays a role that is magnificently instructive and purposive in many respects, but in which it provides no information at all about the origination and the inner possibility of these forms, although it is that with which theoretical natural science is properly concerned.

Teleology, as a science, thus does not belong to any doctrine at all, but only to critique, and indeed to that of a particular cognitive faculty, namely that of the power of judgment. But insofar as it contains *a priori* principles, it can and must provide the method for how nature must be judged in accordance with the principle of final causes; and thus its methodology has at least a negative influence on procedure in theoretical natural science, and also on the relation that this can have in metaphysics to teleology, as its propaedeutic.

§ 80.
On the necessary subordination of
the principle of mechanism to the
teleological principle in the explanation of a thing
as a natural end.

The **authorization to seek** for a merely mechanical explanation of all natural products is in itself entirely unrestricted; but the **capacity**[a] **to get by** with that alone is, given the constitution of our understanding insofar as it is concerned with things as natural ends, not only quite restricted, but also distinctly bounded, since by a principle of judgment that follows the first procedure alone nothing at all can be accomplished toward the explanation of such products, and hence our judging[b] of them must always be subordinated to a teleological principle as well.

5: 418   It is thus rational, indeed meritorious, to pursue the mechanism of nature, for the sake of an explanation of the products of nature, as far as can plausibly be done, and indeed not to give up this effort because it is impossible **in itself** to find the purposiveness of nature by this route, but only because it is impossible **for us** as humans – since for that an intuition other than sensible intuition and a determinate cognition of the intelligible substratum of nature, which could furnish the ground for the mechanism of the appearances in accordance with

[a] *Vermögen*
[b] *Beurtheilung*

286

particular laws, would be necessary, and this is entirely beyond our capacity.[a]

If, therefore, the investigator of nature is not to work entirely in vain, he must, in the judging[b] of things whose concept as natural ends is indubitably established (organized beings), always base them on some original organization, which uses that mechanism itself in order to produce other organized forms or to develop its own into new configurations (which, however, always result from that end and in conformity with it).

It is commendable to go through the great creation of organized natures by means of a comparative anatomy in order to see whether there is not to be found therein something similar to a system, one, indeed, regarding the principle of their generation, without which we would have to settle for the mere principle of judging[c] (which provides no insight into their production), and would have to give up all claim to **insight into nature** in this field. The agreement of so many genera of animals in a certain common schema, which seems to lie at the basis not only of their skeletal structure but also of the arrangement of their other parts, and by which a remarkable simplicity of basic design[d] has been able to produce such a great variety of species by the shortening of one part and the elongation of another, by the involution of this part and the evolution of another, allows the mind at least a weak ray of hope that something may be accomplished here with the principle of the mechanism of nature, without which there can be no natural science at all. This analogy of forms, insofar as in spite of all the differences it seems to have been generated in accordance with a common prototype,[e] strengthens the suspicion of a real kinship among them in their generation from a common proto-mother,[f] through the gradual approach of one animal genus to the other, from that in which the principle of ends seems best confirmed, namely human beings, down to polyps, and from this even further to mosses and lichens, and finally to the lowest level of nature that we can observe, that of raw matter: from which, and from its forces governed by mechanical laws (like those which are at work in its production of crystals), the entire technique of nature, which is so incomprehensible to us in organized beings that we believe ourselves compelled to conceive of another principle for them, seems to derive.

5: 419

[a] *Vermögen*
[b] *Beurtheilung*
[c] *Beurtheilungsprincip*
[d] *Grundriss*
[e] *Urbild*
[f] *Urmutter*

Now here the **archaeologist** of nature is free to let that great family of creatures (for thus must one represent it if there is to be a basis for the thoroughly coherent kinship that has been mentioned) originate from the remaining traces of its oldest revolutions in accordance with any mechanism for it that is known to or conjectured by him. He can have the maternal womb of the earth, which has just emerged from a condition of chaos (just like a great animal), initially bear creatures of less purposive form, which in turn bear others that are formed more suitably for their place of origin and their relationships to one another, until this birth-mother itself, hardened and ossified, has restricted its offspring to determinate species that will degenerate no further, and the variety will remain as it turned out at the end of the operation of that fruitful formative power. – And yet ultimately he must attribute to this universal mother an organization purposively aimed at all these creatures, for otherwise the possibility of the purposive form[a] of the products of the animal and vegetable kingdoms cannot be conceived at

5: 420   all.* In that case, however, he has merely put off the explanation, and cannot presume to have made the generation of those two kingdoms independent from the condition of final causes.

Even the alteration to which certain individuals in organized genera are contingently subjected, where one finds that their altered characteristic is heritable and has been taken up into the generative power, cannot be properly judged[b] as other than an incidental development of a purposive predisposition to the self-preservation of the kind that was originally present in the species, because in the thoroughgoing internal

---

5: 419   * One can call an hypothesis of this sort a daring adventure of reason, and there may be few, even among the sharpest researchers into nature, who have not occasionally entertained it. For it is not absurd, unlike *generatio equivoca*, by which is meant the generation of an organized being through the mechanism of crude, unorganized matter. It would still be *generatio univoca* in the most general sense of the term, insofar as something organic would be generated out of something else that is also organic, even though there would be a specific difference between these kinds of beings, e.g., as when certain aquatic animals are gradually transformed into amphibians and these, after some generations, into land animals. *A priori*, in the judgment of mere reason, there is no contradiction in this. Only experience gives no example of it; rather, according to experience, all generation that we know is *generatio homonyma* and not merely *univoca*, in contrast to generation from unorganized

5: 420   matter, and produces a product that is in its organization itself homogeneous with that which has generated it; and *generatio heteronyma*, so far as our experiential knowledge of nature goes, is nowhere to be found.

   [a] *Zweckform*
   [b] *beurtheilt*

purposiveness of an organized being the generating of its own kind is so closely connected with the condition that it incorporate nothing into its generative power that does not belong to one of the undeveloped original predispositions of such a system of ends. For if one departs from this principle, then one cannot know with any certainty whether several of the elements that are currently to be found in a species are not of contingent, purposeless origin, and the principle of teleology that in an organized being nothing that is preserved in its procreation should be judged to be nonpurposive would thereby turn out to be quite unreliable in application, and valid merely for the original stock (which, however, we no longer know).

Hume makes the objection against those who find it necessary to assume for all natural ends a teleological principle of judging,[a] i.e., an architectonic understanding, that one could with equal right ask how such an understanding is possible, i.e., how the many faculties and properties that constitute the possibility of such an understanding that simultaneously has executive might could themselves have purposively converged in one being.[1] But this objection amounts to nothing. For the whole difficulty surrounding the question about the initial generation of a thing that contains purposes in itself and is comprehensible only through them rests on the further question concerning the unity of the ground of the combination in this product of the manifold of elements **external to one another**; however, if this ground is posited in the understanding of a productive cause as a simple substance, that question, insofar as it is teleological, is adequately answered, but if the cause is sought merely in matter, as an aggregate of numerous substances external to one another,[b] the unity of the principle for the intrinsically purposive form of its formation[c] is entirely lacking; and the **autocracy** of matter in productions that can be comprehended by our understanding only as ends is a word without any meaning.

5: 421

From this it follows that those who seek a supreme ground for the objectively purposive forms of matter without conceding an understanding to it nevertheless happily make the world-whole into a single, all-encompassing substance (pantheism) or (what is only a more determinate explanation of the preceding) into a sum of determinations inhering in a single **simple substance** (Spinozism),[2] merely in order to satisfy that condition of all purposiveness, namely the **unity** of the ground; where by so doing they do, to be sure, satisfy **one** condition

---

[a] *Beurtheilung*
[b] Reading *außer einander* with the first edition, rather than *aus einander* (out of one another) with the second.
[c] *Form ihrer Bildung*; the only candidate for the antecedent of the "its" (*ihrer*) would seem to be "a productive cause."

of the problem, namely that of unity in the relation to the end, by means of the ontological concept of a simple substance, but adduce nothing for the **other** condition, namely its relation to its consequence as an **end** through which that ontological ground for the question should be more precisely determined, and thus by no means answer the **whole** question.[a] And this question remains absolutely unanswerable (for our reason) if we do not represent that original ground of things as a simple substance and its quality for the specific constitution of the natural forms founded on it, namely the unity of an end, as that of an intelligent[b] substance, and its relation to those forms (on account of the contingency that we find in everything that we can conceive of as possible only as an end) as the relation to a **causality**.

§ 81.
On the association of mechanism with the teleological principle in the explanation of a natural end as a product of nature.

Just as the mechanism of nature, according to the preceding section, is not by itself sufficient for conceiving of the possibility of an organized being, but must (at least given the constitution of our cognitive faculty) be subordinated to an intentionally acting cause, the mere teleological ground of such a being is equally inadequate for considering and judging[c] it as a product of nature unless the mechanism of the latter is associated with the former, as if it were the tool of an intentionally acting cause to whose ends nature is subordinated, even in its mechanical laws. Our reason does not comprehend the possibility of a unification of two entirely different kinds of causality, that of nature in its universal lawfulness and that of an idea that limits the latter to a particular form for which nature does not contain any ground at all; it lies in the supersensible substrate of nature, about which we can determine nothing affirmative except that it is the being in itself of which we know merely the appearance. But the principle that everything that we assume to belong to this nature (*phaenomenon*) and to be a product of it must also be able to be conceived as connected with it in accordance with mechanical laws nonetheless remains in force, since without this kind of causality organized beings, as ends of nature, would not be natural products.

Now if the teleological principle of the generation of these beings is

5: 422

---

[a] In the first edition, there is a comma rather than a period here.
[b] In the first edition, "intelligible."
[c] *beurtheilen*

assumed (as cannot but be the case), then the cause of their internally purposive form can be grounded in either **occasionalism** or **prestabilism**.[3] According to the former, the supreme world-cause, in accordance with its idea, would immediately provide the organic formation[a] to the matter commingling in every impregnation; according to the latter, it would only have placed in the initial products of its wisdom the predisposition by means of which an organic being produces more of its kind and constantly preserves the species itself, in which a nature that continuously works at their destruction simultaneously makes good the loss of the individuals. If one assumes the occasionalism of the production of organic beings, then everything that is natural is entirely lost, and with that is also lost all use of reason for judging the possibility of such a product; hence it can be presupposed that no one who cares anything for philosophy will assume this system.

Now **prestabilism** can in turn proceed in two ways. Namely, it considers each organic being generated from its own kind as either the **educt** or the **product** of the lattter. The system of generatings as mere educts is called that of **individual preformation** or the **theory of evolution**; the system of generatings as products is called the system of **epigenesis**.[b] The latter can also be called the system of **generic preformation**, since the productive capacity[c] of the progenitor is still preformed in accordance with the internally purposive predispositions that were imparted to its stock, and thus the specific form was preformed *virtualiter*. Given this, the opposing theory of individual preformation might better be called the **theory of involution** (or that of encapsulation).[4]

5: 423

The champions of the **theory of evolution**, which excepts every individual from the formative power of nature in order to allow it to come immediately from the hand of the creator, would still not have dared to have this happen in accordance with the hypothesis of occasionalism, which would make impregnation a mere formality, since the supreme intelligent world-cause has decided always to form a fruit immediately with his own hand and to leave to the mother only its development and nourishment. They instead declared themselves for preformation, as if it made no difference whether they would have these forms arise, supernaturally, at the origin or during the course of the world,[5] when they would in fact have been spared by occasional creation the multitude of supernatural arrangements that would be necessary in order to preserve uninjured the embryos formed at the

---

[a] *Bildung*
[b] In the first edition, there is a comma rather than a period here.
[c] *Vermögen*

beginning of the world and to save them from injury by the destructive forces of nature during the long time until their development, and would likewise have been spared an immeasurably greater number of such prefigured beings than would ever develop, thereby making so many of these creations unnecessary and purposeless. Yet they would at least have left something to nature in order not to fall into a complete hyperphysics, which could dispense with all natural explanation. To be sure, they still held fast to their hyperphysics, finding even in miscarriages (which one cannot possibly hold to be ends of nature) a marvelous purposiveness, even if this is only aimed at one day striking an anatomist with its purposeless purposiveness and precipitating his astonishment. But they had absolutely no way of fitting the generation of half-breeds into the system of preformation, but had to concede to the male seed, to which they had otherwise conceded only the mechanical property of serving as the first nourishment of the embryo, a purposive formative power which, however, in the case where the whole product is generated by two creatures of the same species, they would not have conceded to either.[6]

In contrast, even if one did not recognize the great advantage that the defender of **epigenesis** has over the other side in the matter of experiential grounds for the proof of his theory, reason would still already be favorably disposed to this explanation because it considers nature, at least as far as propagation is concerned, as itself producing rather than merely developing those things that can initially be represented as possible only in accordance with the causality of ends, and thus, with the least possible appeal to the supernatural, leaves everything that follows from the first beginning to nature (without, however, determining anything about this first beginning, on which physics always founders, no matter what chain of causes it tries).

No one has done more for the proof of this theory of epigenesis as well as the establishment of the proper principles of its application, partly by limiting an excessively presumptuous use of it, than Privy Councilor **Blumenbach.**[7] He begins all physical explanation of these formations with organized matter. For he rightly declares it to be contrary to reason that raw matter should originally have formed itself in accordance with mechanical laws, that life should have arisen from the nature of the lifeless, and that matter should have been able to assemble itself into the form of a self-preserving purposiveness by itself; at the same time, however, he leaves natural mechanism an indeterminable but at the same time also unmistakable role under this inscrutable **principle** of an original **organization**, on account of which he calls the faculty in the matter in an organized body (in distinction

5: 424

from the merely mechanical **formative power**[a] that is present in all matter) a **formative drive**[b] (standing, as it were, under the guidance and direction of that former principle).

§ 82.
On the teleological system in the external
relations of organized beings.

By external purposiveness I mean that in which one thing in nature serves another as the means to an end. Now things that have no internal purposiveness or presuppose none for their possibility, e.g., soils, air, water, etc., can nevertheless be quite purposive externally, i.e., in relation to other beings; but these must always be organized beings, i.e., natural ends, for otherwise the former could not be judged[c] as means. Thus water, air, and soils cannot be regarded as means for piling up mountains, because the latter do not contain in themselves anything at all that requires a ground for their possibility according to ends, thus nothing in relation to which their cause could be represented under the predicate of a means (useful for that end).

External purposiveness is an entirely different concept from the concept of internal purposiveness, which is associated with the possibility of an object regardless of whether its reality is itself an end or not. In the case of an organized being, one can also ask, why does it exist? but one cannot readily ask this of things in which one recognizes merely the effect of the mechanism of nature. For in the former we already represent a causality according to ends for its internal possibility, a creative intelligence,[d] and we relate this active faculty to its determining ground, the intention. There is only a single external purposiveness that is connected with the internal purposiveness of organization and is such that, without raising the question of for what end such an organized being must exist, nevertheless serves in the external relation of a means to an end. This is the organization of the two sexes in relation to one another for the propagation of their kind; for here one can always ask, just as in the case of an individual, why must such a

---

[a] *Bildungskraft*
[b] *Bildungstrieb*
[c] *beurtheilt*
[d] *Verstand*. This term has been translated as "understanding" when it refers to one of the faculties of human cognition; here and in the ensuing sections it will be translated as "intelligence" when it refers to the putative nature of God.

pair have existed?[8] The answer is that this is what here first constitutes an **organizing** whole, although not one that is organized in a single body.

Now if one asks why a thing exists, the answer is either that its existence and its generation have no relation at all to a cause acting according to intentions, and in that case one always understands its origin to be in the mechanism of nature; or there is some intentional ground of its existence (as a contingent natural being), and this thought is difficult to separate from the concept of an organized being: for once we have had to base its internal possibility in a causality of final causes and an idea that underlies this, we also cannot conceive of the existence of this product otherwise than as an end. For the represented effect, the representation of[a] which is at the same time the determining ground of its production in an intelligently acting cause, is called an **end.** In this case, therefore, one can either say that the end of the existence of such a natural being is in itself, i.e., it is not merely an end, but also a **final end;**[b] or it is outside of it in another natural being, i.e., it exists purposively not as a final end, but necessarily at the same time as a means.

But if we go through the whole of nature, we do not find in it, as nature, any being that can claim the privilege of being the final end of creation; and one can even prove *a priori* that whatever could be an **ultimate end**[c] for nature could never, no matter with what conceivable determinations and properties it might be equipped, be, as a natural thing, a **final end.**

If one looks at the vegetable kingdom, one could initially be led by the immeasurable fertility by which it spreads itself over practically every terrain to think of it as a mere product of the mechanism of nature that is displayed in the formations of the mineral kingdom. But a close acquaintance with the indescribably wise organization of the former does not allow us to stop with this thought, but rather leads to the question: Why do these creatures exist? If one answers: For the animal kingdom, which is nourished by it so that it is able to spread itself over the earth in so many genera, then the question arises again: Why do these herbivorous animals exist? Perhaps the answer would be: For the carnivores, which can only be nourished by what lives. But in the end the question is: For what are these, together with all the proceeding natural kingdoms, good? For the human being, for the diverse uses which his understanding teaches him to make of all these creatures; and he is the ultimate end of the creation here on earth,

[a] The words "the representation of" were added in the second edition.
[b] *Endzweck*
[c] *letzter Zweck*

because he is the only being on earth who forms a concept of ends for himself and who by means of his reason can make a system of ends out of an aggregate of purposively formed things.

One could also, with the Chevalier Linné,[9] take the apparently opposite path and say that the plant-eating animals exist in order to moderate the excessive growth of the plant kingdom, by which many of its species would be choked; the carnivores exist in order to set bounds to the voraciousness of the plant-eaters; finally, humankind exists in order to establish a certain balance among the productive and destructive powers of nature by hunting and reducing the number of the latter. And thus the human being, however much he might be valued as an end in a certain relation, would in another relation in turn have only the rank of a means.

If one makes an objective purposiveness of the multiplicity of the genera of earthly species and their external relations to one another, as beings understood as purposive, into a principle, then it is rational to think in turn that there is in this relation a certain organization and a system of all the kingdoms of nature in accordance with final causes. But here experience seems clearly to contradict the maxim of reason, especially in what concerns an ultimate end of nature, which is nevertheless requisite for such a system, and which we cannot place anywhere but in the human being; for in regard to the latter, as one among the many genera of animals, nature has not made the least exception to its generative as well as destructive powers, but has rather subjected him to its mechanism without any end.[10]

The first thing that would have to be intentionally established in an order for a purposive whole of natural beings on the earth would have to be their habitat, the ground and the element on and in which they should thrive. But a more precise knowledge of the constitution of this foundation of all organic generating gives no indication of anything except a cause that acts quite unintentionally, indeed one which is rather destructive of than favorable to the generation of causes of order and ends. The land and the sea do not merely contain monuments of ancient, powerful devastations, that have affected them and every creature on and in them; their entire construction, the strata of the land and the boundaries of the sea, have every appearance of the products of wild, all-powerful forces of a nature working in a chaotic state. However purposively arranged the configuration, the structure, and the slope of the land may now appear for the reception of water from the air, for the channels of springs between different layers of the earth (for various products), and the course of the streams, still a closer investigation of them proves that they have come about merely as the effect of eruptions both fiery and watery, or even of upheavals of the ocean, as far as concerns the first generation of this configuration as well as especially its subsequent reconfiguration together with the destruction of its first organic productions.* Now if the habitat, the maternal soil (the land) and the maternal womb (the sea) for all these creatures yields no signs of anything except an entirely unintentional mechanism for their generation, how and with what right could we demand and assert another origin for those products? Even if the human being was not included in these revolutions, as the most meticulous examination of the remains of those natural devastations seems to prove (according to the judgment of Camper),[11] still he is so dependent on the other creatures that if a mechanism of nature reigning over all the others is conceded, then he too must be included beneath that, even if his understanding was able to save him (at least for the most part) from its devastations.

This argument, however, seems to prove more than it was intended to, namely, not merely that the human being is not an ultimate end of nature and, for the same reason, that the aggregate of organized natural things on earth cannot be a system of ends, but rather that even the products of nature that we previously held to be natural ends can have no other origin than that in the mechanism of nature.

5: 429   But in the solution given above for the antinomy of the principles of the mechanical and teleological explanation of organic natural beings we have seen that since these principles are, with regard to their particular laws (the key to the systematic coherence of which, however, we lack) of formative nature, merely principles of the reflecting power of judgment, which in themselves determine nothing about the origin of these beings, but say only that given the nature of our understanding and our reason we cannot conceive of them except in accordance with final causes, the greatest possible effort, indeed boldness, in attempting to explain them mechanically is not merely allowed, but we are also summoned to it by reason, even though we know that we can never be successful in this attempt because of subjective reasons in the particular manner and limitation of our understanding (and not, say, because the mechanism of generation itself contradicts an origin in accordance with

5: 428   * If the name **natural history** that has been adopted for the description of nature is to remain in use, then one can call that which it literally means, namely a representation of the **ancient** condition of the earth – about which, even though there is no hope for certainty, there is reasonable ground for making conjectures – the **archaeology** of **nature**, in contrast to that of art. To the former belong fossils, just as to the latter belong carved stones, etc. For since we are really constantly if also, as is fitting, slowly working on such an archaeology (under the name of a theory of the earth), this name would not be given to a merely imaginary branch of research into nature, but to one to which nature itself invites and summons us.

ends); and, finally, we have also seen that even the unifiability of the two ways of representing the possibility of nature may well lie in the supersensible principle of nature (outside of as well as inside us), since the representation of it according to final causes is only a subjective condition of the use of our reason when reason would not judge[a] the objects merely as appearances, but rather demands that these appearances themselves, together with their principles, be related to the supersensible substratum in order to find possible certain laws of their unity, which cannot be represented except by means of ends (of which reason too has ones that are supersensible).

§ 83.
On the ultimate end of nature as a
teleological system.

In the preceding we have shown that we have sufficient cause to judge[b] the human being not merely, like any organized being, as a natural end, but also as the **ultimate end** of nature here on earth, in relation to which all other natural things constitute a system of ends in accordance with fundamental principles of reason, not, to be sure, for the determining power of judgment, yet for the reflecting power of judgment. Now if that which is to be promoted as an end through the human being's connection to nature is to be found within the human being himself, then it must be either the kind of end that can be   5: 430 satisfied by the beneficence of nature itself, or it is the aptitude and skill for all sorts of ends for which he can use nature (external and internal). The first end of nature would be the **happiness**, the second the **culture** of the human being.

The concept of happiness is not one that the human being has, say, abstracted from his instincts and thus derived from the animality in himself; rather, it is a mere **idea** of a state to which he would make his instincts adequate under merely empirical conditions (which is impossible). He outlines this idea himself, and indeed, thanks to the involvement of his understanding with his imagination and his senses, in so many ways and with such frequent changes that even if nature were to be completely subjected to his will it could still assume no determinate universal and fixed law at all by means of which to correspond with this unstable concept and thus with the end that each arbitrarily sets for himself.[12] But even if we sought either to reduce this concept to the genuine natural need concerning which our species is in thoroughgoing self-consensus, or, alternatively, to increase as much as possible the

---

[a] *die Beurtheilung . . . angestellt wissen will*
[b] *beurtheilen*

skill for fulfilling ends that have been thought up, what the human being understands by happiness and what is in fact his own ultimate natural end (not an end of freedom) would still never be attained by him; for his nature is not of the sort to call a halt anywhere in possession and enjoyment and to be satisfied. And further, it is so far from being the case that nature has made the human being its special favorite and favored him with beneficence above all other animals, that it has rather spared him just as little as any other animal from its destructive effects, whether of pestilence, hunger, danger of flood, cold, attacks by other animals great and small, etc.;[13] even more, the conflict in the **natural predispositions** of the human being, reduces himself and others of his own species, by means of plagues that he invents for himself, such as the oppression of domination, the barbarism of war, etc., to such need, and he works so hard for the destruction of his own species, that even if the most beneficent nature outside of us had made the happiness of our species its end, that end would not be attained in a system of nature upon the earth, because the nature inside of us is not receptive to that. The human being is thus always only a link in the chain of natural ends; a principle, to be sure, with regard to many ends which nature seems to have determined for him in its predispositions, since he himself makes those his ends; yet also a means for the preservation of the purposiveness in the mechanism of the other members. As the sole being on earth who has reason, and thus a capacity to set voluntary ends for himself, he is certainly the titular lord of nature, and, if nature is regarded as a teleological system, then it is his vocation[a] to be the ultimate end of nature; but always only conditionally, that is, subject to the condition that he has the understanding and the will to give to nature and to himself a relation to an end that can be sufficient for itself independently of nature, which can thus be a final end, which, however, must not be sought in nature at all.[14]

5: 431

In order, however, to discover where in the human being we are at least to posit that **ultimate end** of nature, we must seek out that which nature is capable of doing in order to prepare him for what he must himself do in order to be a final end, and separate this from all those ends the possibility of which depends upon conditions which can be expected only from nature. Of the latter sort is earthly happiness, by which is meant the sum of all the ends that are possible through nature outside and inside of the human being; that is the matter of all of his ends on earth, which, if he makes them into his whole end, make him incapable of setting a final end for his own existence and of agreeing with that end. Thus among all his ends in nature there remains only

[a] *Bestimmung*

298

the formal, subjective condition, namely the aptitude for setting himself ends at all and (independent from nature in his determination of ends) using nature as a means appropriate to the maxims of his free ends in general, as that which nature can accomplish with a view to the final end that lies outside of it and which can therefore be regarded as its ultimate end. The production of the aptitude of a rational being for any ends in general (thus those of his freedom) is **culture.** Thus only culture can be the ultimate end that one has cause to ascribe to nature in regard to the human species (not its own earthly happiness or even merely being the foremost instrument for establishing order and consensus in irrational nature outside him).

But not every kind of culture is adequate for this ultimate end of nature. The culture of **skill** is certainly the foremost subjective condition of aptitude for the promotion of ends in general; but it is still not sufficient for promoting the **will**[a] in the determination and choice of its ends, which however is essential for an aptitude for ends. The latter condition of aptitude, which could be named the culture of training (discipline), is negative, and consists in the liberation of the will from the despotism of desires, by which we are made, attached as we are to certain things of nature, incapable of choosing for ourselves, while we turn into fetters the drives that nature has given us merely for guidance in order not to neglect or even injure the determination of the animality in us, while yet we are free enough to tighten or loosen them, to lengthen or shorten them, as the ends of reason require.

5: 432

Skill cannot very well be developed in the human race except by means of inequality among people; for the majority provides the necessities of life as it were mechanically, without requiring any special art for that, for the comfort and ease of others, who cultivate the less necessary elements of culture, science and art, and are maintained by the latter in a state of oppression, bitter work and little enjoyment, although much of the culture of the higher class gradually spreads to this class. But with the progress of this culture (the height of which, when the tendency to what is dispensable begins to destroy what is indispensable, is called luxury) calamities grow equally great on both sides, on the one side because of violence imposed from without, on the other because of dissatisfaction from within; yet this splendid misery is bound up with the development of the natural predispositions in the human race, and the end of nature itself, even if it is not our end, is hereby attained.[15] The formal condition under which alone nature can attain this its final aim[b] is that constitution

[a] In the first edition, the word "freedom" (*Freiheit*) appears in place of the word "will" (*den Willen*).
[b] *Endabsicht*

in the relations of human beings with one another in which the abuse of reciprocally conflicting freedom is opposed by lawful power in a whole, which is called **civil society;**[a] for only in this can the greatest development of the natural predispositions occur.[b] For this, however, even if humans were clever enough to discover it and wise enough to subject themselves willingly to its coercion, a **cosmopolitan whole,**[c] i.e., a system of all states that are at risk of detrimentally affecting each other, is required.[d,16] In its absence, and given the obstacles that ambition, love of power, and greed, especially on the part of those who are in power, oppose to even the possibility of such a design, **war** (partly of the kind in which states split apart and divide themselves into smaller ones, partly of the kind in which smaller ones unite with each other and strive to form a larger whole) is inevitable, which, even though it is an unintentional effort of humans (aroused by unbridled passions), is a deeply hidden but perhaps[e] intentional effort of supreme wisdom if not to establish then at least to prepare the way for the lawfulness together with the freedom of the states and by means of that the unity of a morally grounded system of them, and[f] which, in spite of the most horrible tribulations which it inflicts upon the human race, is nevertheless one more incentive (while the hope for a peaceful state of happiness among nations recedes ever further) for developing to their highest degree all the talents that serve for culture.[17]

5: 433

As far as the discipline of the inclinations is concerned, for which the natural predisposition in respect to our vocation as an animal species is quite purposive but which make the development of humanity very difficult, nature still displays even in regard to this second requisite for culture a purposive effort at an education to make us receptive to higher ends than nature itself can afford. There is no denying the preponderance of the evil showered upon us by the refinement of taste to the point of its idealization, and even by indulgence[g] in the sciences as nourishment for vanity, because of the insatiable host of inclinations that are thereby aroused: however, there is also no mistaking nature's end of prevailing ever more over the crudeness and vehemence of those inclinations, which belong more to our animality and are most opposed to our education for our higher vocation (the

---

[a] *bürgerliche Gesellschaft*
[b] In the first edition, there is a comma rather than a period here.
[c] *Weltbürgerliches Ganze*
[d] In the first edition, Kant's sentence again continues with only a comma rather than a period here.
[e] The word "perhaps" was added in the second edition.
[f] The word "and" was added in the second edition.
[g] *Luxus*

inclinations of enjoyment), and of making room for the development of humanity. Beautiful arts and sciences, which by means of a universally communicable pleasure and an elegance and refinement make human beings, if not morally better, at least better mannered for society,[a] very much reduce the tyranny of sensible tendencies,[b] and prepare humans for a sovereignty in which reason alone shall have power;[18] while the evil that is visited upon us partly by nature, partly by the intolerant selfishness of human beings, at the same time calls forth, strengthens, and steels the powers of the soul not to be subjected to those, and thus allows us to feel an aptitude for higher ends, which lies hidden in us.*

5: 434

§ 84.
On the final end of the existence of a
world, i.e., of creation itself.

A **final end** is that end which needs no other as the condition of its possibility.

If the mere mechanism of nature is assumed as the basis for the explanation of its purposiveness, then one cannot ask why the things in the world exist; for on such an idealistic system, what is at issue is only the physical possibility of things (which for us to conceive of as ends would be mere sophistry, without any object); whether one assigns this form of things to chance or to blind necessity, in either case that question would be empty. But if we assume that the connection to ends in the world is real and assume that there is a special kind of causality for it, namely that of an **intentionally acting** cause, then we cannot stop at the question why things in the world (organized beings) have

* It is easy to decide what sort of value life has for us if it is assessed merely by **what one enjoys** (the natural end of the sum of all inclinations, happiness). Less than zero: for who would start life anew under the same conditions, or even according to a new and self-designed plan (but one still in accord with the course of nature), which would, however, still be aimed merely at enjoyment? It has been shown above what value life would have if conducted in accordance with the end that nature has set for us, which it contains in itself, and which consists in that **which one does** (and not merely what one enjoys), where we are, however, always merely a means to an undetermined final end. Thus nothing is left but the value that we ourselves give to our lives through that which we do not merely do but also do so purposively and independently of nature that even the existence of nature can be an end only under this condition.

5: 434

[a] *für Gesellschaft, wenngleich den Menschen nicht sittlich besser, doch gesittet machen*
[b] *Sinnenhanges*

this or that form, or are placed by nature in relation to this or that other thing; rather, once an understanding has been conceived that must be regarded as the cause of the possibility of such forms as they are really found in things, then we must also raise the question of the objective ground that could have determined this productive understanding to an effect of this sort, which is then the final end for which such things exist.

I have said above that the final end cannot be an end that nature would be sufficient to produce in accordance with its idea, because it is unconditioned. For there is nothing in nature (as a sensible being) the determining ground of which, itself found in nature, is not always in turn conditioned; and this holds not merely for nature outside of us (material nature), but also for nature inside of us (thinking nature) – as long as it is clearly understood that I am considering only that within me which is nature.[19] A thing, however, which is to exist as the final end of an intelligent cause necessarily, on account of its objective constitution, must be such that in the order of ends it is dependent on no further condition other than merely the idea of it.

Now we have in the world only a single sort of beings whose causality is teleological, i.e., aimed at ends and yet at the same time so constituted that the law in accordance with which they have to determine ends is represented by themselves as unconditioned and independent of natural conditions but yet as necessary in itself. The being of this sort is the human being, though considered as noumenon: the only natural being in which we can nevertheless cognize, on the basis of its own constitution, a supersensible faculty (**freedom**) and even the law of the causality together with the object that it can set for itself as the highest end (the highest good in the world).[20]

Now of the human being (and thus of every rational being in the world), as a moral being, it cannot be further asked why (*quem in finem*)[a] it exists. His existence contains the highest end itself, to which, as far as he is capable, he can subject the whole of nature, or against which at least he need not hold himself to be subjected by any influence from nature. – Now if things in the world, as dependent beings as far as their existence is concerned, need a supreme cause acting in accordance with ends, then the human being is the final end of creation; for without him the chain of ends subordinated to one another would not be completely grounded; and only in the human being, although in him only as a subject of morality, is unconditional legislation with regard to ends to be found, which therefore makes him alone capable

5: 435

5: 436

[a] to what end

302

of being a final end, to which the whole of nature is teleologically subordinated.*

§ 85.
On physicotheology.

Physicotheology is the attempt of reason to infer from the **ends** of nature (which can be cognized only empirically) to the supreme cause of nature and its properties.[21] A **moral theology** (ethicotheology) would be the attempt to infer from the moral ends of rational beings in nature (which can be cognized *a priori*) to that cause and its properties.[22]

The former naturally precedes the latter. For if we would infer **teleologically** from the things in the world to a world-cause, ends of nature must first be given, for which we have subsequently to seek a final end and then for this the principle of the causality of this supreme cause. 5: 437

Much research into nature can and must take place in accordance with the teleological principle without there being cause to inquire into

---

* It would be possible for the happiness of rational beings in the world to be 5: 436 an end of nature, and in that case it would be its **ultimate** end. At least one cannot understand *a priori* why nature should not be so arranged, since at least as far as we can understand this effect would be quite possible by means of its mechanism. But morality and a causality subordinated to it according to ends is absolutely impossible by means of nature; for the principle of its determination for action is supersensible, and is thus the only thing possible in the order of ends that is absolutely unconditioned with regard to nature, and its subject alone is thereby qualified to be the **final end** to which the whole of nature is subordinated. – Happiness, in contrast, is, as was shown in the previous section by the testimony of experience, not even an **end of nature** with regard to human beings in preference to other creatures, let alone a **final end of creation.** Human beings must always make it into their ultimate subjective end. But if I ask about the final end of creation: Why must human beings exist? then the issue is about an objective supreme end, such as the highest reason would require for its creation. Now if one answers: So that beings should exist whom that supreme cause can benefit, then one contradicts the condition to which the reason of a human being subjects even his inmost wish for happiness (namely its correspondence with his own internal moral legislation). This proves that happiness can only be a conditioned end, and that the human being can thus be the final end of creation only as a moral being; as far as his state is concerned, happiness is connected to it only as a consequence, in proportion to the correspondence with that end as the end of his existence.

the ground of the possibility of purposive action that we find in various
of the products of nature. If, however, we would also have a concept of
this, then we have absolutely no further insight into this other than the
mere maxim of the reflecting power of judgment, the maxim, namely,
that if even a single organic product of nature is given to us then, given
the constitution of our cognitive faculty, we can think of no other
ground for it except that of a cause of nature itself (whether the whole
of nature or even only this piece of it) that contains the causality for it
in virtue of understanding; a principle for judging^a by means of which
we are not brought a step further in the explanation of natural things
and their origin, but which does open up for us a prospect on nature
that may perhaps allow us to determine more precisely the otherwise
so fruitless concept of an original being.

Now I say that physicotheology, no matter how far it might be
pushed, can reveal to us nothing about a **final end** of creation; for it
does not even reach the question about such an end. It can thus
certainly justify the concept of an intelligent world-cause, as a merely
subjectively appropriate concept for the constitution of our cognitive
faculty of the possibility of the things that we make intelligible to
ourselves in accordance with ends; but it cannot determine this concept
any further in either a theoretical or a practical respect; and its attempt
does not fulfill its aim of establishing a theology, but always remains
merely a physical teleology, because the relation to ends in it always
can and must be considered only as conditioned within nature; hence
the end for which nature itself exists (the ground for which must be
sought outside of nature), on the determinate idea of which the determinate concept of that supreme intelligent world-cause and thus the
possibility of a theology nevertheless depend, cannot even become a
question.

How the things in the world are useful to one another; how the
manifold in a thing is good for this thing itself; how one even has
reason for assuming that nothing in the world is in vain, but that
everything **in nature** is good for something, under the condition that
certain things should exist (as ends), hence for assuming that our reason
5: 438 can provide the power of judgment with no other principle of the
possibility of the object for its unavoidable teleological judging^b than
the principle of subordinating the mechanism of nature to the architectonic of an intelligent world-author: the teleological view of the world
answers all of this magnificently and extremely admirably. But since
the data and hence the principles for **determining** that concept of an
intelligent world-cause (as the highest artist) are merely empirical, they

^{a} *Beurtheilungsprinzip*
^{b} *Beurtheilung*

do not allow us to infer any properties beyond what experience reveals to us in its effects: which, since it can never comprehend the whole of nature as a system, must often hit upon grounds of proof that (to all appearance) contradict one another as well as that concept, but it can never, even if we were capable of having an empirical overview of the whole system as long as it concerns mere nature, elevate us beyond nature to the end of its existence itself, and thereby to the determinate concept of that higher intelligence.[23]

If one minimizes the problem that a physicotheology is supposed to solve, then its solution seems easy. That is, if one reduces the concept of a **deity** to that of an intelligent being that can be conceived by us, which may have one or more, or even many of the important properties that are requisite for the establishment of a nature corresponding to the greatest possible ends, but not all of them; or if one thinks nothing of making good what cannot be proved within a theory by supplementing it with arbitrary additions, and takes oneself to be authorized, where one has reason for assuming **much** perfection (and what is much for us?), to presuppose **all possible** perfection: then physical teleology can make significant claims to the distinction of establishing a theology.[24] But if it is demanded that we show what drives us and even more justifies us in adding those supplements, then we will seek in vain to find anything that justifies us in the principles of the theoretical use of reason, which always demands that no properties be assumed in the explanation of an object of experience that are not to be found among the empirical data for its possibility.[a] On closer examination we would see that there actually lies in us *a priori* an idea of a highest being, resting on a very different use of reason (its practical use), which drives us to amplify physical teleology's[b] defective representation of the original ground of the ends of nature into the concept of a deity, and we would not falsely suppose that we have produced this idea and a theology along with it by the application of theoretical reason to knowledge of the physical world, let alone proved its reality.

The ancients should not be blamed so severely for having conceived of their gods very diversely, as far as both their capacities and their intentions and preferences are concerned, but for having conceived of all of them, even their chief one, as always limited in human ways. For if they considered the arrangement and the course of things in nature, they certainly found sufficient reason to assume something more than the mechanical as their cause, and for suspecting the intentions of certain higher causes, which they could not conceive except as super-

5: 439

---

[a] In the first edition, this sentence continues with a comma and an "and" rather than concluding here with a period.
[b] The first edition has "theology" rather than "teleology" here.

human, behind the machinery of this world. But since they found the good and evil in this world, what is purposive and what is contrapurposive, to be very mixed, at least as far as our insight goes, and they could not allow themselves to assume for the sake of the arbitrary idea of a[a] most perfect author that there are nevertheless wise and beneficent ends lying hidden beneath this, the proof of which they did not see, their judgment of the supreme world-cause could hardly come out otherwise, so long, that is, as they proceeded quite consistently in accordance with maxims of the merely theoretical use of reason. Others, who wanted to be both physicists and theologians at the same time, thought that they could satisfy reason by taking care of the absolute unity of the principle of natural things that reason demands by means of the idea of a being in which, as a sole substance, all those things together are only inhering determinations; which substance would not be cause of the world, by means of its intelligence, but in it, as a subject, all the understanding of beings in the world would nevertheless be found – a being, therefore, that would certainly not bring forth anything in accordance with ends, but in which all things, because of the unity of the subject of which they are mere determinations, must still necessarily be purposively related to each other even without any end and intention.[b] Thus they introduced the idealism of final causes by transforming the unity of a multitude of substances purposively connected to each other, which is so difficult to produce, from causal dependency **on one** substance into inherence **in one** substance; which system, as **pantheism** if considered from the side of the inhering beings in the world and (later) as **Spinozism**[25] if considered from the side of the single subsisting subject as original being, did not so much solve the question of the first ground of purposiveness as rather nullify it, by robbing that concept of all its reality and making it into a mere misinterpretation of a general ontological concept of a thing in general.

The concept of a deity sufficient for our teleological judging[c] of nature can thus never be produced in accordance with merely theoretical principles of the use of reason (on which alone physicotheology is based). For we either declare all teleology to be a mere deception of the power of judgment in the judging[d] of the causal connection of things, and take refuge in the single principle of a mere mechanism of nature which, because of the unity of the substance of which nature is nothing but the manifold of its determinations, merely seems to us to

---

[a] The first edition here inserts the word "single."
[b] In the first edition, the sentence continues with a comma and an "and" rather than concluding with a period here.
[c] *Beurtheilung*
[d] *Beurtheilung*

contain a universal relation to ends; or, if, instead of this idealism of final causes, we would remain attached to the fundamental principle of the realism of this special kind of causality, then, whether we base the natural ends on many or even just one intelligent original being, as long as we have available for the establishment of the concept of this being nothing but principles of experience, derived from the actual nexus of ends in the world, we can, on the one hand, find no help against the discord with regard to the unity of ends that nature presents in many cases, and, on the other, insofar as the concept of a single intelligent cause is produced only as is justified by mere experience, we will never be able to determine it adequately for any usable theology of whatever sort (theoretical or practical) it might be.

Physical teleology certainly drives us to seek a theology, but it cannot produce one, however widely we may scrutinize nature through experience and however much we may supplement the nexus of ends discovered in it with ideas of reason (which, for physical problems, must be theoretical). What help is it, one may rightly complain, to ground all these arrangements on a great and for us immeasurable intelligence, and have it arrange this world in accordance with its intentions, if nature does not nor ever can tell us anything about the final aim, without which, however, we can form no common reference point for all these natural ends, no teleological principle sufficient for cognizing all the ends together in a single system as well as for forming a concept of the supreme intelligence, as the cause of such a nature, which could serve as a standard for our power of judgment for reflecting upon nature teleologically? In that case I would, to be sure, have an **artistic intelligence**, for various ends, but no **wisdom**, for a final end, which, however, must really contain the determining ground of the former. But in the absence of a final end, which only pure reason can provide *a priori* (since all ends in the world are empirically conditioned, and can contain nothing except what is good for this or that as a contingent aim, and nothing that is absolutely good), and which alone would teach me what properties, what degree, and what relation of the highest cause to[a] nature I must conceive in order to judge it as a teleological system, how and with what right could I arbitrarily expand the very restricted concept of that original intelligence which I can ground on my limited knowledge of the world, of the power of this original being to bring his ideas to reality, of his will to do so, etc., and bring it up to the level of an idea of an all-wise, infinite being?[b] If this were to happen theoretically, it would presuppose omniscience in my-

5: 441

---

[a] Reading, with the first edition, *zur* instead of *der* (of the).

[b] In the first edition, the sentence continues instead of ending here with a question mark, and does not include the phrase "If this were to happen theoretically."

self in order to have insight into the entire nexus of the ends of nature and to be able to think even further of all other possible plans, in comparison with which the present one could be judged,[a] with reason, as the best. For without this complete knowledge of the effect, I cannot infer to any determinate concept of the supreme cause, which can only be found in that of an intelligence that is infinite in every respect, i.e., the concept of a divinity, and thus establish a foundation for theology.

Thus, even with all possible expansion of physical teleology, we can still say, in accordance with the fundamental principle that has been adduced above, that, given the constitution and the principles of our cognitive faculty, we cannot conceive of nature, in the purposive arrangements that have become known to us in it, except as the product of an intellligence to which it is subject. But whether this intelligence may have had a final aim in the whole of nature and its production (which in that case would not lie in the nature of the sensible world) can never be revealed to us by theoretical research into nature; rather, even in the face of all the knowledge of the latter, it remains undetermined whether that supreme cause is its original ground in accordance with a final end throughout rather than through an intelligence determined by the mere necessity of its nature to the production of certain

5: 442   forms (in analogy with that which we call artistic instinct in animals), without it being necessary to attribute to it any wisdom, let alone the highest wisdom combined with all the other properties requisite for the perfection of its product.

Thus physicotheology, a misunderstood physical teleology, is usable only as a preparation (propaedeutic) for theology, and is adequate for this purpose only with the assistance of another principle, on which it can support itself, but not in itself, as its name would suggest.

§ 86.
On ethicotheology.[26]

If it thinks over the existence of the things in the world and the existence of the world itself, even the most common understanding cannot reject the judgment that all the many creatures, no matter how great the artistry of their arrangement and how manifold the purposive interconnections by which they are related to each other may be, indeed the whole of so many systems of them, which we incorrectly call worlds, would exist for nothing if there were not among them human beings (rational beings in general), i.e., the judgment that without human beings the whole of creation would be a mere desert,[b]

---

[a] *beurtheilt*
[b] The phrase "a mere desert" was added in the second edition.

existing in vain and without a final end. But it is not their cognitive faculty (theoretical reason) in relation to which the existence of everything else in the world first acquires its value, so that someone should exist who can **consider** the world. For if this consideration of the world were to allow him to represent nothing but things without a final end, then no value would emerge from the fact that they are cognized; and a final end would already have to be assumed in relation to which the consideration of the world would itself have a value. Nor is it the feeling of pleasure and the amount of such feeling in relation to which we think of a final end of creation as given, i.e., it is not well-being, not enjoyment (whether corporeal or spiritual), in a word it is not happiness by means of which we estimate that absolute value. For the fact that if the human being exists he makes this itself his final aim does not yield any concept of why he should exist at all, and what value he himself has in order to make his existence agreeable. He must already be presupposed to be the final end of creation in order for there to be a rational ground why nature, if it is considered as an absolute whole in accordance with principles of ends, must agree with his happiness. – Hence it is only the faculty of desire, although not that which makes him dependent on nature (through sensible impulses), not that in regard to which the value of his existence rests on what he receives and enjoys; rather it is the value that he alone can give to himself, and which consists in what he does, in how and in accordance with which principles he acts, not as a link in nature but in the **freedom** of his faculty of desire; i.e., a good will is that alone by means of which his existence can have an absolute value and in relation to which the existence of the world can have a **final end**.[27]

5: 443

Further, the commonest judgment of healthy human reason is in complete agreement with this, namely, that it is only as a moral being that the human being can be a final end of creation, if we but direct its judging[a] to this question and give it occasion to investigate it. What does it help, one will ask, that this person has so much talent, even that he is very active with it, and thereby exercises a useful influence on the common weal, and also has a great value in relation to his own state of happiness as well as to the advantage of others, if he does not possess a good will?[28] If one considers what is inside him, he is a contemptible object; and if creation is not to be entirely without a final end, then he, who as a human also belongs to it, must nevertheless, as an evil person, in a world under moral laws, be prepared, in accordance with them, to sacrifice his subjective end (of happiness), as the sole condition under which his existence can be congruent with the final end.[29]

---

[a] *Beurtheilung*

309

Now if we encounter purposive arrangements in the world, and, as reason inexorably demands, subordinate the ends that are only conditional to an unconditioned, supreme end, i.e., a final end, then one readily sees, first, that in that case what is at issue is not an end of nature (within it), insofar as it exists, but the end of its existence, with all its arrangements, hence the ultimate **end of creation**, and in this, further, what is actually at issue is the supreme condition under which alone a final end (i.e., of the determining ground of a highest understanding for the production of the beings of the world) can obtain.

Now since we recognize the human being as the end of creation only as a moral being, we have in the first place a ground, at least the chief condition, for regarding the world as a whole interconnected in accordance with ends and as a **system** of final causes, but, above all, a ground for a **principle** for conceiving, for the relation of natural ends to an intelligent world-cause that is necessary given the constitution of our reason, of the nature and the properties of this first cause as the supreme ground in the realm of ends, and so for determining the concept of it – which physical teleology, which could only produce concepts that are indeterminate and for that very reason unsuited for both theoretical as well as practical use, could not do.

On the basis of the principle of the causality of the original being thus determined we must not conceive of it merely as an intelligence and as legislative for nature, but also as a legislative sovereign in a moral realm of ends. In relation to the **highest good** possible under his rule alone, namely the existence of rational beings under moral laws, we will conceive of this original being as **omniscient**, so that even what is inmost in their dispositions (which is what constitutes the real moral value of the actions of rational beings in the world) is not hidden from him; as **omnipotent**, so that he can make the whole of nature suitable for this highest end; as **omnibenevolent** and at the same time **just**, because these two properties (united as **wisdom**) constitute the conditions of the causality of a supreme cause of the world as a highest good under moral laws; and likewise all of the remaining transcendental properties, such as **eternity, omnipresence**, etc. (for goodness and justice are moral properties),[a] which must be presupposed in relation to such a final end, must also be thought in such a being.[30] – In this way **moral** teleology makes good the defect of **physical** teleology, and first establishes a **theology**; since the latter, if it is to proceed consistently rather than borrowing, unnoticed, from the former, could by itself alone establish

---

[a] The phrase in parentheses was added in the second edition.

nothing more than a **demonology**, which is not capable of any determinate concept.

But the principle of the relation of the world to a supreme cause, as a deity, on account of the moral vocation*a* of certain beings in it, does not do this merely by supplementing the physical-teleological basis for proof, and necessarily making this its ground; rather, it is adequate for that **by itself**, and urges attention to the ends of nature and research into the inconceivably great art that lies hidden behind its forms in order to provide incidental confirmation from natural ends for the ideas created by pure practical reason. For the principle of beings in the world under moral laws is an *a priori* principle in accordance with which human beings must necessarily judge.*b* Further, that if such an intentionally acting world-cause directed at an end exists at all, then that moral relation must be just as necessary a condition of the possibility of a creation as is the relation according to physical laws (if, that is, that intelligent cause also has a final end):*c* reason sees this *a priori* as a fundamental principle that is necessary for it for the teleological judging*d* of the existence of things. Now it comes down only to this: whether we have any sufficient ground for reason (whether speculative or practical) to attribute a **final end** to the supreme cause acting in accordance with ends. For given the subjective constitution of our reason and even how we must always think of the reason of other beings, it can count as certain for us *a priori* that this final end can be nothing other than **the human being under moral laws**, while by contrast the ends of nature in the physical order cannot be cognized *a priori* at all, nor can it be understood in any way that a nature could not exist with such an end.

5: 445

Remark

Consider a person at those moments in which his mind is disposed to moral sensation. If, surrounded by a beautiful nature, he finds himself in peaceful and cheerful enjoyment of his existence, he feels a need to be thankful to someone for it. Or if, on another occasion, he finds himself in the same state of mind under the press of duties which he can and will satisfy only through voluntary sacrifice, he feels a need to have done something that was commanded and to have obeyed an overlord. Or if he has in some heedless way acted contrary to his duty, although without having become answerable to other people, nevertheless a strong self-reproach will speak to him as if it were the voice of a judge to whom he must give account for his action. In a word, he needs a moral

5: 446

---

a *Zweckbestimmung* (literally, "end-determination").
b *beurtheilen*
c The parentheses were added in the second edition.
d *Beurtheilung*

311

intelligence in order to have a being for the end for which he exists, which is the cause of him and the world in a way suitable to this end. Cleverly to dig for incentives behind these feelings would be in vain, for they are immediately connected with the purest moral disposition, since **thankfulness, obedience** and **humiliation** (subjection to deserved chastisement) are particular dispositions of the mind*a* toward duty, and the mind that is inclined to the enlargement of its moral disposition here only voluntarily conceives of an object that is not in the world in order, where possible, to demonstrate its duty toward such an object. It is thus at least possible as well as well-grounded in a moral way of thinking to represent*b* such a purely moral need for the existence of such a being, by means of which our morality acquires either more strength or (at least as we represent it) more scope, namely, by assuming a new object for its exercise, i.e., a morally legislative being outside of the world, without any regard to a theoretical proof, but on a pure moral ground, free from all alien influence (and thus, to be sure, only subjective), on the basis of the mere recommendation of a pure practical reason legislating for itself alone. And even if such a disposition of the mind were only rarely forthcoming, or did not last long, but passed by quickly and without an enduring effect, or even without any reflection on the object represented in such a shadowy image and without any effort to bring it under distinct concepts, still the ground of such a disposition, our moral predisposition as the subjective principle not to be content with natural causes in the consideration of the purposiveness of the world but rather to base it in a supreme cause ruling nature in accordance with moral principles, is unmistakable. – In addition, there is the fact that we feel ourselves forced by the moral law to strive for a universal highest end, but at the same time feel ourselves and all of nature to be incapable of attaining it; there is the fact that it is only insofar as we strive for this that we feel that we can judge ourselves to be in accord with the final end of an intelligent world-cause (if there is one); and there is thus a pure moral ground of practical reason for assuming this cause (since this can be done without contradiction), even if for nothing more than avoiding the danger of seeing that effort as entirely futile in its effects and thereby flagging in it.

5: 447   By all of this only this much is here meant to be said: that although **fear** certainly first produces **gods** (demons), only **reason**, by means of its moral principles, is capable of having produced the concept of **God** (even if one were very ignorant in the teleology of nature, as is commonly the case, or even very dubious, on account of the difficulty of balancing contradictory principles in it by means of an adequately confirmed principle); and that the inner **moral** vocation*c* of human existence has made good that which was wanting in the knowledge of nature, by directing us to conceive of the supreme cause, for the final end of the existence of all things, for which no principle other than an **ethical** principle of reason is sufficient, with properties by means of which it is

---

a In the second edition, *Gemüthsstimmungen*; in the first edition, *Gemütsbestimmungen* (determinations of the mind).
b "to represent" added in the second edition.
c *Zweckbestimmung*

capable of subjecting the whole of nature to its sole aim (for which nature is merely its instrument) (i.e., to conceive of it as a **deity**).[31]

§ 87.
On the moral proof of the existence
of God.

There is a **physical teleology**[a] which gives our theoretically reflecting power of judgment a sufficient basis[b] for assuming the existence of an intelligent world-cause. But we also find in ourselves, and even more in the concept of a rational being endowed with freedom (of its causality) in general, a **moral teleology**, which, however, since the relation to an end together with its laws is determined in us *a priori*, and thus can be cognized as necessary, needs no intelligent cause outside of us for this internal lawfulness, any more than we need to look beyond what we find purposive in the geometrical properties of figures (for all sorts of artistic exercises) to a highest cause which has imparted this to those figures. Yet this moral teleology concerns us as beings in the world and thus as beings connected to other things in the world, upon which this very same law prescribes us to direct our judging,[c] whether as ends or as objects in regard to which we ourselves are ends.[d] Now from this moral teleology, which concerns the relation of our own causality to ends and even to a final end that must be aimed at by us in the world, and thus the reciprocal relation of the world to that moral end and the external possibility of its accomplishment (to which no physical teleology can guide us), there arises the necessary question of whether it compels our rational judging[e] to go beyond the world and to seek an intelligent supreme principle for that relation of nature to what is moral in us, in order to represent nature as purposive even in relation to the morally internal legislation and its possible execution. Thus there is certainly a moral teleology; and this is just as necessarily connected with the **nomothetic** of freedom on the one hand and that of nature on the other as civil legislation is connected with the question of where the executive power should be sought, and with the general question of how reason is to provide a principle of the reality of a certain lawful order of things that is possible only in accordance with ideas. – We will first describe the progress of reason from that moral teleology and its relation to the physical to **theology**, and will sub-

5: 448

---

[a] In the first edition, "theology."
[b] *Beweisgrund*
[c] *Beurtheilung*
[d] In the first edition, "either as ends or ourselves as final end in regard to them."
[e] *Beurtheilung*

sequently consider the possibility and the cogency of this sort of inference.

If one assumes that the existence of certain things (or even only of certain forms of things) is possible contingently, and hence only through something else, as cause, then one can seek the supreme ground for this causality, thus the unconditioned for that which is conditioned, in either the physical or the teleological order (in accordance with the *nexu effectivo* or *finali*).*a* I.e., one can ask: What is the supreme productive cause? or What is the supreme (absolutely unconditioned) end of that, i.e., the final end for the production of this or that of its products in general? – in which case, of course, it is assumed that this cause is capable of a representation of ends, hence that it is an intelligent being, or at least must be conceived*b* by us as acting in accordance with the laws of such a being.

Now if we follow the latter order, then it is a **fundamental principle**, to which even the most common human reason is compelled to give immediate assent, that if reason is to provide a **final end** *a priori* at all, this can be nothing other than **the human being** (each rational being in the world) **under moral laws.*** For (so does everyone judge)

5: 448

5: 449

* I deliberately say "**under** moral laws." The final end of creation is not the human being **in accordance with** moral laws, i.e., one who behaves in accordance with them. For with the latter expression we would say more than we know, namely, that it is in the power of an author of the world to make it the case that the human being always behaves in accordance with moral laws, which would presuppose a concept of freedom and of nature (for the latter of which alone one can conceive of an external author) that would have to contain an insight far exceeding the insight of our reason into the supersensible substratum of nature and its identity with that which makes causality through freedom possible in the world. Only of the **human being under moral laws** can we say, without overstepping the limits of our insight, that his existence constitutes the final end of the world. This is also in complete agreement with the judgment of human reason as it reflects upon the course of the world. We believe that we perceive the traces of a wise relation to ends even in someone evil when we see that the wanton criminal would rather not die until he has suffered the well-deserved punishment for his misdeeds. According to our concepts of free causality, good or evil conduct depends upon ourselves; the highest wisdom in the governance of the world, however, we set in the fact that the motivation of the former but the consequences for both depend upon moral laws. Honoring God consists in the latter, which is thus not inaptly named the final end of creation by theologians. – It should also be noted that when we use the word "creation" we do not mean anything

a According to the nexus of efficient or final causes.
b *gedacht*; in the first edition, *vorgestellt* (represented).

if the world consisted entirely of lifeless beings or even in part of living   5: 449
but nonrational beings, then the existence of such a world would have
no value at all, because there would exist in it no being that has the
slightest concept of a value. If, by contrast, there were also rational
beings, but ones whose reason was able to place the value of the
existence of things only in the relation of nature to themselves (to their
well-being), and were not able themselves to create such an original
value (in freedom), then there would certainly be (relative) ends in the
world, but no (absolute) final end, since the existence of such rational
beings would still always be without an end. The moral laws, however,
have the unique property that they prescribe something to reason as
an end without a condition, thus do exactly what the concept of a final
end requires; and the existence of such a reason, which in the relation
to ends can be the supreme law for itself, in other words, the existence
of rational beings under moral laws, can alone be conceived of as the   5: 450
final end of the existence of a world. If, on the contrary, this is not the
case, then there is either no end at all for the existence of a world in
its cause, or it is grounded in an end without a final end.

The moral law, as the formal rational condition of the use of our
freedom, obligates us by itself alone, without depending on any sort of
end as a material condition;[32] yet it also determines for us, and indeed
does so *a priori*, a final end, to strive after which it makes obligatory
for us, and this is the **highest good in the world** possible through
freedom.

The subjective condition under which the human being (and, according to our concepts, every rational finite being as well) can set a
final end for itself under the above law is happiness. Hence the highest
physical good that is possible in the world and which can be promoted,
as far as it is up to us, as a final end, is **happiness** – under the objective
condition of the concordance of humans with the law of **morality**, as
the worthiness to be happy.[33]

However, given all of the capacities of our reason, it is impossible
for us to represent these two requirements of the final end that is set
for us by the moral law as both **connected** by merely natural causes
and adequate to the idea of the final end as so conceived.[34] Thus the
concept of the **practical necessity** of such an end, by means of the

except what is said here, namely the cause of the **existence** of a **world** or of
the things in it (its substances), which is what is implied by the proper concept
of this word (*actuatio substantiae est creatio*),[a] which does not already imply the
presupposition of a freely acting and consequently intelligent cause (whose
existence we first of all wish to prove).

[a] The realization of substances is creation.

application of our own powers, is not congruent with the theoretical concept of the **physical possibility** of producing it if we do not connect our freedom with any other causality (as a means) than that of nature.

Consequently, we must assume a moral cause of the world (an author of the world) in order to set before ourselves a final end, in accordance with the moral law; and insofar as that final end is necessary, to that extent (i.e., in the same degree and for the same reason) is it also necessary to assume the former, namely, that there is a God.*

* *
*

5: 451

This proof, which one could easily adapt to the form of logical precision, is not meant to say that it is just as necessary to assume the existence of God as it is to acknowledge the validity of the moral law, hence that whoever cannot convince himself of the former can judge himself to be free from the obligations of the latter.ª No! All that would have to be surrendered in that case would be the **aim** of realizing the final end in the world (a happiness of rational beings harmoniously coinciding with conformity to the moral law, as the highest and best thing in the world)ᵇ by conformity to the moral law. Every rational being would still have to recognize himself as forever strictly bound to the precept of morals; for its laws are formal and command unconditionally, without regard to ends (as the matter of the will). But the one requirement of the final end, as practical reason prescribes it to beings in the world, is an end irresistibly imposed upon them by their nature (as finite beings), which reason would subject to the moral law **as** an inviolable **condition**, and would also have universally known in accor-

---

5: 450
5: 451

* ᶜThis moral argument is not meant to provide any **objectively** valid proof of the existence of God, nor meant to prove to the doubter that there is a God; rather, it is meant to prove that if his moral thinking is to be consistent, he **must include** the assumption of this proposition among the maxims of his practical reason. – Thus it is also not meant to say that it is necessary to assume the happiness of all rational beings in the world in accordance with their moralityᵈ **for** morals,ᵉ but rather that it is necessary **through** their morality. Hence it is a **subjective** argument, sufficient for moral beings.³⁵

ª This sentence is translated according to the third edition rather than the first two, which reverse "former" and "latter."
ᵇ *das höchste Weltbest*
ᶜ This note was added to the second edition.
ᵈ *Moralität*
ᵉ *Sittlichkeit*

316

dance with that law, and thereby makes the promotion of happiness, in consensus with morality, into the final end. Now for us to promote this (as far as happiness is concerned) as far as lies in our power to do so is commanded by the moral law, let the outcome of this effort be whatever it will. The fulfillment of duty consists in the form of the earnest will, not in the intermediate causes of success.

Suppose, then, that a person were to convince himself, partly because of the weakness of all the speculative arguments that have been praised so highly, and partly by the weight of the many irregularities that he has encountered in nature and in the world of mores,[a] of the proposition that there is no God; he would still be worthless in his own eyes if on that account he were to hold the laws of duty to be merely imaginary, invalid, and nonobligatory, and were to decide to transgress them without fear. Such a person, even if he could subsequently convince himself of that which he had initially doubted, would still always remain worthless with such a way of thinking, even though he fulfilled his duties as punctiliously as might be demanded of him because of fear or the aim of reward, but without the disposition of reverence for duty.[b] Conversely, if as a believer he follows his conscience[c] uprightly and unselfishly yet nevertheless believes, whenever he considers the case, that if he could ever be convinced that there were no God then he would be free from all moral obligation, then his inner moral disposition could only be bad.

5: 452

We can thus assume a righteous man (like Spinoza) who takes himself to be firmly convinced that there is no God and (since with regard to the object of morality it has a similar consequence) there is also no future life: how would he judge[d] his own inner purposive determination[e] by the moral law, which he actively honors? He does not demand any advantage for himself from his conformity to this law, whether in this or in another world; rather, he would merely unselfishly establish the good to which that holy law directs all his powers. But his effort is limited; and from nature he can, to be sure, expect some contingent assistance here and there, but never a lawlike agreement in accordance with constant rules (like his internal maxims are and must be) with the ends to act in behalf of which he still feels himself bound and impelled. Deceit, violence, and envy will always surround him, even though he is himself honest, peaceable, and benevolent; and the righteous ones

---

[e] *Sittenwelt*
[a] In the first edition, there is a comma rather than a period here.
[b] *Bewußtseyn*
[c] *beurtheilen*
[d] *Zweckbestimmung*

besides himself that he will still encounter will, in spite of all their worthiness to be happy, nevertheless be subject by nature, which pays no attention to that, to all the evils of poverty, illnesses, and untimely death, just like all the other animals on earth, and will always remain thus until one wide grave engulfs them all together (whether honest or dishonest, it makes no difference here) and flings them, who were capable of having believed themselves to be the final end of creation, back into the abyss of the purposeless chaos of matter from which they were drawn. – The end, therefore, which this well-intentioned person had and should have had before his eyes in his conformity to the moral law, he would certainly have to give up as impossible; or, if he would remain attached to the appeal of his moral inner vocation and not weaken the respect, by which the moral law immediately influences him to obedience, by the nullity of the only idealistic final end that is adequate to its high demand (which cannot occur without damage to the moral disposition), then he must assume the existence of a **moral** author of the world, i.e., of God, from a practical point of view, i.e., in order to form a concept of at least the possibility of the final end that is prescribed to him by morality – which he very well can do, since it is at least not self-contradictory.

5: 453

§ 88.
Restriction of the validity of the moral proof.

Pure reason, as a practical faculty, i.e., as a faculty for determining the free use of our causality by means of ideas (pure concepts of reason), not only contains a regulative principle for our actions in the moral law, but at the same time also thereby provides a subjectively constitutive one, in the concept of an object that only reason can think and which is to be made actual by means of our actions in the world in accordance with that concept. The idea of a final end in the use of freedom in accordance with moral laws thus has subjectively **practical** reality. We are determined a priori by reason to promote with all of our powers what is best in the world,[a] which consists in the combination of the greatest good for rational beings in the world with the highest condition of the good for them, i.e., the combination of universal happiness with the most lawful morality. In this final end the possibility of one part, namely that of happiness, is empirically conditioned, i.e., dependent on the constitution of nature (whether it corre-

---

[a] das Weltbeste

sponds with this end or not), and is problematic from a theoretical point of view; while the possibility of the other part, namely morality, with regard to which we are independent of the cooperation of nature, is established *a priori* and is dogmatically certain. For the objective theoretical reality of the concept of the final end of rational beings in the world it is thus requisite not merely that we have a final end that is set before us *a priori*, but also that the existence of creation, i.e., the world itself, has a final end – which, if it could be proven *a priori*, would add objective reality to the subjective reality of the final end. For if creation has a final end at all, we cannot conceive of it except as having to correspond to the final end of morality (which alone makes possible the concept of an end). But we certainly find ends in the world, and physical teleology presents them in such measure that if we judge rationally we will ultimately have reason to assume as the principle for research into nature that there is nothing in nature at all without an end; yet we try in vain to find the final end of nature in nature itself. Just as even the objective possibility of its idea is based only in reason, the final end of nature can and must be sought only in rational beings. The practical reason of the latter, however, does not merely provide this final end, but also determines its concept with regard to the conditions under which alone a final end of creation can be conceived by us.

5: 454

Now here the question is whether the objective reality of the concept of a final end of creation cannot be adequately established for the theoretical requirements of pure reason, if not apodictically, for the determining power of judgment, then at least adequately for the maxims of the theoretically reflecting power of judgment. This is the least that one can expect of speculative philosophy, which undertakes to connect the moral end with natural ends by means of the idea of a single end; but even this little is still far more than it can accomplish.

On the principle of the theoretically reflecting power of judgment we would say: If we have reason to assume a highest cause of nature for the purposive products of nature, whose causality with regard to the latter (the creation) must be conceived of as different from the mechanism of nature, namely as that of an intelligence, then we would have in this original being sufficient reason to think not merely that there are ends everywhere in nature, but also that there is a final end – not to prove the existence of such a being, but at least (as was the case in physical teleology) to convince ourselves that we can make the existence of such a world comprehensible to ourselves not merely according to ends, but only by ascribing a final end to its existence.

But a final end is merely a concept of our practical reason, and can neither be deduced from any data of experience for the theoretical

5: 455 judging[a] of nature nor be derived from any cognition of it. No use of this concept is possible except solely for practical reason in accordance with moral laws; and the final end of creation is that constitution of the world which corresponds only to that which we can give as determined in accordance with laws, namely the final end of our pure practical reason, insofar as it is to be practical. – Now in virtue of the moral law, which imposes this final end upon us, we have a basis for assuming, from a practical point of view, that is, in order to apply our powers to realize it, its possibility, its realizability, hence also a nature of things corresponding to that end (since without the accession of nature to a condition that does not stand within our own power its realization would be impossible). Thus we have a moral ground for also conceiving of a final end of creation for a world.

Now this is not yet the inference from moral teleology to a theology, i.e., to the existence of a moral author of the world, but only the inference to a final end of creation, which is determined in this way. Now that for this creation, i.e., the existence of things, in accordance with a **final end**, there must be assumed, first, an intelligent being, but second, not merely an intelligent being (as is necessary for the possibility of the things in nature that we are forced to judge[b] as **ends**) but also a **moral** being as author of the world, i.e., a God, is a second inference, which is so constituted that one sees that it is made merely for the power of judgment, in accordance with concepts of practical reason, and that as such it is made for the reflecting and not for the determining power of judgment. For we cannot presume to understand that just because the principles of morally practical reason are essentially different from those of technically practical reason in us, they must also be so in the supreme cause of the world if it is assumed to be an intelligence, and that it needs a special and different kind of causality for the final end than for mere ends of nature; hence we cannot presume that in our final end we have not merely a **moral ground** for assuming a final end of creation (as an effect) but also for assuming a **moral being** as the original ground of the creation. But we may well say that **given the constitution of our faculty of reason**, we could not even make comprehensible the kind of purposiveness related **to the moral law** and its object that exists in this final end without an author and ruler of the world who is at the same time a moral legislator.

5: 456 The reality of a highest morally legislative author is thus adequately established merely **for the practical use** of our reason, without determining anything in regard to its existence theoretically. For reason

---

[a] *Beurtheilung*
[b] *beurtheilen*

requires for the possibility of its end, which is in any case imposed upon us by its own legislation, an idea by means of which the obstacle arising from the incapacity for conforming to it given mere natural concepts of the world is removed (adequately for the reflecting power of judgment); and this idea thereby acquires practical reality, even if all means for providing it with theoretical reality, for the explanation of nature and the determination of the supreme cause, are entirely absent from speculative cognition. For the theoretical power of reflecting judgment, the physical teleology from the ends of nature was sufficient to prove an intelligent world-cause; for the practical power of reflecting judgment, this is accomplished by moral teleology by means of the concept of a final end which it is compelled to attribute to creation from a practical point of view. Now the objective reality of the idea of God as the moral author of the world cannot of course be established by means of physical ends **alone**; nevertheless, if the cognition of those ends is connected with that of the moral end, then the former, because of the maxim of pure reason to seek unity of principles as far as is possible, is of great significance for assisting the practical reality of that idea by means of the reality that it already has for the power of judgment from a theoretical point of view.

Now in order to avoid a misunderstanding that can easily arise, it is most necessary to mention here, first, that we can **think** these properties of the highest being only by means of analogy. For how would we investigate its nature, nothing similar to which can be shown to us by experience? Second, that by means of this analogy we only think this being, and do not thereby **cognize** it and attribute anything to it theoretically; for that would be something for the determining power of judgment, from the speculative point of view of our reason, in order to have insight into what the supreme world-cause is **in itself.** But what is at issue here is only what sort of concept we are to form of it given the constitution of our cognitive faculty, and whether we have to assume its existence in order to provide even practical reality for an end that pure practical reason, without any such presupposition, enjoins us *a priori* to realize by the use of all of our powers, i.e., only in order to be able to think of an intended effect as possible. That concept may always be excessive for speculative reason, and the properties that we attribute to the being that is thereby conceived may, if used objectively, conceal in themselves a certain anthropomorphism: yet our aim in using them is not that of determining its nature, which is unattainable for us, but of determining ourselves and our will in accordance with them. Thus just as we name a cause after the concept that we have of its effect (though only with regard to its relation to the latter), without thereby meaning to determine its internal constitution intrinsically by means of the properties that are all that we know about such

5: 457

causes and which must be given to us by experience – e.g., just as we would attribute to the soul among its other properties a *vim locomotivam*,[a] because real movements of the body arise whose causes lie in the soul's representations, without thereby meaning to ascribe to the soul the only ways in which we are acquainted with moving forces (namely, through attraction, impact, repulsion, hence movement that always presupposes an extended being) – so we must assume **something** that contains the ground of the possibility and the practical reality, i.e., the realizability, of a necessary moral final end; but given the constitution of the effect that is expected from it, we can conceive of it as a wise being ruling the world according to moral laws, and in accordance with the constitution of our cognitive faculties we must conceive of it as a cause that is distinct from nature, only in order to express the **relation** of this being transcending all of our cognitive faculties to the object of **our** practical reason, without on that account theoretically attributing to it the only kind of causality of this sort that is known to us, namely an intelligence and a will, indeed without meaning to make an objective distinction between the causality that we conceive in this being itself with respect to what is a final cause **for us** and its causality with respect to nature (and its purposive determinations in general); rather, we can assume this distinction only as subjectively necessary, for the constitution of our cognitive faculty, and as valid for the reflecting but not the objectively determining power of judgment. But when it comes to the practical sphere, such a **regulative** principle (for prudence or wisdom) – namely, to act in conformity with something, as an end, which given the constitution of our cognitive faculties can only be conceived by us as possible in a certain way – is at the same time **constitutive**, i.e., practically determining; for the very same thing which is by no means theoretically determining as a principle for judging[b] the objective possibility of things (the principle, namely, that the only kind of possibility that pertains to our faculty for thinking also pertains to the object) is rather a merely **regulative** principle for the reflecting power of judgment.

5: 458

Remark

This moral proof is not any newly invented argument, but at most only a newly articulated one; for it lay in the human faculty of reason even before its earliest germination, and with the progressive cultivation of that faculty has merely become more developed. As soon as human beings began to reflect on right and wrong, at a time when they still indifferently overlooked the purposiveness

---

[a] a locomotive force, i.e., a power to initiate motion
[b] *beurtheilen*

of nature, taking advantage of it without thinking that to be anything more than the usual course of nature, the judgment must inevitably have occurred to them that it could not in the end make no difference if a person has conducted himself honestly or falsely, fairly or violently, even if to the end of his life he has found at least no visible reward for his virtues or punishment for his crimes. It is as if they heard an inner voice that things must come out differently; hence there must have lain hidden in them the representation, even if obscure, of something they felt themselves obligated to strive for which would not be compatible with such an outcome, or which, if they regarded the ordinary course of the world as the only order of things, they did not in turn know how to reconcile with that inner vocation of their mind. Now they may have represented the way in which such an irregularity (which must be far more enraging to the human mind than the blind chance that one might assume as the principle for judging nature)^a could be straightened out in many if still quite crude ways; yet they could never have thought up any principle of the possibility of the unification of nature with their inner moral law other than a supreme cause ruling the world in accordance with moral laws: because a final end within them that is imposed upon them as a duty and a nature outside them that has no final end but in which that end is nevertheless to become real is a contradiction. Now they could have hatched up a lot of nonsense about the inner constitution of that world-cause, but that moral relation in the government of the world always remained the same, universally comprehensible for the most uncultivated reason as soon as it considers itself as practical even though speculative reason is far from being able to stay in step with it. – Further, in all probability this moral interest would first have aroused attention to the beauty and the ends in nature, which would then have served admirably to strengthen that idea, but could not have founded it, let alone made it dispensable, because it is only in relation to that final end that even the investigation of the ends of nature acquires that immediate interest that displays itself in such great measure in the admiration of them without regard to any advantage to be drawn from them.

5: 459

§ 89.
On the utility of the moral argument.

That, with regard to our ideas of the supersensible, reason is restricted to the conditions of its practical use has the unmistakable utility concerning the idea of God that it prevents **theology** from rising to **theosophy** (in extravagant concepts that confuse reason) or sinking to **demonology** (an anthropomorphic way of representing the highest being), and that it prevents **religion** from lapsing into **theurgy** (an enthusiastic delusion that we can feel other supersensible beings and can in turn have influence on them) or into **idolatry**[36] (a superstitious

---

^{a} *Naturbeurtheilung*

delusion that the highest being can be satisfied by means other than a moral disposition).*

For if anyone would make any concession to the vanity or presumptuousness of the sophistical attempt to determine anything at all with regard to what lies beyond the sensible world in a theoretical way (enlarging cognition), if anyone would pride himself on insight into the existence and the constitution of the divine nature, into its intelligence and will and into the laws of both of these and the properties which flow from them to the world, then I would very much like to know where and at what point he would limit the pretensions of reason; for from wherever those insights come, from there more are certainly to be expected (if only, one supposes, one thinks hard enough). Yet such claims must be limited by a certain principle, not merely because we find that all our attempts at them thus far have gone awry; for that proves nothing against the possibility of a better result. But here no principle is possible except to assume either that absolutely nothing at all can be determined about the supersensible theoretically (except strictly negatively) or else that our reason contains in itself a font of who knows what great and informative knowledge reserved for ourselves and our posterity. – But as far as religion is concerned, i.e., morals in relation to God as legislator, if theoretical cognition of God had to come first, then morals would have to conform to theology, and not merely would an external arbitrary legislation of a supreme being be introduced instead of an internal necessary legislation of reason, but further because of this everything that is defective in our insight into nature would also spread itself to the ethical precept, and thus religion would be made immoral and perverted.[37]

With regard to the hope for a future life, if, instead of making the final end which in accordance with the precept of the moral law we ourselves have to fulfill into the guideline for reason's judgment about our vocation (which can thus be considered as necessary or worthy of being assumed only in a practical relation), we consult our faculty of theoretical cognition, then in this respect the theory of the soul, just like theology above, yields nothing more than a negative concept of

---

* Any religion is idolatry in a practical sense which conceives of the highest being as having properties according to which human beings can be in accord with its will by any means other than morality, which could be an adequate condition by itself. For however pure and free from sensible images such a concept may be from a theoretical point of view, from a practical point of view it is still represented as an **idol**,[a] i.e., the property of its will is represented anthropomorphically.

[a] The first edition reads *Ideal*.

our thinking being, namely, that none of its actions nor the appearances of inner sense can be explained materialistically, therefore that absolutely no informative determining judgment based on speculative grounds concerning its separate nature and the duration or nonduration of its personality after death is possible for our entire faculty of theoretical cognition.[38] Therefore, since everything is left to the teleological judging[a] of our existence from a practically necessary point of view and to the assumption of our continuance as a necessary condition for the final end that is absolutely imposed upon us by reason, the utility (which on first glance certainly seemed to be a net loss) is displayed: namely, that just as theology can never become theosophy for us, so rational **psychology** can never become **pneumatology** as an informative science, yet at the same time is also secured against the danger of lapsing into **materialism**; rather, it is really merely an anthropology of the inner sense, i.e., knowledge of our thinking self **in life**, and as theoretical cognition it also remains merely empirical; while as far as our external existence is concerned, rational psychology is not a theoretical science at all, but rests on a single inference of moral teleology, and its entire use is necessary solely on account of the latter as our practical vocation.

5: 461

§ 90.
On the kind of affirmation[b] involved in a moral proof of the existence of God.[39]

The first thing that is required of any proof, whether (as in the case of a proof by observation of the object or by experiment) it proceeds by the immediate empirical presentation of that which is to be proved or is conducted by reason *a priori* from principles, is that it not **persuade** but **convince**,[c] or at least have an effect on conviction; i.e., what is required is that the basis of the proof, or the inference, not be merely a subjective (aesthetic) determining ground for assent (mere appearance),[d] but rather objectively valid and a logical ground for cognition; for otherwise the understanding is bewitched but not brought to conviction.[e,40] It is that sort of pseudo-proof that is conducted in natural theology, perhaps with a good intention, but with deliberate concealment of its weakness: a whole host of evidence for the origin of natural

---

[a] *Beurtheilung*
[b] *Fürwahrhalten*, literally, "holding to be true"; the modern notion of a propositional attitude might be the closest equivalent to Kant's term.
[c] *überrede, überzeuge*
[d] *Schein*
[e] *überführt*

things in accordance with the principle of ends is adduced, and advantage is taken of the merely subjective ground of human reason, namely its native tendency to conceive of one principle instead of many as long as it can do so without contradiction, and, where only one or several of the requisites for the determination of a concept are found in this principle, to complete the concept of the thing by means of an arbitrary addition of the others. Indeed, if we encounter so many products in nature that are signs of an intelligent cause for us, why should we not think of a single cause rather than many such causes, and indeed conceive of this cause as having not merely great understanding, might, etc., but rather omniscience, omnipotence, in a word, conceive of it as containing the sufficient ground for such properties in all possible things? and why not further ascribe to this single all-powerful original being not merely understanding merely for the laws and products of nature, but also, as a moral world-cause, the highest ethical practical reason, since by this completion of the concept a sufficient principle for insight into nature together with moral wisdom would be provided, and not even the least well-grounded objection can be made against the possibility of such an idea? Now if here the moral incentives of the mind are also set into motion and a lively interest is added to the latter with rhetorical force (of which they are quite worthy), then from that there arises persuasion of the objective sufficiency of the proof and even a healthy (in most cases of its use) illusion that entirely supersedes any examination of its logical acuity and in fact abhors and resists any such examination, as if it were based in a malicious doubt. – Now against this there is nothing to be said, as long as one is considering strictly popular usefulness. But still the separation of this proof into the two different parts that its argument contains, namely that which belongs to physical teleology and that which belongs to moral teleology, cannot and should not be rejected, since fusing the two together makes it hard to recognize where the real nerve of the proof lies and how and in which part it must be reworked in order for its validity to withstand the most acute examination (even if one is compelled to concede the weakness of our rational insight into one part); thus it is a duty for the philosopher (assuming that he takes no account of the claim of sincerity) to unmask even such a healthy illusion, which can cause such confusion, and to separate what belongs merely to persuasion from that which leads to conviction (two types[a] of approval that differ not merely in degree but in kind), in order to exhibit the state of mind[b] in this proof in complete clarity and to subject it to the most stringent and open-minded examination.

5: 462

[a] Bestimmungen
[b] Gemüthsfassung

A proof, however, that aims at conviction can be in turn of two different kinds, either one that would determine what the object is **in itself** or else one that would determine what it is **for us** (human beings in general) according to the necessary rational principles for our judging[a] (a proof κατ’ ’αληθειαν or κατ’ ’άνθρωπον,[b] taking the latter word in the broadest sense to stand for human beings in general). In the first case it is grounded on sufficient principles for the determining power of judgment, in the second merely on sufficient principles for the reflecting power of judgment. In the latter case it can never produce conviction, resting as it does on merely theoretical principles; but if it is based on a practical principle of reason (which is thus universally and necessarily valid), then it can make a sufficient claim of conviction from a purely practical point of view, i.e., moral conviction. A proof, however, **tends to conviction** without actually convincing if it is merely[c] led onto the path to conviction, i.e., if it contains only objective grounds for that, which, although they are not sufficient for certainty, are nevertheless of the sort that do not serve merely as subjective grounds of the judgment[d] for conviction.

5: 463

Now all theoretical grounds for proof suffice either (1) for proof through logically strict **rational inferences**,[e] or, where this is not the case, (2) for **inferences** from analogy, or, if this too does not obtain, then still (3) for **probable opinion**, or finally, what is the least,[f] (4) for the assumption of a merely possible explanatory ground as an **hypothesis**. – Now I say that no grounds for proof tending to theoretical conviction at all can produce any of these sorts of affirmation, from the highest to the lowest, if the proposition of the existence of an original being, as a God, is to be proven in a sense adequate to the complete content of this concept, namely as a **moral** author of the world, through which the final end of creation is given.

1) As far as **logically correct** proof, proceeding from the general to the particular, is concerned, it has been sufficiently demonstrated in the *Critique* that since the concept of a being that is to be sought beyond nature corresponds to no intuition that is possible for us, and thus that its concept itself, insofar as it is to be theoretically determined by synthetic predicates, always remains problematic for us, there is absolutely no cognition of it (through which the scope of our theoretical knowl-

---

[a] *Beurtheilung*
[b] proof based on truth or proof aimed at the person (i.e., *ad hominem*)
[c] The word "merely" was inserted in the second edition.
[d] *des Urtheils*; in the first edition, *des Urtheilens* (of judging).
[e] *Vernunftschlüsse*, often translated as "syllogisms."
[f] This phrase was inserted in the second edition.

edge would be in the least extended) and the particular concept of a supersensible being cannot be subsumed under the general laws of the nature of things in order to infer from the former to the latter – since those principles are valid solely for nature, as object of the senses.[41]

5: 464

2) One can, of course, **think** of one of two dissimilar things, even on the very point of their dissimilarity, by means of an **analogy*** with

5: 464

* An **analogy** (in a qualitative sense) is the identity of the relation between grounds and consequences (causes and effects), insofar as that identity obtains in spite of the specific difference between the things or those of their properties that contain in themselves the ground for similar consequences (i.e., their difference outside of this relation). Thus, in comparing the artistic actions of animals with those of human beings, we conceive of the ground of the former, which we do not know, through the ground of similar effects in humans (reason), which we do know, and thus as an analogue[a] of reason, and by that we also mean to indicate that the ground of the artistic capacity in animals, designated as instinct, is in fact specifically different from reason, but yet has a similar relation to the effect (comparing, say, construction by beavers with that by humans). – Yet from the fact that the human being uses **reason** in order to build, I cannot infer that the beaver must have the same sort of thing and call this an **inference** by means of the analogy. Yet from the comparison of the similar mode of operation in the animals (the ground for which we cannot immediately perceive) to that of humans (of which we are immediately aware) we can quite properly infer **in accordance with the analogy** that the animals also act in accordance with **representations** (and are not, as Descartes would have it, machines), and that in spite of their specific difference, they are still of the same genus as human beings (as living beings). The principle that authorizes such an inference lies in the fact that we have the same ground for counting animals, with respect to the determination in question, as members of the same genus with human beings, as humans, insofar as we compare them with one another externally, on the basis of their actions. There is *par ratio.*[b] Likewise, in the comparison of the purposive products of the causality of the supreme world-cause in the world with the artworks of human beings, I can conceive of the former in an analogy to an understanding, but I cannot **infer** to this property in the world-cause by means of the analogy; because here the principle of the possibility of such an inference is precisely what is missing, namely the *paritas rationis*[c] for counting the highest being as part of one and the same species along with human beings (with regard to their respective causalities). The causality of the being in the world, which is always sensibly conditioned (even its causality through understanding) cannot be transferred to a being that has no generic concept in common with the former except that of a thing in general.

[a] Following the first edition in reading *Analogon*; the second edition has *Anlage*, or "predisposition."
[b] equal reason
[c] parity of reason

the other; but from that respect in which they are dissimilar we cannot **draw an inference** by means of the analogy, i.e., transfer this characteristic of the specific difference from the one to the other.[42] Thus, in analogy with the law of the equality of effect and counter-effect in the mutual attraction and repulsion of bodies, I can also conceive of the community of the members of a commonwealth in accordance with rules of justice,*a* but I cannot transfer the specific determinations of the former (the material attraction and repulsion) to the latter and attribute them to the citizens in order to conceive of a system which is called a state.[43] – Likewise, we can very well conceive of the causality of the original being with regard to the things in the world, in analogy with an intelligence as the ground of the forms of certain products that we call artworks, as natural ends (for this occurs only for the sake of the theoretical or the practical use we have to make of this concept by our cognitive faculty, with regard to the natural things in the world, in accordance with a certain principle); but from the fact that among beings in the world the cause of an effect that is judged*b* as artistic has to be attributed to intelligence we can by no means infer by an analogy that the very same causality that we perceive in humans must also pertain to the being who is entirely distinct from nature in regard to nature itself; because this touches the very dissimilarity in their effects that must be conceived between a sensibly conditioned cause and the supersensible original being, and thus cannot be transferred from the former to the latter. – In the very fact that I am to conceive of the divine causality only in analogy with an intelligence (a faculty with which we are not acquainted in any being other than the sensibly conditioned human being) lies the prohibition against attributing this intelligence in a strict sense to the supersensible original being.*

3) **Opinion** has no place at all in *a priori* judgments; by their means one either knows something as entirely certain or knows nothing at all.[44] But if the given grounds of proof from which we set out (as in this case ends in the world) are empirical, then by their means one cannot form any opinion about what lies beyond the world of the senses, and one cannot grant such rash judgments the slightest claim to probability. For probability is part of a certain series of grounds of

5: 465

---

* One does not thereby lose anything in the representation of the relation of this being to the world as far as either theoretical or practical consequences are concerned. To wish to investigate what it is in itself is a pretension that is as purposeless as it is futile.

5: 465

a *Rechts*
b *beurtheilt*

possible certainty (the grounds of probability compare to the grounds of certainty as parts compare to a whole), in which the insufficient grounds of probability must be capable of being augmented.[45] But since both, as determining grounds of the certainty of one and the same judgment, must be similar, because otherwise they would not jointly constitute a single magnitude (like certainty), one part of them cannot lie within the bounds of possible experience while another lies outside all possible experience. Thus, since merely empirical grounds of proof do not lead to anything supersensible, the defect in the series of them cannot be augmented by anything; thus the attempt to arrive at the supersensible and cognition of it through them does not make the slightest progress, and there is consequently no probability in a judgment about the supersensible made on the basis of arguments derived from experience.

4) If something is meant to serve as an **hypothesis** for the explanation of the possibility of a given appearance, then at least its possibility must be completely certain.[46] It is enough if I forswear knowledge[a] of actuality in the case of an hypothesis (which is still asserted in the case of an opinion that is put forth as probable); I cannot surrender anything more: the possibility of that on which I base an explanation must at least be subject to no doubt, otherwise there will be no end to empty figments of the brain. But to assume the possibility of a supersensible being determined in accordance with certain concepts would be a completely groundless presupposition, since in this case none of the requisite conditions of a cognition which depend upon intuition are given, and thus nothing is left as a criterion of this possibility but the mere principle of contradiction (which can prove nothing but the possibility of thinking, not that of the object which is thought itself).

The result of this is that for human reason any theoretical proof of the existence of the original being as a divinity or of the soul as an immortal spirit is absolutely impossible from a theoretical point of view, even if only to produce the slightest degree of affirmation; and this for the entirely understandable reason that we have no material at all for the determination of the idea of the supersensible, since we would have to derive any such material from things in the sensible world, but nothing of the sort is adequate for such an object, and thus, in the absence of any determination of the latter, nothing is left but the concept of a nonsensible something that contains the ultimate ground of the world of the senses, which does not constitute

[a] *Erkenntnis*

any cognition (as an enlargement of the concept) of its inner constitution.

§ 91.

On the kind of affirmation produced
by means of a practical faith.

If we look merely to the way in which something can be an object of cognition (*res cognoscibilis*)[a] **for us** (in accordance with the subjective constitution of our powers of representation), then the concepts are not compared with the objects, but merely with our cognitive faculties[b] and the use that these can make of the given representation (in a theoretical or a practical respect); and the question whether something is a cognizable entity or not is a question that pertains not to the possibility of the things themselves but rather to our cognition of them.

Now there are three kinds of **cognizable** things: **matters of opinion** (*opinabile*),[c] **facts** (*scibile*),[d] and **matters of faith**[e] (*mere credibile*).[f]

1) Objects of mere ideas of reason, which cannot be represented for theoretical cognition in any sort of possible experience at all, are to that extent also not **cognizable** things at all, hence with regard to them one cannot even **have an opinion**, because to have an opinion *a priori* is absurd on its face and is a straight road to pure figments of the brain.[47] An *a priori* proposition is thus either certain or it affirms nothing at all.[g] Thus **matters of opinion** are always objects of an at least intrinsically possible experiential cognition (objects of the sensible world) that, however, merely because of the degree of capacity that we possess, are impossible **for us**. Thus the ether of recent physicists, an elastic fluid penetrating all other materials (completely permeating them), is a mere matter of opinion, although always still of the sort that could be perceived if the outer senses were sharpened to the highest degree, but which can never be exhibited in any observation or

---

[a] a cognizable thing
[b] This is singular in the first edition.
[c] things that can be opined
[d] things that can be known
[e] *Glaubenssachen*; this expression could be translated as "matters of belief," and in many contexts, especially in the *Critique of Pure Reason*, *Glauben* must be translated as "belief"; it is being translated as "matters of faith" in this section because at 5:469 below Kant will equate it with the Latin expression *res fidei*, which cannot be translated otherwise.
[f] things that are genuinely credible
[g] *enthält gar nichts zum Fürwahrhalten*

experiment.[48] To assume rational inhabitants of other planets is a matter of opinion; for if we could approach more closely to other planets, which is intrinsically possible, we could determine by means of experience whether they exist or not; but we never will come close enough to other planets, so this remains a matter of opinion.[49] But to have the opinion that there are pure, bodiless, thinking spirits in the material universe (if we ignore, as is appropriate, certain actual[a] appearances

5: 468

that have been passed off as such) is fiction, not a matter of opinion at all, but a mere idea left over if one takes everything material away from a thinking being but still leaves it the power of thought. But whether in that case thought remains (something we are acquainted with only in human beings, i.e., only in connection with a body) we cannot determine. Such a thing is a **sophistical**[b] entity (*ens rationis ratiocinantis*),[c] not an **entity of reason** (*ens rationis ratiocinatae*)[d] – for the latter of which it is still possible adequately to establish the objective reality of its concept, at least for the practical use of reason, because the latter, which has its own special and apodictically certain principles *a priori*, even demands (postulates) this.

2) Objects for concepts the objective reality of which can be proved (whether through pure reason or through experience, and whether in the first case through theoretical or practical data for reason, but in all cases by means of intuitions corresponding to the concepts) are (*res facti*)[e] **facts.*** The mathematical properties of magnitudes (in geometry) are of this sort, since they are capable of an *a priori* **presentation** for the theoretical use of reason. Further, things, or their properties, which can be established by means of experience (one's own experience or the experience of others, by means of testimony) are likewise facts. – But what is quite remarkable, there is even one idea of reason (which is in itself incapable of any presentation in intuition, thus incapable of theoretical proof of its possibility) among the facts, and that is the idea

5: 468

* Here I extend the concept of a fact, as seems to me right, beyond the usual meaning of this word. For when the issue is the relation of things to our cognitive capacities it is not necessary, indeed not even feasible, to restrict this expression merely to actual experience, since a merely possible experience is already sufficient for speaking of them merely as objects of a determinate kind of cognition.

---

[a] The word *wirkliche* was added in the second edition.
[b] *vernünfteltes*
[c] an entity of reason rationalizing, i.e., engaging in sophistical ratiocination
[d] an entity reasoned by reason, i.e., rationally inferred
[e] matters of fact; in the first edition, this phrase follows the German word *Tatsachen* rather than preceding it.

of **freedom**, the reality of which, as a particular kind of causality (the concept of which would be excessive from a theoretical point of view) can be established through practical laws of pure reason, and, in accordance with these, in real actions, and thus in experience. – It is the only one among all the ideas of pure reason whose object is a fact and which must be counted among the *scibilia*.[a,50]

3) Objects that must be conceived *a priori* in relation to the use of   5: 469
pure practical reason in accordance with duty (whether as consequences or as grounds) but which are excessive for its theoretical use are mere **matters of faith**. Of this sort is the **highest good** to be achieved in the world through freedom, the objective reality of the concept of which cannot be proved adequately in any experience possible for us, and hence for the theoretical use of reason, but the use of which is nevertheless commanded by practical pure reason for the best possible realization of that end, and which must thus be assumed to be possible. This commanded effect, **together with the sole conditions of its possibility that are conceivable for us**, namely the existence of God and the immortality of the soul, are **matters of faith** (*res fidei*), and are indeed the only ones among all objects that can be so designated.* For although we can have faith in that which we can learn only from the experience of others by means of **testimony**, it is not on that account intrinsically a matter of faith; for in the case of **one** of those witnesses it was still real experience and fact, or presupposed to be such. Further, it must be possible by means of this route (of historical faith) to arrive at knowledge; and the objects of history and geography,[b] like everything else that it is at least possible for us to know given the constitution of our cognitive faculties, belong not among matters of faith but among facts. Only objects of pure reason can be matters of faith in any case, but not as objects of mere pure speculative reason; for then they could not even safely be counted among the matters, i.e., objects, of possible cognition for us. They are ideas, i.e., concepts, for which one

---

* But matters of faith are not for that reason **articles of faith**, if by the latter   5: 469
one means those matters of faith to the **confession** of which (whether internal or external) one can be obligated, the likes of which, therefore, are not contained in natural theology. For, as matters of faith, they cannot (like matters of fact) be grounded in theoretical proofs; thus they are to be affirmed freely[c] and only as such are they compatible with the morality of the subject.

[a] things that can be known
[b] The words "and geography" were added in the second edition.
[c] *so ist es eine freyes Fürwahrhaltens*

cannot secure objective reality theoretically. In contrast, the highest final end that is to be realized by us, that through which alone we can become worthy of being ourselves the final end of a creation, is an idea that has objective reality for us in a practical relation, and is an object,[a] but since we cannot provide objective reality for this concept from a theoretical point of view, a mere matter of faith of pure reason, together with God and immortality, as the conditions under which alone we can, given the constitution of our (human) reason, conceive of the possibility of that effect of the lawful use of our freedom. The affirmation involved in matters of faith, however, is an affirmation in a purely practical respect, i.e., a moral faith, which proves nothing for the theoretical cognition of pure reason, but only for its practical cognition, directed at the fulfillment of its duties, and does not extend speculation or the rules of practical prudence in accordance with the principle of self-love at all. If the supreme principle of all moral laws is a postulate, then the possibility of its highest object and thus also of the condition under which we can conceive of this possibility is thereby also postulated along with it. Now the cognition of the latter does not thereby become either knowledge or opinion of the existence and the properties of these conditions, as a theoretical kind of cognition, but is merely an assumption in the practical use of our reason and the relation that is commanded for its moral use.

Even if we could plausibly ground a **determinate** concept of an intelligent world-cause on the ends of nature, which physical teleology lays before us in such rich measure, the existence of this being would still not be a matter of faith. For since it would not be assumed for the sake of the fulfillment of my duty, but only for the explanation of nature, it would merely be the opinion and hypothesis that is most appropriate for our reason. Now that teleology by no means leads to a determinate concept of God, which to the contrary can be found only in that of a moral author of the world, since this alone provides the final end that we can take ourselves to be only insofar as we conduct ourselves in accordance with that which the moral law imposes on us as the final end, and to which it thus obligates us. Consequently, the concept of God acquires the distinction of counting as a matter of faith in our affirmation only through its relation to the object of our duty, as the condition of the possibility of attaining the final end of that duty; by contrast, the very same concept can still not make its object valid as a fact, because although the necessity of duty for the practical reason is quite clear, still the attainment of its final end, insofar as it is not entirely in our own power, is assumed only for the sake of the

[a] *Sache*

practical use of reason, and is thus not practically necessary like duty   5: 471
itself.*

Faith (as *habitus*, not as *actus*)*ᵃ* is reason's moral way of thinking
in the affirmation of that which is inaccessible for theoretical cognition. It is thus the constant fundamental principle of the mind to
assume as true that which it is necessary to presuppose as a condition
for the possibility of the highest moral final end, on account of the
obligation to that,† although we can have no insight into its possibility   5: 472

---

* The final end, the promotion of which is imposed upon us by the moral law,   5: 471
is not the ground of duty; for this lies in the moral law, which, as a formal
practical principle, guides us categorically, regardless of the object of the
faculty of desire (the matter of the will), hence regardless of any end. This
formal property of my actions, in which alone their inner moral worth consists, is entirely in our power; and I can perfectly well abstract from the
possibility or unrealizability of the ends that I am obliged to promote in
accordance with that law (because only the external value of my actions
consists in them) as something that is never completely in my power, in order
to see only that which is my own doing. Yet the aim of promoting the final
end of all rational beings (happiness, insofar as it is consistent with duty)*ᵇ* is
still imposed precisely by the law of duty. But speculative reason cannot
understand the realizability of this final end at all (either on the part of our
own physical capacity or on the part of the cooperation of nature); rather, on
the basis of such causes, as far as we can rationally judge, it must hold the
assumption of such a success of our good conduct in mere nature (inside and
outside of us), without the assumption of God and immortality, to be un-
founded and empty even if well-intended, and, if it could be completely
certain of this judgment, it would regard the moral law itself as a mere
deception of our reason in a practical respect. But since speculative reason is
fully convinced that the latter can never happen, but by contrast those ideas
the object of which lies beyond nature can be conceived without contradiction, it must acknowledge those ideas as real for its own practical law and the
task that is thereby imposed, thus as real in a moral respect, in order not to
contradict itself.

† It is a matter of trusting the promise of the moral law;*ᶜ* not a promise that is   5: 471
contained in the moral law, but one that I put into it, and indeed on a morally
adequate basis. For a final end cannot be commanded by any law of reason
without reason simultaneously promising its attainability, even if uncertainly,
and hereby also justifying the affirmation of the only conditions under which
our reason can conceive this. The word *fides* already expresses this; and it can
only seem questionable how this expression and this particular idea enter into

---

ᵃ as a habit or disposition, not as an individual act
ᵇ Reading *Pflicht* with the first edition rather than *Absicht* (aim) with the second.
ᶜ The remainder of this sentence was added in the second edition.

or into its impossibility. Faith (simply so called) is trust in the attainment of an aim the promotion of which is a duty but the possibility of the realization of which it is not possible for us **to have insight into** (and the same goes for the only conditions of this that are conceivable for us). The faith, therefore, which is related to particular objects that are not objects of possible knowledge or opinion (in which case, especially if historical, it would have to be called credulity[a] and not faith), is entirely moral. It is a free affirmation, not one for which dogmatic proofs for the theoretically determining power of judgment are to be found, nor one to which we hold ourselves to be obligated, but one which we assume for the sake of an aim in accordance with the laws of freedom; yet not like an opinion, without a sufficient ground, but as **adequately** grounded in reason (although only in regard to its practical use) **for that aim**: for without it the moral way of thinking has no way to persevere in its collision with theoretical reason's demand for a proof (of the possibility of the object of morality), but vacillates between practical commands and theoretical doubts. To be **incredulous**[b] means to stick to the maxim not to believe[c] testimony at all; but he is **unbelieving**[d] who denies those ideas of reason any validity because there is no **theoretical** foundation for their reality. He thus judges dogmatically. A dogmatic **unbelief,**[e] however, is not compatible with a moral maxim governing the manner of thinking (because reason cannot command the pursuit of an end which is known to be nothing but a phantom of the mind); but **dubiety,**[f] for which the lack of conviction on the basis of grounds of speculative reason is only an obstacle, is, because a critical insight into the limits of speculative reason can deprive this obstacle of influence on conduct and substitute for it a practical affirmation that outweighs it.

5: 473

5: 472   moral philosophy, since they were first introduced along with Christianity, and the assumption of them may perhaps seem to be a flattering imitation of the language of the latter. But that is not the only case where this wonderful religion in the great simplicity of its expression has enriched morality with far more determinate and pure concepts than morality itself could previously supply, but which, once they exist, are **freely** approved by reason and assumed as ones that it could have arrived at and which it could and should have introduced by itself.

[a] *Leichtgläubigkeit*
[b] *Ungläubisch*
[c] *glauben*
[d] *ungläubig*
[e] *Unglaube*
[f] *Zweifelglaube*

* *
*

If in place of certain unsuccessful attempts in philosophy one would introduce a different principle and make it influential, then it is very satisfying to understand how and why the former had to go wrong.

God, freedom, and **immortality of the soul** are those problems at the solution of which all of the apparatus of metaphysics aims as its final and sole end.[51] Now it was believed that the doctrine of freedom is necessary for practical philosophy only as a negative condition, while the doctrine of God and of the constitution of the soul, belonging to theoretical philosophy, would have to be demonstrated by themselves and separately in order to be subsequently connected with that which the moral law (which is possible only under the condition of freedom) commands, in order to establish a religion. But one can immediately see that these attempts had to go wrong. For absolutely no concept of an original being determined by means of predicates that can be given in experience and thus serve for cognition can be formed from merely ontological concepts of things in general or of the existence of a necessary being; but that concept which would be grounded on the experience of the physical purposiveness of nature could not in turn provide a sufficient proof for morals and hence for the cognition of a God. Just as little could knowledge of the soul provide a concept of its spiritual, immortal nature, adequate for morals, by means of experience (which we have only in this life). **Theology** and **pneumatology**, as problems for the sciences of a speculative reason, cannot be established by means of any empirical data and concepts, because their concept exceeds all of our cognitive faculties. – The determination of both concepts, the concept of God as well as that of the soul (with respect to its immortality) can only come about by means of predicates which, although they are themselves only possible on the basis of a supersensible ground, must nevertheless have their reality proven in experience; for only in this way can they make possible any cognition of an entirely supersensible being. – Now the only concept of this sort to be encountered in human reason is the concept of the freedom of human beings under moral laws, together with the final end that reason prescribes by means of this law, the first of which is suitable for ascribing to the author of nature and the second of which is suitable for ascribing to human beings those properties that contain the necessary condition for the possibility of both – so that the existence and the constitution of this being who is otherwise entirely hidden from us can be inferred from this very idea.

5: 474

Thus the reason for the failure of the attempt to prove God and immortality by a merely theoretical route lies in the fact that by this

337

route (that of concepts of nature) no cognition of the supersensible is possible at all.*ᵃ The reason that it succeeds in the moral route (that of the concept of freedom), by contrast, lies in the fact that in this case the supersensible that is the ground (freedom), by means of a determinate law of causality arising in it, not only provides matter for the cognition of the other supersensible things (the moral final purpose and the conditions of its realizability), but also demonstrates the fact of its reality in actions, although for that very reason it cannot yield a basis for any proof except one that is valid from a practical point of view (which is also the only one that religion needs).

It remains quite remarkable in this that among the three pure ideas of reason, **God, freedom,** and **immortality,** that of freedom is the only concept of the supersensible that proves its objective reality (by means of the causality that is thought in it) in nature, through its effect which is possible in the latter, and thereby makes possible the connection of the other two ideas to nature, as well as the connection of all three to each other in a religion; and that we thus have in ourselves a principle that is capable of determining the idea of the supersensible in us and by that means also the idea of the supersensible outside us into one cognition, although one that is possible only in a practical respect, of which merely speculative philosophy (which can also provide a merely negative concept of freedom) had to despair: hence the concept of freedom (as the foundational concept*ᵇ for all unconditionally practical laws) can extend reason beyond those boundaries within which every (theoretical) concept of nature had to remain restricted without hope.

* *
*

General Remark on the Teleology

If the question is: How does the moral argument, which proves the existence of God only as a matter of faith for practical pure reason, rank against all the others in philosophy, then the entire stock of the latter may readily be assessed, and it turns out that there is nothing to choose from here, but philosophy itself must surrender all claims for its theoretical capacity in the face of an impartial critique.

All affirmation must ultimately be grounded in fact if it is not to be fully groundless; and the only difference among proofs is thus whether affirmation of the consequence drawn from this fact can be grounded on it as **knowledge,** for theoretical cognition, or mere **faith,** for practical cognition.[52] All facts

---

ᵃ In the first edition there was a comma and an "and" instead of a period here.
ᵇ *Grundbegriff*

belong either to the **concept of nature**, which proves its reality in the objects of the senses that are given (or can possibly be given) prior to all concepts of nature, or to the **concept of freedom**, which sufficiently proves its reality through the causality of reason with regard to certain effects in the sensible world possible by means of it, and which are irrefutably postulated in the moral law. The concept of nature (belonging merely to theoretical cognition) is either metaphysical and completely *a priori*, or physical, i.e., *a posteriori*, and necessarily conceivable only by means of determinate experience. The metaphysical concept of nature (which presupposes no determinate experience) is therefore ontological.

Now **the ontological** proof of the existence of God from the concept of an original being either infers the absolutely necessary existence of the original being from ontological predicates by which alone it can be conceived as thoroughly determinate, or else infers the predicates of the original being from the absolute necessity of the existence of any thing, whatever it might be: for if an original being is not to be derived, the absolute necessity of its existence must belong to its concept, and (in order to represent this) its existence must be completely determined by its concept.[a] Now both requirements were believed to be satisfied by the concept of the ontological idea of a **supremely real being**, and so arose two metaphysical proofs.

The proof based solely on the metaphysical concept of nature (the ontological proof properly so called) inferred from the concept of the supremely real being to its absolutely necessary existence, since (so it held) if that being did not exist, it would lack a reality, namely existence. – The other proof (which has also been called the metaphysical-**cosmological** proof) inferred from the necessity of the existence of any sort of thing (which, since an existence is given to me[b] in self-consciousness, must always be conceded) to its thoroughgoing determination, as a supremely real being: since everything that exists is thoroughly determined, but the absolutely necessary (that is, that which we are to cognize as such, and hence cognize *a priori*) must be thoroughly determined **by its concept**, which is something that can be found only in the concept of a supremely real being. It is not necessary here to expose the sophistry in both inferences, which has already been done elsewhere;[53] it is necessary only to remark that such proofs, even if they are defended with all sorts of dialectical subtlety, can never reach beyond the schools to the public and have the least influence on the merely healthy understanding.

The proof that is founded on a concept of nature, which can only be empirical but which is nevertheless to lead beyond the boundaries of nature as the sum of the objects of the senses, can be none other than the proof from the **ends** of nature, the concept of which, of course, can never be given *a priori*, but only through experience, but which nevertheless promises a concept of the original ground of nature which among everything that we can conceive fits only the supersensible, namely, the concept of a highest understanding as

5: 476

[a] In the first edition, "mere concept."
[b] Reading *mir* with the first edition rather than *wir* with the second; the latter must be a misprint because Kant would have had to use *uns* if he meant "to us."

world-cause – which this proof in fact provides completely according to principles of the reflecting power of judgment, i.e., in accordance with the constitution of our (human) cognitive faculty. – But now whether on the basis of
these data this proof is also in the position to furnish the concept of a **supreme**,
i.e., independent intelligent being as that of a God, i.e., an author of a world
under moral laws, thus a concept sufficiently determined for the idea of a final
cause of the existence of the world: that is a question on which everything
depends, whether we demand a theoretically adequate concept of the original
being for the sake of the whole[a] cognition of nature or a practical one for
religion.

This argument taken from physical teleology is worthy of honor.[54] It produces the same conviction in the common understanding and the most subtle
thinker; and a **Reimarus**, who fully expounded this proof in his still unsur-
passed work with the thoroughness and clarity characteristic of him, has
thereby earned immortal merit.[55] – But how does this proof win such powerful
influence over the mind, leading it to calm and completely yielding agreement,
especially in its judging[b] through cold reason (for the emotion and exaltation
of the mind through wonder at nature could be counted as persuasion)? It is
not the physical ends, which all point to an unfathomable understanding in the
world-cause; for these are inadequate, since they do not satisfy the need of
inquiring reason. For why (reason asks) do all these artful things in nature
exist? why does the human being himself exist, at whom we must stop as the
ultimate end of nature that we can conceive? why does the whole of nature
exist, and what is the final end of such great and varied art? That it be created
for enjoyment, or to be intuited, contemplated, and admired (which if it does
not go any further is also nothing but a particular kind of enjoyment), cannot
satisfy reason as the final end for which the world and the human being himself
exist: for reason presupposes a personal value, which the human being alone
can provide, as a condition under which alone he and his existence can be a
final end.[c] In the absence of such a final end (which alone admits of a determinate concept) the ends of nature cannot satisfy human inquiry, since they
cannot provide any **determinate** concept of the highest being as an all-
sufficient (and for that very reason unique, properly so called, **highest**) being
and of the laws in accordance with which an[d] intelligence is cause of the world.

That the physico-teleological proof is convincing, just as if it were at the
same time a theological proof, thus does not rest on the employment[e] of the
ideas of ends of nature, as so many empirical grounds of proof of a **highest**
intelligence; rather, without noticing it, it mixes into the inference the moral
ground of proof, which is present in and so deeply moving for every human
being, in accordance with which we attribute to the being that reveals itself

5: 477

---

[a] The word "whole" was added in the second edition.
[b] *Beurtheilung*
[c] In the first edition, the sentence continues with a comma here.
[d] *ein*; in the first edition *sein* (his).
[e] Following the first edition in reading *Benützung*, rather than the second, which has
Bemühung (effort).

with such incomprehensible artistry in the ends[a] of nature a final end as well, and hence wisdom (although without being justified in so doing by the perception of the ends of nature), and thus arbitrarily make up the defect that still inheres in that argument. In fact, therefore, only the moral ground of proof carries conviction, and only in a moral respect, assent to which everyone feels most deeply; the physico-teleological argument, however, has only the merit of guiding the mind on the path of ends in the contemplation of the world, and thereby to an **intelligent** author of the world: where the moral relation to ends and the idea of such a moral legislator and author of the world, as a theological concept,[b] seems to develop on its own from that ground of proof, although it is a pure addition.

5: 478

Here things can also be left as they are usually put. For if their separation requires much reflection, then it is usually difficult for the common and healthy understanding to distinguish between the different principles that it mixes together but from only one of which it can correctly make its inference. The moral basis for the proof of the existence of God, however, does not properly merely **supplement** the physico-teleological proof, thereby making it into a complete proof; rather, it is a special proof that **makes good** the lack of conviction in the latter; for the latter proof can in fact do nothing but lead reason in the judging[c] of the ground of nature and its contingent but admirable order, which is known to us only through experience, to the causality of a cause that contains its ground in accordance with ends (and which given the constitution of our cognitive faculties we must conceive as an intelligent cause), and make us attentive to this and thus more receptive to the moral proof. For that which is requisite for the latter concept is so essentially different from everything that concepts of nature can contain and teach that it needs a basis for proof and a proof that are entirely independent of the former in order to state the concept of an original being adequately for a theology and to infer to its existence. – The moral proof (which of course proves the existence of God only in a practical respect although one that is also indispensable for reason) would thus always remain in force even if we found in the world no material for physical teleology at all or only ambiguous material for it. We can conceive of rational beings who see themselves surrounded by a nature that gives no clear trace of organization but reveals only effects of a mere mechanism of raw matter, and who on that account, and given the alterability of some merely contingently purposive forms and relations, seem to have no ground to infer an intelligent author, in which case there would also be no suggestion of a physical teleology; nevertheless, reason, which in this case gets no guidance from concepts of nature, would still find in the concept of freedom and the moral ideas that are grounded upon that a practically sufficient ground for postulating the concept of an original being in accordance with these, i.e., as

5: 479

[a] This is singular in the first edition.
[b] Following the first and third editions; the second edition reads "theoretical" instead of "theological."
[c] Beurtheilung

the concept of a divinity, and for postulating nature (even our own existence) as a final end in accordance with that concept and its laws, and of course with respect to the indispensable command of practical reason. – But now the fact that the rational beings in the actual world find ample material for physical teleology there (although this was not necessary) serves as the desired confirmation of the moral argument, insofar as nature is thus capable of displaying something analogous to the (moral) ideas of reason. For the concept of a supreme cause that has understanding (which is, however, far from sufficient for a theology) thereby acquires reality sufficient for the reflecting power of judgment; but it is not necessary in order to ground the moral proof, nor does the latter serve to supplement the former, which by itself does not refer to morality at all, in order to make it into a proof by means of an inference continued in accordance with a single principle. Two such dissimilar principles as nature and freedom can only yield two different kinds of proof, since the attempt to derive from the former what is to be proved will be found to be inadequate.

If the physico-teleological basis for a proof sufficed for the proof that is sought, that would be very satisfying for speculative reason; for it would give hope of producing a theosophy (for thus would one have to call the theoretical cognition of the divine nature and its existence which would simultaneously suffice for the explanation of the constitution of the world and the determination of the moral laws). Likewise, if psychology sufficed for attaining cognition of the immortality of the soul, it would make possible a pneumatology that would be equally welcome to speculative reason. But no matter how dear these might be to our arrogant lust for knowledge, neither can fulfill reason's wish with respect to theory, which must be based on acquaintance with the nature of things. However, whether the first, as theology, and the second, as anthropology, might not better fulfill their objective final purpose if they were grounded on the moral principle, i.e., the principle of freedom, and hence in accordance with the practical use of reason, is another question, which it is not necessary for us to pursue further here.

5: 480   The physico-teleological basis for proof, however, does not suffice for theology, since it neither does nor can provide a concept of the original being sufficiently determined for this purpose, and one must instead obtain this concept from someplace completely different or else make its defect good by an arbitrary addition. You make an inference from the great purposiveness of natural forms and their relation to an intelligent world-cause; but to what degree of this intelligence? Doubtless you cannot presume to infer to the highest possible intelligence; for to do that it would be necessary for you to see that a greater intelligence than that the evidence for which you perceive in the world is inconceivable: which would mean attributing omniscience to yourself.[56] Likewise, you infer from the magnitude of the world to the very great might of its author; but you will grant that this has meaning only in comparison to your power of comprehension, and that since you do not know everything that is possible, in order to compare it with the magnitude of the world so far as you know that, you cannot infer the omniscience of its author from so small a standard, etc. Thus by this means you cannot arrive at any determinate concept of an original being suitable for a theology; for this can be found only in the totality of perfections united with an intelligence, for which merely **empirical** data can give you*ᵃ* no help at all; but without such a determinate concept you also cannot infer to a **single** intelligent being, but can rather (for whatever purpose*ᵇ*) only assume one. – Now it could certainly well be conceded (since reason has nothing well founded to say against it) that you can arbitrarily add that where so much perfection is found one may as well assume that all perfection is united in a single world-cause, since reason can do better, both theoretically and practically, with a principle thus determined. But you cannot then pride yourself on having proved this principle, since you have only assumed it for the sake of a better use of reason. All complaint or impotent rage over the supposed*ᶜ* enormity of putting into doubt the conclusiveness of your chain of reasoning is idle bluster, which would gladly have it that the doubt that is freely expressed about your argument is a doubting of sacred truth so that the weakness of this argument can be slipped past behind this curtain.

Moral teleology, by contrast, which is no less firmly grounded than physical teleology, but rather deserves preference because it rests *a priori* on principles that are inseparable from our reason, leads to that which is required for the possibility of a theology, namely to a determinate **concept** of the supreme cause as author of the world in accordance with moral laws, and hence to a concept that satisfies our moral final end, for which nothing less than omniscience, omnipotence, omnipresence, etc., are requisite as the natural properties belonging to it which must be conceived as connected with and hence as adequate to the moral final end, which is infinite, and which can thus alone provide the concept of a **single** author of the world that is suitable for a theology. 5: 481

In this way a theology also leads immediately to **religion**, i.e., to **the recognition of our duties as divine commands**,⁵⁷ since the cognition of our duty and the final end which is therein imposed upon us by reason is what could first produce the determinate concept of God, which is thus in its very origin already inseparable from our obligation to this being, whereas even if a determinate concept of the original being could be found by a merely theoretical route (namely, as a mere cause of nature), it would still be difficult or even impossible subsequently to connect this being with a causality according to moral laws ascribed to it by means of a sound proof rather than an arbitrary interpolation, without which, however, that supposed theological concept cannot constitute the foundation for religion. Even if a religion could be established by this theoretical route, with respect to the disposition (which is, however, what is essential) it would really differ from that in which the concept of God and the (practical) conviction of his existence springs from the fundamental ideas of morality. For if we had to presuppose the omnipotence, omniscience, etc., of an author of the world as concepts given to us from elsewhere in order subsequently to apply our concepts of duty to our relation to him, this

---

ᵃ Reading *euch* with the first and third editions rather than *auch* (also) with the second.
ᵇ *Behuf*
ᶜ *vorgeblichen*; in the first edition, *vergeblichen* (vain or futile).

5: 482

would have a strong air of compulsion and enforced submission; whereas if respect for the moral law represents the final end of our vocation to us quite freely, as the precept of our own reason, we will then accept this end and the cause that agrees with its accomplishment into our moral perspectives with the most genuine reverence, which is entirely distinct from pathological fear, and willingly subject ourselves to it.*

If one asks why it is so important to us to have a theology at all, then it becomes clear that it is not necessary for the expansion or improvement of our knowledge of nature and, in general, for any sort of theory, but is necessary in a subjective respect strictly for religion, i.e., for the practical, that is, the moral use of reason. Now if it turns out that the only argument that leads to a determinate concept of the object of theology is itself moral, then this will not merely not[a] seem strange, but also one will not lack anything necessary for the affirmation of the final end on this basis if it is admitted that such an argument demonstrates the existence of God in a way that is adequate only for our moral vocation, i.e., in a practical respect, and that in such an argument speculation by no means proves its strength or extends the scope of its domain. Further, what seems strange, or the apparent contradiction between the possibility of a theology that is asserted here and what was said about the categories in the critique of speculative reason, namely, that they can produce cognition only when applied to objects of the senses, but by no means when they are applied to the supersensible, disappears, when one sees that they are used here for a cognition of God, but not from a theoretical point of view (concerning what his nature which is inscrutable for us might be in itself), but strictly from a practical point of view. – In order to take this opportunity to put an end to the misinterpretation of that doctrine of the *Critique* which is very necessary but which also, to the distress of the blind dogmatists, relegates reason to its bounds, I here add the following[b] elucidation of it.

5: 483

If I attribute **moving force** to a body, thus conceive of it by means of the category of **causality**, then I thereby also **cognize** it, i.e., I determine its concept as an object in general through that which pertains to it (as condition of the possibility of that relation) as an object of the senses. For if the moving

---

5: 482

* The admiration of the beauty[c] as well as the emotion aroused by the so diverse ends of nature, which a reflective mind is able to feel even prior to any clear representation of a rational author of the world, have something similar to a **religious** feeling about them. Hence they seem to act on the mind, by means of a kind of judging[d] that is analogous to the moral, primarily through the moral feeling (of gratitude and veneration toward the cause that is unknown to us) and thus by the arousal of moral ideas, when they inspire that admiration which is connected with far more interest than mere theoretical contemplation can produce.

---

[a] This "not" was added in the second edition.
[b] In the first edition, "accompanying."
[c] In the first edition, "beauties."
[d] *Beurtheilung*

force that I attribute to it is a repulsive force, then (even if I do not yet place another one beside it, against which it acts) it acquires a location in space; an extension, i.e., space within itself; a filling of this space by means of the repulsive forces of its parts; and, finally, the law of this filling (that the basis for the repulsion of the parts must decrease in proportion to the increase in the extension of the body and to the expansion of the space which by means of this force the body fills with these parts).[58] – In contrast, if I conceive of a supersensible being as the **prime mover**, thus conceive of it by means of the category of causality with regard to the same determination in the world (the motion of matter), then I must not conceive of it as existing in some location in space, nor as extended, indeed I may not even think of it as existing in time and simultaneously with other things.[59] Thus I do not have any determinations at all that could make the condition of the possibility of motion grounded in this being intelligible. Consequently, I do not have any cognition of it through the predicate of cause (as prime mover); rather, I have only the representation of something that contains the ground of motions in the world; and the relation of these motions to this something, as their cause, since it tells me nothing else about the constitution of this thing which is the case, leaves the concept of it completely empty. The reason for this is that with predicates that find their object only in the sensible world I can certainly progress to the existence of something which must contain the ground of those predicates, but I cannot progress to the determination of its concept as a supersensible being, which excludes all those predicates. Thus by means of the category of causality, if I determine it by the concept of a **prime mover**, I do not cognize what God is at all; but perhaps it would go better if I took occasion from the order of the world not merely to **think** his causality as that of a supreme **intelligence** but also to **cognize** him by means of this determination of the concept in question, because then the burdensome condition of space and extension would drop out. – The extensive purposiveness[a] in the world certainly forces us to **think** of a supreme cause and its causality by means of an intelligence, but we are not thereby authorized to **attribute** these to it (so, e.g., we think of the eternity of God as existence at all times, because otherwise we could form no concept of mere existence as a magnitude, i.e., as a duration, at all, or we think of the divine omnipresence as existence at every location, in order to make comprehensible to ourselves his immediate presence for things that are outside of one another, yet we do so without being able to attribute any of these determinations to God as something that is known about him).[b] If I determine the causality of the human being with regard to certain products that are explicable only by means of intentional purposiveness by thinking of it as an understanding, I do not have to stop there, but can attribute this predicate to him as a well-known property, and I have cognition of him by this means. For I know that intuitions are given to the human senses, and brought under a concept and thereby under a rule by the understanding; that this concept contains only the common characteristic (leaving out what is particular), and is thus discur-

5: 484

---

[a] *Zweckmäßigkeit*; in the first edition, *Zweckverbindung* (connection to an end).
[b] *etwas an ihm Erkanntes*

sive; that the rules for bringing given representations under one consciousness in general are given to the understanding prior to those intuitions, etc.; I therefore attribute this property to the human being as one by means of which **I have cognition** of him. But now if I would **think** of a supersensible being (God) as an intelligence,[a] then in this respect the use of my reason is not merely permitted, but is also unavoidable; but I am by no means permitted to attribute an understanding[b] to it, and thereby to flatter myself with being able to **cognize** it by means of its property, because in this case I must leave out all the conditions under which alone I have knowledge of an understanding, and thus the predicate which serves only for the determination of the human being cannot be related to a supersensible object at all, and thus what God is cannot be cognized at all by means of a causality so determined. And so it goes with all the categories, which can have no significance for theoretical cognition at all if they are not applied to objects of possible experience. – However, in a certain other respect I can and indeed must conceive even of a supersensible being in analogy with an understanding, although without thereby wanting theoretical cognition of it, namely, if this determination of its causality concerns an effect in the world, which contains an aim that is morally necessary but unobtainable for sensible beings: for in this case a cognition of God and of his existence (theology) is possible merely by means of properties and determinations of his causality thought in him by means of analogy, which in a practical relation, but also **only in respect to this** (as moral) has all the requisite reality. – An ethicotheology is thus quite possible; for morals and their rule can very well exist without theology, but the final purpose that morality imposes upon us cannot exist without theology, for then reason would be at a loss with regard to that final end. However, a theological ethics (of pure reason) is impossible, because laws that reason does not ultimately give itself, and compliance with which it does not produce as a pure practical faculty, cannot be moral. A theological physics would likewise be an absurdity, because it would not expound natural laws, but ordinances of a supreme will; whereas a physical (properly physico-teleological) theology can at least serve as a propaedeutic to theology proper, since by means of the consideration of natural ends, for which it provides us with rich material, it suggests to us the idea of a final end, which nature cannot do; hence it certainly makes palpable the need for a theology that can adequately determine the concept of God for the highest practical use of reason, although it cannot produce it and adequately ground it in its evidence.

[a] *Intelligenz*

[b] *Verstand*; here and in the following sentences Kant seems to be contrasting the determinate concept of human understanding with the indeterminate conception of divine intelligence.

Method of citation and abbreviations

All citations of Kant's published writings, correspondence, posthumous notes and fragments, and lectures, with the exception of the *Critique of Pure Reason*, are identified by the volume and page number of their appearance in the Academy edition of Kant's works: *Kant's gesammelte Schriften*, edited by the Königlich Preußischen (later Deutschen, and most recently Berlin-Brandenburgischen) Akademie der Wissenschaften, 29 volumes (no volume 26) (Berlin: Georg Reimer, later Walter de Gruyter & Co., 1900–). The Academy edition pagination for the translations of Kant's first draft of the introduction (volume 20) and the text of the *Critique of the Power of Judgment* (volume 5) is supplied in the margins of the present volume, although our translation is not based on those editions. In the endnotes, citations to the Academy edition give simply the volume number followed by a colon and the page number. The *Critique of Pure Reason* is cited, as is customary, by the page numbers of the first (A) and second (B) editions of 1781 and 1787. All twentieth-century English translations of the first *Critique*, including Immanuel Kant, *Critique of Pure Reason*, edited and translated by Paul Guyer and Allen W. Wood (Cambridge: Cambridge University Press, 1998), supply that pagination. A passage cited either by "A" or by "B" is found only in the corresponding edition; passages cited by both "A" and "B" occur in both editions.

The *Critique of the Power of Judgment* and its introductions are cited in the following notes by the relevant section number and Academy edition pagination.

The following abbreviations have often been used for other frequently cited works by Kant; any works not included on this list are cited by their complete titles.

Universal Natural History	*Universal Natural History and Theory of the Heavens* (1755)
Only Possible Basis	*Only Possible Basis for a Proof of the Existence of God* (1763)
Beautiful and Sublime	*Observations on the Feeling of the Beautiful and Sublime* (1764)
Form and Principles	*On the Form and Principles of the Sensible and Intelligible World* (inaugural dissertation, 1770)
Pure Reason	*Critique of Pure Reason* (1781 and 1787)

Universal History	*Idea for a Universal History from a Cosmopolitan Point of View* (1784)
Groundwork	*Groundwork for the Metaphysics of Morals* (1785)
Practical Reason	*Critique of Practical Reason* (1788)
Teleological Principles	*On the Use of Teleological Principles in Philosophy* (1788)
Religion	*Religion within the Boundaries of Mere Reason* (1793)
Theory and Practice	*On the Common Saying: That May Be Right in Theory but Is of No Use in Practice* (1793)
Jäsche Logic	*Immanuel Kant's Logic: A Manual for Lectures*, edited by Gottlob Benjamin Jäsche (1800)
R	Reflection (followed by number, as given in vols. 15 through 19 of the Academy edition)

The *Anthropology from a Pragmatic Point of View* (1798) is always cited by its full title, to avoid confusion with the recently published transcriptions of Kant's lectures on anthropology from 1772–73 to 1788–89. These lectures, published in volume 25 of the Academy edition (1997) and not yet translated into English, are cited by the German titles (in all but one case the name of the auditor by or for whom the notes were originally taken) given to them by the editors of that volume. For the sake of symmetry, the titles of Kant's lectures on logic (volume 24), metaphysics (volume 28), ethics (volume 27), and theology (volume 28) are also given by their commonly used German titles. Where an English translation of a passage from any of these lectures exists, that has been cited in the notes. Those translations are found in Immanuel Kant, *Religion and Rational Theology*, edited and translated by Allen W. Wood and George Di Giovanni (Cambridge: Cambridge University Press, 1996); *Lectures on Logic*, edited and translated by J. Michael Young (Cambridge: Cambridge University Press, 1992); *Lectures on Ethics*, edited by Peter Heath and J. B. Schneewind, translated by Peter Heath (Cambridge: Cambridge University Press, 1997); and *Lectures on Metaphysics*, edited and translated by Karl Ameriks and Steve Naragon (Cambridge: Cambridge University Press, 1997).

Kant's correspondence has been cited by the numbers given in the *second* edition (1922) of the correspondence in the Academy edition (volumes 10–13). Where a letter has been included in Immanuel Kant, *Correspondence*, translated by Arnulf Zweig (Cambridge: Cambridge University Press, 1999), that has been indicated by the name "Zweig" followed by the page number of that edition.

Opus postumum refers not to the whole of Kant's posthumous literary remains (volumes 14 through 23 in the Academy edition), but to the specific texts from Kant's last years, drafts of an intended but never completed final work, that are included in volumes 21 and 22 of the Academy edition. A selection of these has been translated in Immanuel Kant, *Opus postumum*, edited by Eckart Förster, translated by Eckart Förster and Michael Rosen (Cambridge: Cambridge University Press, 1993).

Editorial notes

Editor's Introduction

1   Karl Leonhard Reinhold, *Briefe über die Kantische Philosophie, Die Teutsche Merkur*, August 1786, January–August 1787; in revised book form under the same title at Leipzig: Göschen, vol. I, 1790; vol. II, 1792.

2   Letter 313, to Karl Leonhard Reinhold, 28–31 December 1787, 10:513–16, at pp. 514–15; translation slightly modified from Immanuel Kant, *Correspondence*, translated and edited by Arnulf Zweig (Cambridge: Cambridge University Press, 1999), p.272. In two letters earlier during 1787, Kant had announced his intention to begin working on a "Foundations of the Critique of Taste" without intimating any connection between aesthetics and teleology: see letter 300, to Christian Gottfried Schütz, 25 June 1787, 10: 489–90; Zweig, pp. 261–2, and letter 303, to Ludwig Heinrich Jakob, 11 September (?) 1787, 1:493–5; Zweig, pp. 262–3.

3   Baumgarten first introduced the term "aesthetics" in his 1735 dissertation *Meditationes philosophicae de nonnullis ad poema pertinentibus* (Philosophical meditations on some matters pertaining to poetry), § CXVI, and then published the first treatise simply entitled "Aesthetics" in his *Aesthetica* of 1750–58, § 1 of which defines aesthetics as "the theory of the liberal arts, the logic of the inferior faculties of cognition, the art of beautiful thinking and the art of intuitive thinking, analogous to rational thinking," in sum, "the science of intuitive cognition" (*Aesthetica (theoria liberalium artium, gnoseologia inferior, ars pulchre cogitandi, ars analogi rationalis) est scientia cognitionis sensitivae*). The *Meditations* were translated into English as *Reflections on Poetry: A. G. Baumgarten's Meditationes philosophicae de nonnullis ad poema pertinentibus*, by Karl Aschenbrenner and W. B. Holther (Berkeley and Los Angeles: University of California Press, 1954), and have been published in a modern Latin-German edition by Heinz Paetzold (Hamburg: Felix Meiner Verlag, 1983). The *Aesthetica* was printed in a modern Latin edition (Bari: Laterza, 1936) as well as in a facsimile (Hildesheim: Georg Olms, 1961), and selections from it were translated into German in Hans Ruldolf Schweizer, *Ästhetik als Philosophie der sinnlichen Erkenntnis* (Basel: Schwabe, 1973), but it has never been translated into English.

4   This definition of teleology comes from Wolff's Latin *Logica* of 1728 (§ 85). Wolff had completed the series of German works in which he first presented his philosophy between 1714 and 1724 with a whole volume on teleology, *Vernünfftige Gedancken von den Absichten der natürliche Dinge* (Rational thoughts on the intentions of natural things) (Halle, 1724).

5   Kant's very first work, the *Thoughts on the True Estimation of Living Forces* of 1747, essentially his senior thesis at the university in Königsberg, was printed by a publisher who went bankrupt, and never properly distributed.

In 1755, he published a major cosmological work, the *Universal Natural History and Theory of the Heavens*, in which he first presented the theory of the origin of the solar system from a nebular dust cloud, as well as a master's thesis *Meditationum quarandum de igne succincta delineatio* (A succinct outline of some meditations concerning fire) and another Latin thesis, *Principiorum primorum cognitionis metaphysicae nova delucidatio* (A new exposition of the first principles of metaphysical cognition), which gave him the right to work as an unsalaried lecturer (*Privatdozent*) at the university, paid directly by the students who took his courses. These works were followed in 1756 by another one that brought together Kant's philosophical and scientific interests, *Metaphysicae cum geometria iunctae in philosophia naturali, cuius specimen I. continet modalogiam physicam* (The joint use of metaphysics and geometry in natural philosophy, whose first example contains the physical monadology), as well as several German essays on earthquakes. The *Physical Monadology* would be Kant's penultimate work in Latin, the last being his mandatory inaugural address on being appointed to a professorial chair in Königsberg in 1770, *De mundi sensibilis atque intellgibilis forma et principiis* (On the form and principles of the sensible and intelligible worlds).

6 See *Only Possible Basis*, Section 2, Fourth Reflection, 2:108–16; in Immanuel Kant, *Theoretical Philosophy 1755–1779*, translated and edited by David Walford (Cambridge: Cambridge University Press, 1992), pp. 150–7.

7 *Inquiry Concerning the Distinctness of the Principles of Natural Theology and Ethics*, 2:273–86.

8 *Attempt to Introduce the Concept of Negative Magnitudes into Philosophy*, 2:165–204.

9 2:205–56; English translation by John T. Goldthwait (Berkeley and Los Angeles: University of California Press, 1960).

10 London: Robert Dodsley, 1757; second edition with additional "Introduction on Taste," 1759; modern editions by J. T. Boulton (London: Routledge and Kegan Paul, 1958) and Adam Phillips (Oxford: Oxford University Press, 1990). Burke's book was reviewed and described by Moses Mendelssohn in 1758, so its outlines would already have been known to Kant in 1764. Gotthold Ephraim Lessing started but abandoned a translation of it, and Christian Garve's translation of it was finally published in 1773.

11 Georg Friedrich Meier, *Auszug aus der Vernunftlehre* (Halle: Johann Justinus Gebauer, 1752), reprinted in vol. 16 of the Academy edition.

12 *M. Immanuel Kant's Announcement of the Program of his Lectures for the Winter Semester 1765–66*, 2:303–13, at 2:311–12; translation from Walford, p. 297.

13 See especially the transcription known as the *Logik Philippi*, especially 24:344–71, as well as the published handbook to Kant's logic lectures, published only after the end of Kant's career in 1800, and known after its editor as the *Jäsche Logic*, 9:62–3; the latter only has been included in J. Michael Young's edition of Kant's *Lectures on Logic* (Cambridge: Cambridge University Press, 1992), pp. 567–8. See also the early transcription known as *Logik Blomberg*, 24:44–54; in Young, pp. 30–8.

14 Seven complete transcriptions of six of Kant's courses on anthropology from the winter semester of 1772–73, when Kant first gave this course (see his letter to Marcus Herz written at the end of 1773, in which he says that he is that winter, i.e., the winter of 1773–74, giving his course on anthropology for the second time; letter 79, 10:143–6, at p. 145; in Zweig, p. 141) to that of 1788–89 were recently published as volume 25 of *Kant's gesammelte Schriften*, edited by Reinhard Brandt and Werner Stark for the Berlin-Brandenburgischen Akademie der Wissenschaften (Berlin: Walter de Gruyter & Co., 1997). At the end of his career, Kant published his own handbook for these lectures under the title of *Anthropology from a Pragmatic Point of View* (1798; 7:117–333; English translation by Mary J. Gregor [The Hague: Martinus Nijhoff, 1974]). Both the lecture transcripts and the published handbook will be referred to frequently in the notes to the text. For the extensive treatment of subjects in aesthetics in the very first series of Kant's lectures, see *Anthropologie Collins*, 25:162–7, 172–204.

15 The first edition of Baumgarten's *Metaphysica* was published in Halle in 1739; it went through three further editions during Baumgarten's lifetime and three posthumous editions (the last in 1779). Baumgarten's colleague Georg Friedrich Meier, already mentioned as the author of the textbook for Kant's logic classes, also published a German translation of the work in Halle in 1766 (in which he condensed Baumgarten's paragraphs and thus altered the numbering). The text of the *Metaphysica* is reprinted in vols. 15 and 17 of the Academy edition of Kant's works; the material on empirical psychology, §§ 504–699 in Baumgarten's original numbering, is contained in vol. 15, which publishes the notes on those sections that Kant made over a period of years in preparation for his anthropology lectures.

16 Alexander Gerard, *An Essay on Genius* (London, 1774); translated as *Versuch über das Genie* (Leipzig: 1776).

17 See the anthropology lectures from 1775–76, known as *Friedländer*, 25:560; *Pillau*, from 1777–78, 25:788; and the lectures from 1781–82, known as the *Menschenkunde* (Knowledge of mankind) from their full title as first published in 1831, *Immanuel Kant's Menschenkunde oder philosophische Anthropologie, nach handschriftlichen Vorlesungen herausgegeben von Fr. Ch. Starke*, especially 25:1095–1109.

18 Although the earliest surviving record of Kant's intention to use that title does not appear until a letter to Herz of five years later; see letter 120, 20 August 1777, 10:213; Zweig, p. 164.

19 Letter 70, 21 February 1772, 10:129–35, at 129–30; Zweig, pp. 132–3.

20 See the preface to the first edition of the *Critique*, A xxi.

21 The title "Transcendental Aesthetic" was new in 1781, but the theory of space and time and the chief arguments for it were not, having been anticipated in Kant's inaugural dissertation of 1770; see *Form and Principles*, Section 3, §§ 13–15, 2:398–406 (Walford, pp. 391–400).

22 *Critique of Pure Reason*, A 21; in the translation by Paul Guyer and Allen Wood (Cambridge: Cambridge University Press, 1998), p. 156. "Judging" has been substituted for "estimation" as the translation of *Beurtheilung*.

23 See *Logik Philippi*, 24:348–9, 354–5; *Anthropologie Collins*, 25:179; *Anthropologie Parow*, 25:376–7.

24 *Critique of Pure Reason*, B 35–6; Guyer and Wood, p. 173.

25 For this claim, see Paul Guyer, *Kant on Freedom, Law, and Happiness* (Cambridge: Cambridge University Press, 2000), chapter 6, "The Strategy of the *Groundwork*."

26 *Critique of Practical Reason*, 5:160; in Immanuel Kant, *Practical Philosophy*, translated and edited by Mary J. Gregor (Cambridge: Cambridge University Press, 1996), p. 268.

27 See *Menschenkunde*, 25:1069; again, these lectures date from the winter semester of 1781–82, just months after the publication of *Pure Reason*.

28 See below, § 34, 5:285–6, and § 47, 5:308–9. In the lectures, see, e.g., *Logik Philippi*, 24:359; *Anthropologie Collins*, 25:194–5; *Metaphysik L₁* (mid-1770s), 28:251 (in Immanuel Kant, *Lectures on Metaphysics*, translated and edited by Karl Ameriks and Steve Naragon [Cambridge: Cambridge University Press, 1997], p. 67); and *Metaphysik K₂ (Schlapp)*, 28:816.

29 On why there are two introductions to the work, see Section III of this introduction.

30 See the first draft of the introduction, Section V, 20:211, and the published introduction, Section IV, 5:179.

31 Introduction, Section IX, 5:196.

32 See Paul Guyer, *Kant and the Claims of Taste* (Cambridge, Mass.: Harvard University Press, 1979; second edition: Cambridge: Cambridge University Press, 1997) and *Kant and the Experience of Freedom* (Cambridge: Cambridge University Press, 1993).

33 See Section III in both versions of the introduction, 20:206–8 in the first draft of the introduction and 5:176–9 in the published version.

34 See 20:208 and 5:178.

35 First introduction, Section V, 20:211; published introduction, Section IV, 5:179.

36 See Section V in the first draft, 20:214–15, and Section V, 5:182 in the published introduction. The examples of crystallization and reproduction are Kant's own; see §§ 58 and 81 below.

37 First introduction, Section V, 20:216.

38 Published introduction, Section V, 5:185–6.

39 Published introduction, Section VI, 5:187–8.

40 See introduction, Section VI, 5:187.

41 Published introduction, Section VII, 5:189. Kant's idea of "subjective purposiveness" is a criticism not only of the aesthetic theory of the Leibnizian school of Wolff, Baumgarten, and Moses Mendelssohn, who regarded judgments of taste as based on an indistinct perception of the perfection of the world-order in which particular objects fit, but also of the aesthetic theory of the pioneering psychologist and novelist Karl Philipp Moritz (1756–93), who regarded objects of taste as having an intrinsic purposiveness distinct from those of the universe as a whole and also from any purposes of our own, which we enjoy by a kind of sympathy. For references on the Leibnizian theory, see note 19 to the first draft of the

introduction and note 34 to § 15 of the main text, below. For Moritz, see his essay *Versuch einer Vereinigung aller schönen Künste und Wissenschaften unter den Begriff des in sich selbst Vollendeten* (Attempt at a unification of all the beautiful arts and sciences under the concept of that which is perfected in itself), *Berlinische Monatschrift* 5 (March 1785), reprinted in Karl Philipp Moritz, *Werke*, ed. Horst Günther (Frankfurt am Main: Insel Verlag, 1993), Vol. II, pp. 543–8.

42 See first introduction, Section VIII, 20:222–3, 224–5, and published introduction, Section VII, 5:189–90.

43 See the first draft of the introduction, section VIII, 20:225, and the published introduction, Section VI, 5:190.

44 Published introduction, Section VIII, 5:192.

45 Published introduction, Section IX, 5:195–6.

46 See especially §§ 83–4 below.

47 First draft, Section XII, 20:251.

48 See Guyer, *Kant and the Experience of Freedom*, chapter 2.

49 §§, 5:216.

50 § 13, 5:223.

51 § 14, 5:225.

52 See especially § 49, 5:313–17.

53 § 17, 5:235.

54 § 19, 5:237.

55 See especially §§ 46–7.

56 At the start of the eighteenth century, well before Burke, "grandeur" had been established as one of the fundamental categories of aesthetics by Joseph Addison in his famous essays "On the Pleasures of the Imagination," in *The Spectator*, Nos. 411 to 461, Saturday, 21 June to Thursday, 3 July 1712.

57 § 24, 5:247.

58 § 26, 5:251.

59 § 26, 5:254.

60 See *Critique of Practical Reason*, 5:72–8.

61 See § 28, 5:261–2.

62 See § 29, 5:265.

63 For a few examples, see Jean-François Lyotard, *Lessons on the Analytic of the Sublime*, translated by Elizabeth Rottenberg (Stanford: Stanford University Press, 1994); Jeffrey S. Librett, ed., *Of the Sublime: Presence in Question* (Albany: State University Press of New York), with essays by Philippe Lacoue-Labarthe, Lyotard, Jean-Luc Nancy, and others; and Frances Ferguson, *Solitude and the Sublime* (New York and London: Routledge, 1992).

64 General Remark following § 29, 5:267.

65 § 30, 6:279.

66 § 38, 5:290n.

67 § 40, 5:296.

68 § 42, 5:300.

69 As noted earlier, in his lectures on anthropology, Kant frequently refers to Alexander Gerard's *Essay on Genius* (London, 1774), the popularity of

which had been demonstrated by its almost immediate translation into German in 1776.

70 § 49, 5:313–14.
71 § 49, 5:315.
72 § 49, 5:317–18.
73 § 46, 5:307.
74 See for example *Anthropologie Pillau* (1777–78), 25:760–2.
75 § 56, 5:338. The clash between two "commonplaces" seems to be an echo of Hume's debate between two "species of common sense" in his famous essay "Of the Standard of Taste" (1757).
76 § 57, 5:339.
77 § 57, 5:340.
78 § 59, 5:354.
79 § 60, 5:356.
80 R. A. C. Macmillan, *The Crowning Phase of the Critical Philosophy: A Study in Kant's Critique of Judgment* (London: Macmillan, 1912).
81 § 64, 5:371–2.
82 § 65, 5:372.
83 § 67, 5:379; Kant repeats this crucial point at § 75, 5:398.
84 § 70, 5:387.
85 § 78, 5:413–15.
86 § 87, 5:450.
87 See also § 88, 5:457.
88 This is the argument that leads to the postulate of God as the author of the laws of nature in the "Dialectic" of the *Critique of Practical Reason*, 5: 124–5.
89 § 86, 5:444.
90 See *Pure Reason*, A 820–30/B 848–58; *Practical Reason*, 5:134–46; and *Jäsche Logic*, 9:86–7.
91 The French name of this prominent Berlin publisher, a descendant of the Huguenots who had been invited to Berlin after their expulsion from France in 1685, has been variously spelled; the Academy edition of Kant's correspondence uses the form "de la Garde." But since the title page of both of the first two editions of the third *Critique* use the form "Lagarde" (the first lists the publisher as "Lagarde and Friederich," the second as "F.T. Lagarde"), it seems reasonable to suppose that the publisher preferred this form.
92 See R 992, 15:436–7.
93 Letter 315, 10:517–18.
94 Letter 362, 11:48–55; Zweig, pp. 311–12.
95 Letter 385, 11:91.
96 Letter 387, 11:97–98.
97 Letter 391, 11:107–10, at 108.
98 Letter 399, 11:123–4.
99 Letter 400, 11:125.
100 Letter 402, 11:128–9.
101 Letter 405, 11:132.
102 Letter 406, 11:133.

103 Letter 412, 11:143–4.
104 Letter 414, 12:145–6.
105 Letter 415, 11:147–8.
106 Letter 349, 11:12.
107 This hypothesis was originally developed by Michel Souriau, in *Le juge-ment refléchissant dans la philosophie critique de Kant* (Paris: Alcan, 1926), and most fully expounded by Giorgio Tonelli, in "La formazione del testo della *Kritik der Urteilskraft*," *Revue internationale de philosophie* 30 (1954): 463–48. It has most recently been revived by John H. Zammito, *The Genesis of Kant's Critique of Judgment* (Chicago: University of Chicago Press, 1992), pp. 4–8.
108 See letter 413a, not in the Academy edition, but in the 1986 supplement to Kant's correspondence edited by R. Malter and J. Kopper, translated in Zweig, pp. 339–40.
109 Letter 549, 11:394–6, at 396; see Zweig, p. 446. The account given in this paragraph follows Norbert Hinske's "History of the Text" in Immanuel Kant, *Erste Einleitung in die Kritik der Urteilskraft: Faksimile und Transkription*, ed. Norbert Hinske, Wolfgang Müller-Lauter, and Michael Theunissen (Stuttgart-Bad Cannstatt: Fromann-Holzboog, 1965), pp. iii-xii. The translation of the first introduction in this volume is based on this edition.
110 Letter 584, 11:441; see Zweig, pp. 464–5.
111 Riga: Hartknoch, 1794, especially pp. 541–90.
112 *Immanuel Kant's Kritik der Urtheilskraft. Herausgegeben von Benno Erd-mann* (Leipzig: Leopold Voss, 1880).
113 *Immanuel Kants Werke*, edited by Ernst Cassirer in cooperation with Hermann Cohen, Artur Buchenau, Otto Buek, Albert Görland, and B. Kellerman; Volume 5: *Kritik der praktischen Vernunft*, edited by Benzion Kellerman, and *Erste Einleitung in die Kritik der Urteilskraft* and *Kritik der Urteilskraft*, edited by Otto Buek (Berlin: Bruno Cassirer, 1914).
114 Except for the *Critique of Pure Reason*, which uses the pagination of Kant's first ("A") and second ("B") editions, as is customary in secondary literature. That practice for citing *Pure Reason* is followed here.
115 Letter 409, 11:135–40, at 138–9.
116 Letter 419, 11:153–5, at 154.
117 See again R 992, 15:436–7.
118 § 30, 5:279.
119 This was done by J. H. Bernard in his translation, originally published in 1892, and by J. C. Meredith, in his translation of the *Critique of Aesthetic Judgment*, originally published in 1911. In his 1987 translation, Werner S. Pluhar avoids this confusion by using a separate running head for each of Kant's numbered sections, which Kant did not do. Details on all of these translations will be found in the bibliography to this introduction.
120 Letter 374, 15/26 August 1789, 11:73–4. Perhaps he had found a copy of his father's letter to Kant of 6 January 1788, referred to in note 93 above.
121 Letter 379, 11:86.
122 Letter 385, 11:91.

123 Although we may be missing a letter that Kant had written to him on 12 April 1790; see 11:151.
124 Letter 457, 20 October 1790, 11:231–3, at 233.
125 Letter 476, 11:269–72, at 270.
126 Letter 480, 11:275.
127 Letter 494, 11:301.
128 Letter 509, 11:330–1.
129 Letter 516, 11:341.
130 Letter 533 to Lagarde, 11:373.
131 See letters 551, 21 December 1792, 11:397, and 555, 4 January 1793, 11:403–4.
132 Jean Jacques Barthelmy, *Reisen des jungeren Anacharsis durch Griechenland*, translated by Johann Erich Biester, 7 vols. (Berlin: Lagarde, 1789–93). Biester was Kant's longtime editor at the *Berlinische Monatsschrift*, where many of Kant's most important essays, such as the 1793 essay on *Theory and Practice*, were published.
133 *Michel de Montaignes Gedanken und Meinungen über allerley Gegenstände*, 6 vols. (Berlin: Lagarde, 1793–95).
134 Paris, 1793; apparently not one of Lagarde's own publications.
135 Letter 643, 11:529–32.
136 Letter 658 to Lagarde, 12:14–15.
137 See letter 733 from Lagarde, 20 December 1796, 12:141–2.
138 Immanuel Kant, *Practical Philosophy*, translated by Mary J. Gregor (Cambridge: Cambridge University Press, 1996).
139 This was also done by Karl Ameriks and Steve Naragon in their translation of Kant's *Lectures on Metaphysics*.

First Introduction

1 Kant refers to *Groundwork*, Section II, 4:414–15.
2 Here Kant refers to Wolff's famous doctrine that all powers of the soul reduce to different manifestations of a single cognitive power of representation; see Wolff, *Vernünfftige Gedancken von Gott, der Welt und der Seele des Menschen* (Halle: Carl Hermann Hemmerde, 1720, and many later editions), ch. 3. Kant criticized this doctrine at *Pure Reason* A 648–9/B 676–7, as well as in his lectures on metaphysics; see *Metaphysik Dohna*, 28:674–5.
3 In his last major work, the *Morgenstunden* of 1785, Moses Mendelssohn had rejected the single-faculty theory of mind of the Wolffian tradition and instead insisted on three fundamental mental faculties, the faculty of cognition, the faculty of desire, and the faculty of "approval, of assent, the satisfaction of the soul, which is properly quite distinct from desire" (*Morgenstunden*, ch. VII; in Dominique Bourel, ed., *Morgenstunden oder Vorlesungen über das Dasein Gottes* [Stuttgart: Philipp Reclam, 1979], p. 71).
4 Kant refers to his doctrine that the determination of the will by pure practical reason produces a feeling of respect, which is at least partly pleasurable, or a feeling of moral self-contentment, which is wholly pleasurable; see *Groundwork*, Section I, 4;401n., and *Practical Reason*, 5:71–89 and 116–19.

5 The doctrine that the feeling of pleasure or displeasure reflects the relation of an object to the subject rather than the properties of the object by
itself is one of Kant's most entrenched views; see *Observations*, 2:207; R
1780 (1764–8), 16:112; R 1809 (1769–70), 16:123; *Logik Philippi*, 24:344–
5, 358; *Anthropologie Collins*, 25:66; *Anthropologie Parow*, 25:389; *Anthropologie Mrongovius*, 25:1315; *Metaphysik L₁*, 28:245–7; *Metaphysik L₂*, 28:586;
and *Metaphysics of Morals*, 6:211–12n.

6 For a similar list, see *Pure Reason*, A 652/B 680.

7 Kant introduces a precursor to the distinction between the determining
and reflecting uses of the power of judgment, in the form of a distinction
between apodictic and problematic uses of reason, at *Pure Reason*, A 646/
B 674.

8 Here Kant makes explicit the claim, already implied in his note at 20:211–
12, that the possibility of the logical form of a system in our concepts of
nature presupposes the transcendental principle that nature itself is systematic. See previous statements of this view in *Pure Reason*, A 648/B 676,
A 650–1/B 678–9, A 653–4/B 681–2, and A 656/B 684.

9 On the contrast between classification and specification, see *Pure Reason*,
A 653–61/B 681–9.

10 Here of course Kant refers to the "Transcendental Aesthetic" in the
Critique of Pure Reason; see A 19–49/B 33–73.

11 See note 5 above and § 1 of the main text below.

12 For the kind of fallacy that Kant means by "subreption," see *Form and
Principles*, §§ 23–29, 2:410–17, and *Pure Reason*, "On the amphiboly of the
concepts of reflection," A 260–92/B 316–49.

13 Here Kant refers to the section of the *Critique of Pure Reason* entitled "On
the schematism of the pure concepts of the understanding," A 137–47/B
176–87.

14 See Section III and note 5.

15 In many of Kant's early accounts of the experience and judgment of
beauty, he explained our pleasure in beauty as arising from the agreement
of an object with the laws of our sensibility alone; e.g., in the notes on
anthropology, R 711 (ca. 1771), 15:315–16; R 764 (between 1772 and
1775), 15:333; R 851 (1776–78), 15:376; R 856 (1776–78), 15:378; R 878
(1776–78), 15:385; in the notes on logic, R 1793 (1769–70), 16:117; R
1797–99 (1769–70), 16:199; in the logic lectures, *Logik Blomberg*, 24:45;
and *Wiener Logik*, 24:806–7; and the idea remains in Jäsche's edition of
Kant's logic lectures (1800), at 9:36–7. However, the thesis that our pleasure in beauty results from a free play of the imagination that somehow
satisfies the demands of both sensibility and understanding without being
mechanically governed by the normal rules of either, which is to become
Kant's preferred view in the present work, also made its initial appearance
quite early: see e.g., in the anthropology notes, R 618 (1769?), 15:265–7;
R 779 (1773–75), 15:341; R 806, (1773–75), 15:351–8; R 983 (1776–78 or
later), 15:429; and R 988 (1783–84), 15:432–3; in the logic notes, R 1810
(1769–70), 16:123–4; R 1812a (1770–71), 16:125; R 1841 (1775–78), 16:
134–5; R 1845 (1776–78), 16:135; R 1904 (1776–79), 16:153; R 1907
(1780s?), 16:154; R 1909 (1780s?), 16:155; and R 1935 (1790s), 16:161–2;

in the logic lectures, *Logik Philippi*, 24:344 and *Wiener Logik*, 24:810; in the anthropology lectures, *Anthropologie Parow* (1772–73), 25:379–80; *Anthropologie Friedländer* (1775–76), 25:525–6, 560; *Anthropologie Pillau* (1778–79), 25:759–63; *Menschenkunde* (1781), 25:1068–9; in Kant's published *Anthropology from a Pragmatic Point of View* (1798), § 67, 7:240–1. Yet the view that beauty involves agreement with the laws of sensibility alone still appears in Kant's lectures on metaphysics quite late, including *Metaphysik L₂* (1790–91), 28:586 and *Metaphysik Dohna* (1792–93), 28:675. Finally, both views appear in *Metaphysik K₃* (*Vigilantius*) (1794–95), the first at 29:1010 and the latter at 29:1011–12! See also note 18 to the published introduction below.

16 For a precursor of this distinction, see *Metaphysik L₁* (mid-1770s), 28:252.
17 This claim was part of Kant's view on judgments of taste from the outset of his lectures on anthropology in 1772–73; references will be given in notes to § 8 and § 18 of the main text below.
18 See § 15 of the main text.
19 Here Kant refers to the account of aesthetic response and judgments of taste developed by Gottfried Wilhelm Leibniz, Christian Wolff, Alexander Gottlieb Baumgarten, and Georg Friedrich Meier. Leibniz characterized sensory perception as the clear but confused cognition of that which the intellect could perceive clearly in "Meditations on Knowledge, Truth and Ideas," published in the *Acta Eruditorum* in 1684; see Leibniz, *Philosophical Papers and Letters*, tr. and ed. Leroy E. Loemker, 2nd ed. (Dordrecht: D. Reidel, 1969), pp. 291–95. He characterized "Taste as distinguished from understanding [as a] confused perception for which one cannot give an adequate reason" in 1712 notes on Shaftesbury, published in 1715 in the *Histoire critique de la république des lettres* (Loemker, pp. 629–35, at p. 634). He characterized pleasure as the sensory and therefore confused cognition of perfection in an unpublished paper, "On Wisdom" (see Loemker, p. 465), and applied this doctrine to the case of music in the 1714 paper "On the Principles of Nature and Grace," § 17 (Loemker, p. 641), which, unlike "On Wisdom," was widely known in the eighteenth century. Leibniz's characterization of sense perception as well as his incipient theory of aesthetic response were taken over by Wolff in his *Vernünfftige Gedancken von Gott, der Welt, und der Seele des Menschen* (Halle: Renger, 1720), the former at, e.g., §§ 198–9, 214, 278, and 282, the latter at § 404, where he writes that "When we intuit perfection **pleasure** arises in us, which is accordingly nothing other than an intuition of perfection." Baumgarten took over the Leibniz–Wolffian conception of sense perception (*Metaphysica*, § 521) and defined aesthetics as "the science of sensory cognition and presentation" in both the *Metaphysica* (which first appeared in 1739) (§ 533), on which Kant based his metaphysics and anthropology lectures, as well as in his incomplete *Aesthetica* (1750–58) (§ 1), with which Kant may not have been directly acquainted; all the relevant passages are reproduced in Latin as well as translated into German in Baumgarten, *Texte zur Grundlegung der Ästhetik*, ed. Hans Rudolf Schwyzer (Hamburg: Felix Meiner, 1983); see also Baumgarten's 1735 thesis *Meditationes philosophicae de nonnullis ad poema pertinentibus*, §§ 14–15; modern edition by

Heinz Paetzold (Hamburg: Felix Meiner, 1983), and English translation by Karl Aschenbrenner and William B. Holther, *Reflections on Poetry* (Berkeley: University of California Press, 1954). Finally, Baumgarten's disciple Meier, whose logic text was the basis for Kant's logic lectures, published similar views in his *Anfangsgründe aller schönen Künste und Wissenschaften* (Halle: Carl Hermann Hemmerde, 1748) and its abridgment, *Auszug aus den Anfangsgründen aller schönen Künste und Wissenschaften* (Halle: Carl Hermann Hemmerde, 1758), e.g., § 7.

See also note 34 to § 15 of the main text.

20 On Kant's fundamental distinction between concepts and intuitions, restated in this footnote, see *Form and Principles*, § 8, 2:294–5, and *Pure Reason*, A 19/B 33 and A 43–6/B 69–63.

21 Kant will expand upon the contrast between our understanding, which is discursive, that is, does not know objects by either intuitions or concepts alone, but only by applying concepts to intuitions (see *Pure Reason*, A 50–1/B 74–5), and our idea of an intuitive understanding, which we conceive of as knowing objects through concepts that also produce the objects, and therefore does not need intuitions, in § 77 of the main text. Kant's use of this contrast to elucidate the character of human knowledge predates the 1780s; see, e.g., R 1832 (1772–75), 16:131.

22 See again *Practical Reason*, 5:71–82.

23 The note to p. 16 of the preface to the *Critique of Practical Reason* to which Kant refers extends from p. 15 to p. 17 of the original edition, and may be found at 5:9.

24 Kant often repeated this characterization of pleasure solely in terms of its effects: see R 556, which could be from the 1780s but could also be from 1776–79, 15:241; *Anthropologie Friedländer*, 25:459; *Anthropologie Pillau*, 25:785; *Metaphysik L$_1$*, 28:247; *Metaphysik L$_2$*, 28:586; *Metaphysik Mrongovius*, 29:890; *Metaphysics of Morals*, 6:212; and *Anthropology from a Pragmatic Point of View*, § 60, 7:231. However, he also frequently departed from the claim that pleasure and displeasure can be explained only by their effects, and explained pleasure as the feeling of the promotion of life and displeasure as the feeling of a hindrance to life; *Metaphysik Mrongovius*, for instance, follows its statement of the present definition with that explanation (see 29:890–1). Further references to this additional explanation will be reserved for note 3 to § 1 of the main text, where Kant explicitly alludes to it.

25 Here Kant seems to allude to the concept of a figurative synthesis introduced in the second edition of the "Transcendental Deduction of the Categories" in the *Critique of Pure Reason*, B 151.

26 Here Kant alludes to the strategy of his *Metaphysical Foundations of Natural Science* (1786), in which he attempted to derive the laws of Newtonian physics by applying the synthetic *a priori* principles of empirical thought deduced in the *Critique of Pure Reason* to the empirical specification of the concept of substance as matter in motion.

27 Edmund Burke, *A Philosophical Enquiry into the Origin of Our Ideas of the Sublime and Beautiful* (London: Robert Dodsley, 1757; second edition with new "Introduction on Taste," 1759). There are modern editions by J. T.

Boulton (London: Routledge and Kegan Paul, 1958) and Adam Phillips (Oxford: Oxford University Press, 1990). Moses Mendelssohn published an extensive review of the first English edition in *Bibliothek der schönen Wissenschaften*, volume 3, part 2 (1758) (reprinted in Moses Mendelssohn, *Ästhetische Schriften in Auswahl*, ed. Otto F. Best [Darmstadt: Wissenschaftliche Buchgesellschaft, 1974], pp. 247–65), and the book was published in an anonymous German translation, actually by Christian Garve, in 1773.

28 The background to this sentence is Kant's long struggle over the proper use of the word "aesthetic." In the first edition of the *Critique of Pure Reason* (1781), Kant had claimed that the word "aesthetic," which Alexander Baumgarten had introduced into modern German usage as a term for the "science of beauty" in his 1735 dissertation *Meditations concerning some matters pertaining to poetry*, and elevated to the name of a discipline in his *Aesthetics* (1750–8), should not be used in this sense at all, because, taste having only merely empirical principles, there could be no such science. Instead, the term could be used to designate Kant's own study of the contribution of sensibility and its pure form to cognition in general, under the name "Transcendental Aesthetic" (see *Critique of Pure Reason*, A 21n.). In the second edition of the first *Critique*, as Kant came closer to writing the *Critique of the Power of Judgment*, he moderated his criticism of Baumgarten and conceded that the word "aesthetic" might be used in two senses, one of which, a "psychological sense," would connote the study of judgments about feelings rather than of the contributions of sensibility to knowledge in general (*Critique of Pure Reason*, B 35–6n.). Kant was clearly still struggling to define this new sense of "aesthetic" in the present passage as well as earlier in the first introduction (see above, Section VIII, 20:221–3).

29 Here Kant is alluding to the doctrine of "schematism" in the first *Critique*, which holds that judgment must supply an appropriate form of intuition in order to apply (pure) concepts of the understanding to objects of actual experience, but that judgment does not use any special rules of its own in so doing, being instead completely guided by the pure concepts of the understanding on the one hand and the pure forms of intuition on the other; see *Critique of Pure Reason*, A 137–46/B 176–81.

30 In fact, Kant does not divide the "Critique of the Teleological Power of Judgment" as this suggests, but instead places what he intended for the discussion of the "relative purposiveness" of nature into the Appendix on the "Doctrine of Method" in this part of the work. The "Dialectic of the Aesthetic Power of Judgment" to which Kant refers to next follows the "Analytic" of the teleological judgment of internal purposiveness.

Preface and Introduction

1 Here of course Kant refers to the *Critique of Pure Reason*, first published in 1781 and published in a second, substantially revised edition in 1787.

2 Here Kant refers to the *Critique of Practical Reason* published in 1788. Kant began work on this as part of the revisions for the second edition of the

Critique of Pure Reason, but then decided to publish it as a separate work. This decision was made sometime between 7 April 1786, when he wrote to Johann Bering that he would write his systematic metaphysics as soon as he finished the revisions for the second edition of the first *Critique*, and thus envisaged neither a second nor a third *Critique* (see letter 266, 10: 440–2; in Immanuel Kant, *Correspondence*, tr. and ed. Arnulf Zweig [Cambridge: Cambridge University Press, 1999], letter 73, p. 249), and 25 June 1787, when he wrote to Christian Gottfried Schütz that he was within a week of sending the *Critique of Practical Reason* to the printer (see letter 300, 10:489–90; in Zweig, letter 78, pp. 261–2). As Kant's letter of 28 and 31 December 1787, to Karl Leonhard Reinhold makes clear, it was only later in that year, after finishing the *Critique of Practical Reason*, that Kant decided to write the third *Critique*, the present *Critique of the Power of Judgment* (see letter 313, 10:513–16; Zweig, letter 83, pp. 271–3).

3 Kant makes a similar argument about judgment at *Pure Reason*, A 132–4/ B 171–3. See also *Menschenkunde*, 25:1036–7.

4 Here Kant refers to his solution to the third antinomy of pure reason, his version of the conflict between freedom and determinism; see *Pure Reason*, A 444–51/B 472–9, A 491–515/B 519–43, and A 532–58/B 560–86.

5 Kant's reference to p. 16 of the original edition of the *Critique of Practical Reason* refers to 5:9n.; see Kant's footnote to the first introduction, 20:230, and our note 23 thereto.

6 Kant anticipated this distinction by distinguishing between apodictic and problematic uses of reason at *Pure Reason*, A 646/B 674. In his logic notes, the present distinction is also found at R 3287, 16:759, which was written at some time after 1776.

7 For a similar point, see *Pure Reason* A 653–4/B 681–2.

8 At *Pure Reason*, A 681/B 709, Kant argues that we must conceive of the systematic unity of the empirical laws of nature as grounded in a "being of reason" (*ens rationis ratiocinatae*), which we must assume "problematically" rather than "absolutely." This is a precursor of the present idea that we must assume an understanding more powerful than our own for purposes of reflection but not for determining, but in the first *Critique* passage he does not yet argue that we must conceive of this ground of systematicity as an understanding.

9 For Kant's earlier statement of this view, see *Pure Reason*, A 687–92/B 715–20.

10 It is by the specification of the concept of the pure concept of substance as matter as that which is movable in space that Kant introduces the additional, empirical premise that is to be added to the pure principles of understanding in order to arrive at the "metaphysical" first principles of natural science; see the preface to the *Metaphysical Foundations of Natural Science*, 4:476–7.

11 See *Pure Reason*, A 652/B 680.

12 This is a reference to Kant's doctrine of schematism; see *Pure Reason*, A 137–47/B 176–87.

13 For Kant's earlier attempt to reconcile the necessity of natural laws with the contingency of the existence of nature, see his 1763 work *The Only*

Possible Argument in Support of a Demonstration of the Existence of God, Section II, Third Reflection, especially 2:106–8.

14 See Kant's exposition of the laws of classification, specification, and affinity in the Appendix to the "Transcendental Dialectic" of the *Critique of Pure Reason*, A 651–63/B 680–91.

15 See *Pure Reason*, A 655–7/B 683–5.

16 In a rare early (1769–70?) application of this argument to the case of aesthetic judgment, R 1807 states that "Aesthetic [perfection] must bear the mark of the contingent, and thus must not be studied" (16:123).

17 Kant frequently stresses that the feeling of pleasure and pain represents the effect of objects on our own subject rather than objective properties of things. Citations for this claim will be provided in note 2 to § 1 of the main text, where Kant makes it the starting point of his whole analysis of the experience and judgment of the beautiful.

18 In note 15 to the first introduction, above, an extensive list of citations to Kant's earlier statements of this idea has been provided, along with a list of passages showing him to have also considered a simpler view that our pleasure in beauty arises from the agreement of an object with laws of sensibility alone. One early note, which explicitly advocates that beauty arises from the agreement of an object with laws of sensibility, is unusually explicit about what Kant means by this:

In everything that is approved by taste, there must be something that facilitates making distinctions in the manifold (something that stands out); something that promotes comprehensibility (relations, proportions); something that makes interconnection possible (unity); and finally something that promotes the distinction from everything possible.

Beauty has a subjective *principium*, namely conformity with the laws of intuitive cognition; but this does not hinder the universal validity of its judgments for people, if the cognitions are all the same. (R 625 (1769?), 15:271)

It is not clear that Kant's substantive conception of how representations furnished by the imagination can playfully satisfy the expectations of the understanding ever undergoes any major change, even as his abstract characterization of the experience does. Another important early characterization of what actually constitutes the basis for the feeling of pleasure can be found in R 806 (1773–75?), 15:351–8, where Kant notes that "Something pleases: intuition – pleases – facility, constitution, magnitude" (15:351), and later states that "Everything that facilitates our intuitions, by means of which one gently brings the objects of the concepts of the understanding close or gives sensibility to what is intellectual, what yields a free play of our faculties: that pleases subjectively. Appearance, insofar as it corresponds with the idea, constitutes that which is essentially beautiful" (15:354).

Although, as noted in the earlier note, traces of Kant's "laws of sensibility" approach linger in some of his lecture courses into the 1790s, his mature view of the harmony of the faculties is fully formed by 1783–84, when he writes:

How is an objectively valid judgment possible, which yet is not determined by any concept of the object? . . .

If the judgment expresses the relation of all the cognitive faculties in correspondence with the cognition of an object in general, hence expresses only the mutual promotion of the cognitive powers by each other, as it is felt. For in that case then no concept of an object can bring forth such a feeling, but only concepts.

If the judgment is related to the object (and only by means of the concept of it to the subject), yet if at the same time the judgment does not make necessary any determinate concept of any object, nor any relation of it (the concept) to the subject that is determinable in accordance with rules: then it must be related to the object in general through the cognitive powers of the mind in general. For then there is no determinate concept, but what contains the ground of the judgment is only the feeling, through concepts in general, of a movement of all the cognitive powers that is capable of communication. (R 988, 15:432)

Another important statement of what the harmony or free play of the cognitive powers actually consists in may be found at *Anthropologie Parow*, 25:379.

19   Following Joseph Addison (see "On the Pleasures of the Imagination," *Spectator*, Nos. 411–21, especially No. 412, Monday, 23 June 1712), Burke, and numerous other writers (for the classical survey, see Samuel H. Monk, *The Sublime: A Study of Critical Theories in XVIII-Century England* [New York: Modern Languages Association of America, 1935]), Kant divided the aesthetic into the beautiful and the sublime as early as his 1764 work *Observations on the Feeling of the Beautiful and Sublime* (2:207–10) and his 1770–71 logic lectures (*Logik Blomberg*, 24:47). However, there are also many notes in which Kant argued that the sublime was not a matter for a genuine judgment of taste; these will be cited in note 1 to § 23, below. What seems to be an early outline for the present book, written sometime between 1785–89, shows that Kant had by then clearly accepted the division of aesthetic judgment into judgments on the beautiful and sublime; see R 992, 15:436–7.

"Analytic of the Beautiful" (§§ 1–22)

1   Much of the content of the "Analytic of the Beautiful" was developed from 1770 onward in Kant's lectures on logic, where Kant was stimulated by Meier's contrast between logical and aesthetic perfection, and in his lectures on anthropology, which were based on the chapter on empirical psychology in Baumgarten's *Metaphysica* and which responded to Baumgarten's brief presentation of his own aesthetic theory there. References to Kant's early treatments of many of the themes and theses of the "Analytic" will be given in the notes that follow. Kant experimented with a variety of forms for the presentation of this material: see his treatments of the "conditions of taste" in some of the early anthropology lectures, such as *Anthropologie Collins* (1772–73), 25:177–87; *Anthropologie Parow* (also 1772–73), 25:374–80; and *Anthropologie Pillau* (1777–78), 25:778; and in his logic lectures, such as *Wiener Logik* (around 1780), 24:809–10, and the *Jäsche Logik*, which was published in 1800 but was based on much earlier materials (9:39). In Kant's anthropology notes, the earliest note that appears to do anything like sketch out a systematic treatment of taste is R 806, 15:351–8, which could be from as early as 1773–75 but which might also be from as late as the 1780s. Among Kant's logic notes, one that attempts to use the four

headings of quality, relation, quantity, and modality (in that order) to organize a treatment of taste is R 1918, 16:156–7, which might be from the 1780s but could be as early as 1776–79.

2   The argument that aesthetic judgments concern the relation of objects to the human subject rather than properties of the objects themselves, that feelings of pleasure and displeasure express this relation, and that aesthetic judgments therefore concern the pleasure or displeasure that the perception of objects produce in us is the chronological as well as logical starting point of Kant's analysis of aesthetic judgments, and was present in his comments on aesthetics from the outset to the end. See R 630 (1769), 15:274; R 1780 (1764–68?), 16:112; R 1790 (1769–70), 16:116; R 1809–10 (1769–70), 16:123–4; *Observations on the Feelings of the Beautiful and the Sublime* (1764), 2:207; *Logik Blomberg* (1770–71), 25:44; *Logik Philippi*, 24:344–5, 358; *Jäsche Logik*, 9:36–7; *Anthropologie Collins*, 25:66; *Anthropologie Parow*, 25:289; *Anthropologie Mrongovius* (1784–85), 25:1315–16; *Metaphysik L₁* (mid-1770s), 28:245–7; *Metaphysik L₂* (1790–91?), 28:586; and *Metaphysics of Morals*, 6:211–12n.

See also note 5 to the first draft of the introduction, above.

3   In the first draft of the introduction (20:230–1), Kant held that the feelings of pleasure and displeasure could not be analyzed, but could be characterized only by their effects, the desire to remain in a pleasurable state or to remove oneself from an unpleasant one. In a large number of other passages, however, Kant explained pleasure as the feeling that expresses a condition that promotes life and its activity, while the feeling of displeasure expresses a hindrance to life or a check to its activity; this conception is presupposed by Kant's conception of the pleasure in the free play of the cognitive faculties, especially at § 9, 5:219 below. See R 567 (1776–78), 15:246; R 586 (1775–78?), 15:252; R 1838 (1773–75), 16:133; R 1839 (1773–8), 16:133; *Logik Blomberg*, 24:45; *Anthropologie Collins*, 25:167–8, 181; *Anthropologie Friedländer* (1775–76), 25:526, 559–61; *Anthropologie Pillau*, 25:786; *Menschenkunde* (1781–82), 25:1068; *Anthropologie Busolt* (1788–89), 15:1501; *Anthropology from a Pragmatic Point of View*, § 60, 7:231; *Metaphysik L1*, 28:247; *Metaphysik Mrongovius*, 29:891; and *Metaphysik L₂*, 28:586.

4   The thesis that the pleasure which is the basis of the judgment of taste is pleasure not in the existence but in the representation of its object is also an early and constant theme in Kant's thought. See R 550 (1776–78), 15:239; R 557 (1780s? 1776–79), 15:240–1, which is one the few places where Kant helpfully explains that what he means by pleasure independent of the existence of an object is pleasure not dependent on the consequences of that existence; R 988 (1783–4), 15:432–3; R 1931 (1790s), 16:160; *Anthropologie Collins*, 25:177–8; *Anthropologie Parow*, 25:374; *Anthropologie Friedländer*, 25:577; *Anthropologie Busolt*, 25:1499, 1508; *Metaphysik Mrongovius*, 29:892; *Metaphysik L₂*, 28:586; *Metaphysik K₃* (*Vigilantius*) (1794–95), 29:1009; and *Metaphysics of Morals*, 6:211. In several places, Kant adopts the more straightforward view of Shaftesbury that pleasure in beauty is independent of the *possession* of an object: see R 704 (1771?), 15:312, and *Metaphysik Mrongovius*, 29:877–8, 892–3. (For Shaftesbury's view, see the *Moralists*, part II, section II; in Anthony [Ashley Cooper], Third Earl of Shaftesbury,

Characteristics of Men, Manners, Opinions, Times, ed. John M. Robertson [Indianapolis: Bobbs-Merrill, 1964], vol. 2, pp. 126–7.) Finally, Kant occasionally says specifically that beauty is independent of the *utility* of an object: see R 983 (1776–80s), 15:429, and R 1820a (1771–72), 16:127; *Anthropologie Collins*, 25: 177–8; and *Anthropologie Parow*, 25:374.

5 Kant first used this example at *Logik Philippi*, 24:353. Kant apparently drew it from François-Xavier Charlevoix, *Histoire et Description générale de la Nouvelle-France* (Paris, 1744), vol. 3, p. 322: "Iroquois who went to Paris in 1666 and who were shown all the royal houses and all the beauties of this great city admired nothing of this and would have preferred the villages to the capital of the leading monarchy of Europe if they had not seen the Rue de la Huchette, where they were immensely pleased with the grill-stalls that are there festooned with every kind of meat all the time." An allusion to the anecdote is perhaps also to be found at *Metaphysik L₁*, 28:251.

6 This remark has not been traced to any specific passage in Rousseau. But Kant undoubtedly had in mind Rousseau's second discourse, the *Discourse on the Origin and Foundations of Inequality among Men* of 1755; see for example note 7, where Rousseau says that the beauties and luxuries of "capital cities" are purchased at the cost of the "abandoned Countryside"; in *The Collected Writings of Rousseau*, vol. 3, edited by Roger D. Masters and Christopher Kelly (Hanover: University Press of New England, 1992), p. 79.

7 See R 1796 (1769–70), 16:118; R 1891 (1776–78?), 16:150; *Logik Philippi*, 24:346–51, especially p. 348; and *Anthropologie Busolt*, 25:1508. See also note 8 to § 5, below.

8 To this paragraph, compare *Anthropologie Collins*, 25:176; *Logik Philippi*, 24:246; *Metaphysik L₁*, 28:252; *Metaphysik Mrongovius*, 29:891–2; and *Metaphysik Dohna* (1792–93), 28:676.

9 The tripartite division of kinds of pleasure that Kant establishes in this section was another early and constant theme in his thought. See Kant's famous letter to Marcus Herz of 21 February 1771, 10:129–35, at p. 129; R 673 (1769–70), 15:298–9; R 681 (1769–70), 15:303; R 712 (1771?), 15:316; R 715 (1771?), 15:317; R 806 (1776–80s), 15:251–8, at p. 351; R 989 (1785–89?), 15:433–4; R 1487 (1776–78), 15:717–26, at p. 724; R 1512 (1780–88), 15:634–8, at p. 836; R 1513 (1780–88), 15:838–43, at p. 838; *Logik Philippi*, 24:246; *Anthropologie Collins*, 25:167; *Anthropologie Parow*, 25:367; *Anthropologie Pillau*, 25:788–9; *Menschenkunde*, 25:1095; *Anthropologie Mrongovius*, 25:1316, 1332; *Metaphysik L₁*, 28:248–50; and *Metaphysik L₂*, 28:586. For a general account of the concepts of satisfaction and dissatisfaction, see *Metaphysik Mrongovius*, 29:890–1.

10 For Kant's claim that there are not phenomenologically different kinds of pleasure or displeasure but rather different relations of feelings of pleasure or displeasure to their objects, see *Practical Reason*, 5:23, and R 1488 (1775–77), 15:726–9.

11 For similar formulations, see R 1829 (1772–5), 16:130–1; *Anthropologie Collins*, 25:167; *Metaphysik L₁*, 28:250, and *Metaphysik Mrongovius*, 29:892–3.

12 See *Anthropologie Collins*, 25:175; *Menschenkunde*, 25:1108; and *Anthropologie Busolt*, 25:1513.

13 Kant paraphrased this definition at *Metaphysik K₃ (Vigilantius)*, 29:1011.

14 That the judgment of taste is a universally valid judgment about the pleasure produced in the human subject by an object, and beauty that in virtue of which an object produces a universally valid pleasure, was also part of Kant's thinking about aesthetics from the outset. See: R 627 (1769? 1770?), 15:273; R 640 (1769), 15:280–2; R 647 (1769–70), 15:284; R 686 (1769–70), 15:306; R 721 (1771), 15:319; R 1793 (1769–70), 16:117; R 1850 (1776–78), 16:137; R 1854 (1776–78), 16:137; R 1872 (1776–78), 16:145; *Logik Philippi*, 24:346–7; *Anthropologie Collins*, 25:180–1, 197; *Anthropologie Parow*, 25:376, 378, 390; *Anthropologie Pillau*, 25:788; *Menschenkunde* 25:1060–1, 1095–6; *Anthropologie Busolt*, 25:1509; *Anthropology from a Pragmatic Point of View*, § 67, 7:240; *Metaphysik L₁*, 28:249, 251–3; *Metaphysik Mrongovius*, 29:892–3.

15 For specific contrasts between the idiosyncratic validity of judgments of agreeableness and the universal validity of judgments of beauty, see *Logik Philippi*, 24:346–7; *Anthropologie Collins*, 25:181; *Menschenkunde*, 25:1095; *Anthropologie Mrongovius*, 25:1325; *Metaphysik L₁*, 28:248, 250–1, 253; and *Metaphysik Mrongovius*, 29:891–2. An interesting variant of the claim is found at *Menschenkunde*, 25:1108, where Kant says that the agreeable has the approval of some, the beautiful, that of more, and the good, that of all. See also *Anthropologie Busolt*, 25:1513.

16 See the first introduction, 20:224, and note 16 thereto.

17 For the distinction between objective and subjective universal validity, see R 993 (1785–89), 15:437; R 1820 (1771–73), 16:127; and *Metaphysik L₁*, 28:249, 252–3.

18 For a striking variation on this theme, see *Anthropology from a Pragmatic Point of View*, § 67, 7:241, where Kant describes the judgment of beauty as an invitation (*Einladung*) to others to experience the pleasure one has oneself felt in an object.

19 See *Menschenkunde*, 25:1097, and *Anthropologie Mrongovius*, 25:1326.

20 This sentence appears to assert that it is the universal communicability of a feeling, or even the fact of our actual agreement about it, that causes our pleasure in it, rather than that a feeling of pleasure produced by the free play of imagination and understanding in the way that Kant described in the introduction, Section VIII, and is about to describe again. This is not an isolated claim, but one that can be found in a number of Kant's earlier comments, e.g., R 653 (1769–70), 15:289; R 683 (1769–70), 15:304–5; R 701 (1770–71), 15:310–11; R 1791 (1769–70), 16:116; *Logik Blomberg*, 24:45–6; *Logik Philippi*, 24:353–5; *Anthropologie Collins*, 15:179–80; and *Metaphysik L₁*, 28:250–1. Even in the published *Anthropology from a Pragmatic Point of View*, Kant explains the pleasure in the beautiful as pleasure in the fact of agreement with others; see § 69, 7:244; likewise, *Metaphysics of Morals*, 6:212. A rare note in which Kant clearly says that pleasure in a universally "communicable movement of the cognitive powers" is the basis for a judgment of taste without saying that the pleasure is in the fact of this communicability is R 988 (1783–84), 15:432–3. In *Anthropologie*

Mrongovius, which is from around the same time, Kant also argues that our "inclination to taste" (*Geschmacksneigung*) is strengthened by society without saying that the pleasurableness (actually, *Annehmlichkeit*, or "agreeableness") of taste is a product of society; see 25:1326.

21 See R 1812a (1770–71), 16:125; R 1841 (1773–78), 16:134–5; and R 1845 (1776–78), 16:135.

22 For the numerous antecedents to this passage, see note 15 to the first draft of the introduction and note 18 to the published version of the introduction.

23 By this reference to "the critique" Kant clearly means the *Critique of Pure Reason*. For the schematism, see A 137–47/B 176–87.

24 On pleasure as the feeling of life or animation, see note 3 to § 1 above.

25 See the first draft of the introduction, 20:230–1, and note 24 thereto.

26 Compare this to Kant's definitions of the will at *Groundwork*, Section II, 4:467, and Section III, 4:446.

27 See *Practical Reason*, 5:71–89, especially 5:73, where Kant explains that the feeling of respect is both negative, and thus unpleasant, insofar as it strikes down self-conceit, but also positive, or pleasurable, because in so doing it reveals the power of our own practical reason to govern our conduct.

28 In the 1764 *Observations on the Feeling of the Beautiful and Sublime*, Kant said that the sublime "moves" (*rührt*) us while the beautiful "charms" (*reizt*) us (2:209). This is clearly the precursor of a claim like that in the "General Remark" following § 29 of the present work, where he says that "The beautiful prepares us to love something, even nature, without interest; the sublime, to esteem it, even contrary to our (sensible) interest" (5:267). But Kant quickly came to reject the characterization of beauty as "charming," and he took great pains to distinguish the beautiful from the charming from 1769 on. See R 1789 (1769–70), 16:115; R 1806 (1769–70), 16:122; R 1864 (1776–78), 16:140; R 1868 (1776–78), 16:143–4; R 1898 (1776–79), 16:152; *Logik Philippi*, 24:349–51; *Anthropologie Collins*, 25:178–9, 184–5, 196–7; *Menschenkunde*, 25:1098–9; *Anthropologie Mrongovius*, 25:1332; *Anthropologie Busolt*, 25:1509; and *Anthropology from a Pragmatic Point of View*, § 67, 7:241.

29 Up to this point, Kant has argued that our pleasure in the beautiful is a response to the form of purposiveness, or the appearance of purposiveness in the absence of a concept of a specific purpose served by an object. Only at this point does he reverse his formula and assert that beauty is purposiveness of form, where form is to be understood in ordinary spatiotemporal terms. Perhaps because the second thesis is introduced into the argument in this less than explicit manner, Kant does not pause to offer any proper definition of form. In addition to the general definition of form in *Pure Reason*, A 20/B 34, there is a definition of form as "the way in which free (productive) imagination arranges this matter [of sensation] inventively" in *Anthropology from a Pragmatic Point of View*, § 67, 7:240–1. That passage immediately goes on to claim that "only form can lay claim to a universal rule for the feeling of pleasure"; other passages that assert the universal validity of pleasure in response to form include R 627 (1769?

1770?), 15:273; R 672 (1769–70), 15:298; R 1796 (1769–70), 16:118–19; R 1891 (1776–78?), 16:150; *Logik Philippi* 24:348, 351, 360; *Anthropologie Collins*, 25:181; *Metaphysik Mrongovius*, 29:893; and *Metaphysik K₃ (Vigilantius)*, 28:1010–12.

30 It seems preferable to follow the third rather than the first two editions here, given Kant's favorable references elsewhere to Euler's theory of light and color; see *De igne*, 1:378, *Metaphysical Foundations of Natural Science*, 4:520n., and *Anthropology from a Pragmatic Point of View*, 7:156, although in the last place Kant also observes that light rays allow us to pinpoint the location of their sources in a way that sound waves do not, which may be a reference to an advantage of Newton's emission theory of light rather than Euler's wave theory. Leonhard Euler (1707–83), a Swiss mathematician and physicist, was one of the most accomplished scientists in the eighteenth century and was the second president of the Academy of Sciences in Berlin. He presented a popular compendium of his scientific and philosophical views in *Lettres à une princesse d'Allemagne* (1770), first translated into English as *Letters of Euler to a German Princess, on different subjects in Physics and Philosophy*, tr. Henry Hunter, 2 vols. (London: for H. Hunter and H. Murray, 1795). Euler discusses his wave theory of light in Letters XIX–XXXVI (originally written from June to August 1760), vol. I, pp. 83–169.

See also below, § 51 (5:324–5), where Kant argues that in spite of the rapidity of the vibrations of the light or air in the perception of colors or tones, we nevertheless do seem to be capable of judging and not merely sensing them, and thus of experiencing music or color as beautiful and not merely agreeable.

31 In R 733 (1771?), 15:323, Kant argues that "The objects of the senses are alone capable of beauty, because they come closest to pure intuition, since they represent the object through an appearance which contains the least sensation." He immediately went on to emphasize that color detracts from the purity of visual representation: "Hence colors as salient sensations belong more to charm than to beauty." A couple of years later, however, Kant at least once asserted the more plausible view that colors can be part of the *materials* of beauty, i.e., part of what imagination and understanding play with in their free play; see *Anthropologie Parow*, 25:384.

32 Kant attacks an inclination to strong impressions of color as a sign of poor taste in R 713 (1771?), 15:316.

33 Kant also mentions the example of architecture in *Anthropologie Collins* 25:189 (actually an insertion from another transcription, *Hamilton*).

34 This phrase, as well as Kant's reference at *Anthropologie Pillau*, 25:785–6, makes it clear that Kant is referring to the aesthetic theory of the Wolffian school, which defined beauty as the sensory presentation of perfection, where sensory representation is in turn defined as clear but confused perception. See Christian Wolff, *Vernünfftige Gedancken über Gott, die Welt und die Seele des Menschen* (Rational thoughts on God, the world and the soul of man, the so-called "German Metaphysics") (Halle, 1720), §§ 316, 319, 321, 404, 417; Alexander Gottlieb Baumgarten, *Aesthetica* (Frankfurt an der Oder, 1750–58), § 1, and *Metaphysica* (Halle, 1739), Part III,

especially §§ 510, 520–21, 531–33, and 607–8; and Georg Friedrich Meier, *Anfangsgründe aller schönen Künste und Wissenschaften* (First principles of all fine arts and sciences) (Halle, 1748), § 23. Meier, who based his work on Baumgarten's lectures although he preceded Baumgarten's publication of the *Aesthetica*, summed up the tradition when he wrote "that beauty is in general a perfection, insofar as it is indistinctly or sensitively known, nowadays needs no proof." Kant may well have based his conception of this tradition in aesthetic theory on Meier's text rather than a firsthand acquaintance with Baumgarten's, since he draws no distinction between the view of Wolff and Meier that beauty is a perfection known through the senses and Baumgarten's subtler view that beauty is the perfection of sensory cognition itself, i.e., it arises from the distinctive features of sensory as contrasted to intellectual representation. Moses Mendelssohn, whom Kant may also have had in mind in the present section, aligned himself with the tradition of Wolff and Meier in his early *Briefe über die Empfindungen* (Letters on the sensations) (Berlin, 1755; see e.g., the second letter), but synthesized this view with that of Baumgarten, arguing that in a work of art we can enjoy both the perfection of what is represented by the senses and the perfection of the representation itself, in the *Rhapsodie oder Zusätze zu den Briefen über die Empfindungen* (Rhapsody, or supplements to the letters on sensations) that accompanied the earlier work in Mendelssohn's *Philosophische Schriften* (Berlin, 1761).

A number of Kant's earliest logic notes could be read as if they were endorsements of the rationalist view, e.g., R 1748 (1750s), 16:100; R 1753 (1750s), 16:101–2; R 1758 (1750s), 16:104; R 1783 (1764–68?), 16:113; and R 1799–1809 (1769–70), 16:119–23. However, it is more likely that these were simply notes that Kant made in order to expound a view he would be criticizing; certainly Kant rejected the identification of the distinction between sensibility and understanding with that between distinct and confused cognition and therefore distinguished aesthetic response from confused cognition by the early 1770s: see *Anthropologie Collins*, 25: 31–2, and *Metaphysik L₁*, 28:246.

See also note 19 to the first draft of the introduction.

35 See R 5245 (1776–78?), 18:130.
36 There are not many precursors to this distinction in Kant's earlier notes and lectures. One exception is R 639 (1769), 15:276–9, which distinguishes between "the sensibly beautiful" (*das sinnliche Schöne*), which is defined as "a play of sensation or a form of intuition (immediate)," and "the self-sufficient beauty" (*selbstständige Schönheit*), defined as "a means to the concept of the good." Kant also uses the term "self-sufficient beauty" in R 1814 (1770–71), 16:124. But in both of these passages what Kant calls "self-sufficient beauty" seems more like what he here calls adherent or dependent beauty rather than free beauty. See also *Anthropologie Parow*, 25:383–4.
37 The phrase "*à la grecque*" was used to refer to the neoclassical style in architecture and interior decoration that became popular in the second half of the eighteenth century, especially after the beginning of excavations at Pompeii in 1748.

38 At a number of places in his lectures, Kant says that beauty must be distinguished from usefulness but must also be compatible with the usefulness of an object. See *Menschenkunde*, 25:1100–1; *Anthropologie Mrongovius*, 25:332; and *Anthropologie Busolt*, 25:1510.

39 Kant asserted that there is an ideal of beauty as early as *Logik Blomberg*, 24:47, but without any explanation of what he meant. The first attempt at a definition of an ideal of beauty is in *Anthropologie Collins*, 25:99–100.

40 The numerous antecedents for this claim will be cited in note 45 to § 18 below.

41 See *Logik Blomberg*, 24:50–1, and *Anthropologie Mrongovius*, 25:1330–1.

42 According to Pliny (*Natural History*, book 34), the bronze sculpture of a "Doryphorus" or spear-bearer by Polyclitus of Argos (fifth century B.C.), a copy of which was found at Pompeii and can be seen in Naples, was regarded as exemplifying the perfect proportions for a human being; likewise, the bronze cow by Myron of Eleutherae (fl. 480–445 B.C.) was regarded as the model for animal sculpture. This sculpture is thought to be reproduced in a bronze statuette in the Cabinet des Médailles of the Louvre; Myron's "Discobolus" or discus-thrower survives in several Roman copies.

43 Kant made this claim as early as 1769; see R 626, 15:271–3, at p. 271.

44 Kant reiterates this definition at *Metaphysik K$_3$ (Vigilantius)*, 29:1011.

45 See *Logik Philippi*, 24:347, and *Anthropology from a Pragmatic Point of View*. § 67, 7:240.

46 That aesthetic judgment must be based on exemplary models rather than rules was a constant theme in Kant's notes and lectures: see R 1823 (1772–75), 16:129; R 1851 and 1853 (1776–78), 16:137; R 1869 (1776–78), 16:144; *Logik Blomberg*, 24:46; *Logik Philippi*, 24:349; and *Wiener Logik*, 24:807, 812. See also § 47 below.

47 In the Aristotelian tradition, the *sensus communis* was regarded as the mental faculty that recognizes that representations supplied by the different senses belong to a common object. In the Cartesian tradition, and to this extent Kant certainly belongs to the latter, this recognition would require a concept of an object – in Kant's case, the categories or concepts of pure understanding would supply the framework for such a concept. Anyone making a cognitive judgment about an object is bringing these concepts to bear on his sensory inputs, whether he is aware of this or not. Thus even the most common cognitive experience depends upon concepts.

48 The idea of a common sense first appears in Kant's treatments of aesthetics at *Menschenkunde*, 25:1095.

49 Kant introduces the distinction between the reproductive and productive (syntheses of) imagination in the transcendental deduction of the categories in the first edition of the *Critique of Pure Reason*; see A 100–2 and A 118.

50 For similar language, see R 1923 (1780s?), 16:158, and R 1935 (1790s), 16:161–2; see also *Metaphysik Dohna*, 28:675–6.

51 William Marsden (1754–1836) was a distinguished British orientalist, who compiled the first Malay-English dictionary. Kant refers to his *History of*

Sumatra (London, 1783), translated into German as *Natürliche und bürger-liche Beschreibung der Insel Sumatra* (Leipzig, 1785). Kant also cites Mars-den in *Metaphysics of Morals*, § 40, 6:304.

"Analytic of the Sublime" (§§ 23–29)

1   Kant followed the British tradition in distinguishing between the beautiful and the sublime in his 1764 *Observations on the Feeling of the Beautiful and Sublime*; but this work focuses on issues such as the differences in the responses to the beautiful and sublime between the genders, different nations, etc., and has little to offer by way of detailed analysis of either the beautiful or the sublime (see also *Logik Blomberg*, 24:47). Because Baumgar-ten did not address the sublime in his chapter on empirical psychology in the *Metaphysica*, Kant had far less to say about the sublime than about the beautiful in his anthropology lectures and the notes for them, so we have fewer sources for the development of his views on the sublime than for his views on the beautiful. Moreover, when he did address the sublime, Kant often said that because the sublime moves us or stirs our emotions, it is not the subject of an objective and universally valid judgment like the beautiful: see *Anthropologie Collins*, 25:198; *Anthropologie Parow*, 25:388–9, 391; and even *Anthropology from a Pragmatic Point of View*, § 67, 7:241. The first of the anthropology notes that clearly reveal Kant's intention to organize the "Critique of Aesthetic Judgment" around the distinction between the beau-tiful and the sublime are R 992 and 993, 15:436–9; both of these notes are from the late 1780s.

2   See note 3 to § 1 of the "Analytic of the Beautiful," above.

3   For the complex character of the feeling of respect, see *Practical Reason*, 5: 72–3.

4   It may sometimes seem as if Kant holds that only objects in nature may produce the experience of the sublime, but this passage at least tacitly acknowledges that there can be at least a representation of the sublime in art. See also § 52 below, and *Anthropology from a Pragmatic Point of View*, § 68, 7:243.

5   See also *Anthropology from a Pragmatic Point of View*, § 68, 7:242, where Kant draws this distinction as that between responses to size and to inten-sity.

6   In § 30, Kant will say that the judgment on the sublime does not need a separate deduction, because it makes a claim only about our own state of mind, not about any object in nature, and thus its exposition already is its deduction (5:280). So here he must mean only to refer to the further exposition of the sublime in the immediately following sections.

7   On the claim that all ordinary measurement is based on arbitrarily chosen units and is therefore "relative" rather than "absolute," see R 5727 and 5729, 18:338–9, both from the 1780s.

8   Leibniz had famously established that there can be no greatest number; see e.g., *New Essays concerning Human Understanding*, book II, chapter xvii, §§ 1, 3; in the translation by Peter Remnant and Jonathan Bennett (Cam-bridge: Cambridge University Press, 1981), pp. 157–8. Further statements

on this issue can be found in *Die Philosophischen Schriften von G. W. Leibniz*, ed. C. J. Gerhardt (Berlin: 1875–90), I:388, II:304–5, V:144, and VI:629. These references are from Bertrand Russell, *A Critical Exposition of the Philosophy of Leibniz*, second edition (London: George Allen and Unwin, 1937), p. 109.

9   Nicolas Savary (1750–1788), orientalist, Egyptologist, and translator of the Koran; his *Lettres sur l'Égypte où l'on offre le parallèle des moeurs anciennes et modernes de ses habitants*, to which Kant refers, was published in Paris in 1787. The passage reads: "Having arrived at the foot of the pyramid, we circled it, contemplating it with a sort of terror. When considered up close, it seems to be made of blocks of rock, but from a hundred feet, the magnitude of the stones is lost in the immensity of the structure, and they seem very small" (p. 189).

10   This is not to say, however, that Kant thinks there is no sublime in art, or at least no artistic representation of the sublime; see *Anthropology from a Pragmatic Point of View*, § 68, 7:243.

11   Kant gives a similar definition of the monstrous in *Anthropology from a Pragmatic Point of View*, § 68, 7:243.

12   For Kant's account of how the imagination schematizes the concept of magnitude to produce determinate numbers, see *Pure Reason*, A 142–3/B 182 and A 162–3/B 202–4.

13   In *Wiener Logik*, 24:892, Kant says that "one can also count with 4 numerals, as Leibniz did." In his note to the latter passage, Gerhard Lehmann says that Kant may be making a mistaken reference to Leibniz's dyadic system for counting, using 0 and 1; see 24:1022. However, in a transcription of early mathematics lectures made by J. G. Herder, and edited by Lehmann more than two decades after his edition of the logic lectures, Kant correctly ascribes the dyadic system to Leibniz and the tetradic system to Valentin Weigel (1533–88) (see 29:56); Kant presumably got the reference to Weigel from Christian Wolff's *Mathematisches Lexikon* (Halle, 1716). We owe this reference to Frank and Zanetti, pp. 1332–3.

14   Compare this passage to Kant's *Universal Natural History and Theory of the Heavens* (1755), chapter 7, 1:307–8; in the translation by W. Hastie (reprinted Ann Arbor: University of Michigan Press, 1969), p. 137.

15   For this aspect of Kant's treatment of the feeling of respect, see *Practical Reason*, 5:78–9, 87–8.

16   See also *Anthropology from a Pragmatic Point of View*, § 68, 7:243.

17   Kant frequently contrasted what he considered the craven attitude of fear of God's threats and hopes of his rewards with the more noble thought that moral rectitude is intrinsically honorable and therefore pleasing to God; see, among many such passages, *Moralphilosophie Collins*, 27:309–310.

18   Kant refers here to the *Voyages dans les Alpes, précedés d'un essai sur l'histoire naturelle des environs de Genève*, 4 volumes (Geneva, 1779–86) by Horace-Bénédict de Saussure (1740–99), the Genevan geologist and physicist who made the second ascent of Mont Blanc in 1787. A German translation of the whole work was published in Leipzig from 1781–88, and abbreviated as *Nachricht von einer Alpenreise des Herrn von Saussure* in Berlin in 1789.

19 In spite of this comment, Kant was also willing to say that while aesthetic experience does not actually improve (*verbessern*) a person it does refine (*verfeinern*) him; see *Menschenkunde*, 25:1102, and *Anthropologie Mrongovius*, 25:1332.

20 For comparison of this note to an earlier version of Kant's account of the bearing of aesthetics upon our moral development, see the section "On the Utility of the Culture of Taste" (*Vom Nutzen der Cultur des Geschmacks*) in *Anthropologie Collins* 25:187–96.

21 See *Practical Reason*, 5:23.

22 Kant's use of the four headings of the categories here to distinguish between the agreeable, the beautiful, the sublime, and the good differs strikingly from his use of the same four headings to organize the discussions of the aspects of the judgments on the beautiful and the sublime in the "Analytic of the Beautiful" and § 24 of the "Analytic of the Sublime," respectively. For some other examples of the flexibility of Kant's use of this organizing scheme, see *Practical Reason*, 5:66, and *Religion within the Boundaries of Mere Reason*, 6:101–2

23 To the foregoing argument, compare R 1928 (1780s), 16:159; *Anthropologie Parow*, 25:388; *Menschenkunde*, 25:1102; *Anthropologie Mrongovius*, 25:1332; *Metaphysics of Morals*, "Doctrine of Virtue," § 17, 6:443; and *Anthropology from a Pragmatic Point of View*, § 69, 7:244.

24 See note 38 to § 16, above.

25 For some comments on Kant's conception of enthusiasm, see *What Does It Mean to Orient Oneself in Thinking?* (1786), 8:145; *Practical Reason*, 5:85–6; *Religion within the Boundaries of Mere Reason*, 6:53, 83, 101, 174–5; and *Anthropologie Collins*, 25:107–8.

26 For other passages on the contrast between affects and passions, see Kant's handbook *Anthropology from a Pragmatic Point of View*, §§ 73–4, 7:251–3, and the following lecture transcriptions: *Anthropologie Collins* (1772–73), 26:212–18; *Anthropologie Parow* (1772–73), 26:414–26; *Anthropologie Friedländer* (1775–76), 26:589–92; *Menschenkunde* (1781–82), 26:1115–25; *Anthropologie Mrongovius* (1784–85), 26:1353–6; *Anthropologie Busolt* (1788–89?), 26: 1519–27.

27 See *Anthropology from a Pragmatic Point of View*, § 75, 7:253, where Kant says that "The principle of apathy – namely, that the sage man must never be in a state of emotional agitation, not even in that of sympathetic sorrow over his best friend's misfortune – is a quite correct and sublime moral principle of the Stoic school."

28 On astonishment, see *Anthropology from a Pragmatic Point of View*, § 78, 7:261.

29 Kant contrasts the affects of timidity and fortitude in *Anthropology from a Pragmatic Point of View*, § 77, 7:256–8.

30 See *Metaphysics of Morals*, "Doctrine of Virtue," § 34, 6:456–7, where Kant argues that feelings of sympathy are useful only when we can do something for another, for otherwise one just adds to the unhappiness in the world.

31 Kant frequently attacked the idea that human beings could please God by any forms of cult or prayer rather than by actions motivated simply by

respect for the moral law itself; see e.g., *Moralphilosophie Collins*, 27:325–32; *Moral Mrongovius*, 29:627–8; and *Religion within the Boundaries of Mere Reason*, 6:170–75

32 Exodus 20, 4.

33 Kant's repeated use of this term in what looks like an English rather than a German form (*Enthusiasmus*), suggests a British origin. Locke contrasted assent based on reason to that based on enthusiasm in the *Essay concerning Human Understanding*, book IV, chapter XIX, and the first work in Shaftesbury's *Characteristics* is "A Letter concerning Enthusiasm" (in the edition by Robertson, vol I., pp. 5–39).

34 By the "inscrutability of the idea of freedom," Kant usually means the doctrine that we can be certain of the reality of freedom on the practical basis of our awareness of our obligation to comply with the moral law, but cannot give any theoretical explanation of the reality of freedom. See *Groundwork*, 4:459–62; *Practical Reason*, 5:47, where Kant refers to the freedom that is deduced from the moral law as an "inscrutable faculty"; and *Religion*, 6:138, where he says that freedom, as the ground of the moral law, is "inscrutable to us . . . since it is *not* given to us in cognition."

35 Here Kant refers, of course, to Daniel Defoe's *Robinson Crusoe* (1719), which spawned many imitations in both British and German popular literature in the eighteenth century.

36 See note 18 above.

37 See note 27 to the first draft of the introduction. Kant gives page references to Garve's 1773 translation of Burke's *A Philosophical Enquiry into the Origin of Our Ideas of the Sublime and Beautiful*; we will cite the modern edition, edited by J. T. Boulton (London: Routledge & Kegan Paul, 1958), which reprints Burke's second edition.

38 In Burke's original words: "if the pain is not carried to violence, and the terror is not conversant about the present destruction of the person, as these emotions clear the parts, whether fine, or gross, of a dangerous and troublesome incumbrance, they are capable of producing delight; not pleasure, but a sort of delightful horror, a sort of tranquility tinged with terror . . ." (part IV, § vii; Boulton, p. 136).

39 In Burke's original words, with their whole original context: "beauty acts by relaxing the solids of the whole system. There are all the appearance of such a relaxation; and a relaxation somewhat below the natural tone seems to me to be the cause of all positive pleasure. Who is a stranger to that manner of expression so common in all times and in all countries, of being softened, relaxed, enervated, dissolved, melted away by pleasure?" (part IV, § xix; Boulton, pp. 149–50).

40 Kant also made this claim about Epicurus in *Anthropologie Collins*, 25:202 (actually from *Hamilton*). Epicurus (341–271 B.C.) does not appear to assert that all pleasure or pain is corporeal explicitly in the extant writings, but it would not be unnatural to attribute such a thesis to him on the basis of statements like these two, attributed to the lost book "On the End of Life": "10. I know not how I can conceive the good, if I withdraw the pleasures of taste, and withdraw the pleasures of love, and withdraw the pleasures of hearing, and withdraw the pleasurable emotions caused to

sight by beautiful form. 11. The stable condition of well-being in the body and the sure hope of its continuance holds the fullest and surest joy for those who rightly calculate it." Translation by C. Bailey, in Whitney J. Oates, ed., *The Stoic and Epicurean Philosophers* (New York: The Modern Library, 1940), p. 46. Diogenes Laertius (ca. 200 A.D.), in his "Life of Epicurus," says that "Epicurus admits both kinds [of pleasure, those that are static and those consisting in motion] both in the soul and in the body, as he says in the work on *Choice and Avoidance* and in the book on *The End of Life*" (Oates, p. 63); but since Epicurus also says that "the soul is a body of fine particles distributed throughout the whole structure" of a person (Letter to Herodotus; Oates, p. 10), the statement in Diogenes Laertius, which was probably known to Kant, would not have undermined Kant's claim.

Deduction and theory of fine art (§§ 30–53 and remark)

1 In the first edition, the heading "Third Book" (*Drittes Buch*) stood over this title. Kant's manuscript said not "Third Book" but "Third Section: Deduction of Aesthetic Judgments"; the change to "Third Book" was made at the instance of his former student and friend Johann Gottfried Carl Christian Kiesewetter, who was overseeing the production of the *Critique* in Berlin (see Kiesewetter's letter to Kant of 3 March 1790, 11:189). Kant did not see this letter until 18 April, because it had been included with a packet of proofs sent to him from Berlin that he set aside, wanting to read the proofs only once they had all arrived. On 20 April, he wrote to Kiesewetter, saying that the latter's change was quite appropriate (*schicklich*), and asking him to reflect the change in the work's table of contents, which had reflected Kant's original division of the "Critique of the Aesthetic Power of Judgment" into only the two books on the beautiful and the sublime, if there was still time, and "to note the altered title at the end [of the volume] among the errata" (letter to Kiesewetter, 20 April 1790, 11:154). What was printed in this list, however, was not that the original title had been altered, but rather that the new title should be "omitted" (*fällt . . . weg*); see the first edition, list of *Druckfehler* following p. 476. In the second edition, which was based on a corrected copy of the first that Kant sent to the publisher, after numerous delays, on 10 June 1792 (see Kant's letter to François Théodore de Lagarde, 12 June 1792, 11:341), the heading "Third Book" is indeed omitted, nor is the original heading ("Third Section") restored. Nothing in Kant's surviving correspondence indicates how this result, a surprise given Kant's initial acceptance of Kiesewetter's change, came about, although Kant did thank de Lagarde for his "excellent" work on the "printing and correction" of the second edition when he received his copies of it in December 1792 (see his letter to de Lagarde of 21 December 1792, 11:397), so the change may have reflected Kant's intentions, but may also have been simply the result of the printer following the errata list from the first edition. However it came about, the omission of any such heading has confused some into reading the "Deduction of Pure Aesthetic Judgments" as a continuation of the "Analytic of the Sublime"; thus in their

translations both J. H. Bernard and J. C. Meredith continue the title "Analytic of the Sublime" as the right running head throughout the remainder of the "Critique of Aesthetic Judgment." But this is not justified by either of Kant's original editions of the work, both of which use only the title "Part I. Critique of the Aesthetic Power of Judgment" as left and right running heads throughout the entire first half of the book. Nor does it make any sense, since Kant now argues that it is only the judgment on the beautiful and not the judgment on the sublime that needs a deduction.

2 See also *Metaphysik K₃ (Vigilantius)*, 29:1011. As we will see in the discussion of genius (§§ 46–50), there are many passages in which Kant stresses that successful works of art cannot be mere imitations of what has gone before; this is one of the few passages that parallels his present insistence that aesthetic judgments must also be genuine self-expressions and not imitations of the responses of others.

3 While Kant warns against the use of empirical examples of actual conduct for the derivation of moral principles in *Groundwork*, section II, 4:406–8, he stresses the positive role of examples of virtuous conduct in moral education at *Practical Reason*, 5:155–6. In the *Religion*, he stresses that the humanity rather than the divinity of Christ must be emphasized in order for him to serve as an example of realizable moral conduct for human beings (part two, section one, 6:60–6).

4 Kant frequently stressed this point. In addition to the passages cited at note 46 to § 18 of the "Analytic of the Beautiful," see also R 1787 (1766–69), 16:114; *R* 1823 (1772–75?), 16:129; *Wiener Logik*, 24:812; and *Anthropologie Collins*, 25:179–80, 194.

5 Charles Batteux (1713–1780), French aesthetician, whose most famous work, *Les beaux arts réduit à un même principe* (Paris, 1746; German translation as *Einschränkung der schönen Künste auf einer einzigen Grundsatz*, Leipzig, 1751), argues that all beautiful art is an imitation of nature. This view was attacked by Mendelssohn in his essay *Über die Hauptgründsätze der schonen Künste und Wissenschaften* (On the fundamental principles of the fine arts and sciences), in the *Bibliothek der schönen Wissenschaften und der freyen Künste* (Leipzig, 1757), and could have been known to Kant through this essay if not directly. A translation of Mendelssohn's essay appears in Moses Mendelssohn, *Philosophical Writings*, translated by Daniel Dahlstrom (Cambridge: Cambridge University Press, 1997); see p. 170.

6 Gotthold Ephraim Lessing (1729–1781), German dramatist and critic, published numerous works of criticism, including the *Briefe, die neueste Literatur betreffend* (Letters concerning the newest literature), with Friedrich Nicolai and Moses Mendelssohn (Leipzig, 1759–65), and the *Hamburgische Dramaturgie* (as articles, 1767–68; in book form first in Bremen: J. H. Cramer, 1769), but the most famous among his critical works was *Laokoön, oder, über die Grenzen der Malerei und Poesie* (Laocoön, or on the bounds of painting and poetry) (Berlin: Christian Friedrich Voß, 1766). Kant's comment on sculpture at § 51, 5:322 strongly suggests that Kant was familiar at least with *Laokoön*. Kant also refers to Lessing as a playwright a number of times, taking his plays as paradigmatic dramatic successes and arguing that if they do not conform to traditional rules of dramaturgy, that shows the invalidity

of such rules, not the failure of the plays; see *Anthropologie Collins*, 25:196, and *Anthropologie Parow*, 25:388.

7 See also *Metaphysik K₂ (Auszug Schlapp)*, 28:815, where Kant argues that in matters of taste rules cannot be prescribed "despotically," but approval must be free.

8 In addition to the passages cited in note 46 to § 18 of the "Analytic of the Beautiful," see also *Logik Philippi*, 24:359; *Anthropologie Collins*, 25:194–5; *Anthropologie Parow*, 25:378; *Anthropologie Mrongovius*, 25:1279; *Metaphysik L₁*, 28:251; and *Metaphysik K₂ (Auszug Schlapp)*, 28:816.

9 Kant refers here to Hume's essay "The Sceptic," where Hume writes, "There is something approaching to principles in mental taste; and critics can reason and dispute more plausibly than cooks or performers. We may observe, however, that this uniformity hinders not, but that there is a considerable diversity in the sentiments of beauty and worth, and that education, custom, prejudice, caprice, and humour, frequently vary our taste of this kind." See David Hume, *Essays Moral, Political and Literary* (Oxford: Oxford University Press, 1963), p. 165. Hume also refers to the "great resemblance between mental and bodily taste" in "Of the Standard of Taste" (*Essays Moral, Political and Literary*, p. 240). Hume's essays were translated into German as early as 1755 by Johann Georg Sulzer, although this edition did not include "Of the Standard of Taste," which was not published until 1757.

10 The "Deduction of the pure concepts of the understanding," or the "Transcendental Deduction," is at the heart of Kant's analysis of the conditions of the possibility of experience in the first *Critique*. The part of the work which Kant himself said cost him the most effort (A xvi), the deduction, which is found at A 84–130 in the first edition (1781), was extensively rewritten for the second edition (1787); see B 116–169. Kant's aims and success in the deduction of the categories have remained highly controversial; for a survey of some of the problems, see Paul Guyer, "The transcendental deduction of the categories," in Guyer, ed., *The Cambridge Companion to Kant* (Cambridge: Cambridge University Press, 1992), pp. 123–60.

11 This passage clarifies Kant's earlier claims that judgments of taste are simply *a posteriori*; see, e.g., R 623–4 (1769?), 15:270, and *Logik Philippi*, 24:347. An alternative view, that aesthetic judgments are straightforwardly *a priori*, is suggested at *Menschenkunde*, 25:1097. Kant does not seem to have arrived at the present view that aesthetic judgments have both an *a posteriori* and an *a priori* aspect until writing the third *Critique*.

12 See *Menschenkunde*, 25:1095, and *Anthropologie Busolt*, 25:1480.

13 Kant formulates these as "enlightened" "maxims of reason" and "enlarged thought" quite early; see R 1486 (1775–77), 15:706–16, at p. 715; see also R 1508 (1780–84), 15:820–22, which also catalogues various forms of *Unmündigkeit* (immaturity), and thus looks as if it might have been a study for *What Is Enlightenment?* (1784) (see next note).

14 Compare this to Kant's famous definition of enlightenment as "the human being's emergence from his self-incurred minority" (*Unmündigkeit*), where Kant emphasizes that enlightenment depends on the "use of one's own

understanding without direction from another"; *What Is Enlightenment?*, 8:35.

15 Kant makes a stronger claim in *Anthropology from a Pragmatic Point of View* when he says that "choice in terms of this satisfaction [of taste] comes, according to its form, under the principle of duty" (§ 69, 7:244).

16 This section represents Kant's attempt to sort out some of the longstanding issues in his conception of the relation between taste and society. As we saw in note 20 to § 9 of the "Analytic of the Beautiful," Kant had long held the view that our pleasure in something beautiful is actually generated by the fact of our agreement about it, so that this pleasure cannot even exist in the absence of society; see e.g., *Logik Philippi*, 24:254–5; this is to be distinguished, however, from the view that the existence of society is necessary to help us form our taste; that making universally valid judgments of taste is of interest to us only in society, and conversely that the development of taste helps make us sociable (see *Anthropologie Collins*, 25: 187, 191); and that taste and the existence of society can amplify the pleasure that we take in a beautiful object by adding the pleasure of agreement with others to it; for the last point particularly, see *Menschenkunde*, 25:1096–7, and *Anthropologie Mrongovius*, 25:1328. Kant does not give any reason to deny the last claim in this section, although he diminishes its importance on the ground that it is merely an empirical fact about us, dependent on our inclination to sociability, rather than something connected to an *a priori* principle of morality.

17 See R 1931 (1790s? 1776–78?), 16:160.

18 Kant repeats this claim numerous times, including at *Metaphysik L$_1$*, 28: 251 and *Anthropology from a Pragmatic Point of View*, § 67, 7:240.

19 Roucou was a dye obtained from the tree *Bixa orellana* by the native inhabitants of the Caribbean and coastal South America, the use of which for body painting was widely described in both travelogues and pharmacological works of the seventeenth and eighteenth centuries. Cinnabar is the red, crystalline form of mercuric sulphide, applied more broadly to the most common form of mercury ore; the term was also used from at least the fourteenth century to designate the red dye produced from this ore.

20 Kant actually formulated this thought quite early; see R 1820a (1771–2), where he wrote that "Beautiful things indicate that the human being fits into the world" (16:127).

21 See especially the appendix to the "Critique of Teleological Judgment," especially §§ 81–84 and § 87.

22 This section follows the preceding ones without any indication of a major break in the text, but it is clear that Kant is now changing the subject, since he has previously been discussing the interest in natural rather than artistic beauty but now turns to give his theory of art in the next dozen sections. It is not at all clear that these sections should be regarded as a continuation of the "Deduction of Pure Judgments of Taste"; perhaps by dropping the heading "Third Book" above § 30, where the deduction began, Kant meant to lessen the impression that the topic of the following sections is continuous with that of the preceding ones.

23 See R 1892 (1776–78), 16:150, where Kant uses a similar formulation. See also R 2704 (1776–1780s), 16:477, where Kant even suggests that the word *Kunst* (art) comes from *können* (to be able), as well as, from the same period, R 2707, 16:478.

24 Pieter Camper (1728–1789), Dutch anatomist and naturalist. Kant refers to his *Abhandlung über die beste Forme der Schuhe* (Treatise on the best forms for shoes) (Berlin, 1783).

25 Kant first mentions the example of Columbus's egg at R 2705 (1776–1780s), 16:477.

26 On the contrast between art and crafts, see R 963 (1776–78), 15:464; *R* 1866, 16:142–3; *Anthropologie Pillau*, 25:783; and *Anthropologie Busolt*, 25:1493; on the contrast between liberal art and arts for remuneration (*Brodkunst*, literally "art for bread"), see R 2026 (1776–78?), 16:201; and on the concept of the liberal arts more generally, see R 2025 (1776–1780s), 16:200–1.

27 See R 626 (1769?), 15:271–3, at p. 272, and *Logik Philippi*, 24:344.

28 This phrase (*schöne Wissenschaften*) was customary at least within German academic aesthetics, as for example in the title of the work by Georg Friedrich Meier (1718–1777), the chief disciple and popularizer of Baumgarten, *Die Anfangsgründe aller schönen Künste und Wissenschaften* (Halle, 1748–50).

29 Compare R 1485 (1775–77), 15:699–706, at p. 701, and *Menschenkunde*, 25:983, 997.

30 See R 962 (1776–78), 15:423–4; R 1855 (1776–78), 16:138; R 1888 (1776–78), 16:149; *Menschenkunde*, 25:1011; and *Anthropologie Busolt*, 25:1511.

31 Genius was a standard subject in all of Kant's anthropology lectures: See *Anthropologie Collins*, 25:167–70; *Anthropologie Friedländer*, 25:556–7; *Anthropologie Pillau*, 25:781–4; *Menschenkunde*, 15:1055–1066; *Anthropologie Mrongovius*, 25:1310–15; and *Anthropologie Busolt*, 25:1492–9. See also *Logik Philippi*, 24:370; and among numerous reflections, R 899 (1776–78), 15:393; R 921, 921a and 922 (1776–78?), 15:406–11; R 1509 and 1510 (1781–4), 15:823–9; R 1788 (1766–68?), 16:114; and R 1847 (1776–78), 16:136.

32 Kant emphasizes this contrast as early as 1769 at R 621, 15:268–9; see also R 778 (1772–73), 16:340–1; R 812 (1773–75?), 15:360–1; R 922 (1776–78), 15:409–11; *Anthropologie Friedländer*, 25: 556–7; *Anthropologie Pillau*, 25:783–4; and *Menschenkunde*, 25:1056.

33 This contrast between the teachable skills of science and the unteachable talent for genius was a frequent theme in Kant's anthropology lectures: see *Anthropologie Friedländer*, 25:556–7; *Menschenkunde*, 25:1061; *Anthropologie Mrongovius*, 25:1310–11; and *Anthropologie Busolt*, 25:1493–4. See also R 932 (1776–78), 15:413.

34 Here Kant refers to the *Philosophiae Naturalis Principia Mathematica* (Mathematical principles of natural philosophy) published by Isaac Newton (1646–1727) in 1687, in which Newton unified terrestrial and celestial mechanics with his famous axiomatization of the laws of motion.

35 Christoph Martin Wieland (1733–1813), educator and man of letters, friend of Goethe and Herder, editor of the influential magazine *Die Teut-*

sche Merkur from 1773–90; considered along with Klopstock and Lessing one of the most important writers of early German classicism. He remains best known for his novel *The History of Agathon* (1766–67), the first German *Bildungsroman* (novel of an education or character-formation), which became the model for Goethe's two *Wilhelm Meister* books, Thomas Mann's *Buddenbrooks*, and many others, and for the epic *Oberon* (1780). A recent selection of Wieland's critical and theoretical writings is *Freiheit in der Literatur* (Frankfurt: Insel, 1997). Wieland's daughter married Kant's supporter Karl Leonhard Reinhold, and Reinhold became associate editor of *Die Deutsche Merkur*, publishing there his important *Briefe über die Kantische Philosophie* (Letters on the Kantian philosophy) in 1786–87, which greatly assisted the spread of Kant's philosophy.

36 For this contrast, see R 920 (1776–78), 15:405.

37 See R 2569 (1769–70?), 16:420–4.

38 See R 924 (1776–78), 15:411.

39 See *Anthropologie Busolt*, 25:1494–5.

40 See R 1816 and 1818 (1770–71?), 16:126; R 1830 (1772–78), 16:131; R 1935 (1790s), 16:161–2; *Logik Blomberg*, 24:50; *Logik Philippi*, 24:356–7; *Anthropologie Collins* (insert from *Hamilton*), 25:183; and *Anthropologie Parow*, 25:379.

41 Here Kant appears to allude to the argument of Lessing's *Laokoön* (1766), which holds that pain or other forms of ugliness can be described in poetry but not represented directly in painting or sculpture, because beauty is the "first law" of the visual arts (see chapter 2 in *Laokoön*).

42 A large number of texts shed light on what Kant means by "spirit" (*Geist*). See R 817 (1776–78?), 15:364–5; R 933 and 934 (1776–78), 15:414–15; R 926 (1776–78), 15:412; R 932–4 (1776–78), 15:413–15; R 946 (1776–78? 1772?), 16:418; R 943 (1776–78), 15:418–19; R 958 (1776–78), 15:422; R 1485 (1775–77), 16:699–706; R 1824–5 (1772–78), 16:129–30; R 1834 (1772–78), 16:132; R 1844 (1776–78), 16:135; R 1847 (1776–78), 16:136; R 1894 (1776–78?), 16:151; *Anthropologie Collins*, 25:167; *Anthropologie Friedländer*, 25:557; *Anthropologie Pillau*, 25:782–3; and *Anthropology from a Pragmatic Point of View*, § 71B, 7:246.

43 See *Anthropologie Pillau*, 25:782, and *Anthropologie Busolt*, 25:1494.

44 In what follows, Kant gives a German prose translation of these lines by Friedrich II (Frederick the Great) of Prussia:

> *Oui, finissons sans trouble, et mourons sans regrets,*
> *En laissant l'Univers comblé de nos bienfaits.*
> *Ainsi l'Astre du jour, au bout de sa carrière,*
> *Répand sur l'horizon une douce lumière,*
> *Et les derniers rayons qu'il darde dans les air*
> *Sont les derniers soupirs qu'il donne à l'Univers.*

Our text translates Kant's German rather than the French, which he does not himself supply. The lines are the conclusion of Friedrich's poem *Au Maréchal Keith, Imitation du troisième livre de Lucrèce: "Sur les vaines terreurs de la mort et les frayeurs d'une autre vie"* (To Marshal Keith, imitation of the third book of Lucretius, "On the vain terrors of death and fears of another life"); the poem may be found in *Poésies diverses*, epitre XVIII (Berlin: 1762), vol. 2, p. 447, or *Oeuvres de Frédéric le Grand* (1846), vol. 10, p. 203.

45 From the *Akademischen Gedichten* (Academic poems) of Philipp Lorenz Withof, in *Sinnlichen Ergötzungen* (Sensory delights) (Leipzig, 1782), vol. 1, p. 70. Withof (1725–1789), was a professor of medicine in Duisburg and Bergsteinfurt, then professor of history, oratory, and morals in the gymnasium of Hamm and then again at the university in Duisburg. Properly quoted, the line is "The sun streamed forth, as tranquility flows from goodness" (*Die Sonne quoll hervor, wie Ruh' aus Güte quillt*).

46 Kant refers to the frontispiece to *Einleitung in die Naturlehre* (1754) by Johann Andreas Segner (1704–1777), Göttingen physicist and mathematician.

47 In spite of his use of the word "talent" in this passage, in R 949 (1776–78), 15:420–1, Kant explicitly contrasts his account of genius, as involving the use of all our faculties, with the idea of it as a special talent distinct from all other talents offered by Alexander Gerard in his *Essay on Genius* (London, 1774), translated into German by Christian Garve as *Versuch über das Genie* (Leipzig, 1776). Kant also cites this work in *Menschenkunde*, 25:945 and 1055, and *Anthropologie Mrongovius*, 25:1314. For the general point, see also *Anthropologie Pillau*, 25:782; *Menschenkunde*, 25:1060–1; and *Anthropologie Mrongovius*, 25:1313.

48 Kant addressed the topic of this section in numerous passages, including R 671 (1769–70), 15:297; R 1847 (1776–78), 16:136; R 1900 (1776–78), 16:152; *Anthropologie Collins*, 25:175; *Menschenkunde*, 25:1060–2; *Anthropologie Mrongovius*, 25:1313; *Anthropologie Busolt*, 25:1493; and *Anthropology from a Pragmatic Point of View*, § 71B, 7:246.

49 David Hume's greatest literary and commercial success, *The History of England from the Invasion of Julius Caesar to the Revolution in 1688*, was published in six volumes between 1754 and 1762, and in a complete edition in the latter year. The final two volumes of the complete edition, dealing with the Stuart period, were actually the first two published in 1754 and 1757. After several intervening editions, a posthumous edition including Hume's final revisions was published in eight volumes in 1778, and this is the basis for the modern English edition, edited by William B. Todd (Indianapolis: Liberty Fund, 1983), which restores the six-volume format of Hume's original publication. A German translation by Johann Jacob Dusch, also in six volumes, was published in Breslau and Leipzig in 1767–71. In his allusion to Hume, Kant may have had in mind these remarks, from Hume's summary of the state of English arts and letters during the reigns of Charles II and James II: "the productions of literature still wanted much of that correctness and delicacy, which we so much admire in the ancients, and in the French writers, their judicious imitators. It was indeed during this period chiefly, that that nation left the English behind them in the productions of poetry, eloquence, history, and other branches of polite letters; and acquired a superiority, which the efforts of English writers, during the subsequent age, did more successfully contest with them" (1983 edition, vol. VI, pp. 542–3). Kant frequently contrasted

the aesthetic proclivities of the different European nations, from the *Observations on the Feeling of the Beautiful and the Sublime* in 1764 (section IV, 2:243–56) to *Anthropology from a Pragmatic Point of View* in 1798 ("On the Character of Nations," 7:313–15). The present contrast between the French and the English is also suggested at *Menschenkunde*, 25:1062, and *Anthropologie Mrongovius*, 25:1314.

50 Kant frequently experimented with schemes for the classification of the different arts and for the comparison of their merits (which he will take up here in § 53). See R 1485 (1775–77), 15:699–706; *Anthropologie Pillau*, 25:760–1, 783; and *Menschenkunde*, 25:986–95, 997–1003.

51 This claim may come as a surprise after the "Analytic of the Beautiful," but it is in fact an early theme in Kant's thought; see R 1855 (1776–78), 16:138.

52 This contrast was a long-standing theme in Kant's thought: see R 1810 (1769–70), 16:123–4; R 1485 (1775–77), 15:699–706, at pp. 702–3; *Anthropologie Friedländer*, 25:526; *Anthropologie Pillau*, 25:760; *Menschenkunde*, 25:986–90, 997; *Anthropologie Mrongovius*, 25:1279–82; *Anthropologie Busolt*, 25:1465–6; and *Anthropology from a Pragmatic Point of View*, § 71B, 7:246–7.

53 On Kant's concept of the pictorial arts, see also *Menschenkunde*, 25:1000–3.

54 Kant feels some need to apologize for including landscape gardening among the fine arts, but he had included it in his lists quite early; see R 626 (1769?), 15:271–3.

55 For variations on this theme, see R 683 (1769–70), 15:304–5; R 685 (1769–70), 15:305; *Anthropologie Collins*, 25:181–2, 198; *Anthropologie Parow*, 25:378–9, 396; *Anthropologie Pillau*, 25:760–1; *Menschenkunde*, 25:986, 998–9; and *Anthropologie Busolt*, 25:1509.

56 This sentence should be compared with Kant's discussion of Euler's theory of color at § 14, 5:224, where he seems to maintain the opposite.

57 See note 50 to § 51.

58 See *Anthropologie Pillau*, 25:761, and *Anthropology from a Pragmatic Point of View*, § 71B, 7:247–9.

59 The quote is not actually from Cicero, but from Cato the Elder. See *Catonis Fragmenta*, edited by Heinrich Jordan (Leipzig, 1860), p. 80, or Quintilian, *Institutio oratoria* XII, cap. I, I.

60 On music, see also *Anthropologie Collins*, 25:187–96, and *Menschenkunde*, 25:999. There are quite a few passages in which Kant praises music rather than criticizing it because it spreads its pleasure around: see *Anthropologie Collins*, 25:187; *Anthropologie Mrongovius*, 25:1325–6; *Anthropologie Busolt*, 25:1509; and *Metaphysik L₁*, 28:251.

61 See note 39 to the "Analytic of the Sublime," above.

62 In the *Anthropology from a Pragmatic Point of View*, Kant defines an "affect" as "a feeling of pleasure or displeasure in his present state that does not allow a subject to rise to **reflection** (the representation of reason whether one should give himself up to it or refuse it)" (§ 73, 7:251), and states that "Affect is surprise by means of sensation, in which the mind's self-control (*animus sui compos*) is suspended" (§ 74, 7:252).

63   Kant discussed the causes of laughter in *Anthropologie Collins*, 25:139–46, 184–7; *Anthropologie Parow*, 25:380; and *Anthropology from a Pragmatic Point of View*, § 79, 7:262.

64   A port on the Gulf of Khambat on the west coast of India, north of Bombay. Originally opened to the West by the Portuguese, during the seventeenth and eighteenth centuries it was one of the main bases of the British East India Company, and one of the most populous cities in India.

65   Voltaire, *Henriade* (1728), canto VII: *"L'un est doux sommeil et la'autre l'espérance"* (The one is sweet sleep and the other is hope).

66   See note 37 to the "Analytic of the Sublime," above.

67   See also *Logik Philippi*, 24:371.

"Dialectic of the Aesthetic Power of Judgment" (§§ 55–60)

1   Kant had made a similar contrast as early as 1771, when he wrote that "The proposition: *de gusto non est disputandum*, if 'disputing' means the same as to establish positions on both sides by rational grounds, is entirely correct. But if it means that there is [in matters of taste] no rule at all, hence no rightful contradiction, then it is a principle of unsociability, crudeness and even ignorance" (R 706, 15:313). He had already formulated the present distinction between arguing (*streiten*) and disputing (*disputieren*); see *Anthropologie Collins*, 25:180; *Anthropologie Parow*, 25:378; *Anthropologie Mrongovius*, 25:1326; and *Metaphysik L$_1$*, 28:251. Shortly before publishing the *Critique*, he also deployed it in *Anthropologie Busolt*, 25:1509, and after the *Critique* was published he repeated it in *Metaphysik K$_3$* (*Vigilantius*), 29: 1011. It is difficult to believe that in his contrast between the two "commonplaces" Kant was not influenced by Hume's contrast between two "species of common sense," one which says that each person's sentiment is right and the other of which insists that some persons' judgments are to be taken more seriously than others, in "Of the Standard of Taste" (1757); in *Essays Moral, Political and Literary*, pp. 234–5.

2   That is, in §§ 32 and 33.

3   The only place in Kant's notes that anticipates this introduction of the idea of the supersensible to resolve the antinomy of taste is R 992 (1785–89), 15:436–7, clearly a late outline for the *Critique*.

4   See note 19 to the first draft of the introduction and note 34 to § 15, above.

5   For Kant's general account of the nature of an antinomy and the conditions for its resolution, see *Pure Reason* A 405–567/B 432–595; for the specific claim that antinomies are natural illusions that retain their grip on us even after we understand their source, see A 421–2/B 449–50, and for the underlying assumption of the present section, namely that the solution of an antinomy must always involve an appeal to transcendental idealism, see A 490–7/B 518–25.

6   The references in the following clause to the present work (the *Critique of the Power of Judgment*) and to the *Critique of Practical Reason* make it clear that in this initial reference Kant is referring to the *Critique of Pure Reason*. As noted, the "Antinomy of Pure Reason," the second chapter of the second book of the "Transcendental Dialectic" in the *Critique of Pure*

Reason, extends from A 405/B 432 to A 567/B 594. In the *Critique of Practical Reason*, the whole of its dialectic is presented as the solution to an antinomy concerning the relationship between virtue and happiness, which is resolved by the introduction of the highest good as a natural condition which is however made possible by a supersensible ground in God's authorship of nature; see 5:110–48.

7   Kant's general account of ideas of reason may be found in *Pure Reason*, A 310–20/B 366–76.

8   Kant's 1786 work *The Metaphysical Foundations of Natural Science* had attempted to provide a philosophical derivation of the fundamental forces postulated in mechanics, dynamics, and kinematics from the concept of matter and the principles of empirical judgment. After the completion of the *Critique of the Power of Judgment*, Kant became increasingly interested in attempting to give a philosophical account of more specific physical processes such as crystallization, and spent much of his effort in his last years trying to write a book that would be called "The Transition from the Metaphysical Foundations of Natural Science to Physics." His drafts for this never-completed work are included in the materials known as the *Opus postumum*, published as volumes 21 and 22 of the Academy edition; a selection of these materials has been published in English as Kant, *Opus postumum*, ed. Eckart Förster (Cambridge: Cambridge University Press, 1993). A few examples of Kant's interest in the nature of crystallization in this late work may be found at 21:404 (Förster, p. 16); 21:308–9 (Förster, p. 24); 22:313–14 (Förster, pp. 32–3); 21:522–3 (Förster, p. 35); Kant's commitment to the theory of caloric as the explanation for the loss or gain of heat is evident in these passages and many others, especially 22: 147–8 (Förster, pp. 49–50; see also pp. 87–99). Kant discusses the theory of caloric, or "phlogiston" as it was also known, in his lectures on physics (1785), 29:83–4, 118–28; these lectures were based on W. C. G. Karstens, *Anleitung zur gemeinnützlichen Kenntnis der Natur* (Halle, 1783), reprinted at 29:171–590; see chapter XXVI, 29:492–525

9   The minerological term *drusig* refers to crystals lining the interior of a cavity in a rock, as in what is now referred to as a geode; the terms *Druse* and *drusig* were in use in the Saxon mining industry in the eighteenth century.

10   PbS, or lead sulfide.

11   Fe_3O_2, or ferric oxide.

12   "Spar-druses" (*Spardrusen*) would refer to any number of crystals found in geodes, e.g., feldspar; hematite (*Glaskopf*) is apparently another form of pyrargyrite, or ferric oxide; aragonite (*Eisenblüte*) is a low-temperature form of calcium carbonate.

13   See particularly §§ 73 and 81 below.

14   The contrast between intuitive and symbolic cognition was introduced into German philosophy by Leibniz in his "Meditations on Knowledge, Truth, and Ideas" (1684). Symbolic knowledge uses words or other signs "(whose sense appears only obscurely and imperfectly to the mind) in place of the ideas I have of those things"; knowledge is intuitive, "When we can, or indeed insofar as we can ... consider all of its component

notions at the same time" (G. W. Leibniz, *Philosophical Essays*, ed. and tr. by Roger Ariew and Daniel Garber [Indianapolis: Hackett Publishing Co., 1989], p. 25). See also Wolff, *Vernünfftige Gedancken von Gott, der Welt, und die Seele des Menschen*, §§ 316–24.

15 See John Locke, *An Essay concerning Human Understanding*, book II, chapter XXIII, § 2; in the edition by Peter H. Nidditch (Oxford: Clarendon Press, 1975), pp. 295–6.

16 For Kant's definition of theism, see *Philosophische Religionslehre nach Pölitz*, 28:1001; translated in Immanuel Kant, *Religion and Rational Theology*, ed. George Di Giovanni and Allen W. Wood (Cambridge: Cambridge University Press, 1996), pp. 347–8; on anthropomorphism, see *Religion within the Boundaries of Mere Reason*, 6:65n. (Di Giovanni and Wood, p. 107) and 6:168–9 (Di Giovanni and Wood, p. 189), and *Pölitz*, 28:1002 (Di Giovanni and Wood, p. 348) and 28:1046–7 (Di Giovanni and Wood, p. 385–6).

17 At the beginning of the *Anthropologie Collins*, Kant had bluntly asserted that "The entire utility of the beautiful arts is that they set moral propositions of reason in their full glory and powerfully support them" (25:33). However, later in the same lectures Kant already introduced the idea that there is at most an analogy between taste and virtue: "Virtue engages us, not through its use, but insofar as it pleases us. In such a way taste prepares the way for virtue. Taste is an *analogon* of perfection, it is in intuition what morality is in reason. The study of taste is therefore very necessary" (25:195–6). See also *Anthropologie Parow*, 25:387, and *Menschenkunde*, 25:1104. *Metaphysik Dohna*, 28:676 (delivered after the publication of the *Critique*) gives a good statement of the points of difference between taste and morality mentioned by Kant in the next paragraph.

18 This whole section may be compared to the section "On the Utility of the Cultivation of Taste" in *Anthropologie Collins*, 25:187–96, as well as to *Anthropologie Parow*, 25:381–2.

19 Kant apparently could not make up his mind whether he should consider taste as propaedeutic for morality or sound morality as the basis for taste. In his metaphysics lectures in the winter semester of 1794, he apparently reversed the argument of the present section and said the following: "*Artes liberales* are the arts that cultivate freedom. Here the human being, who otherwise is acquainted with nothing except what belongs to sensation, is determined to action by the mere representation of the beautiful and the good (thus through something that carries with it no interest at all). This already indicates a degree of freedom. Among the aesthetic determining grounds of the power of choice there are some that do not sustain enjoyment, but rather the culture of the understanding and of the faculty of reflection. *Liberalis* is that which lets [one] be free, which supports freedom. . . . The beautiful arts are such that they do not coerce approval from people, but leave their judgment free, so that their approval is given spontaneously. In them no rules can be despotically prescribed, they are rather a free play of the imagination; but since this is a great assistant to the understanding, namely in providing intuitions for concepts, it promotes freedom. Here one can never prove beauty in accordance with

universal rules, but only in the work of art, where everyone can give the rule for himself. The classics are therefore in such high repute because they have withstood the gnawing teeth of time. Barbarism has been lifted every time people have begun to take them as examples. Although the beautiful arts belong to sensibility, they still promote freedom, because they are active in the beauty of forms; because they make us free from the impressions of the senses and the productive imagination is free, we are self-creators. Humanity is thus the capacity and the inclination to communicate one's thoughts and feelings" (*Metaphysik K₃ [Auszug Schlapp]*, 28: 815–16). Ultimately it seems that Kant can only believe that the cultivation of taste and the development of morality are mutually reinforcing.

"Analytic of the Teleological Power of Judgment" (§§ 61–68)

1   For Kant's view of Plato's theory of ideas, see *Pure Reason*, A 313–19/B 369–75.

2   See Socrates's criticism of Anaxagoras: "This man made no use of Mind, nor gave it any responsibility for the management of things, but mentioned as causes air and ether and water and many other strange things" (*Phaedo*, 98b–c; translation by G. M. A. Grube, in Plato, *Complete Works*, ed. John M. Cooper [Indianapolis: Hackett Publishing Co., 1997], p. 85).

3   For Kant's account of the geological effects of rivers and seas, see *Only Possible Basis*, 2:128–9, and *Physical Geography* (edited from Kant's notes by F. T. Rink in 1802), 9:296–9.

4   To this paragraph, compare *Toward Perpetual Peace* (1795), 8:363–5. Kant had argued as early as *Only Possible Basis*, 2:131, that it is a mistake to infer immediately from the fact that certain natural conditions seem advantageous to human beings to the conclusion that they have been purposively designed to be so.

5   In the *Only Possible Basis*, Kant had distinguished between the case in which a harmonious diversity of effects arises from a single law, which he held to be characteristic of inanimate nature, from the case in which a harmony of effects arises from distinct types of causation, which he took to be characteristic of animate objects in nature (2:107–8); however, he then went on to argue that our failure to explain everything in nature according to mechanical laws should not be taken as a valid ground for a belief in a supersensible ground of nature, because such a supersensible ground – for which, of course, the work does argue – could clearly achieve all of its intended effects in nature through the mechanical operations of the laws that it institutes as the very conditions of the possibility of nature (see 2: 114–15).

6   In a discussion of the value of learning over material goods, Cicero writes: "Who in truth would consider anyone . . . happier than one who is set free from all perturbations of mind, or more secure in his wealth than one who possesses only what, as the saying goes, he can carry away with him out of a shipwreck. . . . In this connection the remark made by Plato, or perhaps by someone else, seems to me particularly apt. For when a storm at sea had

driven him to an unknown land and stranded him on a deserted shore, and his companions were frightened on account of their ignorance of the country, he, according to the story, noticed certain geometrical figures traced in the sand, and immediately cried out, 'Be of good courage; I see the tracks of men.' He drew his inference, evidently, not from the cultivation of the soil, which he also observed, but from the indications of learning" (*De Re Publica*, I.XVII.28–30; translation from Cicero, *Volume XVI: De Republica, De Legibus*, tr. Clinton W. Keyes [Cambridge, Mass.: Harvard University Press, 1928], pp. 51–3). According to this edition, the saying is also found in Vitruvius, *De Architectura*, VI, 1, where it is attributed to Aristippus (435–366 B.C.) rather than Plato.

7 Kant first used the example of a tree to illustrate problems in explanation at *Only Possible Basis*, 2:114–15.

8 Kant argues that it is only from the case of our own intentional actions that we can originally form the concept of purposiveness in the 1788 essay *On the Use of Teleological Principles in Philosophy*, 8:181. But Kant's example is ancient: Aristotle used the example of building a house in his illustration of the four causes at *Physics*, book II, chapter 3, 195b3–5, 20–21.

9 Kant stresses both the analogy between a living thing and a work of art and the limits of this analogy, about to be explicated, at *Religion*, 6:64–5n., a note which ends with an allusion back to the present argument.

10 For Kant's concept of the nature and limits of mechanical forces, see *Metaphysical Foundations of Natural Science*, "General Observation on Dynamics," especially 4:525, 530 and 532–3.

11 This note could refer to either of the two recent revolutions that Kant had followed with great interest, the American Revolution of 1776–83, or the French Revolution, which was in its early months when Kant wrote the present work. But it would seem somewhat strange for Kant to describe the American Revolution as the transformation of a "great nation" (*Volk*) into a state, since the American population, not all of whom in any case supported the revolution, would not be likely to be thought of as a single "people" or "nation." Several years later, when Kant spoke of the danger of anarchy as destroying the organization of a people before it could be replaced with another, he clearly had the later stages of the French Revolution in mind (see *Theory and Practice*, 8:302n.).

12 For a precursor to this definition, see *Teleological Principles*, 8:181. For later versions of it, see passages in the *Opus postumum*, such as "The definition of an organic body is that it is a body, every part of which is *there for the sake of the other* (reciprocally as end and, at the same time, means). It is easily seen that this is a mere idea, which is not assured of reality *a priori* (i.e., that such a thing could exist)" (21:210; Förster, p. 64; see also pp. 100 and 146).

13 "New Holland" was an eighteenth-century designation for Australia prior to its colonization by the British, so Kant's term "New Hollanders" refers to the aboriginal people of Australia. By "Fuegians" he refers to the aboriginal inhabitants of Tierra del Fuego, Argentina.

14 Here Kant introduces his central argument that once we have been led to introduce the idea of purposive systematicity by our experience of organ-

isms, it is then natural for us to attempt to see whether we might not also see the whole of nature as a purposive system. This idea was anticipated in *Pure Reason*, A 691/B 719. In *Teleological Principles*, Kant argues that the idea of a purpose for the whole of nature, introduced by the analogy between organized beings and human artistic production, has to be "empirically conditioned" by what we actually observe in nature (8:182). This restriction is part of what is expressed in the present work by calling the principle of the purposiveness of nature a regulative rather than constitutive principle.

15 In *Anthropology from a Pragmatic Point of View*, Kant defines an affect as "a feeling of pleasure or displeasure in his present state that does not let [a person] rise to **reflection** (to rational consideration of whether he should give himself up to it or refuse it)" (§ 73, 7:251); in other words, an affect is an emotional state that threatens the ability of reason to control our conduct.

16 Kant frequently discussed the nature of dreams; see *Anthropologie Collins*, 25:101–2; *Anthropologie Friedländer*, 25:528–31; *Menschenkunde*, 25:995–7; *Anthropologie Mrongovius*, 25:1283–8; and *Anthropology from a Pragmatic Point of View*, § 37, 7:189–90.

17 To this entire section, compare Kant's discussion of the "Rules of a Revised Method of Physico-Theology" in *Only Possible Basis*, 2:126–7.

"Dialectic of the Teleological Power of Judgment" (§§ 69–78)

1 Kant alludes here to the account of judgment that he gave in *Pure Reason*, A 131–235/B 169–294.

2 See *Letter to Herodotus*: "The motions of the heavenly bodies and their turnings and eclipses and risings and settings, and kindred phenomena to these, must not be thought to be due to any being who controls and ordains or has ordained them . . . Nor again, must we believe that they, which are but fire agglomerated in a mass, possess blessedness, and voluntarily take upon themselves these movements" (Oates, *The Stoic and Epicurean Philosophers*, p. 13).

3 Democritus of Abdera flourished ca. 460 B.C. Large numbers of titles of his works on nature and causes are reported by ancient sources, but none of his surviving fragments actually expound what Kant here calls the system of causality (see Kathleen Freeman, *Ancilla to the Pre-Socratic Philosophers* [Cambridge, Mass.: Harvard University Press, 1966], pp. 91–120). Aristotle says, "if we look at the ancients, natural science would seem to be concerned with the *matter*. (It was only very slightly that Empedocles and Democritus touched on form and essence)" (*Physics*, book II, chapter 2, 194a18–20; translation by R. P. Hardie and R. K. Gaye in Jonathan Barnes, ed., *The Complete Works of Aristotle* [Princeton: Princeton University Press, 1984], p. 331).

4 In his reference to Spinoza, Kant could have in mind statements like the following from Spinoza's *Ethics*: "I shall show . . . that neither intellect nor will pertain to God's nature. Of course I know there are many who think they can demonstrate that a supreme intellect and a free will pertain to

God's nature. For they say they know nothing they can ascribe to God more perfect than what is the highest perfection in us" (*Ethics*, part one, proposition 17, scholium; in Edwin Curley, ed., *The Collected Works of Spinoza* [Princeton: Princeton University Press, 1985], p. 426); or "*Things could have been produced by God in no other way, and in no other order than they have been produced.* For all things have necessarily followed from God's given nature, and have been determined from the necessity of God's nature to exist and produce an effect in a certain way" (*Ethics*, part one, proposition 33; Curley, p. 436).

5 For further comments on hylozoism, see *Dreams of a Spirit-Seer* (1766), 2: 330, and *Metaphysical Foundations of Natural Science*, 4:544.

6 See *Metaphysik L₁*, 28:275.

7 Kant presumably refers to the strict sense of organization as reciprocal causation described in §§ 63 and 64 above.

8 See *Universal Natural History*, 1:229–30 (Hastie, pp. 28–9).

9 See Kant's account of the empirical conditions for the application of the concepts of possibility and actuality in *Pure Reason*, "The postulates of empirical thinking in general," A 218–35/B 265–87.

10 In *Pure Reason*, Kant distinguishes the human intellect, which requires both intuitions and concepts for knowledge, from an intellectual intuition in which concepts would also give their own objects, at B 145, B 150, A 252/B 308–9, and A 256/B 311–12. For an early statement of the discursive nature of human understanding, see R 1832 (1772–75?), 16: 131.

11 Here Kant refers to the doctrine of the *Critique of Pure Reason* that space is not an aggregate constituted out of regions of space that exist independently of it, as parts, but is rather a whole into which particular regions are introduced only by introducing limits into it; see A 25/B 39.

12 Kant's comment on these terms in *Pure Reason*, A 730/B 758, suggests that it is not clear what the precise differences between them are.

"Methodology of the Teleological Power of Judgment" (§§ 79–91)

1 See David Hume, *Dialogues concerning Natural Religion*, part 5; in Hume, *The Natural History of Religion and Dialogues concerning Natural Religion*, ed. A. Wayne Colver and John Valdimir Price (Oxford: Clarendon, 1976), esp. pp. 192–4. Hume's *Dialogues*, posthumously published in 1779, were translated into German as early as 1781.

2 See Spinoza, *Ethics*, part I, especially propositions 14 and 15 (Curley, pp. 420–1).

3 "Occasionalism" refers to the doctrine of Nicolas Malebranche (1638–1715), according to which only God's actions possess the necessity required for genuine causation, so all events in the world are never more than occasions for God to exercise his constant causal power; see *The Search after Truth* (1674), e.g., book six, part two, chapter 3 (in the translation by Thomas M. Lennon and Paul J. Olscamp [Columbus: Ohio State University Press, 1980], pp. 446–52). "Prestabilism" is a term Kant uses here for the theory of preestablished harmony developed by Leibniz and maintained

in various contexts by followers such as Wolff and Baumgarten, according to which every substance in the world evolves independently of but harmoniously with every other, a reflection of the benevolence God exercised in the original creation of the world of independent substances but which does not require any further intervention on his part. In the present context, Kant is using the names for these general metaphysical doctrines to apply to competing theories of organic reproduction. Leibniz's classical statement of the system of preestablished harmony was first published in "A New System of the Nature and the Communication of Substances, as well as the Union between the Soul and the Body," in the *Journal des savants* 27 June 1695 (see Loemker, pp. 452–59; see also R. S. Woolhouse and Richard Francks, eds., *Leibniz's 'New System' and Associated Contemporary Texts* [Oxford: Oxford University Press, 1997]). For Baumgarten, see *Metaphysica*, §§ 448–65.

4   On the theory of individual preformation, the parent is a mere conduit (hence the term "educt") for preformed individuals, which merely develop (hence the use of the term "evolution" in a thoroughly un-Darwinian sense) in the parent. On the theory of epigenesis or generic preformation, the parent actually produces new offspring which reflect the inheritable characteristics of the parents. Kant makes no suggestion here of the possibility of variation in inherited characteristics, as he does in the preceding section (§ 80, 5:418–19); but such a possibility is not excluded by the theory of epigenesis either; thus it is the theory of epigenesis and not what Kant here calls the theory of "evolution" that would be compatible with the later synthesis of the Darwinian theory of evolution with the Mendelian theory of inheritance. The modern version of the theory of "involution" or "encapsulation" was first advanced by Malebranche; see *Search after Truth*, book two, part one, chapter 7 (in Lennon and Olscamp, pp. 112–24, especially p. 118).

5   See *Only Possible Basis*, 2:115.

6   Locke was fascinated with the subject of miscarriages and half-breeds (see *Essay concerning Human Understanding*, book III, chapter VI, §§ 17, 22–3 [in Nidditch, pp. 448–9, 450–2]), and for this reason is associated with early advocates of what Kant calls "epigenesis."

7   Johann Friedrich Blumenbach (1752–1840), Göttingen professor of anatomy and comparative zoology, author of *Handbuch der Naturgeschichte* (Manual of natural history) (1779) and *Über den Bildungstrieb* (On the formative drive) (1781, new edition 1789), which is the work that Kant owned and to which he here alludes.

8   For Kant's explication of the myth that humankind began from a single couple, see *The Conjectural Beginning of Human History* (1786), 8:110.

9   Carl von Linné (Latin "Linnaeus") (1707–1778), Swedish naturalist and taxonomist, author of the *Systema Naturae* (Stockholm, 1766). Kant apparently has the following passage in mind: "The constitution of nature is revealed in the three natural realms: namely, just as people are not born just for the sake of rulers, but the latter are set in place in order to guard order among their subjects, so one exercises its tyranny over the others for the sake of its grim reward: the plants for the plant-eating animals, the

flesh-eaters over the plant-eaters, and among these again the greater over the lesser, and the human being (as animal) over the greatest. All of this serves only that the balance together with the beauty of the state of nature should continue" (vol. I, p. 17).

10 As early as 1755, Kant had written that "Man, who seems to be the masterpiece of creation, is himself not excepted" from the law of constant creation and destruction in which nature "proves her riches" (*Universal Natural History*, 1:318; in Hastie, p. 150).

11 See note 24 to § 43, above. The works of Camper that seem relevant to Kant's present mention of him are *Demonstrationes anatomico-pathologicae* (Amsterdam, 1760–62) and *Über den natürlichen Unterschied der Gesichtszüge* (On the natural distinction among facial features) (Berlin, 1792).

12 See *Groundwork*, section two, 4:418–19; *Practical Reason*, 5:23–8; and *Menschenkunde*, 25:1081.

13 See *Universal History* (1784), Third Proposition, 8:20–1.

14 To this paragraph, compare *The Conjectural Beginning of Human History*, 8:114.

15 On the "unsociable sociability" of mankind as a spur to progress, see *Universal History*, Fourth Proposition, 8:20–2.

16 For Kant's argument that a secure condition of justice can only be achieved through a worldwide legal order (although a worldwide federation, not a single worldwide government, which in his view would inevitably degenerate into an autocracy), see *Universal History*, Seventh Proposition, 8:24–6; *Theory and Practice*, part III, 8:307–13; *Toward Perpetual Peace*, Second Definitive Article, 8:354–7; and *Metaphysics of Morals*, "Doctrine of Right," § 61, 6:352–3.

17 On the unintended contributions of war to human progress, see *Universal History*, Seventh Proposition, 8:24–5, and *Toward Perpetual Peace*, First Supplement, 8:363–7.

18 See notes 19 and 20 to the "Analytic of the Sublime" and notes 18 and 19 to § 60, above.

19 For Kant's account of the infinite regress of conditions in nature considered as phenomenon, see the third "Antinomy of Pure Reason" in *Pure Reason*, A 444–51/B 472–9.

20 The conclusion that Kant has reached, that a teleology based on the concept of a final end for nature can only be grounded on the moral value of human freedom, was anticipated in the essay on *Teleological Principles* of 1788, which concludes with the following: "And now to draw the sum from all of this! **Ends** have a direct relation to **reason**, whether this is that of another or our own. But if we are to place them in the reason of another, then we must at least base this on our own as an analogue: because otherwise this cannot be represented at all. Now the ends are either ends of **nature** or of **freedom**. No one can see *a priori* that there must be ends in nature, although it can very well be seen *a priori* that there must be a connection of causes and effects in nature. Consequently, the use of the teleological principle with regard to nature is always empirically conditioned. It would be the same with the ends of freedom if this had first to be given objects of the will as determining grounds by nature

(in needs and inclinations) ... But the *Critique of Practical Reason* has shown that there are pure practical principles, by which reason is determined *a priori*, and which therefore give its end *a priori*. If therefore the use of the teleological principle for explanations of nature, because it is restricted to empirical conditions, can never give the original ground of purposive connection completely and adequately determined for all ends, then this must by contrast be expected of a **pure doctrine of the end**, the *a priori* principle of which contains the relation of reason in general to the whole of all ends, and can only be practical" (*Teleological Principles*, 8:182). See also *Religion*, 6:60, and *Anthropologie Busolt*, where Kant states that "Freedom is the highest formal good of the natural condition" (25:1529) – something that can be an end *in* nature although it is not given as an end *by* nature.

21 For Kant's other treatments of physico-theology (his name for the argument from design), see *Only Possible Basis*, 2:116–26; *Pure Reason*, A 620–30/B 648–58; and *Religionslehre Pölitz*, 28:1007–10 (in Di Giovanni and Wood, pp. 352–5).

22 See note 26 to § 86, below.

23 The argument that we cannot use an empirical argument to infer the perfect intelligence of the cause of nature was made by Hume in the *Dialogues concerning Natural Religion*, part 2 (in Colver and Price, see especially pp. 167–8) and part 5 (pp. 190–1).

24 It was because the argument from design could not establish the perfection of God that Kant had already argued in the *Critique of Pure Reason*, without benefit of Hume's *Dialogues* (which did not appear in German until the same year as the publication of the *Critique*), that the physico-theological argument could only prove the existence of God as ordinarily conceived if supplemented by the cosmological argument, which begins from the concept of a perfect being and then – of course, illegitimately – infers its existence from its perfection. See *Pure Reason*, A 628–30/B 656–8.

25 See for example Spinoza, *Ethics*, part one, proposition 18 (Curley, p. 428).

26 For Kant's chief accounts of his moral theology, that is, his appeal to moral considerations to specify the attributes of our concept of God and to provide a practical justification for our belief in his existence, see *Pure Reason*, "The Canon of Pure Reason," A 804–31/B 832–59; *Practical Reason*, particularly 5:124–42; *Religionslehre Pölitz*, 28:1010–11, 1071–1117 (in Di Giovanni and Wood, pp. 356–8, 406–42).

27 For Kant's classical statement that the good will is the only thing of unconditional value, see *Groundwork*, section one, 4:393–7. See also *Moralphilosophie Collins*, 27:344–6 (Heath and Schneewind, pp. 125–7), and such notes as R 7210 (1780s), 19:286, and R 7217 (1780s?), 19:288.

28 *Groundwork*, 4:393.

29 For the suggestion that a good will entitles one to happiness while an evil one disqualifies one, in the eye of reason, from enjoying it, see *Practical Reason*, 5:110. See also note 33 below.

30 For other versions of this argument, see *Pure Reason*, A 815/B 843, and *Practical Reason*, 5:140.

31   Kant frequently stressed that fear of God is an ignoble motive for fulfilling
      the moral law; see *Moralphilosophie Collins*, 27:1425-6 (Heath and Schnee-
      wind, p. 69), and *Metaphysik der Sitten Vigilantius*, 27:556-7, 725-6 (Heath
      and Schneewind, pp. 313, 446-7).

32   For this formulation, see *Practical Reason*, Theorem III, 5:27.

33   See *Practical Reason*, 5:110-11. Here Kant seems to conceive of the highest
      good as the combination of two separate things, the merely natural desire
      for happiness which is subjected to the moral condition of virtue as the
      condition for being worthy of happiness. At other places, Kant seems to
      conceive of the highest good in a more unitary fashion, as the systematic
      distribution of happiness that the moral law itself actually enjoins us to
      seek through its injunction that we treat all persons as ends, thus as agents
      who set and fulfill the ends in the realization of which their happiness lies.
      See *Pure Reason*, A 809-10/B 837-8, and *Theory and Practice*, section I, 8:
      278-89, especially 8:279-80n., as well as notes such as R 7199 (1780s?),
      19:272-4, at p. 272, and R 7242 (1780s), 19:293. Kant's argument that we
      need to postulate the existence of God as the author of *nature* who makes
      nature such that our actions can be effective in it makes most sense if the
      highest good is understood in the second sense: it is because it is only
      rational for us to act if we believe that our actions can succeed that we
      must believe in God if our efforts at morality are not to flag, not because
      we need the promise of an extraneous reward if we have shown ourselves
      by our virtue to be worthy of happiness. And Kant seems to have this
      conception in mind on the next page, when he speaks of the highest good
      as the final end enjoined upon us by the moral law itself: in such a
      formulation, a certain kind of happiness is not merely limited by the moral
      law but is enjoined by it (see also § 88, the third sentence of the first
      paragraph on 5:453 as well as the first paragraph at 5:456). However, in
      the "Remark" following § 88, Kant seems to have in mind his other
      conception of the highest good, on which happiness is a merely natural
      good for which virtue is only the condition of entitlement (see 5:458-9).
      Thus, both of the conceptions of the highest good that are found in Kant's
      other works seem to be at play within the culminating argument of the
      third *Critique*.
         Yet a third position, which Kant does not explicate clearly in any of his
      published works, is that freedom is so important to us that it is only when
      happiness is a product of our own freedom that it can seem really satisfac-
      tory to us. Kant hints at this in *Universal History*, Third Proposition, 8:20,
      but gives particularly clear statements of it in *Anthropologie Mrongovius*,
      25:1334-5, and *Menschenkunde*, 25:1142-3.

34   See *Practical Reason*, 5:111-13.

35   See *Practical Reason*, 5:125-6.

36   For some of Kant's comments on idolatry, see *Religion*, 6:185 and 197-8.

37   Kant argued from the outset of the development of his moral philosophy
      that moral laws must be known independently of and prior to belief in the
      existence of God, and were not dependent upon the will of God; see
      Moralphilosophie Collins, 27:262 (Heath and Schneewind, pp. 55-6).

38   See *Pure Reason*, B 419-20.

39 To this section generally, compare *Pure Reason*, "The Canon of Pure Reason," third section, "On having an opinion, knowing, and believing" (A 820–31/B 848–59); *Practical Reason*, 5:142–6; and *Jäsche Logic*, 9:66–73.

40 On the contrast between persuasion and conviction, see *Jäsche Logic*, 9:73.

41 By this reference to the *Critique of Pure Reason* Kant apparently means to refer to the whole of the third division of the "Transcendental Dialectic," the "Ideal of Pure Reason," which contains his critique of the traditional arguments for the existence of God; see A 567–642/B 595–679. The final reference to principles "valid solely for nature" may be yet another reference to his critique of the physico-theological proof (A 620–30/B 648–58).

42 On proofs by analogy, see *Jäsche Logic*, 9:133.

43 For another use of the image of attractive and repulsive forces in the context of political philosophy, see *Metaphysics of Morals*, 6:232–3.

44 See *Pure Reason*, A 822–3/B 850–1; *Jäsche Logic*, 9:66–7.

45 On probability, see *Jäsche Logic*, 9:81–2.

46 For Kant's view of hypotheses, see *Pure Reason*, A 769–782/B 797–810, and *Jäsche Logic*, 9:84–6.

47 See note 39.

48 Kant was to devote great effort to trying to prove the existence of the ether as a nonperceivable but yet still empirical condition of the possibility of interaction in space and even perception itself in the *Opus postumum*; a selection of his attempts at this proof may be found in Förster, pp. 62–99.

49 For Kant's speculation on the possible inhabitation of other planets, see *Universal Natural History*, Third Part, "On the Inhabitants of the Stars" (1:349–68; not included in Hastie).

50 Here Kant refers to his famous doctrine of freedom as the fact of reason; see *Practical Reason*, 5:29–32.

51 For Kant's most famous statement of this point, see *Pure Reason*, A 3/B 7; see also the second edition note at B 395n., and A 798/B 826.

52 For the contrast between theoretical and practical cognition, see *Pure Reason*, A 633–4/B 661–2; *Practical Reason*, 5:132–46; and *Jäsche Logic*, 9:86–7.

53 Here Kant refers, of course, to his critique of the ontological and cosmological arguments in the *Critique of Pure Reason*, at A 592–620/B 620–48; the gist of his critique of these arguments was already present in 1763 in *The Only Possible Basis*, at 2:71–7 and 155–63. Indeed, Kant had already worked out his critique of the ontological argument in his first purely philosophical work, the *New Elucidation of the First Principles of Metaphysical Cognition* of 1755; see proposition VI, 1:394–5.

54 Kant always held that the argument from design is natural and beneficial, in contrast to the ontological and cosmological arguments, which he scorned as academic sophistries; see *Pure Reason*, A 623/B 651.

55 Kant refers here to Hermann Samuel Reimarus (1694–1768), author of *Die vornehmstem Wahrheiten der natürlichen Religion in zehn Abhandlungen auf eine begreifliche Art erklärt und gerettet* (The foremost truths of natural religion explained and saved in ten treatises) (Hamburg, 1754), *Allgemeine Betrachtungen über die Triebe der Tiere, haupsächlich über ihren Kunsttrieb*

(General observations on the drives of animals, especially their artistic drives) (1760), and, most famously, *Apologie oder Schutzschrift für die vernünftigen Verehrer Gottes* (Apology or vindication for the rational worshippers of God), which was written in 1744 but fragments of which were only posthumously published, by Lessing, under the title *Fragmente eines Ungennanten die Offenbarung betreffend* (Anonymous fragments concerning revelation) in the series that Lessing published in his position as librarian for the Duke of Brunswick at Wolfenbüttel, *Beiträge zur Geschichte und Literatur aus den Schätzen der Herzoglichen Bibliothek zur Wolfenbüttel* (Contributions to history and literature from the treasures of the ducal library in Wolfenbüttel) (1773–81).

56 Again, Kant seems to be thinking of the argument of part 2 of Hume's *Dialogues concerning Natural Religion* (in Colver and Price, pp. 158–72, especially pp. 168–9).

57 Kant stressed that we regard moral laws as divine commands because of our rational insight into their necessity, and do not infer the latter from their divine origin as if we could know that independently of morality; see *Pure Reason*, A 818–19/B 846–7; *Practical Reason*, 5:129; and *Religion*, 6: 153–4. This theme remained one of Kant's most enduring philosophical concerns, and he returned to it in the last phases of the *Opus postumum*, stressing that we formulate the merely subjectively valid idea of God and conceive of our duties as his commands in order to emphasize to ourselves the superiority of our own reason, which is the actual source of those commands, over our mere desires. See *Opus postumum*, e.g., 21:13, 19, 21, 28, and 37 (Förster, pp. 221, 225, 227–8, 232, and 239).

58 Kant expounds his theory of matter as the filling of space by attractive and repulsive forces in the *Metaphysical Foundations of Natural Science*, chapter 2, "Metaphysical Foundations of Dynamics," 4:496–535.

59 *Pure Reason*, B 71–2.

Glossary

The following glossaries list only those terms that are of special significance in this work or whose translation is in some way unusual or controversial. The great majority of words used by Kant, especially the large number of German-English cognates found in the text, are omitted.

German-English

abhängig	dependent
Absicht	aim, intention, point of view
absichtlich	intentional
Abstimmung	coordination
Achtung	respect
adhäriend	adherent (see also *anhängend*)
allgemein	general, universal
Allgemeine, das	the universal (*n.*)
allgemeingültig	universally valid
Allgemeinheit	universality
Allmacht	all-powerfulness
angemessen	suitable
Angemessenheit	suitability
angenehm	agreeable (*adj.*), the agreeable (*n.*)
anhängend	adherent
Anlage	predisposition
Anreiz	stimulus
ansehen	to view
Ansicht	view (*n.*),
ansinnen	ascribe, require of
Auffassung	apprehension
Ausdehnung	extension
befassen	grasp
befriedigen	satisfy
Begriff	concept
Beifall	approval
beipflichten	consent to
beleben	animate

Belebung	animation
Beschauung	viewing
Beistimmung	assent
Beitritt	consent
Beschaffenheit	characteristic, constitution, property
bestimmend	determining
Bestimmung	determination, vocation
betrachten	consider
Betrachtung	consideration
beurtheilen	to judge (*transitive*), i.e., to judge something
Beurtheilung	the judging (of something)
Beweis	proof
Beweisgrund	proof, ground of proof
bewirken	produce, realize
Beziehung	relation
bildend	pictorial (arts), formative
Bildwerk	picture
Boden	territory
Contemplation	contemplation
contemplativ	contemplative
Darstellung	presentation
Denkungsart	mentality, way of thinking
disputieren	dispute (*v.*)
Eigenschaft	property
einhellig	harmonious
Einhelligkeit	unanimity, unison
Einsicht	insight
einsichten	have insight into
einstimmig	in accord
Einstimmigkeit	accordance, consensus
Einstimmung	accord, consensus
empfindbar	sensitive
Empfindung	sensation, sentiment (see also *Sinnenempfindung*)
empirisch	empirical
Endursache	final cause
Endzweck	final end
Erfahrung	experience
Erfahrungs-	experiential
Erfordernis	requirement

erhaben	sublime (*adj.*)
Erhabene, das	the sublime
erkennen	cognize, recognize
Erkenntnis	cognition, recognition
Erscheinung	appearance
erwarten	expect
erweitern	enlarge, expand
Erzeugung	generation, production
Form	form
fordern	demand
freiwilling	of one's own free will
Frohsein	joyfulness
fühlbar	palpable
Fürwahrhalten	affirmation
Gebiet	domain
gefallen	please
Gefühl	feeling
Geist	spirit
gemeingültig	generally valid
Gemüth	mind
Gemüthsart	mentality
Gemüthsstimmung	state of mind
Genie	genius
Genießen	enjoyment
Genuß	enjoyment
Geschicklichkeit	skill
Geschmack	taste
Gesetz	law
gesetzmäßig	lawlike
Gesinnung	disposition
Gestalt	shape, configuration
Gewalt	violence, dominion
Glaube	belief, faith
Glaubensache	matter of faith
Größe	quantity
Grund	ground, basis, reason
Grundsatz	fundamental principle
Gunst	favor
Hang	tendency
Harmonie	harmony

harmonisch	harmonious
Heiligachtung	reverence
Heterogeneität	heterogeneity
Ideal	ideal
Idee	idea
Inbegriff	set, totality
Intelligenz	intelligence
Kenntniß	knowledge
Kraft	power (of something)
Kultur	culture, cultivation
Kunst	art
künstlich	artistic, artistically
letztes Zweck	ultimate end
Lust	pleasure
Luxus	luxury, indulgence
Macht	power
mannigfaltig	manifold
Mannigfalte, das	the manifold
Mannigfaltigkeit	multiplicity, variety
Materie	matter
materiell	material (*adj.*)
Menge	host
Meinung	opinion
Mensch	human being
Mißfallen	dissatisfaction
Mittheilbarkeit	communicability
Mittheilungsfähighkeit	capacity for communication
moralisch	moral
Nachahmung	imitation
nachdenken	think over
Nachfolge	succession
Nachmachung	copying
Naturzweck	natural end
Neigung	inclination
Ohnmacht	powerlessness

Princip	principle
Principium	principle
Qualität	quality
Quantität	quantity
Quantum	quantum
reflectirend	reflecting
Reflexion	reflection
Regelmäßigkeit	regularity
Reiz	charm
Rührung	emotion
Schätzung	estimation
Schicklichkeit	fitness
schön	beautiful
Schöne, das	the beautiful
Schönheit	beauty
Sinn	sense
Sinnenempfindung	sensation
sinnlich	sensible
Sinnlichkeit	sensibility
Sitten	morals, mores
sittlich	moral, modish
Spiel	play, game
Stimmung	disposition, state (of mind)
Stoff	material (*n.*)
streiten	argue
Substrat	substratum
Talent	talent
Tauglichkeit	serviceability, aptitude
Trieb	drive
Triebfeder	incentive
übereinstimmen	correspond, concur
Übereinstimmung	correspondence
überreden	persuade
überschwenglich	excessive
Überschwengliche, das	that which is excessive
übersinnlich	supersensible
überzeugen	convince
unabsichtlich	unintentionally
Ungleichartigkeit	diversity, dissimilarity
Unlust	displeasure

unzweckmäßig	nonpurposive
Urbild	archetype, prototype
urbildlich	archetypical
Urgrund	original ground
Urtheil	judgment
Urtheilskraft	power of judgment
Urwesen	original being
Verbindung	combination, nexus
Vergnügen	gratification
Verknüpfung	connection
Verhältnis	relation
verlangen	require (something) of (someone)
Vermögen	faculty, capacity
Vernünftelei	sophistry
vernünftelnd	sophistical, rationalistic
Vernunfterkenntnis	rational cognition
Versinnlichung	making sensible, sensible rendering
Verstand	understanding, intelligence
verständig	intelligible
Verwandtschaft	kinship, affinity
Vorstellung	representation
Widerstreit	conflict (*n.*)
Wille	will
Willkühr	choice, capacity for choice
willkührlich	voluntary
wirken	act, produce
Wirkungsart	agency
Wohlgefallen	satisfaction
zufällig	contingent
Zufriedenheit	contentment
zumuthen	expect (something) of (someone)
Zusammenfassung	comprehension
Zusammenhang	interconnection
zusammenhängend	interconnected
Zusammensetzung	composition, synthesis
Zusammenstimmung	agreement
Zusammentreffen	concurrence
Zweck	end
Zweckbestimmung	vocation, determination of an end
zweckmäßig	purposive, purposively
zweckwidrig	contrapurposive

Glossary

English-German

accordance	*Einstimmigkeit, Einstimmung*
act (*v.*)	*wirken*
adherent	*adhäriend, anhängend*
affinity	*Verwandtschaft*
affirmation	*Fürwahrhalten*
agency (kind of)	*Bewirkungsart*
agreeable	*angenehm*
agreeable, the	*das Angenehme*
agreement	*Zusammenstimmung*
aim	*Absicht*
all-powerfulness	*Allmacht*
animate	*beleben*
animation	*Belebung*
appearance	*Erscheinung*
art	*Kunst*
apprehension	*Auffassung*
approval	*Beifall*
aptitude	*Tauglichkeit*
archetype	*Urbild*
argue	*streiten*
artistic, artistically	*künstlich*
assent	*Beistimmung*
ascribe	*ansinnen*
basis	*Grund*
beautiful (*adj.*)	*schön*
beautiful (*n.*)	*das Schöne*
beauty	*Schönheit*
belief	*Glaube*
capacity	*Vermögen*
capacity for communication	*Mittheilungsfähigkeit*
capacity for choice	*Willkühr*
characteristic (*n.*)	*Beschaffenheit*
charm	*Reiz*
choice	*Willkühr*
cognition	*Erkenntnis*
cognize	*erkennen*
combination	*Verbindung*
communicability	*Mittheilbarkeit*
composition	*Zusammensetzung*
comprehension	*Zusammenfassung*

concept	*Begriff*
concur	*übereinstimmen*
concurrence	*Zusammentreffen*
configuration	*Gestalt*
conflict (*n.*)	*Widerstreit*
connection	*Verknüpfung*
consensus	*Einstimmigkeit, Einstimmung*
consent (*n.*)	*Beitritt*
consent to	*beipflichten*
consider	*betrachten*
consideration	*Betrachtung*
constitution	*Beschaffenheit*
contemplation	*Contemplation*
contemplative	*contemplativ*
contentment	*Zufriedenheit*
contingent	*zufällig*
contrapurposive	*zweckwidrig*
convince	*überzeugen*
coordination	*Abstimmung*
copying	*Nachmachung*
correspond	*übereinstimmen*
correspondence	*Übereinstimmung*
cultivation	*Kultur*
culture	*Kultur*
demand	*fordern*
dependent	*abhängig*
determination	*Bestimmung*
determination of an end	*Zweckbestimmung*
determining	*bestimmend*
displeasure	*Unlust*
disposition	*Gesinnung, Stimmung*
dispute (*v.*)	*disputieren*
dissatisfaction	*Mißfallen*
dissimilarity	*Ungleichartigkeit*
diversity	*Mannigfältigkeit, Ungleichartigkeit*
domain	*Gebiet*
dominion	*Gewalt*
drive	*Trieb*
emotion	*Rührung*
empirical	*empirisch*
end	*Zweck*
enjoyment	*Genießen, Genuß*

enlarge	*erweitern*
enthusiasm	*Enthusiasm, Schwärmerei*
estimation	*Schätzung*
excessive	*überschwenglich*
expand	*erweitern*
expect	*erwarten*
expect (something) of (someone)	*zumuthen*
experience	*Erfahrung*
experiential	*Erfahrungs-*
extension	*Ausdehnung*
faculty	*Vermögen*
faith	*Glaube*
favor	*Gunst*
feeling	*Gefühl*
final cause	*Endursache*
final end	*Endzweck*
fitness	*Schicklichkeit*
form	*Form*
formative	*bildend*
fundamental principle	*Grundsatz*
game	*Spiel*
general	*allgemein*
generally valid	*gemeingültig*
generation	*Erzeugung*
genius	*Genie*
grasp (*v.*)	*befassen*
gratification	*Vergnügen*
ground	*Grund*
ground of proof	*Beweisgrund*
harmonious	*harmonisch*
harmony	*Harmonie*
heterogeneity	*Heterogeneität*
host	*Menge*
human (*n.*), human being	*Mensch*
idea	*Idee*
ideal (*n.*)	*Ideal*
imitation	*Nachahmung*
in accord	*einstimmig*
incentive	*Triebfeder*
inclination	*Neigung*

indulgence	*Luxus*
insight	*Einsicht*
intelligence	*Intelligenz, Verstand*
intelligible	*intelligibel, verständig*
intentional	*absichtlich*
interconnected	*zusammenhängend*
interconnection	*Zusammenhang*
joyfulness	*Frohsein*
judge (*transitive v.*)	*beurtheilen*
judging (*n.*)	*Beurtheilung*
judgment	*Urtheil*
kinship	*Verwandtschaft*
knowledge	*Kenntnis*
law	*Gesetz*
lawlike	*gesetzmäßig*
luxury	*Luxus*
making sensible	*Versinnlichung*
manifold (*adj.*)	*mannigfaltig*
manifold (*n.*)	*das Mannigfaltige*
material (*adj.*)	*materiell*
material (*n.*)	*Stoff*
matter	*Materie*
matter of faith	*Glaubensache*
mentality	*Denkungsart, Gemüthsart*
mind	*Gemüth*
modish	*sittlich*
moral	*moralisch, sittlich*
morality	*Moralität, Sittlichkeit*
morals	*die Moral, Sitten*
multiplicity	*Mannigfaltigkeit*
natural end	*Naturzweck*
nexus	*Verbindung*
nonpurposive	*unzweckmäßig*
of one's own free will	*freiwillig*
opinion	*Meinung*
original being	*Urwesen*
original ground	*Urgrund*

palpable	*fühlbar*
persuade	*überreden*
play	*Spiel*
please	*gefallen*
pleasure	*Lust*
point of view	*Absicht*
peculiarity	*Eigentümlichkeit*
pictorial	*bildend*
picture	*Bildwerk*
power	*Kraft, Macht*
power of judgment	*Urtheilskraft*
powerlessness	*Ohnmacht*
predisposition	*Anlage*
presentation	*Darstellung*
principle	*Princip, Principium*
produce (*v.*)	*bewirken, wirken*
production	*Erzeugung*
proof	*Beweis, Beweisgrund*
property	*Beschaffenheit, Eigenschaft*
prototype	*Urbild*
prototypical	*urbildlich*
purpose	*Absicht*
purposive, purposively	*zweckmäßig*
quality	*Qualität*
quantity	*Quantität*
quantum	*Quantum*
rational cognition	*Vernunfterkenntnis*
rationalistic	*vernünftelnd*
realize	*bewirken*
reason	*Grund, Vernunft*
recognition	*Erkenntnis*
recognize	*erkennen*
reflecting	*reflectirend*
reflection	*Reflexion*
regularity	*Regelmäßigkeit*
relation	*Beziehung, Relation, Verhältnis*
representation	*Vorstellung*
respect	*Achtung*
require	*erfordern*
require (something) of (someone)	*verlangen*
requirement	*Erfordernis*

require of (someone)	*ansinnen*
reverence	*Heiligachtung*
satisfaction	*Wohlgefallen*
satisfy	*befriedigen*
sensation	*Empfindung, Sinnesempfindung*
sense	*Sinn*
sensibility	*Sinnlichkeit*
sensible	*sinnlich*
sensible rendering	*Versinnlichung*
sensitive	*empfindbar*
sentiment	*Empfindung*
serviceability	*Tauglichkeit*
set	*Inbegriff*
shape	*Gestalt*
skill	*Geschicklichkeit*
sophistical	*vernünftelnd*
sophistry	*Vernünftelei*
spirit	*Geist*
state of mind	*Gemüthsbestimmung, Stimmung*
stimulus	*Anreiz*
sublime (*adj.*)	*erhaben*
sublime (*n.*)	*das Erhabene*
substratum	*Substrat*
succession	*Nachfolge*
suitable	*angemessen*
suitability	*Angemessenheit*
supersensible	*übersinnlich*
synthesis	*Zusammensetzung*
talent	*Talent*
taste	*Geschmack*
tendency	*Hang*
territory	*Boden*
think over	*Nachdenken*
totality	*Inbegriff*
ultimate end	*letztes Zweck*
unanimity	*Einhelligkeit*
unanimous	*einhellig*
understanding	*Verstand*
unintentionally	*unabsichtlich*
unison	*Einhelligkeit*
universal	*allgemein*

universal, the	*das Allgemeine*
universality	*Allgemeinheit*
universally valid	*allgemeingültig*
variety	*Mannigfaltigkeit*
view (*n.*)	*Ansicht*
view (*v.*)	*ansehen*
viewing (*n.*)	*Beschauung*
violence	*Gewalt*
vocation	*Bestimmung, Zweckbestimmung*
voluntary	*willkührlich*
way of thinking	*Denkungsart*
will	*Wille*

Index

actuality, contrasted to possibility, 272–3
Addison, Joseph, 355n56, 365n19
adherent beauty, 114–16
Adickes, Erich, xxxix, li
aesthetic ideas, 192–5, 217–18; and arts of tone, 206; and fine art, xxxiv–xxxv; and genius, 192–5, 225; and sculpture, 199
aesthetic judgment: analysis and concept of, xvii, xxv–xxvi, 24–8, 75–8, 89–127; *a priori* principle of, 39, 43–4, 57, 77, 79, 379n11; based on pleasure, 31–3, 75–7; communicability of, 102–4; deduction of, xvii, xxix, xxxii–xxxiv, xliii–xliv, 160–76, 377n1; dialectic of, 213–28; empirical and pure, 108, 114–16; modality of, 121–7; and morality, xxvii, xxxv, 156–7, 178–82, 225–8, 230, 238, 387n17, 387n19; and perfection, 111–13; quality of, 89–96; quantity of, 96–104; relation of, 105–20; subjective rather than objective, 366n2; and teleological judgment, xxi–xxii, 23–4, 33–5, 43–4, 48, 78–80, 136, 190; universal and necessary validity of, 27, 39, 76–7, 99–101, 159, 160, 162–4, 167–9, 368n14, 368n15; *see also* judgment of taste; taste
aesthetics, xiv; Kant's early view of, xv–xx; connection to teleology, xxvii, xxxi; of judgment, not sensibility, 2–5, 46; meaning of, 24–5, 362n28; *see also* aesthetic judgment; judgment of taste; taste
affectlessness, 154
affects, contrasted to passions, 154–5, 384n62
affirmation, in moral proof of God, 325–38
agreeable, the: contrasted to the beautiful, xxviii, 91–6, 97–8, 99, 102, 107, 121, 149–50, 202, 217, 221, 275n22; and color, 108–9, 202; disagreement about, 108–9, 171–2, 213; contrasted to the good, 93–4, 177–8
agreement, in judgments of taste, xxiv, xxxii–xxxiii, 214–15; *see also* assent; communicability; intersubjective validity; universal validity
America, 251; revolution in, 389n11

Ameriks, Karl E., 358n139
analogy: of anatomical forms, 287; between art and nature, 234, 246, 254–5, 262, 328n, 389n9; between beauty and morality, 226–8, 387n17; and idea of God, 321–2, 328–9; proof by, 327–9
analytic: of the beautiful, xxvii–xxx, xli, xliii, 89–127; of the sublime, xxx–xxxii, xli, xliii–xliv, 128–59; of teleological judgment, xxxvi, xli, 235–55
anatomy, system of, 287
Anaxagoras, 236, 388n2
announcement of lectures (*M. Immanuel Kant's Announcement of the Program for his Lectures for the Winter Semester 1765–6*), 352n12
anthropology: of inner sense, 325; Kant's lectures on: xvi–xvii, xli, 353n14, 353n17, 354n23, 354n28, 356n74, 359n5, 359–60n15, 360n17, 361n24, 365n1, 366n2, 366n3, 366n4, 367n7, 367n8, 367n9, 367n11, 368n12, 368n14, 368n15, 368n19, 368n20, 369n28, 370n29, 370n31, 370n33, 370–1n34, 371n36, 372n38, 372n39, 372n41, 372n48, 373n1, 375n19, 375n20, 375n23, 375n26, 378n4, 379n6, 379n8, 379n11, 379n12, 380n16, 381n26, 381n30, 380n31, 381n32, 381n33, 382n39, 382n40, 382n42, 382n43, 383n47, 383n48, 384n49, 384n50, 384n52, 384n53, 384n55, 384n58, 384n60, 385n1, 387n17, 387n18, 390n16, 393n12, 394n20, 395n33
Anthropology from a Pragmatic Point of View, 360n15, 361n24, 365n2, 368n14, 368n20, 369n28, 369n29, 370n30, 373n1, 373n4, 374n10, 374n11, 374n16, 375n23, 375n27, 375n28, 375n29, 380n15, 380n18, 382n42, 383n48, 384n49, 384n50, 384n52, 384n58, 384n62, 390n15, 390n16
anthropomorphism, 227, 321, 387n16
antinomy: of pure reason, 219–20, 385n5, 393n19; of taste, xxxv, 213–25, 385n1, 385n3; of teleological judgment, xxxvi, 257–61, 296–7

413

Index

Antiparos, cave of, 223
apathy, 375n27
appearances, contrasted to things in themselves, 63, 81, 278
apriority, of judgment of taste, xxxiii, 162–3, 168–9
archaeology, 296n
archetype, of taste; *see* ideal, of taste
architecture, xxx, 110–11, 114–15, 199–200, 370n33
Aristippus, 389n6
Aristotle, xxi, 389n8
art, xvi, xxxiv–xxxv, 182–212; agreeable versus beautiful, 184–5, 203, 225; combinations of, 203; contrasted to handicraft, 183, 381n26; contrasted to nature, xxxvi, 35–6, 50, 78, 182, 185–6, 189–90, 224–5, 245–7, 328n; contrasted to science, 166, 183, 187–8; division of, 197–207, 384n50; and genius, 186–97, 225; interest in, 178–9, 181; meaning of name, 381n23, 381n28; source of principles, 45–6; and the sublime, 136, 373n4, 374n10; ugliness in, 190–1; utility of, 287n17, 387n19
assent, in judgments of taste, 121–4, 159, 162–4, 170–1, 227; *see also* agreement; universal validity
association, law of, 192
astonishment, 375n28; contrasted to admiration, 238; and the sublime, 152, 154
Attempt to Introduce the Concept of Negative Magnitudes into Philosophy, 352n8
attractive forces, 329, 344–5, 396n43, 397n58
attributes: aesthetic versus logical, 193–4; of God, 307–8, 310
autonomy: of aesthetic judgment, 27–8, 162–3; of imagination, 125; and teleological judgment, 257, 261

Barthélemy, Jean Jacques, xlvi, 358n132
Batteux, Charles, 165, 378n5
Baumgarten, Alexander Gottlieb, xiv, xvi, xix, xxiii, 351n3, 353n15, 354n41, 360–1n19, 362n28, 365n1, 370–1n34, 390n3
beautiful, the: in art, 184–6, 198–9; contrasted to the agreeable, xxviii, 91–6, 97–8, 99, 102, 121, 149–50, 202, 221, 275n22; contrasted to the good, xxviii, 91–6, 111, 113, 125, 149–50, 221, 375n22; contrasted to the sublime, xxvii, 49–50, 128–30, 149–54, 157–8, 172–3, 375n22; definitions of, 96, 104, 120, 124, 150; disinterestedness of, 90–1; empirical interest in, 176–8; intellectual interest in, 178–82; object of aes-

thetic judgment, 76; as symbol of the morally good, xxxv, 225–8; *see also* beauty
beauty: adherent contrasted to free, xxix–xxx, 114–16; artistic versus natural, 185–6, 189–90, 246–7; as expression of aesthetic ideas, 197–8; and form, 108–11; of geometrical figures, 238; of humans, xxx, 114–15, 117–20; the ideal of, xxx, 116–20, 372n39; judgment of, as reflecting judgment, xxiv; Kant's early theory of, 359n15, 364n16, 364n18, 369n28, 369n29, 371n34, 371n36; not intellectual, 238; and perfection, 11–13, 29–31, 111–13, 125, 216–17, 220; purposiveness of natural, 251–2, 323; universal validity of, 96–7, 99–101; vague versus fixed, 117; *see also* beautiful, the
Beck, Jakob Sigismund, xlii
Bering, Johann, 363n2
Bernard, J. H., 357n119, 378n1
Biester, Johann Erich, 358n132
birdsongs, 126, 182
Blumenbach, Johann Friedrich, 292, 392n7
Bode, Johann Joachim, xlvi
Burke, Edmund, xv, 38, 158, 352n10, 355n56, 361n27, 365n19, 376n37, 376n38, 376n39

caloric, theory of, 386n8
Camper, Pieter, 182, 296, 381n24, 393n11
caprice, 211–12
caricature, 119n
Cassirer, Ernst, xliii
Cato, Marcus Portius, 384n59
causality: our conception of divine, 321–2, 329, 345–6; efficient, 244–5; final, 35, 233–4, 239, 242–5, 252, 294, 297; freedom as kind of, 333; human conception of, xxxvi; ideal versus real, 244; mechanical versus final, 36–7, 242–4, 250–1, 258–9, 261–2, 277–84, 290–3; of nature and freedom, 81; reciprocal, 244–5, 389n12, 391n7; system of, 263; technical versus moral, 60; varieties of forms of, 71–2
chance, games of, 208
Charlevoix, François-Xavier, 367n5
charm: and the agreeable, 150; contrasted to beauty, 98, 369n28; empirical interest in, 178–9; independence of judgment of taste from, 107–110, 159; and intellectual interest in beauty, 181
Christianity, 336n
Cicero, Marcus Tullius, 205n, 384n59, 388n6

Index

deduction (*cont.*)
377n1; of principle of purposiveness of nature, 71–3; of sublime, 160–1, 373n6
Defoe, Daniel, 376n35
deism, 227
deity, concept of, 305–6, 312; *see also* God
Democritus, 263, 390n3
demonology, 311, 323
demonstration, 218, 238
Descartes, René, xv, 328n
design: argument from (physicotheology), 303–8, 394n24, 396n54; contrasted to color, xxix, 110; in nature, xxvii, xxxvi
despair, 154–5
desire, xvi; connection to faculties of cognition, 11–12, 44–5, 64–6
determining judgment, contrasted to reflecting, xxii, xxiii–xxiv, xxxvii, xlvii, 15, 20–1, 26, 36–7, 47, 50, 66–7, 234, 250–1, 254, 257–8, 259–60, 266–9, 275, 277, 282, 285, 297, 320, 327, 359n7
dialectic: of the aesthetic power of judgment, xxxv, 213–28; of the teleological power of judgment, xxxvi–xxxvii, 257–85
Dilthey, Wilhelm, xlii
Diogenes Laertius, 377n40
discipline, 299–301
disinterestedness: of judgment of taste, xvii, xxviii, 90–1, 95–6, 107–8; in the sublime, 133; in taste and morality, xxvii, 227–8
displeasure, in feeling of sublime, 141–3
distinctness, 28–9
domain, versus territory, in philosophy, 61–3
drawing, 100
dreams, purpose of, 251, 390n16
Dreams of a Spirit-Seer, xliv, 391n5
duty, and judgment of taste, xxxiii, 176, 380n15
dynamical sublime, 143–9

Egypt, 135
emotion: and affect, 154–5; independence of judgment of taste from, 107–11, 159; and the sublime, 128–9
empiricism, of critique of taste, 221
ends: concept of, 105, 277; and the good, 93, 111–12; human ability to choose, 294–5, 299, 302, 314; idealism versus realisms of, 263; in nature, 239–41, 270, 294–303, 339–49; organisms as natural, 242–52, 266–8; and subjective purposiveness, 221–2; translation of Kant's terms for, xlviii; *see also* final end; natural end; ultimate end
Enlightenment, 174, 379n13, 379n14

entertainment, arts of, 184–5
enthusiasm: 375n25, 376n33; and the sublime, 154, 156–7
Epicurus: on causality, 263–4, 390n2; on gratification, 159, 207, 209, 376n40
epigenesis, 291–2, 392n4
error, in judgments of taste, xxxiii, 99, 101, 122, 170n
Erdmann, Benno, xlii
eternity, 310
ether, 331, 396n48
ethicotheology (moral), 303, 308–31, 394n26; restriction of validity of, 318–23; utility of, 323–5
ethics, lectures on, 374n17, 376n31, 394n27, 395n31, 395n37
Euler, Leonhard, 109, 370n30, 384n56
evolution, xxxviii, 287–9, 291–2, 392n4
examples: in morality, 378n3; in taste, xxx, 186–8, 195–6, 372n46
existence: and ends, 105; and interest, 91–2, 95, 176
experience: possibility of, 9n; as a system, 13–15
explanation: contrasted to judging, 21; mechanical versus teleological, xxxvii, 36, 260–1, 264, 271, 281, 286, 290–3
expression: of aesthetic ideas, 194–5; and classification of arts, 197–9, 201; of concepts, 226
eye, purpose and structure of, 37, 40

facts, 332–3
faculties of mind, division of, xiv, xxiii, 11–13, 44–6, 64–6, 82–3; *see also* cognitive faculties; imagination; reason; understanding
faith, 333–6, 338
fatality, system of, 263
feeling: connected with judgment, xxiii, 11–13; faculty of, xvi; and pleasure, xvii; *see also* pleasure
Ferguson, Francis, 355n63
final causes, *see* causality; purposiveness
final end: and faith, 334; of nature and/or world, 250–2, 294, 298–9, 301–4, 307–8, 309–10, 314–15, 318–20, 340, 393n20; and moral law, 335n; of supreme cause, 311–13, 316; *see also* highest good
fine art, *see* art
Fitzgerald, Robert, 65n
force, moving: in body, 344–5; in soul, 322
form: in art, 185, 189, 203; and beauty, 107–11, 128–9, 160, 178–80; of purposiveness, xxix, 106, 39n29
formalism, xxix–xxx, xxxii, xxxiv